OXFORD HISTORY OF
ENGLISH LITERATURE

Edited by

F. P. WILSON *and* BONAMY DOBRÉE

THE OXFORD HISTORY OF
ENGLISH LITERATURE

Edited by

F. P. WILSON AND BONAMY DOBRÉE

(*The titles of some volumes are provisional*)

ENGLISH LITERATURE

IN THE

EARLIER SEVENTEENTH CENTURY

1600–1660

BY

DOUGLAS BUSH

OXFORD UNIVERSITY PRESS

NEW YORK

Oxford University Press, Amen House, London E.C. 4

GLASGOW NEW YORK TORONTO MELBOURNE WELLINGTON
BOMBAY CALCUTTA MADRAS CAPE TOWN

Geoffrey Cumberlege, Publisher to the University

FIRST PUBLISHED 1945
REPRINTED 1946, 1948, 1952

PRINTED IN THE UNITED STATES OF AMERICA

PREFACE

THIS volume is (or was supposed to be) limited to about 150,000 words of text, and many things, as Purchas said of Sir Anthony Sherley's travels, 'are left out not for want of worth, but of roome'. Particular problems of inclusion and proportion are complicated by the necessary effort to maintain a balance between the contemporary and the modern scale of values. In regard to authors who straddle 1600, my normal rule has been to mention but not discuss works written before that date, since these will be treated in the volume on the sixteenth century. Doubtless many readers would prefer to have chapters grouped around men rather than around types of writing and modes of thought, but it is hoped that the present arrangement, though it requires the slicing up of some authors, may contribute to a more philosophic unity; it is at least a continual reminder that most great prose of the period was didactic and utilitarian. It is hoped also, since there is continual occasion for doubt or debate, that the apparent assurance of brevity may not 'sound arrogantly unto present Ears in this strict enquiring Age, wherein, for the most part, Probably, and Perhaps, will hardly serve to mollify the Spirit of captious Contradictors'. As for more fundamental complaints, the author can only admit the general impeachment lodged by Hobbes against the Oxford mathematicians: 'There is within you some special cause of intenebration which you should do well to look to.'

Texts are normally quoted from first or authoritative early editions with no change except that italics are not retained, that contractions are expanded, and that *i, j, u, v,* and *w* are made to conform with modern usage. Titles are given in their original form in the bibliography and modernized in the text and chronological tables.

I must record my gratitude for assistance of various kinds: to the President and Fellows of Harvard College for grants from the Clark Bequest; to the Army Medical Library, the Boston Public Library, the Library of Congress, the Newberry Library, the libraries of the University of Chicago, Columbia University, Cornell University, the University of Illinois, Yale University and Divinity School, and the Harvard Divinity School and

School of Business Administration, for the loan of books; to the
Boston Public Library and the libraries of the Harvard Law
School and the Union Theological Seminary, for the privilege
of consulting books; and to the staff of the Widener and
Houghton libraries for their untiring help over a long time.
The University of Toronto Press and the Cornell University
Press have willingly allowed me to use bits of two small volumes
of mine, *The Renaissance and English Humanism* (1939) and *Paradise Lost in Our Time* (1945).

President Wilbur K. Jordan of Radcliffe College, Professors
J. Milton French of Rutgers University, William A. Jackson,
George W. Sherburn, and A. P. Usher of Harvard, F. A.
Patterson of Columbia, and John W. Spargo of Northwestern
University, Dr. Louis B. Wright of the Huntington Library,
and Dr. C. William Miller of the University of Virginia, have
been good enough to answer queries. For amiable and valuable
criticism of parts of the manuscript I am indebted to friends
and colleagues of Harvard University, Professor Jackson again
and Professors Charles H. McIlwain, James B. Munn, Kenneth
B. Murdock, Hyder E. Rollins, and Theodore Spencer, and to
my friends Professors Warner G. Rice of the University of
Michigan and Arthur S. P. Woodhouse of the University
of Toronto. This large sum of scholarly insurance does not of
course exempt the insured from the common lot of man. Professor F. P. Wilson has been from beginning to end not only
a patient and helpful adviser but an active co-worker to a
degree quite beyond what might be expected of a general editor,
and in matters of critical opinion both he and Professor Dobrée
have shown a tolerant magnanimity. It would be superfluous
if not impertinent to pay tribute to the Clarendon Press, but
I must acknowledge its noble indulgence of my bibliographical
excesses—though a large portion of my wild oats has had to
be ploughed under. Finally, my wife has listened to many
pages and many groans, and has done much to prevent the
multiplication of both.

D. B.

HARVARD UNIVERSITY

CONTENTS

I
THE BACKGROUND OF THE AGE

IT might well dismay the intelligent reader to be informed at the outset that the years 1600–60 were an age of transition. But while every period in history deserves, and doubtless has received, that illuminating label, there are some periods in which disruptive and creative forces reach maturity and combine to speed up the normal process of change. In the history of England, as in that of Europe at large, the seventeenth century is probably the most conspicuous modern example, unless we except our own age, of such acceleration. In 1600 the educated Englishman's mind and world were more than half medieval; by 1660 they were more than half modern. The character and causes of such a transformation are far too complex to be summed up in a formula, but something of its breadth and scope may be suggested by a few more labels—democracy and imperialism, industrialism and capitalism, the advance of pure and applied science and the gospel of progress, the spread of the scientific, secular, and anti-authoritarian spirit through other domains of thought and action.

But this process of change did not begin or end in the years 1600–60, and it took place against a background of continuity and compromise. We encounter the clash and the fusion of old and new on every side, in science and religion, politics and economics, law and literature, music and architecture. It is the impact of modernism upon medievalism which gives the age its peculiar character. Yet the forces of 'modernism' were themselves generally as old as the forces of conservative tradition, and it was in the name of conservative tradition that the great rebellion in politics and religion was conducted. As the quarrel between 'ancients' and 'moderns' developed, champions of modern superiority could appeal to the telescope and the microscope, but otherwise there was hardly any new idea of the century, from the motion of the earth to the motion of the atom, from democracy to absolutism, from the theory of ethics to the theory of prose style, of which the germ at least was not to be found in ancient Greece and Rome. In other spheres, such as the religious, social, and economic, the elements of change had been operating since the Middle Ages. What distinguished the seventeenth century from the sixteenth was not so much the arrival of new ideas and forces as the accumulated and irresistible pressure of old and new ones in potent combination and interaction. Even the belief in a rigorous order of nature, which lies behind 'classical' mechanistic thought, may be regarded as in some sense an unconscious heritage from theology. And the period which transformed scholastic and Calvinistic determinism into a scientific counterpart was also the period of mercantilism and mysticism. Surveying the age and its representative minds, in 1660 as well as in 1600, we may say that normality consists in incongruity.

There were, of course, whole-hearted conservatives and whole-hearted modernists, but even they were aware of a changing world, and a multitude who belonged to neither category were disturbed by violent contrasts and divided loyalties. From Donne to Dryden thoughtful men ask 'What do I know?' Sharing the critical spirit, yet conscious of its destructive results, they seek some valid authority, some standing-ground more firm than that which had served their fathers. Is the edifice of knowledge built by ancient genius the modern man's permanent home or is it his prison? In his view of the universe and God and man, shall he hold by the Bible, Aristotle, and Ptolemy, or by one of the confusing new theories? Or, since very few men were troubled by science, what is the final authority in religious doctrine and discipline, the Church of Rome, the Church of England, the Bible, individual reason, or the supra-rational inner light? In the tremendous matter of the salvation or damnation of souls, can those who possess the truth tolerate the propagation of error? Should Protestants worship God according to a prescribed ritual borrowed from the Scarlet Woman or with austere and spontaneous simplicity? What is the divinely appointed form of church government, episcopal, synodical, or congregational? Are Church and State united or separate, and which is superior? Where does supreme political and constitutional authority reside, in the king, the judges of the common law, or Parliament? Does the tyranny of the sovereign justify armed resistance? Does the tyranny of Parliament justify forcible purging and military rule? Is society an organism actuated by religious motives or an aggregate of individuals actuated by economic self-interest? Is morality founded on right reason and divine precept, or on the current law of the land?

Such a catalogue might be prolonged indefinitely, but these far from theoretical questions will serve to illustrate the permanently unsettled state of the seventeenth-century man's inner and outer world. It is not unnatural that melancholy has been taken as a conspicuous, even a dominant, characteristic of late Elizabethan and Jacobean literature. Its manifestations are infinitely various in kind and degree—Jaques, Hamlet, and Thersites are three out of many dramatic voices—and the causes assigned range from introspection to indigestion, from Puritanism to the plague. Certainly we find much disgust with men and society, much vague bitterness against a world which seems out of joint, against the apparent futility of life. Many young men might have uttered, with a difference, the later judgement of Margaret of Newcastle that there was no employment for heroic spirits under so wise a king as James. The young Sir William Cornwallis and the elder statesman Fulke Greville, to cite only two witnesses, see about them nothing but the corruptions of a sick time. Ancient heroes, Cornwallis declares in his essay on 'Fame', searched for substance, modern men chase shadows: 'we are walking Ghostes'. We of the present, who have had our generation of hollow men, our literature of defeatism, are perhaps especially qualified to understand one side of the early seventeenth century, yet we should be unwise in seeking too much affinity between it and the recent past, since selective and plausible parallels can be and have been drawn between our time and every notable period from Chaucer's to the Victorian.

Jacobean pessimism, like the modern, is commonly taken as a reaction against the optimism of the preceding age, although the writers who hold forth glibly on that text seem to regard the name of Marlowe as sufficient evidence of Elizabethan optimism. In fact, Elizabethan literature, like Victorian literature, was pessimistic enough, and it is permissible to think that 'Jacobean melancholy' has been exaggerated. Against the 'Jacobean pessimism' of Shakespeare's partly Elizabethan tragedies and problem comedies may be set the 'Jacobean optimism' of his dramatic romances. 'There never was a merry World', said Selden, 'since the Faries left Dancing, and the Parson left Conjuring.' But in all ages 'Merry England' has been both a living reality and a nostalgic fiction. Much Jacobean melancholy, like that of our own day, was the fashionable exploitation of what in some men was authentic, and while young intellectuals were nourishing one another's disillusionment, many happy extraverts were singing the madrigals and ballets of Thomas Morley and his fellows. The meditations on the brevity of life, so numerous and so rich throughout our sixty years, are not the rhetorical funguses of an age of decay; they are the seventeenth-century version of the Dance of Death, and they tell rather of immense vitality contemplating its inevitable extinction. If Calvinistic religion had its dark and terrifying side, it also raised the humblest of the elect above the lords of the earth. If astronomical discoveries and speculations bewildered and dismayed some philosophical minds, for others they enhanced the glory of God; and applied science promised the conquest of all nature for the use and benefit of man. If some writers were troubled by the belief that they were living near the end of the world, in a time of general deterioration, the mass of men, from politicians, merchants, and colonizers down to ploughmen, were far too busy to be melancholy. They would have shared the retrospective verdict not of the romantic duchess but of Fuller: 'Indeed all the Reigne of King James was better for one to live under, than to write of, consisting of a Champian of constant tranquility, without any tumours of trouble to entertain posterity with.' And if the latter half of our period was one of war and continued discord, the rebellion and the Commonwealth were the culmination of intense zeal for the establishment of a new era. Altogether, one could make out a strong argument for the Elizabethan age as one of pessimistic gloom and the earlier seventeenth century as one of optimistic recovery.

However, granting the whole period its fair share, and no more, of the melancholy which runs through all English literature, we may illustrate some of its special features and causes in a brief sketch of the changing background. The general political, religious, and economic causes, even the philosophic ones, were all alive in the time of Elizabeth. Political and religious strife was brought to a head by the clear-cut Stuart theory of State and Church, partly because the sovereign's conception of sovereignty had become more rigidly legalistic, and still more because the structure of society and the temper of the nation and

Parliament had changed. The Tudors were skilful in avoiding both doctrinaire theory and open conflict, and were lucky in not having to face the ultimate consequences of active problems, though even Elizabeth in 1601 bowed to a refractory Parliament. Anxiety about the succession and the various other troubles of her last years—among them the execution of Essex, the patron and the national hope of many young literary men—contributed to make the welcome given to James much more than empty adulation. The king, however, always remained a stranger in England, and he was quite incapable of inspiring patriotic devotion to himself and the Crown. His outlook, and that of his son, were dynastic rather than national. Men who recalled the days of the Armada did not feel proud over James's unwearied appeasement of Spain and his sacrifice of the Palatinate, Bohemia, and continental Protestantism—the theme of the bitter 'Tom Tell-Truth' (c. 1622). Yet others could justly rejoice because he had kept the country out of futile and unnecessary war. The domestic problems he inherited were far beyond the grasp of a dogmatic academic theorist, however erratically shrewd he might be, and through a long series of arbitrary acts he contrived to alarm or antagonize almost all the substantial groups in the nation except the orthodox clergy. All classes alike resented the king's extravagance, his attachment to unworthy favourites, and the moral and financial corruption of the court circle. In fairness we should remember that the increasing friction between James (and Charles) and Parliament was caused in part by quite inadequate governmental revenue. And James was wiser than Parliament in his desire for union with Scotland and for more liberal treatment of Catholics, perhaps also in his pacific foreign policy.

It is more difficult to find any evidence of Charles's wisdom. Yet, when Parliament was exasperated beyond endurance, invincible respect for the Lord's Anointed was still shown in the honest efforts to dissociate abuses from the king and fasten them upon his advisers. Even in 1640, when the Long Parliament began to take over royal powers, its aim was to curb the prerogative, not to assert the sovereignty of Parliament. Up to the last the parliamentarians were too instinctively monarchical to contemplate revolution; only step by step were they driven into it. For the most part they did not consider themselves pioneer democrats, they were patriotic—and propertied—Englishmen who appealed to Magna Carta and Bracton in defence of their traditional rights and the traditional supremacy of law. And whatever the modern world owes to the creators of parliamentary government, from the noble and impetuous Eliot to the sober Pym and the rest, the conflict cannot be regarded in terms of black and white. We may perhaps set aside the personal appeal which the royal martyr and sainted cavalier has always made, but we should not forget that all along he had had a large share of legality, if not of equity, honesty, and intelligence, on his side. On the other hand we cannot, as even Milton discovered, idealize the Long Parliament as an assembly of political Galahads, and the behaviour of the victorious army, however strong the provocation, was scarcely in accord with the doctrine of the supremacy of law for which they had fought. When war came, it divided individual souls as well as families and districts. Many men on both sides were happy in seeing only one course before them, but many also had a hard decision to make. It was with broken hearts that the chivalrous Sir Edmund Verney and the philosophic Falkland followed their liege lord.

As events showed, the nation was not prepared for a republic, and it did not get one. If Cromwell had had a free hand, the protectorate would have been a happier era than it was, and in spite of the pressure of conflicting factions he succeeded to a remarkable degree, in a few years, in commanding a new respect abroad and creating order at home. But his foreign policy, based on a mixture of commercial, religious, and imperialistic motives, was expensive, if nothing worse, and domestic order was partly artificial. No amount of beneficent and liberal reform, and there was a good deal, could obscure the fact that the government was not a free republic but a military dictatorship. The greatest of republicans betrayed his anxiety even in eulogizing the Protector. What had been thinly disguised became very clear with the inquisitorial jurisdiction of the regional major-generals. Altogether, experience of the iron hand, the repressive severity of Puritan legislation on manners and morals, the political chaos which attended and followed the brief reign of Richard Cromwell, and the extremities of economic depression, were enough to inspire London itself, the former stronghold of Puritan resistance, with an ardent longing for the return of king, Parliament, prosperity, and the *Book of Common Prayer*.

During these sixty years religious and ecclesiastical questions were increasingly bound up with politics, and they directly touched larger numbers of people and inflamed passions which constitutional issues might leave cool. The Elizabethan compromise from the first had failed to draw in the more resolute Catholics and Protestants. James's tolerant inclinations were frustrated by alarm over Catholic conspiracies and the multiplication of recusants, and the re-enforcement of the penal laws resulted in the Gunpowder Plot, which was to remain in the popular imagination an inflammatory warning of the political dangers of popery. The oath of allegiance (1606), James said in his *Apology*, was a test of civil obedience and, though the oath went beyond the merely civil, it might, but for papal *breves* and Parliament, have been a virtual instrument of toleration. Later years brought comparative relief to English Catholics, and under Charles's French queen Catholicism raised its head at court and won some notable converts. In the eyes of Puritans who dreaded the grim wolf with privy paw, Laud's High Church was Roman in all but name. And in 1641 Lord Falkland, who was no Puritan, declared in Parliament that some bishops were so absolutely, directly, and cordially papists that it was all that £1,500 a year could do to keep them from confessing it.

But Catholicism proved a much less formidable force than Puritanism, which grew from a drop of dissent to an angry flood. At the beginning of 1644 John Greene wrote in his diary that 'now 'tis made a warre almost merely for religion, which I feared'. To intensely serious people, learned and unlearned, who demanded apostolic simplicity, the Church of England with its Romish ritual and hierarchy appeared a very imperfect fulfilment of Reformation ideals. While the word 'Puritan' came to mean many things, it properly denotes firm adherence to the Bible as the sole and sufficient authority in all matters of ecclesiastical government and ceremony as well as of belief and conduct. The Bible and the congregation were for the religious republican or democrat what the common law and Parliament were for his political counterpart, and both effected a revolution by appealing to a remote and somewhat nebulous past against a corrupted present. Theologically, there was for generations little or no difference between Anglicans and Puritans, since the Church of England until the early seventeenth century was largely Calvinistic. The advance of Arminian theology and its association with High Church principles were registered in George Morley's famous answer to the question 'What the Arminians held?'—that they held all the best bishoprics and deaneries in England. Indeed, though Laud was liberal in his theological outlook, through his rigorous insistence on external uniformity and his far-reaching interference in all departments of life, Arminianism was identified with the doctrine of divine right, royal and episcopal, and with the whole Stuart régime. Mrs. Hutchinson was not unwarranted in saying, as the Grand Remonstrance had said, that if any gentleman maintained the good laws of the land, or stood up for any public interest, he was called a Puritan. The union of prelacy and monarchy brought about the union of religious and political nonconformity which finally overthrew both Church and State. But before condemning the motives and methods of Bancroft and Laud and their sovereigns in enforcing conformity, we should remember that our religious tolerance has been largely the by-product of religious apathy, and that the Church, in the conviction of many good men, could not afford to be tolerant when its very survival as a national institution was in danger. As Laud said, in dedicating the *Conference with Fisher* (1639) to the king, the Church of England—which we think of as a serene *via media*—was ground between two millstones, Romanist and Puritan. We must not forget, moreover, the Tudor legacy of disorder, ignorance, inefficiency, and poverty among the mass of the clergy.

During Elizabeth's reign the growing body of Puritans were mostly content to form the left wing of the Church, but in the seventeenth century that position became less and less tenable. At the Hampton Court Conference (1604) James enunciated Stuart policy with a mixture of short-sighted violence and prophetic penetration. His promise to harry Nonconformists out of the land bore immediate fruit in the ejection of a few dozen Puritan clergymen. The sectarian exodus from the Church had begun much earlier—Sir Andrew Aguecheek hated a Brownist—and some people moved to Holland, but the most impressive portents were the voyage of the *Mayflower* (1620) and the 'great migration' of 1630 and subsequent years. The religious origins of Massachusetts illustrate the mingled loyalty and ingenuity of the emigrants and the invincible instinct for

unity and uniformity which was a general heritage. Across the
wide ocean, in 'the savage deserts of America', faithful Englishmen and Christians could maintain the paradox of non-
separating Congregationalism with much less trouble than at
home; they were only separating from the corruptions of the
Church. In England Puritan antagonism to prelacy, which had
long been seething, boiled over in 1640-1. In addition to some
detached and more or less secular Erastians, there appeared
among the warring Puritans three main parties or groups of
parties. The Solemn League and Covenant (1643) signalized
a Presbyterian predominance which was to last for four or five
years. The English Presbyterians wanted a national Presbyterian Church, controlled by the State, with no toleration for
dissent; what emerged, however, was only the shell of a Presbyterian system. Reactionary and *bourgeois* Presbyterianism gave
way before the liberal and flexible Independents, who stood for
toleration and feared parliamentary absolutism, and whose
strength was centred in Cromwell's army. They were able in
1648-9 to purge the House of Presbyterians and execute the
king. The third and much more miscellaneous group comprised the sects and parties which were being born every month,
with varying religious, political, or economic creeds and often
with lunatic fringes. In his *Gangraena* (1646) the Presbyterian
Thomas Edwards listed sixteen recognizable groups and over
two hundred 'errors, heresies, blasphemies' (including the innocent three of Sir Thomas Browne's 'greener studies'), which
had developed in recent years. This burgeoning of sects was of
course the logical outcome of Protestant individualism, and the
centrifugal impulse was stimulated by more immediate causes,
the flourishing of old and new abuses in the Church, the royal
and episcopal campaign for High Church uniformity, and some
experience of what promised to be the equally tyrannous uniformity of Presbyterianism. There was, too, the positive desire,
sometimes partly spurious and fanatical, sometimes deep and
real, for a kind of illumination which the Establishment did not
seem to give. An example of the one kind would be the Fifth
Monarchy men, who were looking—as Milton could look—for
the second coming of Christ. The finest example of the other
was the Society of Friends, which grew so rapidly under the
compelling leadership of the itinerant mystic, George Fox.
    If the fusion and the variety of political and religious problems

made an insoluble tangle, a further important element of complication was the economic. As Peter Chamberlen said, in *The Poor Man's Advocate* (1649), 'None more fond of a King then the English, yet they departed from him to ease their purses, and their Consciences.' The complaints of men of property against arbitrary taxation and other evils were uttered in a succession of stormy Parliaments and, after 1629, were kept alive by such individuals as Hampden. The middle and poorer classes, if they did not win satisfactory relief, at least made their grievances audible through local petitions and through union in secular or religious groups. The Levellers, headed by the brave, much-enduring, and difficult John Lilburne, aimed at political democracy. The communistic Diggers, who represented a more extreme demand for economic and social justice, and other older bodies like the Anabaptists and Family of Love, revived the radical-mystical movement of the Middle Ages. In the seventeenth century, especially after 1640, the breaking-down of things established seemed to open the way for the rebuilding of society, for the realization of perennial dreams of Christian communism. To the eyes of authority the inner light had always looked decidedly red.

While the economic causes of discontent were greatly aggravated by the war and its aftermath, most of them were much older than our period. Apart from such acts of God as the recurring plague and bad crops, the seventeenth century inherited the related evils of enclosures, evictions, unemployment, pauperism, and vagrancy. Behind these and other particular troubles was the general fact of accelerated change in the economic structure of society, both rural and urban. The corpuscular life of the Middle Ages was becoming the fortuitous collision of atoms that we know. There was still the medieval pattern of the small agricultural unit, the self-contained and stable manorial community with its unwritten but powerful law of 'custom'. In the towns the craft guilds were parallel units of corporate life, with authority and traditions which were economic, fraternal, and paternal. But both systems were declining, or at any rate changing, before the advance of capitalistic enterprise and large-scale production (in farming as well as in industry) with their division of labour and division between employer and employed. The result was economic confusion, depressions, much occupational and social disturbance, and widespread distress. Monopolies, which bulk so large in the period, affected everyone from the sovereign or government and actual or would-be monopolists and 'projectors' down to the great body of helpless workers and consumers; one achievement of the interregnum was the virtual abolition of that particular evil. Masses of people were increasingly dependent on the fluctuations of national and international trade. As usual, the poor grew poorer and the rich richer. Economic along with religious motives took emigrants to America. While some men, from Dekker to Winstanley, had a feeling for the poor, economic writers were more concerned with improving the methods of production, with the problems of big business, of a self-sufficient national economy and the balance of trade. If the first forty years of the century can be called relatively prosperous, the decade of the civil war almost ruined agriculture and business, and the decade of the Commonwealth, which brought a measure of recovery, ended amid cries of despair from London and the counties. In the administration of poor relief the Commonwealth, with all its efforts, fell below the years of Charles's personal rule. It was easier to punish multiplying vagrants than to cure unemployment, and harshness had a partly theoretical basis; medieval notions of charity for the unfortunate were more and more being replaced by an economic—and Puritan—view of idleness and poverty as criminal.

The long years of comparative peace under Elizabeth and James, and the dynamic effect of the bullion acquired from America and Spain, made possible the transformation of a country which had lived mainly at the subsistence level into a financial power. The formation of the great trading companies, the expansion of foreign commerce, not merely on the Continent but in the Far East, and the exploration and colonizing of America were both causes and results of the accumulation of capital. The development of woollen and other textile manufactures, and of mining, coal-mining in particular, required capital, credit, technological inventions, and a national and foreign market. During the sixteenth and seventeenth centuries prices rose much faster than rents and wages, and the royal exchequer and the mass of the population suffered alike. But there were vast profits for the capitalist. One obvious indication was the rapid spread of luxury. The Plugsons and Bounderbys might rejoice in progress and prosperity; many others saw greed for money, sinful usury, competitive commercialism, speculative gambling, and reckless extravagance poisoning good old ways. A modern theory has identified the growth of individualistic capitalism with Puritanism, with the illiberal, ascetic, and acquisitive devotion to business and thrift which merits and receives divine approbation. This theory, though congenial to the many who are inclined to believe anything ill of Puritans, has been considerably modified by more recent economic historians, and even the layman can discern large flaws in the equation. At any rate, what had been an agricultural country of self-sufficing local units was beginning to turn into the workshop of the world. While the nobility, gentry, and yeomen were, in their several ways, attached to the land, much of the new money was concentrated in the towns, above all in London. The capital, with somewhat less than 250,000 people in 1600 and somewhat more than 400,000 in 1660, was the one real city—'second to none beyond Seas, a noble Mart', said Robert Burton—and its public and private opulence impressed foreign visitors. But though at the beginning of the century London had almost a monopoly of business, the provincial towns, especially the seaports, were increasing in population and economic importance.

The rise of the commercial and industrial middle class is such a standard feature of every modern century that we may well hesitate to claim it for any one, yet it is in the late sixteenth and the early seventeenth century that we first encounter a solid array of merchants, manufacturers, entrepreneurs, bankers, shipowners, and tradesmen enjoying the prosperity and the consciousness of economic and political power which the war fully revealed—and which Henry Robinson philosophized. The definite emergence of a substantial *bourgeoisie* had of course the most varied social and literary consequences. Men of business bought estates and added new blood and new money, often without the old conception of duties, to the squirearchy; and it was difficult to avoid the stream of titles that flowed so insistently from the royal fountain of honour. On the other hand, the prejudice of the landed classes against commercial connexions relaxed under the most persuasive of arguments. Shares of stock and middle-class dowries were exciting if speculative lures. Younger sons might start better game in the City or abroad than on the paternal and perhaps mortgaged acres. The distinctions of degree had lost much of their rigidity, and economic class-distinctions had not yet hardened, so that there was, in scientific language, a good deal of osmosis. The heralds, if not the moralists, were disposed to see a gentleman in any well-to-do male. Literature is full of complaints about upstarts. All of these social changes, which had begun ages before and were quickened by the growth of industry and commerce, were still further quickened by the war and the mainly middle-class victory.

These changes are mirrored in drama and satire, treatise and sermon, petition and remonstrance, and yet pictures of change are less deeply registered in our memories than the milkmaid and franklin of the Overbury characters, the bovine content of Earle's plain country fellow, and the unchanged countryside of 'L'Allegro', the *Hesperides*, and *The Complete Angler*. The rural world was still so largely feudal that much depended on the character of the landlord and his wife. Many of the nobility and gentry were seduced by the attractions of London, and both James and Charles tried, in vain, to compel them to stay at home; yet many also continued to practise the beneficent doctrine of *noblesse oblige*, to dispense hospitality, charity, and educational and literary patronage. After the Restoration they are found, as before, administering local government and up-holding the *mores* of their communities. The evolution of the impersonal economic order, or disorder, did not extinguish the expression at least of the medieval sense of human and ethical considerations and of the principle of subordinating private gain to public good. Governmental paternalism worked in the old spirit in its constant struggles with the problems created by economic individualism. And if that individualism was partly Puritan, the Puritan principle of the 'calling', in alliance with the old and universal principle of 'degree', was a conservative force. The ambitious might seek to rise in the world and share class privileges, but only antinomian radicals thought of class war.

The universities and schools were not immune from these various kinds of disturbance. In some ways it was good for the country that the proportion of students and graduates should have been so high. The other side of the picture appears in Bacon's repeated objections to the increasing number of schools and the breeding of more scholars and clerics than 'Prefer-ments can take off', which means the breeding of seditious discontent and an inadequate supply of manual workers. Similar views were expressed in 1656 by the thoroughly practical Francis Osborn. Less tough-minded observers, like Robert Burton, lamented the economic plight and social humiliations of many teachers, tutors, and clergymen. Then, while alarms and controversies were frequent in the first four decades, the war brought university education almost to a standstill. Oxford, the king's head-quarters, combined the atmosphere of a court with that of a garrison. Much college plate went to the royal mint, and pious hands destroyed many relics of idolatry. During and after the war parliamentary visitations caused wholesale evictions of scholars, among them a number of our authors.

Further, the political, religious, economic, and social revolution was paralleled by the movement for educational reform, although in this sphere radical zeal did not get much beyond verbal expression, and educational practice followed its traditional course. The founding of schools went on more rapidly after 1600 than it had before. The standard-bearers of secondary education were of course the public and free schools inherited from earlier times, Winchester, Eton, St. Paul's, and the rest. Harrow, chartered in 1571, commenced its activity in 1608, and in 1609 Thomas Sutton was granted letters patent for the Charterhouse. In our period the British Isles possessed what was to be for a long time their full complement of universities: Oxford, Cambridge, St. Andrews, Glasgow, Aberdeen, Edinburgh, and Trinity College, Dublin. While there was much building and rebuilding, the one new college added to an old foundation was Wadham (1610). 'King James his Colledge in Chelsey' (1610), Matthew Sutcliffe's 'Spirituall Garrison', did not live long; and the college established at Durham (1657), in response to pressure from the north, died after a brief but lusty infancy, 'an orphan scarce bound up in its swaddling cloaths'. Since a growing portion of England lay across the sea, we may notice the founding of the Boston Latin School (1635) and of Harvard College (1636); most of Harvard's founders were Cambridge men, and of the early university emigrants to New England a high proportion had belonged to Emmanuel. A survey of the English educational scene should not omit the Inns of Court, which Ben Jonson saluted as 'the Noblest Nourceries of Humanity, and Liberty, in the Kingdome'. They not only fostered the law—and the drama—but provided a finishing school and club for courtiers and the heirs of country gentlemen. Finally, sons of the aristocracy and the upper middle class owed much to private tutors, such as Hobbes and Thomas Young.

The character of school life may be indicated by a summary of the routine at Westminster in the sixteen-twenties, as an alumnus described it. From a quarter-past five, when the boys were roused by a monitor's *Surgite!* for Latin prayers and ablutions, until supper at five, they were almost continuously occupied in repeating rules of Latin and Greek grammar, writing prose and verse in Latin or Greek, translating from one form or language into the other, and analysing the grammatical and rhetorical figures of classical texts. After supper a master might have senior boys in his rooms for the study of extra-curricular things like maps or, in the case of Lancelot Andrewes, for Greek and Hebrew. On Friday the week's lessons were reviewed. On Saturday declamations were held. On Sunday the King's Scholars construed the Greek Testament and wrote verses on the morning sermon. At all times, even on the playing-field, monitors took care that the boys spoke only Latin. The curriculum Milton proposed, which shocks the degenerate modern, becomes much less shocking when judged by contemporary standards of what constituted work, and also by contemporary faith in the efficacy of right methods. University students enjoyed more freedom, though less than they have nowadays; of course they were normally younger. At Cambridge, in Milton's time, the day began with chapel at five. Breakfast was followed by four hours or more of attendance at lectures and disputations, and an hour or two after twelve-o'clock dinner.

If such curricula look forbidding, there were compensations. University students at least had leisure for talk, reading, music, and the less innocent recreations which the 'Lady' of Christ's College hit out against. The same critic later denounced theological students' participation in the dramatic performances which were a traditional feature of academic life, especially on the occasion of royal visits. The herd of undergraduate loafers have generic representatives in Richard Brathwait's *Law of Drinking* and in John Earle's 'A young Gentleman of the University', and particular ones in Christopher Guise and his 'ingeniouse' fellow tipplers at Oxford. And we may remember

Randolph's appeal to a Cambridge landlord to rebuild the fallen Mitre at the students' expense—'We drank like Freshmen all before, But now wee'll drink like Doctors'. Then, as Guise said (and Brathwait amply indicated), *Post vinum Venus*. Dissipation at the universities was one article of faith on which Puritans and Chancellor Laud could agree. And in recalling some facts which temper our impression of educational rigour we should not forget one of supreme importance. Both colleges and schools possessed as masters and dons a remarkable number of personalities, intellectual or temperamental, men like Richard Mulcaster, Thomas Farnaby, John Hales, Sir Henry Savile, Sir Henry Wotton, John Earle, John Wilkins, and the Dr. Kettell whose eccentricities Aubrey recorded. Against Bacon's assertion that at the universities students learned nothing but to believe may be set such a tutor as Joseph Mede (possibly the 'old Damœtas' of 'Lycidas'), who was wont to greet his charges with '*Quid dubitas?* What Doubts have you met in your studies to-day?' Lancelot Andrewes, said Bishop Hacket, frequently took a hand in teaching, and 'never walk'd to Cheswick for his Recreation, without a brace of this young Fry; and in that way-faring Leisure, had a singular dexterity to fill those narrow Vessels with a Funnel'. A later Westminster figure had another kind of dexterity as well; Dr. Busby left his mark upon many distinguished minds and bodies, including Dryden's. And unusual talents might be found in provincial schools—Philemon Holland at Coventry and at Warwick John Owen, whose European fame as an epigrammatist would hardly be inferred from Jonson's description, 'a pure Pedantique Schoolmaster sweeping his living from the Posteriors of litle children'.

It is to two ardent and enlightened provincial schoolmasters that we owe the best accounts of the classical programme and methods. John Brinsley's *Ludus Literarius* (1612) and Charles Hoole's *New Discovery of the Old Art of Teaching School* (1660) are both built on the tradition of Renaissance humanism, the ideal of learned piety. Although Hoole had just translated, with a sympathetic preface, the famous *Orbis Sensualium Pictus* of Comenius, he was little of a Comenian in his major work, and the differences between him and Brinsley are mainly the result of advancing classical scholarship. Both men, like many contemporaries, prescribe Hebrew. The immediate object of secondary education was complete mastery of Latin as a spoken and written medium, and that of course involved close study of the literature. As for the universities, they had begun and continued, in the words of Anthony Wood, 'to noe other end but to propagate religion and good manners and supply the nation with persons cheifly professing the three famous faculties of Divinity, Law, and Phisick'. The traditional dominance of Aristotle and theology was reinforced by the Laudian statutes for Oxford. There had, to be sure, been internal changes, and the scholastic tradition had been modified by Tudor humanism, but the general pattern was still that of the medieval university. The prime purpose of the medieval university, the training of clerics, was still the prime purpose; and the founders of Harvard, while seeking to avoid the ecclesiasticism of Oxford and Cambridge, were moved by the fear of leaving 'an illiterate Ministery to the Churches, when our present Ministers shall lie in the Dust'. Rhetoric and logic were still a practical and professional rather than a vaguely cultural discipline. And the parliamentary committee in 1649 insisted, no less urgently than Laud, on the old rule that only Latin or Greek should be spoken at the universities. If the final test of an educational method is the quality of the minds and characters it produces, then this scholastic and humanistic programme, whatever its shortcomings, can hold its own with any before or since. At all times students were masticating tough food. If there was more concern with grammar and flagellation than with ideals of spontaneity and self-expression, the later careers of the many illustrious victims reveal few traces of cramped intelligence and originality. If accounts of classical teaching sometimes suggest aesthetic and humane deficiencies, the literature of the age amply proves that the classics were an abiding joy, stay, and stimulus to educated readers and writers. And their dynamic power was manifested on a larger stage, in the upholding of both liberty and order in politics and religion.

With this glance at educational orthodoxy we may turn to the current of modernism which accompanied the Puritan ascendancy. The greatest mathematician of the period, John Wallis (1616–1703), recalled his early days at Cambridge (1632–40) as a time when 'Mathematicks . . . were scarce looked upon as Academical Studies, but rather Mechanical'. In 1661 Isaac Barrow, Professor of Greek at Cambridge, complained in a humorous speech that he sat lonesome as an Attic owl cut off

from all companionship with other birds—and in 1663 he became the first Lucasian Professor of Mathematics. Probably
both men exaggerated their isolation, but they bear witness to
a real shift in academic interests. The humanistic tradition of
the Renaissance had not been invariably indifferent or opposed
to science, and in the seventeenth century the rising tide trickled,
if it did not quite flood, into the citadels of learning. Sir Francis
Kynaston, in his account (1636) of his new academy for young
noblemen and gentlemen before they went abroad, provided
for the sciences as well as for languages and courtly accomplishments, and for teaching 'by Demonstration and Experiment'.
Sir Balthazar Gerbier's academy (1649) also included 'experi-
mentall naturall philosophy'. Lord Herbert prescribed for a
gentleman, along with the usual subjects, the serious study of
geography, medicine, anatomy, and botany. Francis Osborn
(1593–1659), in his *Advice to a Son* (1656–8), dismissed most
academic learning as 'but Lumber and Formes' and extolled
mathematics and medicine. Recalling the slender science
possessed by the Oxford of his day, and its popular repute,
Osborn said that 'Not a few of our then foolish Gentry' refused
'to send their Sons thither, lest they should be smutted with the
Black Art'. But scientists had been multiplying, without much
official encouragement, in response to the demands of practical
technology. Gresham College, opened near the end of the sixteenth century, was a home of science, and in 1619 Oxford
received the stimulus of the Savilian chairs. In 1621, the year
in which the Sedleian lectureship in natural philosophy (Aristotle's) was inaugurated, Nathanael Carpenter published his
anti-Aristotelian *Philosophia Libera*. From 1626 at least, Oxford
medical students were expected to acquire some knowledge of
anatomy; the Tomlins lectureship in that subject (1624) may
have revealed a gap.

From about 1640 there was a vigorous campaign for the over-
hauling of both universities and schools. One significant event
was the visit (1641–2) of the great Czech educator, John Amos
Comenius (1592–1670). The Ramist movement had given a
general impulse to empirical thought and educational reform,
Bacon had shown the direction it should take, and the Puritan
middle class was eager for constructive action. Comenius had
devoted himself, partly as an educational reformer and partly
as a builder of international religious amity, to universal

elementary education, in languages as well as in science, on a simplified, realistic, graduated, encyclopaedic, and of course religious plan. His mission in England, the organizing under parliamentary auspices of a pansophic college, was frustrated by public disturbances, the Irish rising in particular, but the breadth of its appeal is indicated by the names of the patrons— Bishop Williams, who had been a friend of Bacon, Archbishop Ussher, Lord Brooke, Pym, Selden, and Sir Cheney Colepeper. Comenius's visit was engineered chiefly by a man who had for some years been propagating his ideas, that indefatigable progressive philanthropist, Samuel Hartlib (c. 1596/1600-62), the friend of Milton and of Boyle and other members of the 'Invisible College' of scientists which began to meet about 1645. Another admirer and sponsor of Comenius was John Durie (1596-1680), a friend of Hartlib and Milton and a zealous worker for the unification of the evangelical churches of Europe. It may be observed that, while Comenius's great aim was not the experimental research of the 'Invisible College', the two lines of thought and activity met in a Baconian preoccupation with 'things', in a return to nature, observation, and experience. Another bond of affinity was the moderate Puritanism of most members of the 'Invisible College' and the majority of Comenius's backers and disciples. Comenius, by the way, seems in 1641-2 to have been offered the headship of Harvard, through one of Hartlib's innumerable friends, the younger John Winthrop.

During the last third of our period Puritan discontent with conventional academic curricula and methods brought forth a flood of pamphlets. One obvious motive was religious antipathy to Anglican tradition and scholastic learning as contrasted with the simple gospel and pure spirituality. That note, familiar in Milton's prose, is heard also in the blasts of Roger Williams, Gerrard Winstanley, and William Dell, Master of Caius College, against a 'Hireling Ministry', a 'Carnal and Antichristian Clergie'. Another aim was practical and scientific education. Hartlib published works by Comenius in 1637 and following years. His friend Hezekiah Woodward issued some Baconian and Comenian tracts in 1640-1. Hartlib published several by Durie in 1642, 1649, and 1650(?). Milton's *Of Education* (1644) and William Petty's *Advice* (1648) were both addressed to Hartlib. Modernist reforms were urged by John

Hall (1649), George Snell (1649), and John Webster (1654). Noah Biggs (1651) and the quack George Starkey (1657) denounced the tyranny of Aristotle and Galen in medicine. Durie, Dell, and others, including James Harrington (1656) and Milton (1659–60), pleaded for popular education as a duty of the State. In partial harmony with Puritan strictures were the anti-academic utterances of Hobbes in *Leviathan* (1651) and of Hobbes's friend, Francis Osborn (1656–8). And we might end with a less polemical item, Cowley's *Proposition for the Advancement of Experimental Philosophy* (1661).

In the body of Puritan tracts Bacon's influence worked directly and also through Comenius, who was himself somewhat indebted to Bacon. In general, Bacon's separation of religion and knowledge, his hostility to the scholastic and humanistic tradition, his positive scientific, empirical, utilitarian, and humanitarian ideals, were translated into practical and pedagogical terms. The Puritan middle class, learned or unlearned, felt a natural impulse to replace the old, abstract, aristocratic, and 'useless' studies with the modern, concrete, popular, and useful. Their watchword was 'the public good', the union of progress and piety. Their utilitarianism might, as in Petty, concern itself only with 'Reall Learning' or, as in Durie, retain the classics, and Hebrew, with less formal grammar. John Hall, a minor poet and essayist, was not illiberal, and in Milton's letter, of course, the Baconian by no means submerged the Renaissance humanist. The hard-headed John Webster, in his *Academiarum Examen*, summed up the Baconian complaints of his time and class with philistine religiosity, and with a scientific and utilitarian zeal which did not forbid the glorifying of astrology and Robert Fludd—a joint in his armour not missed by Seth Ward and John Wilkins in their *Vindiciae Academiarum* (1654). The two Oxonians, though they could not but share some of Webster's views, easily showed that he and Hobbes had overlooked the recent progress of science at Oxford. There were other defences of the universities on traditional lines. Surveying the whole educational controversy, we can see prejudice and wisdom on both sides. In the popularizing of the Baconian gospel, shorn of its original grandiosity, is heard the gritty voice of Mr. Gradgrind and his numerous modern descendants; the human spirit is to be nourished in technical schools. On the other hand, whatever England and Europe owed, and still owe, to the scholastic and humanistic traditions (and most of this volume is a record of their fruits during two generations), they did not provide a satisfactory framework for popular and scientific education, and the claims of the middle class in a commercial and technological world had become insistent. The Puritan and progressive movement had some effect but, like many other advanced ideas of the time, this one was not fulfilled until the nineteenth century.

The reforming impulse was directed also to practical and domestic training for girls, though the private schools of our period, like Mrs. Salmon's at Hackney, which Katherine Fowler and her friend Mary Aubrey (John's cousin) attended, seem to have been devoted more to fashionable accomplishments than to household science. The Reformation had cut off one of the two careers open to gentlewomen, the monastic—Mary Ward's Catholic community (1638–42) and what a pamphlet of 1641 called the 'Arminian Nunnery' of Little Gidding were *sui generis*—and had left only the marital. One matrimonial lure, said Burton, was music, so that a gentlewoman learned that art before she could 'say her *Pater Noster*, or ten Commandements'. Yet the multitude of women who, like Mrs. Donne, 'had yearly a child'—and every other year a death—were more than decorative. In an age when households great and small were relatively self-contained, the wife and mother, like Mrs. Donne's sister, Lady Oglander, or Magdalen Herbert or Lady Mildmay, was perforce a busy and capable manager. In addition to supervising her servants, her family, and any girls who might be committed to her charge, a lady of the manor was likely to combine the functions of estate bailiff, Lady Bountiful, and Mrs. Grundy, and the 'skill in Chirurgery' of Burton's mother. The continual exercise of biological fortitude and of a wide range of practical talents left the average married woman, however intelligent, no great freedom or energy for intellectual culture; and normally she was married when young.

About feminine attainments on the literary and academic side it is difficult to generalize, because the means of education were so varied and uneven and because, from the nature of the case, evidence is somewhat meagre. The ideal woman of Erasmus, More, Ascham, and Sir Anthony Cooke had such representatives in the seventeenth century as Elizabeth Jane Weston (1582–1612), Elizabeth Lady Falkland (1585?–1639), Lady

Anne Clifford (1590–1676), who according to Donne coul
'Discourse of all things, from Predestination to Slea Silk', an
Lady Conway and Lady Pakington, who enjoyed the friendship
and admiration of many eminent divines. But in the feminine
as well as in other spheres there was a change from aristocrat
to middle-class standards, a change by no means peculiar
Puritans. For the common masculine view, which women held
also, of the limited furnishings desirable for the female mind we
have not merely Milton's attitude towards his daughters but,
in addition to books of conduct and courtesy, such documents
as Overbury's popular poem, *A Wife* (1614), and Sir Ralph
Verney's famous letter (1652) to his god-daughter who had
announced her intention of learning Hebrew, Greek, and Latin:
'Good sweet hart bee not soe covitous; beleeve me a Bible (with
the Common prayer) and a good plaine cattichisme in your
Mother Tongue being well read and practised, is well worth all
the rest and much more sutable to your sex.' If Sir Ralph's
precept, however golden, might fail to produce mates 'sutable'
for cavalier husbands, either of the literary or the hunting type
(though he did recommend French), a broader kind of cultivation was increasingly provided for the girls of well-to-do families.
Lucy Apsley, better known as Mrs. Hutchinson, when she was
about seven had eight tutors in languages, music, dancing,
writing, and needlework. And Sir Ralph's letter reminds us
that it would be wrong to infer too much from the epistolary
spelling of such women as Lady Brilliana Harley and Dorothy
Browne, since both sexes and all classes enjoyed a pleasant
orthographic freedom. In general, feminine reading was expected to be pious and elegant rather than classical and solid,
and one prominent part of it comprised books of devotion. On
another level we think of such charming devotees of French
romance as Dorothy Osborne and Mary North.

In the realm of letters the great patronesses, Lady Pembroke
and Lady Bedford, had no worthy successors, but the number of
female authors multiplied. Sidney's sister had done her writing
before 1600. His daughter, the Countess of Rutland, was a poet,
Jonson told Drummond, 'nothing inferior to her Father'.
Sidney's niece, Lady Wroth, published an Arcadian romance.
Lady Falkland wrote a juvenile play or two, translations, and
perhaps a history of Edward II. Elizabeth Countess of Kent
may have contributed indirectly to the production of literature

–at least to the nourishment of two men under her roof, Selden and Samuel Butler—through a popular cookery-book. We acknowledge, if we do not quite understand, the fame of the matchless Orinda, but we prefer to read the letters of Dorothy Osborne, who never dreamed that she would be the best-loved woman writer of the age. If it was natural for women to turn to *belles lettres*, some of them held their own with men in more popular writing. Elizabeth Grymeston's posthumous *Miscellanea* had four editions from 1604 to about 1618; for this pious manual of advice to her son the compiler might have used the title Dorothy Leigh gave to her far more popular book, *The Mother's Blessing* (1616). In 1641 the Amazonian Katherine Chidley published a vigorous justification of Independency in answer to the gangrenous Presbyterian, Thomas Edwards. And finally there appears the Duchess of Newcastle, voyaging through strange seas of Thought, alone.

During our period the lower layers of the reading public were enlarged, and political, religious, social, and cultural lines of cleavage grew sharper than they had been. A shifting of the centre of gravity had results parallel to those which became more obvious in the reign of Anne. The new gentry and the commercial class needed instruction and were prepared to receive what they could absorb of their Renaissance heritage, along with more modern and useful matter. Besides, many men, like Robert Burton, deplored the intellectual and moral decline of the aristocracy and, though such nostalgic lamentations were not new, there was always need to rekindle dying ideals of *gentillesse*. We have abundant evidence of these facts and sentiments in the continued production of books of conduct and courtesy (with such allies as the essay), and in the alterations of scope and tone which reflect a changing society. One large branch of the genre took the form of 'advice to a son', a form exemplified in the brief, Polonian, and popular counsels of Lord Burghley and Ralegh, posthumously printed in 1616 and 1632, and in Francis Osborn's pungently independent book (1656–8). Two interesting treatises have been made available in recent years. One, written partly in the Tower in 1609, was by Ralegh's scientific friend, Henry Percy, ninth Earl of Northumberland. The other (1651) was the work of a more gracious lover of religion and his family, the second Earl of Carbery, Jeremy Taylor's patron; it illustrates a stage in the transition

from learned humanism towards the gentlemanly ideal. And
we should add such cousins of the 'advice' family as the autobiographies of Lord Herbert and others.

Advice to a son was likely to have the more personal and
realistic character of a private testament than manuals addressed
to the public. The moral, civic, and cultural handbook had an
illustrious pedigree, from many ancients down through Italian,
Spanish, French, and English writers, and it filled the gap
between the universities and the world. While the hundreds of
courtesy books of the Renaissance represented some diversity of
aim and emphasis, the central tradition, the tradition most congenial to Englishmen, embodied the solid objects of Christian
humanism, the training of young men of the governing class for
active public life. The best-known work of our period, the
Complete Gentleman (1622, 1634) of Henry Peacham (1578?–
1642?), is often taken as the ideal picture of the cavalier, and it
evidently continued to please the gentry; but, apart from its
modern style, a large portion of the book might have been
written generations earlier. In fact Peacham owes something to
Elyot's *Governor* (1531), and even when he may not be borrowing his outlook is very similar; in his survey of poetry, moreover, he draws upon Scaliger and Puttenham. Peacham's
emphasis on religion and virtue united with good letters and
knightly exercises, his fusion of aristocratic and amateur with
utilitarian standards and motives, his constant appeal to classical precept and example, even the idealist's inevitable strain of
pessimism about the present, all this and more is thoroughly
in the spirit of Tudor humanism. But while the book takes its
place in the long line of treatises on the education of a Christian
prince, there are, of course, marks of a later age and of the
author's own varied interests. His hero is on the way to becoming not so much a statesman or courtier as a public-spirited
country gentleman with cultivated tastes and hobbies. Classical
literature, especially Latin (and neo-Latin), and the Bible form
the literary, ethical, and religious foundation; but Peacham
calls the lengthening roll of English authors—outside of the
drama—and rejoices in the lustre of his native tongue. He takes
account of science, and names Copernicus, though his outline
of cosmology is Ptolemaic. Whatever his particular debts, he
writes with first-hand authority on many subjects, teaching,
writing, music, travel, heraldry (he was a worthy contemporary

of 'Master Guillim'), and fishing. If not a first-hand authority on noble birth, he is as stout an upholder of degree as Elyot; but nobility, as usual, belongs to merit, not merely to rank. As the author of a book on drawing, Peacham can discourse expertly on art and antiquities, and he incorporates sketches, abridged from Vasari, of many Italian painters. Altogether Peacham shows himself an intelligent conservative, a cosmopolitan patriot, a man of zest and flavour. A generation later the hard-boiled Francis Osborn, rewriting Bacon's *Essays*, as it were, for the sceptical age of Hobbes and Butler, repudiated this humanistic ideal in the interest of practical experience, mundane utility and success, and Chesterfieldian *savoir-faire*.

Meanwhile another change in the character of the tradition had been recorded in a whole swarm of books like the *English Gentleman* and *English Gentlewoman* (1630–1) of the prolific Richard Brathwait (1588?–1673). This royalist country gentleman also slighted aristocratic culture, but in order to emphasize pietistic goodness and well-doing. Peacham, Brathwait, and Osborn show in varying degrees the adaptation or adulteration of Renaissance humanism for the benefit of a solidifying squirearchy and middle class. In many other works the stress is on the pious activities of every day, and in the poetic book of conduct there is the significant change from *The Fairy Queen* to *Paradise Lost*. On a lower plane we have—not to mention the cynical satire of Thomas Powell's *Tom of All Trades. Or the Plain Pathway to Preferment* (1631)—such a *vade mecum* for the virtuous apprentice as *An Essay of Drapery: or, the Complete Citizen* (1635) by William Scott, an early Rotarian, and books on common life and family relations which range from William Gouge's earnest and prolix *Of Domestical Duties* (1622) to the well-known works of Fuller and Jeremy Taylor. In such treatises there is more of unexciting good sense, of piety and prudence, sometimes in unctuous excess, than of magnanimous ardour and many-sided culture. But more or less Puritan pictures of the family as a religious commonwealth of busy bees, if they lack the aristocratic virtues, exalt some others—an ideal of marriage, for instance—not always found among their betters. And such families did not live merely on paper, they were the backbone of the nation—though the reader of literature may feel moved to ask, as a modern essayist asked in a parallel connexion, if the backbone should be exposed.

The broad extension of the reading public meant the final establishment of English as the medium not only for popular books, which of course had always been written in that tongue, but for those addressed to the educated. Latin was still the international language of scholarship and thought; without it English science and philosophy would have been much the poorer, and continental workers would have missed the writings of Gilbert and Harvey, Bacon and Hobbes. Bacon's attitude towards 'these modern languages' is familiar. The Latin epigrams and miscellaneous verse of Campion, John Owen, George Herbert, Crashaw, Milton, and many other men, and the works of John Barclay, are evidence of the vitality of the literary tradition. Sir Francis Kynaston tried to make Chaucer readable at home and abroad by translating part of *Troilus and Criseyde* (1635). The *Religio Medici* won its first continental repute in a Latin version, and foreign visitors who called on the aged Milton were seeking the annihilator of Salmasius rather than the English poet. To write in the mother tongue, as Milton said of his English pamphlets, was to forgo European fame and be 'content with these British Ilands as my world'. Yet the tide had long set in the modern direction. From the early sixteenth century even most scientific books had been done in English. Fynes Moryson wrote his big *Itinerary* in Latin but published his translation (1617). The stationers would not hear of a psychological treatise in Latin, so that Burton was compelled to prostitute his muse in English; we might say that she remained a *demi-vierge*. Browne intended to offer the *Pseudodoxia Epidemica* 'unto the Latine republique and equal Judges of Europe' but shifted, happily, to English.

Although the omnivorous Burton groaned over the multiplication of books, the figures look very small in modern eyes. During the period 1500–1630 the annual production of books of all kinds rose from about 45 to about 460, and in what may be loosely classified as 'literature' there was a corresponding advance from a dozen to about 115; of the literary items perhaps a fifth would be broadside ballads. By 1640 the total figure was approaching 600, and works of 'literature' numbered over 150. In the twenty troubled years which followed the number of books of course greatly increased. For various reasons statistics are somewhat uncertain; these are drawn from a tabular survey made in 1938 at the Huntington Library.

All books printed in England, except those issued by the presses of Oxford and Cambridge, were produced by the master-printers in London who belonged to the Stationers' Company, a modern guild called into being, in 1557, by a modern trade. The company controlled, or tried to control, every phase of the business, from the number of apprentices to the number of copies in an impression. Among insoluble problems were surreptitious and piratical printing and monopolies of profitable books. The problem most familiar to the modern reader was the enforcement of censorship. Under the governmental regulations of 1586, books legally published had to be approved by the Archbishop of Canterbury or the Bishop of London (that is, by their chaplains); the licensing of plays for performance and (from 1607) for press was handled by the Master of the Revels and his Deputy. Even in normal times the law was constantly ignored, and in 1640–1 the system broke down altogether before the flood of controversial pamphlets. The attempt of the Stationers' Company and Parliament to revive it in 1643 gave the occasion for Milton's grand defence of liberty.

In 1637 the number of printers in London was limited to twenty, but this, like many other regulations, proved ineffectual, and by 1650 there were about sixty. The centre of publishing and bookselling remained St. Paul's churchyard, though shops began to spread along Holborn and the Strand. From the first, English printers had rarely approached the standard of scholarship, taste, and technical execution set by the great continental printers, and if in the seventeenth century continental work declined, English printing hardly advanced. Most printers were men of business without much interest in literature and without very exacting ideals in mechanical matters. Among exceptions the most notable was Humphrey Moseley, who published many of the chief authors of the period and whose preface to Milton's volume of 1645, for instance, attests his literary zeal and discernment. English printers were still backward in the publishing of classical and especially Greek authors, apart from the common texts, but one illustrious achievement was Sir Henry Savile's edition of Chrysostom in eight folio volumes, which was done at Eton in 1610–13 by the king's printer.

We hear much more about publishing from the author's standpoint. Outside of such staple commodities as Latin grammars, almanacs, and devotional works, the market was usually small and uncertain, and the author suffered accordingly. Everyone knows of the £18 paid for *Paradise Lost* late in the century, and it sold pretty well. There was no royalty system, and rates of payment were low, so that few men could think of living by writing. Gervase Markham's repetitious efforts resulted in his capitulation (1617) and a promise to write no more books on the diseases of cattle. The thrifty Shakespeare gained a competence chiefly from the dividends of his theatrical stock, but the ordinary dramatist received only the price of his plays. A hand-to-mouth playwright like Dekker could supplement his earnings by producing pamphlets perhaps at £3 or £4; a lesser author might be paid £2. However much these sums are multiplied to approximate modern values (and figures on that point have little real meaning), it was not easy for the most industrious free-lance writer, impelled by what Samuel Sheppard called 'a mercenary dizzinesse', to keep far ahead of the catchpole. John Taylor the Water-Poet published his books on travel by subscription; once a host of his 'mongrel' patrons refused to pay and thereby occasioned another pamphlet. A not too reliable hope in the struggle for existence lay in the generosity of more exalted patrons, whose bounty might range from a present in return for a dedication to substantial annuities or such prolonged hospitality as Jonson and Donne received. Literature owed much to Prince Henry, the Earls of Pembroke and Southampton, the Countesses of Pembroke and Bedford, Fulke Greville, Sir Robert Cotton, Endymion Porter, and others, but the new wealth engendered few Maecenases, and the number of needy authors increased. Indeed, our period witnessed a gradual shift from the aristocratic tradition of private patronage towards modern ways. King Charles was the last English sovereign who was a real patron of letters. A large proportion of authors, to be sure, had other means of subsistence and wrote with no serious thought of profit; and of course the gentleman of quality seldom breathed the tainted air of Grub Street. Before we leave this general topic, one speculative consideration may be allowed. When we remember that the population of England was about five million and then look at the list of books produced in the years 1600–60, we may be inclined to transfer the quarrel over the ancients and moderns to the seventeenth and twentieth centuries. We may think of the two hundred million people nowadays whose language is English, and compile a list of the books written in the last sixty years which, according to the best light we have (a dim light, it is granted), seem destined to be alive three centuries hence, and we may wonder if the list would be much longer than the early one, if the best of it would equal the best work of the earlier seventeenth century in quantity or quality.

One explanation of the realistic strength of seventeenth-century literature is the fact that few of its makers were merely men of letters. From King James down to John Taylor most of them led active lives in the workaday world and shared the experience of non-literary men. A multitude of authors held posts in the public service or at court, or were members of Parliament. Many men from Jonson to Bunyan had experience in arms. The civil war and the Puritan ascendancy left hardly any writers undisturbed. Even that man of peace, Izaak Walton, found himself transmitting the royal 'George' after the battle of Worcester. Most literary men of course were on the king's side and, led chronologically by the timorous Hobbes, a number of them crossed over to the Continent, to become royalist agents, to travel, and to pick up French ideas and tastes. The wholesale expulsions and replacements in the universities involved literary losses and some scientific gains. Among non-academic churchmen who lost their preferments were Earle, Fuller, Herrick, and Bishop Hall. Fuller, Chillingworth, John Pearson, and Jeremy Taylor spent some time with royalist armies. William Dell and John Webster, whose educational tracts we have noticed, and John Saltmarsh and Richard Baxter were parliamentary chaplains. But apart from the dislocations and dangers of war, which are not unknown to modern authors, the literary life was subject to other mutations. Perhaps the quickest way of indicating that is to give a partial list of writers who suffered imprisonment, civil or political: Bacon, Sir Richard Baker, Benlowes, Bramhall, Chapman, Cleveland, Sir Robert Cotton, Cowley, Davenant, Lady Eleanor Davies (the widow of Sir John and a troublesome prophetess), Dekker, Denham, Sir Kenelm Digby, Donne, John Everard (King James's 'Dr. Never-out'), Lord Falkland, Mildmay Fane, Sir Richard Fanshawe, Sir Robert Filmer, George Fox, Godfrey Goodman, Thomas Habington, Joseph Hall, Henry Hammond, Sir John Harington, James Harrington, Sir John Hayward, Lord Herbert, John Hoskyns, James Howell, Jonson, Thomas Killigrew,

Sir Roger L'Estrange, John Lilburne (who holds with Fox the record for the number of arrests), Lovelace, Marston, Milton, Geffray Mynshul, Overbury, Richard Overton, Prynne, Ralegh, Selden, Jeremy Taylor, Urquhart, Waller, and Wither.

If on the one hand literature was close to life and action, on the other it was wedded to learning. One reminder of that fact is the medieval 'clerkly' predominance which clergymen still retained. 'All Confess there never was a more Learned Clergy', said the anti-clerical and immensely learned Selden, and their writings were by no means confined to the religious and scholarly but included much of the best poetry of the time. There were clerical mathematicians and scientists like William Barlowe, William Oughtred, John Wallis, Jeremiah Horrocks, and, to represent another area, Thomas Vaughan the alchemist. There was a whole galaxy of literary, scholarly, and scientific bishops—Andrewes, Bramhall, Corbet, Earle, Gauden, Godwin, Goodman, Hall, King, Morley, Pearson, Sanderson, Taylor, Ussher, Brian Walton, Ward, and Wilkins. The three most popular writers on astronomy were clerics, Nathanael Carpenter, John Swan, and John Wilkins. The chief geographers of several generations were relatively untravelled clergymen, Hakluyt and Purchas, George Abbot (later Archbishop of Canterbury), Carpenter again, and Heylyn.

These lists suggest other facts of broad significance. For one thing, relatively little prose can be classified as *belles lettres*. Nearly all the works which we now read as 'literature' were written as contributions to religion, ethics, politics, science, travel, and the other fields of inquiry and instruction. Prose fiction, which bulks so large in the modern output, was represented by a meagre bunch of minor authors; its place, to be sure, was partly filled by innumerable plays, social pamphlets, character-books, and 'Providence' books.

Another broad fact, another legacy from the Renaissance, is the extraordinary versatility of an extraordinary number of men, whatever qualifications we make concerning the amount of knowledge to be compassed at that time. The most obvious Renaissance types are Bacon and Ralegh. And if Ralegh belongs to heroic drama, Sir Kenelm Digby may be called the Ralegh of light opera. Henry Peacham, who pronounced Digby a 'noble and absolutely compleat Gentleman', was himself not only an author of varied parts but a painter, composer, mathematician, and heraldic expert. A somewhat startling footnote to Sir John Harington's undoubted versatility is his solicitation of the archbishopric of Dublin. Joseph Medè, one of many learned college dons, was master of half a dozen sciences and of Egyptian and Semitic lore. Selden's varied learning was proverbial. Among physicians who were not enslaved by what one of them termed 'the fruitless importunity of Uroscopy' were William Gilbert, Mark Ridley, Thomas Lodge, Philemon Holland, Campion, Matthew Gwinne, Henry Vaughan, Sir Thomas Browne, John Collop, Walter Charleton, Martin Lluelyn, Richard Whitlock, and William Chamberlayne. Browne's medical studies and practice did not hinder his exploration of religion, morals, and metaphysics, science and antiquities, and many languages, including Old English. Versatility was almost a condition, or a result, of membership in what became the Royal Society. John Wilkins we shall meet later. Sir William Petty, the founder of political economy, and Sir Christopher Wren live by virtue of the work they did after 1660, but before that date Petty was an Oxford professor of anatomy and the first scientific surveyor of the land of Ireland, and Wren was professor of astronomy at Gresham College and a figure in anatomical and other scientific investigations. What is of more immediate concern to us, there has never been a period in which there were so many good minor poets (in addition to the major ones), so many men of varied pursuits who could turn off good poems.

These few random names remind us that the inevitable but disastrous division of labour had not yet pulverized the learned world into a mass of mutually repellent particles. The various sciences were still 'natural philosophy' and, before 1660, anyone of scientific interests pursued several at once. Moreover, almost all authors, scientists like other men, had had a thorough classical training, and the classical tradition was a unifying and humanizing force. Although the old antagonism between the humanities and science deepened considerably, it was that fine humanist, Sir Henry Savile, the translator of Tacitus and editor of Chrysostom, who founded two important scientific chairs at Oxford; and Hobbes, the scientific materialist and foe of classical libertarianism, began and ended his career with translations from the Greek. Thanks to the humanistic ideal of universality, educated authors—and that means nearly all the

authors we read, except pot-poets and the like—could not
follow one road in hostile ignorance of other roads. It was
difficult for the seventeenth-century writer to be insular, since
his reading was likely to be more European than English. He
was an intellectual citizen of the world, the child of the whole
past as well as of the present. And whatever the rift between
science and the humanities, there was little or none between
scholarship and literature. It is not merely a coincidence that
the earlier seventeenth century is the Golden Age of both learning and literature—and of most other arts and sciences from
music to law. From one point of view it appears as a springtime
of ploughing and sowing, from another as the autumnal harvest
of the Renaissance and Reformation.

Both aspects receive illustration in every chapter of this book.
Here we may record some concrete facts in the cultural background. One landmark is the Bodleian Library, which was
opened, with more than 2,000 volumes, in 1602. Sir Thomas
Bodley (1545–1613), the quondam pupil of Calvin and Beza,
collected much massy divinity but would have no such 'riffe
raffe' as contemporary plays and pamphlets; however, new
books were soon brought in through the agreement with the
Stationers' Company (1610). Bodley's watchful care over every
detail is revealed in his statutes and in his letters to the first
Keeper, Thomas James; he was grievously disappointed by the
matrimonial desires of that able officer, who had seemed 'alienis-
simus from any suche cogitation'. Bodley was zealous both in
giving and in begging. Among the library's multitudinous
benefactors were Ralegh, Sir Francis Vere, William Herbert,
Earl of Pembroke, Sir Thomas Roe, Sir Kenelm Digby, Laud,
Robert Burton, Cromwell, and Selden. The catalogue printed
in 1605 was apparently the second general catalogue issued by
a European public library. Of nearly 6,000 volumes only 36
were in English and only 3 belonged to English literature—
Chaucer's works, Lydgate's *Fall of Princes*, and Puttenham's *Art
of English Poesy*. A religious zeal similar to Bodley's, on the
middle-class level, animated the Manchester clothier and
private banker, Humphrey Chetham (1580–1653), who, says
Fuller, had 'signally improved himself in piety and outward
prosperity'. His bequests included money for a public library
and for the purchase of 'godly English Bookes ... proper for the
edificacion of the common people', to be chained in the local

parish churches. The library at Lambeth and one opened in
1631 at Sion College were of course ecclesiastical. The fine
collection started by Archbishop Bancroft passed to Cambridge
in 1646–7. Archbishop Ussher's library became the property of
Trinity College, Dublin. The most famous of private libraries,
that of Sir Robert Cotton (1571–1631), was at once a symptom
and an instrument of the antiquarian and Anglo-Saxon studies
which were being carried on in all directions. And we must not
omit a man to whom scholars are grateful, the London book-
seller and friend of Milton, George Thomason, who assembled
and dated nearly 23,000 pamphlets, newspapers, and books
issued during the years 1640–61.

The zeal for collecting ranged far beyond books, from the
coins which Laud gave to Oxford (along with manuscripts and
money) to the heterogeneous curiosities of Sir Thomas Browne.
The virtuosity which Restoration wits were to satirize was not
of course altogether critical, and the collector's itch became
a kind of polite aristocratic disease. The many collectors of
rarities were overshadowed by the *magnifico* of the century,
Thomas Howard, second Earl of Arundel (1585–1646). His
friendship and patronage extended from Inigo Jones, Van
Dyck, and Rubens to the antiquarian set; Francis Junius was
his librarian. Personally and through agents Arundel gathered
artistic treasures such as England had not seen before. The
marbles, many of which were given to Oxford in 1667, were
described in Selden's *Marmora Arundelliana* (1628). A connoisseur and patron still more illustrious was King Charles, from
whose accession Horace Walpole dated the first era of real taste
in England. It is not unfitting that we always see him, comely
and calm, on the canvas of Van Dyck, the painter whom he was
able to domesticate in England. Two of the king's most notable
acquisitions were Mantegna's *Triumphs of Caesar* and Raphael's
cartoons.

These various libraries and antiquarian, scientific, and
artistic collections are evidence of cultural breadth and
maturity, of the desire and the means to preserve and study the
past. If in painting (apart from miniatures) and sculpture
original achievement lagged far behind that of the Continent,
the more necessary art of building was, like literature, in active
transition from the medieval to the neoclassical and displayed
a similar hybrid character. The new movement, which drew

its inspiration from Vitruvius and the Italians, had had an early Elizabethan pioneer in John Shute, and it reached its first culmination with the learned architect and stage-designer, Inigo Jones (1573–1652)—'Vitruvius Hoop' the estranged Jonson called him. Though Jones's work and influence, like Wren's, were far-reaching, we identify him with the Banqueting House at Whitehall (1619–22) as we identify his successor with St. Paul's. In domestic architecture Tudor peace and prosperity had inaugurated a change from the baronial castle or fortress to mansions like Theobalds and Holdenby House, and many less palatial manors, planned for spacious dignity and comfort. In his essay of 1625 Bacon has such stately homes in mind, and his ideas on building are a mixture of old and new; for example, he retains the quadrangular form with the great hall, although that semi-public centre of household life was shrinking into the modern vestibule. The altered conditions and purposes of domestic architecture were reinforced by Palladian taste— Jones's state room at Wilton is a famous specimen of interior design—and Elizabethan irregularities were somewhat curbed and co-ordinated without, as yet, the loss of picturesque vitality. With a changing style of life and building came a refinement and luxuriousness of furnishing which made Tudor ways seem primitive. These benefits were not entirely confined to the nobility and gentry; the old timbered houses of London citizens might contain an impressive array of plate and panelling. In literature neoclassical discipline did not readily impose itself upon a vigorous native tradition, but in architecture the native tradition had no exponents who could rival the masterful genius of Jones. The general evolution is illustrated in the Gothic towers and 'high embowed Roof' of 'L'Allegro' and 'Il Penseroso' and the neoclassical palace of Pandemonium which is akin to St. Peter's. Yet the exotic style was, before 1660, the ideal of the few like Wotton and Evelyn; most people preferred English variety to Palladian uniformity. The Englishman's conservatism was manifested likewise in regard to that most personal possession, his garden, and in the more or less unsophisticated manuals of Sir Hugh Platt, Gervase Markham, William Lawson, John Parkinson, Sir Thomas Hanmer, and others. Continental influence was beginning, but only beginning, to extend architectural symmetry and axial design into the formal garden. Sylvester's Eden, for one early example, is dressed 'In true-love-knots, tri-angles, lozenges', yet patterns did not extinguish simple delight in floral profusion, and natural prospects were more satisfying than artificial vistas.

This chapter has outdone the variety of an English garden, but it cannot end without a brief reminder of some intellectual and spiritual attitudes which are fundamental in most authors of the earlier seventeenth century and are alien to most modern minds. The working philosophy inherited by those authors was the Christian humanism which during the Middle Ages and the Renaissance had fused Christian faith and pagan reason into a stable framework of religious, ethical, political, economic, and cultural thought. That tradition, the main European tradition, comes from Plato and Cicero down through Erasmus and others to such men as Spenser, Hooker, Daniel, Chapman, and Jonson —and, though less obviously, Shakespeare. Its central religious and philosophic doctrine is order, order in the individual soul, in society, and in the cosmos. To mention two large elements of that doctrine which we meet everywhere in the seventeenth century, one is the concept of 'right reason', the eternal and harmonious law of God and nature written in every human mind and heart; the other is that of the great chain of being, the hierarchical order which descends from God through angels and men to plants and stones, which at once distinguishes and unites all levels of existence. This orthodox ideology was the foundation of most reflective and imaginative writing up to the Restoration. As we move from 1600 to 1660, however, that traditional orthodoxy is more and more undermined by changing economic and social conditions, by the causes and effects of civil war, by scientific thought, and by various individual rebels of the two kinds especially feared by Henry More, enthusiasts and atheists. At the same time the old religious and humanistic verities are reaffirmed, stoutly or subtly, by such diverse champions as the schoolmasters Brinsley and Hoole, the Cambridge Platonists and Bishop Bramhall, and Milton.

Modern readers and writers, who prefer the brandy of bold rebellion to the brown bread of orthodoxy, resent the endless classical commonplaces to which even Montaigne appeals, but they fail to understand that for the humanist such moral platitudes could be living realities. There is, after all, no unbridgeable gulf between the Polonian creed and the Apollonian. Especially to Englishmen who looked back upon continual war,

change, and confusion, peace, order, and conformity were
precious things. Shakespeare as well as lesser men clings to the
humanistic principles of order. He stands in the centre, not on
or beyond the margins of the normal and ethical. On the other
hand, he does not share that untroubled confidence in the
goodness and greatness of man which we are so often told was
fostered by the Renaissance. That confidence was one element
in Christian humanism, but it was kept in check by a religious
sense of man's littleness and sinful frailty. Shakespeare and the
rest know, as Pico had said, that man may sink to the brute or
rise to the divine. With a simultaneous double vision they see
man as both a god and a beast. That double vision is, to be sure,
the mark of the greatest writers of all ages, especially the
ancients; but the Christian religion intensified the paradox by
exalting man's sense of his divinity and deepening his sense of
bestiality. There is a vast difference between that humanistic
view and the unchecked optimism of the romantic who does not
believe in the fall of man, or the unchecked pessimism of the
realist who is a romantic on all fours. And both of these
extremes, the impulse to see either the god or the beast to the
exclusion of the other, are largely the result of the scientific
movement which in the early seventeenth century began to
inspire such grandiose dreams of the conquest of external nature
as the goal of mankind.

While this religious and ethical view of man and society was
a possession by no means confined to scholarly writers, a still
more universal possession was its macrocosmic complement.
Not merely the soul of individual man but the whole world
is the battle-ground between God and Satan. For nearly
all men, simple or sophisticated, the universe and human life
constitute a divine order with a divine purpose, not an ordered
or a haphazard mechanism. Shakespeare may have been withdrawn far enough from religion to see the natural man acting
in a natural world, yet he is not so far withdrawn, in time or in
temperament, that medieval religious concepts have lost their
imaginative and emotional power over him. And what is plain
enough in Shakespeare is much plainer in the host of writers
more directly in touch with, and intellectually more disposed to
hold fast to, the traditional creed. The modern reader who
would understand seventeenth-century literature must shake
off his habit of believing only what he sees and must try to

realize a world in which man's every thought and act are of
vital concern to God and to his own eternal state, a world interpenetrated by spiritual potencies.

> Millions of spiritual Creatures walk the Earth
> Unseen, both when we wake, and when we sleep.

Of course men could think and act, then as now, in entire
forgetfulness or disregard of divine omniscience and the judgement day, but very few would have denied the major premiss
itself. The consciousness of the immediate presence and active
intervention of God in all the affairs of life and the universe is
even stronger in the seventeenth century than in the sixteenth;
it was heightened by Puritanism and by various forms of more
or less mystical thought. This ultra-religious view of the world
entailed, to be sure, a belief not only in the harmless science of
astrology but in witchcraft, and the practical consequences of
that belief were horrible; yet one could hardly accept God and
His angels without accepting Satan and his. At any rate literature—above the level of such books as Thomas Beard's horrific
Theatre of God's Judgements—was infinitely the gainer from a
conception which was religious, imaginative, and poetical,which
enlarged the human stage far beyond that of merely mundane
and naturalistic motives.

We have remarked already upon the versatility of the seventeenth-century man, his free handling of the most diverse
kinds of knowledge and experience, and that quality has its
transcendental as well as its common significance. The religious
outlook which has just been emphasized was quite compatible
with the toughest realism, for the capacious and flexible mind
of the age could accommodate all the 'humours' which in other
ages are likely to exist in much more imperfect fullness and
harmony. Some peculiar and fundamental characteristics of
seventeenth-century literature arise from the simultaneous em-
bracing of different planes of knowledge and experience or the
habit of immediate and almost unconscious transition from one
to another. That is, in brief, the medieval allegorical instinct.
Ultimately it springs from the religious belief in the divine unity
of all things physical and spiritual, and it works through both
intuition and the formal logic in which all men were trained.
But in the seventeenth century that belief operates in an enlarged terrestrial and celestial world, against a developing

background of philosophic and scientific scepticism, so that the allegorical mode of thought and feeling now appears less instinctive and normal, more eccentric and 'quaint', than it did when its basic assumptions were universal and unquestioned, when the realm of knowledge had not been separated from the realm of faith. The result is 'metaphysical' poetry and prose. As one of the greatest metaphysical writers said, 'thus is man that great and true *Amphibium*, whose nature is disposed to live not onely like other creatures in divers elements, but in divided and distinguished worlds: for though there be but one to sense, there are two to reason; the one visible, the other invisible'.

II

POPULAR LITERATURE AND TRANSLATIONS

1. *Popular Literature*

THE vague term 'Popular' is used here rather than the still more vague 'Miscellaneous' to cover a body of prose and verse which does not belong in other chapters. By far the most popular of all books of course was the Bible, while much fiction in English as well as Latin was certainly not popular in the same sense. But a large proportion of the writing to be surveyed here did mirror the everyday world of the middle and lower classes, and a very large proportion of this popular literature, like the money its authors usually lacked, was concentrated in London.

The walled, mile-square city that Shakespeare knew was in most respects still medieval. Only a few of the buildings that he saw have survived (up to 1939), such as the Tower, the Inns of Court, and 8 of the 114 parish churches. Chaucer would have missed—not very keenly—the crowd of monks and friars, whose two dozen houses had been torn down or put to other uses, and he might have admired the coaches groaning through the narrow, dirty, dark, and ill-paved streets, but he would have been surprised by little except the city's growth in population. Between 1600 and 1660 the population apparently doubled, though the data on which modern estimates are based are uncertain. Throughout that time governmental and civic authorities, unable to cope with the aggravated problems of population and traffic, tried repeatedly and vainly to check the spread of building. There was nothing like city-planning until the great fire gave an opportunity, an opportunity also for replacing timber with brick. The distribution of the inhabitants was in general the reverse of that which, thanks to improved means of transport, prevails in modern cities. The court circle and the well-to-do were likely to live within the city or in Westminster, while the poor and disreputable multiplied in the districts outside the walls and outside of effective control, districts which were the recognized nurseries of vice, crime, and the plague. What is now London was a wide expanse of country containing the 'Twin-sister-Cities' (in Heywood's phrase) of London and Westminster, with suburbs sprawling in every direction, isolated villages, and the beginnings of the modern 'ribbon' development. Within as well as without the walls public services were lacking and conditions were fairly primitive, but at least no one was very far from green grass and trees and flowers, and Moorfields was early laid out as a park. The river not only united London with Westminster and with the theatres and beargardens of Southwark but was still the main thoroughfare of the city. However, the livelihood of the army of watermen was more and more threatened, as John Taylor urgently protested, by the popularity of 'hackney hell carts'. Another kind of rivalry is indicated in Henry Peacham's *Coach and Sedan* (1636).

While the variegated pageant of London life is displayed most fully by the army of playwrights, there are vivid supplements in the writings of the journalists. The best of these, Thomas Dekker (1572?–1632), was of course himself a playwright by vocation, but he found pamphleteering a useful sideline, especially when the theatres were closed. Like Dr. Johnson's luckless acquaintance, Dekker 'lived in London, and hung loose upon society', and being—to echo Nashe—subject to debt if not to deadly sin, he spent a long time (1613–19) in prison. That experience gave authenticity to his prison 'characters' in the fifth edition of *Lanthorn and Candlelight*, called *Villainies Discovered* (1616). In general, the vicissitudes of a precarious existence bore fruit in an extensive and peculiar knowledge of London and, without souring his zest for life, deepened his feeling for the submerged nine-tenths. He had the full-blooded toughness of his age and a tenderness of his own.

One large segment of Dekker's work comprises his pamphlets on the recurring plague, *The Wonderful Year* (1603), the roughly impressive poem *News from Graves-end* (1604), *The Meeting of Gallants* (1604), *A Rod for Runaways* (1625), *London Look Back* (1630), and *The Black Rod* (1630). Only the first and fourth were claimed by him, but the others seem to bear his hall-mark. To think of accounts of the plague is to think of Defoe, but while Defoe writes as a social historian, marshalling his facts and statistics into a sober analysis, Dekker is a reporter, humorist, and poet who, with a mixture of personal emotion and artistic detachment, seizes upon whatever has immediate human interest. Both writers accept the plague as a divine punishment for sin, but the later *bourgeois* moralist does not ring such poetic changes upon the eternal contrasts between health and disease, exuberant vitality and sudden extinction, the marriage-bed and the grave. Dekker is much closer to the medieval and pictorial tradition of the Dance of Death; *The Meeting of Gallants* carries us back, in its setting if not in its quality, to the *Pardoner's Tale*. Dekker's Jacobean imagination is kindled into macabre intensity by the lurid horrors of whole-sale mortality and corruption, yet even the plague does not check his flow of robust humour and racy slang and puns. In *The Wonderful Year*, after visions of the charnel house and crawling worms, come the *fabliau* of the cobbler's wife who made a death-bed confession of her affairs with neighbouring husbands and then recovered, and the anecdote, told with such dramatic verve, of the bold tinker who came sounding through a country town and, to his great profit, buried the Londoner's corpse which the villagers were afraid to approach. In a very different key Dekker speaks out against the people of London who have had the means and the will to escape from the trials of their fellow citizens and have carried the pestilence into the country.

The journalist and the poet appear, in varying proportions, almost everywhere in Dekker's prose. In *The Seven Deadly Sins of London* (1606) the pattern and the fervour of a medieval sermon permit an urban vignette of carts and coaches thundering, people jostling at every corner, hammers beating, tubs hooping, pots clinking, water-tankards running at tilt, porters sweating under burdens, merchants' men bearing bags of money, chapmen skipping out of one shop into another. . . . But the lover of the city from whose womb he received his being, from whose breasts his nourishment, brings no less spontaneity to such a biblical apostrophe as this:

O London, thou art great in glory, and envied for thy greatnes: thy Towers, thy Temples, and thy Pinnacles stand upon thy head like borders of fine gold, thy waters like frindges of silver hang at the hemmes of thy garments. Thou art the goodliest of thy neighbors, but the prowdest; the welthiest, but the most wanton. Thou hast all things in thee to make thee fairest, and all things in thee to make thee foulest; for thou art attir'de like a Bride, drawing all that looke upon thee, to be in love with thee, but there is much harlot in thine eyes. Thou sitst in thy Gates heated with Wines, and in thy Chambers with lust.

Such a passage may lessen our surprise at Dekker's producing a piece of devotional literature, *Four Birds of Noah's Ark*, an attractive distillation of sincere religious feeling, unspoiled innocence of soul, and instinctive sympathy with forgotten men like prisoners and miners. He rarely slips, as authors of prayers may, into unctuousness, and his language reflects without effort the rhythmical simplicity of the Bible and the liturgy.

In the same year, 1609, Dekker published his very different *Gull's Hornbook*. Dedekind's *Grobianus* (1549) had been translated as *The School of Slovenry* by one R. F. in 1605, and Dekker himself had rendered a good deal of it, but, 'not greatly liking the Subject, I altred the Shape, and of a Dutchman, fashioned a meere Englishman'. Although, as he says, his own book tastes strongly of Grobianism in the beginning, his ironical guide to etiquette owes little to the crude Latin poem. Dekker's gull is not a mere nasty boor but an ignorantly pretentious young man from the country who wants to cut a dash as a sophisticated man about town, and whose behaviour is inspired by the one motive of attracting attention to himself. He is at least a cousin of Master Stephen, though Dekker suffers a fool more gladly than Jonson. The London scene is sketched with satirical liveliness in the chapters on Paul's walk, ordinaries, a playhouse, a tavern, and the street. The account of the audience in a theatre, the most detailed and vivid we have, releases the emotions of a much-enduring dramatist. What is now the best known of Dekker's prose works was never reprinted until 1812, though it was revamped for the Restoration world by Samuel Vincent as *The Young Gallant's Academy* (1674).

A journalist on the alert for timely topics could not overlook the 'coney-catching' tribe whose felonious little plans Greene had so profitably exploited. *The Bellman of London* and *Lanthorn and Candlelight*, both of 1608, were and remain popular, for the literature of roguery is always fascinating, and Dekker, if he lacks his customary anecdotal gusto, seldom lacks the unexpected fancy and phrase. He was original, too, in his exposure of literary cozenage and in his sketches of prison life. But he probably had no very expert knowledge of the criminal underworld, and in borrowing, like his contemporaries, from Harman, Greene, and others, he gave a picture less true of Jacobean than of Elizabethan conditions. It is more important that these pamphlets on social cankers spring partly from a

serious impulse which runs through Dekker's hastiest concoc-
tions. A man who abhorred bear-baiting was not likely to be
unmoved by the poverty and suffering of his fellow creatures;
here certainly he had expert knowledge. Many of the ills of a
changing economy, which successive statutes had been trying to
cure, find illustration in Dekker's pages; even the gull has his
social significance. Dekker is very serious in *Work for Armourers*
(1609), which lives up to its motto, 'God helpe the Poore, The
rich can shift'. He denounces all kinds of greed and corruption,
but, though a townsman, he is especially vehement in regard to
enclosures and evictions, and he does not cherish sentimental
illusions about rural virtues. He found country life (in the
Bellman)

ful of care, and full of craft; full of labour, and yet full of penurie;
I saw the poore husbandman made a slave to the rich farmour; the
farmour racked by his landlord: I saw that covetousnesse made
deere yeares when she had fullest barnes; and to curse plentie for
being liberal of her blessings. I had heard of no sinne in the Cittie,
but I met it in the village; nor any Vice in the tradesman, which was
not in the ploughman.

Like Dickens, Dekker is a middle-class humanitarian, not a
radical economic theorist. He sees and hates the rapacious
Bounderbys and Merdles, the 'yea-and-by-nay Cheaters', land-
lords, courtiers, and lawyers, who suck the blood of others.
He is not unlike Dickens also in having no remedy, unless it is
in uprightness and benevolence, and no economic ideal except
security within the existing frame of things, whether the sweet
content and golden slumbers of the poor or the modest affluence
of jolly Simon Eyre and his busy little kingdom. To redress the
injustice of this world he can only call in the next, hell as well
as heaven.

Samuel Rowlands, whose conjectural dates are 1570–1628/30,
is, biographically, little more than a name, though he may be
identical with a cooper and churchwarden of East Smithfield
who lived from 1565 to 1627. At any rate he was a prolific
writer. His first and last and two middle works (1598, 1605,
1618, 1628) were religious and were doubtless inspired both by
current fashion and by the *bourgeois* ideals of virtue which un-
derlie his satires. In *A Terrible Battle between Time and Death*
(1606), a great traditional theme, very real in a plague-
stricken age, raised a hack-poet above his common level. A

fluent version of the old tale of Guy of Warwick (1608) re-mained, like the best comic pieces, a favourite for generations. But Rowlands's main body of work, which gives him his small niche as a painter of manners, is a great mass of satirical epigrams, characters, jests, and anecdotal skits, and a few titles are better than description—*The Letting of Humour's Blood in the Head Vein* (1600), '*Tis Merry when Gossips Meet* (1602), *Look to It, for I'll Stab Ye* (1604), *Humour's Looking Glass* (1605 or earlier), *Democritus* (1607; later *Doctor Merryman*), *Diogenes' Lanthorn* (1607), and a series of 'Knave' volumes (1600?–19/20). Among the later pieces are *The Melancholy Knight* (1615), a burlesque survey of a corrupt age by a man who is at once a Quixotic lover of medieval romance and a far from virtuous malcontent, and *The Bride* (1617), a pleasant defence of marriage. Though his writing is almost wholly in verse, Rowlands's talent is a prose talent, suited for the re-creation of a world of knaves, gulls, fools, and shrews. His topics and jests, vices and 'humours', however old, are given a contemporary London costume, rich in detail if not too rich in variety. If he has what Saintsbury would have called a diploma piece, it might be '*Tis Merry*, an alcoholic discussion of marriage by a widow, a wife, and a maid which is more amusing than Sir John Davies's courtly *Contention* of a few months later, and which is somewhere between the earthy prodigality of Skelton and the dramatic economy of the parallel scene incorporated by the translator in *The Bachelor's Banquet* (1603).

Although literary history generally associates 'popular litera-ture' with London, both logic and the Englishman's traditional attachment to the country warrant a wider view. It might strain logic to take account of such exotic, not to say occult, things as Topsell's *History of Four-footed Beasts* (1607) and *History of Serpents* (1608), but we may notice four writers who have at least one foot in the country, Markham, Breton, John Taylor, and Brathwait. The industrious hack, Gervase Mark-ham (1568?–1637), has perhaps only one toe in literature (by virtue of some miscellaneous writings), since he is identified with numerous manuals for horse-breeders, gardeners, house-wives, and other practical readers, manuals which grew, like popular ballads, by incremental repetition. Yet his useful books were reprinted unceasingly throughout the century and even later (witness Diana Vernon's horror at Frank Osbaldistone's ignorance); they tell or imply a great deal about rural life, and their author deserves mention if only for one enchanting title, *Country Contentments* (1615).

Nicholas Breton (1551?–c. 1623), a stepson of George Gascoigne, combined gentility with professional writing. His several dozen volumes of verse and prose were spread over forty-odd years and ranged from romantic fiction to religion and satire. His euphuistic fluency is sometimes vitalized by religious feeling, a love of nature, a quiet relish for life and character, and a sincere attachment to good old ways. These qualities, the qualities of an amiable essayist, may also soften the edge of his social observations. Breton followed up his successful satire in verse, *Pasquil's Madcap* (1600), with a rapid series in the same vein, but he could never snarl and his indictments of the age were quite general and innocuous. The prose tale, *Grimello's Fortunes* (1604), might have been a serious treatment of the problem of the educated and honest gentleman's finding employment, but Breton is content to apply a soothing salve to what Burton and others regarded as a dangerous sore. The *Merry Dialogue between the Taker and Mistaker* of 1603 (in 1635 called *A Mad World, my Masters*) is an anecdotal exposure of hypocritical selfishness and knavery, but the author is no Timon, and in his dedication to Florio he says: 'The Dialogue is not tedious, nor the matter so serious, but it may passe the musters of a merry humor.' Breton's fondness for the dialogue, by the way, illustrates the effect of that form in retarding the growth of the essay. In general we forget Breton's little sermons and toothless satire and enjoy the pictures of manners and such lively tales as that of the eel and the magpie in *Grimello's Fortunes*. In the realistic, critical, and cynical Jacobean age he irradiated the simple idealism of the age of Lyly—unlike his contemporary, Barnabe Rich (1542?–1617), who turned during these years to sour and angry social pamphlets. Breton is at his lyrical best in *Fantastics* (which was entered in the Stationers' Register and presumably published in 1604) and *The Court and Country* (1618), when he celebrates with loving detail the timeless world of Chaucer's franklin, *The Complete Angler*, and Hardy's Wessex.

A more robustious spirit inhabited the active body of John Taylor the Water-Poet (1578?–1653). The son of a Gloucester 'Chirurgian', he found work in London as one of the tribe of watermen, of whose rights he remained a loyal defender. In 1596–7 he went on the Cadiz and 'Islands' expeditions. In 1612 he published his first book, *The Sculler*, which carried tokens of friendship with Jonson, Breton, and Rowlands; one epigram started a feud with Coryate which Taylor followed up with relentless pugnacity. The first of a number of 'stunts' which made him a well-known character was his 'pennyles pilgrimage' to Edinburgh in 1618, an enterprise not altogether relished by Jonson. For pleasure and profit Taylor made two short visits to Germany and numerous trips, often by water, about England, and, in the absence of Sunday newspapers, printed pamphlets about them. Besides the gossip of travel, and due recording of hospitalities received from provincial knights and mayors, he called attention to the neglect of inland waterways. After many years of life in Southwark, in 1643 Taylor took refuge, like some greater authors, in Oxford. In 1640 he had opened fire, on behalf of King and Church, against Roundheads and 'Amsterdamnable opinions', and in 1645 he broke an old friendship by denouncing Wither as a 'Juggling Rebell'. Taylor's *Works* had been collected in a folio in 1630, and he produced an even greater number of tracts after that date. He may be said to have carried the prose of his admired Nashe into the age of Cromwell, but verse was his favourite medium. For his countless miscellaneous pieces any catch-penny subject would do. He wrote on religion, the plague, the oldest man in England (Thomas Parr of Shropshire), the death of King James, Bishop Andrewes, and other notables, on tobacco, sea-fights, beggars, jails, murder, clean linen, the history of English kings and English drinks. In general he is a *bourgeois* satirist, ready to assail anything from pride to prostitution. We may exclaim, in his own semi-Shakespearian phrase, 'Here's a sweet deale of scimble scamble stuffe', or, to borrow from his abuse of William Fennor,

> Thou art the Rump, the taile, or basest part
> Of Poetry, thou art the dung of Art.

And yet, though Taylor is a man of earth (if his sobriquet allows the term), his voluminous pages reflect a buoyant zest in their author as well as a panorama of the middle and lower levels of English society. He proclaims that he knows 'no forreigne speach', that he is 'an artlesse creature' with 'no learning but the booke of Nature', but he can be as mythological as other self-taught men of the age, and he even mentions Copernicus. He has read ancients and moderns in translation, from Homer and Ovid to Du Bartas and Montaigne, and he praises Philemon Holland. He knows Don Quixote and 'our English sir John Falstaff'. More than once he celebrates the great line of native poets from Chaucer to Shakespeare, Donne, and the rest, and we find him, in 1622, quoting Peter Quince's prologue. The general public might, as Jonson scornfully declared, have voted for 'the Water-rimers workes' in preference to Spenser's (or Ben's), but our picture of the age owes something to the 'home-spun medley of my mottley braines'. Robert Burton possessed fourteen of Taylor's tracts.

A rival to Taylor in slipshod productivity, on a more cultivated plane, was the country gentleman Richard Brathwait (1588?–1673). Though his courtesy-books retain some social interest, his acknowledged works have all been eclipsed by the pseudonymous *Barnabae Itinerarium*, of which two parts, in Latin, were printed about 1636 and the four parts, in parallel Latin and English, in 1638. The doggerel poem (like Hobbes's translation of Homer) lives chiefly in one quotation:

> Where I saw a Puritane-one,
> Hanging of his Cat on Monday,
> For killing of a Mouse on Sonday.

But there are many amusing bits (heightened in the Latin by a sonorous ironical gravity which is often lost in the English), for in his perambulation of provincial England the normally moralistic author becomes an irresponsible and jovial Bacchus, and every other public-house has a casual Ariadne. The jogging journal is better than any of Taylor's travelogues—and a world away from *Poly-Olbion*.

While the first half of our period yielded a large crop of popular tracts from many more or less well-known hackwriters, in the latter half pamphleteering naturally grew more serious and controversial, and much of it belongs to political and religious thought. But one sturdy veteran cannot be overlooked. Henry Peacham (1578?–1642?) is associated with an early book on art and with epigrams and emblems, above all with *The Complete Gentleman* (1622), but in his later years he produced semi-popular essays, some royalist tracts, and several lively pieces on London life. *Coach and Sedan* (1636) has already been mentioned. *The Worth of a Penny, or a Caution to Keep Money* (1641?) had seven more editions in the years 1664–1704. The civilized and serious Renaissance humanist was now old and poor, but he brought unimpaired good humour and vitality to his anecdotal survey of Lady Pecunia's everyday domain. Though he has plenty of classical tags (translated in 1664), he is addressing the middle-class reader, and his quiet colloquial manner represents a step towards the next age. Peacham tapped this vein again in *The Art of Living in London* (1642).

As in the Elizabethan age, the functions of the modern magazine of fiction and the tabloid newspaper were discharged by the broadside ballad. Shakespeare's picture of Autolycus and Earle's character of the pot-poet relieve the historian from a vain effort to describe a vast amount of heterogeneous material, though a lively and instructive chapter might be made of a mere list of titles. 'More solid things do not shew the Complexion of the times so well, as Ballads and Libels', said Selden, whose collection of ballads gave Pepys his start. On the whole ballads changed less in character from age to age than other forms of literature, but there was a steady widening of the gulf between balladist and poet which had developed in the later years of Elizabeth; and with the rapid rise of the newsbooks the proportion of political ballads rose too. Although, as the collections of Pepys and Anthony Wood indicate, the output continued, the Golden Age of the ballad may be said to have ended, like that of the drama, with the beginning of the civil war, or perhaps one should say with the death of the popular laureate (and tavern-keeper), Martin Parker (*c.* 1600–52). For many years, as contemporary allusions prove, Parker ruled as he thought fit the universal monarchy of ballad wit. 'For a peny', said Peacham in 1641, 'you may have all the Newes in England, of Murders, Flouds, Witches, Fires, Tempests, and what not, in one of Martin Parkers Ballads.' Parker could be sensational or didactic, but he was often at his best in humorous songs of wives, husbands, and hussies. And, along with his tuneful and topical genius for popular song, he had a strain of manly poetry in him. He celebrated the worthies of English legend, and one sound-hearted ballad, 'Sailors for my Money', after some sea-changes inspired Campbell's 'Ye Mariners of England'. About 1638 Parker's muse became outspokenly royalist and he was named in the Root and Branch Petition of December 1640 as one of the authors of 'lascivious, idle and unprofitable Books'. He and his friend John Taylor were attacked as 'Papisticall, Atheisticall Ballad makers'. Parker's great contribution to the Stuart and Jacobite cause was 'When the King Enjoys His Own Again' (1643), which Ritson pronounced 'the most famous and popular air ever heard of in this country'. The decline of the old ballad tradition was furthered by parliamentary hostility, and in 1647 Parker transferred his energies to journalism in prose. (The poet received a posthumous accolade when two of his ballads were quoted in *The Complete Angler*.) In spite of vigorous censorship many humble authors like Parker made the ballad a political force during the war and the interregnum. And a sort of trinitarian attachment to King Charles, Venus, and Bacchus was nourished also by the very popular verse of such sophisticated cavaliers as Cleveland, Sir John Mennes, and James Smith.

During the winter of 1620–1, when English interest in continental affairs was especially keen, the regular weekly 'coranto' of foreign news came into being, at Amsterdam. It was the quite natural child of the topical broadside, the occasional news-pamphlet, and the various kinds of official or unofficial dispatches and private letters such as Sir Dudley Carleton, the English ambassador, received from John Hales at Dort or John Chamberlain in London. From 1621 to 1641, with an interval of suppression in 1632–8, corantos confined to foreign news were issued in London; the pioneer publishers were Nathaniel Butter, Nicholas Bourne, and Thomas Archer. Near the end of 1641 the mounting public fever and the collapse of censorship brought the first reports of domestic politics. In the next fifteen years there were over 300 periodicals, of which a fourth appeared but once and only a tenth lasted for more than a year. The first royalist newsbook, issued from Oxford and London, was *Mercurius Aulicus* (1643–5). The three 'grand mercuries', also royalist, were *Mercurius Melancholicus* (1647–9), which was quickly taken over by Martin Parker and later employed John Taylor; *Mercurius Pragmaticus* (1647–50), in which Samuel Sheppard, Marchamont Needham, and probably John Cleveland were the chief figures; and *Mercurius Elencticus* (1647–9), with which the mercurial Sheppard was especially associated. It may perhaps be said—and on better authority than Cleveland's 'characters' of a diurnal-maker and a London diurnal—that the parliamentary newsbooks were on the whole less scurrilous and less clever than the royalist. The first opponent of the *Aulicus* was *Mercurius Britannicus* (1643–6); Needham, in his first parliamentary phase, was its editor in 1644–6. Abler opposition was furnished by the *Spy* (1644) of Durant Hotham, son of the defender of Hull and biographer of Boehme. We may mention also George Wither's *Mercurius Rusticus*, which achieved one number in October 1643, and the *London Post* (1644–5, 1646–7) of John Rushworth, a licenser of the press for a time, whose *Historical Collections* remain useful. The censorship exercised by Parliament and the Stationers' Company from 1643 onward was sometimes vigorous, sometimes ineffectual. After an ordinance of 1649 exterminating newsbooks, only a few official and semi-official journals were allowed; the best known of the former class, *Mercurius Politicus* (1650–60), was edited by Needham, once again a Commonwealth man, who in 1651 had Milton as his supervisor or associate. A new Act of 1653 centralized control of printing in the Council of State, but this too failed, and from 1655 Cromwell handled the problem with as much tolerant indifference as his followers permitted.

While that indispensable manual, the almanac, had no more literary claims than its modern descendants, there were, as there had been since Geoffrey of Monmouth's 'Prophecies of Merlin', great numbers of prognostications related in character to the political ballad and pamphlet. Whether based upon private revelation, astrology, or common sense, whether bona fide or propagandist, these prophecies could affect as well as indicate the climate of popular opinion. King Charles and Laud were disturbed by the ominous success of Lady Eleanor Davies (one of whose judges, after the sibyl's own anagrammatic fashion, turned 'Dame Eleanor Davies' into 'Never so mad a ladie'). In William Lilly's prognostications, 1645–60, the stars consistently favoured the parliamentary side. In quite innocuous ways, moreover, the prophetic habit left its mark upon literature. Breton's *Fantastics* was a 'perpetuall prognostication'. And the mock-prognostication, a type which carries us down to Swift and Partridge, ranged from the social satire of the fool's speech in *King Lear* to that of Dekker's *Raven's Almanac* (1609).

The general astrological colouring of literature and language is much more obvious. The science itself was constantly attacked by rationalists and satirists but, apart from the vagaries of ignorant credulity, it received a qualified adherence from eminent minds. Among active exponents were such early Copernicans as the learned almanac-makers, Edward Gresham and Thomas Bretnor. In any case we cannot feel superior, since astrologers flourish in modern cities. For various reasons there was much less scepticism about witchcraft. It is represented chiefly by Sir Robert Filmer and, most fittingly, by the 'atheist' Hobbes. As late as 1677, in *The Displaying of Supposed Witchcraft*, John Webster, the educational iconoclast (and believer in astrology), displayed, like the Elizabethan Reginald Scot, a limited and peripheral scepticism not directed against the central dogma of evil spirits. Among thorough believers flourishing after 1660 were Jeremy Taylor, Browne, Sir Matthew Hale, Meric Casaubon, Glanvill, More, Cudworth, Isaac Barrow, and Robert Boyle. We cannot go into the literature of witchcraft, much less the painful record of trials and executions, but three statements may be made: that King James's odious repute as a witch-hunter is undeserved; that, as James Howell (a believer) noticed, the civil war brought a recrudescence of witchcraft or prosecution; and that, as most of the names just cited indicate, there was no essential connexion between witch-hunting and Puritanism.

A public conscience which accepted as a matter of course the punishment of witches was shrilly divided on the 'art of whiffing' that Ralegh had helped to make fashionable. Tobacco gave birth to a whole controversial literature of its own and to countless allusions in the satirists, dramatists (with the exception of Shakespeare), and other writers. Some gentlemen, snorted King James in his *Counterblast to Tobacco* (1604), bestowed three or four hundred pounds a year 'upon this precious stinke'. The king used his pen to more effect in raising the duty enormously, but in vain. Barnabe Rich, whose persistent antipathy gave him a multiplying eye, declared in 1614 that London had upwards of 7,000 tobacco shops. Brathwait's *Smoking Age* (1617) contains an illustration of a shop—'the Randevous of spitting', in Earle's phrase—and its puffing gallants; Jonson's Dame Ursula charged the high price of threepence a pipeful, and for adulterated tobacco at that. While we might expect Josuah Sylvester to write *Tobacco Battered*, it seems odd, whatever we allow for some efforts to win royal favour, that popular authors like Rich, Breton, Dekker, Rowlands, and Taylor should cry out against 'Tobacco's stillified stink'. Among the well-known men who showed a recreational or medicinal interest in the subject were Sir John Beaumont, Bacon, Burton, Howell, whose encomium includes the savoury anecdote of King James in a pigsty, and the young William Temple, who stands with the enemy. And one must quote a late and poignant item from the diary of the Puritan divine, Henry Newcome: 'My base heart is but too much concerned with this tobacco.'

One lively legacy from the past was satire on women and marriage, and the best contribution, *The Bachelor's Banquet* (1603), was a rendering, perhaps by Robert Tofte (1561/2–1619/20), of the fifteenth-century satire, *Les Quinze Joies de Mariage*. The book was very popular in its century and the enraptured Swinburne took it, as he well might, for an original composition. With inspired ease and freedom the author turned the old text, which was good, into something better which was completely and racily English. On a much lower level was Joseph Swetnam's *Arraignment of Lewd, Idle, Froward, and Unconstant Women* (1615), which revived the everlasting *querelle des femmes*; much ink was shed in a prolonged battle. To mention one witness to feminine virtues, the humanistic tradition dignified Thomas Heywood's historical compilations about famous women (1624, 1640). Brathwait's bolster lecture, *Art Asleep, Husband?* (1640), is half jestbook and provides a transition to that very popular type of popular literature.

The material in jestbooks was of three principal kinds: detached jests, practical and verbal jokes ascribed to one hero, and comic short stories or *novelle*. Among the collections of detached jests, not to speak of older books that still flourished, were Robert Armin's *Fool upon Fool* of 1600 (enlarged in 1608 as *A Nest of Ninnies*), in which the jests were grouped around half a dozen characters; *Jests to Make You Merry* (1607), by Dekker and George Wilkins; and several compilations (1628–38) by John Taylor. Clever repartee might belong to the alehouse or the humanistic tradition or to both; and some jests and some subjects, such as women, the clergy, and national characteristics, are ageless, though they may change their costume. In the second or 'biographical' class, among the progeny of such crude ancestors as *Eulenspiegel* ('Howleglas') and some English works are *The Merry Conceited Jests of George Peele* (1607) and pieces of rural waggery or *diablerie* like *The Merry Devil of Edmonton* (1608) of Thomas Brewer, *The Pleasant History of Friar Rush* (1620), *Robin Goodfellow, His Mad Pranks and Merry Jests* (1628), and the excellent *Pinder of Wakefield* (1632). Some of these titles and dates only represent, as it were, one of the heroes' nine lives. The prime example of the third class is *Westward for Smelts*, a collection of *novelle* published in 1620 and possibly in 1603; one tale provides an analogue to the wager in *Cymbeline*. The comic *novella* and the biographical jestbook are fused in *Dobson's Dry Bobs* (1607), which, if its racy pictures of provincial and university life had a better basis than practical jokes, would hold a high place in the early history of the picaresque novel.

Some of these jestbooks, various social tracts, books of characters, and such things as *The Bachelor's Banquet* and Breton's *Post with a Mad Packet of Letters*, bring us to the threshold of the realistic middle-class novel. One effort to cross it was *Penny-Wise, Pound-Foolish* (1631), in which Dekker gave a happy ending to a tale of a dissolute Bristol merchant reclaimed by his devoted wife. But the realistic-romantic Deloney had no worthy successor. Nor did the promise of picaresque fiction bear fruit, though a fresh impulse was provided by James Mabbe, who translated in 1622 Mateo Alemán's *The Rogue* (which is cited in *The Religion of Protestants* !), *The Spanish Bawd* (1631), from De Rojas's old *Celestina*, and the *Exemplary Novels* (1640) of Cervantes. The dominant tradition was that of the chivalric, courtly, or pastoral romance, a pattern which combined all the intricate and fantastic loves and adventures that Greek, medieval, and Renaissance authors had evolved. Heliodorus (this in verse), Achilles Tatius, and Longus were translated afresh by William Lisle, Anthony Hodges, and George Thornley respectively, in 1631, 1638, and 1657. 'What Schole-boy,' exclaimed Joseph Hall in 1620, anticipating Macaulay, 'what apprentice knows not Heliodorus?' Caxton's version of Lefevre's courtly tale of Troy, revamped, had at least eight editions in the century and reached its so-called eighteenth in 1738. Foreign romances and those of Greene and Sidney—the *Arcadia* of course was much more than a romance—remained very popular and had many unoriginal imitators: Breton, Emanuel Ford, whose work survived into the eighteenth century, Gervase Markham, Lady Mary Wroth, Sidney's niece, and others. The old British and English heroes, and such newer recruits as Tom a Lincoln (1599–1607) and Tom Thumb (1621)—these last the offspring of Richard Johnson, author of the long-lived *Seven Champions of Christendom*—rubbed shoulders with Palmerin and his sons and Amadis de Gaule, who were naturalized by Anthony Munday between 1583 and 1618. For a symbol of the state of English fiction we might take the title of Brathwait's novel of 1640, *The Two Lancashire Lovers: or The Excellent History of Philocles and Doriclea*; in the tale itself an instinct for native realism is not quite submerged by romantic convention.

While the old romance was dying, or passing into the euthanasia of the chapbook, a new pattern was being woven into the complex web. The arrival of modern French romance is registered in the comments of readers like Dorothy Osborne, in the allusive preciosities of Katherine Philips and her circle, and, more concretely, in translations. In 1620 appeared the first part of the *Astrea* of 'the great and incomparable Urfé, . . . the Painter of the soul'; the work had been entered in 1611. Later comes a series which includes Gombauld's *Endimion* (1639), Gomberville's *Polexander* (1647), La Calprenède's *Cassandra* (1652) and *Cléopâtre* (*Hymen's Praeludia*, 1652–9), Georges and Madeleine de Scudéry's *Ibrahim* (1652), *Artamenes or the Grand Cyrus* (1653–5), and *Clelia* (1655–61), and, in 1657–8, the complete *Astrea* of D'Urfé—not to mention such signs of reaction as Sorel's *Extravagant Shepherd* (1653). At the head of English imitations may stand Sir Kenelm Digby's autobiographical romance written in 1628. In 1648–50 Dorothy Osborne's serious young lover wrote, though he did not print, adaptations from Rosset's *Histoires Tragiques*. But French romance bore its first famous fruit—apart from *Argenis*—in Roger Boyle's *Parthenissa* (1651–69), which is more often named than read and which disappointed even the omnivorous Dorothy. A minor specimen of another kind of fruit, which in the Restoration was to flourish along with pseudo-heroic idealism, was Walter Charleton's anti-Platonic, anti-Puritan, and of course partly Petronian piece, *The Ephesian Matron* (1653?).

French romance had owed something to the Scotsman John Barclay (1582–1621). Barclay's chief works in prose were *Euphormionis Satyricon* (1603–7), a Petronian mixture of episodic adventure, satire, and learned discourses; *Icon Animorum* (1614), a series of essays on national and temperamental types which Thomas May translated as *The Mirror of Minds* (1631); and the extraordinarily celebrated *Argenis* (1621), which was translated in 1625 and again in 1628 (Ben Jonson's version, entered in 1623, was one of Vulcan's victims). As a scholar and, by virtue of his continental birth and background, a man of the world, and as the son of a noted champion of monarchy, Barclay was well fitted to write a book which combined the attractions of a courtly romance with those of a political and didactic *roman à clef*. Owen Felltham expressed the sentiments of the European public, if not ours, when he declared that he read *Argenis* for pleasure and for its 'Wisdome, with Worth, and State-Philosophy'. Barclay's influence in England was shown in Samuel Gott's *Nova Solyma* (1648), Boyle's *Parthenissa*, Brathwait's *Panthalia* (1659), and Sir George Mackenzie's *Aretina* (1660).

The use of Latin and a degree of European fame link Barclay with Joseph Hall (1574–1656). In *Mundus Alter et Idem* (1605?), which was to draw Milton's gibes, Hall utilized the timeless device of the imaginary country that Renaissance exploration had reanimated. Among his many and various antecedents were Plato and Lucian, Marco Polo and 'Sir John Mandeville', Sir Thomas More, Rabelais, and Hakluyt. The picture of an Antarctic land of Cockaigne is a burlesque of credulous travellers and encyclopaedists and ideal commonwealths, and a general satire, in the words of Heylyn, on 'the Vices, Passions, Humours, and ill Affections' of mankind (and womankind); and, finally, the hero's travels form an allegory of the individual life. In Healey's translation, *The Discovery of a New World* (1609?), Hall's ironic restraint gives place to the lusty lingo of Nashe.

One last kind of writing, destined to be a notable phenomenon of the seventeenth and eighteenth centuries, dealt with the imaginary voyage which was not merely terrestrial. The Jules Verne or H. G. Wells who inaugurated the scientific romance was the historian and bishop, Francis Godwin (1562–1633); his *Man in the Moon* appeared in 1638, the year of John Wilkins's lunar treatise. The date of its composition is uncertain, but not its popularity; by 1768 it had gone through some twenty-five editions in four languages, and its range of influence embraced Cyrano de Bergerac. The moon had had earlier visitors, from

those of Lucian (whose *True History* and *Icaromenippus* were included in Hickes's translation of 1634) to Ariosto's Astolfo, but
it acquired a new face and a new actuality through Galileo and
Kepler. Godwin's Spanish hero, after many adventures, finds
himself on St. Helena; he is carried—here we have an idea
Bacon had touched—by a brigade of trained swans to the moon,
sojourns in that utopian climate and society, and returns to earth
in China. The scientific amateur is further revealed in discussions of such topics as the diurnal rotation of the earth and
magnetic force.

Bishop Godwin, however interesting, scarcely counts as a
novelist (though he has a strain of Defoe and, according to Lady
Brilliana Harley, of 'Donqueshot'), and fiction in our sense of
the word was only coming to birth in the seventeenth century.
Both elegant and popular tales were, to be sure, thumbed by
multitudes of readers, from noble ladies down to young John
Bunyan. But the Duchess of Newcastle could affirm in 1656
that she had 'never read a Romancy Book' through and had
scorned such 'foolish Amorosities, and desperate Follies'. And
if the Duchess was individual in this as in other things, there
is the solid negative evidence of William London. In his
Catalogue of the most Vendible Books (1657–8), London warned
gentlemen against sitting down idly with *Sir John Mandeville*
or *Bevis of Southampton*, and he gave romances, poems, and
plays four and a half pages, less than half the space accorded
'physick' or law and very little compared with the twenty-seven
pages of history and the seventy-five of divinity.

2. *Translations*

Translations may well be joined with popular literature, if we
allow the adjective an elastic meaning. From the beginning of
English history the translation of ancient and modern books had
been a main agent in the development of religious and secular
culture and of literary style. To mention only one kind of
writing, of the nearly 500 seventeenth-century books which can
be included in the literature of conduct and courtesy, over 100
were translated. The sixteenth century, with patriotic zeal
for the enrichment of the English mind and the English
language, had produced an immense and heterogeneous body of
translation from the classical and modern languages, but its
work had not all been on the level of North's *Plutarch*, and there

was constant need of more modern or more direct and accurate versions. There were, too, conspicuous gaps; Plato and Greek drama and Dante remained, and were long to remain, almost untouched. The whole *Decameron* first appeared in 1620, in a version of more decorum than fidelity. Machiavelli's two chief works, the *Discourses* and the *Prince*, were first printed in English, very belatedly, in 1636 and 1640, and Patericke's version of Gentillet (1602) might be called belated also, since Machiavelli had been a bogyman for generations. However, our sixty years produced more great and still living translations than any other period in English literary history, and for that very reason we must largely ignore a crowd of notable minor writers and salute a few giants.

By virtue of scholarship, bulk and variety of performance, and nobility of style Philemon Holland (1552–1637) stands at the head of the list as 'the Translator Generall in his Age', although he has, unfortunately, been less reprinted and read than his fellows. After nearly two decades of teaching in Coventry, Holland took a medical degree at Cambridge (1597) and began to practise, but in 1608 he resumed teaching, as a humble usher in the Coventry Free School. His weighty volumes, which drew a groan from Pope, made, as Fuller said, a competent library of historians for a country gentleman—Livy (1600), Pliny's *Natural History* (1601), Plutarch's *Morals* (1603), Suetonius (1606), Ammianus Marcellinus (1609), Camden's *Britannia* (1610), and Xenophon's *Cyropaedia* (1632). Along with the patriotic aims of an Englishman and a literary voyager Holland has a theory of his art, though only hints of it are given in his prefaces. What he calls his 'meane and popular stile' might be taken as a generic representative of the best early seventeenth-century writing. Holland's unusual learning and care chastened his prose without robbing it of colloquial energy, concrete amplitude, and metaphorical colour. His slight but frequent additions are made in the interest of complete and vivid clarity and emotional effect. And the whole tone of his work reflects his Elizabethan veneration for, and sense of contemporaneous intimacy with, the great men and events and the ethical wisdom of antiquity. Pliny's philosophy gave him some qualms, but these were satisfactorily quieted. In his life and in his work Holland was a fine example of the Christian humanist.

Modern literature, including neo-Latin, was not of course a

closed account and it yielded a growing harvest. In addition to
many able and attractive works, such as James Mabbe's, we
have the three supreme translations of John Florio, Thomas
Shelton, and Sir Thomas Urquhart (1611–60?). Shelton's *Don
Quixote* (1612–20) is by far the happiest version of the great book
which he so quickly made available (though popular appreciation did not come quickly); in robust ease, grace, and verve he
stands between the restrained Holland and the extravagant
Florio and Urquhart. This last, we might say, was born to
naturalize in England the exploits of Gargantua and Panta-
gruel, though his work (1653, 1693) had to be finished by
Motteux. The Scottish royalist had many adventures and
troubles, and a mind full of learned quirks and quiddities; one
notorious achievement was the tracing of his pedigree to Adam.
For most English readers Rabelais has taken the very form and
pressure of his eccentric, full-blooded translator, and doubtless
he would have smiled upon the joyous excess to which Urquhart, with the aid of Cotgrave's lustily Rabelaisian *Dictionary*
(1611), carried his verbal gymnastics. Since, however, we can
touch only one of this gallant triumvirate of translators, that
one must be Florio, partly because of his literary prominence in
his day and partly because of his more radical alteration of his
author.[1]

Florio's translation of Montaigne, which seems to have been
urged upon him by the Countess of Bedford, was entered in
1600 and apparently circulated in manuscript before it was
published in 1603. He has in full measure the common sins of
the Elizabethan translator, frequent inaccuracy and the habit
of rendering single words by two or three. He takes both an
Elizabethan and a pedagogical delight in words and com-
pounds, picturesque and dramatic metaphors and proverbs.

---

[1] John Florio (1553–1625/6) was born in London, the son of an Italian Protestant refugee, but his youth was spent abroad. He returned to England to become
a teacher of Italian and published his first lively text-book in 1578. About 1580 he
married Daniel's sister; he married again in 1617. In 1583 he began to work at the
French embassy and by 1594 he was in the 'paie and patronage' of the Earl of
Southampton. In 1604 he entered the service of Queen Anne. Florio had numerous feuds and friendships. Among his literary acquaintances, besides Daniel, were
Hakluyt, Giordano Bruno, Jonson, Breton, John Healey, and Matthew Gwinne,
who helped him with Montaigne's quotations. Another helper was Theodore
Diodati, the father of Milton's friend. Florio's importance in the propagation of
Italian culture and in the enrichment of the English vocabulary was signalized by
his *World of Words* (1598; much enlarged, 1611). He came to poverty and died of
the plague.

To adapt a phrase from the text, the 'volubility' of his 'loose-capring minde' ('la volubilité de nostre esprit detraqué') gives an embroidered exuberance and artifice to the informal simplicity of Montaigne. His expansions, rhetorical or explanatory, not only have a somewhat 'coarsening' effect but may embody personal convictions of the 'resolute' malcontent who in life rubbed many men the wrong way. Such a refracting medium, or re-creation, obviously will not serve the student of Montaigne. Yet Florio's translation surpasses all others, from Cotton's to those of our time, in energy, gusto, and native flavour. Like North and the rest, he passes easily from slang to poetry. At one pole we have 'certaine verball wilie-beguilies, whereat I shake mine eares: but I let them runne at hab or nab' ('certaines finesses verbales, dequoy je secoue les oreilles; mais je les laisse courir à l'avanture'). At the other pole we have a rendering, inspired in diction and rhythm, of Montaigne's fine phrase about the death of Socrates, 'à souffrir l'engourdisse-ment des riches allures de son esprit'—'to endure the benum-ming of his spirits richest pace'. Florio made the *Essais* a rich and racy English book, and the miracle appears all the greater when we remember that neither French nor English was his native tongue. Large claims have been made for Shakespeare's debt to Montaigne and to Florio, but the wide currency of moral commonplaces warrants some scepticism; Florio, by the way, seems to have borrowed from Shakespeare when he turned *un lievre* into 'a seelie dew-bedabled hare'.

All these men and many lesser ones are akin in their robust virtues and faults. Like their fellows of the theatre, they instinctively put ancients and moderns into contemporary English dress. If their authors in consequence lost something of their individual character, they had the infinite compensation of quickened vitality and relevance. For the translators were not dilettantes of leisure but Renaissance humanists with a mission. Then they illustrate, perhaps more clearly than original writers, the linguistic felicity of their age and the lessons that translation helped to teach. Modern English prose is in its first fresh maturity; youthful intoxication with words and ideas is just beginning to receive wholesome discipline (the discipline of Euphuism had not been altogether wholesome). From Caxton and Berners onward there is a frequent and marked contrast between the rhetorical extravagance of translators' prefaces, in which they are striving, on their own, for ornate dignity, and the degree of restraint imposed by their texts. But Elizabethan force and concreteness and figurative prodigality have not been subdued into elegant and abstract flatness. No rigorous canons of propriety have divided the language of prose from the idiom of the street on the one hand or from that of poetry on the other.

What has been said of translations in prose is largely true of those in the other medium, at least for the first third of the century. The qualities of Holland and Florio are fused and intensified in the greatest of poetic translators, George Chapman (1559?–1634).[1] Chapman's *Iliad* (completed in 1612?) and *Odyssey* (1614–15) are among the great heroic poems in the English tongue. Everyone knows of Keats's rapturous discovery, and almost everyone of Arnold's less rapturous verdict on Chapman's Elizabethan fantasticality. Arnold found the translator's diction and syntactical structure appropriate, and recognized his fresh vigour and, with qualifications, his rapidity, but dwelt chiefly on the figurative and intellectual sophistication of a nobly plain original. While Chapman's lack of simplicity and sobriety is obvious, Arnold missed the essential character and causes of his treatment of Homer. Modern scholarship, in partly shifting Chapman's intellectual roots from ancient to Renaissance sources, may have damaged his title to large original erudition (though even Jonson shares whatever kind of guilt is involved), yet it has only confirmed his standing as a Christian humanist who drew philosophic nourishment from Ficino and Erasmus as well as from Plutarch and Epictetus. And he was not a mere transmitter but an individual force. In poetry and drama he carried on a crusade for the humanistic tradition, its aristocratic learning and ethical wis-

[1] Chapman's life seems to have been largely spent in poverty, study, and writing, and much of it is wrapped in 'the shadow of night', to borrow the title of his first work (1594). The faith in nocturnal inspiration he there expressed, taken with Shakespeare's eighty-sixth sonnet and other items, have led some to argue for Chapman as 'the rival poet'. At any rate, as a friend of Marlowe, Matthew Roydon, and Harriot, Chapman was associated with Ralegh's circle. His dramatic career, which began about 1596, reached its height in the tragedies written around Bussy D'Ambois and Byron (1604?–10?). In 1605 Chapman got into trouble, along with Jonson and Marston, over *Eastward Ho*; his friendship for Jonson was to end in a bitter *Invective*. From 1604 to 1612 he was in the service of Prince Henry, whose death he had special cause to lament. His next patron, the Earl of Somerset, soon fell from power (his actual guilt in the Overbury case is uncertain), but Chapman remained sincerely and publicly loyal.

dom, the control of the rebellious passions by the reason and will, the ideal of Stoic strength and completeness. Approaching with religious and medieval fervour the supreme teacher (one who had suffered, moreover, from the 'soule-blind' Scaliger's elevation of Virgil!), Chapman could not but translate Homer into the spirit and language of the creed he held with such strenuous intensity. For him as for Sidney, Spenser, and the rest, the ancient heroes are moral *exempla*. In the noble dedication of the *Iliad* to Prince Henry and, more quotably, in the preface to the *Odyssey*, Chapman sums up his conception of the two epics which begin so significantly with the words μῆνιν and ἄνδρα:

In one, Predominant Perturbation; in the other, over-ruling Wise-dome: in one, the Bodies fervour and fashion of outward Fortitude, to all possible height of Heroicall Action; in the other, the Minds inward, constant, and unconquerd Empire; unbroken, unalterd, with any most insolent, and tyrannous infliction.

The heroical—and Stoical—phrasing and the exaltation of Odysseus show how thoroughly Chapman has made traditional ideas his own. Such a view leads to innumerable and at times large expansions of the text; and some ethical as well as much scholarly aid was furnished by the lexicon of Scapula and the commentary of Spondanus. From the quarrel between Agamemnon (who is subject to irrational passions) and Achilles (who is moved to just anger) to Odysseus's slaying of the wooers, Athene explicitly ministers to the human reason and will by infusing the divine knowledge of virtue. In the simple speech of Nausicaa to her maidens Chapman interpolates eight lines, suggested in part by Scapula, on the man who

is truly manly, wise, and staid;
In soule more rich; the more to sense decaid.

After Odysseus and his men have set foot on Circe's island, the hero's brief expression of despair becomes a homily on the limitations of human knowledge and the need of using one's best powers with trust in the wisdom of God. Thus Chapman is not content with Homer's objectivity but constantly incorporates ethical glosses in the text, a method which extends to the conscious modification of character.

Of course many small additions are metrical, explanatory, and rhetorical, yet even Chapman's figurative conceits may

represent something more than normal Elizabethan taste. He
carries over into 'our sacred Homer' his high and esoteric con-
ception of divine poetry and its essentially difficult symbolism.
He despises 'word-for-word traductions' and defends the ex-
pansiveness incurred in making a foreign author English.
(Jonson, whose hostile marginalia survive in his copy of the
Whole Works of Homer of 1616, may have been one of the critics.)
Chapman avowedly had Latin and French versions before him,
like other translators, and he made increasing if arbitrary use of
Scapula, but charges of inadequate Greek he disposed of in his
notes with his usual confidence in his unique understanding of
Homer. Although he did the last twelve books of the *Iliad* in
fifteen weeks, he was conscientious in revising or rewriting the
parts he had already published, and he tried to meet criticism
by making an effort towards greater fidelity, simplicity, and
smoothness. Many faults remained, and conceits were added,
yet Chapman could justly affirm: 'I have rendred all things of
importance, with answerable life and height to my Authour,
(though with some periphrasis, without which no man can
worthilie translate anie worthie Poet).' And later, when he had
translated the minor poems attributed to Homer and furled
'the proud full saile of his great verse' (if the phrase may be
used without implications), he could proclaim, in words of
more than common significance: 'The Worke that I was borne
to doe, is done.'

    In Augustan days Dryden and Pope did not share the 'in-
credible Pleasure and extreme Transport' which Chapman
aroused in 'the Earl of Mulgrave and Mr. Waller, two of the
best Judges of our Age', although in his own small ventures
Dryden sometimes followed Chapman when Chapman did not
follow Homer, as Pope (who followed Dryden and others in the
same way) pointed out. Chapman's revival came with the
romantic age, but even Coleridge did not better Pope's final
word on the 'daring fiery spirit that animates his translation,
which is something like what one might imagine Homer himself would have writ before he arrived at years of discretion'.
If Homer could return from Elysium to read all the English
renderings, he would surely find in Chapman his truest son,
a man who has fed on lions' marrow; he would rejoice in such
phrases as 'The sea had soakt his heart through', and he might
not disapprove of Chapman's moral emphasis. For, one may

repeat, it is not merely Chapman's poetical genius that gives his erratic versions what Swinburne called their 'indefatigable strength and inextinguishable fire', but the ethical and religious passion which inspires his conception of the 'Promethean facultie', of Homer, and of himself.

Of the lesser translators, some turned to such comparatively neglected classics as Lucan, Persius, Juvenal, and Martial, but the perennial favourites were still Virgil and Ovid. In Virginia George Sandys (1578–1644), treasurer of the company and brother of one of its chief backers, continued his Ovidian labours, with Drayton's friendly encouragement. The complete *Metamorphoses* appeared in 1626. Dryden relied rather too much on his boyish impressions in condemning 'the so-much-admired Sandys' for unpoetical literalness. We may say of his style and tone what can be said, *mutatis mutandis*, of most other translators of the period, that he is about halfway between the fresh colour and freedom of Golding and the conventional correctness of the Augustans. Metrically, Sandys is one of the notable early builders of the closed and balanced couplet. In a commentary, added in 1632, he summed up a venerable allegorical tradition which was soon to be driven underground by critical rationalism, but both the tradition and his book emerged in the romantic age to attract Leigh Hunt and Keats.

In the field of modern literature we encounter, in 1600, a work that no subsequent translator has rivalled, Edward Fairfax's version of the *Gerusalemme Liberata*. Even the *ottava rima* tends to run into distinct couplets. Dryden named Spenser and Fairfax as great masters in our language, and—the supreme tribute!—reported Waller's assertion 'that he derived the harmony of his numbers from *Godfrey of Bulloign*'. The work of the literary ambassador, Sir Richard Fanshawe (1608–66), is less familiar. In addition to graceful versions of Guarini's *Pastor Fido* (1647) and selections from Horace (1652), Fanshawe translated the fourth *Aeneid* (1647) in Spenserian stanzas and made it a warmly passionate poem. His pioneer rendering of the *Lusiad* (1655) displays his vagaries on a large scale but, like his other work, it displays also, as Sir Richard Burton said, the gallant energy of a gentleman, a scholar, and a soldier. From the half-Elizabethan cavalier we may turn to the chief of a group of more elegant translators, Thomas Stanley (1625–78), the historian of philosophy and editor of Aeschylus. Stanley (a pupil of Fairfax's son) wrote some original poems, but the bulk of his work (1647–51) consists of translations from Anacreon, Bion, Moschus, and other small ancients, and from many moderns like Johannes Secundus and Marino. The choice of such authors, and Stanley's 'smooth and genteel' manner, illustrate the changing motives of translators, the dwindling of humanistic and patriotic seriousness into the cultivation of a polite accomplishment.

Such changing motives only stimulated theorizing about the right method of translation. The next age might forget Chapman's protests against literalness but not those of Sir John Denham (1615–69). Denham applauded Fanshawe's rejection of the 'servile path', and in the preface to his Virgilian *Destruction of Troy* (written in 1636, revised and published in 1656) he urged sympathetic and truly poetical freedom. Although, as Dryden said, Denham advised more liberty than he took himself, he did much to mould the theory and practice of translation. Dryden's dislike of Chapman's eccentricity and of Sandys's fidelity we have seen. Jonson's literal rendering of Horace's *Ars Poetica* Dryden labelled metaphrase (and Swinburne violently damned). For an example of 'Paraphrase, or Translation with Latitude', Dryden named the version of the fourth *Aeneid* (1658) which Waller completed after it had been begun by Sidney Godolphin. These translations, moreover, had a significant effect upon prosody. The evolution of the closed couplet had already been forwarded by translators of the ancient elegiac distich like Marlowe and Heywood, by Drayton in his imitation of Ovid's *Heroides*, and by other translators such as Fairfax and Chapman in his *Odyssey*. In the work of Sandys, Jonson, Denham, Godolphin, and Waller we can follow the further development of the Augustan manner in both metre and diction.

The briefest catalogue of religious and philosophic translations illustrates the 'amphibian' character of the period. On the one hand we have Lodge's *Flowers of Lodowick of Granada* (1601), representing a Catholic writer very popular in England; the *Introduction to a Devout Life* (1613) of St. Francis of Sales; the *Boethius* (1609) of 'I. T.', probably a Jesuit, Michael Walpole; Healey's *City of God* (1610) and St. Augustine's *Confessions* by the Catholic Sir Tobie Matthew (1620) and the Protestant

William Watts (1631); five or six new or revised versions of the *Imitation of Christ*, the latest (1654) by John Worthington; Nicholas Ferrar's *Hundred and Ten Considerations* (1638), from Juan de Valdés; a rapid series (1645–62) of the works of Jacob Boehme, chiefly by John Sparrow and John Ellistone; the translations (1644–53) from 'Hermes Trismegistus' and Nicholas of Cusa, the *Theologia Germanica* and other mystical writings, by two popular and earnest preachers, John Everard and Giles Randall, who were obnoxious to both the Court of High Commission and Presbyterians; and, finally, *The Mount of Olives* and *Flores Solitudinis* (1652, 1654) by Henry Vaughan. These translations, and many more, are representative of the widespread European effort, in the face of institutional dogma, strife, and worldliness, to kindle a truly spiritual religion. On the other hand, in addition to Florio's *Montaigne* and Holland's *Pliny* and *Plutarch*, there are such signs of the naturalizing of Stoic or sceptical thought as Lennard's version of Charron's *De la Sagesse* (1607–12?), Healey's *Epictetus* (1610), Lodge's fine translation of Seneca's prose works (1614), Meric Casaubon's *Marcus Aurelius* (1634), the second and third English renderings of Lipsius's *De Constantia* (1653, 1654), and the first translations of Descartes (1649, 1650) and of Hobbes's Latin works (1651, 1656). Some of these names will come up again, but this section must be given mainly to 'the noblest monument of English prose', the great moulder of English literature and life, the Bible unofficially authorized by King James in 1611.

The project of a new translation was the one happy result of the Hampton Court Conference (1604), and the proposal, made by John Reynolds, President of Corpus Christi College, was the one Puritan idea which the king warmly endorsed and carried into effect. Nowadays we are accustomed to co-operation in scholarship and science, but we do not associate great literary work with committees. The Bible, however, was produced by an organization worthy of Salomon's House. The preliminary labour occupied several years. It was divided among nearly fifty translators, who worked in six groups; two met at Westminster and two at each of the universities. To the Westminster committees, whose most illustrious figure was Lancelot Andrewes, were allotted the section from Genesis to Kings and the Epistles of the New Testament. The Cambridge groups were given the section from Chronicles to the Song of

Solomon, and the Apocrypha. Edward Lively, Regius Pro-
fessor of Hebrew, died before the work really began; other
members were John Bois, Andrew Downes, Regius Professor of
Greek, and two eminent Puritans, Laurence Chaderton, Master
of Emmanuel College, and Samuel Ward, who in 1610 became
Master of Sidney Sussex College. The Oxford groups had
charge of the Old Testament from Isaiah to Malachi and of the
Gospels, Acts, and Revelation. Among the Oxonians were
John Reynolds, who died in 1607, Sir Henry Savile, Miles
Smith, and George Abbot, who became Archbishop of Canterbury in 1611. After the first drafts had been circulated for
mutual criticism, a central committee carried out a prolonged
revision; but we do not know how completely the machinery
operated, and there was some unevenness in the work of the
various groups. The translators did not tie themselves 'to an
uniformitie of phrasing, or to an identitie of words, as some
peradventure would wish', and as some modern scholars have
wished; such scruples, they thought, would 'savour more of
curiositie then wisedome' and rather 'breed scorne in the
Atheist, then bring profite to the godly Reader'. Miles Smith
and Thomas Bilson made the final revision and saw the folio
through the press, and to them are attributed the dedication,
preface, and chapter headings. In spite of all this careful
labour, the text was repeatedly revised during the next generation.

The new version was 'more exact' as well as more beautiful
because, though Tyndale and the Genevan group had been
conspicuously learned, the Jacobean translators had at hand
a richer store of oriental and classical scholarship (and fifty
years later Brian Walton's learned band produced the Polyglot
Bible). Then, like the secular translators, they were working at
a singularly propitious season in the history of the language and
of prose style; to appreciate that fact one has only to look into
modern revisions and translations. With a few exceptions, the
translators were not men of literary genius and do not belong to
literature by virtue of their original works. But they had, so
to speak, a collective ear and taste and, above all, they had
intense and reverent zeal. For the Bible is the grand proof in
English that in the greatest writing literary beauty is not a main
object but a by-product. Of course the translators, like their
predecessors, wished to render the book of books in a style

worthy of its Author and His purpose, but the fundamental fact for them and their readers was the infinite importance to every individual soul of God's revelation of the way of life and salvation. 'It is a fearefull thing to fall into the hands of the living God', says the preface, in the one passage which touches eloquence; 'but a blessed thing it is, and will bring us to everlasting blessednes in the end, when God speaketh unto us, to hearken; when he setteth his word before us, to reade it; when hee stretcheth out his hand and calleth, to answere, Here am I; here we are to doe thy will, O God.' Like earlier translators, these men were raised above themselves by the consciousness of their responsibility for making the divine word clear and persuasive to 'the very vulgar'.

Their aim was not to create a new translation 'but to make a good one better, or out of many good ones, one principal good one, not justly to be excepted against'. As a basic English text they took the official Bishops' Bible (1568; revised in 1572). They were to consult the versions of Tyndale and Coverdale; the Matthew Bible (1537), which had combined the work of the two pioneers; the Great Bible of 1539–40 (Coverdale's revision of the Matthew Bible), which Archbishop Parker and his co-adjutors had taken as the basis for the Bishops' Bible; and the Geneva Bible (1560). One special contribution which this last made to the Authorized Version, in addition to many miscellaneous changes, was the correcting of Hebrew names. The Geneva Bible, the first with roman type and verse divisions, had been, and for a generation or more after 1611 continued to be, the popular and the Puritan text, thanks to its size and price and the Puritan colour of its ecclesiastical terms and marginal notes. The Jacobean translators avowedly shunned invidious words associated with both the Puritan and the Catholic traditions. The Catholic version of the New Testament (1582), which had kept fairly close to the Protestant texts, was not prescribed (in fact some of its language was expressly censured), but traces of its learned diction indicate that it was read. The Catholic Old Testament (1609–10) came out too late to be used. And along with all these and foreign translations, and the original Hebrew and Greek, we must remember the language and rhythms of the traditional Vulgate.

The main texture of the Authorized Version was the English of Tyndale and Coverdale. Of the New Testament about nine-tenths remained in the words or the pattern of Tyndale, and he had translated parts of the Old Testament and set the style for the whole. In his fervent desire to 'stablysh the laye people' Tyndale had stressed Saxon simplicity, even to occasional bluntness, though he was capable of both tender feeling and grandeur. Coverdale the preacher inclined to make the rhythms more full and flowing. Thus Tyndale writes (Matthew xxv. 21):

Then his master sayde unto him: well good servaunt and faithfull. Thou hast bene faithfull in lytell, I will make the ruler over moche; entre in into thy masters joye.

The Great Bible brings us almost to the familiar version:

His lorde saide unto him: well thou good and faithfull servaunt. Thou hast bene faythfull over few thinges, I will make the ruler over many thinges: entre thou in to the joye of thy lorde.

On the whole the Jacobean revisers, while eclectic, may be said, like the Bishops, to have carried Coverdale's refinement and elevation of phrase and rhythm to its consummation without losing the plain strength of Tyndale. The partial classicizing of biblical diction had been going on steadily from the Great Bible through the Geneva and the Bishops' Bible, and of course the Catholic New Testament. For instance, from the Bishops' Bible the 1611 version retained, to the improvement of the rhythm if not of the sense, the word 'charity' in the thirteenth chapter of 1 Corinthians; it had been in the Wycliffe translation and was in the Rheims (the Vulgate word was *caritas*), but Tyndale and his successors had used 'love', which returned to the text in 1881.

A few parallels will suggest, however inadequately, both the nature of the changes made and the basic preservation of older readings. It is impossible to illustrate the various kinds and levels of writing represented in the Bible, but there is room for some phrases from the New Testament and one prose poem from the Old. Tyndale renders Matthew v. 13 thus: 'Ye are the salt of the erthe: but and yf the salt have lost hir saltnes, what can be salted ther with?' The Great Bible has: 'Ye are the salt of the erthe: But yf the salt have lost the saltnes, what shalbe seasoned therwith?' The Geneva version, which was followed in 1611, is this: 'Ye are the salte of the earth: but if the salte have lost his savour, wherewith shal it be salted?'

Tyndale's rendering of Matthew vi. 34 is typically plain: 'For the daye present hath ever ynough of his awne trouble.' The Great Bible approaches the familiar reading: 'Sufficient unto the daye, is the travayle therof.' The Geneva reverts toward Tyndale: 'The day hathe ynough with his owne grief.' The final form appears in the Bishops' Bible: 'Sufficient unto the day, is the evyl therof.' Tyndale's phrase in Luke xx. 17, 'The stone that the bylders refused', is kept in the Great Bible and the Geneva; the Bishops' text has 'disalowed', while the Rheims and the King James versions have 'rejected'. In Romans viii. 30, Tyndale and the Great Bible have 'appoynted before'; the Geneva, Bishops', Rheims, and 1611 texts use 'predestinate'. In 1 Corinthians ii. 10 the phrase of Tyndale and the Great Bible is 'the bottome of Goddes secretes'; the Geneva and the Bishops' Bibles, which were followed in 1611, change to the more literal, sonorous, and emotional expression, 'the deepe thinges of God'.

The reader may make his own inferences from such items, and also from these versions of one of the greatest of meditations on mortality. This is the Great Bible:

Remembre thy maker in thy youth, or ever the dayes of adversytie come, and or the yeares drawe nye, when thou shalt saye: I have not pleasure in them: before the sunne, the lyght, the moone and starres be darckened, and or the cloudes turne agayne after the rayne, when the kepers of the house shall tremble, and when the stronge men shal bowe them selves: when the myllers stande styll, because they be so few, and when the syght of the wyndowes shall waxe dymme: when the dores in the stretes shalbe shutt, and when the voyce of the myller shalbe layed downe: when men shall ryse up at the voyce of the byrde, and when all the daughters of musike shalbe brought lowe: when men shall feare in hye places, and be afrayed in the stretes: when the Almonde tree shall florysh and be laden with the greshoper, and when all lust shall passe (because when man goeth to hys longe home, and the mourners go aboute the stretes.) Or ever the sylver lace be taken a waye, and or the golden bande be broken: Or the pot be broken at the well, and the whele upon the cysterne: Then shall the dust be turned agayne unto earth from whence it came, and the sprete shal returne unto God, which gave it. All is but vanite (sayth the Preacher) all is but playne vanyte.

This is the Geneva version:

Remember now thy Creator in the daies of thy youth, whiles the evil daies come not, nor the yeres approche, wherein thou shalt say, I have no pleasure in them:

Whiles the sunne is not darke, nor the light, nor the moone, nor the starres, nor the cloudes returne after the raine:

When the kepers of the house shal tremble, and the strong men shal bowe them selves, and the grinders shal cease, because thei are fewe, and they waxe darke that loke out by the windowes:

And the dores shal be shut without by the base sounde of the grinding, and he shal rise up at the voice of the birde: and all the daughters of singing shalbe abased.

Also thei shalbe afraied of the hie thing, and feare shalbe in the way, and the almonde tre shal florish and the grashopper shalbe a burden, and concupiscence shalbe driven away: for man goeth to the house of his age, and the mourners go about in the strete.

Whiles the silver corde is not lengthened, nor the golden ewer broken, nor the pitcher broken at the well, nor the whele broken at the cisterne:

And dust returne to the earth as it was, and the spirit returne to God that gave it.

Vanitie of vanities, saith the Preacher, all is vanitie.

Many phrases carried over from the Geneva version into the Authorized did not appear in the Bishops' (1572 edition):

Remember thy maker the sooner in thy youth, or ever the dayes of adversitie comme, and or the yeeres drawe nye when thou shalt say, I have not pleasure in them.

Before the sunne, the lyght, the moone, and starres be darkened, and or the cloudes turne agayne after the rayne:

When the kepers of the house shal tremble, and when the strong menne shal bow them selves, when the milners stande styl because they be so few, and when the sight of the windowes shal waxe dimme:

When the doores in the streetes shalbe shut, and when the voyce of the mylner shalbe layde downe, when menne shal ryse up at the voyce of the bryde, and when al the daughters of musicke shalbe brought lowe:

When menne shal feare in hie places, and be afrayde in the streetes, when the Almonde tree shal floryshe, and be laden with the grashopper, and when al lust shal passe: because man goeth to his long home, and the mourners goe about the streetes:

Or ever the silver lace be taken away, and or the golden wel be broken: Or the pot be broken at the wel, and the wheele broken upon the cesterne.

Then shal the dust be turned agayne unto earth from whence it came, and the spirite shal returne unto God who gave it.

Al is but vanitie (sayth the preacher) al is but playne vanitie.

It will perhaps be more convenient than impertinent to add the version of 1611:

Remember now thy Creatour in the dayes of thy youth, while the evil daies come not, nor the yeeres drawe nigh, when thou shalt say, I have no pleasure in them:

While the Sunne, or the light, or the Moone, or the Starres bee not darkened, nor the cloudes returne after the raine:

In the day when the keepers of the house shall tremble, and the strong men shall bowe themselves, and the grinders cease, because they are fewe, and those that looke out of the windowes be darkened:

And the doores shal be shut in the streets, when the sound of the grinding is low, and he shall rise up at the voyce of the bird, and all the daughters of musicke shall be brought low.

Also when they shalbe afraid of that which is high, and feares shall bee in the way, and the Almond tree shall flourish, and the grashopper shall be a burden, and desire shall faile: because man goeth to his long home, and the mourners goe about the streets:

Or ever the silver corde be loosed, or the golden bowle be broken, or the pitcher be broken at the fountaine, or the wheele broken at the cisterne.

Then shall the dust returne to the earth as it was: and the spirit shall returne unto God who gave it.

Vanitie of vanities (saith the preacher) all is vanitie.

Unlike their secular contemporaries, the translators of the Bible erred at times on the side of literalness; Selden, while he pronounced it the best translation in the world, anticipated some future complaints in saying that the Bible was translated rather into English words than into English phrase. Another and more especially modern complaint is that the vocabulary of relatively central words is small in comparison, say, with that of Shakespeare. Then, since the Authorized Version was not in the main a new thing, its language was already somewhat archaic in 1611, and with the lapse of 300 years the significance of many words has altered or grown dim. Finally, when we recall that the first ancient manuscript of the Greek Testament arrived in England in 1628, we realize that the deep but limited learning of the translators, and the century-long effort after clarity and dignity, could not suffice to prevent mistakes and obscurities; and even these have become hallowed, if not intelligible, through immemorial association. But whatever the shortcomings of the old version, it may be doubted if modern accuracy has led more souls to heaven. The history of the

English Bible has been parallel to that of its great ally, the classics; critical scholarship rose as the spiritual and moral fire of the Middle Ages and the Renaissance died down. Like translations from the classics, the Bible became a Tudor and Stuart book, and in being so thoroughly assimilated to the English genius it inevitably lost—again like classical literature —a good deal of its original character and the individual qualities of its various authors; in other words, it was alive. From the opposite standpoint the effect of the Bible upon English writing has sometimes been deplored because, it is said, its spiritual ardours and florid oriental imagery have from the beginning heightened an imaginative, emotional, and pictorial exuberance always in need of restraint. No doubt the Bible has appealed to the non-rational and 'poetical' elements in the English temper, yet it could be made English, as it could be made German, because it was universal; and its concreteness both of spiritual idea and of expression happened to be especially close to the age of Shakespeare. As for exotic and emotional excess, one might point to men from Bunyan to Lincoln whose saturation in the Bible fostered the beauty of simple strength. But to attempt here a formal discussion of the religious and literary influence of the Bible, as of the book itself, would be a predestinate absurdity—*Si monumentum requiris, circumspice.* The all-embracing power of the Bible was of course at its height in the seventeenth century, but that power lasted well through the nineteenth (about the twentieth one hesitates to generalize), and one testimony to the way in which the Bible—and the *Book of Common Prayer*—have interpenetrated English life is the magical language and rhythm of rustic speech in Hardy's novels. In the sixteenth and seventeenth centuries the Bible was, moreover, a radical and revolutionary book; for leftist writers it and the classics had to do in the absence of Marx.

From the Bible we descend for a moment to a chain of foothills, or an ant-hill, which cannot be altogether ignored. Unquenchable zeal went into the effort to provide a national psalter for congregational and domestic singing which would be more satisfactory than that of Sternhold and Hopkins; and the first book printed in the American colonies was the Bay Psalm Book of 1640. The widespread impulse to paraphrase the psalms, which had touched poets like Marot, Wyatt, Surrey, and Buchanan, was greatly stimulated by the growth of

Puritanism and the influx of Protestant refugees. The psalm-singing weaver was not loved by Falstaff and Sir Toby Belch. In the first half of the seventeenth century there was an over-whelming flood of metrical versions of the complete psalter or of selected psalms. In the long list we find such various men as Bacon, Carew, Denham, Joseph Hall, George Herbert, King James (with Sir William Alexander), Henry King, Milton, Sir Edwin Sandys, and especially George Wither and George Sandys. In all this activity, public and private and religious and literary motives might be mixed; Wither objected to the rhetorical trimming of 'easy and Passionate Psalmes'. Of this mass of writing it can only be said that all service ranks the same with God—and with the modern reader.

Milton's earliest attempts at psalmody revealed the influence of a religious translator whose work his own epic was destined to supplant. Josuah Sylvester (1563-1618) is only on the edge of our period, since his translation of Du Bartas had begun to appear in 1590-2 (and his minor writings done after 1600 do not invite comment), but the first collected edition of the *Divine Weeks and Works* was published in 1605, and in the seventeenth-century landscape it stands as a kind of Albert Memorial of encyclopaedic fundamentalism.[1] *La Semaine, ou Création du Monde* (1578) is the largest and, after *Paradise Lost*, probably the best-known relic of the great body of hexaemeral literature of the Middle Ages and Renaissance. In a long but unfinished sequel (1584 ff.) Du Bartas essayed to carry on the history of mankind. The poetical leviathan may be said to have had its ultimate descendants in the numerous sub-literary books of the nineteenth century which provided for an edifying 'Sunday at Home'. The amplified story of the Creation and the youth of the world hit exactly the taste of the mass of people who had more interest in the material than in poetry. Yet the Huguenot poet, a disciple of the Pléiade, captured sophisticated taste as well, and the roll of his French and foreign

[1] At Southampton Sylvester learned French under Hadrian à Saravia (who later had some part in the compiling of the King James Bible), and passed early 'From Arts, to Marts (and Miseries among)'. By 1591 he could subscribe himself 'Marchant-adventurer'. At some time he appears to have been a steward to the Essex family. About 1606 he became a groom of the chamber to Prince Henry; on the Prince's death he published an elegiac volume, *Lachrymae Lachrymarum* (1612). Sylvester was then appointed secretary to the Merchant Adventurers and removed to Middelburg, where he died in 1618, 'having had', according to Henry Peacham, 'very little or no reward at all, either for his paines or Dedication'.

admirers was commensurate with the bulk of his poem. In England there were Sidney, Spenser, Florio, and countless other writers, including King James, a personal and literary friend of Du Bartas. The energetic and grandiose poem was full of picturesque description and narrative, geography and popular science (much of it from Pliny), sound moralizing, and ardently optimistic pietism. The Christian Lucretius rhapsodized about the beneficent harmony of God's creation and, with all the appearance of learned scientific modernity, took a firmly traditional and reassuring stand on the problems of cosmology. His conception of the divine nature and function of poetry sustained him and contributed greatly to the exaltation of the Christian and Platonic Muse. Although many men made partial translations, and many had read or could read the French, it was Sylvester who established Du Bartas for half a century or more as an English classic. While generally faithful to the letter and the spirit of the poem, Sylvester made it more vigorously Protestant. His work became a quarry for poets but, since almost any idea in it may be assumed, *ipso facto*, to be a commonplace, we may be on our guard about the specific indebtedness of Donne, Milton, and lesser authors. Probably one main reason for the poem's eventual eclipse was what had been a main reason for its prestige, the religious medievalism of its scientific substance. Intellectuals did not remain content along the shore with sails of Faith to coast, 'Their Star the Bible; Steer-man th'Holy-Ghost'.

Another reason is indicated in Dryden's famous verdict on the 'abominable fustian' which had rapt him into an ecstasy in his uncritical youth. But Dryden was unwittingly biting the hand that had fed him. Sylvester, both through his own popularity and through his great influence on the poets of the main line, from Drayton and Browne onward, had an enormous effect upon the language of poetry. While his inventive boldness, good or bad, went beyond his original and fostered the taste for what Florio calls 'high-swelling and heaven-disimbowelling words', it was he if anyone who started the process which was to culminate, though not to end, in Pope's *Iliad*, namely, the creating of 'poetic diction'. The ultimate and immediate source of the common devices—Latin idioms and syntax, participial adjectives, generalized descriptive phrases, the use of Latin derivatives in their literal sense, and the like—was of course the Roman poets. And it was Sandys who in his *Ovid*, seeking literalness and compression more than ornament, purged, refined, and canalized the variegated effects of Sylvester. Thus the translators are the clearest index not only of the development of neoclassical versification but of the development of neoclassical poetic diction—which includes the standardizing of much simple English too. Sylvester uses the plainest words like 'fishes' (even 'slippery Fishes') and 'sheep', but the idea of man's sovereignty suggests 'the scaly Nation' and a pretty shepherdess may well drive her 'bleating happiness'. (We may be less sure of William Browne's 'fleecy traine' and 'bleating charge', though Browne can be concrete also.) Sandys likewise has plenty of homely diction but, in harmony with a metaphorical idea, the sea may become 'the wavy Monarchie' or 'that liquid Plain'. Milton in *Comus* uses the Spenserian 'finny drove' because he wants us to see fins moving in the moonlight. Benlowes, among his many echoes of Milton, takes over the phrase because it fits into a compressed catalogue, 'The wing'd, hoof'd, finnie Droves'. Conventional censures of such poetic diction, based on the merely stilted and 'elegant' use of it in late and bad writers (or in early bad writers like Sir William Alexander) are as idle as wholesale condemnations of metaphysical poetry because of its decadent excesses. Indeed, these methods of compression, the generalizing or humanizing references to creatures and things, the literal use of such words as 'obvious', 'error', 'horrid', and the like, these devices might have, originally, the kind of neat precision and surprise achieved by metaphysical wit.

III

THE SUCCESSORS OF SPENSER: SONG-BOOKS AND MISCELLANIES

I

THE first half of this chapter embraces both disciples and congeners of Spenser and some other conservative poets who are not sealed of any particular tribe. Since modern devotees of Donne have seldom grasped the breadth and depth of Spenser himself, they may not be inclined to recognize the claims of generally voluminous inheritors of a divided legacy. Indeed, our first group of poetic friends, of which Drayton came to be the acknowledged head, seem to constitute, in their patriotic and popular principles, a nucleus of conscious or half-conscious opposition to the matter and manner of the intellectuals of their day. But if these poets, and Drummond and Daniel and Greville, were somewhat old-fashioned in their own time, their best work outlives the whirligigs of taste.

Michael Drayton (1563–1631) was not merely the chief heir of Spenser but a younger contemporary of original force who was moulded by the same age and who, without ceasing to grow, remained a stout-hearted Elizabethan. He was born in War-wickshire of yeoman stock and spent many years in the ser-vice of Thomas Goodere and of his brother Sir Henry, whose daughter Anne, later Lady Rainsford, was the 'Idea' of the sonnets and the object of Drayton's continued devotion. (Sir Henry was the uncle and father-in-law of Donne's Sir Henry.) Drayton's life was divided between the country and London. His biography is largely the record of his writings (of the two dozen plays in which he collaborated all but one are lost), and of his relations with patrons, the Gooderes, the Countess of Bedford, Sir Walter Aston, and Edward, fourth Earl of Dor-set. Among his literary acquaintances or friends were Jonson (after a fashion), Shakespeare (who was said to have had the fatally 'merry meeting' with Drayton and Jonson), Chapman, John Stow, Camden, Selden, Izaak Walton, Wither, Davies of Hereford, and especially Alexander, Drummond, 'the two Beaumounts' (Sir John and Francis), Browne, George Sandys, and Henry Reynolds. In the survey of English poets in Drayton's epistle to Reynolds (1627), 'Grave morrall Spencer' is pre-eminent, but six lines of the poem are the finest distillation of Marlowe's 'brave translunary' genius ever written; and poetic autobiography has no more winning picture than that of Drayton's boyish appeal to his tutor to make him a poet. In an age when, said Francis Meres in Falstaffian language, 'there is nothing but rogery in villanous man', Drayton stood out as an example of 'vertuous disposition, honest conversation, and wel governed cariage'.

Like Shakespeare, he was always a man of Warwickshire and of England, not one of a sophisticated London coterie. Native endowment, an ideal of 'noble Poesie', and a devoted craftsmanship which led to both persevering revision and happy experiment, these combined to produce a large body of verse of distinctive flavour and of frequent and varied beauty; many inferior poets have been more readily credited with genius. Drayton was bitterly disappointed by his failure to win James's patronage and, though he had an eye to current fashions and enjoyed great popularity during his lifetime, he came more and more to feel, like some fellow Spenserians, that modern barbarism was deaf to heroic numbers, that 'the worlds coldnesse', as he said in 1619, 'had nipt our flowery Tempe'. We think of Drayton's flavour and beauty as Elizabethan, but actually of course nearly all of his work that we read was Jacobean and Caroline. And in the main it stands as a sweet and wholesome and (to use his own favourite epithet) 'brave' antidote to Jacobean melancholy—or to the common dogma about it. The chief satirical exceptions are *The Owl* (1604) and 'The Moon-Calf' (1627), in which Drayton's anger against public and private corruption fuses the spirit of *Mother Hubberd's Tale* with that of other and older things; and the puzzling 'Shepherd's Sirena' of 1627. Partly satirical, too, was 'The Man in the Moon' (1606), the unfortunate recast of the freshly pastoral and Platonic *Endymion and Phoebe* of 1595. Du Bartas (that is, Sylvester), who had had a finger or two in those mythological poems, may be debited with Drayton's biblical tales, though even these contain some pastoral attractions, and they confirm the abundant evidence of his sober piety.

In the new sonnets of 1602 (eighteen), 1605 (seven), and 1619 (ten), as in some amatory odes of 1619, Drayton carried on the anti-romantic, ironic, and colloquial strain which had shown itself in 1599. In the famous 'Since ther's no helpe, Come let us kisse and part' (1619), manly dignity achieves dramatic tension and dramatic plainness of speech, of a kind nearer to Wyatt than to Donne, and if drama is a little blurred by the abstract personifications that follow, these enlarge our sense of the high power of love, and of the trembling balance, so as to make the final couplet an inevitable surprise.

Drayton was much more prolific as a lover of his country than as the lover of 'Idea', and for us, if not for his own age, the historian is less inviting than the pastoral poet. The most successful of all his works was *England's Heroical Epistles* (1597–9), in which the Ovidian distich had a marked effect in shaping closed and often antithetical couplets. One of Drayton's later biographical and historical narratives, the *Legend of Great Cromwell* (1607), proclaimed its ancestry by finding a place in the last edition of the *Mirror for Magistrates* (1610), although the poet was here turning from the conventions of the tragical complaint to present, not John Foxe's Protestant hero, but a doubtful, and timely, 'Example of a new Mans fortune'. The relatively epical *Mortimeriados* (1596) he rewrote as *The Barons' Wars* (1603). Since he would not wish, as he said of Daniel, 'To be too much Historian in verse', he was not too rigorous in pruning descriptive luxuriance, but, with recent anxieties about civil dissension in mind, he did essay a more historical and epical technique and tone, and changed from rhyme royal to the *ottava rima* of Daniel's *Civil Wars* for the sake of 'Majestie, Perfection, and Solidity'. In 1627 came his most completely epic tale, 'The Battle of Agincourt', which may have been inspired by preparations for the relief of Rochelle. Though vivid, it has never competed with the early ode.

In the group of odes—twelve in 1606 and eight more, chiefly amatory, in 1619—Drayton was indebted to Horace, Skelton, Ronsard, and the Anacreontic tradition, and he was aware of Pindar, Soowthern's poor adaptations of Ronsard, and more popular things, but he was thoroughly English in his virtual creation of what had been a loosely lyrical genre. The two great odes, 'To the Virginian Voyage' and the 'Ballad of Agincourt', both of 1606 and revised of course, were based on Hakluyt and Holinshed, and in

> Holding one stately height,
> In so brave measure,

the poet was giving an Elizabethan version of the heroic songs
of 'Th'old British Bards, upon their Harpes'. His simple, buoyant patriotic fervour, which becomes epic in the mere proper
names of 'Agincourt', is as far from Marvell's 'Bermudas' and
'Horatian Ode' as 'To his Coy Love' is from 'To his Coy Mistress'.

The *Fairy Queen*, the *Principal Navigations*, and Camden's
Britannia (Drayton's chief guide) have a not unworthy companion in

*Poly-Olbion. Or a Chorographical Description of Tracts, Rivers, Mountains,
Forests, and other Parts of this Renowned Isle of Great Britain, with Inter-
mixture of the most Remarkable Stories, Antiquities, Wonders, Rarities,
Pleasures, and Commodities of the same.*

In this vast heroic and panoramic poem the national and local
patriot, the scholar, and the pastoral writer had full scope.
As for the metaphysical poet all experience is one, so for the
sturdy extravert all things British make up a rich and variegated
whole—sheep, birds, country games, saints, and heroes from
Brute and Arthur to Essex and Ralegh. The best translation
of the title is simply 'Merry England'. But the great work,
which had been planned before 1600, found in 1612 and 1622
a public which was outgrowing chorography and lusty river-
nymphs. In his prefaces Drayton defended his 'true native
Muse' against chamber-poets and public lethargy, and in
commending the second part his friends Browne and Wither
saluted the happy pen which in unheroic times upheld Elizabethan virtue. In the nineteenth and twentieth centuries at
least, *Poly-Olbion* has not 'met with barbarous Ignorance, and
base Detraction'.

Drayton had commenced pastoral writing with *The Shepherd's Garland* (1593), which contained the partly Chaucerian
ballad of Dowsabell, and in the revised eclogues of 1606
'Rowland' was still the pupil of 'learned Colin', 'the prime
Pastoralist of England'. In the thirteenth song of *Poly-Olbion*
he had turned from the sottish world to glorify a hermitage, and
if his pastorals became poetry of escape, no escapist was ever
more healthy. 'The Shepherd's Sirena' appeared in 1627 but
seems to have chronological and other affinities with Browne's
Shepherd's Pipe (1614) and Wither's *Shepherd's Hunting* (1615),
and to reflect troubles and resentments; these do not, however,

cloud the central lyric in praise of Sirena, 'Neare to the Silver Trent'. 'The Quest of Cynthia' (1627), like 'The Description of Elysium' (1630), celebrates the sequestered paradise of poetry and nature, in Drayton's own way, through a loving catalogue of observed beauties, but with a simplicity chastened and condensed. The supernatural is still more concrete in the very different 'Nymphidia' (1627). This always popular poem is linked by debt or affinity with Chaucer, Shakespeare, Browne (the first song of the third book), and Herrick, but Drayton's robust fancy and carefree mock-heroic gusto are his own.

Though the poet of the Golden Age had become increasingly conscious of living in an iron age, *The Muses' Elysium* (1630) was his happiest work, in both senses of the word. It was indeed something of a miracle that the veteran of sixty-seven, in spite of his long-proved stamina and flexibility, should display such fertile vigour and such added lightness and grace. Drayton was not, to be sure, a Herrick or a young Milton; his fresh effects were gained rather by the page than by the phrase. But his ripened assimilation of literature old and new had steadily refined his own clear vein of bucolic and poetic enjoyment, and now homely English realism and classical artifice are mingled with more civilized delicacy. In this 'Poets Paradice', this elysium of eternal youth and beauty and song, Drayton possesses his soul. The serene exhilaration of his old age becomes a kind of spiritual vision, a triumph over the ugly world. He died, poor, in the next year, the year of Donne's death (and of Dryden's birth), when rising poets were intent upon ideas and 'strong lines'. In 1637 the man of many collected editions had what was to be his last one until 1748. One wishes that he could have foreseen the noble edition of our day.

Probably no one except the author of *Britannia's Pastorals* (1613, 1616) ever had more than a hazy notion of the doings of his nymphs and swains, of Walla and Tavy, Thetis and Pan, and Riot and Truth and Limos.[1] But if there is much literary

---

[1] William Browne (1590/1?–1643/5?) was educated at Exeter College, Oxford, and the Inns of Court. He joined with several friends in *The Shepherd's Pipe* (1614) and in 1615 he wrote the *Inner Temple Masque*. In 1624 he returned to Oxford and then, according to Wood, took service with the Earl of Pembroke, to whom he had dedicated the second book of *Britannia's Pastorals*. After what may have been a second marriage (1628), he seems to have settled near Dorking.

and romantic tinsel in Browne's pastoralism and in his style, he does at least give us a larger view than Herrick of Devonshire, that blessed plot 'Whose equall all the world affordeth not!' And affectionate observation may beget simple pictures of fields, valleys, rocks, and streams, flowers, singing birds, bees, snails, squirrels (and badgers with the inequality of legs to be rejected by the poet's namesake), maypoles and other rustic festivals, milkmaids, ploughmen, blacksmiths, fishermen, ballad-mongers, the games of children and of fairies. In the seasonal round of work and play, pastoral realism and idealism are mixed. Some shepherds' boys may, like Shakespeare's Dick, blow their nails for cold; another 'lovely' one, taken no doubt from Sidney's *Arcadia*, sits piping on a hill as if his joy would still endure. Naturally the singer of country contentments is something of a primitivist (and in his most elaborate eulogy of the Golden Age he apparently uses Chaucer and Cervantes), yet his vision can be disturbed by thoughts of a decayed navy, of enclosures, rack-rents, and 'The Prelate in pluralities asleepe'.

Like most of the Spenserians, Browne inherited only a slender portion of the master's poetic and humanistic legacy, but he was a literary scholar. While we might take for granted his wide range of classical reading, we might not expect, even in an increasingly antiquarian age, citations from Bede, Geoffrey of Monmouth, Joseph of Exeter, and others; and we may remember his hope of editing Occleve. Browne formally reviews the poets of Italy and France and patriotically winds up with tributes to Sidney, 'Well-languag'd Danyel', and his friends Chapman, Drayton, Jonson, Christopher Brooke, Davies of Hereford, and Wither. Spenser in general seems to occupy a special pedestal. Such poets as Marlowe and John Fletcher are echoed but not named. Like the young Keats, the young Browne was in love not only with nature but with the idea of poetry. As everyone knows, Keats may have recalled the shepherd's boy from the *Arcadia*, the maiden undressing (a passage in the Arcadian style), and, among other things, one of the few lines in Browne in which rhythm counts—'Let no Bird sing!' But the endless flow of pastoral couplets, and the miscellaneous verse, hardly prepare us for the famous poem on the Countess of Pembroke, which has perhaps received sufficient praise in being long attributed to Johson. Yet

Browne is altogether himself in a briefer and more touching epitaph dated in May 1614:

> May! Be thou never grac'd with birds that sing,
> Nor Flora's pride!
> In thee all flowers & Roses spring,
> Mine onely died.

George Wither (1588–1667), that 'most profuse pourer forth of English Rhime', changed, about 1619, from a sort of Browne into a sort of combination of John Taylor and Quarles, and he was popular in all his roles, satirical, pastoral, and didactic.[1] Most of his great mass of religious and journalistic verse and prose, such as the long jeremiad on the plague, *Britain's Remembrancer* (1628), has now only an historical interest, if any, but in his own egoistic and irritating way Wither was a zealous champion of righteousness, liberty, and moderation, a latitudinarian (and anti-Calvinist) Anglican opposed to both Arminian and Puritan dogmatism and intolerance. Though in 1635 he could dedicate his *Emblems* to Charles and the queen, the civil war found him in the other camp. 'Honest George Withers', said Baxter in 1681, 'though a Rustick Poet, hath been very acceptable as to some for his Prophecies, so to others for his plain Country-honesty.' It is the 'Rustick Poet' whose 'homely heartiness of manner' (in Lamb's phrase) appeals to us in his early pastorals, *The Shepherd's Hunting* (1615), written in prison, *Fidelia* (1615)—which included the famous 'Shall I wasting in Dispaire?'—and the belatedly published *Fair Virtue* (1622). Especially in his easy septasyllabics there is simple and pleasant praise of love, the country, poetry, and virtuous independence and content, and it is not out of keeping with the genre and the character of 'Philarete' that he should seek 'How on each object I may moralize'. In later works, as he grew old-fashioned and more didactic, Wither defended his 'lowly stile' and useful matter against the taste for 'Strong-lines' and 'Verball Conceites'.

[1] Wither (or Withers), scion of an old and well-to-do Hampshire family, was at Oxford (?1603 ff.) and had two terms (1614, 1621) in the Marshalsea, on account of *Abuses Stript and Whipt* (1613) and *Wither's Motto* (1621). *Hymns and Songs of the Church* (1623), which was authorized by royal patent for insertion in all metrical Psalm-books, led to a prolonged quarrel with the stationers. Wither became an active officer in the parliamentary army and held minor posts under the Commonwealth, and he wearied Parliament in his efforts to repair his damaged fortunes. In 1660 he was imprisoned for the fourth or fifth time, and for three years, because of an unpublished poem *Vox Vulgi*. He wrote busily to the last.

Another friend of Browne, and perhaps of Wither, William Basse (c. 1583–1653?) occupies a tiny but secure niche through his 'Elegy on Shakespeare', to which Jonson alluded in his lines of 1623 (and which was first printed in Donne's *Poems* in 1633), and through Walton's quoting 'The Angler's Song' 'that was lately made at my request by Mr. William Basse, one that has made the choice Songs of the *Hunter in his careere*, and of *Tom of Bedlam*, and many others of note'. Basse's early 'Urania. The Woman in the Moon' was a mythological satire on women, more mildly humorous than Drayton's 'Man in the Moon', which perhaps inspired it. In his eclogues Basse achieved nothing of distinction, but he gives a picture of a cheerful, stable, rural world, a picture almost untouched by the public problems which had clouded the pastorals of his admired Spenser. As a member of the household of Sir Richard (later Lord) Wenman in Oxfordshire, Basse had a genuine knowledge and love of the country, and his homely flavour is not killed by literary convention and moralizing. He may have written the poem commonly called 'On the Tombs in Westminster Abbey', which has been ascribed without reason to Francis Beaumont.

The golden book of Elizabethan pastoral lyrics, *England's Helicon* (1600, 1614), belongs to the age preceding ours, but some of its better-known pieces, 'In the merry moneth of May' and other love-makings of Phillida and Coridon, are happy reminders of the eternal youth of Nicholas Breton (1551?– c. 1623), a sort of 'Georgian' who could greet the new century with buoyant as well as melancholic humours. In his *Passionate Shepherd* (1604), as in his prose *Fantastics* (1604?), Arcadian idealism and artifice admit authentic, though pleasant, rural realism. The wooer of Aglaia, drawing the conventional contrast between court and country, records the familiar sights of the merry country lad, the fox sneaking through the hedge, the little black-haired cony sitting in the sun to wash her face with her forefeet. The Renaissance pastoral, though it yielded much lovely verse of peculiar fragrance, was always in danger of inanition, but it was not promptly killed by the rational realism of Donne and Jonson. Jonson himself ended his career with the very English *Sad Shepherd*, and even Carew's 'Rapture' started from the first chorus of Tasso's *Aminta*. In the Caroline age the old conventions were quickened by fresh feeling in Drayton and Milton and others. If *Comus* and 'Lycidas' stand apart, the cause is not only Milton's genius but his reviving of the pastoral's concern with great themes, public or private. In Quarles's *The Shepherd's Oracles* (1644-6) that revival was rather a journalistic than a poetical success. On the other hand, the country is the real country in the charming ode to Anthony Stafford by the author of *Amyntas*, Thomas Randolph, and in the less familiar but also charming 'Ode, upon occasion of His Majesty's Proclamation in the Year 1630. Commanding the Gentry to reside upon their Estates in the Country', by the translator of *Pastor Fido*, Sir Richard Fanshawe.

We may pause here to look at the chief of Scottish writers, who was in some degree isolated in body and spirit from current English poetry. Like his friend Alexander, William Drummond of Hawthornden (1585-1649) gave his English allegiance to the author of the *Arcadia* and *Astrophel and Stella*, but he may be counted with the Spenserians by virtue of his smooth fluidity of movement (a movement delicately varied and restrained by the irregularities of the *canzone*) and his pictorial and mythological texture of clear and often vivid colour.[1] As his library and his verse testify, Drummond had a knowledge of French, Spanish, and especially Italian *belles lettres* probably unrivalled in England in the second decade of the century. His special admirations included not only such familiar authors as Ronsard and Desportes, Tasso and Guarini, but the less familiar, like Garcilaso and Marino, and he read many others. When about 1614-15 Drummond characterized the English poets of love (the first four were Sidney, Alexander, Daniel, and Donne), his criterion was Petrarch. His own verses, Jonson told him, 'smelled too much of the schooles and were not after the Fancie of the tyme'. But if he was in part a Jacobean—or half-Elizabethan—Stanley, a bookish artist whom we identify with graceful translation and imitation, his borrowings from diverse poets did receive the

---

[1] Drummond attended Edinburgh University (M.A., 1605), spent several years abroad in study and travel, and in 1610 became laird of Hawthornden. He settled down to a retired life of reading, writing, and, on the side, mechanical invention; he conceived, among other things, of machine-guns and tanks. His chief literary friends were Alexander, Drayton (by letter only), and Jonson, who visited him in the winter of 1618-19. Drummond's first fiancée died in or about 1615; he married in 1632. From 1635 onward he wrote a number of tracts on public affairs, inspired mainly by his royalism and love of peace. His history of Scotland from 1423 to 1542 was printed in 1655. His best piece of prose, *A Cypress Grove* (1623), is noticed in Chapter X.

transforming and unifying impress of his own lucid decorative instinct and reflective melancholy.

Drummond's first publication, the lament for Prince Henry, indicated his devotion to Sidney. In the panegyric on King James, *Forth Feasting* (1617), he remembered Virgil's eclogues and Ronsard's *Le Bocage Royal*. Both poems show skill in regular couplets. Drummond's best work was in the amatory *Poems* of 1616 and the religious *Flowers of Sion* (1623, 1630). The former has such pure literary beauties as the radiant madrigal, 'Like the Idalian Queene', and the *canzone*, 'Phoebus arise'; if we are surprised by an image of unwonted violence,

> Night like a Drunkard reeles
> Beyond the Hills to shunne his flaming Wheeles,

we find that it comes from *Romeo and Juliet*. The ecstasies and pangs of the lover, rather more sensuous than Petrarchan, yield in the second part of the *Poems* to grief for the death of the beloved. 'It Autumne was' embodies the Stoic, Neoplatonic, and Christian *contemptus mundi*, the Neoplatonic vision of the heaven of eternal life and love and beauty, which are elaborated in *A Cypress Grove*. One line, 'O leave that Love which reacheth but to Dust', illustrates both Drummond's Platonism and his use, even in sorrow, of other poets. His desire to live 'Farre from the madding Worldlings hoarse Discords', his philosophic and religious sense of earthly vanity—instincts heightened by his serious illness of 1620—explain the relative originality and depth of *Flowers of Sion*. When, for instance, he rewrites Ronsard's 'Hymne de l'Eternité' as the 'Hymn of the Fairest Fair', he changes Ronsard's half-Epicurean thought into a picture of the Creator and Creation which accords with his own Christian Platonism. In 'The woefull Marie', adapted from Marino's ' *Stabat Mater*', the baroque strain is much subdued, as it is in the fine 'Hymn of the Ascension' and other purely religious poems.

Before we come to the chief heirs of Spenser's religious and moral allegory (and without lingering over the fluent products of Breton's sacred muse), we must give a paragraph to John Davies of Hereford (1565?–1618). Davies, the most famous penman of his day, had pedagogical and literary connexions with many members of the great families, and in *The Scourge of Folly* (1610?) he addressed complimentary epigrams to some two dozen authors, including Shakespeare and Donne. He was associated with Browne, Wither, and Brooke in *The Shepherd's Pipe* (1614). Davies's rough satirical epigrams belong to the semi-popular rather than the classical section of the very large and drab body of verse of that kind. But his main effort went into a series of religious, moral, and psychological treatises or sermons in verse, *Mirum in Modum* (1602), *Microcosmos* (1603), *Summa Totalis* (1607), *The Holy Rood* (1609), and other things. Among his sources were De la Primaudaye's *French Academy*, Mornay's *Trueness of the Christian Religion*, and Agrippa's *De Incertitudine*. In manner Davies was a sort of scholastic Sylvester; one example of eccentric taste is the anatomical mysticism of 'Formosity' in *Wit's Pilgrimage* (1605?). He could achieve the raw material of poetry in describing the plague, in *Humour's Heaven on Earth* (1609), and his 'Picture of an Happy Man' in *The Muse's Sacrifice* (1612) is a respectable religious pendant to Wotton's Horatian poem, but the master (in Fuller's words) of fast, fair, close, and various handwriting was as a poet slow, laborious, diffuse, and flat. There is no answer to his query:

> Busie Invention, whie art thou so dull
> And yet still doing?

Giles Fletcher's *Christ's Victory and Triumph* (1610) is the chief monument of baroque devotional poetry between Southwell and the young Milton and Crashaw.[1] Although Fletcher crowned his prefatory list of 'divine and heroical' poets with those 'two blessed Soules', Du Bartas and Spenser (and King James), he did not seek to embrace their large poetic domain but centred his four cantos around the birth, temptation, crucifixion, and resurrection of Christ. His Spenserianism shows itself in his metrical movement (though his stanza is not Spenser's), in narrative and allegorical imitations like the

---

[1] Giles Fletcher (1585/6–1623) and Phineas (1582–1650) were the sons of Giles Fletcher, M.P., diplomat, and author, who died in 1611, and cousins of John Fletcher the dramatist. Giles was educated at Trinity College, Cambridge (B.A., 1606; B.D., 1619), and became Reader in Greek in 1615. In 1617 he received from Bacon a living which in 1619 he exchanged for another in Bacon's gift, that of Alderton in Suffolk, which he held until 1623—a change made unhappy, says Fuller, by the intractable character of his parishioners. Phineas Fletcher went to Eton and King's College (B.A., 1604; M.A., 1608) and was ordained in 1611. In 1615 he became chaplain to Sir Henry Willoughby and married. In 1621 his patron presented him to the living of Hilgay in Norfolk, which was his home for the rest of his life.

Bower of Vain-Delight, in the borrowing and echoing of lines, phrases, and diction, in the fusing of biblical and pagan story, and in the lusciously Italianate embellishment of heroic virtue. The picture of Mercy suggests Ovid, the Hero of Marlowe and Chapman, and Spenser's Belphoebe and Mercilla; and the 'snowie mountelets' of her breast carry us forward to the Theophila of Phineas's friend, Edward Benlowes. Milton, who in his younger days owed a good deal to both Fletchers, seems to have remembered Giles's handling of the temptation even in the late and austere *Paradise Regained*, but the earlier Christ in the wilderness is modelled on the lover in the Song of Solomon; he has black hair in small curls, 'cheekes as snowie apples, sop't in wine', and (like Belphoebe also) 'two white marble pillars' for legs. He is, moreover, the true Orpheus who conquered hell, and He ascends to heaven like Ganymede. But while Fletcher has not the 'voice of steel' that he craves, his tendency towards soft excess is checked by antithetical 'wit'. His opening stanza is only the first of many series of those paradoxical contrasts which are at the centre of baroque religiosity:

> The birth of him that no beginning knewe,
> Yet gives beginning to all that are borne,
> And how the Infinite farre greater grewe,
> By growing lesse, and how the rising Morne,
> That shot from heav'n, did backe to heaven retourne,
> > The obsequies of him that could not die,
> > And death of life, ende of eternitie,
> How worthily he died, that died unworthily.

Further, especially in the latter half of the poem, sincere if 'naïve' devotion and homely directness triumph over allegory as Christ triumphs over death, and though Giles leaves to his brother the composing of a divine epithalamium, his own 'beatificall' vision inspires a finer ecstasy than Phineas attained at the end of *The Purple Island*.

Phineas Fletcher has his moments of sensuous charm and beauty, but he is perhaps at his best and simplest in the late and private verses of *A Father's Testament*. On the whole he is of coarser grain and less pure spirituality than Giles. His favourite model, in addition to Spenser, was Du Bartas or rather Sylvester, to whom Giles owed little or nothing. Among his models we should perhaps include himself, for he was thriftily repetitious as well as diffuse. Most of his verse was written during the years 1607–12, though published later.

Locustae vel Pietas Jesuitica, and the larger English version, *The Locusts, or Apollyonists* (1627), may have been among the many sources which gave Milton hints for Satan, the infernal council, and Sin, but its poetical quality and its anti-Romanism are closer to *In Quintum Novembris* than to *Paradise Lost. Venus and Anchises* was printed in 1628 as *Britain's Ida* and as a work of Spenser's. Even in an age which allowed some latitude to the clerical muse it might have been awkward to acknowledge a voluptuous addition to the Elizabethan series of Ovidian and Italianate narratives, though Fletcher's warmth is mitigated by touches of humour. With that poem may be placed the unprinted 'Epithalamium' discovered in 1923, which has perhaps more than a family resemblance to the 'Epithalamium' of Johannes Secundus. In 1631 appeared *Sicelides, a Piscatory,* which had been acted at King's College in 1615. The piscatory eclogues in *The Purple Island* (1633) were praised by Walton as the excellent work of an excellent angler, but they are for the most part dull imitations of the pastorals of Spenser and Sannazzaro. *The Purple Island* itself has a pastoral background. On a first encounter with the text and gloss of this notorious poem one may exclaim, like Kipps when he first beheld an anatomical chart, 'Chubes! Chubes!' The medieval theme of 'the castle of the body', which had been grotesque enough in Du Bartas and in Spenser, becomes still more grotesque in becoming more laboriously scientific. Fletcher may be called the Jacobean or Caroline Erasmus Darwin. Since the poem was apparently begun about the same time as *Christ's Victory and Triumph,* we cannot blame the author for versifying Vesalian anatomy and Galenic rather than Harveian physiology. Fletcher's zeal was of course religious and ethical as well as scientific—his book was dedicated to Benlowes and received high tributes from Benlowes and Quarles—and if we survive the anatomy (which attracted James Joyce), we reach a catalogue and a battle of the vices and virtues. It is, however, a static mixture of decorative abstraction and satirical realism. While Spenser at his best can vitalize ethical and religious ideas in his characters and action, Fletcher can only describe emblematic figures.

Francis Quarles (1592–1644) cannot have had many readers

since Lamb, Browning, and Thoreau, but his *Emblems* (1635) was the most popular book of verse of the seventeenth century and his *Enchiridion* (1640-1) the most popular book of aphorisms, and other works were frequently reprinted too.[1] In Horace Walpole's phrase, Milton was forced to wait till the world had done admiring Quarles. Cowley in 1656 censured his biblical narratives and Edward Phillips in 1675 called him 'the darling of our Plebeian Judgments', but less sophisticated comments help to explain his hold on the public. Samuel Sheppard, in *The Times Displayed* (1646), ranked him 'next to Bartas'; according to Fuller, he drank of Jordan instead of Helicon; and Baxter in 1681 said that he 'out-went' Wither in 'mixing competent Wit with Piety'. Such popular fame might, in a later age, have been the reward of facile optimism, but Quarles's first book was *A Feast for Worms* (1620), and he seldom came nearer optimism than in the assertion 'Tis glorious misery to be borne a Man'. His life and outlook were of Puritanical sobriety, though his 'Genius jumpt with' that of his admired friend Phineas Fletcher to the length of one 'vain amatorious poem', *Argalus and Parthenia*. A believer in established order and uniformity, a zealous defender of divine right and 'a true sonne of the Church of England', Quarles nevertheless was not blind to Anglican errors and, holding by the authority of the individual conscience and reason, he could not be intolerant.

We need not then be surprised by the mingled Puritan and Catholic religiosity of Quarles's *Divine Fancies* (1632), *Emblems* (1635), and *Hieroglyphics of the Life of Man* (1638). The emblem, a symbolic picture with a motto and an exposition, had become one of the last European manifestations of a medieval habit of mind. It was born, or reborn, in 1531 with Alciati's collection, drawn largely from the Greek Anthology and other ancient sources. The English pioneer was Geoffrey Whitney (1586). Among the later men interested in emblems were Peacham, Wither, Christopher Harvey, John Hall, and Bunyan. Hoole

---

[1] Quarles was the son of a surveyor-general of victualling for the Navy. He was educated at Cambridge (B.A., 1608) and Lincoln's Inn. In 1613 he went abroad in the train of the Earl of Arundel, who was one of the newly married Princess Elizabeth's escorts. From 1626 to 1629-30 Quarles was in Ireland as secretary to Archbishop Ussher. By 1633 he had retired to his native Essex. In 1640 he was appointed chronologer to the city of London. In that year he wrote *The Virgin Widow* (printed in 1649), an allegorical play about the Church of England. His last four years were given mainly to prose. His widow was left in poverty with nine of their eighteen children.

spoke of the use of emblems in schools. More important was the significance of the emblem in poetry and literature generally, notably in George Herbert and Crashaw, and the emblem poet *par excellence* was Quarles. His plates were taken from two Jesuit emblem books and his verses sometimes echoed theirs. In the preface of *Argalus and Parthenia* (1629) he repudiated 'the tyranny of *strong lines*, . . . the meere itch of wit', but the emblem was an essentially 'metaphysical' device, at once epigrammatic, metaphorical, and concrete. 'Before the knowledge of letters', says Quarles, 'God was knowne by Hierogliphicks; And, indeed, what are the Heavens, the Earth, nay every Creature, but Hierogliphicks and Emblemes of His Glory?' In his penitential dialogues with God, in his earnest *contemptus mundi*, in his dark vision of puny, lustful, and restless man, Quarles is something of an inferior Herbert, a less jerky and vehement Benlowes. The latter, his friend and patron, must have studied him. Both, by the way, see man as a magnetic needle trembling until he comes to rest in God (an image handled by a finer artist, Jeremy Taylor, in his sermon on Bramhall), and both, as poets, have the uncertainty of the needle. Likening death to a long sleep in bed, Quarles asks, 'And why not Wormes as well as Fleas?'

If Quarles did not attempt allegory on a large scale, two later poets, Henry More (1614–87) and Joseph Beaumont (1616–99), outdid Spenser in philosophic and narrative complexity. (Benlowes belongs rather with the metaphysical poets.) More is a metaphysical poet in the general sense of the word. The nature and evolution of his thought are indicated in the tenth chapter, and the reader cannot hope here for a compendious account of 'Psychozoia, or the Life of the Soul', 'Psychathanasia, or the Immortality of the Soul', 'Antipsychopannychia, or the Confutation of the Sleep of the Soul', and 'Antimonopsychia, or Confutation of the Unity of Souls', all published together as *Psychodia Platonica* (1642), and of *Democritus Platonissans, or an Essay upon the Infinity of Worlds out of Platonic Principles* (1646). These and other pieces were collected in *Philosophical Poems* (1647). As a child More had thought *The Fairy Queen* 'a Poem as richly fraught with divine Morality as Phansy', and his debt embraced the *Four Hymns* and other things. However, even the sage and serious and half-mystical Spenser might not have recognized as his poetic chil-

dren such complex and abstract efforts to expound a rational
and ethical Christian Neoplatonism and defend it against
materialism old and new. The most Spenserian and most attractive of these poems is the earliest, 'Psychozoia', which has
the first spontaneous glow of the satisfying revelation the
author's passionately hungry soul had sought and found.
Here, too, in the course of a pilgrim's progress, and in a mood
both earnest and genial, More gives satirical sketches (much
enlarged in 1647) of erroneous and spurious types of religion,
the self-sufficient humanist, the scholastic rationalist, the Calvinistic bibliolater, the sectarian enthusiast, the greasy ecclesiastical authoritarian, Corvino ('Most like methought to a
Cathedrall Dean'), and Pico, the High Church ritualist. Prominent models for this last were the late Archbishop and
Bishop Wren.

To More, Joseph Beaumont—who was Wren's protégé—
might have seemed a ritualist, and to Beaumont, who was later
to attack More's *Grand Mystery of Godliness*, More may already
have appeared as a dangerously latitudinarian individualist.
Beaumont was ejected from his Cambridge fellowship in 1643-
4, along with his friend Crashaw and others, and though he
remained an Anglican or Anglo-Catholic, he had a close
spiritual affinity with the more intense Crashaw. In his
shorter and more inviting poems Crashaw's influence pre-
dominates. Beaumont's mystical instincts received full expression in *Psyche, or Love's Mystery* (1648), a vast allegory of the
soul's pilgrimage through earthly trials to heavenly felicity.
Such a work, in the Spenserian and Fletcherian tradition, bears
some general resemblance to the poems of More, but Beaumont
is rather a pallid reflection of conventional mystical thought
than a spiritual genius like More (or even Benlowes), and
his style is oppressively Marinistic.

We turn back to consider several poets who cannot be
labelled Spenserian, although the first two of them at least
were closer to Spenser in moral temper than some of his direct
and obvious successors. Samuel Daniel would not sing of
knights and paladins in aged accents and untimely words, but
he was akin to Spenser in his Tudor patriotism, humanistic
ideals, and sweetness of tone[1]. Much of his work lies outside

---

[1] Samuel Daniel (1563?–1619) was born in Somerset, and in 1581 entered Magdalen Hall, Oxford, where he studied under his brother-in-law, John Florio. In

of our limits—*Delia* and *The Complaint of Rosamond* (1592),
which Spenser praised, *Musophilus* (1599), that noble defence
of learning and the English tongue, which was dedicated to
Fulke Greville, the patron of his 'Infant Muse', and the
dramas and masques, which contain lyrics of thoughtful beauty.
The Civil Wars first appeared in 1595 and was enlarged, though
not completed, in 1601 and 1609. This patriotic and admoni-
tory work found a sympathetic reader in Coleridge, but most
people have shared the judgements of Jonson, Drayton, and
Henry Reynolds. The author showed his character in his
refusal to taint history with 'fictions, fantasies', in his epic
aspirations, and his philosophic seriousness. In his sober and
solid ethical humanism Daniel stood with Jonson and Chapman and especially with 'the right worthie and judicious
favourer of vertue', his friend Fulke Greville. To Daniel,
Campion's plea for classical metres meant the dead hand, not
the living spirit, of antiquity. With full reverence for Greece
and Rome, he rejoiced in the Middle Ages and above all in 'the
wonderfull Architecture of this state of England, . . . continually
in all ages furnisht with spirites fitte to maintaine the majestie
of her owne greatnes, and to match in an equall concurrencie
all other kingdomes round about her with whome it had to
incounter'. And though his concern is practical, he sees the
literary problem *sub specie aeternitatis*: 'and we must heerein be
content to submit our selves to the law of time, which in few
yeeres wil make al that, for which we now contend, Nothing.'
Daniel's urbane appeal to custom, nature, and judgement, his
sense of historical relativity, may reflect both Greville and
Montaigne; he echoed the latter in the *Defence of Rhyme* and
commended him apropos of Florio's translation.

On one side Daniel's Renaissance consciousness of devouring

1586 he was employed by the English embassy in Paris. In 1585 he had dedicated
his translation of Paulus Jovius's tract on *imprese* to Sir Edward Dymoke, and he was
still attached to Dymoke in 1592; the pair had travelled in Italy, probably in
1590–1, and visited Guarini. Daniel became tutor to William Herbert, third Earl
of Pembroke, and a member of the Countess of Pembroke's literary circle. Before
1599 he became tutor to Lady Anne Clifford and was associated with her mother,
the Countess of Cumberland, and with the Countess of Bedford, through whom, at
the beginning of James's reign, he entered the service of Queen Anne. In 1604–5 he
licensed plays for the Children of the Queen's Revels. He got into trouble over his
own play, *Philotas* (1604), because of its supposed reference to the Earl of Essex.
During 1604–14 he wrote two masques and two pastoral plays for the court. In
1618 he was dismissed by the queen for being friendly with the disgraced Sir Robert
Floud. He died at his farm in Somerset.

time links the eulogy of the Golden Age (1601), taken from Tasso's *Aminta*, with the 'Description of Beauty' (1623), rendered, in no Marinistic fashion, from Marino. But his sense of time is bound up chiefly with the positive ethical values of the humanistic tradition. For good or ill, the past is one with the present and future; they are parts of a continuous whole. The simple fact that 'Man is a creature of the same dimension he was' is the sobering and inspiring text of the *Civil Wars* and the *History of England*, *Musophilus* and the *Defence of Rhyme*, the tragedies, and the noble series of Horatian epistles of 1601–3. These last are signal proofs that it does not ill beseem 'The function of a Poem, to discourse'. Other writers might have saluted the 'hospitable bountie' of Sir Thomas Bodley, who had conquered time by assembling 'The glorious reliques of the best of men'; but only Daniel perhaps could have addressed to the Lord Keeper Egerton, who has won the glory that does not end 'with our breath', a stately poem on the difference between inflexible Law and Equity, 'the soule of Law'. The young Lady Anne Clifford, if she would fulfil the responsibilities of her noble mind and descent, must, like the planets, 'keep the certaine course Of order'. In the more famous epistles to the Countesses of Bedford and Cumberland Daniel achieves the perfect statement of his Christian Stoicism. He knows, to quote the couplet Wordsworth quoted,

> that unlesse above himselfe he can
> Erect himselfe, how poore a thing is man!

He is translating a Senecan phrase which Jonson also translated, in *Cynthia's Revels*, and which the naturalistic Montaigne cited to reject. The inward order of the man governed by right reason is the order upheld by Greville and Chapman, though Daniel's lucid speech and assured poise are wholly classical, free from knots and obscurities. But Daniel's is not an easy academic view of life, he praises no fugitive and cloistered virtue; his grave ethical passion proves its own authenticity and imparts a poetic glow to the prosaic. Similar things might be said of that fine lyric, 'Ulysses and the Siren' (1605). Here, too, the effect is created, not by winged words and subtle overtones, but by moral elevation and straightforward rightness of form and style. Daniel's presentation of the rival claims of sensual ease and honourable toil is in line with Belphoebe's answer to Braggadocchio and other celebrations of heroic effort all the way back to Hesiod and Homer. After one has been stirred afresh by these poems, one does not hesitate to endorse the manly claim offered 'To the Reader' in 1607:

> I know I shalbe read, among the rest
> So long as men speake english, and so long
> As verse and vertue shalbe in request,
> Or grace to honest industry belong.

Contemporary allusions to Daniel inclined to stress honest industry and pure diction more than poetic fire, and by 1675 Edward Phillips could say that his poems were not totally forgotten but that his *History of England* (1612, 1618?) was 'most principally sought after and regarded'. There is small reason now to seek after that unfinished patriotic legacy, and the reader of the *Defence of Rhyme* knows already that Daniel at his best writes the prose of a Jacobean Dryden.

If Fulke Greville, first Lord Brooke (1554–1628), had been born twenty years later, he might perhaps have stood—with Chapman rather than with Donne—in the forefront of the metaphysical movement.[1] What Edward Phillips called his 'close, mysterious and sentencious way of writing' is nearer the metaphysical than the Spenserian manner, yet Greville shows, in *Humane Learning*, a Hobbesian distrust of metaphor, and his normal utterance is of a massive realistic plainness fitted for sober and penetrating thought. In parts of *Caelica*, which was begun under Sidney's inspiration, he wreathed iron pokers into true-love knots, and although, according to Naunton,

---

[1] Greville's friendship with Sidney began at Shrewsbury School and they entered upon court life together, with similar political and literary interests. In 1584 Greville entertained Giordano Bruno. Except in his efforts to get abroad, he enjoyed the special favour of Elizabeth. His public career, which involved at least the usual amount of subservience, came mostly after Sidney's death (1586). Greville represented Warwickshire in Parliament, held various minor posts, was Treasurer of the Navy from 1598 to 1604, and Chancellor of the Exchequer from 1614 to 1622. He received a knighthood in 1603 and a peerage in 1621. He became a wealthy landowner and rebuilt Warwick Castle. He remained loyal to Essex, and his attachment to Bacon, though less warm, survived Bacon's fall. Greville befriended a number of literary men, Daniel, Speed, Camden, and young William Davenant, and he procured the deanery of Westminster for Andrewes. In 1628, a few days after the murder of Buckingham, he was stabbed by a servant (for whom he had provided an annuity) and died some weeks later. Apart from an unauthorized edition of *Mustapha* (1609), all of Greville's longer works, which he assiduously revised, were published after his death. The *Life of Sidney* is discussed in Chapter VII.

he 'lived, and dyed, a constant Courtier of the Ladies', no series of love poems was ever less amorous. For all the Petrarchan and Sidneian fancies, and the omnipresence of Cupid, Caelica, Myra, and Cynthia are something less than shadows, and towards the end they fade away altogether behind religious and philosophical reflection.

In the wholly philosophical 'treaties' of *Humane Learning, Wars, Monarchy,* and *Religion,* and *An Inquisition upon Fame and Honour,* Greville often treads on the margin of poetry. But for the strong tradition of the didactic poem, indeed, he might have made prose the medium for his essays or counsels, civil and moral, as he did in his 'Letter to an Honourable Lady' concerning the duties of marriage. While Greville's career and ideas may sometimes suggest Bacon's *Essays* and *Advancement of Learning,* he sees at once further and more darkly. And while, in the earnestness and final orthodoxy of his Christian humanism, he is allied with his friends Sidney and Daniel, with Spenser and Jonson, and especially with the Stoic-Platonic Chapman, he is a Jacobean courtier and statesman whose idealism must overcome a tough-minded realism. With a mind and character too complex, sceptical, and experienced to rest in the normal humanistic assurance of truth, he gropes uncertainly through the illusions of the Many towards the infinite and ultimate One. 'I know the world and believe in God', he wrote in 1613, and the phrase is a partial clue to his works. As he says in his *Life of Sidney,* Greville found his 'creeping Genius more fixed upon the Images of Life, than the Images of Wit', and he addressed 'those only, that are weather-beaten in the Sea of this World, such as having lost the sight of their Gardens, and groves, study to saile on a right course among Rocks, and quick-sands'. All about him he sees change, chaos, and corruption. Learned ignorance and blind presumption, disguised by the specious diversity of modern verbal knowledge, have obscured and blighted man's sense of the divine and of the true ends of life. Self-will, the lust for power, has set up false gods. And Greville, like so many Christian humanists before him, seeks to recall men from sinful 'pride of minde' to humility and obedience, to re-establish the sovereignty of religion, reason, and order in the individual soul and in society. But whereas Calvin and Machiavelli, starting, one might say, from similar premisses, had moved confidently along widely divergent roads, it is Greville's difficulty, and the source of his gloomy strength, that he has a good deal of the one along with something of the other.

The same ideals are presented, through examples of 'the high waies of ambitious Governours' and through the sometimes noble and perplexing choric odes, in *Mustapha* and *Alaham*, two treatises cast in the form of Senecan dramas. (The treatises were in fact, Greville tells us, overgrown choruses.) *Mustapha* may have had a number of sources; the main source of *Alaham* is a tale found in the *Itinerary* (1510) of Ludovico di Varthema and in the *novelle* of Bandello and Belleforest. The closet dramatist was not merely a closet philosopher. He burned a play on Antony and Cleopatra, written apparently about 1600, because it revealed too clearly his reaction to the disgrace of his kinsman Essex; and many lines in the other tragedies might have been given a topical application.

A bolder courtier who lacked Greville's capacity for self-preservation, and whose career is too familiar to need an outline, was Sir Walter Ralegh (1552?–1618). So much of Ralegh's verse was written before 1600, the canon is so very uncertain, and his concentrated and poignantly individual poems are so famous, that we may limit ourselves to a few bald facts about a few of the pieces printed after 1600. 'Conceipt begotten by the eyes', published in the *Poetical Rhapsody* of 1602, begins in the manner of the song sung to Bassanio but passes into Ralegh's characteristic brooding on the vanity and mutability of man and the world. That direct and bitter blast on the same theme, 'The Lie', appeared in the 1608 edition of the same anthology. 'What is our life? a play of passion', which, like 'The Lie', has been attributed to several authors, embodies the theme again, in the favourite Elizabethan image of a stage-play; this real epigram Orlando Gibbons made into one of the greatest of madrigals (1612). 'Give me my Scallop shell of quiet' was printed first in Anthony Scoloker's *Daiphantus* (1604) and later in Ralegh's *Remains*; it seems to be charged with the writer's fierce feeling about his trial and death-sentence of 1603, and some odd conceits which grow out of the thematic metaphor scarcely mar its powerful intensity. The still more familiar 'Even such is time' is enveloped in complications. A few days after Ralegh's execution men were quoting lines said to have been written by him the night before it, and the eight lines we know were printed in 1619 in a volume called *A Happy Husband* as 'By Sir W. R., which he writ the night before his execution'; in 1628 they appeared as 'The Authours Epitaph, made by himselfe' in Ralegh's *Prerogative of Parliaments*. They were also printed, without the final couplet, in *A Help to Memory and Discourse*, a book entered in November, 1619, which had a second impression in 1621; and these six lines (with small variants as usual) are a last and appropriate stanza in the manuscript text of a love poem of six stanzas beginning 'Nature that washt her hands in milke'. On the whole, there seems good reason to accept the well-authenticated tradition and to suppose that on his last night Ralegh remembered lines he had written before and added the concluding prayer.

A personality more akin to Drummond than to the volcanic and glamorous Ralegh was Sir John Beaumont (1583?–1627), the elder brother of the dramatist, and a friend and partial disciple of Drayton and Jonson. In 1606, by the way, he was indicted for recusancy soon after Jonson and Lodge. Beaumont's modest position in the history of the heroic couplet was consolidated by the classical 'good sense' of his verse-essay, 'To his late Majesty, concerning the True Form of English Poetry', though he said little which had not been said, as he suggests, by King James, or by Jonson (or by Puttenham, who gave sanction for various later phenomena, from half-Hobbesian rationalism to poems shaped like lozenges). Beaumont's metrical importance has been somewhat diminished by modern recognition of the large number of men who were moulding the couplet, but he did display unusual regularity and smoothness. Nearly all of his verse was written in that form, the mythological and mock-heroic *Metamorphosis of Tobacco* (1602), *Bosworth-Field* (1629), a narrative of the kind cultivated by Drayton and Daniel, most of his classical translations, and sacred and occasional poems. Some of these pieces, such as 'Of True Liberty' and the elegy on his son, are the work of a poet and bear out Anthony Wood's report of him as 'a Person of great knowledge, gravity and worth'.

The line of Spenserian poets from which we have wandered does not of course sum up 'the influence of Spenser'. On the technical side that was felt by all poets, though none but Milton inherited Spenser's full conception of the scope and function of poetry.

2

The Golden Age of English music and song is so rich, especially after 1600, that the historian is lucky in having one pre-
eminent representative of the united arts in Thomas Campion
(1567–1620) who, unlike his fellow composers generally, wrote
his own words.[1] Apart from the masques, his principal works
were the *Poemata* of 1595 (enlarged in 1619); *A Book of Airs*
(1601), edited by his friend Philip Rosseter, who composed the
music and apparently the words of the second half of the
volume; *Observations in the Art of English Poesy* (1602); *Two Books
of Airs* (1613–15?); *Third and Fourth Book of Airs* (1617?); and
A New Way of Making Four Parts in Counterpoint (*c.* 1618?).
Campion's early poetic evolution gives a special significance to
the prefatory words in the first *Book of Airs*: 'What Epigrams
are in Poetrie, the same are Ayres in musicke, then in their
chiefe perfection when they are short and well seasoned.'

Campion has been commonly held guilty of a belated and
unfortunate aberration in his supposed plea for classical metres.
Daniel was the first of many critics who did not altogether
understand Campion's not altogether lucid argument, and his
great reply, happily enough, was not always strictly relevant.
Campion, though he got himself into awkward corners, was not
viewing the problem with quite the confused simplicity of some
earlier classicists. (That is not a reference to 'the Areopagus',
since no amount of scholarly reiteration can create a literary
club out of Harvey's and Spenser's ironical allusions to Sidney
and Dyer.) While modern English verse was still in its uncertain
infancy, there had been extremists who wished to take over
classical metrics *in toto*, and moderates like Harvey and Puttenham who were looking for an English and accentual equivalent
of the quantitative system. Campion was a more sophisticated

---

[1] Campion was born in London, of well-to-do parents who died when he was
a boy. He proceeded from Peterhouse to Gray's Inn and, if his Latin poems are
reliable evidence, he led a free life about town. In 1591–2 he seems to have been
with Essex's expeditionary force in France, probably in the troop of Robert Carey
(the autobiographer). Campion's first printed poems appeared, like Daniel's, in
the surreptitious edition of *Astrophel and Stella* (1591). Between 1602 and 1606 he
took a medical degree, presumably abroad, and henceforth practised in London.
At some time between 1595 and 1619 he appears to have become a Catholic. In
1607 he wrote a masque for the wedding of Lord Hay (or Hayes) and in 1613 three
masques, one for the queen and two for the weddings of the Princess Elizabeth and
the Countess of Essex. Campion had a small and apparently innocent part in the
intrigues which resulted in Overbury's death.

moderate and a poet. He did not want English hexameters, which had had such 'passing pitifull successe', but, in place of reliance on syllable-counting and rhyme as the principles of verse, he urged more exact handling of iambic and trochaic feet and various substitutions. And although he shared the Renaissance scholar's contempt for unlettered scribblers, he wrote rather as a musician than as a neoclassicist, and was moved less by classical authority than by a technician's desire to achieve a flexible and fruitful compromise between quantitative discipline and the accentual genius of the English language. It was that desire which led him in his songs, nearly always with felicitous results, to couple his 'Words and Notes lovingly together'. When we read his verse all through, our pleasure may in the end be clouded by some sense of thinness and monotony, for his amatory world is small (though he also wrote some fine religious lyrics), but it must be remembered that the reader gets less than half of the poet-composer's effect. When we read Shakespeare's lyrics we do not have their original music in mind, it is true, but we do have the whole background of the plays.

If Campion's quantitative experiments yielded only one triumph, 'Rose-cheekt Lawra, come', the pragmatic value of his theories, as of Bridges's, consisted in the tuning of his own ear and others' to more delicate and subtle devices of lyrical artistry. We prefer the emotional and imaginative wealth, the natural magic, and the apparent spontaneity of Shakespeare, but there is still room for 'When to her lute Corinna sings', 'Follow your Saint, follow with accents sweet', and many other jewels of pure art or artifice which carry no trace of the everyday world (and Shakespeare has his share of artifice too). Yet Campion owes much to the popular tradition; it appears in varying degrees of refinement from 'Jacke and Jone they thinke no ill' to 'There is a Garden in her face'. On the classical side, Campion has such Horatian echoes as 'The man of life upright', but he gave his chief study to Catullus and Martial. Like Jonson, and like Herrick and Carew, Campion may be at his best when romantic and classical inspirations are fused and evoke an atmosphere of contrived but potent magic. 'The fayry queen Proserpina' of the early 'Harke, al you ladies that do sleep' is a sister of Titania and of Chaucer's 'Proserpina, and al hire fayerye'. The passions of the Roman lyrists are subdued and altered in Campion's ideal dream-world of love. His most obvious and familiar paraphrase of Catullus, 'My sweetest Lesbia let us live and love', loses the poignant actuality of the original and becomes detached, reflective, serene. Propertius apparently suggested one of Campion's finest openings:

> When thou must home to shades of under ground,
>   and there ariv'd a newe admired guest,
> The beauteous spirits do ingirt thee round,
>   white Iope, blith Hellen, and the rest,

but the richly mythological and emotional vision, the contrast between radiant love and vitality and the darkness of death (a classicist's parallel to 'A bracelet of bright haire about the bone'), this dwindles, as Propertius himself can dwindle, into the conventional hyperbole of a sonneteer.

While Campion the poet cannot be separated from Campion the musician, the former ranks higher among lyrists than the latter among composers. As a maker of graceful tunes within a fairly narrow range, he is not to be numbered with the great galaxy, Byrd, Wilbye, Morley, Dowland, Weelkes, Gibbons, and many other men; indeed, the plenitude of English musical genius within one generation is probably unmatched in the history of music. Campion exploited that one of the several chief forms of lyrical composition which gave most prominence to the words, namely, the 'ayre'. This form, inaugurated by Dowland in 1597, was quickly established by Dowland himself, Morley, and Robert Jones, and by Campion and Rosseter, in their books of 1600–1. It was in 1601 that the older madrigal reached its climax in *The Triumphs of Oriana* that Morley edited. The madrigal was 'a composition for two or more unaccompanied voices singing in combination, all the voice parts being of equal interest and mainly designed from the same melodic material'. The themes and moods of the madrigal ranged from the grave to the merry, its structure from the intricacy of Byrd's 'Though Amaryllis dance in green' to the air-like simplicity of Gibbons's 'The Silver Swan'. The madrigal, with its normal complexities of fugal succession and repetition, could hardly be carried beyond a single stanza or be followed by hearers intent upon the words. The air, on the other hand, was a melody for one voice, usually accompanied by the lute, but sometimes by the bass-viol or by other voices, and the same melody was repeated for each stanza. The ballet was a composition for combined voices which was less complex than the madrigal and kept much of the clear-cut regularity of dance music; its obvious characteristic was the 'fa-la' refrain. There were of course many other forms, from Byrd's majestic liturgical music to catches like that of Sir Toby Belch. But this paragraph is only the briefest reminder of the manifold and not yet fully explored relations between music and lyrical poetry and of the place of music in English life throughout our period. To ignore the great mass of music in manuscript circulation, there were printed, in the forty years before 1630, about ninety collections of madrigals, airs, canzonets, and ballets; of madrigals alone there were nearly a thousand. We do not need the evidence of Morley and Peacham and others to prove that the glory of English composition was accompanied by a knowledge of music more widespread than it has ever been since. And if the lyric ever had a bird-like note, the Elizabethan and Jacobean lyric had. 'For Poetry (like honesty and olde Souldiers)', said Dekker in *News from Hell*, 'goes upon lame feete, unlesse there bee musicke in her.' But in later lyricism, even in Herrick, the intimate relation between song and music did not survive in its old full-throated ease.

Those useful scapegoats, the Puritans, have traditionally been made responsible for extinguishing music along with the other joys of Merry England, but in recent decades the charge has at least been modified. Puritans did frown upon church music which savoured of popish profaneness; they would have agreed with Bacon that 'the curiositie of division and reports, and other figures of Musick, have no affinitie with the reasonable service of God, but were added in the more pompous times'. The Puritans' real crime against music was their abolition of the liturgy and the ecclesiastical establishments which were the great nurseries of the art. In the cultivation of secular music many Puritans, from the elder Milton (who contributed to *The Triumphs of Oriana*) and his illustrious son down to the obscure, took their full share. Even William Prynne, Edwards's chief rival as the voice of Presbyterian rigour, commenced his harangue, in *Histriomastix*, against 'lascivious, amorous, effeminate, voluptuous Musicke' with the assertion: 'That Musicke of it selfe is lawfull, usefull, and commendable; no man, no Christian dares denie, since the Scriptures, Fathers, and generally all Christian, all Pagan Authors extant, doe with one consent averre it.' We may (with due regard for Purcell)

ascribe the general decline of music during the century in part
to such various causes as helped to blight lyrical verse, from
national disunity and economic and social change to the growth
of science and satire. But one cause was the internal evolution
of music itself—the shift of emphasis from the vocal to the
instrumental by which the English genius was largely shorn of
its strength; the shift, encouraged by Puritanism, from religious
to secular music; the development of operatic recitative; and
so on. There was in general a movement away from bold
imaginative freedom towards regularity which was roughly
parallel to the movement in verse associated with Waller and
Denham; one representative of the new tendencies was Henry
Lawes.

The sketch of Campion must serve to suggest the kind of
lyrics, amatory, pastoral, religious, and miscellaneous, which
fill the long array of song-books, and we may turn for a moment
to the miscellanies which, while they may contain songs for
music, belong to literature proper. During the period 1601–60
there were some thirty-five volumes of English verse which can
be called miscellanies, and about seventy-five wholly or mainly
in Latin and other foreign languages. The connexion between
the academic muse and the Crown is indicated by the fact that
sixty-five of these learned effusions appeared before 1642, five
in the years 1643–59, and five in 1660; one humbler volume
which obscures all the rest is the *Justa Edouardo King* (1638).
The mainly or wholly English collections included the elegiac
volumes in honour of Jonson (1638) and Lord Hastings (1649);
several books, like Cotgrave's *Wit's Interpreter* (1655), offered as
guides to amorous and courtly expression; the unique *Annalia
Dubrensia. Upon the Yearly Celebration of Mr. Robert Dover's
Olympic Games upon Cotswold Hills* (1636), which had among its
contributors Drayton, Randolph, Jonson, Felltham, Basse,
Mennes, Marmion, and Heywood; and the volumes of unkind
satires upon *Gondibert* published by Denham and others.

Apart from their varying intrinsic worth, the more general
anthologies provide an index of changing taste. Davison's
Poetical Rhapsody (1602), which reached a final edition in 1621,
was the last predominantly Petrarchan and pastoral collection;
it has many lyrics from the song-books, and a number of poems
reveal a crystallizing conception of the ode. In 1640 we come
to *Wit's Recreations*, the first of a long line of anthologies which

owed their success to a mixture of poetry, ribaldry, and royalism, and of which the chief fathers, or grandfathers, were Sir John Mennes and the Reverend James Smith. The stationer assured the readers of *Musarum Deliciae* (1655) that 'Plain Poetry is now disesteem'd, it must be Drollery or it will not please'. Among further fruits of Puritan domination were *Choice Drollery* (1656), *Wit and Drollery* (1656), *Wit Restored* (1658), *J. Cleaveland Revived* (1659), and, in 1660, more patent broadside reminders of political change in *Rats Rhymed to Death* and its second edition, *The Rump*. Along with these things may be mentioned the 'Sack-inspired Songs', first collected in 1661, of 'the English Anacreon', Alexander Brome (1620–66). A less slipshod anti-Puritan nostalgia animated the Reverend Abraham Wright, who put together the partly clerical *Parnassus Biceps . . . Composed by the best Wits that were in both the Universities before their Dissolution* (1656). Most of the well-known poets included, Donne, Jonson, Wotton, Herrick, Randolph, Corbet, Cartwright, King, and others, did not appear at their best or in good texts, but the book is an attractive and representative collection of amatory, elegiac, royalist, and miscellaneous verse. If *Parnassus Biceps* was transitional in a retrospective way, Joshua Poole's *English Parnassus* (1657) is a small landmark in the development of Augustan neoclassicism. In a short prefatory discourse on poetry, one 'J. D.' (possibly Dryden), who knows Sidney and Campion and especially Puttenham and Daniel, lays down general and particular rules for attaining regularity and correctness in versification and style. On the whole the Restoration and the eighteenth century did not cherish the religious or—apart from drollery—the secular verse of the earlier seventeenth century, though a number of things survived. For instance, Jacob Tonson, in re-editing Dryden's *Miscellany* in 1716, included about a hundred poems by Drayton, Wither, Donne, Jonson, Corbet, Carew, Suckling, and Marvell, and broadside and popular ballads, drawn from *Parnassus Biceps* and other anthologies and from less obvious sources. But while some twenty-five of the pieces—mainly not those of the poets named—were reprinted in other books of the earlier eighteenth century, the old material does not seem to have made an appeal in 1716. We have, however, leaped far beyond our period and must turn back to survey the exponents of 'modernist' poetry, classical and metaphysical.

IV

JONSON, DONNE, AND THEIR SUCCESSORS

WITH a heterogeneous crowd of poets behind us, we arrive at the customary division of the rest into the schools of Jonson and Donne, cavalier and metaphysical. The dichotomy is sound enough to be useful, and false enough to be troublesome, since lines and planes which at times seem quite divergent do in fact often meet. The impossibility of a clear-cut grouping is epitomized at the start in the much-discussed question whether certain poems were written by Jonson or by Donne; and their contemporaries and successors, indifferent to posterity's need of distinct labels, drew in varying proportions from both masters. On this point it may be said once for all that the names of Jonson and Donne stand not only for their actual and demonstrable influence but for the whole set of traditions and conditions which worked upon their fellows as well as upon themselves. Both poets rebelled, in their generally different ways, against pictorial fluidity, decorative rhetorical patterns, and half-medieval idealism, and both created new techniques, a new realism of style (or new rhetoric), sharp, condensed, and muscular, fitted for the intellectual and critical realism of their thought. But while Donne—'Wit's forge and fire-blast, meaning's press and screw', in Coleridgean phrase—hammered out an irregular personal instrument, it was typical of Jonson that he should, among other things, have had a large share in the development of the regular heroic couplet, 'the bravest sort of Verses'.

I

Jonson, the first great English theorist and practitioner of neoclassicism, the first really direct, learned, deliberate, and single-hearted heir of antiquity, gave poetry a new charter through his dynamic assimilation of the main tradition of the past.[1] His non-dramatic verse, bulky and varied though it is,

---

[1] Benjamin Jonson (1572–1637) was the grandson of a gentleman of the Scottish border and the son of a clergyman who died in 1572. His mother married a master bricklayer of Westminster. Jonson had a few years (until about 1588) at Westminster School and always remained devoted to his master, Camden. Some experience in bricklaying and in service in Flanders, and his marriage in 1594—his wife was to receive intermittent devotion—bring him to the stage; his first role was

we may regard as a minor part of a dramatist's output, but he apparently did not. Nearly all Jonson's poems, apart from the songs in plays and masques, were occasional, and for the purpose of this sketch may be divided into three groups: epigrams, lyrics, and reflective pieces. Nowadays we are perhaps inclined to skip the main body of epigrams, in spite of the author's pronouncing them 'the ripest of my studies'. The epigram was one of the favourite genres of the European Renaissance, and in Elizabethan and Jacobean England it had such exponents as Campion and John Owen in Latin, Sir John Davies, Guilpin, Bastard, Harington, Weever, Donne, Peacham, Parrot, Davies of Hereford, Rowlands, and Jonson's despised Heath. In most

that of actor. In 1598 he was listed by Francis Meres among tragic dramatists, but his first great extant play, of that year, was *Every Man in his Humour*, in which Shakespeare acted. In 1598 also Jonson was tried for killing an actor; he pleaded self-defence and claimed benefit of clergy. While in prison he was converted and 'therafter he was 12 yeares a Papist'; but he assisted official inquiries into the Gunpowder Plot and did not suffer when charged with recusancy (1606). In 1600–1 he exchanged dramatic blows with Marston and Dekker in the 'war of the theatres'. With the accession of James began Jonson's career as purveyor-in-chief of masques and entertainments for the court, and *Sejanus* (1603) inaugurated a great series of plays, *Volpone* (1606), *Epicoene* (1609), *The Alchemist* (1610), *Catiline* (1611), and *Bartholomew Fair* (1614). In 1605 Jonson was in trouble, along with Chapman and Marston, over the anti-Scottish satire in *Eastward Ho*. In 1612–13 he was abroad as tutor to young Walter Ralegh. Jonson collected his plays, masques, epigrams, and *The Forest*, his best writings up to 1612, in the folio *Works* of 1616. For a decade after 1616 he wrote no plays. In 1618–19 he made his pedestrian journey to Scotland. His dignity as a scholarly artist was confirmed by Scottish tributes and an honorary degree from Oxford (1619). But his later years were not too happy, for various reasons—a fire (1623) which destroyed many of his books, notes, and unpublished manuscripts; poverty, ill health, and, in 1628, a paralytic stroke; the failure of *The New Inn* (1629) and most of his other dramatic 'dotages'; the sporadic character of King Charles's favour; and an old feud with Inigo Jones which culminated in 1631. But Jonson could always study and he had, as always, many more friends than enemies. There were, or had been, people of rank like the Countess of Bedford, Lord d'Aubigny (with whom he lived for some years), the Earl of Pembroke and other men and women of the Sidney connexion, and the Earl of Newcastle; men of learning and affairs like Bacon, Camden, Cotton, Hoskyns, Edward Hyde, and Selden; and men of letters from Shakespeare, Donne, Chapman, and Beaumont and Fletcher to Herrick, Carew, Suckling, Sir Kenelm Digby, Richard Brome and others. The early gatherings at the Mermaid tavern were succeeded by those at the Old Devil, 'the Sun, The Dog, the triple Tunne' (in Herrick's phrase), and, later still, in Ben's sick-room. He was the privileged dictator and oracle of a whole tribe of younger writers who were proud to be called his 'sons'. Jonson was buried in the Abbey. Among the contributors to *Jonsonus Virbius* (1638), a volume of thirty-three elegies, were Lord Falkland, Sir John Beaumont, Henry King, Thomas May, Habington, Waller, James Howell, Sidney Godolphin, Cleveland, Jasper Mayne, Cartwright, Felltham, Marmion, and John Ford. In 1640–1 Digby edited a second volume of *Works*, containing later plays, masques, and non-dramatic verse, and *Timber* and *The English Grammar*.

of these writers the epigram inclined more or less towards social satire and a popular manner. Certainly none was so serious, complete, artistic, and original a disciple of Martial as Jonson, and none was such a Roman epigrammatist in temper, for Jonson the playwright and even Jonson the lyrist may be said to see and think and feel in terms of the epigram. His satirical epigrams, like those of his contemporaries, are interesting chiefly as acrid pictures of manners. They show what they helped to train, their author's caustic eye, tough vigour of language, and rhetorical resource and economy, but they are less distinguishable from other men's work, and less attractive to most readers, than the addresses and compliments to titled and literary patrons and friends. And much better still, in their masculine tenderness, are the epitaphs on his daughter and son and on the child actor, Solomon Pavy, which enshrine the most felicitous of all Jonson's adaptations of Martial.

A reader fresh from *Timber* may well expect to find in Jonson less of the ardent lover than of the confident and competent artist for whom love is a part of his *métier*. A strong, not to say cynical, head and a firm hand rule his heart and his senses. 'All extremes I would have bard', he says in his prescription for the ideal mistress, a prescription based on Martial and on the idea of love as a courtly game 'Neither too easie, nor too hard'. ' 'Twas an ingeniose remarque of my lady Hoskins', says Aubrey, 'that B. J. never writes of love, or if he does, does it not naturally.' The moral of 'Still to be neat, still to be drest' (a version of a post-classical epigram first printed by Scaliger in 1572) is only half-true of Jonson's amatory verse. Yet artistic feeling, if not love, refined and ordered in a pattern of delicate strength, gives to his best lyrics a cool, assured poise, an idealism at once artificial and rational, hardly less compelling in its way than emotional intensity. The most familiar example, 'Drinke to me, onely, with thine eyes', is one of those perfect poems which somehow seem to have always existed, but the geometrical conceit is woven out of scattered threads in the Greek prose of Philostratus. Similarly, in the songs derived from Catullus, 'Come my Celia' and 'Kisse me, sweet', there is more courtliness than passion, and no hint of the metaphysical fourth dimension. In Jonson's code of urbane gallantry the lady (if not a patroness) is something below a Petrarchan divinity, and her lover is decidedly not a worm. And impersonal detachment enables the poet, despite 'My mountaine belly, and my rockie face', to grow old gracefully. 'A Celebration of Charis' begins in the tone of *vers de société* and does not lose its hold upon realistic rhythm and language even in the fourth part, that ecstatic vision which recalls Lodge's 'Rosalind' and Spenser's *Prothalamion*,

> See the Chariot at hand here of Love
> Wherein my Lady rideth!

The triumphal divinity of this first stanza rises out of Ovid's *Amores*, and the enchanting mistress of the last out of the tomb of Martial's Erotion, but for once a rich inner fire fuses the mythological and the physical, and the metaphysical too. If the reader of *Timber* is prepared for the classical qualities of Jonson's amatory art, the reader of the *Conversations* may not be prepared for the metaphysical treatment of love, either in the broad or the special meaning of the term. Yet it is not the Roman poets but Lucian, Macrobius, and many allegorical mythographers who furnish the conception of love in the 'Epode' as 'a golden chaine let downe from heaven'. Nor is it mere fancy that glows in the conventional decorative setting of *The Hue and Cry after Cupid*:

> At his sight, the sunne hath turned,
> Neptune in the waters, burned;
> Hell hath felt a greater heate:
> Jove himselfe forsooke his seate:
> From the center, to the skie,
> Are his trophæes reared hie.

When love as a cosmic force, or as viewed against a cosmic background, is described in 'witty' and intellectual images and argument, the 'metaphysical' result is more obvious. That kind of writing Jonson at least approaches, notably in the three amatory elegies which he probably wrote when inspired by Donne's 'The Expostulation'. But Jonson's strength of judgement normally keeps his 'wits great over-plus' within mundane bounds ('Metaphors farfet hinder to be understood, and affected, lose their grace'); and when he uses the figure of the compass, it is to suggest Selden's circle 'Of generall knowledge'.

Of those three 'metaphysical' elegies which can safely be ascribed to Jonson, the first, ' 'Tis true, I'm broke!', is largely a mosaic drawn from Seneca's *De Clementia*. Even Ben's conversational censures of Drayton, Du Bartas, and Beaumont took the form of phrases from Quintilian. To a man saturated in ancient and especially Latin prose and verse, modern continental literature, Renaissance or baroque, meant correspondingly little, apart from humanistic neo-Latin, handbooks of mythology, and the like. It was to be expected that Jonson should rank as the first great disciple of Catullus in England, though he was, or thought he was, much better qualified for discipleship to Horace, Horace the satirist, moralist, lyrist, and critic; the *Ars Poetica*, which he so baldly translated, and commented upon, was part of his being. Ben's assimilation of Martial has been noticed already. But it would need a volume to cite his borrowings from the classics and, when he has learned the lessons of their wisdom and craftsmanship, he remains their peer and contemporary, not a tame 'classicist' but his own very English self. With even more than the serious Renaissance poet's usual reverence for learning and scorn for half-educated writers and their public, Jonson insists that the ancients are 'Guides, not Commanders'. The artist, the imitator of normal nature, must bring critical independence to the integration of ancient and modern experience, as, in his diction, he should fuse 'the eldest of the present, and newnesse of the past Language'. Reacting against Elizabethan vagaries of matter, form, and style, Jonson demanded, and unceasingly strove for, the ageless classical virtues of clarity, unity, symmetry, and proportion; in short, the control of the rational intelligence. His poems are wholes, not erratic displays of verbal fireworks, and false taste always pronounces such writing 'barren, dull, leane'. The curt phrase, 'Shaksperr wanted Arte', which only bardolaters have resented, is probably nearer Ben's considered judgement than the lapidary generosity of his noble tribute in verse. We are hardly surprised to hear that he wrote all his poems 'first in prose, for so his master Cambden had Learned him'. If the fact symbolizes and partly explains the prosaic element in most of Jonson's poetry, it suggests too his colloquial tone and idiom and clear, tough intellectual fibre. As the most influential of recent classicists has said, 'to have the virtues of good prose is the first and minimum requirement of good poetry'. That does not mean that one could readily summarize the prose content of such lyrics—more Elizabethan than Jonsonian—as those two in *Cynthia's Revels*, the silvery 'Queene, and Huntresse, chaste, and faire', and the exquisitely modulated song of Echo, 'Slow, slow, fresh fount, keepe time with my salt teares'. And while Jonson is no bird-like songster, the classicist who would write as he drinks, 'In flowing measure, fill'd with flame, and spright', can also warble such native wood-notes wild as 'The faery beame upon you' and 'The owle is abroad, the bat, and the toad'.

But Jonson's classicism was far too deep and genuine to expend itself on mere technique. His broadest and noblest statement of the ethical and didactic function of poetry is given, with special reference of course to the stage, in the dedication of *Volpone* to 'the Two Famous Universities'. Recalling the ideal poet of Strabo and Horace, and the ideal orator of Cicero and Quintilian, Jonson affirms 'the impossibility of any mans being the good Poet, without first being a good man', and if he falls short of Milton in religious fervour of utterance, he is wholly sincere. He goes on, in words which link him with Milton, Spenser, and Sidney and a host of other men, to elaborate the Renaissance ideal of the poet as the supreme instructor of youth and age, 'the interpreter, and arbiter of nature, a teacher of things divine, no lesse then humane, a master in manners', who 'can alone (or with a few) effect the businesse of man-kind'.

Such words, amplified in many passages from ancient and modern humanists in *Timber*, express the solid and positive essence of Jonson's classicism. And his ethical view of poetry, which on the one hand supports his satire, on the other animates a great deal of soberly reflective verse. The hundred and first epigram, a genial and gracious invitation to supper, leads up, as it were, to what is a kind of apostolic consecration, 'An Epistle answering to one that asked to be Sealed of the Tribe of Ben'. Such bread-and-butter epistles as 'To Penshurst' and 'To Sir Robert Wroth' bring weight and dignity (and Martial and Virgil's second *Georgic*) to the celebration not only of the country but of the good old ways of feudal life and pure religion breathing household laws. Seneca furnishes a large part of the epistle to Sir Edward Sackville. As we might expect from Jonson's devotion to Seneca, his central creed is rooted in Stoic magnanimity and inward order, the virtuous strength 'Here in my bosome, and at home' which preserves the individual soul among

> such as blow away their lives,
> And never will redeeme a day,
> Enamor'd of their golden gyves.

And with these Arnoldian lines 'To the World' may be placed

the manly and beautiful epitaph on Vincent Corbet (a modern parallel to the younger Pliny's philosopher Euphrates), who exemplified 'A life that knew nor noise, nor strife'. Jonson is nowhere more explicitly didactic, and seldom more truly poetical, than in the early 'Epode', or in one strophe at least of the Senecan ode of a generation later ·which inaugurated the strictly Pindaric form in English:

> It is not growing like a tree
> In bulke, doth make man better bee;
> Or standing long an Oake, three hundred yeare,
> To fall a logge, at last, dry, bold, and seare:
> A Lillie of a Day,
> Is fairer farre, in May,
> Although it fall, and die that night;
> It was the Plant, and flowre of light.
> In small proportions, we just beauties see:
> And in short measures, life may perfect bee.

These rhythms seem to have been in Wordsworth's mind when he wrote the 'Intimations of Immortality', and the relationship underlines the difference between two ages and two men; Jonson could not see radiant clouds of glory or touch thoughts too deep for tears, but neither could his stout rationality lapse into bathetic extravagance.

And yet, finally, Jonson's serious thought and feeling do not always move on the plane of Stoic ethics. The modern reader, when confronted, in writers of the Renaissance tradition, with pieces of salty wit alongside devotional poems, is given to assuming that the latter are only the conventional pietisms of essentially emancipated minds. But the Renaissance mind did not run on a single track, and we should have a mistaken view of Jonson—and of many other poets—if we ignored rare but authentic moments of confessional humility, faith, and aspiration:

> Good, and great God, can I not thinke of thee,
> But it must, straight, my melancholy bee?

The 'great lover and praiser of himself' and 'contemner and Scorner of others' can pray, like Herbert, 'Use still thy rod'. The lover of sack and canary, who had nocturnal visions of Tartars and Turks, Romans and Carthaginians, fighting about his great toe, could also entreat 'My Maker, Saviour, and my Sanctifier' that he might be truly glorified 'Among thy Saints'.

Swinburne, in whose critical vocabulary 'gods' and 'giants' were roughly equivalent to 'Apollonian' and 'Dionysian', gave to Ben the supremacy among English giants that Shakespeare held among English gods—and 'No giant ever came so near to the ranks of the gods'. With all his fervent praise, Swinburne (who of course was assessing the whole body of Jonson's work) represents the main line of nineteenth-century romantic criticism. The flowers of Jonson's growing 'have colour, form, variety, fertility, vigour: the one thing they want is fragrance'. In recent decades critical noses have been in great indignation at the thought of poetical fragrance, and of magic and wonder and mystery, and Jonson has risen on the wave of the anti-romantic reaction. We still praise the 'rational' virtues Swinburne praised, but with a less easy assurance that they are of an inferior kind. Our increasing respect for Jonson's classical art, our unwillingness to call his genius talent, is doubtless a sign of increasing sanity. The light that never was on sea or land has become an intoxication and a poetaster's dream; we want poetry which is dry, not damp. But our dislike of romantic excesses, such as the embarrassing parts of Wordsworth's ode, still leaves unharmed the great poetry of Jonson's own and slightly later days, from 'Full fathom five' to 'The Retreat', and of those worlds the clear-eyed, robust, concrete Jonson has at most partial glimpses. His achievement is a strong, massive, and symmetrical pyramid, if not 'a Star-ypointing' one; and we may perhaps cancel the qualification when we return to his individual and enduring beauties, or think, with Swinburne, of the 'something heroic and magnificent in his lifelong dedication of all his gifts and all his powers to the service of the art he had elected as the business of all his life and the aim of all his aspiration'.

Among all Jonson's disciples the only real heir of his Renaissance humanism, the ethical and scholarly solidity of his art, was the young Milton. The rest, in their various ways and degrees, and with varying responsiveness to the metaphysical fashion, cultivated such patches of the Jonsonian garden as amatory, complimentary, elegiac, and epigrammatic verse. The most versatile, the most classical (in a limited sense), and the least metaphysical was Robert Herrick (1591–1674).[1] While

---

[1] Herrick's father, a London goldsmith, died in 1592. We know nothing of the boy's bringing-up until 1607, when he entered upon a ten-year apprenticeship with

Herrick praised very few English poets, he bestowed a number
of tributes upon Jonson. A large proportion of his verse, as of
Jonson's, belongs to the genre of the epigram, in its broad
classical meaning, and he has some moralizing epistles on
country contentment in the vein of Jonson (and of Horace,
Tibullus, and Martial). But the Jonsonian stream has run thin;
in other words, the bricklayer has given place to the goldsmith's apprentice, the master of filigree. In Herrick Renaissance neo-pagan and belated Elizabethan united to form a pure
artist, who would rather see his book dead than not perfected,
whose poetic creed is to live merrily and trust to good verses,
and who in a troubled age is largely content to mirror or create
a timeless epicurean Arcadia. With full recognition of the
vigorous and even crude masculinity which shows itself often
enough, we might call Herrick not so much a son as a daughter
of Ben. Apart from the serious Jonsonian realms which the
disciple scarcely enters, there is a difference as well as a likeness
between Ben's lyrics of manly gallantry and courtly idealism
and Herrick's 'Carkanet' of more richly artificial fancies offered
to a bright but indistinct procession of dainty mistresses. (We
may remember, by the way, his classical apology: 'Jocond his
Muse was; but his Life was chast'.)

Herrick refines his commonplaces with a loving and individual subtlety in the use of words and rhythms. An amorous
trifle can be almost transcendentalized by one startling, half-
metaphysical, and triumphant phrase, 'That liquefaction of her
clothes'. Jonson's 'Still to be neat, still to be drest', with its
plainness of generalized statement, makes its impression as a
well-turned whole. Herrick's 'Delight in Disorder' has the
feminine particularity of a dressmaker, and the phrases are a
succession of delicate or delicately mock-heroic paradoxes which

his wealthy uncle, Sir William Herrick, a goldsmith also. He broke loose in 1613 to
go up, at a late age, to Cambridge (B.A., 1617; M.A., 1620). After 1620, or 1617,
he apparently lived in London, writing in the sunshine of Jonson and the other
wits and of such courtiers as Endymion Porter. He had given up notions of the law,
and in 1627 we find him going to the Isle of Rhé as chaplain to the Duke of
Buckingham. In 1629 Herrick became vicar of Dean Prior in the diocese of Exeter
and bade a formal 'Farewell to Poetry'; happily he did not abide by his sober
resolution. He was ejected from Dean Prior in 1647 and seems to have spent the
next fifteen years chiefly in London. A volume of his poems had been entered in
1640, but it was not until 1648 that *Hesperides* (with *Noble Numbers*) appeared; he
wrote hardly anything thereafter. In 1662 Herrick was restored to his old living.
He died in the same year as Milton and Traherne.

turn a woman into a dainty rogue in porcelain, and one whose roguishness is not limited to her costume. (It is pleasant to find that Herrick's earnest bishop, Joseph Hall, had spoken in a sermon of 'a loose lock erring wantonly over her shoulders'.) Among the countless sensuous or sensual conceits and metrical experiments that the cool-hearted poet lays on the altar of love, there are a few poems to which consummate art gives the semblance of passion, poems which enshrine the ideal attitude of the cavalier. In

> Bid me to live, and I will live
> Thy Protestant to be,

a formal symmetry and texture of unwonted strength may recall Jonson, but the inspired wit of 'Protestant' is Herrick's. And in the novel setting, at once rich and homely, of 'The Night-piece, to Julia'—which has metrical and other affinities with Ben's 'The faery beame upon you'—Julia is not the mere possessor of lacteal breasts and hairless legs but a divinity of nature whom glow-worm and moon are alike happy to serve.

Whether Herrick remembers pseudo-Ausonius or Catullus or another, in 'Gather ye Rose-buds while ye may' (perhaps the most popular lyric of the century) or the radiant 'Corinna's going a Maying', his variations on the brevity of youth and love express more sentiment than passion. When he rings these changes on universal Renaissance themes, and when he tells us of himself and his pride in his craft, Herrick is conscious of course of his descent from Anacreon, Catullus, Horace, Tibullus, Propertius, Ovid, and Martial, though his thumb-nail painting on ivory owes much of its tone to modern continental imitators of the ancients and to Jonson. What is most obvious in Herrick's classicism is not the mythological symbols (which dwindle in stature without quite losing their ideal quality), nor the technical discipline that has won him such urbane simplicity, but a degree of saturation in the atmosphere of Roman life which has no comparable parallel unless in the purple eloquence nourished at Golden Grove. If we read him as he wished to be read, 'When Laurell spirts 'ith fire', we see the incumbent of Dean Prior (who looked like a Roman emperor) 'Drinking wine, & crown'd with flowres', performing or prophetically receiving the ancient rites of burial, pouring libations to his household gods, promising a cock to Aesculapius on behalf of his maid Prue. In this imaginative escape from 'lothed Devonshire' Herrick cannot very well be a frigid academic classicist. The genuineness of his feeling is attested on every other page by his fusion of native and classical lore, a fusion happily avowed in his title *Hesperides*. The Anglican cleric worships his Lares while he trolls a bowl of North-down ale and crickets sing on the hearth. The Theocritean, Ovidian, and Marlovian invitation 'To Phillis to love, and live with him' is purely English. 'To the Maids to walk abroad' mingles mythological tales with wedding-smocks, posies, gloves, and ribbons. In the epithalamia we have Hymen's torch, Juno, and filleted door-posts along with the bride's garters, the bridegroom's points, and the sack-posset.

Herrick's bookish, idyllic, and realistic pastoral verse has a charm often more 'fresh and fragrant' than that of his many mistresses. The 'free-born Roman' is also 'Robin Herrick'. The priest of Cupid and Bacchus inhabits a country rectory with his faithful Prue, his cock, hen, goose, lamb, cat, and spaniel (he does not mention the pig he taught to drink out of a tankard), and he can enjoy, or at least praise, the frugal diet of 'Pea, or Bean, or Wort, or Beet'. At times he abhors the currish people about him and impales luckless individuals in epigrams, and he exults in returning to London after his 'long and irksome banishment' in 'the dull confines of the drooping West'; but he gained enduring fame in his parish, and real affection for 'the Countries sweet simplicity' went to the making of his half-English, half-classical pictures of the seasonal round of work and play. Herrick's volume of 1648 was no more remote from public affairs than the works of other poets published about that time, but none offered such an open challenge to the spirit of civil war:

> I sing of Brooks, of Blossomes, Birds, and Bowers:
> Of April, May, of June, and July-Flowers.
> I sing of May-poles, Hock-carts, Wassails, Wakes,
> Of Bride-grooms, Brides, and of their Bridall-cakes. . . .

So, 'in time of "the breaking of nations" ', we have what goes onward the same though dynasties pass, the sports of Christmas and Twelfth Night, the 'tough labours, and rough hands' of Devon harvesters ('the Lords of Wine and Oile'!), and the glorified Maying of that 'sweet-Slug-a-bed', Corinna. It was inevitable, too, that a lover of rural lore, a neo-pagan, and an artist in miniature should be one of the last to sing of 'The Court of Mab, and of the Fairie-King'. And we should not forget that the sophisticated poet could write 'The mad Maid's Song'.

The two final lines of the fourteen which compose 'The Argument of his Book' relate to hell and hopes of heaven, and the arithmetical proportion may serve as a critical statement concerning *Noble Numbers*. Herrick was not deeply disturbed by the conflict between soul and sense which harassed and inspired some greater contemporaries, and he was not alone in feeling small compunction about printing 'unbaptized Rhimes' and divine poems together; both God and the shy virgin may read his sinful book without harm. There is no need to question the sincerity, whatever the limitations, of Herrick's religious sentiment, and it was only natural that some of his most attractive devotional pieces should be expressions of mundane content and thanksgiving.

Herrick's poems were too sensuously and smoothly Elizabethan for an age of 'strong lines'. They circulated in manuscript and were reprinted in contemporary and later miscellanies and song-books, but anonymously, and his book was not reissued as a whole until 1823. The poet himself did not begin to emerge from obscurity until the end of the eighteenth century, and did not win real fame until the later nineteenth, and then an overdue debt was possibly overpaid. In recent years he has been either disparaged or ignored by critics who, having been weaned on a pickle, are not inclined to suck 'on countrey pleasures, childishly'. Herrick's conception of poetry, which many distinguished minor artists have held, did not require that a lyric or epigram should be an assault upon the Absolute, and we need not feel unduly guilty if we are charmed by a singer of such civilized grace. Nor is Herrick always lacking in seriousness. Witness such things as the 'Apparition of his Mistress calling him to Elysium', or the noble numbers addressed to Endymion Porter on his brother's death, where he is less remote from Catullus than in his amatory verse:

> Sunk is my sight; set is my Sun;
> And all the loome of life undone:
> The staffe, the Elme, the prop, the shelt'ring wall
> Whereon my Vine did crawle,
> Now, now, blowne downe; needs must the old stock fall.

And we should do more justice to the simple beauties and pieties of *Noble Numbers* if we had not heard the deeper and more personal note of the greater souls of Herrick's time.

Thomas Carew (1594/5–1639?) is akin to Herrick in some central qualities but he is distinguished by his narrow range, his courtly reserve, and his metaphysical strain.[1] Two-thirds of his poems deal with love. Among the occasional poems the largest group is obituary, and two of these would alone indicate the divided allegiance of a 'son of Ben', the beautifully simple 'Epitaph on the Lady Mary Villiers' and the Donnian elegy on Donne, one of the most significant essays in criticism that the age produced. We are reminded of Jonson also by two pleasant pictures of country-house life, 'To Saxham' and 'To my friend G. N. from Wrest', which are especially welcome from a poet of Whitehall. While in Carew as in other men the influence of Jonson and of Donne cannot be completely differentiated, it is safe to say, in spite of hints of condescension towards Father Ben and of the fervent tribute to Donne's anti-classical originality, that without Donne Carew's best poems would have lost much but that without Jonson he would not have been a poet at all. He could use Donne's ideas and phrases, and he could give to the poetry of love a half-metaphysical tone and edge through realistic, cosmic, and religious images, but he had very little of Donne's glancing wit, intensity, learning, and intellectual pressure. Carew was essentially—and mainly at second-hand, through Jonson—a classical amorist. Even in the 'Elegy' Donne is a priest of Apollo with Promethean breath, and Carew owes some of his amatory felicities to the ideal value of mythological reference. To him as to his fellows, of course, Jonson the humanist is quite alien, and the qualities of Jonson's love poetry become in transmission less robust and more precious. Sophisticated gallantry, poise, and grace, and a strain of chivalric idealism partly conceal the sensual or cynical core,

---

[1] Carew was the son of the lawyer Sir Matthew Carew. He graduated from Merton College in 1611 and, after a sojourn at the Middle Temple, held a secretaryship under Sir Dudley Carleton (a relative by marriage) in Italy (1613) and at The Hague (1616). He was dismissed in 1616 for slandering Sir Dudley and Lady Carleton. He went to France in 1619 in the train of Sir Edward (later Lord) Herbert. In 1628 Carew received his first post at court. Among his literary friends were Edward Hyde, James Howell, Suckling, and the men to whom he addressed epistles in verse: Jonson, George Sandys, Thomas May, Walter Montagu, Aurelian Townshend, and Davenant. Carew's masque, *Coelum Britannicum*, was presented and printed n 1634. His *Poems* appeared in 1640.

and passion is controlled, or the want of it almost supplied, by elegant symmetry of form, by an urbane and impersonal refinement of the traditional and normal in both feeling and expression. (Yet elegance may admit unexpected realistic force, as when—to go outside the amatory verse for a phrase Keats may have remembered—Carew sees the widowed Countess of Anglesey 'Glutting' her 'sorrowes'.)

No Elizabethan sonneteer praised, persuaded, or chided a mistress with more extravagant conceits than Carew, and his success varies with his restraint. 'Ask me no more where Jove bestowes' is his most perfect, though not his most typical, lyric because conventional Petrarchan ideas and images are strengthened and ordered by Jonsonian discipline and just touched by metaphysical vibrations, so that one man's eulogy of one woman becomes a grandiose pattern of transcendental beauty and love. Even 'The Complement' is raised above its luscious Italianate kind through being firmly moulded. 'A Rapture', the most elaborate of the poems in which sensual passion spoke out undisguised, is far more fleshly and pictorial than Donne's most wanton elegies, yet the piece is also a serious attack, in the name of ' Nature ', upon ' Honour ' or the laws of orthodox morality. No doubt there is a gulf between the stately 'Song' and 'A Rapture', and no doubt most of Carew's amatory verse was closer in spirit to the latter, but the 'Song' and some other things enable us to understand how at moments the libertine courtier might become aware of his

> restlesse Soule, tyr'd with pursuit
> Of mortall beautie, seeking without fruit
> Contentment there.

We remember also the story of his summoning John Hales once too often for a death-bed repentance and absolution, and we may include a pious along with a poetic and musical impulse behind his quota of Psalms.

In contrast with Carew, whose 'Muse was hard bound', the author of that phrase, Millamant's 'Natural, easy Suckling', was the first of 'The Mob of Gentlemen who wrote with Ease'.[1]

---

[1] Sir John Suckling (1609–42), a scion of an old Norfolk family, passed from Cambridge to Gray's Inn, travelled during 1628–30, was knighted on his return, and in 1631–2 served under Gustavus Adolphus. At home again, Suckling became, says Aubrey, 'the greatest gallant of his time, and the greatest gamester, both for bowling and cards, so that no shop-keeper would trust him for 6d.' He is said to have invented cribbage. Suckling drew some gibes with the gorgeous costuming of

In 'A Sessions of the Poets' (which, by the way, can have owed
no more than a hint to Boccalini's *Ragguagli di Parnaso*), he is
complacently conscious of his amateur status:

> He loved not the Muses so well as his sport;
> And prized black eyes, or a lucky hit
> At bowls, above all the Trophies of wit.

And it is that Suckling whose lucky hits at verse we prize, 'Why
so pale and wan fond Lover?', "Tis now since I sate down before
That foolish Fort, a heart', 'Out upon it, I have lov'd Three
whole days together', and above all, of course, the daintily
robust 'Ballad: Upon a Wedding', which according to tradition
was written for the marriage of Roger Boyle, Lord Broghill, and
Lady Margaret Howard in January 1641. Suckling's poetical
bent is partly indicated in his allusions to Jonson's vanity and
laboriously learned brain and to Donne as the unrivalled lord of
wit. The one clear imitation of Ben—'Hast thou seen the Down
in the Air . . .?'—turns the ecstatic praise of Charis into satire,
while the pervasive spirit of Donne goes beyond such obvious
echoes as 'Oh! for some honest Lovers ghost'. It is chiefly the
cynical strain of the young Donne that Suckling carries on, with
a lighter flippancy and with some notes suggestive of the French
libertins—though the friend of Hales and Falkland, and the
author, whatever his motives, of *An Account of Religion by Reason*
(and some private letters as well) was not merely the frivolous or
sensual man about town who wrote most of the verse. But when
Suckling chooses to think in verse, he seldom rises above the
simple, lucid, and witty exposition of conventional naturalism;
he feels no need of reconciling soul and body, love and desire.
He writes repeatedly 'against fruition' not because the con-
queror of Bridget and of Nell subscribes (unless in his plays) to
the fashionable 'Platonics', which in fact he ridicules, but
because the chase is a titillating refinement of ultimate pleasure.

For us, to think of the cavalier spirit is to think first of Richard
Lovelace (1618–56/7), and it is hard to believe that his two
most familiar lyrics were rescued from oblivion by Bishop Percy
and that Scott, misquoting the shorter one, assigned it to Montrose.[1] As soldier, courtier, lover, poet, scholar, musician, and

both his play *Aglaura* (1637–8) and the troop he led to Scotland in the first Bishops'
War (1639). In 1641 he was involved in the 'first army plot', escaped to France,
and died there—according to one tale (Aubrey's), by suicide. His *Fragmenta Aurea*
appeared in 1646.

[1] Lovelace, the son of a Kentish knight and soldier, was educated at the

connoisseur of painting, the 'extraordinary handsome' Lovelace exemplified the tradition of Sidney and Castiglione, and not least in service of his prince. While we can enjoy a number of his courtly and miscellaneous poems, among them such unexpected things as 'The Toad and Spider' and the Anacreontic and Horatian 'Grasshopper', fame has rightly fixed upon the few lyrics in which Lovelace struck a simple, sincere, and perfect attitude. In them, with an idealism untouched by the sceptical or cynical, he enshrined the cavalier trinity, beauty, love, and loyal honour. 'To Althea, from Prison' (which perhaps owes a hint to Voiture's 'Dans la prison') might almost be called a royalist broadside, refined and ennobled without loss of masculine spontaneity. The flawless 'Going to the Wars' is Jonsonian in its ordered brevity and completeness; we may remember, by the way, that Lovelace was the first literal translator of Catullus. The other famous and less famous poems show, with the extreme unevenness of a gentleman amateur, the more characteristic influence of Donne and continental fashions. Like other poets of his time, including his kinsman Stanley, Lovelace illustrates very often the pernicious anaemia of the secular metaphysical muse, the dwindling from cosmic audacities into pretty, laboured, and eccentric artifice. The radiant Elizabethan vision of Gratiana dancing hovers between inspired *naïveté* and fantastic sophistication. But Lovelace is linked also with Ralegh and Sidney and Wyatt, rather than with Carew and Suckling, by a grave nobility of mind, and he views the overthrow of his king and the established order with the sober and selfless dignity of 'To Lucasta, From Prison'.

A modern addition to the roll of cavalier poets is Sidney Godolphin (1610–43), Suckling's 'little Sid', the admired friend of Falkland, Hyde, and Hobbes. Though retired, bookish, and 'melancholique', 'of so nice and tender a composition' that he would turn back from a ride if the wind were against him, Godolphin was a member of Parliament and, like Falkland, one

Charterhouse, where Crashaw was his contemporary, and at Oxford (M.A., 1636). His life as courtier and country gentleman was interrupted in 1639–40 by the Bishops' Wars, and in 1642, when he presented the Kentish petition to the Commons, by a brief imprisonment in the Gatehouse. There he wrote 'To Althea, from Prison'. He spent much of the years 1643–6 abroad. In 1648 he was again imprisoned, for ten months. *Lucasta* appeared in 1649; the identity of the lady has not been established. Lovelace's fortune had gone in the king's cause and he passed his remaining years in obscurity, though probably not in the extreme penury reported by Aubrey and Wood. Another volume was issued after his death.

of the first volunteers and early victims of the war. Like Falkland, too, he wrote elegies on both Jonson and Donne, and in
the distinctive manner of each; the compressed and critical
tribute to Jonson, 'The Muses fairest light in no darke time',
was long ascribed to Cleveland. Such lyrics as 'Or love mee
lesse, or love mee more' combine fastidious clarity of style and
sound with a strain of metaphysical pregnancy and paradox,
the 'strong' quality that Suckling reproved. Godolphin's grave
thoughtfulness is illustrated on another plane in 'Lord when the
wise men came from Farr', or in the celebration of Donne not as
the wit and rebel but as the 'Pious dissector' of hearts and sins
who gave 'a religious tincture to our feares'.

The poetical claims of such sons and heirs of Jonson as
Richard Brome, James Howell, and Jasper Mayne are not very
urgent, and Lord Falkland's poems are of interest chiefly as
personal and metrical documents. Some other men cannot be
overlooked. The most familiar poem of the dramatist Francis
Beaumont (1584?–1616) is one of his two epistles to Jonson from
the country, about the convivial gatherings at the Mermaid; if
he wrote the long *Salmacis and Hermaphroditus* (1602), he added
an unusual degree of humour to the luxuriant Ovidian convention. The pastoral, erotic, and festive verse of the short-
lived and much-praised Thomas Randolph (1605–35) was
rather too facile and unoriginal for the convenience of either
the anthologist or the historian; among the courtly and metaphysical poets he remained the precocious undergraduate,
though we can still feel his genuine delight in the country.
Bishop Corbet (1582–1635), who, if not quite the Friar Tuck of
Aubrey's sketch, lacked the Stoic sobriety Jonson honoured in
his father, is for ever identified with 'Farewell rewards and
Fairies', that robustly nostalgic lament for a Catholic Merry
England blighted by Puritanism. And Corbet's chaplain,
William Strode (1602–45), is also virtually a man of one poem,
the gracious little conceit 'I saw faire Cloris walke alone'.

Strode's *Floating Island*, produced at Oxford in 1636 in honour
of the king and queen, may be said to have sunk, though it
employed the talents of Inigo Jones and Henry Lawes, but the
next night's play, *The Royal Slave*, staged by the same pair, was
a resounding success. Its author, William Cartwright (1611–
43), like Corbet and Strode, was a Christ Church man, and 'the
most florid and seraphical Preacher in the University', a scholar

and wit beloved by a multitude of men from King Charles
down. But the poet disappoints expectations aroused by Jonson's unwonted encomium, 'My Son Cartwright writes all like
a Man'. His lustre, indeed, grew dim after 1660. A disciple of
Jonson and, in a lesser degree, of Donne, he seldom rose above
smooth and skilful imitation, whether in his courtly compliments and elegies or in his amatory ardours. One Platonic
stanza of 'To Chloe who wish'd her self young enough for me'
attracted the possessive admiration of Coleridge. Cartwright's
commendatory poems are somewhat more critical than the
mass of their kind (such as the fanfare which accompanied his
own volume of 1651), and, if he exalts John Fletcher's sophisticated art at the expense of Shakespeare's 'Old fashion'd wit', he
is taking a step towards Dryden, or one of several Drydens.

2

Most of the courtly lyrists, major as well as minor, live chiefly
and on the whole not undeservedly in anthology pieces, and
these perhaps give a stronger impression of family resemblance
than of the individual flavour which even the slighter poets may
possess. The endless problems of authorship which envelop
fatherless or many-fathered poems supply concrete evidence for
a degree of homogeneity among the writers who went to school
to Jonson or Donne or both. At the same time, the cultivation
of wit made for less obvious homogeneity than had characterized the choir of Elizabethan singers. So far we have been concerned with Jonsonian cavalier poets, and the frequency with
which the name of Donne and the word 'metaphysical' have
occurred illustrates the impossibility of any clear-cut distinction
between two 'schools'. Indeed, one sometimes thinks of grouping the lyrical poets, and some others, as disciples of Donne who
felt the influence of Jonson and disciples of Donne who did not.
Yet even that suggestion reminds us that the influence of Jonson
was by its very nature less palpable as well as less seductive.
Before we come to the major metaphysical poets—and partly
by way of avoiding a prolonged anticlimax at the end of this
chapter—we may notice a reasonable number of small poets who
are mostly nearer to Donne than to Jonson or who cannot be
given any very precise label.
    These remarks make an odd prelude to the name of Shake-
speare, though the word 'notice' is prudentially appropriate for

a reference to that fascinating enigma 'The Phoenix and the Turtle', which was printed in Robert Chester's *Love's Martyr* (1601), along with poems on the same theme by 'Ignoto', Marston, Chapman, and Jonson (who·was represented by the 'Epode' and its appendages). Lesser mysteries of another kind, now cleared up, have obscured the fame of the lawyer, scholar, and wit, John Hoskyns (1566–1638). For nearly three centuries portions of his tract on rhetoric lay unrecognized in Jonson's *Timber* and some later text-books, and his 'Absence, heare thou my Protestation', a poem printed anonymously in Davison's *Poetical Rhapsody* (1602), was assigned to Donne; Saintsbury was almost ready to go to the stake for Donne's authorship. Sir Henry Wotton (1568–1639), the friend of Donne and Walton and the eulogist of *Comus*, wrote like a greater Dyer in one famous poem, the Horatian 'Character of a Happy Life', which Jonson had by heart, and like a lesser Carew in his other famous piece, the lyric on the Queen of Bohemia, 'You meaner Beauties of the Night'. One of Wotton's unsuccessful rivals for the provostship of Eton, Sir Robert Aytoun (1570–1638), the cultivated courtier and friend of Jonson, Hobbes, and 'all the witts', was the first notable Scotsman to use English. The sober dignity of his amorous complaints can be quickened by neat wit and occasional humour, and Dryden pronounced them 'some of the best of that age'.

In the next generation we have such definitely metaphysical lyrists as the 'poore & pocky' Aurelian Townshend (1583?–1651?), who for a time travelled with Lord Herbert, and Sir Francis Kynaston (1587–1642), whom we have met before as an educational 'projector'. Townshend produced two masques in 1632, but he lives in a handful of lyrics like 'Victorious beauty', and 'Though regions farr devided', in which manly gallantry and wit are wedded to manly music. Kynaston is less restrained and less musical; but once at least, though avowedly heart-whole, he is touched by the authentic spark and rivals Carew in symmetry if not in finish:

> Do not conceale thy radiant eyes,
> The starre-light of serenest skies,
> Least wanting of their heavenly light,
> They turne to Chaos endlesse night.

The soaring fire which in this age was distributed with such pentecostal generosity seldom kindled William Habington

(1605–54), author of the popular *Castara* (1634). This Catholic poet hardly belongs to any school, as his concentration on the sonnet indicates, and his sincere glorifying of chaste love separates him from both 'Platonic' and more candid amorists. Although he could anticipate Lovelace with 'In the chaste Nunn'ry of her brests', his self-consciously edifying muse was inclined to be dull, if not sublunary (to echo the phrase of Donne that he borrowed), and less attractive than what he deplored, 'loose coppies of lust happily exprest'. But his soul could spread her wings in such religious poems as *Nox nocti indicat Scientiam*.

The largely metaphysical texture of this chapter may permit the juxtaposition of the blameless Habington and the noseless Sir William Davenant (1606–68). Though hailed by Suckling as Donne's successor, Davenant does not reveal any special allegiance. His famous song, 'The Lark now leaves his watry Nest', is a compliment more cavalier and Elizabethan than metaphysical. Still less metaphysical is the very different *aubade*, 'O Thou that sleep'st like Pigg in Straw, Thou Lady dear, arise'. But Davenant at his best has both a large masculine energy of imagination, as in 'Wake all the dead! what hoa! what hoa!' (in *The Law Against Lovers*), and a distinctive vein of thoughtful sobriety. He was, or was to be, a signal actor and sufferer in the royalist cause, yet in 'The Soldier going to the Field' he strikes more than the conventional notes:

> And, for the sport of Kings, encrease
> The number of the Dead.

In such things as the 'Song. Endymion Porter and Olivia' and 'The Philosopher and the Lover to a Mistress Dying' the time-worn theme of love and death becomes metaphysical, though the grave dignity of tone and movement belong rather to the poet of *Gondibert* than to the metaphysical manner.

A greater cavalier than Davenant, or than Lovelace, was James Graham, Marquis of Montrose (1612–50), whose 'My dear and only Love', written probably in 1642, was the most fervent of all expressions of royalist devotion. But in a larger way it was, in the words of the hero's best biographer, 'the song of a man who has at last found assurance, the confession of a soul which has a vision of a noble purpose, and holds no risk too high in its attainment':

He either fears his Fate too much,
    Or his Deserts are small,
That puts it not unto the Touch,
    To win or lose it all.

From the gallant and glamorous man of action we turn for
a moment to an attractive man of books, Thomas Stanley
(1625–78). His few original lyrics show a tinge of Donne
through the predominant graceful artifice of foreign models and
cavalier convention. Though himself rather a moon than a
sun, Stanley had a number of poetical satellites, kinsmen, and
friends. One relative was William Hammond (1614–?), whose
Poems (1655) are not distinctive. One friend was the vigorous
and versatile John Hall (1627–56), author of a precocious
volume of essays, *Horae Vacivae* (1646), *Poems* (1647), a tract on
the reformation of the universities (1649), the first English
translation of Longinus (1652), and other things. Herrick
saluted the young Apollo, and Henry More commended at
length his 'Satyrick Flail'. Hobbes, who esteemed the young
man's talents, might have welcomed an 'Epicurean Ode' linking metaphysical passion with atomism, and Traherne might
have liked his 'Pastoral Hymn'. What Saintsbury calls the
poet's 'Gold *dust* only ... but *gold* dust' may be assayed, too, in
'The Call' and 'The Lure', which bring fresh feeling to the
theme of love and passing time.

The older James Shirley (1596–1666), whose plays over-
shadow his other work, was praised by Stanley as 'dearest
Friend', and he in turn praised the high yet clear and terse and
innocent muse of Stanley. Shirley the lyrist was a smooth Jonsonian cavalier with some touches of wit, a sort of Carew without Carew's genius. His long *Narcissus*, which had been entered
and presumably published in 1618, was, in his *Poems* of 1646,
one of the last facile products of Elizabethan Ovidianism. But
Shirley was the last of the Elizabethans in a stronger way. In
that noble dirge in *The Contention of Ajax and Ulysses* (1659) the
greatest of medieval and Renaissance commonplaces is treated
with an unabashed exaltation of traditional metaphor and statement in which we just hear the Augustan note:

   The glories of our blood and state,
      are shadows, not substantial things,
   There is no armour against fate,
      Death lays his icy hand on Kings. . . .

Many small voices are not inaudible. The clergyman Thomas Pestell (1585–1667) especially imitated Sir John Beaumont and praised Donne as the 'Prince of Wits' and 'The late Copernicus in Poëtrie'. Thomas Beedome (1613–41?), in his *Poems Divine and Human* (1641), and the physician John Collop (1625–*post* 1660), in *Poesis Rediviva* (1656), could on religious themes strike genuine sparks of metaphysical fire. Martin Lluelyn (1616–82), Oxonian, cavalier, and later physician, in *Men-Miracles* (1646) displayed fanciful humour and rural realism along with metaphysical wit, and real intensity of thought and feeling in his Anglican and royalist carols. Mildmay Fane, Earl of Westmorland (1602–66), a relative of Marvell's Lord Fairfax, in his musing 'on Natures Book' in *Otia Sacra* (1648) was more preoccupied than Marvell or his friend Herrick with religious 'Mysterie'. Robert Heath, in his amatory and miscellaneous *Clarastella* (1650), was less advanced in his astronomy than Pestell; in 'Seeing her Dancing' (which recalls Jonson, Lovelace, and others) Heath compares his lady to the sun— 'We know it goes though see no motion'—and elsewhere he declares that Copernicus 'Was drunk sure or on shipboard'. Edward Phillips, by the way, in 1675 ranked Herrick with Heath.

We may end this catalogue of a few out of many minor or sub-minor poets with a respectful bow to two illustrious women. The Duchess of Newcastle (1623?–74) had, like Petulant, a pretty deal of an odd sort of a small wit and, like Petulant, she relied altogether on her parts. What tribute can be paid to her, however, may be better bestowed upon her *Life* of the Duke than upon such scientific, metaphysical, and moral effusions as her *Poems and Fancies* and *Philosophical Fancies* (1653). The other and less eccentric woman was a poetic disciple of William Cartwright and the first real English poetess, Katherine Philips (1632–64). The matchless Orinda's circle of admired and admiring literary friends, intimate or remote, included—besides Cartwright, the 'Prince of Phansie', who died in 1643— Cowley, Henry Vaughan, Jeremy Taylor, Sir Charles Cotterell (translator of La Calprenède), and the Earls of Roscommon and Orrery. Thanks largely to Gosse's imagination, we have a mental picture of Mrs. Philips as something between Madame de Rambouillet and Mrs. Leo Hunter. There is no evidence for a salon, or for anything more than a sincere portion of the

fashionable Platonism which turned good friends like Mary
Aubrey and Mrs. Owen into Rosania and Lucasia, and enveloped Mr. Philips and other men in similar celestial hues.
Orinda's Platonism, if somewhat Frenchified, was particularly
a heritage from Cartwright. As Keats perceived, she has her
poetic moments; the most familiar example is 'To my Excellent
Lucasia, on our Friendship'. But we recognize Orinda's individuality and her blameless renown more willingly than we
read her verse.

3

Metaphysical poetry has had no later critic of such generalizing power and rational sanity as Dr. Johnson, but nowadays
it would be said, not without justice, that Johnson's somewhat
blunt insight was focused largely upon degenerate extrava-
gances and that he missed the essentials of the metaphysical
genius, its philosophic depth and breadth, its pregnant use of
homely, realistic, and trivial as well as learned imagery, its
fusion of the colloquial and the cosmic, of levity and seriousness,
of irony and sublimity, above all the fusion of thought and feeling (a critical idea enunciated by the despised Grosart in his
edition of Crashaw), the assimilation by a rich and active
sensibility of widely different elements of experience into a
stimulating, suggestive, and, in a sense, 'unfinished' whole.
The simple label for this mode of thinking and feeling is of
course 'wit', the *callida iunctura*—not quite in the Horatian
meaning—of ideas and objects apparently dissimilar and un-
related. And while metaphysical writing is a matter of general
texture, its special mark is the metaphysical conceit, which is
likely to be more logical and functional in its purpose and in its
many hooks of disparate association than the merely fanciful
and ornamental conceit (though this, we may forget, had its
own functional logic too). Something was said at the end of the
first chapter about the intellectual conditions which, along with
the revolt against Elizabethan convention, developed the
metaphysical sensibility—the survival, into an age of critical
and realistic scepticism, of the medieval philosophic and allegorical conception of the unity of all things physical and
spiritual in the universe, a conception partly supported and
partly disturbed by the new science. In religious metaphysical
poetry that conception may retain its philosophic wholeness

and solidity. In secular verse it may often become a flickering
ghost of its old self, a mental habit or technique cut loose from
philosophic totality and applied to heterogeneous and tangential objects and emotions.

Approached from another direction, metaphysical poetry
appears as the complement of the anti-Ciceronian movement
in prose. That movement, characterized a little less briefly
in later pages, may be summed up as a revolt against the flowing
oratorical period and the established verities which it commonly expressed, and an attempt to create a medium fitted to
render the realistic questionings, complexities, and diversities of
private experience in a world of changing values. These same
words might obviously be used of metaphysical verse. It
expresses, not the result of thought and feeling, but the process,
the 'naked thinking heart', not single-minded assurance but
conflict and tension. Both the allegorical and the realistic impulses lead away from 'general nature' to particulars, and this
tendency is strengthened by the knowledge that—to give an
enlarged sense to George Herbert's advice on preaching—
'particulars ever touch, and awake more then generalls'. A
standard critical term of the age for such 'witty', condensed,
and difficult writing was not the 'metaphysical' which Johnson,
following Dryden and others, made current, but 'strong'. While
the term was more commonly used of verse, Richard Busby's
elegy on Donne, for example, reports Puritan complaints
against Donne the preacher as 'a strong lin'd man'.

The metaphysical movement proper may be said to have
started openly, if the adverb is not paradoxical, with Chapman's
Shadow of Night (1594) and subterraneously with the satires,
elegies, and 'songs and sonnets' which Donne was writing
about the same time and which circulated widely in manuscript. Some of Chapman's later non-dramatic writings were
Ovid's Banquet of Sense (1595), a truly and uniquely metaphysical
departure from the type of Venus and Adonis; the elaborately
didactic and digressive continuation of Marlowe's Hero and
Leander (1598); Euthymiae Raptus, or the Tears of Peace, dedicated
to his patron Prince Henry in 1609; Andromeda Liberata (1614),
an unfortunate attempt to link Neoplatonic doctrines of love
with the marriage of the Earl and Countess of Somerset, but
published, we may remember, before their trial (though
Chapman always remained a loyal believer in the Earl's

innocence); and miscellaneous poems and translations. The great versions of his revered Homer have already been noticed.

The reading of Chapman's works confirms Anthony Wood's description, 'a Person of most reverend aspect, religious and temperate, qualities rarely meeting in a Poet'. In his first dedication Chapman began to expound the conception of poetry which he pursued with religious and solitary devotion to the end of his ill-rewarded life. In poems as well as plays the Christian Platonist and Stoic glorified truth and wisdom and the complete and heroic soul of the 'Senecall man' that rules over perturbation and passion and is proof alike against the corruptions and the assaults of the world. As a Christian humanist, with a prophetic and mystical fervour of his own, Chapman stands, not with Donne, but in the line of poets less occult than himself, Spenser, Daniel, Jonson, and Milton. Swinburne pronounced Chapman, among other things, a Theognis rather than a Homer not yet come to years of discretion; he might have discerned something Pindaric or Aeschylean. In Chapman the ethical and didactic gospel of Renaissance humanism was heightened and strengthened, and darkened, by an avowed and passionate belief in the learned and esoteric obscurity of divine (and nocturnal) inspiration. In the nature of his revolt against conventional Elizabethan style Chapman was less close to Jonson than to Greville and Donne. The impression he leaves is best conveyed in his own words, from the fine epistle to his friend Thomas Harriot (1598):

> O had your perfect eye Organs to pierce
> Into that Chaos whence this stiffled verse
> By violence breakes: where Gloweworme like doth shine
> In nights of sorrow, this hid soule of mine:
> And how her genuine formes struggle for birth,
> Under the clawes of this fowle Panther earth.

While Chapman has a lucid gnomic strain, his characteristic texture is tough and knotted with emblematic images and symbols sought for their philosophical and functional expressiveness, and, as in many poets of our own day, these tend to become a semi-private code. Yet Chapman works in a great tradition and his symbols are not merely personal and miscellaneous, nor are they, like Donne's, largely realistic, scholastic, and scientific; much of his imagery comes, along with his ethical ideas, from such favourite authors as Plutarch, Epictetus, Ficino, Erasmus, and the allegorical mythographer Natalis Comes.

Chapman's most attractive poem is *The Tears of Peace*, and, though he is here more plain and less muscle-bound than usual, comparison with the straightforward clarity of Daniel's *Musophilus* would lead to a fair definition of metaphysical poetry. In the induction the spirit of Homer presents the lady Peace mourning over the strife and chaos that prevail among men who prize outward more than inward worth, and the body of the poem is a dialogue on that text between Peace and the poet. Contemplating a blind and sordid world of ambitious men of action, ignorant idlers, and self-seeking intellectuals, Chapman passionately urges the claims of divine learning, not the erudition of 'a walking dictionarie' but 'the rich crowne of ould Humanitie', the sovereign empire of the soul over 'the bodies mutinous Realme'. And the soul is not mere reason, it is from God and should aspire to its true sphere 'Where burns the fire, eternall, and sincere'. This image reminds us that in Chapman generally flashes of pure fire often break through the blanket of the dark in unforgettable phrases, from 'The downward-burning flame, Of her rich hayre' in *Ovid's Banquet of Sense* to the celebration of the Redeemer and condemnation of the soul which

> for nothing takes
> The beauties that for her love, thou putt'st on;
> In torments rarefied farre past the Sunne.

But Chapman had a too conservative humanistic message to be the leader of a poetic revolt, and it was Donne who gave utterance to the discontents and libertine consolations of the intellectuals who had outgrown the old verities and old ideals.[1]

[1] John Donne (1571/2–1631) was the son of a prosperous London business man, John Donne (d. 1576). His mother was the daughter of John Heywood and the granddaughter of Sir Thomas More's sister, Elizabeth Rastell; she saw to it that Donne had a Catholic upbringing. After some years at Oxford and, probably, at Cambridge too, he was entered at Thavies Inn (1591) and Lincoln's Inn (1592–4), and proceeded to combine omnivorous study with the life of a young man about town. He travelled abroad, perhaps in 1595–6, and took part in Essex's Spanish expeditions of 1596 and 1597. Most of his satirical and amatory poems seem to have been written during the fifteen-nineties; according to Jonson, Donne wrote 'all his best pieces err he was 25 years old'. In 1597–8 he was made secretary to Sir Thomas Egerton, the Lord Keeper. By this time he had doubtless become at least

Chronology, however, excludes from this volume the definitely early poems and, where chronology is uncertain, logic must put with them the rest of the short poems concerned with love and women, including whatever ones were addressed to Mrs. Donne. All these of course we cannot forget in reading Donne's other works and the work of his disciples, but our direct interest is limited to *The Progress of the Soul*, a number of occasional pieces, the two *Anniversaries*, and the divine poems, an uneven and arbitrary but considerable slice.

The Progress of the Soul, Donne's longest satire though but an introductory fragment, was hardly intended for print, as we may infer from its matter and the use of the same title for *The Second Anniversary*. According to Jonson's account, which is perhaps more familiar than Donne's text, the fable was to carry 'the soule of that Aple which Eva pulled' through 'all the bodies of the Hereticks from the soule of Cain & at last' lodge it 'in the body of Calvin'. Internal evidence, however, indicates that the final habitation of the heretic soul was to have been the body of Queen Elizabeth, and prudence may have suggested the substitution of Calvin. In 1601—the poem is dated 16 August of that year—Donne still had an emotional

a nominal Anglican. What promised to be a brilliant worldly career was blasted by a secret marriage (December 1601) with Lady Egerton's niece, Anne More. Her father, Sir George, procured Donne's imprisonment and dismissal. Thenceforth, until 1615—though difficulties were eased after 1608, when Sir George opened his purse-strings—Donne and his increasing family were more or less dependent upon various patrons. For a time, about 1605–7, he seems to have assisted Thomas Morton in the latter's polemics against Rome. One patron of indirect poetical importance was Sir Robert Drury, with whom Donne was abroad in 1611–12. During this middle period of his life he wrote *Biathanatos* (printed in 1646) and published two other prose works, *Pseudo-Martyr* (1610) and *Ignatius his Conclave* (1611), and the two *Anniversaries* (1611, 1612). Donne had been a member of Elizabeth's last Parliament in 1601 and was M.P. for Taunton in 1614. In 1615, when all secular doors seemed to be closed, he was ordained. The *Essays in Divinity* (published in 1651) belong to this time. From 1616 to 1622 Donne was Reader in Divinity to the Benchers of Lincoln's Inn. His wife, who had borne twelve children and lost five, died in 1617, and the widower and 'careful father' became an ascetic recluse, 'crucified to the world'. A good part of 1619–20 Donne spent abroad, with Lord Doncaster's embassy to Germany. In 1621 he was appointed Dean of St. Paul's by King James, and three years later he became vicar of St. Dunstan's in the West, where he had Walton as a parishioner. A serious illness in 1623–4 gave birth to the *Devotions*. During the plague of 1625 Donne lived in Chelsea with his old friend Magdalen Herbert, now the wife of Sir John Danvers. Both as a young wit and courtier and as a divine he had a wide circle of notable friends, many of them Jonson's friends also. Most of Donne's poems were first printed posthumously in 1633 and later years. His sermons, mostly posthumous too, and other prose writings are discussed in Chapter X, his paradoxes in Chapter VI.

attachment to Catholicism, but his animus against the queen and the world in general was more than religious. Six months previously the Earl of Essex, his former commander, who for some time in 1599–1600 had been confined at York House, the Lord Keeper's residence, had attempted the rising that brought him to the scaffold, and many people, especially of the younger generation, forgot the earl's criminal folly and saw only a relentless old queen extinguishing the brightest hope of a brave new world. But that, if it counts, is merely one of many facts and feelings behind Donne's 'sullen Writ, Which just so much courts thee, as thou dost it', and in some five hundred lines he does not carry his tale very far towards Elizabeth or Calvin; nor does heresy as such come into it. After lodging in the apple and a mandrake, the soul is taken through the bodies of a sparrow, a fish, and other creatures down to an ape and Adam's daughter, the sister and wife of Cain. Being Donne's, the whole is much less effective than the parts, and what De Quincey likened to Ezekiel and Aeschylus remains a satirical extravaganza. A serious text, the entire relativity of good and evil, is plainly stated in the abrupt conclusion, though it has not been worked out. The poem is obviously another product of Jack Donne's conventional libertine naturalism. One impression left is of nature red in tooth and claw, but that is submerged in a kind of brutal sexuality; the young man who in a few months was to marry for love dwells with mingled gloating and loathing upon a succession of animal couplings.

After Jonson's epitaphs, his sober and weighty epistles to men and his moderate flatteries of women, one may not be inclined to linger with Donne's 'Epicedes and Obsequies' and the larger body of 'Letters to Several Personages', in which intellectual ingenuity is so seldom fused with feeling, not to mention the letters to the Countess of Bedford, in which ingenuity and feeling are so seldom restrained by taste. There could be no personal sorrow in Donne's most elaborate poems on death. Having won the patronage of Sir Robert Drury with a funeral elegy on his fifteen-year-old daughter, whom he had never seen, Donne made further payments in the two *Anniversaries* written and published in 1611 and 1612, *An Anatomy of the World* and *Of the Progress of the Soul*. A critical as well as amusing introduction is provided by the exchange of comments with Donne that Jonson reported to Drummond (their positions

might have been reversed if the topic had been Jonson's
apotheosis of Venetia Stanley!):

> that Dones Anniversarie was profane and full of Blasphemies
> that he told Mr Donne, if it had been written of the Virgin Marie
> it had been something to which he answered that he described the
> Idea of a Woman and not as she was.

Lady Bedford and others seem to have shared Ben's opinion,
and Donne himself was somewhat embarrassed.

But Elizabeth Drury is a symbol of all the vitality, goodness,
order, and symmetry of the childhood of the world, and her
death is a symbol of all the corruption and disorder, external
and internal, which have grown to a head in the old age of
nature and the race. One passage has been quoted a thousand
times of late years, partly perhaps because it would not be
easy to find many parallels, as the *locus classicus* for the scientific
unsettling of the Jacobean mind:

> And new Philosophy calls all in doubt,
> The Element of fire is quite put out;
> The Sun is lost, and th'earth, and no mans wit
> Can well direct him where to looke for it.
> And freely men confesse that this world's spent,
> When in the Planets, and the Firmament
> They seeke so many new; they see that this
> Is crumbled out againe to his Atomies.
> 'Tis all in peeces, all cohaerence gone;
> All just supply, and all Relation.

But these lines are not in the spirit of the scientific modernism
of Donne's age, and along with the facts and speculations of the
new science go old science, pseudo-science, and fable. Donne
is, in some degree like Spenser, a man of half-medieval outlook
whose traditional faith in the divine order of the world has been
shaken. But whereas Spenser, though deeply afflicted by the
apparent sway of Mutability, tries to reaffirm a half-medieval
belief in a divine plan of evolution, Donne, aware of newer
problems, is wandering between two worlds, that of cosmic unity
and that of meaningless disorder and decay, and he cannot
resolve the conflict. He is no longer the ruthless naturalist of
The Progress of the Soul, and he assumes and asserts the absolutes
of virtue and religion, yet our dominant impression is hardly
of clear-eyed faith in the religious dignity of man, and man,
rather than his macrocosmic setting, is the real theme. In the

Second Anniversary a puzzled and pessimistic anatomizing of the world gives way to a religious *contemptus mundi*, joy in the release of the imprisoned soul, and the celebration of heavenly knowledge. Three passages are especially famous. One is on the fallacious weakness of earthly 'sense, and Fantasie'. Another is the pure and eloquent vision of 'her pure, and eloquent blood'. In the third, beginning 'Thinke then, my soule, that death is but a Groome', Donne awakens his peculiar 'metaphysical shudder' as he contemplates the languor of the death-bed which is

> but unbinding of a packe,
> To take one precious thing, thy soule from thence.

Donne's intellectual and colloquial substance, manner, and movement are of course a world away from the mythological and pictorial *Cantos of Mutability* (though the total result is not more moving). The texture is woven of direct 'prosaic' statement and complex conceit. The tone ranges from the realistic and earthy to the image of the moon shipwrecked on Teneriffe (an image so breath-taking that we forget the idea it illustrates), or the more abstract sublimity of 'As till Gods great *Venite* change the song'. And the degree of poetic vitality varies also. In both *Anniversaries* Donne's central theme, the tragic contrast between divine perfection and human frailty and corruption, is not seldom obscured by the network of particulars.

The religious poems written before Donne took orders were more or less impersonal and artificial. His great religious poetry came after his wife's death (1617), in the nineteen 'Holy Sonnets', the 'Hymn to Christ, at the Author's last going into Germany' (1619), and the lyrical products of the illness which inspired *Devotions*, 'A Hymn to God the Father' and the 'Hymn to God, my God, in my sickness'. Though marriage with Anne More may have polarized Donne's wandering passions, marriage with the Church of England did not altogether heal some fundamental discords and conflicts in his intense and restless nature. If the philosophic doctrine of the relativity of truth helped to open the doors of the Church, it also left them ajar. 'Show me deare Christ, thy spouse, so bright and clear', Donne could write, two or three years after his ordination, in a sonnet discreetly omitted from his collected *Poems*. But his chief torments were not those of the philosophic mind and the relations of faith and reason. It is the emotional tension of the 'naked thinking heart' which gives such unique force to the later religious poems. The contrast, set forth at large in the *Anniversaries*, between divine goodness and human weakness is now felt in wholly personal terms. The stage, or rather the battle-ground, is not the macrocosm but that 'little world made cunningly Of Elements, and an Angelike spright' which is John Donne, not Donne the consecrated preacher but Donne the man facing his Maker. And over all hangs the lurid shadow of death—'What if this present were the worlds last night?' Donne has, indeed, only one theme, his sins and his salvation, 'Despaire behind, and death before', and the abysses of sin and death are more constantly vivid to his imagination than is the abyss of God's love and mercy. His

> devout fitts come and go away
> Like a fantastique Ague.

His anguished cries are composed of contrition, fear, and hope, of passionately humble entreaty and almost imperious demand:

> Batter my heart, three person'd God . . .

> But sweare by thy selfe, that at my death thy sonne
> Shall shine as he shines now, and heretofore;
> And, having done that, Thou haste done,
> I feare no more.

Medieval learning is still there—'At the round earths imagin'd corners'; the newer geography is there—lying on his sick-bed, Donne sees himself as a map explored by his physicians; and wit is still his natural medium, but it is purified by fire, and paradoxical antitheses are dissolved in the blood of Christ.

The religious experience revealed in Donne's poetry is as limited in range as it is intense. If he kindled the religious poets who followed him, he kindled poetry which embodied central religious elements lacking in his own, from the practice of the Christian life to contemplative vision. No one can fail to recognize Donne's extraordinary spirituality and extra-ordinary expressive power, yet we may (or may not) feel that his experience and utterance are so peculiarly personal and so restricted that he is, as *religious* poet, much more remote from us than his chief successors.

Most of Donne's finest poetry is concerned with himself in relation to women or with himself in relation to God (two prime causes of 'love melancholy'), so that the body of his secular and religious verse forms in some respects a consistent whole. Our glance at one portion of it, therefore, can hardly avoid reference to Donne's enormous modern vogue, a vogue which has been the main single factor in effecting the modern revolution in taste. While Donne had long been familiar to scholars, it was about 1920–5 that he became the idol and shibboleth of intellectual poets, critics, and undergraduates. The fundamental reason was genuine recognition of his unique quality. Some other reasons were strong but partly accidental. In the first place, Donne's speech and rhythms fascinated a generation which was itself reacting against 'poetical' writing. Secondly, according to the standard dogma of our time, Donne embodied the unified sensibility which Milton was to split up and which modern poets have been seeking to regain. Thirdly, Donne's supposed modernity of outlook, his disillusioned cynicism, his sexual candour, his subtle scepticism, and, for some, his final turning to authority, all this, especially when half-misapprehended, harmonized perfectly with the mood of what used to be called the post-war world. Such reasons, good and less good, combined to exalt Donne to a place beside Shakespeare. If, surveying Donne's poetry as a whole, unexcited and unexciting moderation were to raise its voice in a minority report, it might suggest that the greatest artists dominate and unify experience and that Donne's fragments of experience remain fragments, that his sensibility is not unified but multiple; that readers who regard poetry as a *magister vitae* may find him unsatisfying; and that, if Donne inhabits the inmost mansion of poetry, nearly all the Greeks and Romans and many great modern poets must be cast into outer darkness. The poet and critic whose authority did much to establish Donne on his throne predicted, in 1931, that the critical orthodoxy of the future would not be the orthodoxy of the immediate past. The fulfilment of that prophecy— the minority report might continue—was coming about through natural causes before 1939, and will have been hastened by the war. We may well return to the first and wisest judgement, that Donne is 'the first poet in the World in some things'.

Although Jonson represented critical theory as well as poetic practice, his influence, as we have seen, is seldom found 'pure', and the strongly individual followers of a more infectious and dangerous example were even less likely to be homogeneous.

As the early phenomenon of Chapman reminds us, Donne was merely the most compelling exponent of a mode of apprehension and expression which would have shown itself in some similar way if he had never been born. That is not to minimize his potent influence: it is only to say that the degree of unlikeness among the poets who are called metaphysical—Lord Herbert, George Herbert, Crashaw, Vaughan, King, Cowley, Marvell, Cleveland, Benlowes, and others—forbids our defining metaphysical poetry simply in terms of Donne. All but one of his chief successors were religious poets, and neither spiritually nor even technically are Herbert, Crashaw, and Vaughan very much like their supposed progenitor.

4

No one turned so completely away from human to divine love as the author of *The Temple* (1633).[1] Herbert may not electrify the nerves and the imagination so often or so startlingly as Donne, but, instead of Donne's fevered preoccupation with death, Herbert has a far more truly religious preoccupation with everyday fulfilment of the divine will here and now. The one thrills the non-religious reader, the other may not, very much. If a prime essential of metaphysical poetry is inner tension, no writer has more than the man whose manuscript was 'a picture of the many spiritual Conflicts that have past betwixt God and my Soul, before I could subject mine to the will of Jesus my Master: in whose service I have now found perfect freedom'. There were in the first place the conflicting claims of God and the great world. By his mother's wish and his own, Herbert had been early dedicated to the Church, but his university career and his experience as Public Orator gave new strength to worldly ambition in a young man not unnaturally disposed,

[1] George Herbert (1593–1633), the fifth son of Richard and Magdalen Herbert, and the younger brother of Lord Herbert of Cherbury, sprang from an ancient, distinguished, and martial family of the Welsh border. His father died in 1596 and he grew up under the watchful eye of his gifted mother, the friend of Donne; she married Sir John Danvers in 1609 and died in 1627. Herbert won distinction at Westminster School and at Trinity College, Cambridge (B.A., 1612; M.A., 1616). He became a fellow, a Reader in Rhetoric (1618), and during 1620–7 was Public Orator to the University. In or before 1626 he was ordained deacon and for some time he lived with relatives and friends, unsettled in mind and more or less ill in body. In 1629 he married Jane Danvers. In 1630 he was appointed rector of Bemerton, near Salisbury, and was ordained priest. His English poems, which had circulated in manuscript, he sent, just before his death, to his friend Nicholas Ferrar, to be either printed or burned.

in the words of the reverent but honest Walton, to put 'too great
a value on his parts and Parentage'. So 'he enjoyed his gen-
tile humor for cloaths, and Court-like company, and seldom
look'd towards Cambridge, unless the King were there, but
then he never fail'd'. The death of King James and other
patrons, Herbert's own inward wrestlings, his mother's counsel
and probably Donne's, brought him back to his original resolve,
but the years following his diaconal ordination did not apparently bring the peace of single-hearted assurance. There
may have been lingering doubts or regrets over the step taken;
certainly there was still much struggling to make the will of a
proud and passionate Herbert bend gladly, to attain a satisfying
consciousness of being a true child and servant—and guest—of
his Master. That consciousness did come, and so irradiated
his brief and humble pastorate at Bemerton that the life as well
as the works of 'Holy Mr. Herbert' remained an inspiration for
his century. There are poems, like 'The Odour' and 'The Call',
which express that profound serenity; and a happy sense of
vocation fills the prose 'character' of the country parson, *A
Priest to the Temple*. Yet even at Bemerton, where he wrote perhaps the larger half of *The Temple*, failing health stirred painful
thoughts of unfitness and futility and magnified his tender
apprehension of a 'shrivel'd heart' and 'Thy distance from me'.
Thus in part Herbert's career was not unlike Donne's, though
Herbert was spared some of his elder's special difficulties. A
closer parallel would be with his other friend, Nicholas Ferrar,
who in 1625 had turned his back upon auspicious worldly prospects to fulfil his deepest desires by establishing a religious
community at Little Gidding.

  This short and simple outline has taken roughly chronological
form, but one cannot impose chronology or any logical pattern
upon the variable and recurrent moods of a sensitive soul. As
Aldous Huxley has said, Herbert is the poet of 'inner weather',
in the full English sense of the metaphor. That is one element
in his peculiar intimacy and honesty. With all his sophisticated
art, he seems unaware of an audience, so that we rather over-
hear him than read him. The Puritan Baxter said in 1681:
'Herbert speaks to God like one that really believeth a God, and
whose business in the world is most with God.' He is less than
himself when he addresses others, in the homespun gnomic
counsels of 'The Church-Porch', which reminds us of the

Outlandish Proverbs, and in the historical panorama of 'The Church Militant'.

We may partly distinguish two poets in Herbert. There is, first, the parish priest of early seventeenth-century England who revered his Church as a chaste mother neither 'painted' nor 'undrest'; who deplored the worm of schism eating away the English rose and (to the disturbance of the Cambridge licenser in 1633) saw Religion standing

> on tip-toe in our land,
> Readie to passe to the American strand;

who celebrated with loving particularity and complete security of belief the meaning of God's temple and worship. It is this poet who can be fully appreciated, in Coleridge's words, only by 'an affectionate and dutiful child of the Church'; and it is to Herbert's writings and life that we owe much of our picture of the order, strength, and beauty of seventeenth-century Anglicanism at its best. But church-bells are heard beyond the stars, and the Anglican parish priest merges with the larger poet, with the very human saint who gives fresh and moving utterance to the aspirations and failures of the spiritual life. This is the Herbert we know through 'Aaron', 'Discipline', 'The Collar', 'The Pulley', and many other poems in which he strives to subdue the wilful or kindle the apathetic self. His principal themes are those 'two vast, spacious things . . . Sinne and Love'. There is nothing soft in the poet who seeks to engrave divine love in steel; and a catalogue of gratuitous, untempered, and short-lived sweets leads up to the magnificent contrast of the disciplined soul that 'never gives'.

As the Anglican merges with the greater poet, so the 'quaint' writer merges with the metaphysical. Herbert had his share of the age's passion for anagrams and the like, which Addison was to condemn as 'false Wit'. But the poet who could shape a poem in the physical likeness of 'The Altar' or 'Easter Wings' had, even more than most of his fellows, a functional sense of metre and rhythm. The technical experimentalist and master was, we remember, a skilled and devoted musician. The movement of his verse, taut or relaxed, can suggest all his fluctuating moods, from self-will or weakness to joyful surrender and assured strength. He moves from this world to the world of spirit 'As from one room t'another', or dwells simultaneously in both, and it is in keeping with that habit of mind, and with metaphysical origins in general, that many of his poems should be allegorical anecdotes, transfigured emblems. Apart from some of his fine dramatic openings, Herbert does not attempt the high pitch of Donne's 'Divine Poems'. His great effects are all the greater for rising out of a homely, colloquial quietness of tone; and peace brings quiet endings—'So I did sit and eat'; 'And I reply'd, *My Lord*'. Though the friend and admirer of Donne (and of Bacon), Herbert did not cultivate scholastic or scientific imagery; nature and everyday life, the Bible and the liturgy were his chief sources. The highest truth, as he said more than once, must be plainly dressed. In spite of his classical learning and his Latin and Greek verse, he avoided the common surface classicism of his time. Of the elements of a deeper classicism, if we care to use that name, he had muscular density, precision, deceptive simplicity, and a dynamic sense of form. At times his structure may be a winding stair, but it is all built of seasoned timber.

In contrast with the English and untravelled Herbert, who moved only from Cambridge to Bemerton, a combination of outward circumstance and inward compulsion made the physical and spiritual life of Richard Crashaw a long pilgrimage to Loreto.[1] His father, a vigorous Puritan clergyman from Yorkshire, a disciple of Perkins (and a friend of Selden and Ussher), described the Pope as Anti-Christ even in his will. Although the Protestantism of the young Richard Crashaw's poems on the Gunpowder Plot approached the young Milton's, by 1634

---

[1] Richard Crashaw (1612/3–49) was born in London; his father, the Rev. William Crashaw, was preacher at the Temple. He was educated at the Charterhouse (1629–31) and at the High-Church Pembroke College, Cambridge (B.A., 1634). In 1635 he became a fellow of Peterhouse, the most Laudian of the colleges. Along with teaching he pursued his favourite avocations, poetry, music, and painting. His poetic friends were Cowley and Joseph Beaumont. Crashaw may have been the 'R.C.' who contributed a Latin poem to the volume of elegies on Edward King (1638). He was a frequent participant in the religious life of Little Gidding. By 1639 he must have been ordained; he was described as a poetic and ravishing preacher. He quitted Cambridge in January 1643, before being formally ejected by the Puritans. The details of his subsequent movements are obscure. He was in Holland in 1644, and perhaps at Oxford. In 1645, apparently, he entered the Roman communion. In 1645–6 he lived in Paris, in association with Cowley and other exiles, including the Countess of Denbigh and Queen Henrietta. Crashaw journeyed to Rome, where he suffered from poverty, ill health, and, in spite of the queen's patronage, from neglect. In 1647 he was in the service of Cardinal Pallotta, who in 1649 gave him a post at Loreto. Here he died. *Steps to the Temple* had appeared in 1646 and been much enlarged in 1648. Among the additions in *Carmen Deo Nostro* (Paris, 1652) were ll. 85–108 of 'The Flaming Heart'.

he had become a thorough High Churchman, and in 1635 he
was rebuking both Puritanism and the kind of anti-papal
hostility upheld by his father (who had died in 1626) and even
by his friend Nicholas Ferrar. But there is little or no positive
Romanism in his poems, and the 'Hymn' to St. Teresa was
'writt when the author was yet among the protestantes'.
Possibly, if he had not been uprooted and exiled by the war,
Crashaw might have remained an Anglo-Catholic like Ferrar,
and like Joseph Beaumont and a fellow-exile, Dr. Cosin, the
Master of Peterhouse, who were uprooted at the same time.
Yet the Italianate and Spanish intensities and excesses of
Crashaw's poetry suggest a temperament which could not have
found full 'Catholick contentation' in the *via media*, even on its
High level. It was characteristic of his intellectually simple
faith that, when in Paris he wrote the relatively muscular poem
urging the Countess of Denbigh to become a Catholic, the
problem appeared merely as one of 'Resolution in Religion',
'Twixt life & death, twixt in & out'.

Crashaw holds a place between Herbert and Vaughan
mainly because of chronology and convenience. He possesses
none of the stigmata of the true metaphysical poet, inward
conflict and tension, philosophic and analytic complexity of
mind, a colloquial, realistic, and non-pictorial manner and
texture. It is difficult to see any real affinity with Donne, or a
tangible debt to Herbert that goes much beyond the little poem
on him and the title *Steps to the Temple*. Both Donne and Herbert
knew the continental languages, but their poetry remained
largely English in character. Crashaw is the one conspicuous
English incarnation of the 'baroque sensibility'. The religio-
aesthetic creed and culture of the Counter-Reformation affected
all the arts, and indeed aimed at mixing and transcending
them, in its effort to make the five senses portals to heaven.
The elements of the revival most stimulating to the artistic
imagination were the clash and fusion of extremes in the
human and divine, the pictorial and the abstract, in the joys
and agonies, the spiritual splendour and the mean estate, of
Christ, the Virgin, and the pantheon of saints and martyrs.
Poetry took on a new and bizarre intricacy of sensuous decoration and symbolic metaphor, a kind of form—or formlessness—
which sought a unity deeper and higher than the classical
through emotional and impressionistic multiplicity. German

exponents of *Geistesgeschichte* have pursued the ramifications of 'barock' as Browne pursued the quincunx, with a heavier foot and with equally spacious and elliptical logic, but for us the simplest definition is 'poetry like Crashaw's'. Its motto might be 'Over-ripeness is all'. Crashaw's abundant revision always led to further elaboration and rarely to improvement.

In the *Epigrammatum Sacrorum Liber* of 1634 Crashaw expressly turned away from the traditions of the genre (though not from classical myth) to follow chiefly the Jesuit epigrammatists in treating religious themes while restricting himself to the New Testament. The completely religious character of the volume was only the most obvious sign of the direction its author was to take. We find, not a theologian or thinker, or a troubled soul like Donne or Herbert, but a secure, single-hearted worshipper whose feeling for the central paradoxes of faith does not lessen his sense of the human values in the story of the Son of Mary. And, in spite of the general hard and 'witty' brevity imposed by the form, there are not a few hints of sensuous fancy, the association of gold and purple and roses with the new-born or the crucified Christ, the endless variations on tears, and a version of the popular conceit on the water changed to wine—*Nympha pudica Deum vidit, & erubuit.*

Among the early secular poems in *Steps to the Temple* are sober, half-Jonsonian epitaphs and the more artificial 'Wishes. To his (supposed) Mistress' and 'Love's Horoscope', in which idealism takes a half-cavalier or half-Donnian form. Among translated pieces we might expect two Psalms, if not the *Dies Irae*, to be near Crashaw's heart, and his dilution of such great originals is not altogether insignificant. For all his skill in Latin and Greek verse Crashaw is one of the most unclassical, and uncertain, of English poets. The nature of his real artistic roots is partly suggested by two re-creations, 'Music's Duel' (*ante* 1634?), the uniquely expressionistic elaboration of the Jesuit Strada's popular Latin poem, and 'Sospetto d'Herode' (1637?), a highly charged rendering of the first book of Marino's epic on the Slaughter of the Innocents. The Jesuits and Marino both contribute to the famous or notorious 'Weeper' (*ante* 1634?), which offers a severe though not a final test for appreciation of Crashaw and baroque religiosity. Mary Magdalene is draped in rope upon rope of 'Her richest Pearles, I meane thy Teares'. The subject was familiar, even in English, and for the

contemporary reader who knew Sidney's *Arcadia* and the
sonneteers, Southwell and Giles Fletcher, and the emblem-
books, there would be little surprise in the individual conceits,
fantastic as they are, but no English poet had produced such a
concatenation. And their extravagance is heightened by bits
of grotesque realism too familiar to quote.

Crashaw was to go far beyond Marinism in power of vision
and symbol, but even in his greater poems he generally hovered
between the organic unity of baroque inspiration and a dazzling spray of associated images, and the reader who lacks a
special temperament or a knowledge of the symbolic code may
sometimes think of the dreams of a convert who has eaten rich
food and slept on his back. Crashaw's words and details are
not vague as modern romantic poetry can be, nor even esoteric,
since they grow out of a precise ritual and out of the European
Catholic tradition, but we may not have patience to find the
controlling motive, and at times the poet himself may have lost
it. At times, too, he is capable of relatively simple beauty like
the opening of 'On the Assumption', and the most startling
thing in that amazing rosary, 'The Weeper', is the couplet:

> Nowhere but heere did ever meet
> Sweetnesse so sad, sadnes so sweete.

There is some resemblance in 'naïve' conceits between Milton's
most Italianate poem, the 'Nativity', and Crashaw's 'Hymn' on
the same theme, though Crashaw is thinking more of the child
in the manger. 'The Glorious Epiphany' is nearer to Milton
in part of its substance; here, in a manner very different from
the 'Hymn' and of course from Milton, Crashaw develops a
threefold contrast, physical, historical, and spiritual, between
natural and supernatural light.

Another of Crashaw's irregular odes or ecstasies, 'To the
Name Above Every Name, the Name of Jesus', is not unlike
the 'Epiphany' in symphonic multiplicity but is more central
and typical in its purely devotional passion. The reader probably comes back most often to the strong and simple 'Hymn' to
St. Teresa, and to the sequel, 'The Flaming Heart', in which
cool ingenuity becomes incandescent. The author of the preface of 1646 spoke truly of 'the Quintessence of Phantasie and
discourse center'd in Heaven . . . the very Outgoings of the
soule'. The 'Poet and Saint' of ascetic life and luxuriant imagination, who seeks fulfilment in the pain and joy of divine

annihilation, and freedom from years in Eternity, has little to
do with this earth and common experience. He is

> Drest in the glorious madnesse of a Muse,
> Whose feet can walke the milky way;

a beautiful angel beating his luminous wings in a richly coloured
Catholic heaven. His nests and spices and wounds and blood,
whether we like them or not, have along with their Latin
warmth a degree of ritualistic remoteness and abstractness.
But the 'strong wine of Love' is a heady drink which, to put
to illegitimate use another phrase from the preface, may give
birth to the 'prodigious issue of tumorous heats and flashes'.
It is almost inevitable that a poet striving to express the in-
expressible should seem, at least, not to know the difference
between gold and gilt, between spiritual vision and verbal
intoxication. One who can soar and burn can also sink and
melt. Though the mystic's instinct for erotic imagery has a
long tradition behind it, not merely the uninformed or unsympathetic reader may be embarrassed by the kind of religious
emotion which hails the Virgin as 'rosy princesse' and St.
Teresa as 'My Rosy Love'. And the feeling may not entirely
vanish even when, so to speak, Murillo gives way to El Greco:

> By all thy brim-fill'd Bowles of feirce desire
> By thy last Morning's draught of liquid fire;
> By the full kingdome of that finall kisse
> That seiz'd thy parting Soul, & seal'd thee his. . . .

The question whether an indisputable poet is also an indisputable mystic cannot be settled by rule of thumb, and perhaps
does not need to be settled. But one may feel uneasy when the
authentic motives of adoration and self-surrender issue in an
undisciplined fervour which has never been rational and never
ceases to be sensuous and excited; and one may think that
larger and clearer glimpses of the One were granted to the
quiet Vaughan.

While Crashaw's short life was an ascent, by way of Rome,
to the rosy heaven of Christ, the Virgin, and the saints, the soul
of Henry Vaughan, during much of his long sojourn on earth,
was meditating, to borrow Crashaw's language,

> her immortall way
> Home to the originall sourse of Light & intellectuall Day.[1]

[1] Henry Vaughan (1621/2–95) came of an old Welsh family of Brecknockshire,

There is perhaps no more signal example than Vaughan's of spiritual and poetical rebirth. The *Poems* of 1646, which opened with a tribute to Jonson and Randolph and indirectly acknowledged the influence of Donne, were the efforts of a 'weak striver' in fashionable modes, and readers did not need to be assured that the amatory fire was 'but Platonick'. The chief exceptions to tame artifice were bits of nature, especially 'Upon the Priory Grove', and the urban realism of the convivial piece on the Globe tavern. *Olor Iscanus* (1651) showed more feeling and substance in the celebration of the Usk and in satirical epistles and elegies on friends killed in the war, and gave testimonies of literary admiration in the verses on the 'dark shades of deep Allegorie' in Gombauld's *Endymion*, and on John Fletcher, Cartwright, Mrs. Philips, and Davenant. But the author of *Silex Scintillans* (1650) had already disowned his secular muse. As he made clear in the preface to the enlarged edition of 1655, he had come to look upon 'idle verse' as the fruit of vanity and spiritual sickness. A number of causes, later augmented by severe illness and by the death of his wife, contributed to his 'conversion'—the personal and public distresses of prolonged civil and religious strife, the influence of his brother Thomas, the death of his brother William in 1648, and deep study of the Bible, the book which, having brought him home, did there show him that pearl he sought elsewhere. The special agent of spiritual and poetical quickening to whom

a county once inhabited by the Silures; hence the appellation 'Silurist' on most of his title-pages. He entered Jesus College, Oxford, apparently in 1638, along with his twin brother Thomas (whose mystical strain was to become more occult than Henry's). After two years or more he was sent to London to study law. When war broke out he served on the royalist side under Sir Herbert Price; he alludes to this experience in his poems. The period of his medical study is uncertain, but he practised for a few years at Brecknock and during the rest of his life at Newton-by-Usk. Vaughan was twice married. We have some late letters from him to John Aubrey, his cousin.

Half of Vaughan's first volume (1646) was occupied by a rendering of Juvenal's tenth satire. *Olor Iscanus* ('The Swan of Usk'), published in 1651 with a preface dated 1647, contained original verse (some of it later than 1647), translations from Ovid, Ausonius, Boethius (who is echoed in 'The Retreat'), and the Polish Casimir, and prose essays from Plutarch and others. Vaughan's great poetry appeared in 1650 and 1655 in the two parts of *Silex Scintillans* ('Sparkling Flint'). An inferior volume of verse, *Thalia Rediviva*, was printed in 1678. Of Vaughan's compilations of religious prose, mainly translated, the most original parts were the devotional meditations in *The Mount of Olives* (1652) and 'Primitive Holiness', a life of St. Paulinus of Nola, in *Flores Solitudinis* (1654). He also translated a medical treatise, *Hermetical Physic* (1655), from the alchemist Nollius.

Vaughan avowed his great debt was 'The first, that with any effectual success attempted a diversion' of worldly and licentious poetry into the religious channel, 'the blessed man, Mr. George Herbert, whose holy life and verse gained many pious Converts, (of whom I am the least) . . .'.

In such a case 'influence' is an inadequate term, but it may be said for what it is worth that, of the 129 poems in *Silex Scintillans*, over 50 bear traces of *The Temple*, and that many other echoes have not been recorded. Herbert sometimes suggests the theme, spirit, and form of whole poems; more often he supplies single words, phrases, and ideas, many of which are embedded in quite different contexts. But, whether taken over or transformed, these things are, as Dowden said, less an appropriation than an inheritance. On the artistic side, Vaughan could follow his master in developing his own intimate, reflective colloquialism, though he more seldom attained to Herbert's technical mastery of structure and rhythm. The inward affinity is more important. As Herbert contains in himself two poets, the Anglican priest and the spiritual struggler, so in Vaughan there are the Herbertian religious poet and the timeless (but no less Christian) Neoplatonist. Since it is the latter and larger Vaughan that we cherish, his generally inferior expressions of evangelical experience are likely to be neglected. Yet the very high proportion of these, the author's view of all his 'Sacred Poems' as a body of 'ordinary Instructions for a regular life', his echoing not only of Herbert but of Felltham's *Resolves*, and his considerable devotional prose, all this testifies to an everyday religious effort which explains, not the magic, but the strength and centrality of his richest intuitions of the invisible. The God of 'deep, but dazling darkness' is also God the Father. Over and over Vaughan celebrates the redeeming love of Christ; still more constantly—and even in his epitaph—he laments his sinful or frozen heart and prays for a regenerating breath of divine grace. 'Certaine Divine Raies breake out of the Soul in adversity, like sparks of fire out of the afflicted flint.' Vaughan's consciousness of spiritual failure is not so specific and dramatic as Herbert's, but it is none the less real in a poet who strives for 'a true, practick piety', 'for perfection and true holyness, that a door may be opened to him in heaven'.

Vaughan's great poems are those in which the door is opened —'The Retreat', 'The Morning-Watch', 'Peace', 'And do they so?' 'The Dawning', 'The World', 'Man', 'Ascension-Hymn', 'They are all gone into the world of light', 'The Night', 'The Waterfall', 'Quickness', and others. Whatever his various debts, in such utterances Vaughan had in some sense to make his own way, both as seer and as writer, and even a less unequal poet could hardly sustain the transcendental note without sinking. But, although relatively few poems are perfect wholes, in them and in many lines and passages, the vital gold shot from an unthrift sun, Vaughan has a peculiar quiet power unlike that of any other poet. His central theme, of course, is the traditional idea, especially attractive to his age, of the exiled soul's longing to return to its heavenly home, the world of light. The theme is not merely nostalgic. Though imprisoned in flesh, and in the darkness of earth, the soul, in its 'little inch of time in this life', may enter into the kingdom of heaven, in the true sense of Christ's words, by regaining the unsullied vision of 'Angell-infancy', by re-creating, so to speak, God's primal intention, by recognizing His immanence in all things, the 'prolusions and strong proofs of our restoration laid out in nature, besides the promise of the God of nature'. Even in such an ostensible imitation of 'The Church-Porch' as 'Rules and Lessons', the voice of Vaughan is clear:

> There's not a Spring,
> Or Leafe but hath his Morning-hymn; Each Bush
> And Oak doth know I AM . . .
>
> Thou canst not misse his Praise; Each tree, herb, flowre
> Are shadows of his wisedome, and his Pow'r.

Flowers and fallen timber, blades of grass and the 'poor highway herb', stones ar.d stars that 'nod, and sleepe', singing birds and crowing cocks, the 'gilded Cloud' and the waterfall, dew and rain and the seed growing secretly, all the letters of the divine alphabet proclaim 'The great Chime And Symphony of nature'. Life is 'A knowing Joy' in ordered harmony, 'A quickness, which my God hath kist', and death is only a rebirth in the fullness of knowledge and joy.

To think of nature and intimations of immortality is to think of Wordsworth (who apparently never saw Vaughan's poems) and of other nineteenth-century poets, but the fundamental difference has already been emphasized. Vaughan does not indulge in any romantic glorification of childhood and he is

thoroughly Christian in studying God in the secondary book of
His works as well as in His word. We feel nothing spurious in
a poet whose religious awareness of the Many gives not only a
poignant reality but a positive direction to his quest of the One,
the 'one, who never changes, Thy God, thy life, thy Cure'.
'The World', which begins with such casual sublimity, as one
might say 'I saw John Brown the other night', and which returns at the end to 'the Ring' and God, is for the most part
a melancholy picture of earth-bound, deluded man. Vaughan's
understanding of human restlessness and weakness, his Christian
faith and Christian effort do not dull his feeling for the mystery
of existence, but they do prevent his losing himself in soft
idealism or naturalism. His moments of intense contemplative
vision are not moments of auto-intoxication or escape. His
steady white light, the shadow of God, is not the damp and
flickering gleam of romantic gropings towards a vague infinity.
Indeed, Vaughan's fusion of Neoplatonic mysticism with
orthodox Christianity could hardly be found, in quite this
form, except in his own age, in such men as John Smith or
Sir Thomas Browne or the twin brother whose Hermetic and
other mystical studies nourished a somewhat erratic faith in
the divine unity of creation. And even these are only partial
parallels to Vaughan.

Thomas Traherne (1637/9-74) was the latest born and, in
his immediate effect, is perhaps the loveliest vision far of all
the religious hierarchy.[1] Those who think that his fame has
shone somewhat the brighter for being belated would not deny
his authentic lustre and significance. Traherne has all the
excited urgency of a man who has been vouchsafed a spiritual
revelation which he must share. The gradual process of his
discovery, or rediscovery, is vividly set forth in the autobiographical third *Century*. His whole quest and message are comprised in 'felicity', of which he had found the magical secret in

---

[1] We have few facts about Traherne. He was the son of a Hereford shoemaker
and was educated, probably by a well-to-do relative, at Brasenose College, Oxford
(B.A., 1656; M.A., 1661; B.D., 1669). In 1657 he was presented to the living of
Credenhill in Herefordshire and seems to have divided the next ten years between
Oxford and his cure. Then he became chaplain to Sir Orlando Bridgeman, who
was Lord Keeper from 1667 to 1672, and who took Traherne with him when he
retired to his house at Teddington. There Traherne died.

Manuscripts of the poems and *Centuries of Meditations* first turned up in a London
bookstall in 1896–7 and were printed by Bertram Dobell, who discovered their
authorship.

himself and in nature, in the Bible and in philosophy. Childlike
innocence, love, and joy are man's natural endowment, but if
that 'first Light' is lost, as in the unnatural course of common life
it well may be, it can be regained. Man can recover his primal,
God-like state by shunning the false aims and values of the
world and by cleaving to the simple, universal, incorruptible
things, the goodness and glory of God, mankind, and all creation, the 'illimited field of Variety and Beauty' in earth and sky
and sea, flowers and grains of sand, orient and immortal wheat,
and 'Especialy Ones self', the whole outer and inner world in
which God is daily revealed to those who love and seek Him.
Thus reborn in love and 'the highest reason', man ceases to
be a distracted, futile creature and is filled with beatific power,
peace, and happiness. Through his soul and his senses he reigns
in communion with God, and his life here and now links Eden
with eternity.

The *Centuries of Meditations* are generally ranked above the
poems, since it is the poet who is chiefly given to prosaic stumb-
ling and incoherent diffuseness, but the two portions of his
work are as like in substance and manner as prose and verse can
be. Both prose and verse are all 'News', a series of mainly
lyrical variations on Traherne's one great theme. The briefest
account of it may suggest close kinship with Vaughan, and the
two have some instincts in common, though the list of essential
differences is on the whole a list of Traherne's defects. His
normal prose is less angular and muscular than Vaughan's and
has a winning candour and simplicity; in its higher flights it
often reminds one of the florid rhapsodist Peter Sterry. Traherne's poetry is, artistically, like a bright fountain crossed with
bars of shadow. In verse a concern for direct expression, a
deliberate avoidance of 'curling Metaphors' and 'painted
Eloquence' was not enough, and far less often than Vaughan
was Traherne able to roll all his sweetness up into one ball.

The undisciplined quality of his verse reflects the undisciplined quality of his temperament and his religious experience.
Vaughan, though here and there he touches men like his
brother and Boehme, stops short of 'enthusiasm'. Traherne
does not. He is 'all light and life and love' and, instead of being
a sad and sober alien, he exuberantly possesses the glorious
earth. When we dip into Traherne we find pure refreshment,
even inspiration, in his ardent love of God and goodness, his

exaltation of the divinity of man, his unspoiled faculty of wonder and joy, his eager and sensitive apprehension of common and unregarded beauty, and perhaps we should be grateful for that and not ask for more. The trouble is, for some readers, that even these positive qualities lose something of their virtue in the absence of others.

Traherne was of course a devout Christian and Anglican and he did not apparently perceive how far the Christian centre of gravity could shift in himself. He writes, in all sincerity, about sin, but one does not feel that evil to him is a reality, an inescapable fact of life and religion. And that blind spot in his 'Infant-Ey' explains both the strength and the weakness of his work. Whatever spiritual trials Traherne had gone through before he won felicity, in his ecstatic writings he seems to be far removed from the inward struggles of the restless Donne, the passionate and choleric Herbert, the 'proud and humorous' Vaughan, even the supposedly serene Browne who has Lucifer and the battle of Lepanto raging within him—or we might think of the ardours and torments of Gerard Manley Hopkins. Traherne enjoys 'the Hony even without the Stings'. And after prolonged reading we may feel, behind all his very genuine spiritual and sensuous fervour, a degree of poverty and monotony, a lack of true religious humility, a large element of facile, expansive, emotional optimism, the kind of optimism which in the next generations passed easily into deistic sentimentalism. Traherne was a master of philosophical learning, and in his *Roman Forgeries* and infinitely richer *Christian Ethics* he showed an awareness of the world of men (in the latter book of Hobbes), yet in the poems and *Centuries* his mind and nature seem to have little edge or toughness. He does not escape the peculiar danger of Neoplatonists, a nebulous idealism; there is a great difference between him and the Cambridge Platonists with whom he is often linked. Neither as Christian nor as philosopher does Traherne seem quite mature; he hardly graduates from songs of innocence to songs of experience. Even when, in being childlike, he does not hover on the brink of childishness, he may in the end repel a little through that remote 'unhumanity' which also belongs to the soul and the world of the child.

We drop back, chronologically and in some respects poetically, to take account of Edward Benlowes (1603/4–76), whose *Theophila* (1652), though as a 'Heroick Poem' of 'Spiritual

Warfare' it belongs with the works of Joseph Beaumont and
Henry More, represents metaphysical religious poetry *in excelsis*
and *in extremis.*[1] In style Benlowes is the Cleveland—or the
Urquhart—of 'divine and Christian Poesie'. Oppressed by the
sway of atheism and sin 'in this Dotage of the World' and by
national strife, he sought to awaken man's sense of himself as
'the Image of his Maker', above the beasts and just below the
angels. His poem pictures the soul's ascent to God 'By Humi-
litie, by Zeal, by Contemplation', by the three mystical ways,
'Purgative, Illuminative, and Unitive'. Benlowes can be very
moving in his religious and philosophic vision of life as a point
between eternities of space and time and between Nature and
Grace, of the soul's triumph over 'the World, Hell, and her
own Corruptions' and of her ecstatic union with the One. But
the poetic eagle whom Davenant saluted flies too near the sun:

> Heav'ns Paths are traceless, by Excess of Light;
> O're-fulgent Beams daz'd Eyes benight.
> Say Ephata, and Clay's Collyrium for my Sight!

Though Benlowes as a captain of horse was said (by Samuel
Butler, to be sure) to have given allegorical names to his
accoutrements, he can affirm partly Hobbesian principles:

Now 'tis Judgement begets the Strength, Invention the Ornaments
of a Poem; both These joyn'd form Wit, which is the Agility of
Spirits: Vivacity of Fancie in a florid Style disposeth Light and Life
to a Poem, wherein the Masculine and refined Pleasures of the Understanding transcend the feminine and sensual of the Eye: From the
Excellencie of Fancie proceed grateful Similies, apt Metaphors, &c.

The alarming hints in this are more than borne out in the text.
Benlowes has all the metaphysical qualities, homely realism
and far-fetched learning, general and scientific, indubitable
'wit', intensity of thought and feeling; but with a basic texture
resembling that of Donne's *Anniversaries* are blended such other

[1] Benlowes, the heir of a wealthy Catholic family, went from Cambridge to
Lincoln's Inn, made the grand tour (about 1630), and settled on his Essex estate to
cultivate poetry and the arts. He had become a Protestant, apparently after his
return from abroad. He encouraged or helped scholars and men of letters, among
them Phineas Fletcher, Quarles, Alexander Ross, James Howell, and Fuller.
His various benefactions, parliamentary fines (he seems to have shared in the
royalist rising of 1648), the burning of his house in 1653, and other drains on his
fortune, including litigation during 1657–66, reduced him by degrees to poverty.
Dr. John Fell described him as 'the most helpless creature in the world'. In the
penurious obscurity of his last years at Oxford he may have found the kind of peace
he celebrated in the final cantos of *Theophila*.

elements as emblematic epigrams, the excited staccato of traditional satire, and something of Crashaw's baroque lusciousness. He becomes grotesque because of his peculiar vocabulary and syntax ('Poets have Legislative Pow'r of making Words'), his constant, sudden, and violent juxtaposition of images, and his complete lack of 'Judgement'. There is hardly a stanza in the long poem which is not vivid, hardly one which is not more or less odd, and the reader who finishes the soul's quest of grace and glory feels as if he had been riding on the rims over an endless timber bridge. Granting the difficulties of the mystic who 'doth Inexpressibles expresse', we may say, with appropriate exaggeration, that Benlowes is every other inch a poet. As a sample of his non-mystical best, this might be set beside Nashe and Marvell:

> Deaths Serjeant soon thy courted Helens must
>   Attach, whose Eyes, now Orbs of Lust,
> The Worms shall feed on, till they crumble into Dust.

One of Benlowes's marked characteristics is the 'conveying', with little or no change, of phrases and longer bits from other writers. It is not perhaps a surprise that he borrows from Jonson and Randolph and Quarles, from Donne's 'Hymn to Christ', *Second Anniversary*, and sermons, from Cleveland (among other things the first line of 'To Fuscara'), and that, in drawing upon Sylvester, he uses twice the notorious image of the periwigged woods; but it is a surprise, in this poem and at this date, to find at least over a score of clear and sometimes prolonged echoes of Milton—ten or more from *Comus*, six from the 'Nativity', and the rest from 'On Time', 'L'Allegro', 'Il Penseroso', and 'Lycidas'.

5

As George Herbert stands at the head of the metaphysical religious poets, so his eldest brother, Lord Herbert of Cherbury (1583–1648), is the first disciple of Donne on the secular side.[1]

[1] Edward Herbert was at Oxford from 1595 to 1600, and while there married his cousin. In the next two decades he frequented the court and the society of Jonson and the wits, lived at home (he was made sheriff of Montgomeryshire in 1605), and had much travel and adventure abroad. At all times he was a student. In 1619 he went to France as ambassador (with Thomas Carew in his train), and he held that post, with an interval, until 1624. He had been one of James's early flock of knights, and in 1629 he was created Baron Herbert of Cherbury. His later years were rendered unhappy by the war and ill health. He tried to keep neutral but had to surrender Montgomery Castle in 1644, and in 1645 he submitted to Parliament

In his elegy on Donne, where he falls far short of the critical discernment of his friend, 'my witty Carew', he testifies his admiration for his master's pregnant originality. In general, Herbert is scornful of the sensuous clichés of the 'old Poetry' of 'Our vulgar wits', and he partly reveals his own instinct when he intellectualizes traditional forms like the sonnet and madrigal, when—unlike Carew in 'The Complement'—he turns the Italianate catalogue of the female body into a series of cosmic images, or when he adds to the chorus of lamentation for Prince Henry the elegy which led Donne to write 'Looke to mee faith' in order 'to match Sir Ed: Herbert in obscurenesse'. On the other hand, Herbert has little of Donne's personal intimacy, glancing wit, everyday realism, recondite learning, verbal and metrical power, and cynical or passionate dramatic force. He rarely raises his voice above a studied and almost prosaic quietness, and his diction is so simple that one is surprised at the effort of comprehension his close and sometimes knotted texture requires. All these negatives indicate that Herbert is not an immediately compelling poet, in the ordinary meaning of the term. Whereas Carew's perfectly moulded and generalized 'Ask me no more' casts such an hypnotic spell that we hardly observe what the words mean, the 'Elegy over a Tomb', one of Herbert's best and simplest pieces, has the true metaphysical effect of 'unfinality', of insisting that it be understood.

Herbert was unique among the metaphysical poets in being a figure of real importance in the history of philosophy. He could philosophize the age's sense of passing time and mortality, or work out a satire on kingship and aristocracy with complex boldness of thought, but most of his poetical thinking revolved around love. Like Donne, he outdoes the Petrarchans in glorifying love and his mistress with argumentative hyperbole, but, as we might expect of the philosopher if not of the autobiographer, he is far more of a Platonist. Three poems called 'Platonic Love' and one called 'The Idea' (this last

and received a pension. If not one of the most admirable characters of the age, he was certainly one of the most energetic, versatile, and complex. In later chapters of this volume Herbert appears as historian, autobiographer, and in his major role as philosopher. His poems circulated chiefly in manuscript and were not published until 1665. One defiance of the times is dated 1644, and there are other late pieces, mainly Latin, but nearly all of the English verse seems to have been written between 1608 and 1631.

written at Alnwick during the first Bishops' War!) are only the most obvious marks of a serious and abstract analysis of love as an avenue to knowledge, liberty, unity, and eternity, a light in darkness, a religion, and a mysterious magnetic force. The most elaborate and most famous proof that there is feeling blended with Herbert's dry cerebration is the 'Ode upon a Question Moved, Whether Love Should Continue For Ever?' Donne in 'The Ecstasy' urges that love, however exalted, must express itself by descending to the level of the body. Herbert's lover, when his mistress fears the extinction of love in death, argues, with Sidney's Pamela, that 'eternall causes' cannot 'bring forth chaunceable effects', that love must transcend the limitations of earth and time. Here if anywhere Herbert approaches the consummate in phrase and rhythm, and his concluding image of the stars may be mentioned along with 'Else a great Prince in prison lies'. In love poetry of the age Platonism is often only a veneer—and even Donne's has been questioned—but perhaps those Platonists who recognize the flesh can be said to vindicate their idealism.

Henry King (1592–1669), son of the bishop who ordained Donne, was himself the executor of his 'most dear and incomparable Friend' and wrote an elegy on that 'Rich Soul of wit and language'.[1] He also paid elegiac tribute to Ben Jonson. One layer of King's verse includes mainly Donneish amatory wit, in both lyrical and couplet form. Another is best represented by 'Tell me no more how fair she is', in which artifice gains a Jonsonian neatness, dignity, and grace. At the top are those poems, such as 'The Legacy' and 'The Surrender', in which death or destiny inspires moods and images with something of 'that awful fire' that once burned in Donne's 'clear brain'. Of these last the great example, one of the few great elegies which are elegies, is of course 'The Exequy', on the poet's young wife. Reading his other obituary poems, which make up two-fifths of his work, we should never guess that he was quite capable of this. Donne's name is linked with it merely as a shorthand description of the poetical medium, the

---

[1] King was educated at Westminster and at Christ Church, Oxford (B.A., 1611; M.A., 1614). He rose through a series of preferments to the bishopric of Chichester (1642). In 1643 he was ejected and led a migratory life, in dependence on various friends, until the Restoration restored him to his see. About 1617–18 he had married Anne Berkeley, who became the mother of six children and died, 'scarce' twenty-four, about 1624. King's poems were first collected in 1657.

realistic blend of emotion and poignant wit, that was available. But it is Henry King whose love and Christian faith find utterance here. Donne himself has no expression of real grief to compare it with and, though he might have conceived a bit like

> And a fierce Feaver must calcine
> The body of this world like thine,

it may be doubted if he could have written an elegy of such selfless devotion, such climactic unity, such simple and yet richly suggestive clarity, and such a magnificent movement:

> But heark! My Pulse like a soft Drum
> Beats my approch, tells Thee I come;
> And slow howere my marches be,
> I shall at last sit down by Thee.

The contemporary fame of John Cleveland (1613–58) was much greater even than Cowley's, and it has shrunk even more.[1] His name now calls up the bee that

> tipples Palmestry, and dines
> On all her Fortune-telling Lines,

the doom of a Scottish Cain, and perhaps several characters in prose, two of them on London 'diurnals', which mark the adaptation of a popular genre to political uses. In the seventeenth century there was a large audience not merely for the author of the dazzling 'Fuscara' and the genial 'Mark Antony' but for the royalist wit and satirist *par excellence*, the gadfly of Presbyterians and shirtless Scots. While the poetry of Milton, Crashaw, Vaughan, King, and even Lovelace failed to sell, Cleveland received an almost unanimous chorus of eulogy and went through some twenty editions, editions often swollen with that final kind of tribute, the products of other men's 'Clevelandism'. The war, in raising Cleveland's royalist fervour and

---

[1] Cleveland was the son of a Yorkshire clergyman who had moved to Leicestershire. He was a contemporary of Milton and Henry More at Christ's College, Cambridge (B.A., 1631; M.A., 1635). He became a fellow of St. John's (1634) and a Reader in Rhetoric. In 1640 he opposed the election of Cromwell as M.P. for Cambridge. In 1643, apparently, he retired to Oxford, though not formally ejected from his fellowship until 1645. As judge-advocate at Newark (1645–6), he held that town against the Scots. For some years thereafter he moved about in dependence on friends. During 1647–9 he probably had a hand in *Mercurius Pragmaticus* and perhaps in other journals. In 1655–6 he suffered a short imprisonment at Yarmouth, on vague charges, and was released after a manly appeal to Cromwell. He died at Gray's Inn. The first edition of his poems appeared in 1647.

satirical ferocity to boiling-point, gave him as a poet one deep
emotion. He would scarcely have been heard of if he had only
continued the serious extravagance of the elegy on Edward
King or the unique sobriety of the elegy on Jonson. In his
amatory verse, apart from the subdued piquancy and fresh
charm of 'Upon Phillis', Cleveland surpassed all strong-lined
men in weaving complex tissues of the prettily or boisterously
fantastic. 'His Epithetes', says Fuller in 1662, in one of his few
useful summaries of critical opinion,

were pregnant with Metaphors, carrying in them a difficult plainness, difficult at the hearing, plain at the considering thereof. His
lofty Fancy may seem to stride from the top of one Mountain to the
top of another, so making to it self a constant Level and Champian of
continued Elevations.

Cleveland has no feeling but the joy of the game and, as *l'homme
moyen sensuel*, he can turn the hose of common sense or mockery
upon the idealistic sparks of the cavalier and metaphysical
tradition. His far-fetched and twisted wit might be condemned
by Dryden, but his robust levity and irreverence helped to form
the spirit of the Restoration, most obviously of course through
his friend and disciple, Samuel Butler.

The metaphysical impulse might seem to have had its death-
throes in Cleveland, but it had a euthanasia in Abraham
Cowley (1618–67), who carried his personal charm and fame
into the fairly congenial age of the Restoration.[1] Yet by 1700
Cowley's great lustre had somewhat faded among the critical,

[1] Cowley, a middle-class Londoner, was educated at Westminster (1628?–36)
and Trinity College, Cambridge. He became a fellow in 1640. Among his Cambridge friends were Crashaw, whom he later assisted in Paris, and especially William Hervey (d. 1642). Like Crashaw, Cowley anticipated his ejection and early
in 1643 repaired to the court at Oxford. During 1644?–54 he was in France as
secretary to Jermyn and the queen and he went on several missions as a royalist
agent. He returned to England in 1654, was imprisoned in 1655, and on his
release took up the study of medicine (M.D., Oxford, 1657). The preface to his
Poems of 1656 contained some words on submission to authority which were not to
be forgotten, and it remains uncertain whether, as Sprat said, Cowley had been
masking continued royalist activity or had been really convinced of the necessity
and wisdom of accepting the Cromwellian régime. In 1659–60 he was again in
France. After the Restoration he was reinstated in his fellowship and given land
by Queen Henrietta, a reward possibly commensurate with what seemed his
dubious loyalty but not with his hopes. Henceforth he led a retired life at Barn
Elms and Chertsey, busy with books and botany and writing his familiar essays.
He had been one of the first men nominated for the Royal Society but, though
interested in its work, he did not become a fellow. Cowley's funeral was more
splendid than any mere man of letters had received before.

and he was foreordained to hold an eminence both bad and good at the head of Johnson's *Lives of the Poets*. He was one of the few men who felt all three of the major influences in poetry, Spenser, Jonson, and Donne. *Poetical Blossoms* (1633) was the work of a boy who had been enchanted by Spenser and knew other Elizabethans (including Golding); this astonishingly precocious volume was enlarged and reached a third edition in 1637. At Cambridge Cowley wrote three plays, a pastoral he had begun at school, a Latin comedy, and *The Guardian* (1642), which was revamped as *Cutter of Coleman Street*. In 1643 he discharged a vigorous broadside, *The Puritan and the Papist*. He paid part of his tribute to Donne in *The Mistress* (1647). The *Poems* of 1656 contained 'Miscellanies' (among these were 'Of Wit', the elegies on Hervey and Crashaw, the gay 'Chronicle' of mistresses, and the Anacreontics), *The Mistress*, the Pindaric odes, and the unfinished religious epic *Davideis*, which provided a main text for the important preface. Some more verse and the familiar essays appeared in 1663 and 1668.

The essays have been enjoyed since the early eighteenth century, and in recent decades Cowley the poet has, at a distance, followed the great metaphysicals back into favour. He deserves critical respect, for he was a very clever, versatile, learned, self-conscious, and serious artist, a mirror, if not a profound interpreter, of the new rationalism of the English and the European mind. It is characteristic of both his nature and his position that in him the Christian humanist was not extinguished by the scientific modernist, nor metaphysical wit by neoclassical good sense. He remains a writer of more interest to the student of intellectual and literary history than to the reader of poetry. Much of his work suffers from lack of intensity, from both prosaic flatness and oratorical magniloquence, and from the incessant play of unfelt and uncontrolled wit, wit that is more tangential and coolly analytical than dynamic and passionate. As we go through the eighty-four poems of *The Mistress* we may admire the endless ingenuity employed to embroider the prescribed themes of metaphysical and cavalier lovers, but we seldom have any other reaction. Donne's fever of the bone has become a case of measles. If any poem makes an impression, it is 'Against Hope', and that is not mainly amatory. Unlike most other men of the age, Cowley offers no inevitable pieces to the anthologist. Roman influence is stronger in him than in any of the metaphysical amorists, though Ovid may only have encouraged rhetoric and antithetical conceits. But when Cowley 'Translated Paraphrastically' some Anacreontic poems, his wit was restrained by his model and his want of depth was an advantage, so that he produced charming cameos of vivacious neatness. In later paraphrases of Martial and others the same quality appeared, with some dilution. In temper, of course, Cowley was supremely Horatian.

The innocently and happily epicurean poet had an itch to be 'the Muses Hannibal'; the Alps of the religious epic he had essayed at Cambridge, but *Davideis* can best be treated along with other things of its kind. The odes, Pindaric and miscellaneous, constitute the most impressive portion of Cowley's work. Beginning with free translation of Pindar, he went on to imitation; though not the first English imitator, he created the genre for the next hundred years and more. Cowley was much too good a scholar to be ignorant of the Pindaric structure, but he wished to develop a looser form suited to the English genius, and he recognized, more clearly than many turgid followers, that the 'Pindarique Pegasus' 'flings Writer and Reader too that sits not sure'. The interest of the odes varies between the topical and the poetical. 'Brutus', which could not fail to be related to Cromwell, was not quite cancelled out by the *Vision* of 1661. The celebration of Hobbes's overthrow of the Stagirite is a poem, since Cowley can be stirred by ideas, and the ode is one obvious clue to his absorption, however incomplete his grasp, of recent thought. 'Life' begins on the Hobbesian level but rises higher. Determinism appears in 'Destiny'. Cowley was destined to celebrate the Royal Society, and his last grandiose ode is an historical document which lives chiefly in the image of Bacon as the Moses of the new science denied admission to the promised land, an image, by the way, which the poet had earlier applied to 'Reason. The Use of It in Divine Matters'. In these and other more or less ambitious odes there are bits of noble thinking and writing, yet hardly any poem stands out as compelling or completely good. The once admiring Dryden came to see that Cowley 'cou'd never forgive any Conceit which came in his way; but swept like a Drag-net, great and small'. Here, as in most of his work, 'nimble-footed Wit' is joined with 'smooth-pac'ed Eloquence', but 'strong Judgment' is not always in command of 'unruly Phansie'. For one of many illustrations there is

the fantastic and prolonged mythological conceit which opens
the ode 'Upon Dr. Harvey', though the poem settles down into
a sober eulogy of science. The elegies on William Hervey and
Crashaw have the exaltation of the odes, or rather more than
that, thanks to the unwonted strength of deep feeling. The
poet's mind is almost purged of artifice as he recalls the high
soul of his 'dearest Friend' and their days and nights of intellectual companionship. The elegy on Crashaw, after the fine
and famous beginning, lapses—if it is a lapse—into literary
criticism akin to the preface of 1656, but soon soars up again in
an impassioned Anglican tribute to the Catholic poet and saint.
There is emotion also, of a different kind, in the late 'Hymn.
To Light'. Cowley is not, like Vaughan, contemplating the
white radiance of eternity so much as the dome of many-
coloured glass. As country gentleman and as virtuoso, and in
a mood both serious and happy, he enjoys 'All the Worlds
bravery that delights our Eyes'.

Two odes, 'The Muse' and 'Of Wit', are critical essays in
verse which almost epitomize the poetical evolution of Cowley's
age, the shrinking of a large, deep, and lofty vision of poetry
and life into an ideal of rational congruity and decorum. And
Cowley himself reflects part of the process. In real metaphysical
poetry wit and feeling were fused by the heat and pressure
of inner tension; they remained separate and relatively shallow
and narrow in Cowley, whose cool critical temper was still
further cooled by Hobbesian rationalism. The poet was an
essayist in more than his essays. He was not born for exile and
secret service but for a time of moderation and security; and in
spite of his troubles and his constitutional melancholy—'When
all's done, Life is an Incurable Disease'—one would hardly guess
from a cursory glance at his writings that he had ever been
driven from an academic retreat. Instead of being a poet who
wrestled with experience Cowley was a man of letters who produced 'literature' for a social group. In most of his mature work
he was both the enfeebled grandson of Donne and the enfeebled
grandfather of Dryden. 'Not being of God, he could not stand.'

While the great religious poets, after Herbert, were not
strictly heirs of Donne, and secular wit ran more or less to seed
in Cleveland and Cowley, the finest flower of secular and serious
metaphysical poetry was Andrew Marvell (1621–78).[1] Marvell

[1] Marvell's father was a clergyman, 'facetious, yet Calvinistical', who in 1624

united in himself, with an independent moderation of his own, a fresh, muscular, agile, and subtle metaphysical wit and the rationality, clarity, economy, and structural sense of a genuine classic, the cultured, negligent grace of a cavalier and something of the religious and ethical seriousness of a Puritan Platonist. To this rare combination of gifts were added, moreover, a feeling for nature at once particular and general, earthly and unearthly, and an individual sensitivity and suppleness of rhythm. In some of these qualities, and in his response to the claims of both contemplative solitude and public affairs, Marvell had a degree of affinity with his friend Milton, whose early poems he was among the first to echo and to whose epic he gave homage in 1674. He owed of course a prime debt to Donne and Donne's disciples, perhaps a small one to such *libertins* as Saint-Amant, and some other tinctures in his elixir are implied in his praise of Lovelace and of Jonson. These classical and metaphysical, continental and English, epicurean and Puritan, civilized and simple elements are mingled in varying proportions in Marvell's poems and, except in his style, they are not always fused. The Christian and the Platonist are not very close to the passionate lover, nor the poet of gardens to the future political satirist—and 'The Coronet', with its quiet antitheses between thorns and poetic garlands, divine humility and human pride, is a religious sacrifice of all poetry.

One piece in particular stands apart from the rest, the

became preacher and master of the alms-house at Hull and was drowned in 1641; his devoted life received the praise of Fuller. From 1633 to 1641, as undergraduate and then as Scholar of Trinity, Marvell was at Cambridge, the Cambridge of Cowley and Crashaw, John Sherman and Whichcote. He had a brief Catholic phase and was recalled to Anglicanism by his father. From 1642 to 1646 he travelled abroad, perhaps as a tutor. During 1651–2 he was tutor to Lord Fairfax's daughter at Nun Appleton House in Yorkshire, where much of his best poetry was presumably written. He had sympathized with the king and the king's cause, but he passed from acceptance to admiration of Cromwell. In 1653 he became tutor to a ward of Cromwell's; this post took him to Eton and led to a valued acquaintance with Hales. During 1657–9 he was assistant in the Latin secretaryship to Milton (now no longer active), who had strongly recommended him in 1653. According to Edward Phillips it was Marvell who protected Milton at the Restoration. As member for Hull, Marvell served in Parliament, with exemplary zeal and probity, from 1659 until his death. His political satire of this period lies beyond our limits, but we may notice one famous work, *The Rehearsal Transprosed* (1672), written in support of toleration and against the intolerant Samuel Parker. None of Marvell's important early poems was printed in his lifetime. The first collection was published in 1681, ostensibly by his widow, though she was a legal fiction.

'Horatian Ode upon Cromwell's Return from Ireland' (1650), the only English poem, except some of Milton's sonnets, in which the tone of Horace's heroic odes is recaptured with original strength. The Puritan general, called by his active star from a life 'reserved and austere', makes one with Hannibal and Caesar. (Marvell echoes the version of Lucan by the Tom May whom, in this same year, he sped to a republican grave.) The full though critical recognition of Cromwell's personal greatness gives place for a time to the execution of the king (and here, too, Marvell remembers Lucan). To put this famous passage beside Lionel Johnson's poem on King Charles is to realize the difference between classical and a common kind of post-romantic art, between hard, dry, outwardly cool, and even witty precision and rich, damp, nebulous words and music which are poured directly upon the reader's feelings. But the final weight of the ode, as of 'The First Anniversary' (1655), is on Cromwell as an instrument of national and divine order.

To come to a more characteristic body of writing, the relatively formal and uneven and over-long 'Upon Appleton House' suggests comparison with the impersonal and mundane rationality, the plain, straightforward sententiousness, of *Cooper's Hill*, the 'classical' landmark of ten years earlier. Marvell can summarize history, as it concerns the Fairfax estate, and can celebrate the devout lives of the former nuns, but his range of reference and sensibility is much wider than Denham's—from 'The hatching Thrastles shining Eye' and the kingfisher, 'the Saphir-winged Mist' of twilight, to 'Mexique Paintings', 'The Circle in the Quadrature', and *Gondibert*. His wit plays, with mingled lightness and seriousness, upon the ways of man and, in a happy passage which parallels 'The Garden', upon his own secure and easy intimacy with birds and trees. Marvell's reading 'in Natures mystick Book' stops well on this side of Vaughan and Traherne, but his capacity for sensuous self-identification with natural things has a touch of the old symbolic and religious concept of nature as the art of God which appears in so many philosophic writers from Plato to Sir Thomas Browne. Marvell is of course too unconscious of a message to be a Meredithian Melampus, and his poems of nature, like his others, are written in

> short but admirable Lines,
> By which, ungirt and unconstrain'd,
> Things greater are in less contain'd.

In 'Upon Appleton House', 'The Nymph Complaining for the
Death of her Fawn' (if this have any ulterior meaning, it may be
an Anglican's grief for the stricken Church), 'The Picture of
Little T. C. in a Prospect of Flowers' (even if this ends with a
hint of nature's cruelty), and the 'Mower' poems, Marvell
reveals an enjoyment, at once fresh and subtle and sophisticated, of natural simplicity, the 'wild and fragrant Innocence'
which 'Luxurious Man' has spoiled. The best example, 'The
Garden', is not the mere idyllic ecstasy of a romantic primitivist
or escapist; the rhythmic variations themselves suggest complexity. Even in the moment of apparent surrender, when the
creative mind suddenly transforms the universe into Virgil's
viridi umbra,

> Annihilating all that's made
> To a green Thought in a green Shade,

the detached intelligence is there to criticize what it creates.
Marvell is aware that he is a man in the world of men, that
a golden holiday is not, though it may approach, a mystical
vision.

Being a sincere and rational Christian who is not subject to
auto-intoxication, Marvell can link nature and religion without
confusing them. In 'Bermudas' the tropical luxuriance of an
island paradise is rendered with such clean (yet magical) strokes
that it becomes a fit Puritan temple 'where to sound his Name',
the very home of primitive Christianity, and the music of 'An
holy and a chearful Note' is as simple as the chime of the falling
oars. (Marvell may have re-created items from the chromato-
graph at the beginning of Waller's 'Battle of the Summer
Islands', or from Captain John Smith's *General History of
Virginia,* or he may have drawn upon the Bermudan memories
of his Eton host, John Oxenbridge, or he may have got hints
from a source mentioned in the following chapter.) It is a long
way from this Puritan canticle to dialogues between Thyrsis and
Dorinda and Clorinda and Damon, yet in the midst of pastoral
tinsel we are surprised by 'Heaven's the Center of the Soul' and
the sudden query prompted by a tinkling fountain:

> Might a Soul bath there and be clean,
> Or slake its Drought?

Another poem develops, not in the Shelleyan vein, the parallel
between the life-cycle of a drop of dew and the soul, that drop

from 'the clear Fountain of Eternal Day'. Marvell may not, like Vaughan, thirst to return (his favourite epithet is 'green', not 'white'), but his Christian Platonism is genuine.

The Platonism of the first lines of 'A Dialogue between the Soul and the Body' is about half-way between Vaughan and the passage in Donne's *Second Anniversary*; the lines are more firmly rhythmic than Donne's and hence seem less disturbed and disturbing. Yet Marvell is serious enough, and his emphasis is ethical. Though fancy may cherish a garden as love's best retreat 'When we have run our Passions heat', in more sober mood the poet confronts the active and interwoven desires and ills of flesh and spirit. The 'Dialogue between the Resolved Soul and Created Pleasure' springs also from an old tradition, which carries us from the ancient fable of Hercules, Pleasure, and Virtue down to Cowley's 'The Soul'. Here the nature that Marvell could revel in has lost its divine innocence and become the multiple foe of man's integrity. In both poems Marvell treats his ethical problem with relative directness, which does not mean that he eschews bold and homely images. The 'Tyrannic Soul', the body complains,

> impales me so,
> That mine own Precipice I go.

The resolved soul declares:

> I sup above, and cannot stay
> To bait so long upon the way.

Yet, next to the stanza on the flesh-imprisoned soul, probably the most stirring lines are a moral statement as plain as similar things in *Comus* or as Daniel's 'Ulysses and the Siren':

> Earth cannot shew so brave a Sight
> As when a single Soul does fence
> The Batteries of alluring Sense,
> And Heaven views it with delight.

The poems so far mentioned would not be what they are if Donne had not written, but they are almost all remote from him in theme and feeling and music. The one which bears the clearest marks of Donne is the strange and high 'Definition of Love'. It might have started, though Marvell's antitheses of steel are his own, from Cowley's 'Impossibilities', or from the complaint of Sidney's love-stricken Philoclea, who appeals to the stars and laments that, whereas in others hope kindles love, 'in me despaire should be the bellowes of my affection: and of all despaires the most miserable, which is drawen from impossibilitie'. On Marvell's as on other metaphysical lovers 'Loves whole World . . . doth wheel', and the poem is made up of philosophic and verbal paradoxes, of realistic, cosmic, and geometrical images. On the other hand, its thoroughly metaphysical thought and feeling are welded with a classical clarity, rightness, and inevitability of evolution, detail, and rhythm which attain something like grandeur:

> Therefore the Love which us doth bind,
> But Fate so enviously debarrs,
> Is the Conjunction of the Mind,
> And Opposition of the Stars.

It is a somewhat similar blending of the metaphysical and the classical which makes 'To his Coy Mistress' stand out as it does even in such an age of love poetry. In the great body of Petrarchan sonnets, and in the lyrics from Anacreon and Theocritus down to Marlowe and Jonson and Herrick, Carew and Cleveland and Cowley (whose 'My Diet', with its tracts of years and 'vast Eternity', may have been in Marvell's mind), the 'persuasion to love', whether sober or sportive, generally moved on one plane. But when seriousness has gone as far as it can, it can be both heightened and restrained by self-mocking irony. In Marvell's first paragraph emotion is so interpenetrated with apparent levity that hyperbole, being hypothetical, becomes rational. More concretely and gaily than in the sombre 'Definition of Love', the poet sees the whole world of space and time as the setting for two lovers. But wit cannot sustain the pretence that youth and beauty and love are immortal, and with a quick change of tone—like Catullus's *nobis cum semel occidit brevis lux* or Horace's *sed Timor et Minae*—the theme of time and death is developed with serious and soaring directness, until wit takes over to weave its antitheses of macabre irony. (Among many variations on his ancient text, one wonders if Marvell remembered Herbert's 'Church-Monuments'—'How tame these ashes are, how free from lust'.) In the third paragraph traditional directness soon gives way again to bold metaphysical images, expressive now of consummated love's triumph over time. Throughout, the most complex reverberations are set up by simple words in a simple pattern and a simple tune, a tune carried, to be sure, with Marvell's peculiar *brio*. And throughout

we are aware, as we are never aware in Donne, that the poet
is a classical artist whose lucid wit is under severe though unseen
control and always subordinated to the dominant theme, so
that the lyric possesses a cavalier grace and poise, beyond the
cavalier level.

Marvell's unique quality and his chronological position
might appear to contradict what the names of Cleveland and
Cowley imply, and might suggest that metaphysical poetry
could have had a second birth. Some modern critics have
affirmed that the fruitful metaphysical movement was crushed
by the deadening power of Milton, although the influence of
Paradise Lost did not begin to work until long after metaphysical
wit had died of its own excesses and of the steadily rising
reaction associated with Waller and Denham. There is the
further fact that Marvell's perfect poems of the years around
1650, poems which united something more than the sweetness
and strength of the official neoclassical pair, were not collected
until 1681. But the poet's own career is itself proof of the radical
change in the climate which had nourished the metaphysical
genius. His satirical instinct had appeared, not too happily,
at the very beginning—his first victim was that *corpus vile*,
Richard Flecknoe—and it ultimately extinguished the metaphysical. The heir of Donne became, as political satirist, the
chief heir of Cleveland, the admirer of Rochester, and, in spite
of mutual dislike, the father of Dryden.

6

This chapter has been concerned with two of the three principal currents in poetry, and of these two the more conspicuous
was the metaphysical. It is of course far more distinct to us
than it was in the seventeenth century, when many men were
loosely credited with wit and learning or 'strong lines'. Even
Dryden's later censures took in only Donne and the notorious
Cowley and Cleveland. Carew, and Crashaw's English poems,
had only one edition after 1660; Herbert's popularity was more
pious than poetical; Vaughan was almost, and Traherne quite,
unknown; and Marvell's early poems, when printed in 1681,
were overshadowed by his satires. Apart from Carew's early
elegy on Donne, there was not much critical appreciation of the
qualities we prize. On the other hand, increasing distaste for

extravagance was coupled with increasing esteem for the virtues represented by the mediocre pair who happened to lead the return to the main tradition of European neoclassicism, 'those Standard-bearers of Wit and Judgment, Denham and Waller', in the phrase of Alexander Brome. If Milton's full poetic fruition had not been postponed, he might have been the standard-bearer. As it was, the classicism of Waller and Denham was only the ghost of Jonson's. Yet Dryden, himself a true heir of Renaissance humanism, often and generously acknowledged his age's debt to the Dioscuri:

But the Excellence and Dignity of it [rhyme], were never fully known till Mr. Waller taught it; He first made Writing easily an Art: First shew'd us to conclude the Sense, most commonly, in Distichs; which in the Verse of those before him, runs on for so many Lines together, that the Reader is out of Breath to overtake it. This sweetness of Mr. Wallers Lyrick Poesie was afterwards follow'd in the Epick by Sir John Denham, in his Coopers-Hill: a Poem which your Lordship knows for the Majesty of the Style, is, and ever will be the exact Standard of good Writing.

Dryden and others were not wholly unaware that the smoothing process had begun before Waller and Denham, and Waller himself, Dryden recorded, looked back to Fairfax as his master. In addition to Fairfax a crowd of poets contributed more or less to the development of the closed and balanced couplet, for instance, Marlowe, Sylvester, Heywood, Drayton, Hall, Sir John Beaumont, Drummond, Jonson, George Sandys, Henry King, who praised Sandys and could sound an Augustan note himself, Lord Falkland, Godolphin, Cartwright, and others. As some of these names suggest, much reflective, occasional, and commendatory verse took this form. Many of the names represent translation, especially from Latin and from the elegiac distich; something was said in Chapter II of that chain of stylistic and prosodic evolution. Translation was one link between Waller and Denham, and between them and their precursors and successors. Over half of Denham's non-dramatic verse was in that kind, much of it from Virgil; and Waller had a share in Godolphin's version of the fourth *Aeneid*. Of Denham's Virgilian paraphrases, done in 1636, the two revised portions which were printed show freer treatment of the original along with a stricter handling of the couplet. One sample of antithetical neatness is 'Darkness our Guide, Despair our

Leader was', which Dryden sharpened into 'Night was our
Friend, our Leader was Despair'. There are, incidentally, bits
from Virgil in *Cooper's Hill.*

No poetical reputation of the seventeenth century has been so
completely and irreparably eclipsed as that of Edmund Waller
(1606–87).[1] Whereas Cowley and Cleveland can still give
pleasure, Waller's name calls up scarcely more than two lyrics
of attenuated cavalier grace, 'On a Girdle' and 'Go lovely
Rose', and a dim memory of much complimentary and occasional verse. He had, like Samuel Rogers, the prestige of
wealth, culture, and wit, but Rogers was never celebrated as
the standard-bearer of a new poetical movement. Probably the
most significant crystallization of all the tributes paid to Waller
was the equating of his name, in the Soame-Dryden 'translation' of Boileau (1683), with that of Malherbe (which was, by
the way, rather more logical than the substitution, for Villon,
Marot, and Ronsard, of Fairfax, Spenser, and Davenant). And
assuredly the most succinct was Thomas Rymer's heading:
'Chaucer refin'd our English. Which in perfection by Waller.'
Francis Atterbury, in his preface to the *Second Part of Mr.
Waller's Poems* (1690), praised the poet's avoidance of mono-
syllabic excess like Donne's and of run-on lines, his making
pauses in sense and metre coincide, his good and new rhymes,
in short, the harmonious 'dance of words' which we associate
with the balanced and antithetical half-lines of the closed
couplet. Even in this preface, by the way, Atterbury appealed
to Roscommon, Dryden, and Milton as men who had resented

[1] Waller, the son of a country gentleman of wealth and ancient name, attended
Eton, had a brief sojourn at Cambridge, and seems to have commenced his parliamentary career at sixteen. In 1631 he married an heiress, apparently for love;
she died in 1634. During 1636–9 Waller paid poetical homage to Lady Dorothy
Sidney ('Sacharissa'), who married Lord Spencer in 1639. Waller was, like
Cromwell, a cousin of John Hampden, but in politics he held in the main to the
constitutional royalism of which his friend Falkland was the finest representative.
'Waller's Plot', a scheme to seize London for the king, was exposed in 1643. Waller,
who did not play a noble part (though he was less base than Clarendon made out),
escaped with banishment and a heavy fine. He married again and spent seven
years abroad, with Evelyn and with the English exiles in Paris. His early verse,
which had circulated in manuscript, was first collected in 1645, the year of Milton's
first volume. In 1651 Waller was pardoned by Parliament and allowed to return
home. The poetical superiority of his panegyric on Cromwell (1655) over his
welcome of Charles II occasioned a famous display of his ready wit. In 1661 he
joined the Royal Society and returned to Parliament, where he made frequent
pleas for religious toleration. His tombstone at Beaconsfield proclaimed him
inter poetas sui temporis facile princeps.

or broken the tyranny of rhyme, and in later years he turned highly critical of Waller.

Apart from his importance in the history of style and technique, and half a dozen slight amatory pieces, there is little attraction in Waller. Any public or private occasion could release a stream of his lucid rhetoric and, seen through that medium, all occasions appear about equally significant, whether 'Of a War with Spain, and a Fight at Sea' or 'Of Tea, Commended by her Majesty'. In the former we have a couplet about Cromwell as Jove transferred from an earlier poem 'To the King, on his Navy'. Classical myth, which had been and in Milton was still to be a rich inspiration, is everywhere, and everywhere is of the true Augustan coinage, smooth, polite, and pallid. And though, as a member of the Royal Society, Waller took a modest interest in the habits of toads and the generation of insects as well as in the improvement of the English language, the scientific ideas in his verse do not go very far; they, like his mythology, dwindle into material for courtly gallantry. (Since there is so little to put to Waller's credit, perhaps we should remember that he greatly enjoyed Chapman's *Homer*.) Of the last verses of Waller's old age one couplet remains famous, a sombre version of a conceit he had once used in addressing the sick Amoret:

> The Soul's dark Cottage, batter'd and decay'd,
> Let's in new Light thrô chinks that time has made.

He may have remembered the phrase in Fuller's 'Life of Monica', 'her soul saw a glimpse of happinesse through the chincks of her sicknesse-broken body' (or perhaps a passage in Sylvester's 'Sixth Day of the First Week'); at any rate comparison with Fuller suggests the loss involved in the whole poetical mode that Waller stood for. For us he remains a fluent trifler, the rhymer of a court gazette. But we need not deny that 'he added something to our elegance of diction, and something to our propriety of thought'.

Waller and Denham may have met as early as 1635–6; they admired each other's work, and Denham in particular supplies evidence of imitation as well.[1] The critical decision, said

---

[1] Sir John Denham (1615–69) was born in Ireland, where his father was Chief Baron of the Exchequer. He spent several years (1631–4) at Oxford, but gave more time to dice, cards, and dreaming than to study. He entered Lincoln's Inn in 1634 and was called to the Bar in 1639. He had married in 1634. He won

Dr. Johnson, following Dryden and Pope, had identified Waller
with sweetness and Denham with strength, strength, as Johnson
explained, in the sense of conciseness. Denham resembled
Davenant, whose *Gondibert* he burlesqued, in being a cavalier of
irregular life with an instinct for regular verse and moral reflection which made him a harbinger of the new era. He had ribald
affinities with Sir John Mennes and Thomas Killigrew, but his
historical significance rests on his graver work. One minor
piece, 'The Progress of Learning', is a sober historical survey,
a world removed from Fanshawe's mythological and allegorical
canto on the same subject (1647), which opens with an appeal
to 'Spencers Ghost', or from George Herbert's witty 'Church
Militant'. Yet Denham can feel the great question of his age:

> Through Seas of knowledg, we our course advance,
> Discovering still new worlds of Ignorance.

With such an outlook Denham was naturally inclined to religious toleration, and, though he wrote a manly poem in praise
of the dead Strafford, he was not such a blindly devoted royalist
but that he could condemn tyranny with an eye on Charles I.

Cooper's Hill (1642), while not the first topographical poem,
was the first in which description was mainly an excuse for
reflection. Windsor suggested a review of English history, the
Thames a royal stag-hunt (which took some details from Waller
and perhaps gave some to *Gondibert*), Runnymede, and the
relations of king and subjects. The topics are not unskilfully
articulated and the texture of the poem has a massive plainness
and economy; conceits are eschewed, though 'turns' and antitheses are numerous enough. Denham's couplets are bolder
and less monotonous than Waller's. The four famous lines on
the Thames, which were among the additions of 1655, were

fame with his play *The Sophy* (1641) and especially with *Cooper's Hill*, which was
piratically published in 1642. Denham fought on the king's side and lost some of
his property to George Wither, whose life he was said to have saved later by a
stroke of wit. Both abroad, during 1648–52, and afterwards at home, he worked
for the royalist cause. In 1660 he became Surveyor of Works; among the results
of his tenure of office were Burlington House, Greenwich Palace, and improved
pavements in London. He was knighted (1661) and received grants of land and
money. In 1661 he was elected M.P. and in 1663 a member of the Royal Society.
He married again in 1665. For a time he lost his mind; the cause was probably his
own early excesses rather than, as contemporaries thought, his young wife's becoming the Duke of York's mistress. He recovered enough to write a fine elegy on
Cowley and to pay the first tribute to *Paradise Lost*. He was buried in the Abbey
beside Cowley.

probably indebted to Cartwright's elegy on Jonson and may also
have owed something to a poem Denham echoed elsewhere in
Cooper's Hill, Randolph's tribute to Felltham, which is quoted
below in Chapter VI. But Denham achieved a neat compact-
ness which made his quatrain long admired as the acme of the
qualities it described:

> O could I flow like thee, and make thy stream
> My great example, as it is my theme!
> Though deep, yet clear, though gentle, yet not dull,
> Strong without rage, without ore-flowing full.

This is indeed a thoroughly classical ideal, the ideal which in
our time has been summed up as 'fullness in the concise and
depth in the clear'. Unhappily, many of Denham's successors,
and not only in the dreary topographical genre, carried further
his tendency to confuse the grandeur of generality with the
obvious, the plain with the flat.

Metaphysical poetry, if we ignore its rich results, may be said
to have only held back for a time the wave of European neoclassicism that had reached its first crest in Jonson. And though
Denham and Waller deserved some of the credit they received
for curbing eccentricity and moulding versification, they were
but superficial signs of a larger movement. That movement
was far from being merely literary and neoclassical, for its
dynamic—and desiccating—symbols are the names of Descartes
and Hobbes. Nor is it altogether paradoxical, after mentioning
one of those names at least, to say that the slow rise of the closed
couplet to dominance implied in some measure the rise of a
collective sense of political, social, and philosophic order. In
literature that sense of security was attained partly by turning
back from troubled explorations of the individual soul to the
accepted sententiousness of public occasions and general experience. And in the antithetical balance of lines and half-lines,
as in Denham's apostrophe to the Thames, we see, as some
modern critics have observed, the bold and questioning 'wit' of
the earlier seventeenth century coming under the control of the
moderating 'judgement' which aims, not at the conflict of
opposites, but at the rational mean between them.

V

THE LITERATURE OF TRAVEL

IN the early seventeenth century people travelled, according to their means and station, in their own carriages, on horseback, and on foot. As literary representatives of these several classes we might think of Bacon stopping his coach to stuff the notorious hen with snow, of Fuller loading his saddle-bags with antiquarian notes, and of Ben Jonson and John Taylor the Water-Poet walking up to Scotland. Stage-wagons had been on the road in Elizabeth's time, but stage-coaches did not come into use until the reign of Charles I. Though roads and conveyances slowly improved, a long journey required a good reason, a stout heart, and a resilient frame. Business kept many people in motion, from royalty to beggars and highwaymen, but travel in Britain for the sake of travel was relatively rare and its literary fruit still rarer. However, there was a marked increase of books on county antiquities, topography, and resources, and ample evidence of affection for the English scene appears in such poems as *Britannia's Pastorals* and the encyclo-paedic *Poly-Olbion*. In the course of thirty-five years John Taylor made many journeys by land or water, chiefly around England, and published pamphlets about them from 1617 onward. A unique item in the literature of travel and of 'Merry England' is Will Kemp's infectious account (1600) of his dancing a morris from London to Norwich. But our attention must be given to a few of the numerous travellers who recorded their observations of the Continent, the Near and the Far East, and America. As one of them says, 'the nature of man, by an inward inclination, is alwaies inquisitive of forraine newes; yea, and much more affecteth the sight and knowledge of strange, and unfrequented kingdomes, such is the instinct of his naturall affection'.

Throughout the Middle Ages the motives of pilgrim, ecclesiastic, scholar, business-man, diplomat, soldier, and mere tourist had led multitudes to surmount the difficulties and dangers of foreign travel. For Protestant Englishmen of the sixteenth and seventeenth centuries all these motives except the first were operating with greater urgency than ever. The political and commercial conditions of Europe, combined with the ideals of Renaissance humanism, gave a new importance to study of the history, policy, language, and manners of foreign countries as a preparation for public service and international trade. Many a young man, as Wood says of Overbury, 'travelled for a time, and returned a most accomplished Person'. Sometimes a tutor like Ben Jonson or Hobbes went along. A Polonian letter of advice from an elder was a frequent preliminary, and a frequent sequel was the writing of a report, which might serve as an informal equivalent of a modern Civil Service examination. While the grand tour developed as a privilege or obligation of sons of the nobility and gentry, such as Evelyn, it was shared —thanks to patron or parent—by such others as Inigo Jones and Milton. These names remind us that Italy was still attractive for antiquities, architecture, art, and music, and the liberal University of Padua enjoyed scientific and legal renown among transalpine students; but the sun of Italian humanism had set. From the early seventeenth century onward, as travellers' manuals and the royalist migrations testify, France was more and more recognized by Englishmen as the centre of thought, business, fashion, accomplishments, and vice. Another country of growing interest to Englishmen, through religious and military ties and commercial rivalry, was the Netherlands.

Variety of motives meant variety of literary reactions. On the one hand, the affected traveller who picked up his clothes and his behaviour everywhere was a stock figure for satire, and the Elizabethan fear of moral and religious contagion was still a reality, a somewhat lurid reality in Joseph Hall's *Quo Vadis?* (1617). Moreover, if at home a traveller's physical safety was not a matter of course, still less was it so for a Protestant Englishman in many parts of Europe. On the other hand, in the minds of philosophic travellers and essayists from Robert Johnson and Dallington and Bacon to Peacham and Howell and Harrington, the cultural advantages of travel far outweighed the dangers. Serious travellers kept journals and, if ambitious too, wrote them up when they returned to England, where they could buttress their first-hand observations with solid borrowings from foreign works, ancient and modern, of history and cosmography. While the great mass of travel literature was a by-product of trade, exploration, and colonizing, three of the best-known books were written by independent and disinterested globe-trotters, and our brief survey may begin with them.

Fynes Moryson (1566–1630) was a Cambridge man, Thomas Coryate (1577?–1617) an Oxonian, and William Lithgow (1582?–1645?) was, as patriot and stylist, a worthy fellow-countryman of Sir Thomas Urquhart's. (Scotland, says Lithgow, is 120 miles longer than England; he paced out the distance.) When we contemplate a map of Europe and the Orient not yet embraced by the paternal arms of Thomas Cook, it quickens the pulse to think of these resolute travellers who let no toil or danger subdue their desire to see the world, and whose peripatetic economy reveals such a mixture of romantic wander-lust, pedagogic zeal, and *bourgeois* thrift. Fynes Moryson's journeys were made in the last decade of the sixteenth century. His *Itinerary* (1617) combines lyrical praise of travel with sage practical advice and, along with substantial information on the serious subjects every gentleman should know, gives especially full details about life and manners in various countries (including Ireland). But the modern reader relishes most the more personal items. When French highwaymen rob Moryson they miss the money he has cannily hidden in a box of ointment and a ball of thread. Sober and prudent as he is, curiosity leads him into tight places for the pleasure of getting out of them—which he does, through his skill in disguise and in foreign tongues. Posing as a Frenchman he visits Bellarmine at the Jesuit College in Rome; as a German he inspects a Spanish fort. He preserves the purity of his faith by dodging the Holy Stairs, he flits about Italy to escape the sacramentary census at Easter, and in Jerusalem he avoids attendance at Mass by feigning ill-ness. On such occasions we share the narrator's modest pride in his own ingenuity.

Moryson's normal warmth of anti-Catholic feeling becomes incandescence in William Lithgow. His title, *Rare Adventures and Painful Peregrinations* (1632), gives the reader a foretaste of an aureate style which often soars into passages of execrable verse. Yet there is also much straightforward narrative and descrip-tion of frequently vivid intensity. Lithgow has a dour nature, embittered by Spanish tortures, and he takes his joys as well as his sufferings rather grimly. But dogged determination and 'ambitious curiosity' drove on his 'paynefull feet' and 'fatigated corps' for nineteen years over 36,000 miles, exclusive of journeys by water. Historically, Lithgow's chief claim to attention is the fact that he was the first Briton to give a first-hand if inadequate report of Greece and the Aegean.

A happier gusto inspired the wanderings of 'the Hiero-solymitan Syrian-Mesopotamian-Armenian-Median-Parthian-Persian-India-Legge-strecher of Odcomb in Somerset, Thomas Coryate'. He traversed a good part of the Continent in 1608 and walked home from Venice; before setting off for India in 1612 he hung up his well-worn shoes in his father's parish church. From the court of the Great Mogul at Ajmere Coryate wrote home to his old friends of the Mermaid tavern, 'Right Generous, Joviall, and Mercuriall Sirenaicks'. But his 'pan-craticall and athleticall' health did not survive his continued exertions, and at Surat in 1617 English merchants 'laid his rambling Brains at Rest'. Coryate's 'sesquippledan verboo-juice' (to quote another ink-hornist wanderer, Mr. Polly) is not, like Lithgow's, chronic and gritty, it is the occasional and oratorical effervescence of vitality. He had been a notable Grecian at Oxford and he mastered a number of oriental languages. Not only did he honour the Mogul (and embarrass Sir Thomas Roe) with a speech in Persian but, a more remarkable feat, worsted a termagant Indian laundress in a duel of Hindustani Billingsgate. What has survived of Coryate's eastern journal shows a pioneer interest in antiquities of the Levant, including the ruins of Troy. *Coryate's Crudities*, an account of his earlier European travels, appeared in 1611, with a prolonged salvo of mock-commendatory poems from dozens of the wits, whose jocosity was mixed with affectionate admira-tion for the 'single-soled, single-souled, and single-shirted Observer'. Coryate gobbled up a good deal in his five months' travel. The gibe provoked by his zeal in copying inscriptions, that he was 'a tombe-stone traveller', he disdained, but he promised to pay more attention to affairs of state in his next book. Along with careful descriptions of the conventional sights he records such Italian devices as 'wooden flaps' for use against flies, umbrellas for use against the sun, and those implements unique in Europe, table forks. One of the glories of Venice, which his predecessors have not described, Coryate investigates with scientific innocence, namely, the courtesans who are truly if oddly said to be 'famoused over all Christendome'. These elegant sirens, by the way, rarely have children, as 'the best carpenters make the fewest chips'. But Coryate is interested in higher things, buildings and books and scholarship, and his comments, like those of other English travellers, display a mixture of cosmopolite and patriot. He would gladly spend his old age in lovely Mantua if the Italians were not idolaters and—this is an echo of Lucian—if the very smoke of Odcombe in Somerset were not dearer than the fire of all other places under the sun.

The East was visited by more sober and affluent tourists. George Sandys's *Relation of a Journey* (1615), a richly illustrated and popular book which was of use to authors like Bacon, Milton, and Browne, combined first-hand and second-hand information about the present and past of the Graeco-Roman East. In 1628–9 Thomas Herbert (who in his old age was to write a memoir of his attendance upon the captive King Charles) traversed Persia in the suite of the English ambassador. His graphic picture of the land and its people (1634) was in later editions increasingly submerged under bookish erudition. Sir Henry Blount's *Voyage into the Levant* (1636) showed unusual appreciation of Turkish virtues. Thus the multiplication of visitors and residents and books of travel gradually reduced oriental legend to fact, but without dispelling the glamour that still remains for us. Knolles's opening phrase proclaimed a great reality, 'the glorious Empire of the Turkes, the present terrour of the world', an exotic, splendid, sensual, and barbaric civilization united by a crude and powerful religion against divided Christendom. There was the Holy Land, from which sacred relics had once been transported to Italy by angels, and there was the whole classical Orient, from which antique marbles were now being transported to England by agents of the Earl of Arundel. The romantic and realistic attractions of eastern geography, history, and ethnology are attested not only by travellers' narratives but by such books as Fuller's *Holy War* (1639) and *Pisgah-Sight of Palestine* (1650), not to mention *Paradise Lost* and *Paradise Regained*.

Then 'the wealth of Ormus and of Ind' had opened up a more prosaic but even more potent vision of the East as an unlimited field for commercial enterprise, a vision translated into actuality by the formation of the great trading companies. Thomas Mun, economist and champion of eastern trade, was not concerned with history or manners but with drugs, spices, raw silk, indigo, and calicoes. Indeed, the silk trade was the occasion of the ambassadorial journey in which Thomas Herbert took part. Romance and realism are mingled in the strange careers of the brothers Sherley—'Quæ regio in terris', exclaims Purchas, 'Sherlii non plena laboris?'—and of the numberless traders who turn up in Syria, India and the Indies, and Russia, bargaining as shrewdly though not so securely as if they were in Cheapside. They faced not only the normal dangers of travel but, to condense one of Purchas's spacious headings, Turkish treachery, Portugal hostility, Moorish and ethnic perfidy, Dutch malignity, ignorant and malicious calumny. Abundant information about all aspects of the East was contained in the narratives and reports of diplomats like Sir Thomas Roe, chaplains like William Biddulph and Edward Terry, and many sailors and business-men who could write vivid descriptions of what they saw and did. Roe's journal and correspondence give a clear impression of his vigorous character and ability and of the difficulties he overcame as the first English ambassador at the court of the Great Mogul (1615–19). Although he shares with Sir James Lancaster the title of founder of British India, Roe urged the East India Company to confine itself to trade and avoid military entanglements.

But the greatest of eastern travellers, perhaps the ideal traveller of the whole period, was that middle-class man of business, the astonishing Peter Mundy (1596?–1667?). From 1608 until 1656 Mundy was in almost perpetual motion, and in 1647, when he did not know he was to make a third voyage to India, he reckoned that he had covered more than a hundred thousand miles and had been preserved from a thousand dangers. Mundy always hated 'waistinge of meanes' at home and always 'had a Mind to see Farther First'. He never gratified his desire to go round the world, but he saw or lived in most parts of Europe and Asia and adjacent islands. His huge journal, copiously illustrated with drawings, was begun in 1620, when he returned overland from Constantinople, and broken off in 1667. It first reached print, in six volumes, in the present century. Though mainly in the form of disconnected notes and almost completely impersonal, the record displays a rare combination of gifts, laconic prose, a scientific concern for accuracy, invincible fortitude and good humour, and an alert and insatiable curiosity about every aspect of the world.

Mundy is interested in geography and the stars (he cherished a telescope); books of travel, philosophy, and science; birds, fish, animals, and people; clothes, scenery, and wholesome 'chucculatte'; religious rites and grisly executions (in the East and in Restoration London); the building of the Taj Mahal and of 'Pel Mel'; trade and languages; music in the Cathedral of Seville and at feasts at Agra. Did ever any other traveller's ears, when his eyes were on dancing girls, record that Indian music seems to lack thirds and fifths? And in farthest Asia the tireless nomad recalls England, which excels all countries in the world 'both For conveniency and delightt', and all English counties, we feel, give place to Cornwall.

East and West meet in the pages of Purchas, and voyages in both directions were made with partly similar motives, sometimes by the same navigators. (Davis and Baffin, whose names are perpetuated on the map of northern Canada, were both killed in the East.) It was of course the commercial desire for a shorter route to the East which sent ship after ship and 'many of the best sort of men' in search of a North-West Passage. In the exploring of the American coast early dreams of a waterway to the Pacific did not vanish with the acquisition of such tangible commodities as tobacco, whale-oil, fish, and furs. But while the East encouraged the establishment of nothing more than trading posts, the virgin spaces of America invited colonization. The vision of Hakluyt and Ralegh inspired others, and during the seventeenth century hundreds and then thousands of people left England—not to mention undesirables who were sent—to obtain land and security or religious and political freedom, or to achieve 'the Conversion of Salvages to Christianytie'. 'The first and last thing therefore in this Virginian argument considerable, is God; that is, whether we have Commission from him to plant, and whether the Plantation may bring glory to him.' Because of the large and novel issues involved from the beginning, and the ultimate results, the story of early colonizing in America is by far the most important branch of the heterogeneous literature of travel. But that story of dissension and failure, of perseverance and courage, of miseries and triumphs, needs no recounting here.

In the nature of the case America did not attract cosmopolitan tourists, though one whom we have met already, George Sandys, combined official and Ovidian labours in Virginia.

Mere wanderlust did not send Ralegh to the Orinoco or drive men into strange seas where 'The ice did split with a thunderfit', or even to face the discomforts and dangers of Virginia and New England. Early reports on America, written for London backers and prospective settlers, were highly practical, even in their eulogies of natural resources, but accounts of exploration, of Indian manners, and of the colonists' struggle to survive, could never be dull. One happily dramatic incident is the arrival of Lord De la Warr bringing salvation to the despairing remnant of Jamestown settlers who had just embarked for home. Some narratives have an accidental importance, like the several concerning the storm which cast Sir George Somers and Sir Thomas Gates upon 'the Ile of Divels', otherwise 'the still-vex'd Bermoothes'. Apart from storms, Bermuda appears in the accounts of Strachey and Jourdain as an earthly paradise, with fruits ripening in a continual spring and with a supply of ambergris; and another story, that of Richard More's party landing in Bermuda in 1612, contains, along with a similar picture of the islands, the description of men rowing and the singing of a Psalm of thankfulness—all of which carries us forward from *The Tempest* to Marvell's lovely lyric. For contrast we might transport ourselves to the frozen north described by Luke Fox, Thomas James, and others; and to think of the north is to think of that darkly vivid narrative of Hudson and his loyal followers being set adrift by mutineers.

But since we can notice only one writer on America, we must take the one whose commonplace name might stand as a symbol of English enterprise in all parts of the globe, and who has long enjoyed popular fame by reason of his extraordinary career, his vigorous personality, and his unwearied labours in person and in print on behalf of Virginia and New England, Captain John Smith (1579/80–1631). Modern scholarship has dealt more or less severely with Smith's romantic autobiography, but the reader of literature may be allowed to take untroubled pleasure in the tale of the Lincolnshire apprentice who ran away to seek adventures and found plenty in soldiering on the Continent; whose three single and victorious combats with Turkish heroes won a royal reward; who escaped from captivity with the aid of a pasha's wife, the first of four ministering angels in the life of an attractive bachelor; who was made a slave, killed his master, and after long wanderings returned to England, a veteran of twenty-four. During 1607–9 he was active in Virginia, as both administrator and explorer. Comparison of his narratives with other evidence indicates a degree of masterful ambition and jealousy, yet Smith did much to carry Jamestown through the first distresses caused by inexperience, factions, famine, disease, and Indians. We have no good ground for doubting the story that he was saved from death, when captured by the Indians, through the intercession of Pocahontas. A less celebrated but unforgettable item in the expansion of Britain is the picture of Captain Smith as guest of honour at an Indian banquet, with thirty naked damsels dancing before him—a sort of analogue to Sir Calidore and the Graces, except that the Indian nymphs, after vanishing, returned to swarm upon the Captain crying 'Love you not mee?'

In 1614 Smith made a successful voyage to New England; a second attempt (1615) was frustrated by storms and pirates and ended in another of his difficult escapes. Though he had much less actual experience of New England than of Virginia, he was during his retirement even more zealous in advertising the northerly region; it was he who established its name. The Pilgrims preferred Smith's helpful books to his company. Much of his own and others' earlier writings was gathered up in his *General History of Virginia, New England, and the Summer Isles* (1624). In 1626 he published a manual for seamen. In 1630 appeared the *True Travels, Adventures, and Observations of Captain John Smith, in Europe, Asia, Africa, and America*, and in the year of his death the indefatigable champion of colonization issued his last appeal to 'men that have great spirits and small meanes', *Advertisements for the Unexperienced Planters of New England, or Anywhere*. Whatever discounting may be done, Smith's career, like that of not a few contemporaries, is an astonishing mixture of the romantic and the prosaic. If he had been cast up on an island he would have been Robinson Crusoe. And along with practical knowledge, sagacity, and energy, Smith had devotion to a cause. We could not ask for a sturdier piece of eloquence than this declaration concerning the American settlements:

By that acquaintance I have with them, I may call them my children, for they have bin my wife, my hawks, my hounds, my cards, my dice, and in totall my best content, as indifferent to my heart as my

left hand to my right; and notwithstanding all those miracles
of disasters have crossed both them & me, yet were there not
one English man remaining (as God be thanked there is some
thousands) I would yet begin againe with as small meanes as I did
at the first.

This chapter, brief as it is, cannot end without a paragraph
in honour of the toiler who first printed many of these narratives. Samuel Purchas (1577–1626)—his name was pronounced
'Purkas'—never travelled 200 miles from his birthplace in
Essex, but a lifelong passion for geography made him a master
of the globe. His first book, *Purchas his Pilgrimage* (1613), appealed to its generation by virtue of its main design as a survey
of the peoples and religions of the world, and also as an encyclopaedia of geography and history. Its success enlarged the
compiler's circle of learned or travelled acquaintances, and the
friendly offices of Hakluyt, Ralegh, Sir Dudley Digges, Sir
Thomas Smith, and others contributed to the enlarging of the
work. For the first edition Purchas drew upon 700 authors; in
the end the list was nearly doubled. If King James's delight
in the book is a dubious recommendation for modern readers,
we may remember that the *Pilgrimage* (along with related items
in the *Pilgrims*) kindled Coleridge's dreams of Xanadu, and that
bits of it passed into the accounts of eastern religions in the
fourth book of *The Excursion*. Purchas's next plan—to pass by
the long jeremiad, *Purchas his Pilgrim* (1619)—was nothing less
than a history of the world as it was contained in the whole
body of the literature of travel, and he laboured almost single-
handed, in the face of domestic sorrows and physical and
pecuniary disabilities. The result was the largest English work
yet printed in England; the four folios of *Hakluytus Posthumus or
Purchas his Pilgrims* (1625) occupy twenty volumes in the modern
reprint. Among the editor's countless sources were his own
Pilgrimage and his manuscript collections, the papers left by
Hakluyt, and the archives of the East India Company; some
narratives that came in late were added to the fourth edition
(1626) of the *Pilgrimage*. The *Pilgrims* inevitably fell short of its
grandiose scheme. It was neither a well-edited series of documents, like Hakluyt's, nor a coherent history. The reproduction
of much printed matter necessitated the abridging, often in-
judicious, of many new and valuable narratives, and the compiler's verbose rhetoric and obtrusive pietism remain a liability.

Thus Purchas suffers in comparison with his great predecessor, yet he has hardly received just praise for the gathering and preserving of materials which would otherwise have been lost. And while he was not, like Hakluyt, an active patriot and promoter of voyages, he had something of Hakluyt's vision; he arranged the story of earlier exploration as a prologue to the swelling act of the imperial theme, the colonizing of America.

Although this survey has given only hints of the mass and variety of the literature of travel, a few general observations may be made. In the first place, if at times we incline to regard the early seventeenth century as wholly absorbed in introspection, we should think of the multitude of robust extraverts, merchants, sailors, and travellers, who were going about their lawful or unlawful occasions all over the seven seas. It is their narratives which compose the island epic. We find, too, the conscious or unconscious beginnings of imperialism (if the word may be used with little or nothing of the meaning it has for modern liberals). Along with the large dreams of such men as Hakluyt, Purchas, and Captain John Smith may be mentioned one small item: Thomas Gage's *New Survey of the West Indies* (1648) was used by Cromwell and later by Colbert to mould public opinion in favour of their West Indian policy. Then, if we incline to regard this period as one of rhetorical and poetic prose, we should remember that the authors of records of travel were mostly plain men with utilitarian aims who produced a great deal of good plain prose without knowing it. Further, in a more immediate and popular way than the scientists, and in frequent co-operation with them, travellers helped to enlarge the known world and actual knowledge and to emancipate their age from legend. As in the past, the spirit of travel and maritime discovery continued to affect every kind of imaginative and reflective literature, from drama and epic to sermon, but our period shows a marked advance upon the sixteenth century in geographical range and accuracy. Finally, although travel for general scientific purposes was not really organized until after 1660, the possibilities of such work were made manifest by the achievements of the earlier independent travellers and commercial explorers.

VI

ESSAYS AND CHARACTERS

1. *Essays*

SINCE the essayists as a group reveal an early and deliberate concern with style, we may take a preliminary glance at the nature of prose in general. Literary history has given currency to the notion that prose writing before 1660 was largely ornate and poetical, and that a plain, workaday, modern style was first inaugurated after the Restoration, chiefly through the efforts of the Royal Society to develop this along with other elements of its Baconian heritage. To correct that vulgar error we have only to think of the vast bulk of plain writing in books of travel, history, biography, politics, economics, science, education, religion, and much popular literature. Plain prose was the natural medium for most kinds of utilitarian writing, and most writing was utilitarian. That old and vigorous tradition was steadily reinforced, moreover, by the needs and demands of a rapidly expanding public. We may grant, to be sure, that the prose of the Restoration achieved a more coherent form and texture, a more civilized ease and urbanity, but we must acknowledge that Dryden and his fellows represented a culmination rather than a beginning. We must acknowledge, too, that the civilizing process, in prose as well as in poetry, was a levelling process which gained some virtues at the cost of some others, and we may be glad that it was not completed in our period.

Such a movement was necessary because Elizabethan prose, while it encouraged both poetic elevation and homely raciness, had not become a tempered and reliable instrument. Along with the general circumstances and purposes which nourished plain prose in the seventeenth century, one special and self-conscious motive, which came over from the Continent, left few intellectual writers untouched. Although by 1600 English prose, even in Hooker, had scarcely attained Ciceronian maturity, there ensued a repetition of the phenomenon which had taken place in imperial Rome, a reaction against the rotund, balanced, oratorical period and in favour of a concise, flexible,

semi-colloquial style. If the ultimate theoretical sanction was
derived from Aristotle, the stylistic models were Seneca and
Tacitus and the editor of both, the chief reviver of Stoic thought,
Justus Lipsius. The 'Attic' style of the anti-Ciceronians was not
of course uniform; it ranged from the 'libertine' naturalness
of Montaigne or Burton to the weighty condensation of Bacon
and Jonson or the clipped, pointed sententiousness of Hall or
Felltham. But with all its theoretical and individual differences
the movement as a whole implied the recognition of a changing
world in which the accepted verities were less secure than they
had been, and it embodied a philosophic desire for a more
realistic, arresting, and subtle expression of both general ideas
and private experience. Hence the simplicity of the new style
or styles was not always simple. Like the parallel manifestation
in verse, the Senecan style had its 'metaphysical' tricks of antithetical and epigrammatic patterns, abrupt surprises, and
ingenious images, and it did not meet with unanimous approval.
Breton's *Characters upon Essays* was commended for its 'Lipsian
stile, terse Phrase', but Earle—though he later deleted a remark which did not leave his own withers unwrung—censured
his 'selfe-conceited Man' as one who preferred 'Lipsius his
hopping stile, before either Tully or Quintilian'. And Milton
jeered at Hall for making 'sentences by the Statute, as if all
above three inches long were confiscat'. Dr. Kettell's judgement of Seneca's style, recorded by Aubrey, was more critical
than quotable. Senecan or Lipsian prose, loose or curt or a
mixture of both, was frequently wedded to Stoic thought, and
among the offspring of the marriage were the English essayists,
whose moral didacticism and studied informality made them
the natural exponents of the new modes.

We think of the essay as one of the late courses in the banquet
of literature. It presupposes a class of readers who possess
economic and social security and who can appreciate rational
reflection upon civilized manners and morals. While Plato and
Cicero and Horace have contributed to the spirit and sometimes
to the form of the modern essay, the classical prototypes are the
moral works of Seneca and Plutarch. Seneca's *Epistles to Luci-
lius*, as Bacon observed, 'are but Essaies,—That is dispersed
Meditacons, thoughe conveyed in the forme of Epistles'. The
essay absorbed many other tributaries, the formal treatises and
often formal letters of medieval and Renaissance humanists

and the academic exercises of generations of students, the private commonplace books which almost all serious readers kept, and the published collections, ancient and modern, of anecdotes, aphorisms, and didactic discourses. And behind all these things was the inexhaustible treasury of classical literature as a whole. Then although the essay tended in its very nature to be secular in tone, it long bore traces of the religious homily and devotional meditation. These various kinds of writing were themselves being carried on in our period, so that a working definition of the essay must be both comprehensive and arbitrary. The genre was at any rate a natural expression of the heightened self-consciousness of the seventeenth-century mind.

The essay was born when Montaigne retired to his tower to take stock of himself and thereby of all human experience, and the evolution of his essays epitomizes the general evolution of the form from the commonplace book to independent reflection. Bacon's went through a partly parallel development, though he never approached nor apparently wished to approach the spacious freedom and intimate personal candour of the first and greatest of modern essayists.[1] While the two men naturally had some common roots, they were far apart in

[1] The life of Bacon (1561–1626) is both too full and too familiar to be summarized. As the younger son of Elizabeth's first Lord Keeper and of one of the learned daughters of Sir Anthony Cooke, he had, except in the pecuniary way, a fortunate heritage and background. At Trinity College, Cambridge, he first rebelled against the tyranny of Aristotle. He was attached to the embassy in France (1576–9), became an 'utter barrister' in 1582, and entered Parliament in 1584. He soon established a solid reputation in the House and in committees, and through his letters of advice on state affairs. Bacon's opposition to the court (1593) won him the queen's ill will, which, with the coolness of his uncle and cousin, the two Cecils, long delayed his legitimate advancement. He took an active share in the prosecution of Essex, who had been his friend and over-zealous patron. This episode has, rightly or wrongly, told against Bacon's character perhaps even more than his later judicial disgrace. But Bacon had early conceived both a personal and a sincerely patriotic distrust of the earl's violent ways, and the two had fallen apart. After many disappointments he got his foot on the official ladder; he became Solicitor-General in 1607, Attorney-General in 1613, Lord Keeper in 1617, and Lord Chancellor in 1618. In 1603 he had been knighted, 'gregarious in a troop', and he received the title of Baron Verulam in 1618, of Viscount St. Alban in 1621. (At no time was he 'Lord Bacon'.) In the year of his last honour the prosecutor of Essex and Somerset and Ralegh, and the rival of Coke, became himself the scapegoat of a lax judicial system and of parliamentary hostility to the government. Bacon admitted the accepting of presents but defended the justice of his decisions, apparently with reason, since few if any seem to have been reversed. Apart from the question of moral obtuseness in this matter, Bacon ranks among the greatest minds in English legal history. After his fall he retired to his estate of Gorhambury

temperament and outlook, and Bacon, after borrowing Montaigne's title, seems to have gone his own way. To the general recognition of the tentative character of the essay Bacon added his special belief in the suggestive virtues of the aphoristic style. The ten 'Essays' of 1597 were merely groups of related apophthegms transcribed from the commonplace book. That Bacon was aware of a more fluid form is sufficiently indicated by other early writings, and when his own and the public's interest in his book led to extensive revision and enlargement he inclined to the looser, more 'methodical' and persuasive style which he had brought to maturity in the *Advancement of Learning* and which was nearer to the established manner of the essay. Although in their final state (1625) his essays remained strongly aphoristic in texture, the discontinuity and abstract severity of the early *sententiae* had been increasingly unified and relieved by expatiation and by interpolated examples and quotations, and enriched by metaphor and cadence. There was, however, only a little relaxing of Bacon's cool objectivity. That, while partly inherited from his chosen models and the commonplace book, represents also the attitude of the scientific analyst who does not gossip and ramble, whose mind is a dry light. Even in his reflections on adversity the fallen Lord Chancellor's pen betrays no momentary quiver; the essay might have been written by a cloistered sage. It is Bacon's impersonality and Tacitean brevity, rather than grandiloquence, which make his style seem less familiar than it is. Though his name suggests full-dress stateliness, he was the theoretical and practical leader of the anti-Ciceronian movement in England, and the groundwork of his prose is reinforced homespun. And along with his genius for pithy and proverbial expression goes a full share of the 'wit' of his age; many of his opening phrases remain as arresting as those of Donne's poems.

Of the fifty-eight essays in the final edition, more than half

and was able to rally his indomitable powers to carry on his private studies and writing.

The *Essays* of 1597 included ten short essays, *Meditationes Sacrae*, and *Colours of Good and Evil*; the edition of 1612 contained thirty-eight essays, nine enlarged from 1597 and twenty-nine new ones; the final edition of 1625 had fifty-eight. Before 1625 there were reprints, some unauthorized, of the earlier editions. The Latin translation of the *Essays* was edited by Bacon's chaplain, William Rawley, in *Operum Moralium et Civilium Tomus* (1638).

Henry VII and the philosophic and scientific works are discussed in Chapters VII and IX.

deal with public life or public affairs, and the statesman or courtier has at least a finger in many others, including such varied pieces as those on truth, marriage, love, and friendship. In 'Of Vicissitude of Things', Bacon touches, greatly, the great Renaissance chord of mutability, and then shrinks back upon the actualities of religious strife and war. Of his countless biblical allusions many permit a political application and some have it forced upon them; the comparison of the kingdom of heaven to a mustard-seed illustrates the difference between extent of territory and real power. Bacon reveals to us the interests, problems, and modes of thought of the ruling class of his age, but the artist who is wedded to the mundane and temporal has given hostages to fortune. We are, to be sure, vaguely aware of some wholly admirable counsels of moral wisdom and public and private virtue (especially in the volume of 1612), but we are much more strongly impressed by an atmosphere of 'business', of cold-blooded expediency, and sometimes of unscrupulous self-interest. While Montaigne's chief concern is in man sitting upon his 'owne taile', Bacon's is in man sitting in an office chair. Obvious reasons for a degree of moral obtuseness are at hand in the facts of his own world and career and in the influence of his favourite authors. But a more fundamental explanation of Bacon's choice and treatment of themes appears in the second book of the *Advancement of Learning*. There he deplores philosophers' preoccupation with abstract ethics and their neglect of the basic material of morality and policy, that is, ordinary human nature as it operates in the various circumstances of the active life. The several lists of particular desiderata which he proceeds to give make a fair table of contents for the *Essays*. In spite of Bacon's disclaimer, in a dedicatory epistle to Andrewes, the essays were not merely the casual recreation of a busy life, they were to a great extent an integral part of the *Instauratio Magna*, an appendix—as innumerable borrowings remind us—to the *Advancement*. Bacon wished to fill a gap in practical psychology and ethics, to contribute to that realistic knowledge of the genus *homo* without which the individual cannot prescribe for his own needs nor the statesman for the needs of society.

Thus it is not simply the limitations of the essayist's mind and heart which lead him to see life so much in terms of tangible success and failure. Even when he reveals a Jonsonian world of politic knaves and gulls he can claim a philosophic purpose. In the *Advancement* he notes the lack of serious studies of professional frauds and vices, a kind of knowledge which is 'one of the best fortifications for honesty and vertue that can be planted', and he pays tribute to 'Macciavell & others that write what men doe and not what they ought to do'. At the same time, in his expert dissection of human egoism, Bacon may forget the ends of honesty and virtue, and the essays are, morally, something of a jumble. The two elements which appear in harmonious innocence in the title *Essays or Counsels, Civil and Moral* appear in Machiavellian or Hobbesian nakedness in the distinction made in the *Advancement*: 'Againe, morrall Philosophye propoundeth to it selfe the framing of Internall goodnesse: But civile knowledge requireth onelye an Externall goodnesse: for that as to societye sufficeth.' These psychological and utilitarian motives keep Bacon's *Essays* in the category of admired books rather than among the well thumbed and beloved. Everyone has read them, but no one is ever found reading them. Yet, if he is less generous and companionable than the other great essayists, we should remember what he was and was not trying to do. And we rejoice all the more when Machiavelli, or a Machiavellian Samuel Smiles, gives way to the Jacobean lover of beauty or royal magnificence in the loving particularity of the essays on gardens, building, or masques and triumphs, and much more still when flashes of poetic phrase and intuition light up Truth and Death and other noble themes. For all his narrowness or obliquity of vision, his tense, athletic prose reflects his unquenchable vitality and his eager curiosity about the earthly doings and experience of man.

Before we leave Bacon a less familiar collection of short discourses must be mentioned. That interest in allegorical mythology which is patent to every reader of the *Essays* and the *Advancement of Learning* received full expression in the popular *De Sapientia Veterum* (1609), which Sir Arthur Gorges translated as *The Wisdom of the Ancients* (1619). Here Bacon, not without a note of apology, allows his philosophic mind and poetic fancy to play around some thirty characters of classic myth. In part he takes over the methods and materials of the mythographers, but his interpretations, whether new or old, are adapted to his own special view of science and civil and moral knowledge. It is easy to guess what the herald of modern science makes of

Prometheus or of Oedipus unriddling the Sphinx (Cupid is less obvious as the natural motion of the atom), or what the statesman makes of Cassandra and Typhon. Thus if *The Wisdom of the Ancients* represents Bacon's less modern side (though he was by no means the last exponent of allegory), it is also, except in the character of its initial texts, a twin volume to the *Essays*.

From the standpoint of general fame the early history of the essay is a picture of a whale followed by a school of porpoises, but before Bacon published the genuine essays of his second edition the form had been more or less ably handled by a number of men. We can take account of only one, the first exponent of the more personal and informal essay, Sir William Cornwallis (1579?-1614).[1] Cornwallis's *Essays* (1600-1) were published when he was only a little past twenty and, if it were not for references to his youth, we might think so sage a moralist, so disillusioned a critic of society, was a lean and slippered pantaloon. He has got beyond adolescent follies but he is still only crawling through the darkness of 'Opinion' towards 'the Land of light'. 'I write therefore to my selfe, and my selfe profits by my writing.' In a decayed and corrupt world men must seek guidance and strength from within. To himself and others Cornwallis preaches a Stoicism which is really, if not very explicitly, Christian. But Stoic rigour is modified by compromises between abstract and practical morals, by the attitudes of an Elizabethan Englishman, and by the inconsistency of youth. How, for instance, is ambition to be shunned by a young man of his time, how is the contemplative life to be reconciled with the duty of public service? 'I must choose the active course, my birth commands me to that.'

The sources of Cornwallis's wisdom are largely classical. Plato (read in Latin) is the supreme philosopher, and he sometimes inspires flights above the Stoic level. But Cornwallis owes most to Seneca and Plutarch, and of their disciple Montaigne he had acquired some knowledge in a translation (probably

---

[1] After an early marriage and a not too studious sojourn at Oxford, where he knew Overbury (whom he later introduced to 'Robin Carr'), Cornwallis served with other young gentlemen in Essex's Irish campaign (1599) and received one of the Earl's over-generous knighthoods. He seems to have been too discreet, or too busy with authorship, to be drawn into Essex's rising. He rivalled his friend Donne in fathering children. In 1603 he was given a post at court and he had some experience in Parliament. He died just after his father, Sir Charles, was sent to the Tower for furnishing John Hoskyns with an anti-Scottish speech.

Florio's unpublished manuscript). It is not the sceptical or naturalistic Montaigne who attracts him, but the man, the nobleman, who makes moral philosophy doff its gown and speak courageously, who puts 'Pedanticall Schollerisme' out of countenance and shows that 'learning mingled with Nobilitie, shines most clearly'. Along with aristocratic morality Cornwallis upholds aristocratic standards of culture, the amateur ideal of Montaigne and Renaissance courtesy books. And, though he is chiefly concerned with individual man, he expounds the traditional view of 'degree' as the frame of the social fabric. But he is aware that gentlemen's bodies may contain slavish minds and, standing between Diogenes and Carlyle, the apologist of order can imagine a naked assemblage from which pre-eminence has vanished with clothes.

Like other early practitioners Cornwallis has a critical consciousness in regard to the scope and spirit of the essay. Ancient writers of short discourses and even Montaigne, he thinks, went beyond the proper limits of the genre. He himself avoids both schematic and unduly loose writing and aims at the familiar level—'Montania and my selfe . . . doe sometimes mention our selves'. Though he respects Cicero the moralist he dislikes the tradition of Ciceronian rhetoric. In spite, however, of his attachment to the concise Tacitus and Seneca, he inclines to the discursive manner of Montaigne. His normal style is a colloquial but dignified 'plainenesse' (his own word), with occasional touches of both solemnity and journalism.

Cornwallis's two posthumous volumes, *Essays or Rather Encomions* and *Essays of Certain Paradoxes* (1616), represent a different genre. The facetious or ironical encomium was a classical device, analogous to the mock-epic, which the Renaissance revived, notably in Erasmus's *Praise of Folly*. This kind of encomium was related to the paradox, which also had a long and varied pedigree. A form sanctioned by Cicero was made witty and lively by Ortensio Lando, whose *Paradossi* (1543) were everywhere imitated. The paradox could not fail to attract men brought up on academic disputations and touched by the current of scepticism. It might be called the *enfant terrible* of the essay family. The author takes a holiday from truth and moral responsibility in order to amuse and stimulate his readers by a display of dialectical ingenuity and rhetorical wit in the proof of any thesis, however contrary to reason or convention. The

paradox was especially alluring to disillusioned young intellectuals, in the grey time around 1600, as a counterpart in prose to
the overworked satire and epigram. The brilliant exponent of
the paradox and the somewhat similar 'problem' was Donne,
whose chief activity in this field belongs to the years 1598–1602.
His pieces, circulating in manuscript, were treasured by Wotton
and other friends, though they were not published until 1633,
after his death. The paradox was a weapon made to Donne's
hand. His half-playful, half-serious questioning of accepted
ideas about man and woman, society and the universe, is a link
between the 'cynical' poet and the troubled preacher. Cornwallis knew Lando's work, and acquaintance with Donne,
which probably began about 1600, may have stirred him to
emulation of his more learned, acute, intense, and speculative
friend. Though his *Essays* proper include some *jeux d'esprit*,
Cornwallis lacks the light touch and edged wit that irony demands, and he cannot readily divest himself of his sober moral
principles. Whereas Donne attacks some articles of the Stoic
creed, Cornwallis's 'Prayse of Sadnesse' (that is, 'Seriousness')
becomes another exposition of the Stoic ethical ideal; and his
eulogy of debt—despite his painful experience—rises, with
eloquence more restrained than that of Panurge, to contemplation of the ordered system of nature. Some of his paradoxical material was borrowed from abroad.

Possibly the paradox, and certainly the developing 'character', did something to relieve and diversify the gravity and
abstractness of the moral essay. Some authors who used both
forms, like John Stephens (1615) and Geffray Mynshul (1618),
distinguished between the decorous plainness of the essay and
the mannered wit of the character; others, like Nicholas Breton
and Sir William Cavendish—the pupil of Hobbes and friend of
Bacon—in his *Horae Subsecivae* (1620), made a conscious or
unconscious fusion of the two. In Breton's *Fantastics* (1604?) the
'characters' of the seasons, months, and hours, for all their
balanced itemizing, resemble the 'Nows' of Leigh Hunt. And
Breton's *Characters upon Essays, Moral and Divine* (1615), though
dedicated to Bacon, treat wisdom, learning, and similar themes
in the pattern and pointed style of the character. Such variations, however, did not carry the essay very far towards informal
flexibility. The *Horae Vacivae* (1646) of the young John Hall
(1627–56), which received unusual commendations from the

literary, was largely in the Baconian tradition. If any writer before 1660 fulfils our notion of the familiar essayist, it is that versatile ex-schoolmaster, Henry Peacham (1578?–1642?), in *The Truth of our Times: Revealed out of one Man's Experience, by way of Essay* (1638). Peacham has of course an eye to the good of the commonwealth, from manners to agriculture, and he is a preacher of moderation, but he writes to please himself. Whether his theme is God's providence or fashions in dress, schools or authorship or liberty or travel, he sets forth his serious convictions with easy, intimate discursiveness and with a store of reminiscence and anecdote—a Holborn sempster's report of the fantastic price of neck-bands, a boyhood memory of Tarlton's acting, the capture of a continental town. A 'character' of a plain country fellow reminds us of Earle's, but Peacham's farmer, in 1638, grudges the payment of ship-money. We are not reminded of Bacon's essay on friendship when we read of those acquaintances who, on a chance encounter, exclaim, 'Good Lord, are you alive yet?' The familiar essayist's capital is personality and style, and Peacham has something of both. His industrious and unprosperous career has given a touch of disillusionment to his wide experience and sturdy good sense. He is 'living in the last age of the world, wherein all iniquity and vice doth abound'. But Peacham's interest in life is not dulled by pessimism and is quickened by some special antipathies, for Nonconformists in particular. His book is a small landmark in the history of the essay and it remains enjoyable on its own account.

The didactic motives of so much secular prose make it hard to distinguish the essay from kindred forms, and it is almost impossible to separate the religious essay from its congeners. Even within fairly strict limits we find such various names as Breton and Brathwait, Joseph Hall and Fuller, and Drummond and Browne, but here we may pass by these men of many books for a less prolific author. If the essays of Cornwallis partake of the 'resolve', Owen Felltham's *Resolves, Divine, Moral, Political* (1623?) often approach the pure essay.[1] Like Cornwallis and

---

[1] The facts of Felltham's life (1602?–68) are obscure. He was the son of a man of some property in Suffolk. He visited the Low Countries probably before 1627; the literary result appeared much later. He was acquainted with the London wits and contributed poems to Long's translation of Barclay's *Argenis* (1625), *Annalia Dubrensia* (1636), Randolph's *Poems* (1638), and other books. Before 1641, perhaps about the time of his father's death (1632), Felltham took service with the Earl of

the rest, Felltham upholds wisdom and the amateur ideal of culture against mere knowledge and pedantry. He defends the practice Burton censured, quoting without naming one's authors; to do otherwise would be 'for a Gentleman . . . a little pedanticall', especially in an essay, 'which of all writing, is the neerest to a running Discourse'. Books are Felltham's delight and recreation, not his trade. His praise of poetry has an intimate warmth which reminds us that he was a poet in his own right. (Of late years he has regained his title to a lyric long ascribed to Suckling, 'When, Dearest, I but think on thee'.) As a devout Anglican and royalist, who could look back on Charles the First as 'Christ the Second', Felltham was a man of piety but not a pietist. His essay on Puritans illustrates his fundamental reverence for 'the beauty of order' in the Church, in society, and in the individual. Although he seeks the *via media* in all things —except the love of God and hatred of evil—and although the commonplaces of religion and morals are his staple article, he can, more than most didactic essayists, make virtue sound exciting and moderation adventurous. Felltham's harmony of Christianity and Stoicism is tempered and sweetened by a love of life and literature, by philosophic charity and undogmatic good sense. His moralizings on death and mutability and vainglory, as well as his Christian Stoicism, carry us forward, if not to *Urn Burial*, at least to *Christian Morals*. Thomas Randolph in his eulogy summed up the qualities of thought and style which the age increasingly admired:

> I mean the stile, being pure, and strong, and round,
> Not long but Pythy: being short breath'd, but sound.
> Such as the grave, acute, wise Seneca sings,
> That best of Tutours to the worst of Kings.
> Not long and empty; lofty but not proud;
> Subtile but sweet, high but without a cloud,
> Well setled, full of nerves, in briefe 'tis such
> That in a little hath comprized much.

But the pointed style does not exclude homeliness or metaphysical wit. 'A bounded mirth, is a Pattent adding time and happinesse to the crazed life of Man.' 'When the Husband and the Wife are together, the World is contracted in a Bed.' And

---

Thomond at Great Billing, Northamptonshire, and spent the rest of his life as steward of the estate. He died in London. Some details about the enlargements of the *Resolves* are given in the bibliography.

with Felltham's Christian faith and pagan reason is blended a strain of the Platonism which we encounter everywhere in the period. Earthly music awakens thoughts of 'a higher Diapason'. For Felltham as for Marvell and others the soul is 'manacled' by the flesh. We are not surprised to find that Vaughan often echoed him, and it was the poet in Felltham who saw 'Eternities Ring' and the soul as 'a shoot of everlastingnesse'.

While the infant essay was taking its first uncertain steps in various directions, its parents, the aphorism and the commonplace book, were still moving along the familiar paths. The tradition of Machiavelli, Guicciardini, and Bacon was carried on in Robert Dallington's *Aphorisms Civil and Military* (1613) and Ralegh's posthumous *The Prince, or Maxims of State* (1642); the moral tradition of humanism in the *Aphorisms of Education* (1654) of Sir Henry Wotton (1568–1639); and both 'Piety and Policy' in the very popular *Enchiridion* (1640–1) of Francis Quarles, who borrowed a good deal from Bacon and Machiavelli. The aphorism usually remained impersonal but was handled somewhat loosely, perhaps because few men had Bacon's or Jonson's gift for massive compression. It was such a natural outgrowth of the commonplace book (or vice versa), entered so largely into the texture of the essay, and was itself treated in such various ways, that it can scarcely be distinguished as a special type of writing.

The commonplace book *par excellence* is Jonson's *Timber: or Discoveries*, which was posthumously published in the folio of 1640–1 edited by Sir Kenelm Digby. The collection was apparently made in Jonson's later years, since the fire of 1623 had destroyed 'twice-twelve-yeares stor'd up humanitie, With humble Gleanings in Divinitie'. He seems to have contemplated publication, though he left the material in no very clear arrangement. The longer pieces of the latter part constitute a sort of draft for a treatise on the art of writing and on types of literature. The first part is a much less homogeneous body of observations which range from isolated *sententiae* to miniature essays and which deal mainly with such aspects of life, thought, and learning as we find in the essayists—though Jonson damns that tribe, 'even their Master Mountaigne', for rushing into print with undigested reading. Thus *Timber* is a visible link between the commonplace book and the essay. It is also a link between a learned poet's reading and his method of poetic composition.

A commonplace book was not as a rule an original product, and the title-page of *Timber* indicated its character. Modern research has traced about four-fifths of the material to its sources. Jonson's chief creditors were the two Senecas and Quintilian (with Heinsius for a good deal of literary theory), but he drew more or less from other ancients and from such moderns as Vives, Erasmus, Machiavelli, Lipsius, John Hoskyns, and Bacon. The moving eulogy of the fallen Lord Chancellor apparently came almost verbatim from Hobbes's manuscript translation of the letters of the Italian scholar, Fulgenzio Micanzio, to the first Earl of Devonshire. Of the four passages on life and conduct cited in the standard edition of Jonson in proof of his sterling honesty and fearlessness, his searching insight and fine economy of words, three and a half are borrowed. Even ostensibly personal bits may be translated. Yet such facts by no means contradict such praise. Jonson's choice of authors and items reveals hardly less of his mind and temper than if the book were wholly original. 'He invades Authours like a Monarch, and what would be theft in other Poets, is onely victory in him.' Then, while there is much translation and paraphrase, there is also much recasting and condensed analysis, with comments and illustrations from Jonson's own store of experience. 'And such his wit,' as Falkland said in *Jonsonus Virbius*, 'He writ past what he quotes.' Finally, apart from occasional traces of Latin diction or idiom, Jonson's prose is no less masculine and pithy, and more naturally crisp and colloquial, than Bacon's. The writers he borrowed from had borrowed from others, and they often lacked the pregnant force which makes his moral reflections arresting.

The book may, therefore, be justly accepted as a portrait of the compiler, a man too independent and too sincere to put down what he has not weighed or does not believe. If, for instance, the wise remarks on the right attitude towards the ancients are derived from Vives, or those on 'Custome of speech' and good style from Quintilian, they none the less represent Jonson's own fundamental faith and practice. The tribute to Bacon's oratory, or the censure of Shakespeare's facility, gains rather than loses when we read the originals in Seneca, for we realize that Jonson's scale of values is not set by personal prejudice or by fashion, that he speaks with the authority of a central and living tradition. Everywhere we see the critical inheritor and the active exponent of the aristocratic and practical wisdom of Renaissance humanism, the poet who is not merely an artist but a philosophic citizen vitally concerned with questions of private and public conduct, with education and government, with the whole range of moral and cultural ideas. Jonson's moral utterances are less well known than his literary dicta, but the latter, with all their judicious breadth and good sense, were recorded by the neoclassical theorist, the former by the man and the strongly Stoic humanist. If the one group of observations explains the disciplined art of his poems and plays, the other explains their rational sobriety and weight.

To this heterogeneous but far from exhaustive survey of the essay family one important member is still to be added. From antiquity to the present the letter has been an elder sister, if not a twin, of the essay. During the Middle Ages and the Renaissance the art of letter-writing was assiduously cultivated as a branch of rhetoric. Writers in the vernaculars, like Guevara and Pasquier, inherited from the humanistic tradition a didactic aim and a rhetorical method. In England in the early seventeenth century the literary epistle, like the essay itself, was breaking away from didactic formalism and approaching the genuine familiar letter. Joseph Hall (1574–1656) invited Prince Henry to observe that his *Epistles in Six Decades* (1608–11) inaugurated 'a new fashion of discourse, by Epistles; new to our language, usuall to others'. But we cannot give heed to his clerical, anti-Romish, and Senecan exhortations when livelier authors are frisking before us.

Nicholas Breton's *Post with a Mad Packet of Letters*, published in 1602 and later enlarged, went through many editions. Breton was aware of 'Latine, French, Italian, and Spanish, Bookes of Epistles'—indeed he imitated one of Guevara's letters—and presumably also of the popular middle-class formularies of William Fulwood and Angel Day, but he changed 'the complete letter-writer' into literature. In his compound of moralizing, satire, and romantic love, and his euphuism, he was a sort of lighter and less didactic Lyly. But to these conventional elements Breton adds novel situations and motives and fresh bits of humorous realism in background, characterization, and

expression. In fact, though he treats essay themes, from education and travel to love and marriage, he comes closer to epistolary fiction than to the essay. And, unlike the aristocratic and
philosophic essayists, Breton makes a distinct appeal to the
moral and mercantile interests of the middle-class reader. As
late as the sixteen-seventies, when for a generation French pre-
ciosity had dominated the English letter-book, a compiler still
found Breton worth pilfering.

The supreme epistolizer of the age was James Howell
(1593?–1666). He 'came tumbling out into the World a pure
Cadet, a true Cosmopolite; not born to Land, Lease, House or
Office'. Both as a man of business, in connexion with Sir Robert
Mansell's glass factory, and as a minor diplomatic envoy, Howell
enjoyed—the word is not colourless—extensive travel; he became an expert linguist and an authority on foreign countries.
He had a wide acquaintance among literary and public men,
including Sir Kenelm Digby, who claimed to have cured him
of a wound by his powder of sympathy. In 1626 he became
secretary to Lord Scrope, Lord President of the North, and in
1627 a member of Parliament. Shortly after being sworn Clerk
of the Council in August 1642, Howell was arrested by parliamentary order, probably because of royalist activity during the
previous decade. The eight years of incarceration (1642–50) were,
until his appointment as Historiographer Royal in 1661, the most
settled period of his career and turned him into a professional
author. He had already published a political allegory, *Dodona's
Grove* (1640; enlarged later), and *Instructions for Foreign Travel*
(1642). There followed dozens of political pamphlets and miscellaneous and philological works. Howell lives, of course, in
the *Epistolae Ho-Elianae*, the four books of which appeared in
1645, 1647, 1650, and 1655. Whether or not he used actual
letters, the necessitous and thrifty author drew freely upon his
own and other men's works, and especially no doubt upon
his note-books, for the more solid portions of his masterpiece,
such as the virtual articles or essays on the religions, wines, and
languages of the world, the unity of creation, and the theory
of the habitable moon. Howell's Oxford education had never
been 'any burden or encumbrance' to him, and the chances
and changes of his life had provided him with one kind of
capital, a fund of varied experience and observation.

The first letter, originally prefixed to the second book,

indicates his knowledge of epistolary authors and manuals, and his dislike of neo-Latin commonplaces and French affectation and emptiness. The true familiar letter, he says (after Seneca), should have the naturalness of talk but should not lack substance and ideas. Howell's letters live up to his theory. Like Leigh Hunt, he was a tricksy sprite for whom stone walls did not a prison make. The bulk of his work deals with the course of English and continental affairs and with the life and manners of continental countries and cities. There are few names, events, or topics which do not come in somewhere and do not give an impression of immediacy. Howell's eager curiosity embraces ship-money, Platonic love at court, and the disease of witty preaching; Spinola and Galileo; the siege of Rochelle and the glories of Venice. Whatever charges of inaccuracy or shallowness the historian may lodge against him, it is to Howell that we owe our most vivid pictures of the Overbury trial, of Gondomar stalking in to King James to ejaculate 'Pyrats, Pyrats, Pyrats', of Prince Charles's difficult courtship of the Infanta, of Buckingham rising on the fatal day and cutting a caper or two—these and many other incidents great and small are sketched with the dramatic instinct of a journalist. We see Ben Jonson at the supper table betraying his 'Roman infirmity' of self-praise, or Lord Leicester bearing up stoutly through thirty-five healths at a Danish banquet and departing, unlike his royal host, on his own legs. Something is always putting Howell in mind of a good anecdote, like the Earl of Kildare's ingenuous explanation that he would not have burned a church if he had not thought the bishop was in it. Then there are some famous and more serious tales, of the anchorite, the pied piper of Hamelin, and the white-breasted bird of the Oxenhams.

Like all good essayists, Howell reveals his own character. Our true cosmopolite is glad to return 'to the sweet bosom of England' and breathe again the smoke of London. His mercurial spirit has its saturnine moods, but misfortunes cannot submerge a man so interested in life—one who, moreover, looks back to that illustrious Armorican dynasty of the Howells. Mercurial and mundane gusto is carried, quite sincerely, into his religion, even if his devotional schedule does not suggest Celtic kinship with Henry Vaughan; he can address his Maker every day in a different language 'and upon Sunday in seven'. With Sir Thomas Browne Howell rather pities than hates

Turk or infidel. If he hates any, it is those schismatics 'that puzzle the sweet peace of our Church, so that I could bee content to see an Anabaptist go to Hell on a Brownists back'.

2. *Characters*

It was not an accident that the birth or rebirth of character-writing coincided with that of the essay, since both forms were engendered by the same social and cultural conditions. The character, like the essay, appeared late in antiquity. Theophrastus was an elder contemporary and probably a teacher of Menander; in other words, his *Characters* were written when Athens was shrinking from a state into a cultured suburb, when the new comedy was devoting itself to the realistic portrayal of urban manners and types of character. In the second place Theophrastus was the pupil of Aristotle and his successor at the Lyceum. His characters, in part the diversions of a philosopher and scientist, in part dramatic footnotes to his serious works, might serve as illustrations of Peripatetic ethics. The vices that he pictures, flattery, surliness, arrogance, and the like, constitute lapses from the rational standards of civilized behaviour. (If Theophrastus wrote characters of virtues they are not extant.) The formal pattern is simple. It is a paragraph which begins with a brief definition of a vice, proceeds with a series of descriptive and narrative items that show a representative of it in his everyday conduct, and ends when the author chooses to stop. In manner, as Richard Flecknoe said in his *Enigmatical Characters* (1658), 'tis more Seneca than Cicero, and speaks rather the language of Oracles than Orators'.

Of course informal sketches of individuals or types are as old as literature and were produced in our period as in every other, for instance in 'coney-catching' tracts and in epigrams, and the long line of character books may be said to have been inaugurated by Breton's very un-Theophrastian *Fantastics* (1604?). But the Theophrastian *descriptio* itself had been a traditional branch of rhetoric and hence of writing generally, so that seventeenth-century characters were new chiefly in being exploited in a more standardized and wholesale way. Besides this living tradition of the usually isolated character, many other circumstances combined to give a fresh welcome to the Greek pattern after Casaubon brought out his edition and translation of Theophrastus in 1592. The persistence of the allegorical mode of conceiving character and of medieval forms of social satire; the use of character-sketches as *exempla* in sermons; the growth of psychological studies and the medical, psychological, and dramatic doctrine of 'humours', fortified by Horatian precepts regarding dramatic types; the love of aphorisms, proverbs, and paradoxes; the general attachment to classical models, particularly in satire and epigram; the desire for realistic treatment of actual life and manners which had achieved fuller expression in social pamphlets, satires, and plays than in the modern medium of prose fiction; the popularity and the limitations of the essay; the eagerness to apply a formula which could be both didactic and entertaining; and perhaps one may add literary men's consciousness of aristocratic cultural standards and of the disturbing pressure of commercial, professional, and religious groups—these were some main reasons for the enormous vogue of character-writing in the seventeenth century.

The formal introduction or revival of the Theophrastian character had been accomplished before the appearance in 1616 of John Healey's translation of Theophrastus, and, for such an imitable type of writing, the Greek model was not essential. Some writers echoed Theophrastus, but not a great deal, partly because they were concerned with a different world and partly because they soon outgrew his deceptively simple technique and style. Indeed the first seventeenth-century characters have already left Theophrastus behind. More than one of the conditions listed above would suggest that the genre ought to have been introduced by Ben Jonson, and it was. In the sketches of the dramatis personae prefixed to *Every Man out of his Humour* (1600), and in some full-fledged characters in *Cynthia's Revels* (1601), we have objective catalogues of particular habits, though without the abstract definition, and plain statement mostly gives way to satirical and figurative wit. The subjects, moreover, are social rather than ethical types. Jonson may have been conscious of his favourite Martial as well as of Theophrastus.

The first formal collection, *Characters of Virtues and Vices* (1608), was the work of that inevitable pioneer, Joseph Hall.[1]

---

[1] Joseph Hall (1574–1656), after a distinguished career at Emmanuel College, Cambridge, received a meagre benefice from the Drurys. He first emerged from professional obscurity in 1608, when he became a chaplain to Prince Henry. His further advancement was crowned by his appointment in 1618 as one of the

The most obvious resemblance to Theophrastus is that of Hall's twenty-six (originally twenty-four) characters all but one or two deal with ethical types. In his choice of some identical subjects and in a number of details Hall evidently has Theophrastus in mind. In method he is only partly Theophrastian. The Greek characters are brief, bare, and lively photographic reports; Hall, in his longer and solider pieces, can use the external, local, and specific, but much of his realism is of the generalized kind excogitated in the study. And with dramatic objectivity he continually mingles comment and interpretation, so that his vices are not free from abstraction and his virtues are almost wholly abstract. In treating virtues Hall would get no help from Theophrastus, though he had some English predecessors. Finally, Hall does not adhere to Theophrastian plainness of expression. 'Our English Seneca' is always a conscious stylist, and especially in the characters of vices he strives for epigrammatic and antithetical wit and point, the 'lesse grave, more Satyricall' manner apologized for in the proem. Hall urges that Christians may learn good lessons from heathen wisdom and pays tribute to 'that ancient Master of Morality' whom he follows 'with an higher and wider step'. Quite often, too, he reminds us of his revered Seneca and of Plutarch. Hall's moral and religious aim contributes to both his relative heaviness and his subtlety of delineation. The characters of virtues, except in their sustained formality of structure, might be extracts from his *Meditations* or sermons. But in the depiction of vices Hall could pretty well hold his own with the wits, and his phrases, unlike theirs, do not cry out for footnotes. The author of *Virgidemiarum* here wields the scourge or the scalpel with an occasional forgetfulness of his didactic purpose which the reader willingly condones. Hall's *Characters* received the unusual honour of a French translation in 1610.

king's representatives at the Synod of Dort. He was made Bishop of Exeter in 1627 and in 1641 was translated to Norwich, but in 1643 he was forced into retirement by parliamentary sequestration. Although a moderate Low Churchman, Hall had vigorously defended episcopacy against the Smectymnuans and Milton. He had been intimate enough with Donne to be remembered in his will, and in his later days he had some association with Sir Thomas Browne. Apart from his sermons and numerous devotional works, Hall was one of the most versatile and experimental of literary clerics: witness his satires, *Virgidemiarum* (1597–8), the prose satire, *Mundus Alter et Idem* (1605?), which was noticed in Chapter II, and the *Epistles* and *Characters*. He was, too, an important exemplar of Christian Stoicism and Senecan prose.

When so sincere a moralist as Hall could yield to the satirical allurements of the form, it was to be expected that young men of letters would go farther. One 'W.M.' put a set of characters into a framework in *The Man in the Moon* (1609). But the witty character was definitely established by Sir Thomas Overbury and 'other learned Gentlemen his Friendes'.[1] The first bunch of twenty-one characters, by Overbury and others, was added to the second impression of his poem *A Wife* (1614), and the number was rapidly enlarged, mainly, it would seem, by the work of professional authors rather than 'gentlemen'. The chief names are John Webster, the dramatist, who on good grounds is now assigned thirty-two of the characters added to the sixth edition (1615); Dekker, who is thought to have done the six pieces on a debtors' prison added to the ninth edition (1616); and John Donne, whose character of a dunce and 'Essay of Valour' were the last pieces added (1622). The final total was eighty-two. There were several reasons for the great popularity of the book—the characters, the much-praised and much-imitated poem (itself a sort of character), and, when the news broke, the tragic scandal of Overbury's death, which was the theme of many broadsides.

The Overbury group had cleverness and variety of matter, they made the character thoroughly English, and set the standard for that kind of writing, but they brought little to the genre which was actually new. Both their technique and their subjects represent a selective exploitation of existing elements. They largely avoid Hall's didacticism and generalized satire, but they carry on his mingling of fact with comment and carry much further his epigrammatic and conceited wit. In other words their method was very close to that of Jonson, a friend of Overbury's, who to all these negative and positive qualities had

[1] Sir Thomas Overbury (1581–1613) was an able and ambitious courtier of literary tastes. The first chapter of his life included Oxford and the Middle Temple. He became the friend and adviser of Robert Carr, later Earl of Somerset (to whom, as we have seen, he had been introduced by his old Oxford friend, Cornwallis), and for some years he forwarded and shared his patron's prosperity at court. When he opposed Carr's marriage with Frances Howard, Countess of Essex, the combined hostility of the countess, the Howards, and the king brought him to the Tower, where he was poisoned. The story leaked out and a trial followed (1615–16). The earl and countess were convicted but their lives were saved by the king; the lesser flies, as Howell calls them, were executed. The case has as many dubious as unsavoury elements. Overbury's poem, *A Wife*, was entered in December 1613, a few months after his death.

added a notable amount of pungent observation. Indeed in most of their work the Overbury group may be called lighter and more flippant Jonsons. In subject-matter they much prefer the English social types of Jonson to the ethical types of Hall and Theophrastus, and the idealistic portraits which furnish such an attractive wing in the Overbury gallery have precedents in Jonson as well as in Hall. Of course all these elements from native realism to puns were familiar in the less formal and more popular character-sketches of pamphleteers and preachers.

To say this is not to detract from the writers' real originality in re-creating their instrument and playing so many lively tunes upon it. Our chief interest in their work is in the broad cross-section it gives of early Jacobean society, male and female, high and low, bad and sometimes good. The point of view is mainly satirical, because young men about town and men of letters seldom look amiably upon the academic, professional, and commercial *bourgeoisie* or upon Puritans. Yet the writers do not spare their own class; if university pedants have too much learning, the courtier, the 'Inns of Court man', and the gentleman of town and country may have too little. As a rule, however, the authors' intellectual and social attitude is not very seriously philosophic. They take their world as they find it and are more concerned with discovering victims for their wit than with diagnosing social ills. One exception is the prison characters probably written by Dekker and written within the walls he knew so well. While these too keep up a rattle of witty musketry, they have besides touches of the poignant realism and human sympathy which distinguish Dekker from many of his contemporaries.

One principle of the early character is summed up in the nursery tag: when he is good he is very, very good, and when he is bad he is horrid. The painter, unless he happens to be John Earle, does not mix black and white but lays on each colour with single-hearted gusto. There are in the Overbury collection a dozen idealistic characters, and seven of them, including the best ones, are among those assigned to Webster. 'An Excellent Actor', a reply to John Stephens's 'A Common Player', is a gracious and dignified portrait possibly drawn from Burbage. The famous prose lyric, 'A Fair and Happy Milkmaid', which Walton so happily remembered, may, like Elizabethan pastoral verse, be too Arcadian for some tastes—bits of it are in fact taken from Sidney's book—but that fault, if it be one, cannot be charged against 'A Franklin', a sturdy pillar of a paternal rural economy.

From 1614 onward every warbler had the tune by heart and only a few names can be mentioned here. One, which attests more clearly than Hall's the mutual debt of character and sermon, is that of the great Puritan preacher, Thomas Adams. Earlier in this chapter the mingling and the merging of the character and the essay were illustrated by reference to such men as Breton, Stephens, and Mynshul, and other developments will be noticed as we go on. But the best of all character-books, Earle's *Microcosmography* (1628-9), does not owe its primacy to formal innovations; in some outward and inward ways it is more Theophrastian than any of its kind.[1] To a mode of writing which encouraged the brittle and flashy, Earle, without loss (and with better control) of wit and satirical edge, added the element of quiet contemplation, so that his best pieces, which are numerous, become essays; though impersonal, they reveal the mind and heart which charmed his friends. Like Felltham, and like his associates at Great Tew, Earle is a liberal and cultivated divine who loves the beauty of order in the individual and in Church and State. He condemns the irrational eccentricity of the blunt man and the sceptic, and the irrational conformity of the vulgar-spirited man and the mere formal man; and he contrasts the shallowness of the 'Young Raw Preacher' with the humane solidity of the 'Grave Divine', who 'is a Protestant out of judgement, not faction'.

A number of Earle's characters are more or less direct replies to those of the Overbury group, and comparison shows at once

[1] As one of the younger lights of Oxford, John Earle (1600?–65) was a member of the choice company which forgathered at Great Tew. In 1641 he became tutor to Prince Charles and the attachment lasted till his death. As a 'malignant' he was soon deprived of his preferments and he lived abroad for sixteen years. In exile he translated the *Ecclesiastical Polity* and the *Eikon Basilike* into Latin; the manuscript of the former was accidentally destroyed but the latter was published. At the Restoration Earle was made Dean of Westminster, then Bishop of Worcester and later of Salisbury. His personal character and his efforts on behalf of persecuted Nonconformity won the admiration of such men as Baxter.

Unlike his 'staid man', Earle wrote some verse in his younger days. The first edition of *Microcosmography* (1628) contained fifty-four characters; twenty-three were added in the fifth edition (1629) and one in 1633. The seventeenth-century editions were anonymous, though the authorship was early known. The book reached its 'eighth edition' in 1664, the year when the Overbury collection attained its seventeenth. Two unnumbered editions of Earle had been issued in 1650.

the difference between shooting at a haystack target and critical and sympathetic analysing of actions and motives. The Over-burian 'Old Man' is merely a tedious, stubborn, offensive nuisance. Earle's 'Good Old Man' is not a sentimental idealiza-tion, but he has wisdom and dignity along with his Polonian defects. In the 'Mere Scholar' the man of the world is only scoring points and produces a conventional caricature. Earle, a don who excels in academic satire, presents in his downright scholar a worthy ancestor of Dominie Sampson; his manners are not those of a courtier, but 'his fault is onely this, that his mind is somewhat too much taken up with his minde'. The melancholy man, though an unwontedly philosophic figure in the Overbury collection, is a catalogue of symptoms. Earle defines a discontented man in an arresting phrase, 'one that is falne out with the world, and will bee revenged on himselfe', and cuts immediately to 'The roote of his disease . . . a selfe-humouring pride'. Whether praising or blaming, Earle is not content to report what a character does or is, he asks why.

Earle unites all the virtues of the tradition, the dramatic observation and ethical reason of Theophrastus, the moral and religious seriousness and interpretative habit of Hall, the epi-grammatic wit and English realism of the Overburian writers. And these qualities are broadened and deepened by insight, wisdom, kindliness, and humour, especially remarkable in a young man. Like Theophrastus's boor, the 'Plain Country Fellow' stands dumb and astonished in contemplation of a good fat cow, yet Earle brings humorous truth and sympathy to the picture of an immortal Hodge, a brother of Tennyson's northern farmer—but not of the peasant of modern fiction, since he has 'reason enough to doe his businesse, and not enough to be idle or melancholy'. Earle's book lives up to its title; it is a minia-ture human comedy. And, like his own contemplative man, 'Hee lookes not upon a thing as a yawning stranger at novelties; but his search is more mysterious and inward, and hee spels Heaven out of earth'. Earle's child, a charming addition to the normal range of subjects, is a child of tears and laughter who is not made unreal either by a hint of Neoplatonism or by Shake-spearian irony: 'his Drums, Rattles and Hobby-horses' are 'but the Emblems, & mocking of mens businesse'. It is indeed Earle's enveloping irony which gives even slight sketches and trivial items a philosophic largeness of suggestion. A 'Pot-Poet'

is not merely a bibulous and ridiculous balladmonger; it is
scarcely hyperbole to say that the whole tragicomic contrast
between what man is and what man would be is implicit in the
phrase, 'sitting in a Bawdy-house, hee writes Gods Judgements'.

The English character had begun with a wide extension of
the Theophrastian range and method, and our survey may end
with a work which unites character, aphorism, injunction,
essay, and biography in what is essentially a comprehensive
conduct-book, Fuller's *The Holy State* (1642).[1] The first, second,
and fourth books deal in the main with family relationships,
occupations, and the governing class respectively, and the fifth
with 'the profane state' from the harlot and witch to the traitor
and tyrant. The formal division between sheep and goats had
precedents in Hall and in Breton's *The Good and the Bad* (1616),
but Fuller's entire and practical didacticism sets him apart from
the normal Theophrastian tradition and compels abandonment
of the Theophrastian pattern. The essays or 'General Rules' of
his third section, in themselves a book of conduct and courtesy,
consist of strings of maxims elaborated in comment and anecdote, and the same method is used in the characters, so that
dramatic realism and satirical analysis give way to good counsel.
The addition of numerous separate *exempla* is prompted by
Fuller's interest in biography and by the instinct of a popularizer. Altogether *The Holy State* answers the plea made in the
Advancement of Learning for studies of 'the proper duty, vertue,
challenge, and right, of every severall vocation, profession, and
place', and much of its inspiration comes from Bacon, the
thinker and essayist who had translated abstract philosophy into
terms of modern utility, and from William Perkins, the theologian who had taught family and social duties and ministered

---

[1] Thomas Fuller (1608–61) was the son of a clergyman and the nephew of two
prominent ecclesiastics. He was at Cambridge in the period of George Herbert,
Taylor, and Milton. His actual or nominal connexion with his University, of
which he published a *History* in 1655, covered seventeen years. A successful minis-
terial career, which brought him to the Savoy Chapel, was interrupted by the war.
In 1643 he took refuge in Oxford, then served as chaplain with Hopton's army, and
stayed a while at Exeter, where he printed the first volume of his popular *Good
Thoughts* (1645). After some years of wandering Fuller found peace in the rectory
of Waltham Abbey (1649), and was allowed to do a good deal of preaching in
London. With one of his patrons he went to The Hague to welcome Charles II—
his sole foreign travel. He became a royal chaplain and regained old preferments
but did not enjoy them long. Fuller's chief works in biography and history are
noticed in the following chapter.

to the individual conscience. And, of course, Fuller is never far from the Bible.

To those whose affection for him is solidly based on Lamb and choice extracts it may seem blasphemous to say that *The Holy State*, read as a whole, is extremely dull. But it is of great interest as a literary and social document. We noticed in the first chapter how the aristocratic courtesy book adapted itself to the needs of the country gentry and prosperous commercial class; and Fuller, like Brathwait (whom he frequently echoes), is a conspicuous exemplar of classical and Christian humanism reduced to the plane of philistine common sense and rather pedestrian obligations and virtues. For one aspect of the matter there is his view of 'degree' as the framework of society. From the king, 'a mortall God' embodied to perfection in Charles, down to the household servant, all creatures, including the lay patron with livings in his gift, have their place and duties. This traditional theory, most familiar to us in the speech of Shakespeare's Ulysses, is a law of nature more readily appreciated by the upper than by the lower classes. Fuller, accepting the divine and feudal scheme without question, labours to heighten his readers' sense of responsibility to God and especially to man, but he points out, with a characteristic mixture of piety and worldly wisdom, the chances of an individual's overleaping the bars of caste. A younger brother, though divinely ordained to be a younger brother, may with divine help win fame and fortune in war, in business, at court, or by marriage. The sturdy yeoman, by thrift and enterprise, may become a gentleman. While the contemporary scene cast some dark shadows over his buoyant pages and particularly over his preface, in 1640–2 Fuller saw only dimly that his static, comfortable world of mutual obligation and trust, of pure and unenthusiastic religion breathing household laws, had long been changing from a fact, if it ever was a fact, into an ideal; and it was soon to be shaken so violently that Clarendon, a not unprejudiced witness to be sure, was to trace the corruptions of the next age to the break-up of family ties and traditional *mores* in the civil war.

In general, there is a large difference in tone between the magnanimous *sententiae* hallowed by humanistic tradition and the proverbial wisdom of Fuller. 'Knowing that knotty timber is unfit to build with, he edifies people with easie and profitable

matter.' Never a man's thought in the world keeps the road-
way better than his, but fertility in platitude is equalled by the
fertility of fancy which turns platitude into epigram. At his
best Fuller crystallizes common sense in unforgettable phrases:
'They that marry where they do not love, will love where they do
not marry'; 'one is not bound to believe [of the controversial
divine] that all the water is deep that is muddy'. Coleridge's
dictum, that wit was the stuff and substance of Fuller's intellect,
has often been used to set him as an amiable gargoyle in an
isolated niche of quaint eccentricity. But no small share of his
writing is quite plain and direct and, moreover, wit was a
quality of mind and style almost universal in his time, not least
among preachers, though Fuller's wit was perhaps more
homely and spontaneous, and certainly was less integral, penetrating, and serious, than that of many contemporaries. Magistrates and ministers, Fuller says, should be 'metamorphos'd
from all lightnesse to Gravity', but in his case the process was
never completed. George Fox would, not without reason, have
called him a great lump of earth, and Fuller would, not without
reason, have pronounced Fox an arrogant trouble-maker. But
Fuller's writings as a whole leave us in no more doubt of his
fundamental earnestness than of his fundamental limitations.
If in guiding his readers to heaven he was fascinated by many
good things along the road, at any rate he did not get too far in
advance, and as a preacher a child of this world is sometimes
more effective than the children of light.

   In this account of character-writing we have had to pass by
many more or less readable but not especially significant books.
The rapid exhaustion of the character proper and the increasing
flexibility of the form in time allowed the name to cover almost
anything. The early authors started a number of hares which
produced large and doubtfully legitimate families. Early
characters of Puritans lead on to the religious and political in-
vectives of the civil war and interregnum. Early sketches of
places develop into such extended but lively things as Felltham's *Brief Character of the Low Countries* (1652), Marvell's
'Character of Holland' (1653 or earlier) in verse, and Evelyn's
Character of England (1659). And of course the normal kind of
character was always being written, though it never recovered
the quality of Earle. But we have met the chief representatives
of the genre in the century, with the exception of the later

Butler, and, viewing the immense output, we must be content with microcosmography.

In the course of this chapter we have, inevitably, seen almost as much of the essay's parents and aunts and uncles as of the growing child. One title of Francis Osborn's partly indicates the variety of kinship—*A Miscellany of Sundry Essays, Paradoxes, and Problematical Discourses, Letters and Characters* (1659). While the numerous writers would yield a respectable anthology of familiar essays, the definite emergence of the pure type comes after 1660, with Cowley. The old traditions of the impersonal religious homily and the impersonal humanistic discourse did not encourage the essayist to speak freely of his own experience and of the small matters of everyday life. If the great French essayist had done so, the great English one had not. Montaigne was widely read, but his actual influence is hard to estimate; it is fairly clear, for instance, in the young Cornwallis and in the early unpublished essays (1652–3) of Sir William Temple. We cannot ascribe all the qualities of the essayist's temper, which many Englishmen of our period possessed, to the study of Montaigne, but certainly he would support the writers who preached rational moderation and urbane, gentlemanly culture, and who aimed at a colloquial, personal manner.

Since the early essay springs so directly from Renaissance humanism it is more seriously and solidly didactic and ethical, more aristocratic and masculine in its appeal, than the papers of Steele and Addison. Our essayists are always striving to re-express, chiefly for the educated ruling class, the eternal verities of moral and civil wisdom as these had been laid down by the ancients. They teach Stoic control of the passions rather than the solution of domestic problems, the management of a state rather than of a fan, the knowledge of man rather than of London. But if most essayists of the age carried heavier guns than most of their successors, their readers did too. And didactic seriousness was more or less mitigated by touches of personal reminiscence, wit, humour, satire, and a frequent vein of poetry. Unlike Montaigne, the early essayists rarely scrutinize the fundamentals of orthodox religion and morality. Following the Tudor humanists, they take these as fixed and labour to uphold tradition, order, and authority—as, to be sure, Montaigne did also, in his own way. But at the end of the period we have such a significant portent as Francis Osborn, that disillusioned rationalist who was akin to Samuel Butler. (In that, while 'wanting the Engines of Learning', he endeavoured 'to shake the Pillars of the Schooles', Osborn was akin to the Victorian Butler as well.) Another sceptic, of greater moral earnestness than Osborn, but a disciple of Bacon, Montaigne, and especially Charron, was Richard Whitlock, author of *Zootomia* (1654), a combination of 'anatomy', essays, and characters.

The vast popularity of the character, wit's descant on the plainsong of the essay, did a good deal to check the growth of the more learned and contemplative form. The evolution of the two was roughly parallel and we have observed their tendency to merge. Both widened their scope to take in almost any kind of writing, and in both the original preponderance of *utile* over *dulce* diminished. The essay and the character alike embodied ideals of rational, civilized behaviour and culture. These ideals were a traditional and international inheritance, yet in England they continued to be nourished by a vigorous and heterogeneous individualism. In contemporary France the same ideals and the same literary forms suffered from the dominance of a standardized and overcivilized minority. Montaigne had no worthy successors; the genuine essayist could hardly live in the close air of the *salon*. And while the English character-writers painted the rich variety of street and farm, study and tavern, La Bruyère, though he began by translating Theophrastus, analysed members of the *beau monde*.

VII

HISTORY AND BIOGRAPHY

Hᴵꜱᴛᴏʀʏ, said Ciccro, in words often repeated—and with emblematic elaboration in the frontispiece to Ralegh's *History
of the World*—is 'testis temporum, lux veritatis, vita memoriae,
magistra vitae, nuntia vetustatis'. For the humanists of the
Renaissance, who werc so preoccupied with the education of
rulers, history was philosophy teaching by examples. In the
long list of English translations from the classics in the sixteenth
and early seventeenth centuries the works of ancient historians
and moralists together far outweigh other kinds of litcrature.
By 1600 many minor historians and some major ones had been
turned into English, and in that year Philemon Holland's *Livy*
announced a translator who combined nobility of style with a
new standard of scholarship. Among his later translations
were Suetonius (1606) and Camden's great antiquarian work,
Britannia (1610). Heywood translated Sallust in 1608, with a
preface taken from Bodin's *Methodus ad Facilem Historiarum
Cognitionem*. The industrious Edward Grimeston rendered many
modern works and, in 1633, Polybius. In 1629 Hobbes commenced his literary and anti-democratic career with a version
of Thucydides, a version more faithful to the author's style than
the smooth periods of Jowett. Tacitus had been done in the late
years of Elizabeth, and his high prestige both as a stylist and, in
Donne's phrase, as 'the Patriarch, and Oracle of States-men'
is attested by such admirers as Bacon (who pointed out to Elizabeth Sir Jqhn Hayward's Tacitean 'felony'), Jonson, and the
essayists Cornwallis and Robert Johnson. The names of Hayward and Tacitus remind us that historians suffered from royal
and official fear of propaganda and that in 1627–8 the first
incumbent of Fulke Greville's chair of history at Cambridge
was silenced because his lectures on the *Annals* seemed to havc
a contemporary bearing.

The classical historians, along with such moderns as Comines,
Machiavelli, Guicciardini, Bodin, and Sarpi, contributed to
raise both the critical and the artistic level of English historiography. The simple method of the Tudor chronicler had been
to start with Brute, or with Creation, and come down with

increasing patriotic fervour through English history. We have links between old and new in the chronicles of the two tailors, the plain-sewing of the not very critical John Stow (1525–1605) and the stylistic embroidery of the more critical John Speed (1552?–1629); the latter had the practical and scholarly help of such men as Greville, Camden, and Cotton. The old ways died hard. Even the scientific Camden, not to mention the late and unscientific Fuller, clung to the annalistic method. The *Chronicle of the Kings of England* (1643) by Sir Richard Baker, that unfortunate old knight who commenced author in the Fleet prison, was eyed askance by scholars, but it continued, with many enlargements, to satisfy generations of country gentlemen like Sir Roger de Coverley. For us the persistence of medievalism (which is partly classical too) is more of a virtue than a defect. Clio was still in possession of her throne. The historian was a man, often a man of action, with a temperament, not a cloistered and impersonal card-index. The conception of history as epic story and drama, not as scientific diagnosis, of individual men rather than social and economic forces as the causes of events, of God working out His will in human and especially in English affairs, all this meant that history had not yet been entirely robbed of its traditional poetry.

The great example of this conception is Ralegh's *History of the World* (1614), the huge fragment of a work which, like the *Instauratio Magna* and *The Fairy Queen*, only Elizabethan energy could conceive. The *History* was written, moreover, by a man who had been a soldier, sailor, colonizer, statesman, courtier, and chemist, as well as an author, a man now prematurely old and broken, and confined in the Tower under a suspended sentence of death. Ralegh was not a scholar but he had always been, as Naunton said, an indefatigable reader whether by sea or land, and in this task he had some helpers, Robert Burhill the orientalist (according to Aubrey), and Ben Jonson for 'a peice . . . of the punick warre' (according to Jonson); and tradition includes other names. There were also the usual short cuts; the first four chapters on the Creation were indebted to commentaries on Genesis like that of Benedict Pererius. Even so the book is a monument of Ralegh's own labour and learning and literary power. Its vast scope grew out of its kinship with the medieval encyclopaedia or 'mirror' and the literature *de casibus virorum illustrium*, and the book of advice to princes. All these motives were unified by Ralegh's desire to show the working of Providence from the beginning of the world and to come down through British history—though not too far down. However, the death of his young patron, Prince Henry, and no doubt his increasing restlessness of soul and body, led him to break off at 168 B.C. Prudential flattery of James proved vain. Ralegh's daring to publish a book when 'civilly dead', his saucy censuring of princes, and his anti-Spanish feeling, only roused his captor's animosity.

Matthew Arnold, contrasting Thucydides' examination of Greek legend with Ralegh's speculations on the waters above the firmament and the site of paradise, found the modern critical mind in the ancient historian. Ralegh's notion of the origins of human history and of natural philosophy in general may have been less modern than that of a few of his contemporaries, yet his premisses and modes of thought appear in too many later men to warrant our regarding his attitude as an anachronism. On the other hand, within the limits set by his entire acceptance of Scripture, Ralegh brings critical reason to the scrutiny of all human authority, historical, Aristotelian, patristic, and scholastic, and his mind works more freely when he leaves the Bible and the chosen people for profane history. In comparing Roman with English soldiers or showing the advantages of control of the sea he writes with the plain force and sagacity of an experienced commander, and his admiration for the great generals of old is mingled with a quite natural and contemporaneous sense of professional kinship. As a spacious narrative compiled from the classical historians, Plutarch and the rest, this part of the book lived longer than the first, yet the theological and metaphysical passages have their interest for the student of ideas. In Ralegh's own century his work was popular from the beginning and was esteemed by such various persons as Ussher and Elizabeth of Bohemia, Cromwell and Montrose, Milton and Joseph Hall, and even the exacting Peter Heylyn.

Ralegh's view of history is not so much classical, ethical, and 'prosaic' as it is medieval, religious, and poetic. In the great drama of the rise and fall of kings and empires the head of the 'school of atheism' sees everywhere the hand of God, who casts down the mighty from their seats. The sweeping panorama of God's judgements especially commended the *History* to Puritans and republicans in the seventeenth century, and it still stirs the imagination. Allied with that is the conception of mutability in the lives of nations and of men, and Ralegh touches the great theme with spontaneous and masculine beauty of phrase and rhythm. The gallant man of action is haunted by thoughts of time and age and death,

towards which we always travaile both sleeping and waking: neither have those beloved companions of honour and riches any power at all, to hold us any one day, by the promises of glorious entertainments; but by what crooked path so ever wee walke, the same leadeth on directly to the house of death: whose doores lie open at all houres, and to all persons. For this tide of mans life, after it once turneth and declineth, ever runneth with a perpetuall ebbe and falling streame, but never floweth againe: our leafe once fallen, springeth no more, neither doth the Sunne or the Summer adorne us againe, with the garments of new leaves and flowers.

It is not the new science, for all Ralegh's knowledge, which darkens his broodings over the frailty and brevity of life. His words are in the spirit of Homer and Catullus and Ovid, still more of *Everyman* and the Dance of Death and 'To-morrow, and to-morrow, and to-morrow. . . .' And what gives these commonplaces their special poignancy is that Ralegh (like Petrarch, for instance) is sincere but not secure in his *contemptus mundi*. We read knowing that he was to make one last effort to regain honour and riches and taste 'the false and durelesse pleasures of this stage-play world', knowing too how soon his pride, cruelty, and ambition were to be covered all over with those two narrow words, *Hic jacet*.

Another work of grandiose sweep and sometimes epic power was Richard Knolles's *General History of the Turks* (1603). The provincial schoolmaster was inevitably a compiler from secondary sources, but he had a fiery vision of God using the might of Islam to punish the sins of Christendom. His fame in his own century was confirmed by the praise of Dr. Johnson, Southey, and Byron, and he would receive more than honourable mention here if this volume were, like his, a folio of twelve hundred pages. As it is, we must turn to political history of more mundane inspiration than that of Ralegh and Knolles. Of the various accounts of English sovereigns the only one that we now read is Bacon's *History of the Reign of Henry VII* (1622), a work which, though stripped of its authority, still commands the admiration of historical specialists. This book, the first fruit of enforced leisure after his fall, was Bacon's own partial and hasty fulfilment of a larger design, a history of the Tudor age, which in the *Advancement of Learning* he had held out to other writers as a worthy enterprise (and which Daniel fell short of). He had in fact written a fragment which Speed was able to quote in discussing Henry in his *History of Great Britain* (1611). The groundwork of Bacon's book was furnished by Polydore Vergil, through the medium of Edward Hall. To Cotton's manuscript collections he was indebted for supplementary materials, from Fabyan's 'London Chronicle', Bernard André's account of Henry, and various documents; and he made full use of the Rolls of Parliament. Selden praised him, with Camden, for going to such records. Bacon added his considered theory of history, his political and legal experience and insight, his imagination (especially in speeches on the classical model), and his style. His concentration on kingcraft may now appear somewhat narrow, and he has erroneous and fanciful details, yet he far excels his predecessors in his artistic and coherent picture of events and still more in his analysis of Henry's policy. As 'a perfect and peremptory royalist' and as a fallen Chancellor, Bacon wished to gratify James, but he said truly that he had not flattered his subject, and his sensitive master could hardly have relished some of the facts and comments. While Bacon occasionally refers to God's providence, his political didacticism is not in the moralistic tradition. The Henry of modern research is a less Machiavellian ruler than Bacon saw; in that altered light, however, the book only reveals the more of its author.

The great monument of historical memoirs, Clarendon's, was begun in our period but belongs to the next. Some lesser examples are the attractive sketches of Elizabethan courtiers and statesmen which make up Sir Robert Naunton's *Fragmenta Regalia* (written about 1630 and published in 1641); Sir Anthony Weldon's account (1650–1), according to Heylyn and others a libellous account, of the courts of James and Charles; and the product of Thomas May's political conversion, *The History of the Parliament* (1647). The formidable mass of miscellaneous records we must pass by, though some of them will come into the discussion of autobiography. And we can only mention the definite arrival of a new standard of antiquarianism in the first volume (1655) of the *Monasticon Anglicanum* compiled by Roger Dodsworth and Sir William Dugdale, and of a new type of county history in Dugdale's *Antiquities of Warwickshire* (1656).

We cannot leave history, however, without a glance at one general topic which touches many authors and illustrates the background of contemporary politics as well as the rise of the critical spirit in historiography. That is the slow death of the matter of Brute, New Troy, and Arthur. In the Middle Ages Geoffrey of Monmouth's 'lies' about Arthur might be attacked, but for the most part the Trojan dynasty stood firm. The later scepticism of the Italian Polydore Vergil drew protests from generations of patriotic chroniclers. The strength of traditional feeling is seen in the discretion with which Camden, the great pioneer of historical criticism, indicated his doubts concerning Brute. Speed, in his review of the long controversy, declared that a renowned Christian nation should follow other countries in repudiating descent from 'Venus that lascivious Adulteresse'. The less emotional Selden, annotating *Poly-Olbion*, could argue for Brute 'but as an Advocat for the Muse' and speak of 'the Arcadian deduction of our British Monarchy'. Critical acid ate steadily into the roots of romantic legend, though poets were loath to relinquish stories which had lived so long in the hearts of Englishmen, stories which now, said Drayton, 'the envious world doth slander for a dreame'. But the tradition involved more than literary sentiment. During the Middle Ages the tale of Arthur's empire and prophecies of his return had had political significance, and that they were made a part of Henry VII's dynastic propaganda we are reminded by the name given to his eldest son. In the latter part of the sixteenth century imperialistic, commercial, and antiquarian zeal revived the idea of the Tudor house as the true Arthurian line—an idea writ large in *The Fairy Queen*. After the prolonged anxiety about the succession, the union of England and Scotland evoked a fresh outburst of salutations in pageantry and in books to the second Arthur and second Brute. Shakespeare, Bacon, Jonson, Warner, Campion, Alexander, Drayton, Drummond, and other men of letters celebrated the sovereign who was, in Speed's phrase, the 'Inlarger and Uniter of the British Empire; Restorer of the British Name'. But this wave of 'British' feeling ebbed as James's reign wore on and loyalties became divided between king and

Parliament. Against the theory of divine right parliamentary champions not only cited such medieval precedents as Magna Carta but held that in the Saxon period supreme power belonged to the people. Such an appeal to a remote past, however inaccurate at times, had been made possible by the researches of many scholars into all phases of early and especially Saxon history, legal, political, ecclesiastical, archaeological, and linguistic. Though the Society of Antiquaries did not survive James's antagonism, the library of Sir Robert Cotton might be called the Trojan horse from which emerged the men who overthrew, or provided the means of overthrowing, the walls of prerogative. Such notable students of legal history as Coke, Selden, and Sir Henry Spelman were, indeed had to be, collectors of manuscripts. To cut short a matter we cannot pursue, 'Saxon' sentiment, allied as it largely was with the rising opposition to the Crown, hastened the death of British legend, while royalist sentiment helped to prolong its life.

Milton had reason to feel more keenly than most men the pressure of conflicting claims, and his view of English origins, as of more urgent problems, underwent changes. He gave up the long-meditated Arthurian epic, but he cherished much old lore in his imagination. In the *History of Britain* Milton was sympathetic towards Brute and early 'poetic' fable but quite sceptical about the historical Arthur. Writing in the decade after 1646—though the *History* was not published until 1670—with his eye on his own times, Milton found both British and Saxons incapable of maintaining true liberty; what virtues the latter had they lost, the former never had any, and God punished a sinful and servile nation with successive conquests. In general Milton combined a feeling for romantic story (if not monkish) with critical use of both the standard chroniclers and original sources. Incidentally, his effort at condensed narrative and characterization of persons confirms his expressed preference for Sallust over all the Latin historians.

Thus in historiography at large, apart from a few late and unimportant items, our period witnessed, to quote Stow's excited phrase about Polydore, the final cashiering of threescore princes, the definite separation of legend and history. Romance was banished from text-books. Henceforth the story of Britain was to begin with Julius Caesar, a more substantial descendant of Venus than Brute.

The form and spirit of early biography, as of almost every kind of literature, were born of the marriage of classical and Christian traditions. Plutarch supplied the most winning ancient model for the handling of material and, what was even more attractive to the Renaissance humanist, a conception of biography based, like the 'character', on ethical principles. Then there were the motives and methods inherited from the vast body of medieval lives of saints, ecclesiastics, and exemplary rulers; when the main object was to glorify an illustrious servant of God and show readers what heights a human soul could attain, classical rationality might give place to credulous *naïveté* and an individual portrait to an ideal pattern. Medieval biography yielded many notable exceptions, however, and a vivid modern one was Roper's *Sir Thomas More*, written about 1556 and first printed at St. Omer in 1626. A typical 'saint's life' composed in our period was John Duncon's *Lady Falkland* (1648). One is at a loss to classify Urquhart's unique panegyric of the admirable Crichton. Another important biographical tradition was that represented by the long succession of works in verse deriving from Boccaccio's *De Casibus Virorum Illustrium*, which mirrored the lives of great sinners struck down by the hand of God, and great men brought low by the turn of Fortune's wheel or through a defect of character. An example of that dramatic conception was Cavendish's *Thomas Wolsey*, which, though written about 1556–7 and circulated in manuscript, was first published in 1641, in garbled form, as a timely object-lesson.

In the *Advancement* Bacon lamented the deficiency of lives, and the century grew active in filling the gap; but during our period biography, like the essay, was only detaching itself from related forms and much of it was 'impure'. Since we must fix upon writers who still are or ought to be generally read, we can only mention a work which, if judged by its positive effect, might rank as one of the greatest books ever written in English, the *Eikon Basilike* (1649), the spiritual autobiography, or Dr. Gauden's skilful pseudo-autobiography, of the royal martyr. And our general criterion must be strained at the outset, since it is a question how many people have read a famous piece of what Bacon would call 'Ruminated History', the *Life of Sir Philip Sidney* by Fulke Greville, Lord Brooke. This was written apparently about 1610–12, perhaps revised later, and published in 1652. Greville was writing not a 'Life' but a 'Dedication', a partly autobiographical grand testament, to be prefixed to his own works, the exercises of his youth which owed much to Sidney's influence. He was also salvaging what he could of the formal history he had contemplated and abandoned when the younger Cecil refused him access to state papers. The larger portion of the digressive book—and this no doubt is what repels readers, in spite of the frequently noble matter and style —is taken up with detailed analysis of the political, religious, and commercial forces which have kept Europe in turmoil. This analysis is given partly as Sidney's, since he had laboured and died for his ideal of England as the militant champion of European Protestantism. The sections dealing with Sidney himself narrate only a few episodes and are rather a *laudatio* than a life. Sidney appears in dim or dazzling outline as the perfect hero of a tragic drama, a statesman-saint, one of God's elect. Whatever we deduct for retrospective idealization, it is a testimony to both men that Sidney, fine as he was, should have inspired such deep devotion in a nature so toughly critical as Greville's. But the survivor of a great friendship is not erecting a mere private monument; it is to be 'a Sea-mark' for the nation. A disillusioned statesman whose world seems out of joint, Greville turns to the past and holds up Sidney as the image of England's ancient vigour, the symbol of a great epoch and a great race that are gone. He repeatedly contrasts 'those active times', 'the ancient greatness of hearts', with the 'decrepit', 'effeminate', corrupt, and self-seeking age in which he lives. Such pessimism is more than sentimental nostalgia. Elizabeth, as Greville describes her, had faults along with her lustrous virtues, but she made England a great power, she did not lavish money on favourites, she did not scheme to enlarge her prerogative, she did not resort to new taxes, impositions, and proclamations without the consent of Parliament. It was just as well that Greville's history was incomplete and posthumous.

At the opposite pole from Greville's are two other famous and smaller and livelier memorials. They contain only one element of biography, but that element is the quintessence, for the books are Drummond's *Conversations with Ben Jonson* and Selden's *Table Talk*. Drummond's notes were recorded in 1619 and first printed in full in 1833. Since almost every sentence has been quoted again and again, perhaps one general observation will be enough. We recognize Ben's aggressive critical mind, in the candour of dishabille, and yet, without setting up a Jonsonian image akin to the Stratford bust, we may at moments almost wish the notes unwritten. The visit Jonson paid in 1618–19 to the 'widowed' recluse of Hawthornden must have been something like that of Heracles at the house of Admetus— or possibly that remark is proof of the unfortunate effect the book has had. While his host's character and cellar may have tempted Jonson to throw his considerable weight about, the *Conversations*, for all their objectivity, must be a selection conditioned and heightened by Drummond's reaction to a more robust personality. Many spicy items, along with the final comments on Jonson's egoism and infinite thirst, linger in memories that have forgotten the more truly Jonsonian wisdom of the *Discoveries* and the plays and poems. Although we are thankful that Jonson was not Goethe and Drummond not Eckermann, we must acknowledge that the book has contributed more than anything else to establish, in place of the magnanimous Renaissance humanist and poet, the popular picture of a burly, arrogant, swashbuckling toper and scabrous gossip. If Jonson were only the man Drummond saw and heard, he would scarcely be the commanding figure in English literature that he is. To say that is not to say that his prime virtues were humility and abstemiousness.

The hard-headed John Selden (1584–1654) was a friend of Jonson's and in some ways not unlike him. His *Table Talk*, a record made by his secretary during the last twenty years of his life, was published in 1689, the year in which his principles triumphed. Apart from his acquaintance with the wits and his notes on *Poly-Olbion*, this is his one title to admission into a history of English literature. 'The chief of learned men reputed in this Land' (in Milton's phrase) enjoyed European fame, but only the most resolute investigator now looks into his numerous important works on constitutional, ecclesiastical, and oriental law and antiquities. It is both the special praise and the partial limitation of the *Table Talk* that it records, in crisp, colloquial English, the interests and the clear workings of a great legal and political mind. What we call 'life' comes in abundantly, but through the back door, in the homely similitudes and racy anecdotes employed to elucidate knotty political and ecclesiastical problems. In spite of its contemporary focus the book is a shrewd and pregnant commentary on the unchanging motives and attitudes of men, particularly of those men who will not let well enough alone but must upset ordered liberty, peace, and learning. But the *Table Talk* can only be mentioned here; some pungent quotations appear in other places.

Thomas Fuller's best-known books, *The Holy State* (1642), *The Church History of Britain* (1655), and *The History of the Worthies of England* (1662), all show him as biographer, historian, and antiquary, and in these congenial roles he does not cease to be a preacher and essayist. Something was said of *The Holy State* in the last chapter. The biographical sketches with which Fuller seasoned his moral counsels in that book are what appeal to the modern reader, who, like Aguecheek, cares not for good life. One needs no great knowledge of St. Hildegard to relish such a phrase as 'God who denied her legs, gave her wings'. The biographies are didactic examples of the various social and vocational types, and they are also the expanded anecdotes of a talker who is happier with actual persons than with ideal abstractions. And didacticism might be strained in justifying the account of Paracelsus. Even scholars shun the works of Fuller's admired Perkins, but that faithful minister's emphasis on the word 'damn' has left a doleful echo in every ear. The author's normal charity does not extend to Joan of Arc, who, along with the woman of Endor, exemplifies 'the Witch'. And, as a lifelong devotee of John Foxe, he takes Milton to task for some harsh words about the Marian martyrs.

In the two larger works, for which Fuller gathered material over many years, 'the true Church Antiquary' had full scope for his talents. The *Worthies* is among other things a dictionary of national biography, a series of county histories, a topographical and historical gazetteer, a guide-book, and a dictionary of proverbs. Fuller's house of many gables is built on the foundations laid by Camden, Speed, Stow, and others. Portions of his subject had been treated by such antiquarian topographers as Norden, Richard Carew, William Burton, and Fuller's friend Dugdale. Foxe supplied Protestant martyrs and Bishop Godwin bishops. Fuller was conscientious, according to his light, in trying to check authorities. Besides, he jogged indefatigably about the country to inspect public records, manuscripts, places, and buildings, and to question natives and surviving relatives. As he remarked of one of his creditors, John Pits, 'It is hard to say whether his hands took more pains in writing, or feet in travelling . . .'. Considering the difficulties of research at the time, and the vicissitudes of Fuller's life, we can respect as well as enjoy his monumental labour of love. He had five objects before him: the glory of God, the preservation of dead men's memories, the furnishing of examples for the living, the entertainment of readers, and some honest profit for himself. Not all these objects have been sought by the austere makers of modern biographical dictionaries, nor could they avow that they had 'purposely interlaced (not as meat, but as condiment) many delightful stories'. The *Worthies* is a lineal descendant of the medieval encyclopaedias. Apart from the lists of sheriffs and gentry, we skip at our own risk, for Fuller's best goods may be under the counter. Thus we read, to the greater glory of God, about the Vicar of Bray; the use of malt to make drink in Derbyshire ('a master-piece indeed'); the marriage customs of Lapland; Devonshire strawberries and cream; the Dunmow flitch; a volume of treatises found in the belly of a cod at Cambridge on Midsummer Eve, 1626; the bones of the carp, which are as dichotomous as Peter Ramus. . . . It mars our image of Fuller to have him leaving the virtues of tobacco to those who know them.

But such random items, which give a pleasant unexpectedness to all his works, are 'the Leakage and Superfluities of his Study'. His chief labour went into the biographies, and these display the honesty, humanity, individuality, and 'quick Jocundity of style' that are not unexpected. Many of Fuller's phrases and anecdotes—the preaching of Hooker and Travers, the wit-combats of Shakespeare and Jonson—have long done service for the literary historian; so has the tale of Ralegh's cloak, though it has been honourably retired. Yet the combination of preacher, antiquarian, and essayist is not enough to make a good biographer. We can excuse the omission of many modern writers (for early ones Fuller had the help of 'bilious Bale' and others) and even of some eminent divines; and, knowing his deep sense of the 'long Winter of woe and misery' brought on by the civil war, we do not wonder at the absence of parliamentary leaders. Fuller's prime limitation, which is also a prime source of his peculiar charm, is intellectual immaturity. It is this which separates him from most of the great divines of his age; and it is perhaps not irrelevant to observe that Fuller does not possess the classics in anything like the same degree as his fellows. We justly praise his moderation in a time of strife, but we may feel that his comprehension of the issues involved is not quite adequate. In the *Worthies*, while he can apply common sense, Protestant common sense, to saints' legends, he has small understanding of literature or philosophy. As a rule he hastens, like the modern popular biographer, from perfunctory comment to biographical fact, character, and anecdote; and if he is often amusing, even illuminating, he can also be exasperatingly trivial. His concern is with men, not ideas, and his heterogeneous learning remains an external, unphilosophical, antiquarian hobby. Our staunch royalist may be called a biographical Leveller. Bacon gets little more space than Charles I's dwarf, and Shakespeare a third as much as the unicorn's horn. Fuller appreciates piety or oddity better than genius, and one of his very best sketches is that of Thomas Coryate.

He says, disarmingly, that if he has overlooked any public benefactors, their names are written in the Book of Life. A similar broad plea must extenuate brief mention of the *Church History*. Fuller's best writings are only slices of Fuller, and what has been said of him already would be repeated with slight variations and a fresh store of choice phrases. The *Church History* begins with the Druids and ends in 1649. The closing account of the death and burial of King Charles is a fine example of the simple eloquence Fuller can command when deeply moved. In the earlier part of the book the antiquarian holds sway, in the latter we have a moderate Anglican's picture of his own troubled age. In 1651 he had traversed part of the ground in editing and writing some sketches for the first important collection of lives in English, *Abel Redevivus: The Lives and Deaths of the Modern Divines*. Though Fuller is a rambling annalist, not a philosophic historian, and though he sees churchmen more clearly than the Church, he does a good deal, between the lines as well as in them, to explain the hold of the Anglican tradition. Incidentally, Peter Heylyn would not have been pleased to know that he would live in common memory, not as a learned author, but as the man who censured Fuller— and was eventually seduced into friendship by his victim's indomitable good humour.

Ecclesiastical biography in the seventeenth century began

with a work of distinction, Sir George Paule's *John Whitgift* (1612), but the quality and the fivefold achievement of Izaak Walton (1593–1683) have given him undisputed pre-eminence.[1] Accident, seconded by modest inclination and a genius for friendship, turned Walton into a semi-professional biographer. When Sir Henry Wotton died in 1639, leaving unwritten the life of Donne he was to have prepared for a collection of Donne's sermons, Walton fulfilled the task. The memoir of 1640, composed in haste under pressure, was revised, enlarged, and issued separately in 1658. The projected publication of *Reliquiae Wottonianae* 'begot a like necessity' of commemorating Wotton (1651); this biographical introduction was enlarged in 1654. Personal interest in Hooker had led Walton, about 1626, to begin collecting notes on him and, at the request of Archbishop Sheldon, he produced a life (1665) as a corrective to Gauden's work (1662). His life of Herbert (1670) was a free-will offering, written chiefly to please himself. At a still more advanced age Walton was persuaded to do a life of Robert Sanderson (1678; revised 1681). We can only lament that his notes for the life of Hales remained notes.

Walton was Donne's parishioner and friend and a friend of Wotton, and his were the earliest lives of these men. Herbert he had seen once; Hooker, of course, he had never seen. Sanderson he knew well. For Herbert he had the accounts of Nicholas Ferrar (1633) and Barnabas Oley (1652); for Hooker the sketches in Fuller's *Church History* and *Worthies* and Gauden. But biographical materials in print were of little use and Walton was indebted mainly to his own conscientious research. His most valuable sources were his episcopal friends, Thomas Morton, Henry King, Ussher, George Morley, and others. First-hand or oral information was fortified by general reading and by examination of records and documents. When Walton

---

[1] Walton was the son of an alehouse-keeper in Stafford. He was apprenticed to a London sempster, a relative, and, though a dabbler in verse, he prospered in business. His life was as uneventful as that of his companion in Winchester Cathedral, Jane Austen; his one adventure was the transmitting of a jewel of Prince Charles's after the battle of Worcester. Walton was acquainted with a number of literary men, from Jonson and Drayton to the angler-poet Charles Cotton. His ecclesiastical connexions were multiplied through his two marriages (1626 and 1647) and through the friendships he cherished. After the Restoration Walton lived chiefly with his friend George Morley, Bishop of Worcester and later of Winchester, who made him his steward, and during his last years with his clerical son-in-law in and near Winchester.

felt uncertain of his facts he said so, and occasional mistakes in detail were not the result of carelessness. His desire for accuracy, in contrast with the usual vagueness of his predecessors and contemporaries, is shown in his use, and his increasing use, of dates. Then his subjects were all authors and he drew upon their writings, notably Herbert's. He quoted letters and, though he might telescope passages in a way not endorsed by modern scholarship, he did not falsify the essential impression. Significant incidents were sometimes dramatized through speeches remembered (perhaps with the aid of a diary), reported, or invented in accordance with the biographer's understanding of the situation. Finally, the successive editions give proof of Walton's zeal, both biographical and literary, in their continual enlargements and changes in expression. His 'artless Pensil' laboured for perfection of phrase and rhythm, and no academic rhetoric mars his limpid simplicity. He is nearer to Attic prose than many scholarly writers of his age, yet he rises easily into poetry.

Of Walton's heroes Wotton alone was a man of the world, and even he had taken orders on becoming Provost of Eton. In treating his five clerics Walton is always didactic—and digressive—but not always in the same way. The predominance of either private or semi-official intentions explains the purely biographical handling of Donne and Wotton as individual worthies; the devoutly elaborate picture of Herbert as the ideal country parson, intended, like Oley's, as a 'serious call' to Restoration clergymen; and the historical sketches, in the lives of Hooker and Sanderson, of the Church of England's increasingly difficult struggles with Puritan nonconformity. The tragicomic story of Hooker's marriage and of Mrs. Hooker and her family is, it has been lately shown, a tissue of error and prejudice—possibly because the aged biographer's High Church informants wished to discredit the authenticity of the last books of the *Ecclesiastical Polity* and felt the need of discrediting Mrs. Hooker first. Even if this theory is true, the Tory churchmen may have accepted floating tales in good faith, and there is assuredly no reason to doubt Walton's. In all his writings he shows himself one of those staunch and simple-minded Anglicans who saw history with the eyes of a bishop and could not regard other views as much better than perverse wickedness. But if he be accused of uncritical bias, or of 'an holy Lethargy' of memory, he also helps us to appreciate in their best purity the power and the beauty of the feelings he shared.

Modern readers are less disposed to quarrel with Walton the historian than with Walton the hagiographer or 'sentimental churchwarden'. He is charged with excessive idealization and with re-creating five different men in the likeness of that placid primitive Christian, Izaak Walton. But the charges must be qualified. It is true that Walton's prime virtue is his own personality, which irradiates every page. No English biographer invests his heroes with Walton's peculiar aura of dignity, piety, and peace, a kind of unearthliness which makes the biblical parallels seem quite natural—and there is abundant evidence outside of Walton that the stormy century contained many such persons and havens of quietude. But the path to heaven lies through this world, and Walton has not a little of the gift of Fuller and Aubrey, the eye for picturesque and apparently trivial detail. And Walton's reverence for the beauty of holiness is not incompatible with a very individual compound of wit, humour, and irony; at times, as in the account of Mrs. George Herbert's widowhood and remarriage, he is so blandly innocent that we are not quite sure how to take him. Then it must be an inattentive reader to whom the courtly and cosmopolitan Wotton and the 'timorous and bashful' Sanderson look alike, or the spiritually serene Hooker and such spiritual wrestlers as Donne and Herbert. In venerating the men he wrote about, in dwelling on their strength rather than their weakness, Walton was in the tradition of Plutarch—whom he knew—as well as the authors of saints' lives. At the same time, even if it is to enhance their later glory, he does not let us forget the youthful sins of Donne, the aristocratic pride of Herbert, and the worldly ambitions of both; and the most candid biographer could hardly find serious faults in Hooker and Sanderson, or perhaps many in the more worldly Wotton. As a mere friend of Dr. Donne, Walton may not have grasped the complexities of his nature so fully as we do nowadays, but he tried to see men as God would see them at the day of judgement.

We may glide from biography into autobiography by way of *The Complete Angler* (1653), since Walton avows that 'the whole Discourse is, or rather was, a picture of my own disposition'. (There is a poignant nostalgia in that parenthetical phrase, added in 1661.) But the historian falters in trying to say something of a book which has been second only to the Bible in popular fame. Against a rural background and in a partly holiday mood Walton fills in the portrait of the artist which the reader of the *Lives* can draw in outline. A love of angling is an outward and visible sign of an inward and spiritual grace, of a gentle, contemplative benignity of soul which abhors dissension and loves good old ways, whether in the choice of bait or ballads or barley-wine or the worship of the Creator. We may remember that this prose hymn of contentment in simple and eternal things appeared a few weeks after Cromwell expelled the Long Parliament. Walton's motto is 'Study to be quiet', and in his mind the piety of primitive Christians is linked both with angling and with 'the happy days of the Nations and the Churches peace'. It would hardly have strained seventeenth-century etymology to identify 'angler' and 'Anglican'. If at times the nature of his theme betrays him into unctuousness, we still feel, to echo Dr. Butler's praise of the strawberry, that doubtless God could have made a better man than Walton, but doubtless God never did. Of piscatory lore, practical and theoretical, he was of course a devoted if not always reliable master, and he proves the honourable estate and antiquity of angling with a brave show of frequently Brownesque learning and logic. Was it not the vocation of four of the Apostles and the avocation of Perkins, Whitaker, Nowell, and Wotton? Are not fish-hooks mentioned in Amos and Job? Walton's colloquial and poetic pastoral is the most homespun of idyllic day-dreams, the most substantial of poems of escape. He is as conscious, and as sincere, an artist as Theocritus or Virgil; only such an artist could have given the lyrics of Marlowe and Ralegh their perfect and foreordained setting. There was a mass of country literature before Walton and there has been a great mass since, yet he may be said to have had no predecessors and no successors. His mellow vision of field and stream, of lambs frisking and children gathering lilies and cowslips, of anglers thanking God for the 'Sweet day, so cool, so calm, so bright', or making good cheer in clean inns with lavendered sheets—the vision that is for ever England—is Walton's own creation.

Along with the universal and timeless autobiographical impulse, such special motives as an accentuated self-consciousness (which on the religious plane was expressed in many Puritan diaries), the antiquarian spirit, the habit of the commonplace book, and the practice of writing 'advice to my son', these inspired a multitude of records compiled for private or public perusal which contain the most varied kinds of material. Among these always valuable and nearly always very readable documents we have, for instance, the hodge-podge jotted down in 1602–3 by that lover of sermons and gossip, the lawyer John Manningham; Lady Hoby's chronicle (1599–1605) of domestic duties and pieties; the little sketch, written in 1609 and printed in 1647, by the typical Tudor humanist and diplomat, Sir Thomas Bodley (1545–1613), who could well afford to be brief, since the Bodleian Library 'will testifie so truly and aboundantly for me, as I neede not be the publisher of the dignitie and worthe of mine owne Institution'; the record of Oxford life (1626–40) by Thomas Crosfield; the diary (1625–43) of the clerical collector of satires, John Rous; the fragmentary journal of the masterful *grande dame* and master-builder, Lady Anne Clifford (1590–1676); the journals of those two fine specimens of the royalist country gentleman, Sir John Oglander (1585–1655) and Sir Henry Slingsby, who was executed in 1658; the memorials of his family and himself by a third admirable representative of the type, Gervase Holles (1607–75), whose life was for the most part 'nothing els but a varied scene of infelicity'; the diary (1647–9) of the devout and thrifty Yorkshire yeoman, Adam Eyre; the laconic diary of Sir William Drummond, the poet's son, which pictures the life of a young Scottish laird in 1657–9; and, to make an end, the diaries of the Puritan Nehemiah Wallington (1598–1658) and of Archbishop Laud. Wallington incorporated a pamphlet of thirty pages on the sufferings of Prynne, Burton, and Bastwick, an affair to which Laud gave less than thirty lines. In Laud's diary, and in the history of his troubles written in the Tower, we can read the tragedy of a high-minded but legally minded ecclesiastical dictator.

The more formal autobiographies, whatever their historical value, seldom approach those of seventeenth-century France. In the *Memoirs* (published in 1683) of Sir James Melville (1535–1617) the brightest bit is the famous picture of the rival queens and rival women. There is more flavour in the autobiography and diary of that wise, sturdy, and scholarly servant of God and the kirk, James Melville (1556–1614). The learned and upright antiquarian, Sir Simonds D'Ewes (1602–50), contributed much to our knowledge in his annalistic review of his life, his 'sweet and satisfying studies', his family, and current history. One might find parallels to the memoirs of Blaise de Monluc in the *Commentaries* (printed in 1657) of Sir Francis Vere (1560–1609), chief of 'the fighting Veres' and schoolmaster of military leaders, and in the narrative (printed in 1637) of Colonel Robert Monro, a follower of the great Gustavus more modest, pious, and intelligent than Dugald Dalgetty. Captain John Smith's autobiography has been noticed among books of travel, though some sour critics would put it with fiction. As an obvious if not very literary text around which to group some other autobiographies one might take the degree of their authors' consciousness of God's special favour. The royal shipbuilder, Phineas Pett (1570–1647), was sustained by the belief or the hope that what Fulke Greville and commissions of inquiry regarded as graft would be rightly understood in heaven. Arthur Wilson (1595–1652), servant of the Earls of Essex and Warwick, minor dramatist and historian, wrote *Observations of God's Providence in the Tract of my Life*, which is a much more mundane, active, and robust chronicle than the title might suggest. Better known than these men is Robert Carey, first Earl of Monmouth (1560?–1639), whose memoirs were written about 1627 and printed in 1759. Whether in pursuit of the Armada or of thieves on the Scottish border or of preferment at court, he was always happily aware of God's help, though he relied more upon his horse in the most notorious action of his life—posting from the death-bed of his queen and kinswoman to be the first to salute King James. Carey's book gives a candid, complacent, varied, and vivid picture of himself and his 'stirring world'.

All of these adjectives except the first may be applied to a much more famous book, the autobiography of Lord Herbert of Cherbury (1583–1648), written when he was past sixty and first printed by Horace Walpole in 1764. It ends in 1624, with the end of the author's public career. If Carey was a sort of Rosencrantz-Hotspur, Herbert deserves Sir Leslie Stephen's appellation of Bobadil-Kant. He carried the satisfying assurance of divine protection even into a street brawl. Herbert rationalized or romanticized his martial, duellistic, and amatory bravado by a naïve appeal to the traditional code of chivalry. His swashbuckling vanity would hardly suggest that he could make important contributions to philosophy, poetry, and history, not to mention his diplomatic and military services. But he does now and then betray his intellectual interests in his plea for more practical and scientific education, in his outline of natural theology, and in the notable account of the divine sanction invoked and bestowed upon the publication of *De Veritate*.

A less solid philosopher than Herbert, but a much finer knight-errant, was the handsome, charming, versatile, and unique Sir Kenelm Digby (1603–65), a wandering planet whose orbit one crosses at every turn in the period. Digby's *Private Memoirs*, first printed in 1827, were written in 1628 to vindicate the clouded reputation of his beautiful wife, Venetia Stanley, and to celebrate an 'heroical' love ordained by the stars. He tells, in the form of a *roman à clef*, the truly romantic story of their attachment and their individual adventures from the time they were playmates until Sir Kenelm showed that love had not sapped his energies by winning in 1628 'a glorious victory' over a French and Venetian fleet at Scanderoon. Whatever gossip might say, and it said a good deal, about the bride's experience —her situation may have furnished the plot for Shirley's *The Wedding*—the marriage in 1625 proved to both lovers a reward for all their misfortunes. Lady Digby's death in 1633 was lamented in a shower of poems by Jonson, Felltham, Habington, and others. The *Memoirs* end of course before the period of Sir Kenelm's philosophic, scientific, and political activity, though 'Theagenes' is a student throughout his wanderings.

It is perhaps the stars which bring together here the autobiography of the high-souled, speculative, and eccentric inventor of the powder of sympathy and that of 'the thrice noble, chaste, and virtuous,—but again somewhat fantastical, and original-brain'd, generous Margaret Newcastle'. The two might have made a good match, but the duchess had an idol, whose *Life* she was to write. In it and in the earlier and briefer account of herself in *Nature's Pictures* (1656), she appears in her most lucid and attractive mood, and whatever we think, with Bridget Elia, of her 'intellectuals', we respect the qualities of her heart. Besides the analysis of her own character the duchess gives a picture of the aristocratic woman's breeding and mode of life.

Personal letters, mostly printed in modern times, have survived in sufficient bulk and variety to illustrate intimately every aspect of human nature and manners in a period of colour and candour. There are such shrewd and racy gossips as that disappointed but invincibly witty seeker after court preferment, Sir John Harington, whose masterpiece is his account of the entertainment given the King of Denmark, and John Chamberlain, whose letters (1597–1626) afford the best single panorama of a grasping and violent age. We have the official or private correspondence of such public men as Bacon, Sir Henry Wotton, whose letter about *Comus* everyone knows, and Cromwell, whose despairing appeal to his infallible Scottish brethren almost everyone knows. And we have the 'conceited' reflections of Donne, the tortured farewells of Ralegh, and the manly and sometimes moving simplicity of a later inhabitant of the Tower, Sir John Eliot. Then there are such letters as those of the Verneys, the Oxindens, and the Peytons which, like contemporary diaries, reveal both the apparently unshakable solidarity of old county families and the disintegrating effect of the civil war; the letters of Lady Katherine Paston to her son William at Cambridge (1624–7) and of Lady Harley to her 'Deare Ned' at Oxford and in London (1638 ff.), full of winning motherly solicitude in regard to temporal and eternal welfare; the voluminous exchanges between Lady Conway and Henry More, with their tale of bodily and spiritual pains and consolations; and the scientific and medical bulletins from the philanthropist and 'general artist', Samuel Hartlib, to Robert Boyle. In both of these last series, by the way, we have glimpses of the ubiquitous and mercurial Digby. The correspondence of Hartlib and John Worthington, the minor Cambridge Platonist, is another mirror of philosophic interests; it includes much praise of the angelic Dr. More, and some attempts at settling the question whether good angels appear with beards.

But, since we have noticed elsewhere the dubious 'letters' of James Howell and can linger with only a single exponent of the informal art, we may take an unpretentious woman, one who thought the noble authoress of Newcastle overbold and a little distracted. At Christmas, 1654, Dorothy Osborne (1627–95), daughter of a gallant and impoverished royalist and niece of Francis Osborn, married William Temple, the future statesman and author. Nearly all her extant letters, first printed in full in 1888, were written during 1653–4. Both families had objected and urged more advantageous matches—one of Dorothy's suitors was a son of the Protector—and marriage seemed remote or even hopeless; meetings were few and correspondence was surreptitious. At times Dorothy confessed herself 'a walking missery' and begged Temple to break off the engagement; at the best she could only preach stoic patience to herself and her lover and repeat her assurances of eternal loyalty. When obstacles were finally overcome, smallpox marred her beauty just before the wedding, but this Argalus and Parthenia lived happily ever after. There was ample time to fulfil that early wish which sounds so much like Donne: 'ffor god sake when wee meet let us designe one day to remember old story's in, to aske one another by what degree's our friendship grew to this height tis at. . . .'

Dorothy's letters live as a picture of provincial life, as a 'Romance Story' less artificial than her beloved and inexhaustible *Cléopâtre* and *Grand Cyrus*, and as the unaffected, wise, sad, and humorous revelation of one of the most loving and lovable feminine characters in English history. 'All Letters mee thinks should bee free and Easy as ones discourse, not studdyed, as an Oration, nor made up of hard words like a Charme.' We see her waylaying the carrier in the hope of a letter from her lover; escaping from tedious visitors and managing relatives to write to him and hit off their characters with shrewd strokes; playing shuttlecock with her companion, Jane; sitting up with her sick father; exchanging horticultural courtesies with Sir Samuel Luke; going out in the evening—this is a few weeks after the publication of *The Complete Angler*—to listen to the girls on the common as they sit and sing ballads, until they dash off after straying cows. Most of the time Dorothy is 'buried alive' in Bedfordshire, but she takes the waters at Epsom—though her 'spleen' is of the heart—and on a rare visit to London she has her picture drawn by 'Mr. Lilly', calls on the other Mr. Lilly, the astrologer, and even, duly masked, frequents the park and the new Spring Garden. 'Are not you in some fear what will become on mee? these are dangerous Courses.' We may look far to find another such individual mixture of Juliet, Rosalind, and Jane Austen.

While the sixteenth century was far from barren, it is in the seventeenth, through its multitude of autobiographies, diaries, and collections of letters, that we first become really and fully acquainted with the character, life, and background of many men and women both eminent and ordinary. It is axiomatic that no autobiography can be dull and, incomparably rich as the period is in more formal literature, this large body of informal records of actual experience, exciting or humdrum, is perhaps the most fascinating portion of its legacy. Formal works of history for the most part are naturally much less attractive, though parts of Ralegh are familiar and parts of Knolles and some other authors ought to be. In the field of biography and memoirs, a good many books were written in a modern manner by men conversant with court life and with Tacitus and Suetonius, Comines and Machiavelli, but the biographer whom we chiefly read was at least as typical of his century, and much closer to the supreme biographies of the world, in his naïve faith in God, virtue, and great men.

VIII
POLITICAL THOUGHT

THE political revolution gave birth to Gilberts and Harveys—and Fludds—but it found no Bacon; and, on the royalist side, Clarendon was no Hooker or Burke. Much of the most vital thinking was done in the courts of law, in Pym's lodgings, and on the floor of the House of Commons, or, later, in the quarters of Ireton and Cromwell, and at all times by multitudes of known or nameless people in manor and shop, church and conventicle. As we observed in the last chapter, the parliamentary leaders, like their opponents, appealed to constitutional theory and precedent, but their own instincts and the exigencies of circumstance made their procedure more empirical than doctrinaire; though speeches and remonstrances might contain political wisdom, they had a special and practical purpose. On the other hand, the great literary champions of republicanism and absolutism, Milton and Harrington and Hobbes, were more or less academic theorists, and the Levellers and Diggers and other groups were more intent upon building ideal states in the immediate future than upon philosophic analysis of the immediate past. Yet if the revolution brought forth no single author to whom we might turn for a view of the whole movement (and only an omniscient Deity could have filled that role), there is, in the writers mentioned and in the innumerable tracts of many less famous but important men, so large and diverse a body of active thinking that the historian of political philosophy is almost overwhelmed, and an historian of literature, with a chapter at his disposal, is reduced to the merest outline of some main currents in monarchical and revolutionary writings. Three general facts may be noticed at the outset. Up to about 1640–2 political thought, with relatively few exceptions, may be said to follow a pattern of constitutional monarchism more or less akin to that of Bodin; the next decade brings forth with startling rapidity every kind of parliamentary, popular, and radical opposition. Secondly, while personal factors on both sides hastened the revolution, its seeds had been dormant in all English constitutional history, in a vaguely legal conception of royal government which endangered the subject's legal rights. Thirdly, political thinking was conditioned at every turn by religion; to the very complex problem of the 'two kingdoms' of Church and Crown were added the further complications which followed the overthrow of both.

King James, and England, would have been happier if he, the most learned of English sovereigns, had been a professor at Oxford, uttering words that did not matter, instead of ruling in one of the most critical periods in modern European history. The bases of political thought had been altered by the Renaissance, Reformation, and Counter-Reformation, and by economic and social change, and Protestant England was the inevitable laboratory for the test of democratic theory. James, who had early learned that a Scottish presbytery agreed as well with monarchy as God and the devil, and whose methods had been fairly successful in Scotland, was not aware that in crossing the border he was entering not only another country but another era. He had set down his theory of kingship in black and white before he came to the English throne. The theory appeared in its most attractive form in *Basilikon Doron* (1599), a book of advice for Prince Henry. This picture of the benevolent despot, the father and shepherd of his people, was in the tradition of the ideal prince perpetuated by many Christian humanists before and after Erasmus, a tradition which satisfied Shakespeare and was upheld by Bacon, Filmer, and others, including the fiery Eliot. But the theory, even if James had lived up to it, did not commend itself to the new generation of common lawyers and business-men and some country gentlemen. Besides, James acted rather in the spirit of a more realistic treatise, *The True Law of Free Monarchies* (1598). Here, and in later homilies to Parliament, he enunciated an Hebraic, Roman, and—in a one-sided sense—feudal doctrine of sovereignty such as no Tudor would have dreamed of asserting. James always stresses a ruler's obligations, but the degree of their fulfilment is to be judged by God alone. The crown is inherited as a piece of family property; the king is the absolute master of the lives and possessions of his subjects; his acts are not open to inquiry or dispute, and no misdeeds can ever justify resistance. James had moved far from his quondam tutor, Buchanan, and beyond Bodin. The ultimate sanction for this doctrine was the theory of divine right evolved as an answer to the Catholic claim that the Pope had the right to depose heretical monarchs and release subjects from their allegiance. More important than any treatise of James's was the oath of allegiance (1606), which broke Catholic power in England by dividing Catholics against themselves and which offered the first effective challenge to the revived claims of Rome. To this question, which for many years embroiled all learned Europe, James devoted three-fourths of his own political writing (1607–15), and he enlisted such distinguished helpers as Andrewes, Donne, and Casaubon. Whatever the subtle casuistry of Catholic apologists, the plain fact was that treason and assassination could be justified by good authority, and Protestants could only go one better and appeal to God Himself as the sole maker and breaker of kings. Yet Englishmen might be justly alarmed when such a supra-mundane theory was invoked in domestic affairs, when God's lieutenant claimed to be above Parliament and the law, above all restraints except his own inspired will. The public temper was indicated by the outcry over the definitions of sovereignty in Dr. Cowell's *Interpreter* (1607), but James, though he reluctantly suppressed the indiscreet book, remained much more ready to suppress free speech in Parliament.

The best representatives of royalism in its early and comparatively unphilosophical phase were Bacon, Ralegh, and Fulke Greville; their Elizabethan outlook was not quite adequate for the reign of James. Bacon shared his master's theory of the powers and duties of the ideal prince and did not share the Commons' new notions of their powers and duties or his great rival's notions of the powers and duties of the common-law courts. Yet Bacon had once been bold enough to oppose Elizabeth and he was not unaware of a changing climate, and if James had listened to his counsels of compromise as well as to his endorsements of the prerogative the later crises might have been less violent. In regard to the Church, Bacon had long seen the necessity of internal reform and conciliation of the Puritans, and his ecclesiastical tracts were in demand in 1640–1. His insight was perhaps the clearer because he was 'a sincere if unenthusiastic Christian of that sensible school which regards the Church of England as a branch of the Civil Service, and the Archbishop of Canterbury as the British Minister for Divine Affairs'. Bacon's ideas on the general problems of politics are familiar, thanks to the *Essays*, and they are in the main more shrewd than exalted. A successful nation is a successful individual writ large. The humanist's traditional view of the State as an harmonious organism of divine institution is almost lost in the political physician's scientific knowledge of that body's chemistry and diseases and of useful prescriptions, such as foreign war, for continued good health. If Bacon sometimes appears a little old-fashioned in his Machiavellian nationalism as well as in his royalism, he is modern enough when, in the twenty-ninth essay and elsewhere, he gives hints of the economic basis of political power which Harrington was to take over and develop.

As later supporters of constitutional monarchy and a reformed episcopacy we might name Hyde, Falkland, and Selden. Hyde belongs to the next age, and Falkland's political faith was expressed in the House and in the field. John Selden (1584–1654), of whom we had a glimpse in the last chapter, was an anti-clerical whose Erastianism merits, still more than Bacon's, C. D. Broad's witty judgement quoted in the last paragraph. He early aroused ecclesiastical ire with his *History of Tithes* (1618), yet episcopacy was bound up with monarchy, tradition, and culture, and Selden's chief abhorrence was reserved for upstart sectaries and the Presbyterians whom he tormented in the Westminster Assembly with his learned barbs. The two words *Scrutamini Scripturas* 'have undone the World'. 'The Puretan would be judged by the Word of God: If he would speak clearly, he means himself, but he is ashamed to say so.' Selden was religious, after a fashion, but true Anglican light without heat has often been suspect, and more fervent contemporaries may be excused for seeing Hobbesian infidelity in the play of his cool, mundane intelligence. 'They talk (but blasphemously enough) that the Holy Ghost is President of their General-Councils, when the truth is, the odd man is still the Holy-Ghost.' Selden was rather an emancipated liberal than a high-souled patriot, though in his early reply to Grotius, *Mare Clausum* (printed in 1635), he interpreted the freedom of the seas in terms of 'Rule, Britannia'. The first article of his creed, if not anti-clericalism, was the contract between sovereign and people, but his understanding of that stopped far short of the Puritans'. While his profound knowledge of the common law was enlisted in the struggle to curb the prerogative, and he went to prison along with other parliamentary leaders, Selden was at times regarded, not without reason, as a friend of the court. 'The Parliament-men are as great Princes as any in the World, when whatsoever they please is Priviledge of Parliament.' Selden was too detached and judicial to be a partisan, and he withdrew from the public stage before Charles's execution. 'The wisest way for men in these times is to say nothing.' By temperament a scholar and man of the world, a martyr 'unto the fire *exclusive*', he served the difficult cause of rational moderation with energy and honesty. His latitudinarian position in the midst of warring parties is typified in the conflicting accounts of his death. According to one (Aubrey's), Selden dismissed a clergyman on being rebuked by his friend Hobbes for his feminine courage; according to another, he denied admission to Hobbes and received the ministrations of his friend Archbishop Ussher.

We have a further example of the difficulties of a moderate constitutionalist in Philip Hunton (1604?–82), a country parson who published *A Treatise of Monarchy* in 1643 and in 1657 became Provost of Cromwell's short-lived college at Durham. Hunton sees the English monarchy as fundamentally limited and mixed, a masterpiece, in fact, of architectural wisdom. There is an avowed gap in the chain of argument whenever the question of resistance comes up, since the frame of government provides no constituted judge of a monarch's excesses, which involve a private and moral rather than a legal verdict. (Seventeenth-century notions of a competent judge ranged from the Deity of King James and Hobbes to Lilburne's common jury.) Although nothing can justify violence against a king's person, his agents may be justly opposed by Parliament in the defence of its own rights and the community. Hunton ends by proposing concessions on both sides which, he optimistically thinks, would heal 'the wofull dissention of the Kingdome' and reunite the three estates. But Hunton's distinctive merit is not merely his lucid analysis of past and present theory, it is his prophetic recognition of the corporate character of sovereignty, in England 'the king in Parliament'. The tract was fittingly reprinted, twice, in 1689.

It was the misfortune of Sir Robert Filmer (d. 1653) to have his *Patriarcha: or The Natural Power of Kings* (1680) ridiculed by Locke and to be viewed thenceforth through a distorting lens. But he was, after Hobbes, the ablest defender of absolutism or rather, perhaps, the most acute critic of the logical bases of the democratic doctrines of freedom, popular sovereignty, the contract, in short, all merely man-made sanctions and natural rights. Apart from *Directions for Obedience to Governors* (1652), Filmer's best expositions of his ideas were given in critiques of other writers, Hunton (*The Anarchy of a Limited or Mixed Monarchy*, 1648), Aristotle (1652), and Hobbes, Milton, and Grotius (*Observations concerning the Original of Government*, 1652). Filmer sees democrats as the heirs of the temporal claims of the papacy: 'Monarchy hath bin crucified (as it were) between two Theeves, the Pope and the People.' The corner-stone of his own theory is the moral obligation of obedience. The State is the macrocosm of the family. All government is arbitrary; the only question is who shall exercise it, and God and scriptural history, reason and nature have once for all established the absolute monarch, the magnified *paterfamilias*, as the only real sovereign. No group has the moral authority of a sovereign, and representative government, strictly considered, is only a legal fiction. Naturally Filmer finds anarchy in Hunton's limited and mixed monarchy and in his final appeal to private judgement. Milton makes a king a tyrant or a mere executive of the law instead of the agent of equity, and makes 'the people' only 'the sounder and better part', the judge of that part being apparently the army. Naturally, too, Filmer admires Bodin and rejoices in Hobbes's view of the rights of sovereignty, but he deplores the artificial theory of an original state of nature and a contract.

What hope of compromise there was in ideas of constitutional monarchy became more and more unreal as tension increased, and only extreme views on both sides could win a hearing. Hobbes's *Elements of Law* was circulating in 1640, the year of the impeachment of Strafford and Laud.[1] In 1642, the year

---

[1] In an autobiographical Latin poem of 1672 the bold thinker and timorous man said that his mother's alarm over the Armada had brought on the twin birth of himself and fear. At Oxford (1603–8) Hobbes, like Bacon, did not enjoy the scholastic curriculum (though his psychology and ethics were to bear the marks of Aristotle's *Rhetoric*), and he found solace in maps and books of travel. He was forty or more when he chanced upon Euclid and fell in love with the method of demonstration. After leaving Magdalen Hall, Hobbes entered, as tutor and companion, upon a fortunate connexion with the Cavendish family which, with interludes (1629–30, 1641–53), lasted for the rest of his life. At some time between 1621 and 1626 he was a sort of philosophic secretary to Bacon. As a tutor Hobbes made three continental tours (1610, 1629–30, 1634–7). His modernist thinking was stimulated by intercourse with Galileo and with Father Mersenne, whose cell was

of the outbreak of war, the first Latin edition of *De Cive* was printed at Paris. In 1651, two years after the king's execution, came the much less cool and much more famous *Leviathan*. All three books were developments of the same central ideas. Some malicious contemporaries said that Hobbes's absolutist doctrine could be used to justify a Cromwell as well as a Stuart, and doubtless it could, though hardly in 1640 or even 1651. That the real menace was much larger than any immediate problem Hobbes's best critics in his own time discerned, whatever their partial misconceptions of the man and his thought. The apostle of absolute sovereignty—and of an absolute law of duty—may be called not only a father of both the *laissez-faire* and the totalitarian State but, in a still deeper and broader way, an author and symbol of the disintegrating individualism which has been as much as anything the definition of the modern world.

the nerve-centre of European philosophy, and Hobbes himself began 'to be numbered among the philosophers'. He led the royalist migration to Paris (1640) and lived there for eleven years, in renewed association with the French intellectuals. For a time he was mathematical tutor to Prince Charles. When Paris became uncomfortable for an anti-clerical, Hobbes returned to England (1651) and submitted to the government. After the Restoration his pregnant wit made him a favourite at court. In addition to the Cavendishes, Bacon, Mersenne, and Gassendi, Hobbes had many more or less close friends, such as Jonson, Lord Herbert, Petty, Hyde, Selden, members of Lord Falkland's circle, Sidney Godolphin, Waller, Davenant, Cowley, Dr. Harvey, Sir Kenelm Digby, and Aubrey. This last incomparable authority reports among other things that the philosopher was not drunk more than a hundred times in his long life, and that he was accustomed to shut himself up and sing for the good of his health. During his last twenty-five years Hobbes was embroiled, for the most part unhappily, in controversies with Bishop Bramhall, Seth Ward, John Wallis, and Boyle. He was in bad odour and, he thought, for a time in real danger on account of his religious opinions. Hobbes had begun his career with a translation of Thucydides (1629), and one of the tireless old man's latest works was a translation of Homer (1673–5). He died in 1679.

Hobbes had arrived at some of his main scientific notions in the 'Short Tract on First Principles' written probably in 1630 and certainly before 1636, but first printed in 1889. In 1641 he wrote *Objectiones* to Descartes's *Meditationes* which indicated the fundamental antithesis between the two chief thinkers of the age. The *Elements of Law, Natural and Politic*, after circulating in manuscript for ten years, was printed (1650) in imperfect form in two parts, *Human Nature* and *De Corpore Politico*. Hobbes's other principal works were: *De Cive*, 1642 (enlarged 1647; translated as *Philosophical Rudiments concerning Government and Society*, 1651); *Leviathan*, 1651 (Latin version, 1668); *De Corpore*, begun about 1642 and printed in 1655 (English version, *Elements of Philosophy, the first Section, concerning Body*, 1656); two replies to Bramhall, *Of Liberty and Necessity* (pirated 1654) and *Questions concerning Liberty, Necessity, and Chance* (1656), and a third published in *Tracts* (1682). *Behemoth*, on the causes of the civil war, was finished about 1668 and published in *Tracts* (1682); surreptitious editions had appeared in 1679.

Necessity—in the common if not the Hobbesian sense—compels us to postpone to the next chapter Hobbes's scientific and ethical thought, which deals with body or matter and with the human body, man. The third part of his *Summa* comprised the science of the artificial body politic. In its outlines Hobbes's political theory is or seems to be very lucid and yet, even on some central doctrines (not to mention assumptions and implications), it is not always easy to distinguish between what the philosopher meant and what early and modern critics have taken him to mean, and to attempt a brief summary is to draw out leviathan with a hook.

In the state of nature, when all men are roughly equal in ability and power, and self-preservation is the only law, they are, from a desire for gain, safety, or glory, perpetually at war, every man against every man. Every man has a right to everything, and force and fraud are the cardinal virtues, so that life is 'solitary, poore, nasty, brutish, and short'. Nothing, however, can be unjust, for 'Where there is no common Power, there is no Law: where no Law, no Injustice'. But nature and reason lead men, from self-interest, to seek peace and for the sake of peace to surrender natural rights by making a contract among themselves. Since self-interest, however, may dictate the breaking of covenants, there must be

some coërcive Power, to compell men equally to the performance of their Covenants, by the terrour of some punishment; greater than the benefit they expect by the breach of their Covenant; and to make good that Propriety, which by mutuall Contract men acquire, in recompence of the universall Right they abandon: and such power there is none before the erection of a Common-wealth.

Men's only way of attaining peace and security, therefore,

is, to conferr all their power and strength upon one Man, or upon one Assembly of men, that may reduce all their Wills, by plurality of voices, unto one Will: which is as much as to say, to appoint one Man, or Assembly of men, to bear their Person; and every one to own, and acknowledge himself to be Author of whatsoever he that so beareth their Person, shall Act, or cause to be Acted, in those things which concern the Common Peace and Safety; and therein to submit their Wills, every one to his Will, and their Judgments, to his Judgment. This is more than Consent, or Concord; it is a real Unity of them all, in one and the same Person, made by Covenant of every man with every man, in such manner, as if every man should say to every man, *I Authorize and give up my Right of Governing my self, to this Man, or to this Assembly of men, on this condition, that thou give up thy Right to him, and Authorize all his Actions in like manner.* This done, the Multitude so united in one Person, is called a COMMON-WEALTH, in Latine CIVITAS. This is the Generation of that great LEVIATHAN, or rather (to speak more reverently) of that *Mortal God*, to which we owe under the *Immortal God*, our peace and defence.

Having established his State (the case of conquest we may leave out), Hobbes proceeds to define the rights and obligations of sovereign and subjects. The basis of sovereignty is not divine right but mundane utility and security. The covenant by which men surrender their rights to the sovereign is made among themselves and not between them and him, so that they are the authors of all his actions and nothing that he does, however iniquitous in itself, can be called injustice or a breach of the covenant. While answerable to God, the sovereign cannot justly be opposed or called to account by his subjects. Nor may anyone resist him on the ground of a superior covenant with God, 'for there is no Covenant with God, but by mediation of some body that representeth Gods Person', and that is the sovereign, 'Gods Lieutenant'. The sovereign controls foreign policy, the means of peace and defence, the laws governing property, legislation, the judicature, the choice of administrative officers, rewards and punishments, censorship, in fact everything. If, says Hobbes, the notion had not prevailed in England that sovereign power was properly divided among the King, Lords, and Commons, there would have been no civil war. Since sovereign power is unlimited power (for otherwise the power imposing limitations would be sovereign), it follows that Hobbes cannot find much to say of the liberty of subjects. Their welfare depends upon the sovereign's recognition that it is bound up with his own. Although sovereignty comes originally from the people it never reverts to them, and the obligation of complete obedience lapses only when the sovereign becomes incapable of affording protection. It may be observed that the adoption of Hobbes's regular if perfunctory alternative, an assembly, would turn his absolute monarchy into a socialist State.

Hobbes's conception of sovereignty was born of a troubled time, and the war and its aftermath only intensified his passionate desire for peace and order. The measure of that desire is the measure of the sacrifices his theory entails. The sovereign power he creates 'is as great, as possibly men can be imagined to make it. And though of so unlimited a Power, men may fancy many evill consequences, yet the consequences of the want of it, which is perpetuall warre of every man against his neighbour, are much worşe.' Thus in the lines, and often between them, the apparently detached theorist issues a realistic invitation to unwind the thread of argument and consider how quickly, with the overthrow of central authority, civilization may revert to barbarous anarchy. Contemplation of chaos led Machiavelli to believe that only a despot could establish order, but that artificial order was a stepping-stone to his ideal of organic order, a republic on the Roman model. Hobbes begins with a kind of democracy, created by fear, in order to establish a despotism maintained by coercion. He does praise the moral virtues, and allows almost involuntary glimpses of some faith in human goodness, but normally he builds upon the egoistic passions, above all the desire for power, of the natural man, and these passions can be restrained only by the public sword. The philosopher who sees man as a mechanism must perforce create a greater machine to control him. Or, to put the case in another way, the philosopher who, like Augustine and Calvin, has little confidence in man's character and reason, has to create an absolute and arbitrary deity, a human one.

Hobbes's picture of the state of nature and the evolution of society and government was not offered too seriously as historical anthropology but as logical theory, 'an imaginary state', in the language of Stillingfleet's *Irenicum*, 'for better understanding the nature and obligation of Laws'. In politics Hobbes's method was a mixture of the deductive and the empirical. While parliamentary speakers and writers, and many royalists, constantly invoked history and custom in support of their first principles, Hobbes—after his early Aristotelian and Thucydidean period—was temperamentally and prudentially disinclined to take an historical view. When he did come to analyse the causes of the war in *Behemoth* (finished about 1668 and published in 1682), he showed more prejudiced acuteness than historical breadth and insight. Like the theocratic foe of his impious *Leviathan*, Richard Baxter, Hobbes abhorred the ideas of republican liberty nourished by the study of ancient history. He had translated Thucydides (1629) in order, he said, to show his fellow citizens the folly of democracy. 'And by reading of these Greek, and Latine Authors', he declares in *Leviathan*, with unwonted warmth of feeling,

men from their childhood have gotten a habit (under a false shew of Liberty,) of favouring tumults, and of licentious controlling the actions of their Soveraigns, and again of controlling those controllers, with the effusion of so much blood; as I think I may truly say, there was never any thing so deerly bought, as these Western parts have bought the learning of the Greek and Latine tongues.

Hobbes returns to the charge repeatedly in *Behemoth* and, since his censure of the intellectual deadness of Oxford and Cambridge is well known, it is of some interest to find him, especially in the later and less familiar book, making hostile acknowledgement of the rebellious ideas developed there: 'The Universities have been to this Nation, as the Wooden Horse was to the Trojans.' When he inveighs against admirers of the ancient republics Hobbes is doubtless thinking not only of the dissenting clergy whom he loathed but of such men as Milton (who is named in *Behemoth*, along with Salmasius, as an exponent of good Latin and ill reasoning) and Harrington.

Harrington, the historical student, remarked that 'Leviathan affirms the Politicks to be no ancienter then his Book *De Cive*'. Although Hobbes regarded himself as an independent pioneer, commentators have pointed out affinities and roots all the way back to Aristotle's *Rhetoric*. What made Hobbes such an original and formidable force was, first, the coherent clarity of his total philosophic design; secondly, the utilitarian, secular, and scientific spirit of his selective reinterpretation of old ideas, even the golden rule; and, thirdly, the relentless logic with which he broke through tradition in pushing principles to their conclusions. Like all parties and individuals, he professed to derive his doctrines from reason and Scripture (and he could quote the Bible as profusely and aptly as any Puritan), but much of the strongest opposition came from men whose appeal to the same complementary authorities was in the tradition of Christian humanism. Hobbes's view of the contract and of the State as an artificial construction, his complete subordination of the individual to the State (or, one might also say, his complete individualism), his equating (as it appeared) of justice and truth not with right reason but with *de facto* civil authority, his whole pragmatic and legalistic scale of values and

motives, all this was nearly as abhorrent to royalists as to
parliamentarians and republicans. Though Milton did not
join in the hue and cry, his widow told Aubrey that he had
disliked Hobbes and said that 'their interests and tenets did
run counter to each other'. The corner-stone of Christian
humanism was the 'true liberty' which Bramhall defined as
'the elective power of the rational will'; Hobbes's metaphysical
determinism, when he did not ignore it, was an inconvenient
factor in his own political thought, since it might have been
difficult to explain away the 'necessity' of the rebellion. On all
counts many men for generations shared Bramhall's vehement
opinion that Hobbes's doctrines were 'pernicious both to piety
and policy, and destructive to all relations of mankind, between
Prince and Subject, Father and Child, Master and Servant,
Husband and Wife; And that they who maintain them obsti-
nately, are fitter to live in hollow trees among wild beasts, than
in any Christian or political Society'. To mention only some
notable names which come into this book, there were, besides
Bramhall and Baxter, such diverse opponents of Hobbes's
political and ethical theory as Filmer and Harrington, Cudworth and Traherne—and of course Alexander Ross. But
Hobbes's impact upon the Restoration mind, and upon
European thought at large, is beyond our limits.

Two much-quoted items, however, emphasize an especially
provocative side of Hobbes's doctrine, his undisguised anti-
clericalism and what appeared to be disguised atheism. One is
Warburton's martial picture: 'The Philosopher of Malmsbury
was the Terror of the last Age, as Tindal and Collins are of this.
The Press sweat with Controversy: and every young Churchman militant would try his Arms in thundering upon Hobbes's
Steel Cap.' The other is Pepys's quietly impressive jotting of
3 September 1668: *Leviathan* 'is now mightily called for', and
the price has quadrupled, 'it being a book the Bishops will not
let be printed again'. A reader vaguely aware of Hobbes's
outlook may be surprised to find that half of *Leviathan*, and
parts of his other political works, are concerned with religious
and ecclesiastical matters. Yet it can be argued that the
problem of Church and State is really the central problem of
Hobbes's political philosophy. In his theory subjects are
excused from obedience to the sovereign only when 'obedience
is repugnant to the Lawes of God', and, since his view of that

exception differs widely from post-Reformation thought, he is bound to complete his survey of civil duty by showing what the laws of God are. He grants that the truths of faith are above the reason, and that that may be a sin which is not a crime; yet the kingdom of Christ is not of this world and, though Hobbes calmly decides what is necessary for salvation, it is this world that concerns him. For the individual, since thought is free, the question is one of outward conformity. The civil law is the public conscience and the measure of good and evil actions. In brief, as Selden put it (and as Henry Parker had been urging in his Erastian tracts), 'All is as the State pleases'. In Hobbes's words,

Temporall and Spirituall Government, are but two words brought into the world, to make men see double, and mistake their Lawfull Soveraign. . . . There is therefore no other Government in this life, neither of State, nor Religion, but Temporall; nor teaching of any doctrine, lawfull to any Subject, which the Governour both of the State, and of the Religion forbiddeth to be taught.

As for Hobbes's own religious opinions, he may have been a conforming atheist or a deist, or he may have regarded himself as a sufficiently good Christian, according to his own peculiar definition.

Whatever the storm raised by Hobbes's ideas, his intellectual powers were acknowledged by such hostile judges as Bramhall, Milton, and Harrington. While condemning his political theory, Harrington avowed his firm belief 'that Mr. Hobbs is, and will in future Ages be accounted the best Writer, at this day, in the World: And for his Treatises of Humane Nature, and of Liberty and Necessity, they are the greatest of New Lights, and those which I have followed and shall follow'. The root of Hobbes's style is of course his scientific and materialistic thought; his doctrines could hardly have assumed the vesture of Milton or Browne. No member of the Royal Society achieved a plainer, stronger, clearer texture of exposition and argument than Hobbes brought to perfection in *Leviathan*. In the last paragraphs of that book he indicates how deliberately he has avoided ornament and cultivated the bare, athletic, and often epigrammatically homely style of a rational man talking to men; at the same time he is a thinker preoccupied with the discrimination of meanings. For a man of his cool intelligence, irony is a potent weapon;

witness the Swiftian comparison of bees and ants with men, or the more than ironic exposure of the religious ' Kingdom of Darkness'. And we still enjoy the sight and sound of Hobbes's dichotomizing blade as it shears through layer after layer of illusory idealism:

The force of Words, being (as I have formerly noted) too weak to hold men to the performance of their Covenants; there are in mans nature, but two imaginable helps to strengthen it. And those are either a Feare of the consequence of breaking their word; or a Glory, or Pride in appearing not to need to breake it. This later is a Generosity too rarely found to be presumed on, especially in the pursuers of Wealth, Command, or sensuall Pleasure; which are the greatest part of Mankind. The Passion to be reckoned upon, is Fear; whereof there be two very generall Objects: one, The Power of Spirits Invisible; the other, The Power of those men they shall therein Offend. Of these two, though the former be the greater Power, yet the feare of the later is commonly the greater Feare.

If we grant that Hobbes's style was the easier of attainment because he was not burdened with a very complex or imaginative mind, we must grant also that he was not merely a thinking-machine, that his emotions, however seldom revealed, were deeply involved.

The Puritan revolution proceeded without taking as much account of Hobbes as he took of it. Whatever the force of economic factors, the mother of the movement, and of modern democracy, was the Reformation, with its evolving principles of free inquiry and the priesthood and equality of all believers. Its unacknowledged grandmother was Catholic, since farther back were the medieval principles of the popular origin of sovereignty, the contract between ruler and people, and the right of resistance or even of tyrannicide; and the third of these had lately been given a special prominence by such Jesuits as Cardinal Bellarmine, Mariana, and Robert Parsons. But the immediate background was the powerful re-expression of popular rights by the monarchist Huguenots and others who had the added impetus of Protestant individualism. The English Puritans of the seventeenth century, with their intense religious, millenarian, and iconoclastic zeal, their conviction of God's guidance of His chosen people, went far beyond their predecessors in both word and deed and in both religious and political spheres. The story in all its stages and aspects is much too complex to be simplified. The logical jurist Calvin could be quoted in support of submission to an absolutism like that of King James or Hobbes, and also in support of resistance on the part of the people's legal representatives (witness the plea of Milton's Samson that he had not rebelled as a mere private person), and of any individual's resistance to commands contrary to the law of God. The course of Protestant thought made these large exceptions stronger than the general rule. That development had been epitomized in the writings of John Knox and the result summed up in Buchanan's *De Jure Regni apud Scotos* (1579), a book odious to English royalists throughout the seventeenth century.

The period 1646-60, the second and more difficult phase of the revolution, witnessed the efforts of the victors, increasingly disunited by faction, sect, and theory, to decide what was to be done with the king, with Parliament, with the army, and with the Church, and to establish a working form of government. In the prolonged struggle between Parliament and the army, which may be roughly, but only roughly, equated with Presbyterianism and Independency, the old ideal of legality was kept alive chiefly by the Levellers. Colonel Pride delivered Cromwell from parliamentary opposition in 1648, and in 1653 the Lord, after a fashion, delivered him from Sir Henry Vane. But Presbyterian and parliamentary, royalist and Leveller theories were only drawn closer together and driven underground, and Vane, though he retired, was not subdued. To a chaotic nation ruled by force he offered the brief *Healing Question* (1656), a plea that men of goodwill should be assembled for the planning of a new constitution. The tract is a link between Leveller proposals and Milton's *Ready and Easy Way*.

Similarly the abolition of episcopacy and the Church of England, if it put an end to some troubles, introduced many others. Puritans hopelessly divided among themselves had to find new answers to insoluble questions both new and old. On the general problem of Church and State, logic and history suggested three possibilities: the direct or indirect subordination of civil to religious authority; the Erastian subordination of religious to civil authority; and the coexistence of civil and religious powers with separate jurisdictions. Here we touch upon the Puritan version of a paradox fundamental in Christian and Catholic thought from the gospels and Augustine to

Suarez, the instinct of people who live and think in religious terms to segregate the spiritual and the secular. There was a practical necessity for reconciling membership in the realm of grace with membership in the realm of nature and man, and the tendency both to fuse and to separate which appears in the Puritan espousal of business, Baconian science, and all kinds of progressive reform, is conspicuous in political thinking. Then, too, from 1640 onward, Puritans of all colours were compelled to face what had been the Anglican problem, the fact of Non-conformity, of aggressively antagonistic diversity. Was there to be a Presbyterian establishment without toleration for dissent, a Puritan national Church with limited or unlimited toleration, or entire liberty of conscience without an establishment?

The origins, motives, and problems of religious and political democracy were so complicated and so closely interwoven that it would need a volume of this size to outline the history of even the last third of our period, and to try in a few pages of a literary history to notice a few of the many writers, ideas, and parties which might be called representative is to suggest a set tableau of a simple pattern. In fact, not only was it a time of kaleidoscopic multiplicity, but the labels, platforms, and aline-ments of individuals and parties, while retaining a basic con-sistency, were continually shifting under the pressure of events. As a microcosmic individual illustration of the historian's diffi-culties, though happily not of the prevailing quality of political ethics, there is the career of the astute journalist, Marchamont Needham (whose newspaper, *Mercurius Politicus*, was officially censored by Milton at least from March 1651 to January 1652). Needham was a political Vicar of Bray who wrote in turn for Parliament, for the king, for the Commonwealth, and, long after 1660, for the government against Shaftesbury. Inciden-tally, two of his substantial works, *The Case of the Commonwealth* (1650) and *The Excellency of a Free State* (1656), Needham ran as editorial serials in his paper in 1650–1 and 1651–2.

The particular articles of Milton's political creed were in the main no more original than other men's, but, because of his personality, the course of his growth, and the nature and con-sistency of his first principles, the significance of his theory is greater than the sum of the parts. After his initial monarchism he was diverted to other problems, and the early stages of his political evolution can only be inferred. In the *Tenure of Kings*

and Magistrates (February 1649), following Buchanan and the
rest, Milton arrived at the doctrine of popular sovereignty and
the revocable contract between king and people. The *Tenure*
and *Eikonoklastes* (1649) were steps towards the thorough
republicanism which Milton maintained, in tones ranging from
exultation to despair, in the two *Defences* (1651, 1654) and
A Ready and Easy Way to Establish a Free Commonwealth (1660).
He shared the common attachment to a 'mixed' government,
but painful experience, his loss of faith in bishops, monarch,
Parliament, army, people, and even Cromwell, led him through
progressive modification of the relative power to be given to
the component parts of the mixture, so that he emerged with a
republic predominantly 'aristocratic', an oligarchy of the wise
and good. For the republican framework was only a means
towards the holy community which inspired the hopes of Milton
and other Puritans. And in his campaign on diverse fronts
Milton was the chief exponent of the dynamic idea of Christian
liberty inherited from Luther and Calvin and much enlarged
in the process of transmission, much enlarged, indeed, in the
process of Milton's own development. As he showed most fully
in the *Christian Doctrine*, Christian liberty meant, in brief, the
advance of the regenerate man from restrictive, external subjection under the Mosaic law to the positive, inward, and
voluntary freedom of service and self-direction attained through
faith in the gospel of Christ. The obvious revolutionary
impulses in that idea were manifested by a number of progressive thinkers, such as Milton and Roger Williams. For the
classically minded Milton, however, the aristocratic distinction
between regenerate and unregenerate coalesced with the aristocratic principle of ancient republicanism and Renaissance
humanism, so that he thought in rational and ethical as well
as in religious terms and saw the rule of the saints as the rule
of philosopher-kings. On the other hand, his thought was too
religious to permit of that segregation of the order of grace and
the order of nature which Williams and others accepted, and
that—reinforced by his deepening distrust of the mass of mankind—made it impossible for Milton to accompany radical
Puritans into complete democracy with its secular doctrine of
natural rights. But he did, especially in the *Treatise of Civil
Power in Ecclesiastical Causes* (1659), go a long way in upholding
the extreme Independent doctrine of complete freedom of

the Church and the private conscience from civil jurisdiction.

From 1640 onward a swarm of tracts made clear the strength and intelligence of the popular party and also, very quickly, the wide divergences of political and religious opinion within its ranks. During 1603–40 the battle had been waged for the authority of the common law and the curbing of the prerogative, but it could not stop there. The traditional 'high court of Parliament' was changing, half unconsciously, into the supreme law-maker. The theory of parliamentary sovereignty was first set forth by the bold and able Henry Parker, notably in his *Observations upon Some of His Majesty's Late Answers and Expresses* (1642). In the interest of public safety Parker not only endorsed the recall of authority delegated to the king, when that authority was abused, but went on to claim for Parliament the supreme and final interpretation of law, even an arbitrary power above the law. Among the many vigorous replies was Bishop Bramhall's *Serpent Salve* (1643). An influential Presbyterian statement of 1643 was Prynne's *Sovereign Power of Parliaments*, which, with the author's usual barrage of documentation, enforced a view similar to Parker's. But Presbyterianism, though now entering upon its period of predominance, was the rightist party of the revolution, and in the next few years it showed itself too intolerant in its religious policy, too *bourgeois* in its economics, too much attached to parliamentary power (and to the Scotch), and, finally, too royalist, to satisfy or control the liberal and progressive Independents and the radical Levellers.

The Presbyterian plan for regimented uniformity was soon disturbed by the five Independent divines who wished to continue their congregational practice, and whose plea, carried from the Westminster Assembly into print early in 1644, focused debate upon the first principles of toleration and liberty. The religious side of the controversy is noticed later in this book; on the political side it was no less significant. Roger Williams (1603/6–83), whose invincible individualism had been proved in New England, and such Levellers as Lilburne, Walwyn, and Overton, were predestined spokesmen for the political radicalism latent in the doctrine of Christian liberty and in the mode of thought, already observed, which permitted the segregation of the spiritual and the secular. It was to be expected that the idea of the priesthood and equality of believers, which had been strong enough to overthrow an ancient ecclesiastical hierarchy and establishment, should be extended to the civil sphere as well and to the complete separation of Church and State. But while that idea led Millenarians to the rule of the saints, and Milton to aristocratic republicanism, it led both the strongly religious Williams and the less religious Levellers to a thoroughly democratic and secular view of religious and political liberty and equality and the natural rights of the natural man. Such concepts as reason and the law of nature, which for men like Hooker and Bishop Bramhall were bulwarks of established authority, could be used by Williams, the Levellers, and Milton—as they could by Hobbes in his way—in their rational or religious hostility to custom and the dead weight of antiquitarian tradition. Williams, of course, is one of the few thinkers on record who have had the opportunity to put theory into practice.

The Levellers, a left wing or temporary ally of Independency, were the one genuinely democratic party which played an important part in the revolution. Their intellectual and literary strength was embodied in such men as the scholarly merchant, William Walwyn, an antinomian in whom critical rationalism was warmed by spiritual and humanitarian charity; the tough libertarian and satirist Richard Overton, whose 'mortalist' heresy gave him some kinship with Milton and more with Hobbes; and the army officer Edward Sexby, later notorious as a plotter against Cromwell and as the author of *Killing No Murder* (1657). But the popular and picturesque Leveller hero was the stalwart, fearless, and irrepressible Lieutenant-Colonel John Lilburne (1615?-57).[1] If Walwyn was the keen and ironic (and prolific) Socrates of the party, and Overton its Thomas Paine, Lilburne might be called a religious Wilkes-Mirabeau. His power came from the merits of his cause, his personality and challenging martyrdoms, and his journalistic gift for making abstract questions concrete and dramatic. 'With Coke's "Institutes" in his hand', says Sir Charles Firth,

---

[1] Lilburne, a younger son of a country gentleman, was apprenticed to a London draper. In 1638 he was severely punished for circulating such 'seditious' pamphlets as those of Bastwick and Prynne. He fought well in the parliamentary army, 1642-4, but refused to take the Covenant. Thenceforth, throughout a career punctuated by imprisonments, Lilburne battled for popular rights, and his own, against vested interest and authority. Unlike some of his Leveller associates, he had always been religious, and in his last years he became a Quaker.

'he was willing to tackle any tribunal.' The hold that 'Honest John' and 'Freeborn John' had over the public was shown in the petitions on his behalf and the demonstrations at more than one acquittal. It was said that his writings were quoted 'as statute law' in the army. Lilburne was the champion of the lower middle class against bishops, king, Lords, Commons, lawyers, Presbyterians, Independents, and Cromwell. He abhorred arbitrary power whether it was held by an individual or a group.

In opposition to the claims of king, Parliament, and army the Levellers stood for the supremacy of law, a written constitution, and the rights of man. During 1647 their adherents multiplied in and outside of the army. The army as a whole was at odds with Parliament, and the soldiers, already discontented over arrears in pay, grew more and more restive and suspicious while their generals as well as Parliament negotiated with the captive king and delayed the settlement of a constitution. One highlight in the picture is the army debates of 1647–9 between the 'grandees', Cromwell, Ireton, and others, and the Leveller 'agitators' or delegates who represented the rank and file of the army. In the discussion of the franchise, for example, Ireton spoke for the substantial classes, and vaguely anticipated Harrington, in his insistence upon a property qualification. And, though the individualistic Levellers had no quarrel with private property, Colonel Rainborough put the doctrine of natural rights into the famous statement that 'the poorest he that is in England hath a life to live, as the greatest he'. The Leveller platform, set forth with variations and qualifications in successive *Agreements of the People* (1647–9) and other documents, included manhood suffrage, biennial or annual Parliaments, re-apportionment of constituencies and other electoral changes, legal, judicial, and penal reforms, the abolition of commercial monopolies, the substitution for tithes and indirect taxes of a direct tax on real and personal property, the restoration of enclosed lands, free schools, maintenance for the poor and infirm, and of course liberty of conscience. Most of these proposals were destined to be adopted sooner or later. We may in fact wonder how the Levellers' appeals to reason and principle could arouse opposition; but we may remember that these democratic doctrinaires, being ahead of their time, did not always face the actualities of national dissension which Cromwell did see and had to meet. Also, the Levellers, after curing sores that Parliament had neglected or avoided, would have established a *laissez-faire* government with explicitly limited powers. Although the movement failed, its principles were to remain or reappear in English and American political thought. But we must turn to some less realistic programmes engendered in various quarters, in particular those of the 'True Levellers' or Diggers and of James Harrington.

In the sixteenth and seventeenth centuries manifold causes brought about a European revival of ancient utopian writings and gave birth to many new ones, from More's to the *Christianopolis* (1619) of J. V. Andreae and Campanella's *Civitas Solis* (1623). In revolutionary England, when so many imaginations were kindled by millenarian dreams, a great mass of political, social, religious, educational, and scientific literature was more or less utopian in spirit, even if it usually lacked an exotic costume. Before the revolutionary yeast had fermented two very different Utopias appeared, the strongly practical scheme of social reform incorporated in Burton's preface to his *Anatomy*, and the *New Atlantis* of Bacon, whose technological paradise had a setting of romantic geography and courtly pomp. Without unduly stretching the word 'utopian', we might include next the exuberant seventh Prolusion of Bacon's first great disciple, the young Milton. In 1641 the full-fledged Baconian, Samuel Hartlib, addressed his *Description of Macaria* to Parliament. Macaria was a kind of prismatic mirage which shone before the zealous projector to the end of his life. In that kingdom co-operative planning improves production, develops trade and plantations, and encourages medical research. As the titles of many of his tracts indicate, Hartlib wanted to reform everything, education, religion, husbandry, the Virginian silk-worm, and the commonwealth of bees. One bee that buzzed in his bonnet was the notion of a central clearing-house which would co-ordinate every branch of human activity, from odd jobs to matrimony. In connexion with Hartlib it may be observed that the influence of J. V. Andreae was felt in England at least through the work of his friends Comenius and John Durie, and in the educational and religious Utopia, *Nova Solyma* (1648), of Samuel Gott.

The evolution of political theory outlined in the preceding part of this chapter might be epitomized in two titles. The

sixteenth century ended with Thomas Floyd's *Picture of a
Perfect Commonwealth* (1600), which, as its large debt to Elyot's
Governor implies, was in the old humanistic tradition of the
ideal prince; and our period ends with *The Ready and Easy Way
to Establish a Free Commonwealth*, the bitterly disillusioned outcry
of the greatest of all the Christian humanists and utopian
idealists who had taken part in the revolution. But a significant
change in the scope of political thought became conspicuous
after the war and may be illustrated through two representative
and individually important figures, Gerrard Winstanley (1609–
post 1660) and James Harrington. Winstanley was the spokesman and, along with William Everard, the active leader of the
'True Levellers' who in 1649–50 tried to assert the rights of the
rural populace against the lords of the manors by tilling common ground in Surrey and elsewhere. The Digger movement
failed, but some of Winstanley's ideas were to be revived by
such men as Robert Owen and Henry George, and in recent
years he has been honoured as the champion of the forgotten
man. Magna Carta had been a victory for the barons, and in
the late civil war the middle classes had made good their
economic, political, and religious claims against the feudal,
royalist, and Anglican régime. The lower classes, however,
were not sharing the fruits of the revolution, and Winstanley
insistently proclaimed that fact. Like some contemporaries,
such as Lilburne, he dated economic, legal, and ecclesiastical
tyranny from the Norman conquest. In the dedication of *The
Law of Freedom in a Platform* (1652) he puts two alternatives
before Cromwell, either to 'set the Land free to the oppressed
Commoners, who assisted you, and payd the Army their wages',
or merely to 'remove the Conquerors Power out of the Kings
hand into other mens, maintaining the old Laws still'. If
Cromwell follows the latter course, then his wisdom and honour
are blasted for ever and he will either lose himself 'or lay the
Foundation of greater Slavery to posterity' than he ever knew.
Winstanley has been called Marxist in his economic reading of
history and the class war, but he would have preferred to be
placed in the long line of Christian communists who had
pleaded for the under-dog since the Middle Ages. Quiet, happy,
and unswerving obedience to the inner light led Winstanley,
not to private mystical ecstasies, but to humanitarian effort.
He was of course unrealistic in dreaming of a society rooted in

equality, reason, and brotherly love, not corrupted by property and the possessive instinct, and enjoying freedom of conscience and free practical education.

The proletarian and mystical Winstanley and the high-born and rational author of *Oceana* (1656) have some affinity in their emphasis upon economic and agrarian problems and the principle of rotation in public office.[1] Harrington is a feudal landowner with a touch of the Leveller and Digger about him, and a Renaissance amateur who has caught the spirit of the scientific lawgivers of his age and who in fact invokes the name of Harvey. He has the humanistic conception of the State as an organism like the individual man, with its passions similarly ruled by reason, an 'Empire of Lawes, and not of Men'; he seems to pay more than lip-service to the Christian view of a divine pattern for human society, and in his frequent appeals 'Unto God in the Fabrick of the Common-wealth of Israel' he evidently accepts the special authority of the Bible; yet he is commonly credited with a very secular outlook. As a hard-headed realist he writes in the inductive tradition of Bacon and especially Machiavelli, 'the onely Polititian of later Ages', 'the sole retreiver' of 'ancient Prudence'. Bacon and Machiavelli had harped upon a string which they had not perfectly tuned, 'the ballance of Dominion or Propriety'. Harrington's aim is to demonstrate the working of economic law, to analyse the economic dislocation which had caused the civil war, and, since the commonwealth is still in a plastic state, to provide an economic and political constitution which shall prevent

[1] James Harrington (1611–77) was the eldest son of Sir Sapcotes Harrington. In 1629 he entered Trinity College, Oxford, where he is said to have had Chillingworth as his tutor, but the period of instruction must have been brief. Harrington left without a degree, was admitted to the Middle Temple in 1631, and spent some time in foreign travel. His observations, especially in Holland and Venice, made him a political scientist and a republican. Except for his attendance upon Charles in the Scottish expedition of 1639 and during most of the king's captivity, Harrington led a private life. *Oceana* appeared in 1656 after being held up, it seems, by Cromwell, and quickly provoked controversy. Harrington actively reiterated his views in print and, during the winter of 1659–60, at the much publicized Rota Club. He even dragged his agrarian theory into translations of Virgil (1658–9). With the Restoration Harrington's status altered. Imprisonment (1661) caused both physical and mental derangement from which he never entirely recovered. Among the friends of his later years were Aubrey, Marvell, and Henry Neville, author of the Harringtonian *Plato Redivivus* (1681). The first collected edition of his works was that of the notable John Toland (1700), who had edited Milton's prose in 1698. Toland printed for the first time Harrington's most compact statement of his doctrine, *A System of Politics*.

such violent disturbances in the future. Like Hobbes, whose theories he opposes, Harrington is a master of clear logic and of a plain and sometimes lively style. But while Hobbes largely ignored history (except in *Behemoth*), Harrington, like Machiavelli and many men of his own time, used the historical method in combination with abstract principles. He draws constant examples from Roman and Greek history because his heart, like Machiavelli's, is in the ancient city-state, which he tries in countless ways to reproduce; the only modern government which approaches perfection is that of Venice. Whether his inspiration be philosophy or only tact, Harrington has his republic created by a strong man, 'Olphaus Megaletor', otherwise Cromwell. The imaginative title and framework of his Utopia, in addition to their protective value, unite romantic suggestions of fortunate isles with the imperialistic optimism of a citizen of a self-consciously maritime nation.

Harrington's most fundamental idea has already been touched upon. Ignoring the social contract employed by both republicans and royalists, he defines types of government not in purely political terms but according to the distribution of property among the several classes of people. For him, in his age, property consists chiefly in land, and one of the stable blessings of Oceana is its rural and agricultural economy. When the nobility and clergy possess most of the land, as they did in the Middle Ages, monarchy is possible. But the early Tudors imposed checks upon the old nobility and enabled the gentry and middle class to acquire land and grow strong, so that 'the dissolution of the late Monarchy was as natural as the death of a man'. Equality of estates causes equality of power, and equality of power means a commonwealth; a republican government is now the only kind which squares with economic facts. The main fact, the altered centre of economic gravity, Harrington was not the first to recognize, but he was the first thorough diagnostician. The constitution proposed in *Oceana* is to further and preserve the harmony achieved by organizing the political power of the natural aristocracy of country gentlemen. Thus Harrington was by no means a complete democrat; and, though he touched upon commercialism, his personal and historical instincts tied him to the land. However, what he understands as 'popular government' comes nearest to the interest of mankind, and the reason of popular government comes nearest to right reason. A perfect government is that which affords no cause or means of sedition, and a popular government alone satisfies that need. It rests on two principles, an agrarian law which ensures the perpetual distribution of land and prevents it from being inherited and accumulated by the few, and reform of the electoral and parliamentary system which keeps new blood circulating through the body politic. 'An equal Common-wealth', then, '. . . is a Government established upon an equall Agrarian, arising into the super-structures or three orders, the Senate debating and proposing, the people resolving, and the Magistracy executing by an equal Rotation through the suffrage of the people given by the Ballot.' When he comes to religion Harrington, like Hobbes, puts ecclesiastical laws in the power of the magistrate and sees in papal and Puritan claims the cause of endless disorder and war. Like Hobbes, too, he would have a national Church, since 'a Common-wealth is nothing else but the National Conscience'. His Church, however, is organized on a voluntary basis, with an elected (but learned) ministry, and he insists that liberty of conscience is bound up with civil liberty, though he would exclude Jews, papists, and idolaters from toleration.

While Harrington acquired supporters in Parliament and outside, both his theoretical and his practical ideas were vigorously attacked and satirized. Among his critics were Cromwell, Marchamont Needham, Dr. Henry Stubbe (who later assailed the Royal Society), the younger Matthew Wren, Richard Baxter in his *Holy Commonwealth* (1659), and Milton in the *Ready and Easy Way* (though Milton's aristocratic republicanism—and his view of Cromwell—had something in common with Harrington's). But Harrington's basic doctrines became generally accepted commonplaces; the roll of his admirers included Locke, Hume, and, in the nineteenth century, Coleridge and Wordsworth and the Utilitarians and Radicals. Yet his main influence, direct and indirect, was felt most strongly in the American colonies, first in leaders like Penn and in the constitutions of Carolina, New Jersey, and Pennsylvania, and then, more effectually, in the movement for independence and the formation of the union. Harrington's theory of the economic balance of power had led him to predict the American Revolution and, along with that inspiring prophecy, such men as John Adams made much of the property qualification,

written constitutions, a double-chamber system with checks
and balances, rotation of office, and the ballot. To the French
Revolution and its aftermath Harrington also contributed,
partly through his own writings and partly through English
and American applications of his doctrines. If *Oceana* is not
now one of the living classics, probably the essential reason is
that Harrington's Utopia is not only doctrinaire but somewhat
drab and dusty; he wrote, not unnaturally, with a passion for
external peace and order, but the greatest political thinkers have
had a broader, more positive, and more humane vision of life.

In no kind of writing of our period, naturally, does the clash
of old and new appear in such bold relief as in political thought.
Yet nowhere is the difference between old and new harder to
define, and both terms may be applied at once to the ideas and
the individual writers on all sides of the great controversial
questions. Of the many paradoxical phenomena of the age
the only one that can be emphasized here is the change,
accomplished in the course of a Puritan revolution, from a
religious to a secular view of the State and society. However
secular the outlook of men like Bacon, Selden, and Hobbes,
they had no great influence. The Bible was the common
source which linked together King James and Filmer, Milton
and all the Puritans, the millenarian and antinomian sects, the
more or less secular Harrington, and even Hobbes, who is in
his way the best of all proofs of the power of Scripture. But
though the ideals of Christian liberty and the holy community
provided the religious dynamic of the political revolution (and
had their most logical issue in Winstanley's religious communism), some Puritan parties stood for the complete separation of Church and State, and the most thoroughly democratic,
secular, and modern theories of government came not only from
the Levellers but from the intensely religious Roger Williams.

Finally, since this is a history of literature, it may be observed
that this large body of political writing, though it dealt so much
with abstract ideas, was mostly addressed to the middle classes
and displayed as a whole a steadily increasing power of popular
appeal. And though much of what was most effective has paid
for its effectiveness by dropping below our horizon, there
probably never was a period in English history when the
heterogeneous battalion of minor political authors wrote so
ably—and there again we may think of the Bible.

IX

SCIENCE AND SCIENTIFIC THOUGHT

ALTHOUGH science had been advancing steadily for many centuries, we think of the seventeenth as having given birth to the modern world. And in that age Englishmen made even larger contributions to the European movement than they had in the period from 1200 to 1600. The greatest single discovery, that of William Harvey (1578–1657), was described in lectures in the year of Shakespeare's death and in print in 1628. The result of his revolutionary demonstration was, he told Aubrey, 'that he fell mightily in his practize, and that 'twas beleeved by the vulgar that he was crack-brained; and all the physitians were against his opinion, and envyed him'. However, as his friend Hobbes said, he lived to see his doctrine established. While Harvey's chief debt was to continental anatomists, in mathematics and astronomy Englishmen of the seventeenth century had behind them the distinguished work of Recorde, Dee, Thomas Digges, and William Gilbert (1540–1603). Gilbert's *De Magnete* (1600) laid a solidly scientific foundation, and more than a foundation, for the study of magnetism and electricity. He looked back to the thirteenth-century Petrus Peregrinus and, in his conception of the earth as a great magnet, looked forward to Newton. Thomas Harriot (1560–1621), the friend of Ralegh and the scientific sun of a notable circle, was an eminent mathematician and made telescopic observations contemporaneously with Galileo. John Napier's invention of logarithms (1614), in the famous phrase of Laplace, doubled the lifetime of astronomers. From the end of the sixteenth century onward Gresham College was a centre of practical and theoretical science. The two universities, whose scholastic darkness drew complaints from Bacon, Milton, Hobbes, and many lesser men, produced, if they seldom trained, a multitude of mathematicians and scientists. Among them, to add some more names, were Edward Wright, Henry Briggs, William Oughtred, Edmund Gunter, John Pell, and Jeremiah Horrocks. The Savilian professorships in geometry and astronomy, founded at Oxford in 1619, provided a stimulating current, and with the arrival thirty years later of her own John Wilkins and some illustrious Cantabrigians, for once Oxford became, involuntarily, the home of a winning cause. Throughout our period English and continental men of science followed one another's work closely, and between some there was personal acquaintance or correspondence.

These are only a few out of the scores of scientists who, in England as in Europe at large, made the seventeenth century one of unparalleled achievement. From being a cultural outcast science became a respectable and finally a dominant interest which attracted hosts of amateurs, including aristocrats and obscure business men. Ralegh, Bacon, and, when he first turned to science, Sir Kenelm Digby, were relatively isolated figures; by the time of Evelyn science was a major preoccupation of the virtuoso. The most various causes contributed to the scientific movement: the accident of genius; the critical impetus and the body of new knowledge inherited from the sixteenth century; Bacon's eloquent and timely propagation of new ideals; the middle-class and Puritan reaction against traditional academic learning and in favour of useful studies; the general Protestant approval of scientific research for the glory of God and the service of man; the popular appeal of experiment and invention to both utility and curiosity; and the pressure of countless technological problems created by the growth of an urban population, of industry and manufacturing, of domestic and foreign commerce and transportation. The debt of navigators to science, for example, received quaint acknowledgement from Captain Luke Fox, who named some north-western islands, after his friend and patron, 'Brigges his Mathematickes'.

Along with this great forward movement in the sciences, and sometimes represented by the same persons, we have the old pseudo-sciences which, with or without the help of occult mysticism, were flourishing with unabated vigour. Sufficient reminders of this often murky penumbra of science are the names of Robert Fludd (1574–1637), William Lilly (1602–81), Nicholas Culpeper (1616–64), Elias Ashmole (1617–92), and Thomas Vaughan (1621/2–66). Judicial astrology was repeatedly attacked and defended. Critical minds from Ralegh and Bacon onward, even if they dismissed vulgar notions of astrology, could retain some belief in the influence of the stars. Medicine, biology, and chemistry were still more or less mixed with astrology, fantastic pharmacology (the royal touch retained its virtue far beyond our period), animism, and alchemy. Ancient or Paracelsian notions of primary elements and principles, and the qualitative conception of matter, stood in the way of scientific analysis, though experiment and 'Hooke's microscope' were soon to sweep away many cobwebs. Since Bacon is so often made the scapegoat of credulity, we may remember that Gilbert, Kepler, Descartes, and others were not immune from unscientific ideas. Boyle, for instance, stopped the bleeding of his nose with 'some moss of a dead man's skull'. After Harvey's, doubtless the most celebrated if not the most valuable medical discovery was Sir Kenelm Digby's 'powder of sympathy'; its miraculous efficacy was first publicly proclaimed in 1658. That versatile dilettante showed his really scientific capacity in his treatise on bodies (1644) and his lecture to the Royal Society on the vegetation of plants (1661). In general, the mixture of the fabulous or occult with the scientific was in part a natural legacy from medieval science, in part it was sustained by the persistent conviction, rational or mystical, of the unity between God and all His works.

In the sixteenth and seventeenth centuries, while science was extending man's knowledge of nature and the heavens more rapidly and radically than exploration had been extending his knowledge of the globe, there ran, side by side with enthusiastic optimism, a deep current of disillusionment. One early and long-lived manifesto of 'obscurantism' was Agrippa's *De Incertitudine et Vanitate Scientiarum et Artium atque Excellentia Verbi Dei* (1530). Bacon, in a defence of learning which was by no means otiose, put first 'the zeale and jealousie of Divines', and he constantly sought to guard himself and science against the charge of atheism. (On the other hand, it was a not insignificant fact that many English men of science were clerics.) In all ages any ray of scientific light may alter the focus of religious and humanistic vision, or enlarge the area of enveloping darkness, and in the seventeenth century the most disturbing light was astronomical. New observations and deductions, combined with old and new speculations, slowly effected a great change in the traditional picture of the universe and of man's place in it; some of the various literary repercussions we have met already.

The subject is difficult to handle briefly, since in recent years no part of the background of English literature has been more

fully investigated; our attention shall be given primarily to three
men who are conspicuously great writers. Bacon, though he
touched everything, may represent study of the outer world,
Burton study of the inner, and Hobbes a new and alarming
approach to both. Sir Thomas Browne, though a genuine
scientist and perhaps for many of us the supreme writer, must
here realize, in a sense, his modest ambition 'to be but the last
man, and bring up the Rere in Heaven'.

I

While Bacon has always occupied a throne, the extent of his
realm and authority has been subject to many mutations. He
outshines the normal scientific recluse by virtue of his literary,
legal, and political eminence, the dramatic quality of his
career, and the real or apparent puzzles in his character which
have attracted so many biographers. Then when we look at the
philosopher and his monumental collected works Bacon seems
to bestride his age like a Colossus. Standing between the
medieval and the modern world, he pointed along the road
civilization was to take in the following centuries. His scientific
ideals had been proclaimed and practised by other Englishmen, of whom Gilbert was the most influential, but they did not
stand in the Baconian pulpit under the Baconian sounding-
board. If he himself was the father of no important specific
contributions to science, he was the godfather of many, and his
strictly scientific thought has more significance than the conventional estimate allows.

While Bacon's predominant passion was natural science, he
was a man of the Renaissance who, unlike many of his critics,
never lost sight of the whole range of knowledge. *The Advancement of Learning* (1605) is the most attractive of his philosophic
works because it is the most broadly comprehensive and humane,
because its strength and vision are least impaired by dead technicalities, and because it is, with the *Essays*, the great example
of his English prose. The other major work, the *Novum Organum*
(1620), though confined to the philosophy and methods of
science, embodies, like the *Advancement*, a criticism of the past
and a programme for the future, and we may consider Bacon's
ideas under these two headings rather than in relation to particular books or to his own elaborate classification of knowledge.
The *Instauratio Magna*, as he outlined it in the *Distributio Operis*

prefixed to the *Novum Organum*, was to comprise six parts. The first was fulfilled with relative adequacy in *De Augmentis Scientiarum* (1623), the enlarged Latin version of the *Advancement*. The *Novum Organum*, though incomplete, represents the second part, which was to teach the right method of investigating nature, a combination of the empirical and the rational; the title was a challenge to the Aristotelian tradition. For the rest we turn from torsos to *disjecta membra*. In the third part, which includes the natural histories and the *Sylva Sylvarum*, observations of natural phenomena were to be assembled as material for the new method of study. The fourth part, represented by a preface, was to give examples of its operation. In the fifth part, again represented by a preface, Bacon intended to report what he had himself discovered by more conventional methods, without the help of his special induction. This fifth part would lose its value with the completion of the sixth, which was to expound the new philosophy and methodology in full and describe the results of its application to all the natural phenomena of the universe. The fulfilment of this part Bacon left to posterity. Thus the *Instauratio Magna* is linked with *The Fairy Queen* and *The History of the World* as the partial accomplishment of an impossibly vast design.

As a destructive critic, a mouthpiece for the modern world's declaration of independence, Bacon has only one rival, Descartes (1596–1650), and Bacon, in addition to his priority, is more compendious and arresting. The *loci classici* are, next to the *Essays*, probably the best-known parts of Bacon's writings. The first is the discussion, in the first book of the *Advancement*, of the three principal vanities or distempers of learning (along with a series of 'peccant humours'). Bacon arraigns in turn the rhetorical discipline of medieval and Renaissance humanism, the study of words instead of matter; the medieval scholastic discipline, still dominant in the universities, which has also ignored nature and kept mankind in a desert of barren rationalism; and, thirdly, fallacious pseudo-sciences like astrology and alchemy. Then in the first book of the *Novum Organum* Bacon classifies the four kinds of 'idols' which colour what ought to be the dry light of the scientific mind and interfere with the true investigation of nature. Idols of the tribe are the erroneous modes of thought and feeling instinctive in the human race; idols of the cave arise from an individual's temperament and background; idols of the market-place from the loose language of common intercourse, which perpetuates traditional errors; and idols of the theatre from false systems of philosophy and wrong demonstrations. These categories are not entirely distinct; one notion, or one person, might appear in them all. Bacon is always a great phrase-maker, but here he is something more. His analysis of the permanent sources of uncritical credulity may now seem simple, and historically it was novel in its philosophic breadth rather than in its particular ideas, yet it is a landmark in the intellectual development of mankind, and to the individual reader in any age it gives that sense of illumination and growth which is the proof of great writing.

Like most men, Bacon is more vulnerable in his plans for the future than in his criticism of the past. We have been made so familiar with his defects that it might be idle to rehearse the common charges against him, however valid some of them are, if the case of Bacon did not, *mutatis mutandis*, illustrate that of many other philosophic minds of his 'crepuscular' age. In the first place he did not recognize the degree to which his own mind was affected (not wholly for ill) by the several 'distempers' of learning. Without the rhetorical tradition Bacon's prose would not be the powerful instrument it is; rhetorical and scholastic ways of thought lie behind his dream of a scientific *Summa* and run through his terminology and technique; and, finally, he was not untouched by the pseudo-scientific attitudes he condemned. In the *Novum Organum* Bacon is inspired by such sublime confidence in the novelty and rightness of his ends and methods that he drives his triumphal chariot forward over all Aristotelians and others (including Gilbert) who stand in his way, yet many illustrations for his idols can be found in his own writings, the natural histories in particular. However, as we have seen, most leaders of science retained uncritical notions along with their scientific obedience to observed fact, and in this age it was both inevitable and wise that the body of traditional lore should be preserved until it could be properly sifted.

In the second place Bacon did not know enough. We should never guess from his survey of knowledge that the preceding century had witnessed a scientific advance on all fronts. In medicine, for instance, he either did not know or did not appreciate the work of his personal physician, Harvey; Harvey was not unaware of the Lord Chancellor's philosophy. In astronomy Bacon was intelligent enough to criticize existing theories and ignorant enough to accept a pre-Aristotelian idea of spiral motion revived by Telesio. Yet he can hardly be blamed for his hostility to the Copernican hypothesis; even in later years a choice among the three major cosmological patterns, Ptolemaic, Copernican, and Tychonic, might be difficult not only for non-mathematical laymen but for a mathematician like Pascal. Here we approach a realm which Descartes ruled but which was *terra incognita* on Bacon's intellectual map; in some other realms superiority is reversed. An Aristotelian by the accident of training if not by inclination, Bacon missed that Platonic mathematical tradition which was such a fertilizing current in Renaissance thought. Besides, the deductive character of mathematics was repugnant to him. These are only a few items from the list of his blind spots, a list which would provide a fair set of topics for a history of science in the Middle Ages and Renaissance. But we should not forget that if Bacon had never read or written a word of natural philosophy, his achievements in other fields, from literature to the law of equity, would have made him a great figure, and we who find disparagement so easy appear beside him as anaemic pygmies.

Thirdly, there are the weaknesses of the inductive method which was to revolutionize civilization. The method starts from Bacon's doctrine of 'forms' and 'simple natures'. Simple natures are the relatively few physical properties, heat, colour, and the like, possessed by the heterogeneous bodies which make up the natural world. Behind each simple nature is a more generic form, residing in the constituent elements of bodies; and the discovery of these fundamental forms, the learning of the alphabet of nature, is the great end of science. As for the method, Bacon rejects deduction and 'simple enumeration' of affirmatives. To discover the form of heat he first assembles tables of positive, negative, and variable examples. The problem then is to find such a nature as is always present or absent with heat, always increases or decreases with it, and is a particular case of a more general nature. By progressive elimination of false alternatives from his tables Bacon arrives at the one remaining *sine qua non* which must be the form desired, that is, motion. The more difficult part of the inductive process, the establishment of exact scientific criteria for the method of exclusions, he recognized but never described. In general, he is not always clear or explicit and, since his views changed on some points, not altogether consistent. The experimental method in itself was of course very old and Bacon's elaborate superstructure, it is customary to say, was to prove more significant in the history of inductive logic than in the history of science, and was not of much value for Bacon's own end, the discovery of forms. Modern philosophic critics stress the fallacious ideas of card-indexing all nature, of uncontrolled experimentation, of co-operative research which can be carried out by mechanical industry and leaves no room for individual inspirations, inspirations, moreover, which have generally sprung from a very few experiments or even deductions. But many working scientists of Bacon's century, like Robert Hooke, praised the intellectual 'Engine' of 'the incomparable Verulam', and thought, as some men of science do now, that he had made a notable statement of the principles of scientific method. The reading of his works is enough to qualify the conventional charges. Bacon does not ignore hypothesis, for example, in the 'First Vintage concerning the Form of Heat' (his imaginative labels reveal both the scholastic and the poet), and elsewhere he frequently suggests experiments for the testing of hypotheses. And these facts with others—such as his consciousness that his method must be perfected as discovery advanced, or his very effort to guard the scientific mind from idols—imply allowance for the work of individual genius.

Blanket dismissals of Bacon's positive scientific thought are in part the result of misplaced emphasis, in part they are reactions against the panegyrical tradition of the French Encyclopaedists, Macaulay, and other laymen, and in part they are inherited from an age which accepted a strictly mechanical and materialistic view of the universe as the *ne plus ultra* of scientific philosophy. Tried, rather hastily, by this standard, Bacon seemed to belong to another world than Galileo and Descartes and to deserve banishment to the medieval lumber-room. More recent scientific thought has retreated, or advanced, from that mechanical absolutism, and some eminent philosophers of our time, including Whitehead, who have given Bacon serious and unprejudiced study, treat him with respect. This renewed but more intelligent admiration does not rest merely on the innumerable soundly scientific precepts scattered through Bacon's works, but rather on the scientifically prophetic penetration exhibited in his doctrine of forms and simple natures. The conception is not nullified by errors in the inductive method. A form is both an essence and a structural law, the mechanical condition or means of producing the physical property. Hence to discover forms is to understand the unity underlying diverse aspects of matter and also to have the power of intelligently producing the simple natures corresponding to the forms. Then by different combinations of simple natures, based on a knowledge of forms and latent structure, the scientist can transmute one substance into another, can ultimately control all the phenomena of nature. Bacon condemns the theories and methods of the alchemists but not their object, and modern science, with truer knowledge, has gone far in the same direction. If, as some writers say, the control of phenomenal recurrence is the only concern, the very definition, of the scientist, Bacon, whatever his particular shortcomings, is one of the pioneers of modernism. Further, as these summary remarks have indicated, Bacon represents a transitional phase of escape from the medieval qualitative conception of matter, and from the teleological animism of Renaissance thinkers, to something like the kinematical view. At the same time, whether from 'Aristotelian' insight or want of mathematical capacity, he generally stops short of the chief pitfall of 'classical' mechanism, the identification of reality with a kinematical pattern. If Bacon is not altogether in the direct line which leads from Kepler and Galileo to Newton, he is, by his fusion of a limited mechanism with dynamism, a link between Campanella and Leibniz.

Bacon is not, then, historically negligible as a scientific thinker, but his great claims upon us are more familiar. His scientific deficiencies did not essentially weaken the force of his message for his time, the substitution of humble, critical interrogation of nature for the arbitrary concepts of traditional authority, abstract reason, and the unaided senses. It was not an insignificant thing that a great lawyer, judge, and statesman should take up the cause of natural science, and Bacon did more than any other individual except Descartes to create a favourable intellectual climate. He not only summoned men to research, he brought the Cinderella of science out of her partial obscurity and enthroned her as the queen of the world. No one any longer could be deaf to the scientific and humanitarian gospel of experiment, invention, utility, and progress. The traditional view of human history was static or deteriorationist; Bacon made it dynamic and optimistic. He transferred the Golden Age from the mythical infancy of man to an attainable future. He was the chorus of the scientific drama, the Moses, in Cowley's great image, who led his people to the edge of the promised land. If we say that such changes would have occurred without Bacon, we must say also that the discoveries of Galileo and Newton would have been made if those men had never lived.

And the office of spokesman required gifts no less distinctive than the practical discoverer's. The works of Gilbert and Harvey, if we read them, may make some of Bacon's technical discussions look immature, but to whom other than Bacon can we go for a comparable synthesis of the forces and motives which were changing the character of civilization? His voice, moreover, would have lost much of its power if he had not been one of the great masters of the language whose permanence he doubted. His deliberate aim, set forth in the *Parasceve* and elsewhere, Dr. Rawley summed up when he said that Bacon 'did rather drive, at a Masculine, and clear, Expression, than at any Finenes, or Affectation, of Phrases'. Happily Bacon's conception of scientific and philosophic prose did not run to drab bareness. He was able to combine the homely and pithy stock of pure English idiom and diction with the pointed pregnancy of Tacitus, without losing the massive dignity of the Ciceronian period. His virtues are not of course a mere matter of word and rhythm. Shelley, who manifested his devotion from *The Necessity of Atheism* to *The Triumph of Life*, coupled Bacon and Plato as poet-philosophers, citing especially the *Filum Labyrinthi* and the essay 'Of Death'; and he might have added such passages as the conclusion of the first book of the *Advancement*. Bacon is a scholar and a poet, a thinker and a wit, a realist and a dreamer. His noble eulogies of learning and the quest of truth, his infinite faith in the power of man, his vision of a new era and of himself as the torch-bearer, these things still quicken even the unsympathetic reader's pulse.

We may be unsympathetic because three centuries of progress

have made it clear that the conquest of external nature is an inadequate goal, that, as Shelley said in one of his un-Baconian moods, 'man, having enslaved the elements, remains himself a slave'. Not that Bacon contemplated such an end. 'Only let the human race recover that right over nature which belongs to it by divine bequest, and let power be given it; the exercise thereof will be governed by sound reason and true religion.' Such words fall on our ear as a piece of tragic irony. But if scientific power was to override the assumed safeguards, Bacon himself cannot be cleared of all responsibility. His separation of the realms of knowledge and faith, and of external and internal morality, was all the more damaging for not being cynical. His personal religion, whatever its limitations, inspired some beautiful and sincere utterances, and he would have been shocked at a hint that he was less than a good Christian, but the whole drift of his scientific and ethical thought was towards empirical, irreligious naturalism. He wished, with a reverent acknowledgement of faith, to exclude theological and intuitional idols from the temple of science, and in doing so he virtually denied the validity of a religious view of the world. If religion was outside the sphere of knowledge, it was outside the sphere of reality. Thus, while not condemning inquiry into first causes, Bacon left such problems to be settled by revelation and applied himself to the study of things. To machinery and material progress he sacrificed, in a large and noble way, to be sure, that scale of spiritual and ethical values which the best minds of antiquity, the Middle Ages, and the Renaissance had striven to make prevail. He not only brought philosophy down to earth, he confined it within the four walls of a laboratory in which Plato and Aquinas, and Shakespeare and Milton, would have suffocated. That is why, though we recognize Bacon's intellectual power and our vast debt to him, we do not go back to his works for vital nourishment.

2

Bacon's successors and disciples, however, had no such feeling. His eloquent statement of the claims and methods of experimental science received the praises not merely of his own countrymen but of continental thinkers and scientists from Descartes, Mersenne, and Gassendi to Huygens, Leibniz, and

Vico. Bacon did 'ring a bell to call other wits together', and the bell was heard outside the domain of science. Within that domain we can notice only two illustrations of his influence. The first is the birth of what in 1662 became the Royal Society. Co-operative research, one of Bacon's feasible dreams, had its most sumptuously imaginative, and staggering, presentation in *The New Atlantis* (1627). Apart from general tributes to Bacon, before and after the formal inception of the Society, we have the familiar testimony of such men as Cowley, Sprat, Glanvill, Wallis, and Oldenburg to the potent inspiration of the Baconian ideal. The Society may be said to have been born in or about 1645, during the war, with the meetings at Gresham College of a group of professional and amateur scientists interested in experiment; divinity, state affairs, and news were barred from discussion. But 1645 is a nominal date, since these meetings grew out of the earlier activities of the scientific professors of Gresham College; they for years had been co-operating with one another and with men concerned in practical and especially nautical enterprise, and when Bacon's influence was felt, it furnished a grandiose sanction for a movement already vigorous and fruitful. With the migration of some leading members to Oxford (1648 ff.), the centre of gravity shifted. At Oxford the group developed in numbers, organization, and éclat. Including the ex-Londoners and new members, there were John Wilkins, John Wallis, Jonathan Goddard, William Petty, Robert Boyle, Seth Ward, Robert Hooke, Thomas Willis, Lawrence Rooke, Christopher Wren, and others. It was a constellation of varied scientific genius. By 1660 the centre of gravity had moved back to London and Gresham College, and towards the end of that year the Society was formally established.

The Society was a concrete symptom not only of the rising spirit of scientific inquiry but of the practical ideals of an especially Puritan middle class conscious of the new needs of a new world, ideals which were finding simultaneous expression in pamphlets on educational reform. Most of the ten original members of the London group whom we know—Wilkins, Wallis, Goddard, and others—were moderate Puritans and parliamentarians. Theodore Haak, whom Wallis later credited with having suggested the London meetings, was employed by the Westminster Assembly. Wallis was a secretary to the Assembly, and, as Hobbes did not fail to remind him after the Restoration, used his mathematical skill in deciphering royalist code-messages during the civil war. Wilkins, Wallis, Ward, Petty, and Goddard were appointed by Parliament, during the years of Independent domination, to administrative or professorial posts at Oxford (1648–51). Even the Royal Society of 1662 had a strong Puritan tinge. There were general affinities between Baconian science and rational Puritanism: impatience of traditional authority and useless learning; the critical and empirical instinct; the ideal of action rather than contemplation; belief in utility, progress, and reform, in the study of God's creation and in 'works' as a religious and humanitarian duty and pleasure; and—what is not really inconsistent with that—the disposition to segregate the religious and the secular, the divine and the 'natural'. The minutes of the Royal Society amply attest its utilitarian consciousness of the multiplying technological and economic problems of an age of expansion. It goes without saying that this active Puritan and middle-class sympathy with science contained no suspicion of the irreligious philosophy associated with Hobbes. And, lest this paragraph seem to say too much, it may be added that not all scientists were Puritans.

As a lively and literary representative of the manifold interests of the Royal Society we may take John Wilkins (1614–72), probably the chief moving spirit in its development.[1] His first book (1638) was one of the seventeenth century's numerous speculations regarding the moon as an inhabited globe; the notion of a plurality of worlds had been in men's minds since antiquity, but it gained new life with the new astronomy. In the preface Wilkins twice invoked the learned and judicious Verulam as the champion of observed fact against ancient authority. For particular ideas, though he was well read in the literature of astronomy, he was especially indebted to Cam-

---

[1] Wilkins was a grandson of the noted Puritan divine, John Dod, and was educated in the strongly Puritan Magdalen Hall. After a few years as an Oxford tutor and country vicar, he held several chaplaincies. In 1648 he was made Warden of Wadham College, in place of an ejected royalist. In the Oxford phase of the Royal Society's growth Wilkins's enthusiastic leadership was the prime factor. In 1656 he married Cromwell's sister. In 1659 he was appointed Master of Trinity College, Cambridge. On losing this post shortly after the Restoration, Wilkins achieved a second and ecclesiastical career which ended with the bishopric of Chester (1668–72). He was a friend of Whichcote and other Cambridge Platonists, and of Evelyn. He died 'ready for the Great Experiment'.

panella's *Apologia pro Galileo.* In his *Discourse concerning a New Planet* (1640) Wilkins was replying in part to the stout Aristotelian 'fundamentalist' of the age, Alexander Ross, who in a life of multifarious controversy made up in thunder what he lacked in lightning. Whatever Wilkins's deficiencies, by modern standards, he did more than any other Englishman of his time to popularize the Copernican doctrine, and perhaps did something to undermine the scientific authority of Scripture. We cannot follow his many ideas, original or borrowed, which include mechanics and microscopy, a chariot for flying to the moon and 'an Ark for submarine Navigations', but even this meagre notice may serve to register the new type of curious, forward-looking, scientific amateur and also the spirit of cooperative inquiry which drew such men together.

Wilkins's *Ecclesiastes* (1646) was one of the signposts in the history of plain preaching, and we must mention his *Essay towards a Real Character and a Philosophical Language* (1668), which was sponsored by the Royal Society. In the preceding twenty years many other scientific men had been interested in creating a medium of communication free from the defects and difficulties of Latin and other existing languages and from the cloudiness of traditional terminology. This preoccupation with a universal language resulted, like the modern campaign for Basic English, from the growing consciousness of the dangerous ambiguities latent in words, in the idols of the market-place and theatre, and from the desire for a vocabulary which would designate things with the accuracy needed for experimental and mathematical science. (We find after the Restoration the belief that vague and metaphorical language contributed to sectarian divisions; and the Cambridge Platonists were censured by a Baconian bishop for dealing in nothing but words.) With such ideas and motives scientists from Bacon onward sought plainness of expression, and the strong bare style of Hobbes was the inevitable and climactic instrument of mechanical materialism. Science was, to be sure, only one of many large forces at work. We must reckon with the general advance of rationalism, the growth of the middle-class public and of utilitarian writing, Puritanism and the Bible and religious and political controversy, and, within the province of style, the anti-Ciceronian movement and the neoclassical consciousness of Elizabethan aberrations.

3

Our other example of Bacon's influence, if not of baldly scientific prose, is *Pseudodoxia Epidemica* (1646), commonly known as *Vulgar Errors*, though the errors scrutinized were not merely vulgar. Sir Thomas Browne (1605–82) was still more curious, versatile, and learned than Wilkins, but he looked backward and upward more often than forward.[1] One link with Wilkins is the fact that Browne's first two books were successively opposed by Alexander Ross. Since the Romantic Age the *Pseudodoxia* has acquired a reputation not in accord with the author's design or with the respect in which he was held by his scientific contemporaries. In the seventeenth century as in other periods we find critical and uncritical attitudes side by side and often in the same person, but there is a difference between mere compilations of the marvellous intended to entertain or edify and the cautious sifting of traditional lore. Bacon had repeatedly desiderated, and attempted to supply, 'a Kalender of popular Errors . . . chiefly, in naturall Historie', and Browne's book was a scientific treatise addressed to the learned and challenging 'the Goliah and Giant of Authority'. His introductory chapters, however loose and antiquarian in comparison with Bacon's dynamic analysis, may be called a restatement of the Baconian idols, a protest against credulous and passive acceptance of tradition. If we are conscious of passing from Bacon

---

[1] Browne was born in London and educated at Winchester (1616–23) and Oxford (1623–9). After a brief period of professional work he continued his medical studies at Montpellier, Padua, and Leyden (1631?–34?). For a time he lived in Yorkshire, where he wrote *Religio Medici*. In 1637 he settled at Norwich to practise his profession. In spite of his wish that mankind might procreate like trees—a wish not endorsed by Sir Kenelm Digby and James Howell—Browne married (1641) and had a dozen children. He followed with paternal and scientific interest the travels and medical researches of his son Edward, and upon 'honest Tom', who sojourned in France and then entered the navy, he lavished advice ranging from underwear to the heroic examples 'in your beloved Plutark'. Browne was the physician and friend of Joseph Hall, Bishop of Norwich in 1641–7. He corresponded with Henry Power, Evelyn, Ashmole, Lilly, Dugdale, Oldenburg, Aubrey, and others. Why he did not become a member of the Royal Society we do not know. Although a royalist in sympathy, Browne never let public disturbances interrupt his varied studies and experiments, the collecting of books and rarities, and meditations on all things below and above the moon. He testified at a trial of witches in 1664, but the charge that his evidence was the decisive factor in their condemnation—a charge repeated by his editor as late as 1939—has been shown several times to be unwarranted. Browne was knighted in 1671, on the occasion of a royal visit to Norwich, the uniquely generous mayor effacing himself in favour of the town's most illustrious citizen. His other works are discussed in Chapter X.

to Browne when we reach 'the last and common Promoter of false Opinions, the endeavours of Satan', on the other hand Browne is more scientific and sceptical than Bacon when he discusses some notions already touched in *Sylva Sylvarum*: for instance, that coral is soft under water and hardens in the air; that a salamander can live in and extinguish fire (if ancient tradition is true, says Bacon, the creature has a very close skin and some very cold 'virtue'); that the chameleon lives on air (Bacon makes air its 'principall Sustenance' but admits flies as well). In the examination of these and other arresting items in his encyclopaedia, Browne appeals to critical authority, reason, and experience; of these criteria only the last is strictly Baconian. But Browne was in fact a tireless observer and experimenter. And when a whale was thrown upon the coast of Norfolk he verified his notion of spermaceti; in later years he was able, through his son, to test the belief that 'the Ostridge digesteth Iron'—after swallowing a nugget the bird died 'of a soden'. But in the settling of a more commonplace problem, the reputed inequality of the badger's legs, the mere report of the senses appears, happily for readers, to count less than abstract and almost metaphysical logic. Many exotic and 'occult' traditions were less readily verifiable by experience, and in this un-Baconian realm Browne of necessity relied upon reason and the weighing of authorities. Over many years he had gathered bits of strange learning from countless books, both the standard ones and, preferably, the remote and unfamiliar, and his antiquarian instinct could enjoy what his scientific reason denied. In regard to the great astronomical problem Browne had natural Ptolemaic velleities, but his real position was a not unscientific agnosticism. In general, he tried to keep his mind and his book abreast of modern science. He admired Gilbert and Harvey and Galileo, and knew something of Descartes, even if he did not fully comprehend their methods and significance.

The modern reader cares less for Browne's critical intentions than for his uncritical lapses, the variety and oddity of his matter, the piquant contrast between most of the topics and the polysyllabic arguments woven about them, and the continual revelation, even in this factual and impersonal book, of the author's temperament. Browne wished that the huge project had been undertaken by 'some co-operating advancers', but we rejoice that the stream of learning wound through his mind and not a committee's. He is a wit and a humorist in every sense of the words. We are not accustomed in modern books of science to an unobtrusive irony which can make jokes with quiet solemnity and touch religious mysteries with a reverent smile. 'We shall not, I hope, disparage the Resurrection of our Redeemer, if we say the Sun doth not dance on Easter day.' In the qualified recommendation of Oppian, which many critics have quoted, Browne may be wholly serious; we cannot be sure. One predominant and medieval strain in the book is certainly serious. Unlike Bacon, Browne does not bow to the Deity and pass on. For him science and religion are inseparable, or rather, science is still a part of religion. He looks with scientific detachment for scientific facts, but those facts have a divine aura, not of utility, about them. Although in the *Pseudodoxia* Browne is moving on the level of sober exposition and argument, his characteristic overtones are often heard, or seem to be heard. Even the badger's legs, we feel, illustrate the rational symmetry of the Creator's work, and the dance of the elephants at Germanicus's show—after which they 'laid them down in the Tricliniums, or places of festival Recumbency'—not only proves their possession of joints but touches a chord, in some ears, of the universal harmony.

This sketch of the Baconian tradition may end with a reminder of the optimism it embodied. In the quarrel of the ancients and moderns science, especially applied science, led the van of modernism and progress. Bacon even minimized the difficulties of his own induction in his earnest efforts to banish despair and all the other obstacles which stood between man and the conquest of nature, and his message owed something of its emotional force to his sense of man's actual misery as well as of his potential grandeur. For Spenser undiscovered America had been an imaginative justification of his medieval fairyland; for the young Donne, it was a woman's body; for Bacon, and for Browne in his Baconian moods, America is the symbol of the unknown world to be revealed by science. The present and not the classical past is the ripe maturity of the race. Bacon, Browne, and Milton, in their several ways, are expressly seeking to repair the ruins of Adam, to restore man's forfeited heritage, and Bacon and the earlier Milton, along with the members of the 'Invisible College', may stand as representatives of unbounded faith in the power of man and in the future.

4

When we turn from the possibilities of applied science to the facts and speculations of pure science, from the relief of man's estate to the state of his soul, the picture is less uniformly bright. The doctrine of progress was indeed one answer to scientific and other kinds of pessimism, but, though it was to prove victorious in the long run, it did not in the years 1600–60 win immediate and universal acceptance. At the same time the cautions registered in the first chapter, against the exaggeration of melancholy, may be reaffirmed here. We remember the philosophic doubts and distresses of a relatively small number of sensitive writers and forget the large number, not necessarily less sensitive, whose emotions were as little involved in cosmological ideas as ours have been in the doctrine of relativity.

Within the field of astronomy proper, educated people were confronted by three major theories (all ancient in germ) of the solar system: the so-called Ptolemaic theory of a central earth around which the heavens turned, a system much patched with 'Cycle and Epicycle, Orb in Orb'; the more economical hypothesis of Copernicus, as corrected by the telescope and the orbital laws of Kepler; and, thirdly, the popular compromise of Kepler's master, Tycho Brahe, who made the earth the centre of the universe and of the orbits of the moon, sun, and sphere of fixed stars, the sun being the centre of the orbits of the five planets. The difficulty was that all three theories 'saved the phenomena' and that a critical decision required exceptional command of mathematical science; most of us would have the same difficulty to-day if we did not take the facts on trust. Modern writers have often classified men of the period as sheep or goats on the strength of their attitude towards the Copernican doctrine, but some men's dissent or agnosticism might be based on sounder knowledge of the conditions of the problem than some other men's conventional acceptance. In any case the matter cannot be thought of as a simple choice between two alternatives; and, if it could, the common alternatives would be the Copernican and Tychonic systems, since the Ptolemaic lost ground steadily in the seventeenth century. Then came Descartes's theory of vortices which, though purely speculative, won great favour. In addition to these general cosmic theories there were particular problems, above all that of the diurnal rotation of the earth. This idea was accepted in England earlier than on the Continent, by Gilbertian Tychonists as well as Copernicans. Conservatives might dismiss one, two, or all three of the motions Copernicus ascribed to the earth, but even they could hardly get over some facts of observation, the appearance of new stars and other phenomena which demolished for ever the Aristotelian and Christian conception of changeless and incorruptible heavens. In obvious ways the new astronomy might disturb traditional beliefs and habits of mind. It contradicted the testimony of the senses, the authority of Aristotle and Ptolemy, and the still more authoritative assumptions of the Bible and Christian doctrine. On the other hand, it was supported by the scientific principles of simplicity and harmony and, with telescopic aid, by the senses; classical authority was no longer sacrosanct, and ingenuity could explain away apparent conflict with the Bible.

Yet what we call the new astronomy, with reference to strictly scientific theory and observation, was only one factor in shaking traditional orthodoxies. There was the revival of ideas which, though of ancient origin and largely theoretical, were generally linked with the results of astronomy—a world extending through infinite space; not merely our one solar system but others like it; not one but possibly many inhabited planets. Such speculations, of which Bruno was the best-known exponent, might be more damaging to theological and humanistic doctrine than astronomical science proper. In a universe of universes, with no centre or circumference, earth and man, small enough before, shrank into insignificant dots and divine Providence into a *nominis umbra*. For a philosophic layman's reaction we may take a passage from Drummond's *A Cypress Grove* (1623), a passage which contains some of his numerous echoes of another troubled mind:

The Element of Fire is quite put out, the Aire is but Water rarified, the Earth is found to move, and is no more the Center of the Universe, is turned into a Magnes; Starres are not fixed, but swimme in the etheriall Spaces, Cometes are mounted above the Planetes; Some affirme there is another World of men and sensitive Creatures, with Cities and Palaces in the Moone; the Sunne is lost, for, it is but a Light made of the conjunction of manie shining Bodies together, a Clift in the lower Heavens, through which the Rayes of the highest defuse themselves, is observed to have Spots; Thus, Sciences by the diverse Motiones of this Globe of the Braine of Man, are become Opiniones, nay, Errores, and leave the Imagination in a thousand Labyrinthes. What is all wee knowe compared with what wee knowe not?

But the cosmological ladder, like the Darwinian, could always be used for climbing either up or down. The telescopic or speculative picture of a vast universe might induce buoyant optimism as well as profound pessimism. In 1576 Thomas Digges, contrasting an infinite universe with 'this litle darcke starre wherein we live', could not sufficiently admire the wonderful frame of God's work, and his attitude was typical of the scientist and Christian in the seventeenth century. Then on the metaphysical plane there might be additional support for optimism. Bruno and his fellows were only making an astronomical extension of what a distinguished philosopher of our day has described as the 'principle of plenitude'. This complex of ideas was very old. Along with the conception of God as the One, the absolute, transcendental, self-sufficient Idea of the Good, there was the conception, also Platonic, of the fecund Demiurge who could not but manifest Himself to the fullest extent by creating the visible and temporal world of the Many. The latter conception, always present but continually repressed or evaded in the medieval period, asserted its strength during the Renaissance. And if our earth was, by dialectical necessity, the best of possible worlds, then, since existence and diversity were good in themselves, a world of worlds was still better. But what intoxicated Bruno overwhelmed Pascal.

Another phase of the conflict between pessimism and optimism is illustrated in another set of theological and philosophical ideas of equal antiquity. Primitive man had lost his first innocence and happiness, and the Hebraic and Christian conception of the Fall had early coalesced with the pagan idea of progressive degeneration from the Golden Age. Christian humanists might celebrate man's dignity and his divine gift of reason, but the whole history of the human race and the physical world was one of increasing exhaustion and corruption. Wherever man looked, he could see nothing constant except the remote and incorruptible heavens—and then came astronomy to report that the heavens themselves were subject to mutation and decay. Two significant continental treatments of the great theme were Loys Le Roy's *De la vicissitude ou variété des choses en l'univers* (first edition dated 1575, 1576; translated into English 1594) and Justus Lipsius's *De Constantia* (1584; translated 1595, 1653, 1654, 1670). Le Roy, however, found in change the inspiring evidence of God and human progress, and to the distresses of war and circumstance Lipsius opposed the precepts of Christian Stoicism. In England, John Norden gave a picture of change and decay in his poem *Vicissitudo Rerum* (1600), but did not follow his model, Le Roy, to the optimistic conclusion. The most elaborate argument for progressive deterioration was *The Fall of Man, Or the Corruption of Nature Proved by the Light of our Natural Reason* (1616), by Godfrey Goodman (later a bishop and secret Catholic). The St. Cyprian of his age sees a microcosm and macrocosm alike succumbing to decay, and miserable man's only hope is in turning from the contemplation of external things to God.

Allied with this belief in decay was the belief that the world, having had its two thousand years of nature and two thousand of Mosaic law, would end with the two thousand years of the Christian dispensation. In the sixteenth and seventeenth centuries men could say, with Donne, that of this 'last houre we have heard three quarters strike, more then fifteen hundred of this last two thousand spent'. By 1658 scientific optimism had risen high, but Dr. Browne the scientist could meditate in his richest style on the vainglorious ambition of modern men, born in this setting part of time, to raise a lasting monument. Izaak Walton, in 1665, thinks of Hooker as one of the saints grown rare 'in this weak and declining Age of the World'. The false modern emphasis on the bold confidence and rebellious energy of the Renaissance has ignored the great mass of writing which perpetuated Hebraic, classical, and medieval pessimism, and the religious or naturalistic pessimism inherent in life itself was reinforced by this belief in a dying world and by the paralysing effects of science and of sceptical and conflicting philosophies. It is of course the emotional and imaginative realization of these ideas which awakens the greatest strains in Renaissance literature. From Sackville to Spenser, from Shakespeare, Ralegh, and Donne to Browne and Shirley, men are haunted by the spectres of devouring time and change, the brevity, misery, and vanity of life, the littleness of man in the cosmic panorama. Even Alexander, in his vast and unreadable

Dooms-day, can achieve one great line, 'To scorne Corruption, and to mocke the Dust'.

This body of great writing, whether immediately affected by science or not, was more or less in the medieval and classical tradition, and to old pessimism old answers could still be made. Spenser tried to convince himself that the apparent sway of mutability was really a divinely ordered evolution towards the changeless stability his heart desired. Du Bartas, in Sylvester's very popular translation, combined old-fashioned science with a fervent faith in the providential beneficence of God and the universal harmony of His creation. In a world of flux Shakespeare saw at least the heroic individual as something more than the quintessence of dust. The complex and sceptical Donne took his stand on the Rock of Ages. Drummond and later men climbed out of the slough of despond on the ladder of Christian Platonism. Concerning the specific problem of human deterioration or progress other men spoke with conviction on the modern side. Ben Jonson, following Vives, declared that nature was not exhausted, that she could still equal or surpass her former productions. The great answer to pessimists like Goodman was George Hakewill's *Apology of the Power and Providence of God in the Government of the World. Or an Examination and Censure of the Common Error Touching Nature's Perpetual and Universal Decay* (1627). This comprehensive and reassuring work was welcomed to the extent of two more enlarged editions in 1630 and 1635. Surveying the physical world, human attributes and powers, and the fruits of civilization, Hakewill finds no proof that either nature or man is suffering from decrepitude. His argument is a mixture of old and new, of the religious and the scientific, and his witnesses range from Lucretius, Ovid, Philo, and Boethius to Du Bartas, Bodin, Lipsius, and Ralegh. Like Spenser, Hakewill sees behind mutability a divine order and constancy. Like Le Roy (whom he cites), he expounds a cyclical theory of progress, denies the essential superiority of ancient genius and achievement, attributes decline to human sloth, and calls upon his generation to work with courage and hope. Where Hakewill's assertion of religious and philosophic optimism left off, the Baconian gospel of scientific progress began, and men whose uncertainties were not insoluble might be cheered by one or other or both. Hakewill's book had a visible effect on seventeenth-century thought, from the young Milton's

Naturam Non Pati Senium (1628) and *Seventh Prolusion* (1631?) to the defence of the Royal Society and the culmination of the quarrel over the ancients and moderns.

5

Since we have been concerned with astronomy we may enter Robert Burton's house of many mansions by way of 'a digression of the Ayr'.[1] Probably no passage in all the literature of the time gives the modern reader a more vivid picture of the intellectual confusion caused by the new astronomy than Burton's galloping survey of the multitudinous theories which were, in more than one sense, in the air—the substance and movements of the heavens and heavenly bodies, the appearance of new stars and the problem of change and decay, 'that main paradox, of the Earths motion, now so much in question', the plurality of worlds, and kindred ideas. We are left, like the author, 'almost giddy with roving about'. Faced with such an array of opinions and authorities—and Burton knows them all— he quotes one against another but refuses to commit himself. His attitude is one of interrogative, ironical, Lucianic scepticism. Like the Deity of *Paradise Lost*, he is moved to laughter at quaint opinions wide, at the theorists' desperate efforts to save appearances; obviously Burton does not feel the spiritual distress of some men. His conclusion is more in the vein of Milton, or Browne, than of Lucian; these mysteries God will reveal in His own good time.

The popularity of the *Anatomy* lapsed during the eighteenth century, in spite of Sterne's notorious thefts and Dr. Johnson's notorious devotion. A strong revival began with the beginning

---

[1] The life of Robert Burton (1577–1640) was even more uneventful than that of Browne. He was born in Leicestershire (of which county his brother William wrote a *Description*, 1622), entered Brasenose College in 1593, was elected a Student of Christ Church in 1599, and graduated in 1602. He lived at Christ Church for the rest of his life, never travelling 'but in Map or Card'. He took the degree of B.D. in 1614 and in 1616 became vicar of St. Thomas's in Oxford. He also held a Lincolnshire living (1624–31) and about 1633–4 received a benefice in his native county from his patron, Lord Berkeley. Burton's bust in Christ Church Cathedral, put up by his brother, bears the epitaph he had himself composed: 'Paucis notus, paucioribus ignotus, hic jacet Democritus Junior, cui vitam dedit et mortem Melancholia.' The *Anatomy of Melancholy*, first published at Oxford in 1621, won great popularity and was revised and enlarged by the author in five more editions, the last being posthumous. Burton contributed Latin verses to numerous Oxford anthologies and in 1606 wrote a Latin comedy, *Philosophaster*, which was acted at Christ Church in 1618; it was first printed in 1862.

of the nineteenth century and there has been no subsequent lapse. In the appreciative tradition of that period Burton's book, like Browne's *Pseudodoxia Epidemica*, was commonly regarded as a mine of amusing oddities. A more historical view received impetus from Sir William Osler. Burton was writing a serious scientific treatise on abnormal psychology, and though his large orbit includes many epicycles and eccentrics, he moves on steadily to his goal. His thousands of Latin tags, while sprinkled more thickly than in most contemporaries, were not quaint pedantry in a bilingual age, and they are an unceasing reminder that Burton was a Renaissance humanist for whom the ancients had given final expression to all the commonplaces of experience. The quotations from countless authorities, now mostly forgotten, on psychology and other sciences were of course no less relevant than a modern psychologist's citations from Freud or Pavlov. Yet the old view of the *Anatomy* was not wholly wrong. If Burton's intention and in part his execution warrant putting a traditional bedside book into a chapter on science, nevertheless, sitting between Bacon and Hobbes, he appears as a kind of gargoyle between the two spires of the cathedral of English scientific thought. He exemplifies, it has been said, all three of Bacon's classes of false philosophy, the sophistical, the empirical, and the superstitious. His attitude towards problems of the inner and outer world is that of the layman, a layman of infinite learning, zest, curiosity, and common sense. He has no integrated scientific and critical principles, no forward-looking philosophy, one might almost say no historical sense; ancients and moderns are all contemporaries, living together in the happy isle of Burton's study. But since we read Burton for fun, as we seldom read Bacon or Hobbes, these deficiencies cannot be fatal.

Nothing shows his quality better than the long 'Satyricall Preface' in which Democritus Junior explains his pseudonym and purpose and, from his college window, surveys the mad world as it reels or rushes by. Given an invincible sanity and clarity of vision—and Burton has affinities with Lucian, Chaucer, Erasmus, Rabelais, Montaigne, and Shakespeare—no satire can be more effective than the mere cataloguing of what men feel and do, their carnal and worldly lusts, the fantastic objects, public and private, that they pursue, the follies and crimes they commit in the pursuit, the whole topsy-turvy scale of values and motives which society disowns and maintains. 'If it be so that the Earth is a Moon, then are we also giddy, vertigenous and lunatick within this. sublunary Maze.' From the panorama of life as it is Burton turns to consider what it might be, and it is characteristic of his common sense that his Utopia is not a chimerical commonwealth but a practicable improvement on what already exists. His proposals range from broad streets to hospitals and pensions for the aged and infirm, from the thorough cultivation of all land to the abolition of monopolies, from the suppression of extravagance in building and dress to the curing of idleness, 'the *malus Genius* of our nation'.

But though Burton is here and everywhere a realistic satirist, a detached observer of the human comedy, he is much more than that. He does not, like some modern psychologists, worship a párticular idol of the cave, nor does he start with the tacit invocation, 'Now, Muse, let's sing of rats'. His subject is the soul, body, and whole life of man, and he writes as both a divine and a physician. The *Anatomy* proper begins with a contrast between the original endowment and felicity of 'Man, the most excellent and noble creature of the World, the principal and mighty work of God', and the present miseries, inherited from Adam, of the wretched being who is in many ways inferior to the lower animals. That contrast is seldom absent from Burton's mind and, since he feels as well as thinks, it is tragic as well as comic. His fundamental postulate is 'that all the world is melancholy, or mad, dotes, and every member of it'. 'Being then it is a disease so grievous, so common, I know not wherein to do a more generall service, and spend my time better, then to prescribe means how to prevent and cure so universall a malady, an Epidemical disease, that so often, so much crucifies the body and minde.' Melancholy had been studied ever since Galen, and among Burton's English predecessors, medical and spiritual, were Timothy Bright (1586), Thomas Wright (1601), and the Puritan divine, Thomas Adams (1616). For us it matters not that Burton's technical knowledge was of a kind soon to be, or in some quarters already, outmoded—the four humours; natural, vital, and animal spirits; the vegetal, sensible, and rational soul; the two parts of the rational soul, understanding and will; and so on. Nor would any modern reader except a

SCIENCE AND SCIENTIFIC THOUGHT

psychologist complain because Burton begins with 'God a cause' and proceeds through 'A Digression of the nature of Spirits, bad Angels, or Devils, and how they cause Melancholy', to sections on witches and magicians and the influence of the stars. Like Shakespeare's, Burton's wisdom, got 'by melancholizing', is not of the laboratory and transcends text-books. For him religion and science are mingled and both are interpenetrated with a profound sympathy for deluded, erring, suffering humanity.

If Burton sees man's headaches and hallucinations against a cosmic and divine background, it does not detract from the emotional power of his vision of life, and he is none the less realistic in his treatment of natural causes, old age, heredity, diet ('I finde Gourds, Cowcumbers, Coleworts, Mellons, disallowed, but especially Cabbage'), constipation, 'Venus omitted' ('Intemperate Venus is all out as bad in the other extream'), bad air, immoderate exercise, solitariness, and idleness. No topic recurs more often than the last, for no man knew better the torments of *accidia* than one who wrote 'of melancholy, by being busie to avoid melancholy'. Then come the irascible passions and perturbations of the mind, sorrow, fear, shame, and the rest. In all ranks of society discontents and cares may be so grievous that if we had foresight and choice 'we should rather refuse, then accept of this painful life'. The concupiscible passions include ambition, covetousness, self-love and pride (if the earth is but a little star, 'wher's our glory?'), excessive devotion to learning and study; here follows a gloomy and angry 'Digression of the misery of Scholars'. It would be hard to find in modern text-books any mental disorder that Burton does not touch, and nowhere does he forget, as the divine or the physician alone might forget, the interrelations of body and mind. As for the lawful cures of melancholy, described in the second part, they range from prayer and sober Christian and Stoic precepts through the study of everything from the fine arts to geography and down to cathartics, bleeding, and cordials (including, from Sandys's *Relation*, the Turkish 'drink called Coffa'). Although not himself a wine-drinker, Burton declares that there is no relief so powerful and apposite as 'a cup of strong drink, mirth, musick, and merry company'. The English scene comes to life in advice for trippers and in the recitals of traditional games and country pleasures. And we think of Justice Shallow as well as of

Izaak Walton when we read of old companions sitting by the fire or in the sunshine, remembering ancient matters which happened in their younger years.

Doubtless the section on love-melancholy is the most famous, and doubtless not for its Platonic pages. The follies and torments of love, especially 'Heroical love', clearly belong to his subject, but our celibate divine apologizes for venturing upon such a theme. The length and the liveliness of this part, however, testify to the half-irresponsible exhilaration with which a born essayist and raconteur frisks 'in this delightsome field'. He still draws upon the doctors, but chiefly upon the whole body of historical and imaginative literature, the obscure along with the familiar ancients, medieval and modern authors in Latin and the vernaculars. Ovid and Montaigne, St. Chrysostom and Aretino, and hundreds more furnish grist for the capacious mill. Among English writers Chaucer is most often quoted; others are Sidney, Spenser, Marlowe, Shakespeare, Bacon, Jonson, Daniel, Drayton, Wither, even Samuel Rowlands—Burton's library was not dusty. There is no less variety in the endless catalogue of examples, from the story of the beautiful Lamia to the Rabelaisian or Skeltonic picture, joyously transcribed by Keats in a letter, of an idealized mistress as she really is. Burton understands every phase of 'this Trage-comedy of Love', but he remains as skittishly detached as in astronomical matters. Twelve unanswerable arguments for marriage are followed by twelve unanswerable arguments against it. "Tis an hazard both waies I confess, to live single or to marry.' If all remedies for passion fail, 'the last and best cure of Love Melancholy, is, to let them have their desire'. Here as elsewhere Burton's descriptive analysis is frequently in line with modern psychology, but his case-histories are enveloped in a mixture of romance and realism, humour and wisdom, which is a world away from the technical jargon and narrowly physiological objectivity we are accustomed to.

So far Burton has been enlarging upon traditional branches of his complex subject, but his last one, religious melancholy, has not, he says, been generally recognized as a distinct species, and he has no pattern to follow. However, some authorities divide 'Love Melancholy into that whose object is women; and into the other whose object is God'. Throughout his study rational moderation has been Burton's criterion and prescription, and this last topic is dichotomized into 'Excess and Defect, Impiety and Superstition, Idolatry and Atheisme'. The diagnosis of both enthusiasm and scepticism (including diatribes against Catholics and Puritans) has historical interest, but the last pages deepen our understanding of the author. When he contemplates the causes and cure of religious despair the assured and angry Anglican becomes the wise and compassionate physician of afflicted souls. The prime agency of the devil, particular griefs and misfortunes, much pondering on ominous biblical texts and on the doctrine of election and reprobation, the consciousness of sin, the fear of God's wrath, all reinforced by the thunders of the pulpit—these things work upon neurotic introverts until they hear the howls of the damned and smell the eternal fire. To such people, and there were many in old and New England, Burton addresses his sermon, an earnest appeal to shun whatever aggravates their terrors, to seek the counsel of good physicians and divines, enjoy honest recreations, and dwell on thoughts of God's infinite love and mercy.

I can say no more, or give better advice to such as are any way distressed in this kind, then what I have given and said. Only take this for a corollary and conclusion, as thou tendrest thine own welfare in this, and all other melancholy, thy good health of body and mind, observe this short precept, give not way to solitariness and idleness. Be not solitary, be not idle.

Even a summary sketch of Burton cannot fail to suggest his sanity of mind and largeness of heart, his love of life and of human beings, his capacity alike for robustious or bitter laughter and for sensitive exploration of the darker places of the soul. His matter is never dull, but more than half of our pleasure is in his manner, the revelation of himself. He would have written in the international language—as Browne intended to write the *Pseudodoxia*—if the mercenary stationers had not shied at a Latin treatise. While feeling grateful for that blessing, we may wonder how such a scholar happens to be conspicuous not only in his own period but in the whole range of English prose for colloquial naturalness, garrulous spontaneity, and juicy vigour. Burton has his moments of eloquence (and he wrote passable verses which Milton may have read), but he is not, like some famous contemporaries, a poet in prose. No English author, however, certainly no author of a long didactic work, has more variety of tone on the prose level. His flood of slangy, proverbial, and picturesque language is nearer to Nashe and Dekker than to Cicero or Seneca. Burton piles up all the critical complaints which might be brought against his irregular, homespun writing, but his self-depreciation is really a satire on other men's affectations, and he did not fail to revise his style in successive editions—though he did often fail to verify his references and to catch multiplying misprints. His book was 'writ with as small deliberation as I do ordinarily speak', he says, and to his own accounts of his prose style may be added Anthony Wood's report of his talk:

I have heard some of the Antients of Christ Church often say that his Company was very merry, facete and juvenile, and no Man in his time did surpass him for his ready and dextrous interlarding his common discourses among them with Verses from the Poets or Sentences from classical Authors. Which being then all the fashion in the University, made his Company more acceptable.

6

Burton represents, in his loose and eccentric fashion, the religious and ethical assumptions of Renaissance humanism. It is something of a shock to turn from him to his long-lived contemporary, Thomas Hobbes (1588–1679), the plain and orderly exponent of extreme materialism. In the last chapter we surveyed what was for his own age and posterity the most vital part of his philosophy, the political; here we are concerned with his scientific and ethical thought. These last two parts are related to each other and both, especially of course the ethical theory, condition Hobbes's political thinking. As we have partly seen, his contemporary reputation, before as well as after 1660, resembled that of Machiavelli or Nietzsche (though atheism and libertinism did not have to wait for the supposed sanction of the decorous philosopher); to traditional orthodoxy he appeared, in the words of an obituary broadside, as 'the Bugbear of the Nation'.

Since Bacon stands for concrete experimental induction and Hobbes for abstract deductive logic, the common view is that the ex-Chancellor's amanuensis was not, in Hobbesian language, moved by a contiguous mind. Yet, however different their normal methods, the two were not so far apart in their aims and principles, in their hostility to most Greek philosophy and to Aristotelian scholasticism and in their debt to both; in their attempt to systematize all human knowledge; in their laying hold of science as the key to truth; in their ideal of utility and power as the end of knowledge; in their conception of reality as more or less mechanical and of sense-impressions as subjective; in their dismissal of final causes and separation of the realms of knowledge and faith; and in their extension of naturalistic principles from the physical to the moral and social worlds. It depends on which end of the telescope we look through whether we call them the first English apostles of modern empirical realism or the last of the scholastic nominalists. For both descendants of Ockham, and especially for Hobbes, the new science was at hand to serve the doctrine of the particular.

Although the problem of knowledge was the great problem of the seventeenth century, epistemology had not yet become the sacred cow of philosophy. The tyranny of authority, the deceitfulness of the senses, even the weakness of reason, had been made clear, notably by Bacon, but, apart from Lord Herbert, few men, however intent on finding a sure guide through the labyrinths of opinion and error, went behind the senses and reason—and revelation—to inquire into the processes and grounds of knowledge. (From our standpoint that is not altogether a loss, since it means that philosophy was still in the main a branch of literature and not written in technical language.) Bacon combined the old faculty psychology with some more scientific ideas. To his division between supernatural and natural knowledge corresponds the division, borrowed from Telesio, of the soul into rational and animal. The immaterial rational soul, a direct gift of God to man, has for its instrument the animal soul, a corporeal substance, which man shares with the beasts. This dualism approaches that of Descartes, and still more Cartesian is Bacon's repeated hint of the subjectivity of the sensible qualities of objects. But theoretical psychology was not a major interest for Bacon, it was for Descartes; and Hobbes, like Descartes, put the problem of knowledge in the forefront of his thinking. However plain its gaps and short-cuts, no philosophic system has been more closely integrated than Hobbes's around one central principle. That principle, as everyone knows, is motion, and the word transports us from the medieval to the modern world. In the dedication of *De Corpore* Hobbes paid tribute to Galileo as 'the first that opened to us the gate of Natural Philosophy Universal,

which is the knowledge of the Nature of Motion'. Hobbes conceived of himself as effecting for psychology and moral and civil
philosophy what Galileo had done for physics and Harvey for
physiology, the substitution of realistic facts for speculative un-
realities. A similar enterprise had been a part of the *Instauratio
Magna*, but Hobbes's scientific orientation was more advanced
than Bacon's.

Hobbes was the founder of modern empirical psychology, and
psychology was the foundation of his system. His chief accounts
of it are contained in the 'Short Tract' of 1630 (?), *Human
Nature* (1640; published in 1650), *Leviathan* (1651), and *De
Corpore* (1655). Philosophic knowledge differs from empirical
knowledge in having to do with concepts, propositions, and
conclusions, but there is no conception in a man's mind which
has not at first, totally or by parts, been begotten upon the
organs of sense. All of the sensible qualities 'are in the object
that causeth them, but so many several motions of the matter,
by which it presseth our organs diversly. Neither in us that are
pressed, are they any thing else, but divers motions; (for motion,
produceth nothing but motion).' Nor can there be any cause of
motion except in a body contiguous and moved. Thus all of the
sensible qualities are but phantasms of the observer, not properties of the object. When the phantasm remains after the object
is removed, the decaying sense-impression is fancy or imagination or memory. Emotions are also motions. If the motion
from without quickens and helps the vital motion of the heart,
the result is pleasure; 'and when it hindereth, it is Pain,
Trouble, Grief, &c.' The small beginnings of motion, not yet
translated into action, are 'endeavour'. Endeavour towards or
away from a particular object is appetite or aversion. All the
passions of the mind consist of appetite or aversion except pure
pleasure and pain, which are a certain fruition of good or evil.
Since the appetites and aversions of either an individual or men
in common are not uniform but fluctuate, men, and beasts also,
have deliberation, an alternate succession of appetites, aversions, hopes, and fears. The last and decisive appetite in deliberation is the will. The act of appetite, however, could not
but follow appetite and its cause, so that such a liberty as is free
from necessity is not to be found in the will either of men or of
beasts, though both have the liberty or power to do what they
will.

The general principles by which Hobbes explains the inner world of man and the world of terrestrial nature hold good for the planetary system. He accepts and comments at length upon the ideas of Copernicus, Kepler, and Galileo, but he avoids trouble by limiting the sphere of inquiry as he had already limited psychology. Since our conceptions are necessarily finite, it makes no difference what we think about the magnitude, beginning, duration, and singleness or plurality of the world, or about the nature of God. Such questions must be left to the authorized ministers of God and that means, in England, to the king; thus, as Sir Leslie Stephen remarked, 'Charles II apparently was to decide whether the world had a beginning'. But Hobbes seems to be sincere and consistent rather than cynical, and in his attitude towards supernatural knowledge he resembles not only Bacon but less questionable metaphysicians. However different his premisses, aims, and sanctions, he is not altogether remote from Aquinas or from many religious thinkers of his own time, including his mighty opposite, Milton; for, like Milton and others, Hobbes does not wish men to be distracted by vain speculation from the performance of their duty here and now.

Despite his belated introduction to geometry Hobbes tried to give his system a scientific basis. One instance is the atomic or rather the corpuscular theory. Science had been moving in that direction since the fifteenth century, and our period opened with Nicholas Hill's *Philosophia Epicurea, Democritiana, Theophrastica* (Paris, 1601); near the end came Walter Charleton's *Physiologia Epicuro-Gassendo-Charltoniana* (1654). Bacon did not formally accept the atomic theory; in fact he expressly rejected it because it implied the existence of a vacuum and the unchangeableness of matter. Yet, as an anti-Aristotelian, he gave special and repeated praise to Democritus and his fellows who had 'removed God and Mind from the structure of things, and . . . assigned the causes of particular things to the necessity of matter'. And Bacon himself more than once expounded a corpuscular motion akin to that of Descartes. Hobbes ignored Democritus and had little to say of Lucretius, except in criticizing his argument for a vacuum, but he was in the mechanistic current of Galileo, Gassendi, the chief reviver of Epicureanism, and Descartes, and corpuscular motion was essential to his system. Of course everyone knew ancient speculative atomism in its Lucretian form, and the more scientific recent theories were familiar to a number of men, including Digby and Browne. Even Cudworth, Hobbes's great antagonist, accepted atomism as 'unquestionably true', while he abhorred the atheism traditionally linked with it.

Another basic principle of modern science was the distinction between primary and secondary qualities. In the customary view, that of the philosopher as well as the layman, the sensible qualities of objects, colour and the like, were what they seemed to be, inherent properties possessed by those objects as the Creator made them. The new science changed all that. The senses and the Aristotelian categories no longer furnished accurate criteria. Primary qualities were those which could be scientifically measured, such as space, time, number, force, velocity. The ordinary world ceased to be intelligible to the layman. What had been the solid facts of external nature became sensations in the mind of the observer which could not be quantitatively measured and were therefore scientifically negligible. This conception had been adumbrated by Bacon, but its historical development was the work of Galileo, Descartes, and Hobbes; Hobbes seems to have reached his view independently. The real world, the world of science, was a mathematical mechanism of bodies, vast or minute, moving in space and time in accordance with natural laws. In such a world man himself, a mere aggregate of secondary qualities, was, logically, an insignificant stranger, a superfluous accident. His spiritual experience, like the beauty and diversity of nature, was reduced to the deterministic motion of bodies. Nor was there much room for God, except as the First Cause of motion—and only the initial cause. The celestial machine did not need the compelling hand of Providence, since Galileo and others had exploded the Aristotelian idea that motion required the continuous application of force. Aristotelian and Christian teleology gave way to a chain of physical causes and effects.

Descartes, like Galileo a mathematical genius in his own right, was concerned far more than Galileo with the general problems of philosophy, and he tried to keep God and mind from being drawn into the widening vortex of mechanistic thought. To material substance he assigned the mathematical properties of the world of bodies and to thinking substance the non-mathematical properties. But it was inevitable that the materialistic cat should swallow the spiritual canary, and in this operation Hobbes was the ruthlessly efficient cause. That uncompromising logician would have no Cartesian dualism, no admission of the immaterial and occult. As Copernicus had transformed the pattern of the universe by including the earth in the question Ptolemy had asked of the heavenly bodies, so Hobbes transformed the pattern of man's inner and outer world by including *res cogitans* within *res extensa*. Nothing exists except body, and its attributes are extension and motion. The mind, or nervous system, and the processes of mental experience are not separate from the physical world; they consist, like everything else, of bodies in motion. Man is, though not in the medieval sense, a microcosm. And for Hobbes even the primary qualities of mathematical science, space and time, are consequences of motion, phantasms in the mind of the percipient. Thus the wheel of subjectivity comes full circle. The world of sensible qualities, itself an illusion, is both the cause and the object of perception in an observer who is one of that world's aggregates of non-qualitative particles. Thanks to Hobbes's clarity and relentless consistency (of aim if not of method), one of his unintentional achievements was the exposure of the defects of pure materialism.

There is some initial difficulty in regarding a world emptied of everything but bodies in motion as the material for ethical and political philosophy, but the man who squared the circle was equal to that. Some ethical implications in his psychology have already appeared, and they can be only briefly supplemented here. Hobbes's individual and social ethics are founded on what he takes to be man's fundamental impulse, self-preservation. All men strive towards this end, and pleasures and pains arise from the satisfaction or frustration of this motive. Even 'altruistic' feelings and acts are prompted by and minister to the sense of power. While unceasing endeavour towards a goal may be conceived as a kind of motion, external and internal, there is little real connexion between Hobbes's physical psychology and his ethics. His materialism is chiefly useful in guarding his wholly naturalistic man from any intrusive religious and idealistic motives. But even the naturalistic ego seeks peace in the interest of security, and in moments of deliberation the creature of passions, appetites, and egocentric will recognizes the utility and practical necessity of reason. However, as we have seen,

reason aims only at self-preservation and power, and deliberation is only a succession of conflicting appetites and aversions.
The last and victorious one is the will, the victory being merely
the inevitable effect of an inevitable cause. Hobbes, like Milton,
views life as a race; instead, though, of Milton's 'immortall
garland' he sees 'no other Goal, nor other Garland, but being
formost'. The will, in Milton's tireless and passionate exposition, is an ethical faculty and entirely free; reason is the *recta
ratio* planted by God in the individual soul which teaches man
the divine will, the moral law, the absolute values of good and
evil, the control of his own passions and appetites. Hobbes's
scale of values is not absolute but relative; those things are good
which man desires, they are good because he desires them. The
beliefs and ideals of traditional religion and ethics are unreal
'universals'; nor can the consistent nominalist, despite his own
strong conviction of duty, furnish philosophic support for the
moral law as good in itself. Hobbes's doctrine is a mixture of
bold realism and unrealistic dogmatism. In ethics and science,
as in politics, he was a kind of secular Calvinist.

Thus within the half-century which saw promulgated the teaching of Bacon and Hobbes, there appears in high relief the contrast
which was to be worked out at large in philosophy and literature
in the following centuries, including our own. Bacon's natural
man is an emancipated slave who is being inducted into the rule
of a kingdom, who may rejoice as he contemplates the infinite
potentialities of his dominion over nature. From this demigod
we turn to the natural man of Hobbes, who is a slave to his own
and others' passions and whose only hope of escape from the
jungle is the establishment of an absolute external authority.
Incidentally, Hobbes's picture of naturalistic egoism was in part
a reply to persistent dreams of a mythical Golden Age, and it
was to have a large share in evoking new pictures of a future
Golden Age of natural benevolence.

Even this brief sketch of scientific thought has revealed the
most fervent optimism and the most melancholy pessimism side
by side. But the acceptance of both man's grandeur and his
misery, the double vision of a god and a beast, had been a
central fact in religious humanism ever since Plato and Cicero,
and a temperate faith in the human reason and will was far
too strong to be quickly overthrown. Indeed when we survey
English thought during our period we see that the mechanistic

revolution was largely confined to the brain of Hobbes. English men of science from Bacon to Newton were generally more practical than metaphysical and could remain more or less devout Christians, and not all foreigners were atheists. But while Bacon's sincere tributes to the Creator's glory—the tributes, so to speak, of a junior partner—helped to keep him immune from attack, the more obviously dangerous Galileo, Descartes, and Hobbes, despite their sincere or prudential concessions to orthodoxy, were in their several countries vigorously assailed. The greatest champion of the eternal verities of Christian humanism, if not directly anti-Hobbesian, was Milton. Another, as we saw above, was Bishop Bramhall. Since his polemics receive one contemptuous sentence in the *Dictionary of National Biography*, it may not be amiss to observe that Hobbes's determinism (which the philosopher in his ordinary pragmatic thinking commonly and conveniently ignored) cracked under the bishop's formidable spear. Hobbes was driven to the virtual admission that he could give no reason or evidence for necessity, and he fell back upon a religious dogma, the assertion of God's foreknowledge, a dogma which of course Bramhall accepted, though he stoutly rejected the equating of foreknowledge with necessitarian decrees. The later Cambridge Platonists also saw that the new Democritean and Protagorean philosophy did not merely 'nibble at Moses' but was destructive of the whole religious and ethical order of antiquity and Christianity. If we consider what was at stake we may think twice before dismissing the 'obscurantist' defenders of Christian humanism, especially since mechanistic thought, however valuable for the immediate problems of science, did not prove to be an ultimate explanation of reality. Of the army of religious writers to be reviewed in the next chapter, some were concerned with piety and salvation and some with ecclesiastical and sectarian problems, and many were unaware that scientific reason was undermining the citadel of truth; but many of the best minds were striving, in the tradition of Christian humanism, to uphold a religious view of man and the world by reasserting the divinity of reason.

X

RELIGION AND RELIGIOUS THOUGHT

MORE than two-fifths of the books printed in England from 1480 to 1640 were religious, and for the years 1600–40 the percentage is still higher. In Jaggard's *Catalogue* of 1619 nearly three-fourths of the books are religious and moral; in William London's *Catalogue of the most Vendible Books in England* (1657–8) the space given to works of divinity equals that occupied by all other kinds together. Grotius and Casaubon declared, in the middle of James's reign, that there was little or no literary scholarship in England, that theology was the only interest of educated men. Religion, it does not need to be said, was a main and often intense concern of greater multitudes of people during our period than in any other before or since, and in many ways it profoundly affected the lives of those who were not especially devout.

In an age in which God and Satan, heaven and hell, were radiant or lurid realities, there was a sincere and insatiable demand for devotional and hortatory works, and English Protestantism had to create a new religious literature or re-create the old. The endless repetition and application of the central truths of faith and practice corresponded to the endless re-expression of the commonplaces of ancient ethics, and in some authors the two roads ran together. The appetite for counsels of piety and warnings against sin grew with the middle-class and Puritan public, but churchwomen in castle and hall likewise meditated over such handbooks in the intervals between good works, finding them a support against the pangs of widowhood or of matrimony. The type of book and its individual variations hardly need to be described, and at any rate cannot be here, but some bald figures may suggest the extent of the spiritual awakening. Next to the Bible the best-sellers of our period were such books as John Norden's *Pensive Man's Practice* (1584), which had gone beyond forty impressions by 1627; Arthur Dent's *Plain Man's Pathway to Heaven* (twenty-five editions, 1601–40, and many later ones); John Dod's *Plain and Familiar Exposition of the Ten Commandments* (nineteen editions, 1603–35); Lewis Bayly's *Practice of Piety* (1612?), which achieved some fifty reprints during the century (and a sixteenth French edition in 1684), but which did not save the episcopal author from the royal displeasure. The books of Dent and Bayly, by the way, were the meagre dowry of Bunyan's first wife, and the former contributed to *Mr. Badman*. Sir John Hayward's historical works were less popular than his *Sanctuary of a Troubled Soul* (two parts, 1601?–7). Other books of the kind were Michael Sparke's *Crumbs of Comfort* (1623?), which had forty-one editions by the middle of the century; the allegorical *Isle of Man* by Richard Bernard, one of the forerunners of Bunyan (sixteen editions, 1626–83); Dr. Daniel Featley's *Ancilla Pietatis* (eight editions, 1626–56); and Dr. Cosin's *Collection of Private Devotions* (five editions, 1627–38; tenth edition, 1719), which aroused Puritan feeling. In the latter years of the period, to pass by Jeremy Taylor's very popular manuals, we meet three books destined for a long life in English and other languages, Baxter's earnest exhortations, *The Saints' Everlasting Rest* (1650) and *A Call to the Unconverted* (1657), and the cooler handbook of Christian ethics, *The Whole Duty of Man* (1658), attributed to the prolific Richard Allestree. In the same decade we have the first writings of George Fox and Bunyan, and the *Sancta Sophia* (1657) compiled from the works of the Catholic mystic, Augustine Baker (1575–1641). To these must be added many kindred items and a large body of translations, especially of Catholic writings old and new. And when sermons were printed they made an immense supplement; people denied the privilege of hearing could be privately moved by discourses on *The Back-Parts of Jehovah* and *Bowels Opened*. The quantity and the popularity of such books are facts which speak for themselves. And, moreover, as direct appeals to the heart and conscience, they form a great mass of normally plain writing.

We must observe one other branch of religious literature, a branch once large and heavily laden but now long withered—unless it can be said to have flowered again in psycho-analysis. Foxe had given Protestants an inspiring collection of saints' lives, which remained a favourite book of the seventeenth century (though literature reveals an abiding attachment to the Catholic saints), but many men recognized, with Fuller, that 'in Case-Divinity Protestants are defective. For (save that a Smith or two of late have built them forges, and set up shop) we go down to our enemies to sharpen all our instruments, and are beholden to them for offensive and defensive weapons in Cases of Conscience.' Hence Fuller's praise of the great William Perkins (1558–1602), who 'brought the schools into the Pulpit, and unshelling their controversies out of their hard school-terms, made thereof plain and wholsome meat for his people. . . . An excellent Chirurgeon he was at joynting of a broken soul, and at stating of a doubtfull conscience.' Almost every divine had his portion of the same impulse and, whatever learning might be invoked, a practical and popular aim dictated such works of casuistry as those of Perkins, Ames, Joseph Hall, Sanderson, Fuller, and Jeremy Taylor.

I

It is hardly possible to exaggerate the importance of the sermon in the seventeenth-century world. 'The Religion of England', wrote Evelyn in his satirical tract of 1659, 'is Preaching and sitting stil on Sundaies.' Queen Elizabeth, believing that wherever two or three were gathered together the devil of sedition was among them, had been content with a very limited supply of sermons for her people. But a preaching ministry was one of the Puritans' great ends and a similar zeal, with a sacerdotal emphasis, inspired the Anglo-Catholic movement. According to Selden, 'To preach long, loud, and Damnation is the way to be cry'd up', and the brimstone sermons which moved James Howell to gibes might, as Burton testifies, have distressing effects upon the neurotic. But hell was not the main theme of the amiable and popular Fuller, for instance, and from Andrewes onward the great preachers celebrate holy joy. Then what we mean by the power of the press was still largely concentrated in the pulpit, and did not vanish even after the press had become a potent force in controversy. People are governed by pulpits more than the sword in times of peace, said King Charles in 1646, and possession of the public ear was a prime necessity for both parties in the religious and constitutional struggle. One example is the stir caused by the order (1627) for printing the sermons of Sibthorp and Manwaring on passive obedience. Thus in addition to his office as a guide to salvation, a preacher of repute combined the attractions of a modern journalist, publicist, and lecturer. He was also akin to the modern actor. A London or university audience, even a village congregation, had its squad, large or small, of theological and dramatic critics; Baxter warned preachers against the insidious consciousness of that fact, and Taylor urged that men should not come to church 'as into a Theatre'. The critical attitude was quickened by the taking of notes on sermons, which was, as Brinsley, Hoole, and others indicate, an established educational practice—a practice which enabled the pious Sir Simonds D'Ewes to escape from the 'desperate atheism' of his childhood and become 'a rational hearer' in his teens. Girls like Lucy Apsley and Katherine Fowler also memorized or took down sermons, though Sir Ralph Verney thought it as indecent for women to scribble as to speak in church. For the persistence of the habit in later life there is the diary of John Manningham, or the less familiar journal of the unhappy Edward Wingfield in far-off Jamestown.

While the sermon had the unique character of a divine message, and carried the obligation of close scrutiny of the inspired text, it was also a highly developed literary form, the product of an unbroken oratorical tradition which went back to the ancients. Its own special traditions of rhetoric and logic —the open and the closed hand, according to a common phrase— had been revivified by the powerful influence of Ramus and codified in such books as Keckermann's *Rhetoricae Ecclesiasticae*. It was natural that the preaching of men of all religious categories—except ranters—should have a generic likeness, but there were tribal and individual differences. Many great Puritan preachers from Perkins to Baxter, such men as Laurence Chaderton (1537/8–1640), the first Master of Emmanuel College, Arthur Hildersam (1563–1632), and 'Decalogue Dod' (1555–1645), were disposed, from choice, not ignorance, to favour the presentation of truth in her naked purity, not bedizened with human and profane learning (and some Anglicans shared that view). But there is just the opposite contrast between the Puritan Thomas Adams and the Anglo-Catholic Lancelot Andrewes; and Manningham complained that the Puritan John Reynolds quoted an author for every sentence, almost every syllable. Whatever his particular method, the preacher had scope for his whole range of gifts, spiritual, intellectual, literary, and histrionic. The sermon was at once a sophisticated and a popular kind of literature and on both accounts it was a sensitive index to changing fashions in homiletic technique and in prose style, so that the variety of sermon literature is commensurate with its bulk. In these pages we must ignore dozens of eminent preachers and shall look at only four men, Adams, Andrewes, Donne, and Taylor.

Thomas Adams, whose wit and fancy Southey praised, was an heir of the silver-tongued Henry Smith and the sulphur-tongued William Perkins, and he was touched by both Euphuism and Senecanism (he speaks of Lipsius's style and often quotes Seneca).[1] In his *Mystical Bedlam* (1615) and *Diseases of the Soul* (1616) Adams was a lively exponent of the 'character' as a homiletic device—and recreation. The latter piece (called *The Soul's Sickness* in the *Works*) is 'a discourse divine, morall, and physicall' which reminds us of Burton; Adams is akin to Burton too, and to Latimer, in his mixture of sympathy for the poor and satire upon their oppressors.

Almost any sermon exhibits Adams's mastery of all the popular resources of the City and Puritan preacher. *The City of Peace* opens with a figurative and biblical character of Peace. Then peace is likened to a city, to London. The city of peace has walls of unity and concord; four gates, innocence and patience, benefaction and satisfaction, which correspond to Bishopsgate, Ludgate, Aldgate, and Cripplegate; and so on. The body of the sermon consists in the realistic and hortatory amplification of the *exemplum*. The method is not strictly allegorical, but it springs from the allegorical habit of mind which produced Latimer's sermons on the card, Bernard's *Isle of Man* (Adams uses this phrase), and the poetical treatments of the castle of the body. Some other suggestive titles are *The Gallant's Burden*, *The White Devil or the Hypocrite Uncased* (1612), *The Spiritual Navigator Bound for the Holy Land*. Whether or not an entire discourse rests upon an allegorical frame, the texture of Adams's sermons is rich in vivid and usually homely metaphor and pointed wit. But his sole and fervent aim is to rebuke sin

---

[1] After graduating from Cambridge (B.A., 1601/2; M.A., 1606) Adams became a preacher in Bedfordshire. Then he held a living in Buckinghamshire and, from 1618 to 1623, the preachership of St. Gregory's under St. Paul's Cathedral. By 1629 he was in charge of St. Benet's, Paul's Wharf. He was also an occasional preacher at Paul's Cross and Whitehall. Adams was chaplain to the Chief Justice of the King's Bench, Sir Henry Montagu (later the first Earl of Manchester), who himself compiled a moral, religious, and at times mystical volume, *Contemplatio Mortis, & Immortalitatis* (1631). It may be added that in dedications Adams addressed William Earl of Pembroke, Lord Ellesmere, and others rather as friends than as patrons. His voice is last heard in 1653, speaking of his 'necessitous and decrepit old age'. Many of his sermons appeared separately, and his *Works* in 1629.

and preach the gospel, and his tricks, including the rhetorical *schemata* of which he is one of the last exponents, are only means of arousing the sluggish conscience: 'all our preaching is but to beget your praying.' There is very little of the theological erudition and argument which make so many contemporary sermons crabbed reading, and Adams's secular quotations, though they range from numerous classics to Montaigne, John Owen, Chapman, and Sylvester, are handled discreetly—one may say ingeniously when Ovid's lines about a woman's feigned resistance are applied to the soul and the body. Adams is, then, an earnest preacher, a cultivated scholar, a topical humorist and satirist, and he can write of a summer morning and the lark in a lyrical vein half-way between Breton and Taylor. But for quotation we take two passages on death. The first, from *God's Bounty*, may be set beside Browne:

It is a foolish dreame, to hope for immortalitie and a long-lasting name, by a monument of brasse or stone. It is not dead stones, but living men, that can redeeme thy good remembrance from oblivion. . . . Onely thy noble and Christian life makes every mans heart thy Tombe, and turnes every tongue into a pen, to write thy deathlesse Epitaph.

The second passage comes from *The Sinner's Mourning Habit*:

Dust, the matter of our substance, the house of our soules, the originall graines whereof we were made, the top of all our kinred. The glory of the strongest man, the beautie of the fairest woman; all is but dust. Dust; the onely compounder of differences, the absolver of all distinctions: who can say, which was the Client, which the Lawyer: which the borrower, which the lender: which the captive, which the Conquerer; when they all lie together in blended dust?

Adams's schematic generalities may be set beside this characteristic elaboration of particulars in the fifteenth of Donne's *LXXX Sermons*:

The dust of great persons graves is speechlesse too, it sayes nothing, it distinguishes nothing: As soon the dust of a wretch whom thou wouldest not, as of a Prince whom thou couldest not look upon, will trouble thine eyes, if the winde blow it thither; and when a whirle-winde hath blowne the dust of the Church-yard into the Church, and the man sweeps out the dust of the Church into the Church-yard, who will undertake to sift those dusts again, and to pronounce, This is the Patrician, this is the noble flowre, and this the yeomanly, this the Plebeian bran?

It may be a shock to turn from Adams's moving common-places to a bit of Andrewes's Easter sermon (1617) on Matthew xii. 39–40:[1]

They [the Pharisees] would see a Signe. The answere is negative, but qualified. There is in it, a *Non*, and a *Nisi*: *Non dabitur*, none shalbe given them. Indeed none should: They were worthy of none. Yet saith He not, *Non* simply. His *Non*, is with a *Nisi*, *Non dabitur, nisi*; it is with a limitation, with a *but*: *None, but*, that. So, that: So, one shalbe. In the *Non*, is their desert: in the *Nisi*, His goodnesse: that, though they were worthy none, yet gives them one, though.

The quotations from Adams represent only a slight elevation above his normal manner, and the quotation from Andrewes, which represents no great exaggeration of his normal manner, reads like a parody of the Lipsian and Senecan 'hopping style'. In about two-thirds of the texture of his *XCVI Sermons* (1629) Andrewes is condensed, jerky, and difficult. The reasons are partly personal, partly not. Nearly all of Andrewes's extant sermons were delivered before the court, many of them in series on the great festivals of the Christian year, and 'the first great preacher of the English Catholic Church' was addressing an audience of theological connoisseurs. While Adams seeks always to awaken the sinner and arm the Christian warrior for combat in a world of evil, Andrewes, the biblical and patristic scholar, devotes himself to acute, exact, learned, and impersonal exegesis of his text, squeezing out the last drop of meaning from every word. He declares that 'The onely true praise of a Sermon is, some evill left, or some good done, upon the hearing of it', and his Lenten discourses are full of practical piety, but in the majority of his sermons Andrewes seems to take for granted all that Adams makes the basis of his religious and moral appeal.

---

[1] Lancelot Andrewes (1555–1626) was born in London of middle-class parents. In 1571 he followed Spenser from Mulcaster's school to Pembroke Hall, Cambridge. He was ordained in 1580–1 and some years later became a chaplain to Whitgift and to the queen. From 1589 to 1605 he was Master of Pembroke Hall. He was made Dean of Westminster in 1601, and held successively the bishoprics of Chichester (1605), Ely (1609), and Winchester (1618). Throughout James's reign Andrewes was a prominent figure at court and served in various secular capacities, in spite of his ecclesiastical, devotional, and scholarly preoccupations. He was revered for his learning as well as for his preaching and his sanctity. Andrewes was a friend of Hooker, apparently, and of Bacon, Camden, Selden, Casaubon, Grotius, Junius, and other foreign scholars, and of George Herbert, and his beneficiaries were innumerable. His death was lamented in verse by Milton and Crashaw. Andrewes's share in the Authorized Version was mentioned earlier, and his place in the philosophic establishment of the Church of England is indicated below.

Moreover, the profane literature that Adams so freely draws upon Andrewes almost completely avoids. We may conclude that the Jacobean *stella praedicantium* has sunk altogether below our horizon.

Yet the persevering reader, unless he is too hard, or too soft, for all religious exposition, may come to qualify his first impressions. If he is chilled by Andrewes's severe and 'witty' intellectualism, he must grant that the preacher's mind is always working, and that he demands the same close attention as a jurist or a metaphysical poet. If Andrewes seldom approaches the ecstasies of Donne—we may not enjoy his juggling with 'the seasons' (Christmas, 1623) after Donne's great rhapsody—he has nothing of Donne's extravagance and auto-intoxication. If he seems to lack fire, its frequent brief flashes, analytic or emotional, are all the brighter for habitual repression. Whatever his fame owed to his delivery, Andrewes explicitly disparages the arts of the pulpit, the 'blazes' which 'make us a little sermon-warme for the while' but later 'flitt and vanish': 'It is the evidence of the Spirit, in the soundnesse of the sense, that leaves the true impression.' We feel beneath the austere surface what is more apparent in the famous little book of *Devotions* or *Preces Privatae* (translated 1647–8), the sincerity, gentleness, and power born of a disciplined purity of soul, of a life devoted to the contemplation and forwarding of the Christian ideal and heritage. The sermons do not lend themselves to anthologizing but, to speak of the more obvious literary attractions, a hasty glance may miss the bits of vivid paraphrase and imaginative re-creation which light up rigorous exegesis. Witness the account of Mary Magdalene at the tomb (Easter, 1620), or the religious masque made out of the eighty-fifth Psalm (Christmas, 1616), or the passages, like the following from the same sermon, in which Andrewes shares his visions of Christian joy, visions none the less intense for their logical articulation:

And even so then let there be. So, may our end be as the end of the First Verse in peace; and as the end of the Second, in Heaven. So, may all the blessings that came to mankind by this meeting, or by the birth of Christ (the cause of it) meet in us and remaine upon us: till, as we now meet together, at the Birth; So we may then meet in a perfect man, in the measure of the fulnesse of the age of Christ: As meet (now) at the Lambes yeaning; so meet then, at the Lambes marriage; be caught up in the cloudes (then) to meet Him, and there to reigne for ever with Him, in His Kingdome of Glorie.

2

In obvious ways the experience, character, and genius of John Donne (1571/2–1631) set him apart from other seventeenth-century divines. While they were almost born churchmen, the saintly ascetic of St. Paul's was a lily that had risen out of red earth. Walton's parallel was St. Augustine, the brilliant rhetorician, worldling, and sinner transformed into a mighty champion of Christ and the Church. Donne may have exaggerated the stains of his libertine youth, but at least it was not the youth of Andrewes or Taylor. He had been a wit and gallant, a sensual and cynical poet, a student of sceptical and naturalistic thought, a traveller, a soldier, and a member of Parliament. He had known the pleasures of the court and, though 'undone' by his marriage, he continued to cherish hopes of worldly advancement; and after years of penurious dependence, he could not trust his own motives if he yielded to persuasion and took orders. Walton's 'higher hand' which 'at last forced him' into 'this sacred service' was not God, as we might think, but King James, though we may believe that Donne did not become a priest until he was convinced of his own sincerity and vocation. Then there was his Roman Catholic descent and background, which had from the beginning contributed to his sense of being an outlaw and rebel. He had his 'first breeding and conversation', according to the one famous phrase in *Biathanatos*, 'with men of a suppressed and afflicted Religion, accustomed to the despite of death, and hungry of an imagin'd Martyrdome'. Further, his early training at the hands of Jesuits left a permanent impress upon his mind and modes of thought. Like other divines, he went through the classical, patristic, and scholastic mould, but none perhaps absorbed so little from the classics, none so fully assimilated the technique, if not the philosophic totality, of scholasticism. And while some contemporaries had a knowledge of Spanish religious literature, and some of science, Donne was acquainted with both worlds. With many other liberal conservatives, he seems to have accepted Tycho's geocentric system, but Copernicus and the rest added something to his consciousness of intellectual and spiritual insecurity. Finally, Donne remained a poet. There are many general and specific parallels in substance and manner between the sermons and both the religious and the secular verse—normal avoidance of flowing and balanced rhythms, realistic immediacy of reference, dramatic instinct and power, analytic and eccentric wit, abstruse learning, casuistical argument, a strain of the morbid and macabre and sexual, and above all the passionate personal cry which gives fire to the chief religious poems and is heard through much of the prose. While critics' frequent ignorance of all sermons but Donne's has somewhat exaggerated his idiosyncrasies, nevertheless his 'cloth' was not of conventional cut; he might seem to have been the ugly duckling in the ecclesiastical brood. In their own time Donne was a smaller figure than Lancelot Andrewes, but modern opinion—partly of course on account of Donne's poetry—has much more than reversed their positions.

Before we come to the sermons, some 160 in number, the minor works must be noticed. After *Pseudo-Martyr* (1610), a defence of the oath of allegiance made, says Walton, at the king's request, Donne relaxed in *Ignatius his Conclave* (1611), a satire on Loyola and the Jesuits in the tradition of the Senecan and Erasmian skits on Claudius and Pope Julius and of more recent things. In *Biathanatos* (which may be later than its conjectural date, 1608) Donne was openly, and in the eighth 'Problem' evidently, aware of Kepler, but *Ignatius* contains his first precisely datable reference to the new astronomy; Galileo's *Sidereus Nuncius* had appeared early in 1610 and Donne had doubtless learned of it, like King James, through the prompt agency of his friend Wotton.

In *Biathanatos*, for which Donne had a fondness, though he never published it, he offered a qualified apology for suicide which ran counter to the main tradition of Christian thought. Neither the subject nor the learned casuistry is now inviting, but the book grew out of personal affliction and debate and it represents a stage in the evolution of Jack Donne into Dr. John Donne. The author said it was written by the former, not the latter, yet sober questioning of the law of nature and right reason, an appeal to the conditional and relative, was bound to end either in libertine naturalism or in surrender to the supreme law of God and His quickening grace, and Jack Donne already sees the light of nature as the moon, or fires and tapers, compared with the sun of God's word.

A very directly personal document, also composed under affliction, though in a time of much greater worldly and spiritual security, is the *Devotions* (1624). This book, which can be read as a consecutive whole, is the best introduction to Donne's religious prose and religious temper. What Walton called 'a Sacred picture of Spiritual Extasies' was the product of a dangerous illness, the record of a journey through the valley of the shadow. Donne's thoughts and feelings, linked in a triple chain (with an intricate system of smaller links) of 'Meditations upon our Humane Condition', 'Expostulations, and Debatements with God', and 'Prayers, upon the severall Occasions, to him', constitute a kind of allegorical interweaving of physical and spiritual sickness as he sinks down towards the grave and then, not without fear of relapse, returns to health. The theme brings out all Donne's special characteristics, his preoccupation with sin and death, his acuteness of psychological analysis, his keen awareness of the tension between his soul and the world, the originality of his wit, the troubled and sometimes lurid power of his imagination, the essential simplicity, despite its complex and learned surface, of his religious faith—and, it may be added, a degree of monotony and repetitious expansiveness and, in the emphasis on his sinfulness, something of the masochistic exhibitionism commonly associated with Puritan enthusiasts. If, allowing for the special circumstances of his book and his life, we compare the *Devotions* with, say, Andrewes's prayers, we feel at once Donne's brooding, agitated egoism and unrestraint.

Donne's earliest extant sermon was preached before the queen in the year of his ordination, 1615; his last, *Death's Duel*, of which Walton gives such a dramatic account, in February 1631. (The famous title was stolen by the publisher from an obscure poem which was entered before but printed after the sermon.) Having delivered that final challenge to the everlasting worm, the preacher returned home to begin his elaborate arrangements for his end. During his ministry Donne had enjoyed the admiration of his royal patron, of the grave Benchers of Lincoln's Inn (once the frisky companions of his youth), of 'the Representative Body of the whole Clergy of this Nation', and of countless miscellaneous auditors like his worshipful biographer. Walton describes his method of preparing for the pulpit:

The latter part of his life may be said to be a continued study; for as he usually preached once a week, if not oftner, so after his Sermon he never gave his eyes rest, till he had chosen out a new Text, and that night cast his Sermon into a form, and his Text into divisions; and the next day betook himself to consult the Fathers, and so commit his meditations to his memory, which was excellent.

Some enthusiastic ministers and their hearers preferred extempore or 'inspired' preaching, but sentiment in general, while opposed to the reading of sermons, put less faith in Pentecostal visitations, and most Puritans and Anglicans preached from a more or less memorized manuscript or from notes. Donne, who condemned extempore preaching and praying, though he regarded the preacher as the mouthpiece of the Holy Ghost, seems commonly to have written out his sermons sooner or later after their delivery.

Donne's sermons conform in varying degrees to such patterns as that of Keckermann. There are as a rule three main parts: invention, or analysis of the natural divisions of the text; disposition, or amplification of these divisions with arguments and illustrations from the Bible, the Fathers, and later theologians; and the drawing together of the several lines into a general or specific application. For example, on 29 January 1626 Donne preached at St. Paul's from the sixty-third Psalm: 'Because thou hast been my helpe, Therefore in the shadow of thy wings will I rejoyce.' In these words he sees

the whole compasse of Time, Past, Present, and Future; and these three parts of Time, shall be at this time, the three parts of this Exercise; first, what Davids distresse put him upon for the present; and that lyes in the Context; secondly, how David built his assurance upon that which was past; (*Because thou hast been my help*) And thirdly, what he established to himselfe for the future, (*Therefore in the shadow of thy wings will I rejoyce*).

Reading scraps of Donne's sermons in anthologies, with our modern indifference to homiletic art, we miss the order and clarity of the total design. (Incidentally, Donne is given, like Andrewes, to the use of sonorous and repeated key-words as welding rivets.) In the same way, intoxicated by soaring passages of rich poetic imagery, we may forget that the groundwork of the sermons consists of sober exposition and good counsel, in prose which has special affinities with Seneca and the Senecan Tertullian. Matters of doctrine Donne expressly makes secondary to exhortation, edification, 'and a holy stirring of religious affections', and by his definition most of Andrewes's sermons would approach 'lectures'. We are not surprised to find Donne telling the Benchers of Lincoln's Inn that his favourite parts of the Bible are the Psalms and Paul's epistles, or to see that next to the Bible he quotes St. Augustine.

Donne's unusual experience and temperament give his sermons their special note of anguished contrition, unrest, and ecstasy. In the *Devotions* (*Expostulation* iii), St. Paul's fear takes hold of him, that when he has preached to others, he himself should be a castaway. So, whether openly or not, Donne's preaching is strongly personal. Though he discourses of ecclesiastical dogmas and traditions, we seem to hear not so much the authoritative voice of the Church as it speaks through Andrewes, but that of a man appealing to men. What is more important, as one of his best critics has said, we do not feel in Donne, as we do in St. Paul, God speaking to man, but rather man speaking to God. Walton saw him—and Lord Falkland gave a similar account in verse—

preaching the Word so, as shewed his own heart was possest with those very thoughts and joys that he laboured to distill into others: A Preacher in earnest; weeping sometimes for his Auditory, sometimes with them: always preaching to himself, like an Angel from a cloud, but in none; carrying some, as St. Paul was, to Heaven in holy raptures, and inticing others by a sacred Art and Courtship to amend their lives; here picturing a vice so as to make it ugly to those that practised it; and a vertue so, as to make it be beloved even by those that lov'd it not; and, all this with a most particular grace and an unexpressible addition of comeliness.

The picture confirms our impression, which does not at all reflect upon Donne's entire sincerity, that in the pulpit he was by nature something of a theatrical spellbinder. He had his spark of the peculiar burning intensity of Paul and Augustine, and he evidently shared with them 'a delight, and a complacency, and a holy melting of the bowels, when the congregation liked' his preaching. In his illness his sensitive conscience reproaches him with sinning 'in my ostentation, and the mingling a respect of my selfe, in preaching thy Word'.

Like many other men of his century, Donne is often called a mystic. Some rationally minded moderns, of course, regard any religious sentiment or belief as 'mystical' and, moreover, the word is often employed when a better word would be 'misty'. So far as there are definable criteria for authentic historical mysticism, Donne was not a mystic. But, like many other men, he had a temperament inclining to the mystical, and on occasion could speak the mystical language that was in the air. In 'A Valediction: of the Book' and 'To the Countess of Bedford' Donne says, and his sermons give a larger meaning to the words, that 'all Divinity Is love or wonder' and that 'Reason is our Soules left hand, Faith her right'. Such utterances might be a prelude to mysticism, but there are obvious elements in him, mostly inherited from Jack Donne, which impede his ascent to supra-rational fusion of self with Deity. For one thing, he lacks the desire. He accepts mortal limitations, as a Christian warrior rather than a man of contemplative vision; and one doubts if he *loved* God in the mystic's sense. Then there remained a strong consciousness of the body, and a strongly egoistic personality, which he might strive to subdue and reconcile with God but which he could not wholly extinguish or surrender. With such forces were combined the actuality, the pressure, and the fascination of the mundane world which, both as a man and as a poet, Donne felt so intensely and sought continually to escape from. At prayer he can be distracted by the memory of his youthful wantonness, or even by a straw under his knee, a noise in his ear. If the religious imagination is the faculty by which we unite the broken and dispersed images of the world into an harmonious poetic symbol, it may be thought that Donne has a much stronger sense of parts than of wholes, of the concrete than the abstract. Thus the idea of the infinite extent of God's mercies, or the infinite duration of eternity, becomes intelligibly and intensely vivid when rendered into concrete and imaginative particulars in a beautiful rhythmic spiral of ascending clauses; and yet, as the passages end, we are perhaps less conscious of God than of this world.

A further impediment is Donne's reason, not so much the humanistic 'right reason' of the divines who established the *via media* (though he frequently insists upon the rational element in religion), but the restless, inquiring reason of the instinctive sceptic—if this last word may be used in a very limited and quite unmodern sense. Donne had realized the winding and craggy approach to truth. He had, with intellectual detachment, refused to make a decision until he had digested the whole body of controversy regarding Roman and Anglican claims. And even in the sermons the old demon of uncertainty may raise its head, not seriously to disturb his faith, but to ask what human knowledge is perfect and secure. Such a man, with such relics of self and earth and universal flux about him, could seldom if ever get up into the watch-tower of mystical illumination and insight. It is, then, with all the more passionate abandon that Donne flings himself at the foot of the Cross. For all the learning with which he fortifies and embellishes his sermons, and all the elaboration of minute points of doctrine, his central faith is not much more complex than General Booth's. Whatever his nominal text, his one invariable theme is 'inquietum est cor nostrum, donec requiescat in te'—which is not to say that Donne achieved the altered will and final certitude of Augustine.

To the modern mind, sceptical in a way that Donne never was, the churchman's complete theological orthodoxy, his upholding of rigorous and Erastian uniformity within the Church, and his evangelical emphasis, ought to appear less respectable than Milton's independent creed, though it is Milton who attracts all the missiles. However, the modern student has not been much concerned with Donne's religious thought but rather with the literary qualities of prose and verse which happen to treat religious subjects. The religious reader, indeed, may be somewhat repelled by a preacher whose imperfectly controlled energy is so much more emotional and imaginative than philosophical. It is not an historical accident or oversight that Donne, with all his personal and literary distinction, has not been commonly counted a major figure among the fathers of the English Church. If that is for some a minor point, there is the fact, or opinion, that we can read Donne's sermons without much religious quickening and, in spite of the personal accent, without a sense of intimacy; we get both from almost any page of the layman Sir Thomas Browne. The answer is certainly not that Donne was insincere, or that he never found what he believed to be full satisfaction in the Church, but perhaps that, being the kind of man he was, he obtained full satisfaction for parts of his nature by virtually suppressing other parts. In the seventy-ninth sermon we read:

Even in spirituall things, there may be a fulnesse, and no satisfaction, And there may be a satisfaction, and no fulnesse; I may have as much knowledge, as is presently necessary for my salvation, and yet have a restlesse and unsatisfied desire, to search into unprofitable curiosities, unrevealed mysteries, and inextricable perplexities: And, on the other side, a man may be satisfied, and thinke he knowes all, when, God knowes, he knowes nothing at all; for, I know nothing, if I know not Christ crucified, And I know not that, if I know not how to apply him to my selfe, Nor doe I know that, if I embrace him not in those meanes, which he hath afforded me in his Church, in his Word, and Sacraments; If I neglect this meanes, this place, these exercises, howsoever I may satisfie my selfe, with an over-valuing mine own knowledge at home, I am so far from fulnesse, as that vanity it selfe is not more empty.

These words contain much of the burden of Donne's preaching, and they suggest some of the conflicting elements in his mind and temperament. He had never undergone a religious 'con-version', though his marriage and the loss of his wife had comparable effects. Donne had always been intellectually religious, and marriage and circumstances altered his mode of life rather than his creed. But his soul did not grow freely and naturally from a seed into a spreading tree; it was both mature and somewhat twisted when transplanted, and in putting forth some new roots it lost some old ones. Other men might no doubt arrive at a similar position without being warped, and Donne's own religious evolution was a gradual and not a sudden process; yet there is something forced and unnatural, something which often marks the religiosity of the converted worldling and intellectual, in his eager acceptance of authority and his eager quest of salvation, in his narrowness and his note of excess. In reading Hooker, Taylor, Browne, the Cambridge Platonists, and Milton, we know, whatever their defects may be, that we are in contact with the whole man, the normally ripened man. In reading Donne we may feel that the preacher who plays so wonderfully upon our sensibilities has gained satisfaction at the cost of full-ness, and that our satisfaction in him remains incomplete.

3

The metaphysical style, which was so well adapted to the paradoxes of faith, was a European phenomenon. In England it ran throughout our period but was especially strong in the first half of it. Andrewes and Donne, the greatest Anglo-Catholic preachers of the age, were, though very different, the chief exemplars. In prose as in verse wit involved not merely verbal tricks and surprises but the linking together of dissimilar objects, symbols, and ideas philosophized and fused by intellectual and spiritual perceptions and emotions, weighted by frequently abstruse or scientific learning, and made arresting by pointed expression. Along with the general and philosophic causes behind this mode of thought and feeling, there were the general stylistic influences represented by Euphuism and Senecanism and, for preachers, the example of some of the Fathers and their scholastic and schematic successors. On the other hand, a host of Puritan preachers, and some Anglicans—such as Herbert, the young friend of Andrewes and Donne—preferred a 'Scriptural and Christian Plainness'. That quality, to be sure, was not a fixed absolute. For Donne 'the Holy Ghost is an eloquent Author', abundant though not luxuriant, and, far from being low and homely, outdoes all the figures and tropes of classical poetry and oratory. For most Puritans, as John Downame put it, 'the holie Ghost in penning the Scriptures hath used great simplicitie and wonderfull plainnesse, applying himselfe to the capacitie of the most unlearned'. But this view did not exclude imagery and other popular and effective devices.

The cult of plainness, then, did not begin after 1660. Preaching was affected by the general causes which nourished plain writing: the extension of the middle-class reading public, the rapid growth of the varied literature of knowledge, the still more rapid growth of popular controversy in politics and religion, and the antiquarianism of Camden, Richard Verstegan, and William Lisle, which carried on, with patriotic and primitivist zeal, the sixteenth-century campaign for Saxon purism and clarity. We have observed already the multitude of devotional books. Perkins's Ramist manual for preachers was frequently reprinted throughout the century. Sir William Vaughan's *Golden Grove* (1600) included a plea for homiletic simplicity. Bacon's reverberating attack on Ciceronian rhetoric (1605) was aimed partly at the pulpit. Some twenty years later Owen Felltham, a notable Senecan, urged the cultivation of a 'pleasingly-plaine' pulpit style, 'kemb'd I wish it, not frizzled, nor curl'd'. When Ussher was in Oxford in 1642, his plain preaching 'quite put out of countenance that windy, affected sort of Oratory, which was then much in use, called *floride* preaching, or strong lines'. And with Ussher may be grouped

Hall and Hammond and Sanderson, Hales and Chillingworth. John Wilkins, a moderate Puritan, urged plainness in his *Ecclesiastes* (1646), a popular handbook for preachers; and it might be taken as allegorical that this father of the Royal Society was the father-in-law of Tillotson. There were, then, many important champions and exponents of plain preaching, and their cause was destined to triumph. But our last pulpit orator, who shared with the witty preachers the censures of the Restoration, is the great representative of the decorative school and one of the greatest masters of English prose, Jeremy Taylor. Like so many other writers of his age, he was rediscovered by Coleridge, Lamb, and Hazlitt, although, unlike some others, he had never been lost.[1]

Taylor's first publication (1638), an anti-Romanist sermon delivered at Oxford on the anniversary of the Gunpowder Plot, and dedicated to the archbishop, was a thorny argument which contained no budding roses, though it showed a pacific dislike of force. His second book (1642) was an academic defence of episcopacy such as might have been expected from a young divine nurtured in the school of Laud. His *Discourse concerning*

---

[1] Jeremy Taylor (1613–67) was the son of a Cambridge barber of some education. He attended the new Perse School and had a distinguished career at Gonville and Caius College (1626–35). We do not know if he was acquainted with such Cambridge contemporaries as Milton, Fuller, Crashaw, Whichcote, and Henry More; More at any rate he knew later through the Conways. As a substitute preacher at St. Paul's (which had lost Donne in 1631), the young man made such a name that Laud, watchful for recruits, sent him to Oxford to ripen in a favourable climate. In 1636 Taylor became a fellow of All Souls, whose warden was Gilbert Sheldon. During 1638–42 Taylor was rector of Uppingham. He married in 1639. In 1642 he received from Oxford the degree of D.D. by royal mandate. For some time Taylor was attached as chaplain to the king's household, but in 1645 he was captured by parliamentary troops before Cardigan Castle. Soon after his release he found protection with the Earl and Countess of Carbery at Golden Grove in Carmarthenshire, and spent most of the next decade there. During this time he produced much of his best work. Taylor sometimes preached in London, and became a friend of Evelyn. He suffered imprisonment in 1655, it is not clear why. In 1657 he inscribed his *Discourse of Friendship* to Katherine Philips. In 1658 Lord Conway gave him a lectureship at Lisburn in Ireland. Taylor welcomed the Restoration by dedicating to the king his large and long-incubated work of casuistry, *Ductor Dubitantium*. In 1660 also came *The Worthy Communicant* and Taylor's nomination to the see of Down and Connor. His episcopal career was made unhappy by friction with the Presbyterian clergy. As Vice-Chancellor of the University of Dublin, Taylor accomplished a good deal of reorganization. In 1663 he delivered his oratorical swan-song, the funeral sermon on Archbishop Bramhall. His own death (1667) was the occasion of a fine (and biographically valuable) sermon by his friend Dean Rust. Taylor was buried in the cathedral he had built in Dromore.

Prayer Ex tempore (1646) was a bold criticism of the new *Directory for Public Worship* and, enlarged in 1649 as *An Apology for Authorized and Set Forms of Liturgy*, was boldly dedicated to the king just before his execution. In this, along with a deep loyalty to the Church of England, there are hints of a broadening mind. Taylor sees the unity of the Catholic communion being destroyed by the contentiousness which 'makes every schoole point, become our religion'. And he upholds 'a latitude of Theologie, much whereof is left to us, so without precise and cleere determination, that without breach either of faith or charity, men may differ in opinion'.

These words might stand as the text of his first vital book, *The Liberty of Prophesying* (1647), a book which offended his royal master, though its liberalism was not un-Laudian. In dedicating a collected edition of 1657, Taylor denied any inconsistency on the ground that his plea for liberty of conscience was based, like his plea for episcopacy, on Scripture and antiquity, but the natural development of his mind was quickened by the 'common calamity' and his 'private Troubles'. Although he lamented that, cast upon the shore of Wales by the storm which had wrecked the Church, he had written almost without books, he did bring a weight of learning to his account of the difficulties of scriptural interpretation and the errors and disputes of the councils, Fathers, and later theologians. As a whole the work is the best example of Taylor's earlier prose, lucid, sober, unadorned, and animated by deep and sad conviction. His argument is, in brief, that all Christians agree on the few fundamentals of faith which are plainly revealed in the Bible; that nothing is necessary to salvation except belief in the Apostles' Creed and a good life; that the endless disagreements which lead to persecution turn upon unnecessary points that cannot be solved; and that there is accordingly no real excuse for intolerance and strife if men will only seek God with their best reason, with humility, and with charity. Taylor may have owed something to talk with Chillingworth in Oxford days, or to *The Religion of Protestants*. Writing ten years later, when the Presbyterians and Independents are dominant, Taylor is less preoccupied with Rome and more conscious of sectarian divisions, but he stands with Chillingworth and others in his latitudinarian principles and in his appeal to Scripture and reason. Yet we should not make the liberal High Churchman too broadly or loosely Protestant. In the twenty-second of his *XXVIII Sermons* (1651) he says: 'The Church of England had reason to separate from the Confession and practises of Rome in many particulars, and yet if her children separate from her they may be unreasonable and impious.' And, like most other liberals, Taylor is not of course an advocate of freedom in the modern sense. 'Whatsoever is against the foundation of Faith, or contrary to good life and the lawes of obedience, or destructive to humane society, and the publick and just interests of bodies politick, is out of the limits of my Question, and does not pretend to complyance or toleration.' Finally, for Taylor as for Chillingworth, the operations of reason are circumscribed by the premiss that 'there is no greater probation in the world that a proposition is true, then because God hath commanded us to believe it'.

Holy Living (1650) is, with Fuller's *Holy State* (1642), the best-known example of the religious, moral, and domestic branch of the literature of conduct. Such books had a pedigree stretching back through writers like William Gouge, Joseph Hall, Sir William Vaughan, and William Perkins into the early Middle Ages. *Holy Living* was dedicated to Taylor's patron, Richard Vaughan, Earl of Carbery, nephew of the author of *The Golden Grove* (1600) and himself the author of a courtesy book. In the epistle Taylor pictures the desolation of the Church, which creates all the more need for private guidance, and repeats his constant plea, the sufficiency for membership in Christ of the essentials of faith and a holy life. In the text he covers the usual range of personal and social topics, the care of our time, the uses of prayer (prayers are furnished for every kind of person and occasion), sobriety and temperance, chastity (a subject on which Taylor is more candid than many divines), humility, modesty, contentedness in all estates, the duties of inferiors and superiors, the exercises of piety and charity. Such a table of contents explains modern neglect of the book; and the style, though not the plain, workmanlike instrument of *The Liberty of Prophesying*, has achieved the copious, limpid flow without much of the richness that we associate with Taylor.

A strain of melancholy other-worldliness runs through *Holy Living*, and its most sustained piece of eloquence is an incidental prelude to the full orchestration of *Holy Dying* (1651). Lady Carbery, for whom this book was written, and Taylor's wife had just died, so that personal grief entered keenly into his contemplation of mortality and his precepts of faith and patience. 'Death is nothing but the middle point between two lives.' To us *Holy Dying* makes a much stronger appeal than its predecessor. Its compelling theme awakens in Taylor the qualities he shares with Browne and Shakespeare and the rest, with the authors of the moralities and the many works *de contemptu mundi*. He could command, and know that he commanded in others, all the ideas and emotions which had gathered about the supreme fact in antiquity and in sixteen centuries of Christian faith, and the devout rhetorician rings the solemn changes on them all. His book has nothing of the subtle and individual intellectualism of Donne's *Devotions*. Taylor's power is his capacity for feeling and expressing the great commonplaces. Even his circling repetitiousness has the effect of heightening the physical and spiritual frailty, the inescapable misery, of puny man, of multiplying mirrors in a labyrinthine charnel-house, and, though we pay less heed to this, of multiplying the evidences of God's chastening love and mercy.

With the Christian and—for want of a better word—medieval elements in Taylor's imagination is fused the classical, in a distinctive manner and degree. He extols the ancient philosophers and poets, especially the Greeks, even in the preface to his life of Christ, *The Great Exemplar* (1649). In *Holy Dying*, Christ's command to Peter to walk on the water recalls a parallel in the *Tusculan Disputations*; a sentence on administering the eucharist to the sick contains an echo of the *Satyricon*. Whatever he owes to commonplace books, Taylor's mind dwells so willingly in the world of the Caesars and the East that casual images, involving no proper names, keep us in a half-ancient atmosphere. It was not in Wales that he thought in terms of consulships and saw 'a wilde boar destroy our vineyards', or orchards planted to 'feed our Nephews', a filleted beast bound to the altar, gladiators, pirates, labouring galley-slaves, the tents and triumphal chariots of conquerors. He describes maternal cares and coddling with what is surely first-hand domestic knowledge, and then turns to a father's pride in a son who has speared a lion. Taylor's occasional consciousness of something wrong—'I speak in the stile of the Roman greatnesse'—happily does not check his imaginative realization of the timeless facts of life and death and the vain ambitions of man. Further, the counsels of the Christian priest are con-

tinually philosophized by the ethical wisdom of the pagans—
Seneca (whom Donne disparaged as the oracle of moral men),
Plutarch, Cicero, and a host of others. (High on Taylor's
allusive list, if not on the conventional roll of moralists, are
Petronius and Martial.) Taylor's instinctive fusing of the two
great bodies of truth, natural and revealed, is wholly in
keeping with the tradition of Christian humanism. In him
as in other men, like Milton, it is based on the great principle
that, in his own words, the 'Christian Religion in all its
moral parts is nothing else but the Law of Nature, and great
Reason'.

Like *The Fairy Queen* and *Paradise Lost*, *Holy Dying* may be
viewed as an interwoven series of variations on contrasting
themes, God and man, heaven and hell, good and evil, light and
darkness, health and disease, life and death, and—when they
are not united—Christianity and paganism. These contrasts are
carried out in the rich imagery that has kept alive a book which,
its author says, 'needs no Apology for being plain'. Much of it is
plain, to be sure, and even the most ornate passages are pure
and simple in diction and, however solemn, almost lightly fluid
in rhythm. Taylor's mature prose is as remarkable for its
natural and sensuous images as Donne's is for the lack of them.
He is stirred by pomp and circumstance, by ancient Rome and
the Escurial, and his love of life has its obverse expression in
pictures of the corruptions of the grave; but his characteristic
imagery is common and fresh as the morning—water, wind,
flowers, the lark, the partridge, the stars, and above all the light
of the sun. The sun gilds the fringes of the clouds and dancing
atoms; the wanton young man 'dances like a bubble, empty and
gay, and shines like a Doves neck or the image of a rainbow'.
Taylor's closest affinity, temperamental and didactic as well as
artistic, is with Spenser. This is the most famous simile in
Taylor:

But so have I seen a Rose newly springing from the clefts of its hood,
and at first it was fair as the Morning, and full with the dew of
Heaven, as a Lambs fleece; but when a ruder breath had forced
open its virgin modesty, and dismantled its too youthful and unripe
retirements, it began to put on darknesse, and to decline to softnesse,
and the symptomes of a sickly age; it bowed the head, and broke its
stalk, and at night having lost some of its leaves, and all its beauty, it
fell into the portion of weeds and outworn faces.

And this is Spenser:

> The whiles some one did chaunt this louely lay;
> Ah see, who so faire thing doest faine to see,
> In springing flowre the image of thy day;
> Ah see the Virgin Rose, how sweetly shee
> Doth first peepe forth with bashfull modestee,
> That fairer seemes, the lesse ye see her may;
> Lo see soone after, how more bold and free
> Her bared bosome she doth broad display;
> Loe see soone after, how she fades, and falles away.

It is the divine, and not the lay poet, whose visual and decorative fancy obscures his serious intention.

Taylor's sermons (mostly published in 1651 and 1653) are similar in purpose and character to *Holy Living* and *Holy Dying*. He disclaims novel speculations in favour of 'the sincere milk of the word' and 'the greater lines of Dutie'. Even in the grand funeral orations on Lady Carbery, Sir George Dalston, and Archbishop Bramhall, daily practice is not forgotten. Although Taylor was not quite orthodox on original sin and got himself into trouble with *Unum Necessarium* (1655), the theology of the sermons is the simple, and splendid, pattern which had served preachers ever since Paul. Life is a battle which at every moment, with God's aid or the devil's, we are winning or losing. By grace, repentance, and unceasing effort we are delivered alike from the old covenant and the bondage of sin into Christian liberty, love, and joy. The two supreme incentives are the terrors of hell and the bliss of heaven. The elaboration of these ideas offers the inevitable and suggestive contrasts. 'Now between these two states of naturall flesh, and heavenly spirit, that is, the powers of darknesse, and the regions of light, the miseries of man, and the perfections of God, ... there is a middle state; the Kingdome of grace wrought for us by our Mediator, the man Christ Jesus.' Like all preachers, Taylor makes much of the atonement, but his special emphasis is indicated in the title of his 'holy romance', *The Great Exemplar*. The pulpit and evangelical fervour do not forbid classical embroidery. The subject of epicurean intemperance brings forth allusions in clusters, and even a summary of the central mysteries of faith (at the beginning of *The Spirit of Grace*) contains an Anacreontic phrase.

Classical quotations and references of course do not make classical writing. The simile of the river and the brook, from the

sermon on Lady Carbery, was quoted by Arnold as an example
of the genius of poetry rather than the intelligence of prose,
and, to emphasize Taylor's provincial note, he cited Bossuet.
Whether or not we endorse the verdict, we should remember
that purple patches quoted by critics or assembled in anthologies give a distorted view of Taylor's pulpit style, as they do of
Donne's. The figurative and poetical element is not large in
proportion to the bulk of relatively plain writing. It is that
element, however, which offended Restoration divines and
which chiefly attracts us. Taylor's fancy may lapse into old-
fashioned quaintness, as when he describes the stomach in terms
of a castle with ovens and cooks or when he employs euphuistic
natural history. But his imagination may take wing from any
one of his common themes, life and death, time and eternity,
the worm that dieth not, and the mercy that is inexhaustible.
We cherish him most in the typical quiet moods which reveal
his love for the familiar things of nature, the sea, rivers, and
springs, clouds, refreshing rain, and the sun—or 'the Sun of
Righteousness'—which gives light and life. For Taylor, as for
other men of his time, the rays of the sun come from a Platonic
heaven. If we sinners do our best, God, 'in stead of being a con-
suming fire, shall become to us the circle of a glorious crown,
and a globe of an eternall light'. The preacher has a special
tenderness for those 'little images and reflexes' of God, children,
lambs, roses and 'the softest stalk of a violet', 'the little birds and
laborious bees', the lark struggling bravely against the wind.
Though he can depict the pageant of terrestrial nature and the
cosmic order with panoramic vision, he enjoys 'the beauty of a
little prospect from a hill'. And since Taylor has been accused
of ignoring all but the well-fed, it may be added that he often
contrasts virtuous poverty with sinful wealth and is aware of the
oppression and 'the needs of the poor man, his rent day, and
the cryes of his children'.

Sometimes the familiar is combined with the remote, bizarre,
or romantic. Men of pharisaical religion 'are stiffe as Isicles,
and without flexure as the legs of Elephants'; Taylor must have
missed Browne's triumphant arguments. Faint prayers are laid
aside in heaven 'like the buds of roses which a cold wind hath
nip'd into death, and the discoloured tawny face of an Indian
slave'. Finally, besides what may be called two-dimensional
images, there are rarer ones which have a kind of strangeness

added to their beauty and are quintessential, magical poetry, though they depend for their full effect on their homiletic point, as not all the elaborate similes do. Perhaps the best of them spring from the preacher's poignant sense of the allurements of the world and the flesh for men who 'look after white and red, and the weaker beauties of the night'—

. . . but as the fires die and desires decay, so the mind steals away and walks abroad to see the little images of beauty and pleasure, which it beholds in the falling stars and little glow-wormes of the world.

And while Taylor, like Spenser, is firmly on the side of the resolved soul, our memory (to borrow further examples from Pearsall Smith) retains the image of the libertine who, full of 'wine, and rage, and pleasure, and folly', goes 'singing to his grave', and we forget 'the severities of a watchfull and a sober life'; we remember 'the harlots hands that build the fairy castle' and not 'the hands of reason and religion' which must pull it down.

4

We turn now to some aspects of religious controversy and to philosophic attempts to find a broad and solid *via media* in a world unsettled by both religious dissension and scientific thought. The general situation was outlined in the first chapter, and even here we cannot go very far into the complex problems and the mass of strong and sometimes noble writing they called forth. At any rate those problems all spring from one two-sided question, 'What are the grounds of inward faith and of external authority'?

The construction, or reconstruction, of the Church of England was the work of men like Whitgift, Bancroft, and Laud, who in their increasingly coercive policy received increasing support from their several sovereigns. On the side of apologetics it was Andrewes, the successor of Hooker and Jewel, who established for our period the Anglo-Catholic, High Church, or Arminian position. Earlier generations of Anglicans had naturally stressed their Protestant remoteness from Rome; now that the time of active revolt was past, a larger view was possible. The Church of England was defended as a true Catholic Church, purified from the accumulated inventions and abuses of Rome, perpetuating the apostolic succession and the doctrines, rites, and organization authorized by Scripture, by three

creeds, by the first four general councils, and by the Fathers of
the first five centuries. If that sounds uninspiring to the secular
mind, it may be remembered that Anglo-Catholicism, though
it lost some popular and international roots, meant nevertheless
the restored vitality of a body of traditional thought and feeling,
ecclesiastical, philosophic, and mystical, without which the
great religious poetry and much great prose could not have been
written. In maintaining the continuity and Catholicity of the
Church of England against the great champion of Rome,
Cardinal Bellarmine, Andrewes deployed his judgement of
fundamentals, his powers of acute reasoning, his exact learning, and sometimes edged wit, with such success that the
task of later apologists was mainly amplification. Historical
buttresses were to be erected by the learned Ussher, Sir Henry
Spelman, Sir Roger Twysden, and others, who broadened the
ecclesiastical impulse inherited from the nationalist and Protestant antiquarian movement of the sixteenth century.

In the controversies with Rome one particular question was
forced to the front. The papal bull of 1570 had put both the
English government and English Catholics in a dilemma, and
that was sharpened a generation later by the Gunpowder Plot.
In addition to the Englishman's inveterate dislike of foreign and
ecclesiastical intervention and his well-founded fear of Catholic
treason, more philosophic arguments were raised by King
James, Andrewes, Donne, and others in defence of the oath of
allegiance (1606). Defence of the oath was of course bound up
with the divine right of kings, which was the only adequate
theoretical answer to the papal claim of deposing and dispen-
sing power. If we recoil from the frequent servility of Jacobean
and Caroline churchmen, we should remember that they shared
the common dread of civil disorder and the common reverence
for the throne, and that in fact if not in theory the Church of
England was a new institution, struggling to maintain itself
against enemies abroad and multiplying enemies at home, and
depending for support upon the Lord's Anointed. It was wholly
natural that many churchmen should have deserved the tribute
Sir John Harington paid to Andrewes, that his sermons tended
'to raise a joynt reverence to God and the Prince, to the
spirituall and civile magistrate, by uniting and not severing
them'.

In theology our period witnessed very important reactions to the Calvinism of the Elizabethan Church. Against Calvinistic rigours 'our late Arminians', to quote Robert Burton, 'have revived that plausible doctrine of universall grace, which many Fathers, our late Lutherans and modern Papists do still maintain, that we have free-will of our selves, and that grace is common to all that will beleeve'. According to Fuller, the Dalmatian Archbishop of Spalatro, who was in England during 1616–22, was the first to use 'Puritan' in a doctrinal sense, as opposed to Arminian. While the original meaning of 'Arminian' was theological (and in that sense Milton was the greatest of Arminians), the word became for Puritans the odious label of the High Church and royalist party. Stages in the Anglican movement towards Arminianism are represented by the effective opposition of the elderly Peter Baro and the younger clergy, notably Andrewes, to Whitgift's Calvinistic Lambeth Articles (1595); by the Synod of Dort (1618–19), where John Hales bade good night to John Calvin; and by the storm that arose over Richard Montagu's *Appello Caesarem* (1625). Although many Anglicans, from King James down, retained more or less of Genevan theology (and Hales, it has been said, did not bid good morning to Arminius), the Deity of Anglican thought became more benevolent and rational. One factor in the process was the influence of Grotius.

At the same time, in both old and New England, Calvinism itself was undergoing a change. Much of the emotional power of the creed had come from its dogmatic picture of God as Absolute Will, an inscrutable Jehovah of whom not even human reasonableness and justice could be predicated, since His will, as the almost omnipotent Perkins said, 'it selfe is an absolute rule both of justice and reason', and what He wills 'thereupon becomes reasonable and just'. The doctrine reminds us that Calvin was an heir of Scotus and Ockham. But a group of younger Calvinist theologians, of whom the chief was Perkins's pupil, William Ames (1576–1633), could no longer be content to prostrate themselves before a Deity whose decrees were so far beyond human understanding. In his *Medulla Sacrae Theologiae* (1623; translated 1642), a standard text-book on both sides of the Atlantic, Ames sought to give Calvinist dogma an intellectual and rational foundation. Perkins himself had planted seeds which, watered by men of such influence as Ames, John Preston, and Richard Sibbes, flowered into the great doctrine of the covenant. According to that legalistic conception, mankind from Adam downwards had shared in contracts with God. The original covenant of works was the moral law of nature which should have enabled Adam to walk uprightly. But Adam fell, and with Abraham God made the covenant of grace, by which He undertook not only to save believers but to supply the grace or power of belief which would make salvation possible. That covenant still holds, and modern men have the additional surety of Christ the mediator. Thus God's willingness to be a partner with His creatures proved His essential rationality, benevolence, mercy, and forethought for the progressive capacity of man. The covenant helped to resolve the terrible uncertainties of election and reprobation and gave a reasonable basis and incentive for virtuous effort. Such a doctrine, in reinterpreting Calvinism (while trying to shun Arminianism), in enlarging man's powers and reducing the element of arbitrary grace, has affinities with the more liberal and amiable principles of the mainly Puritan group of Cambridge Platonists, with those of the Oxford latitudinarians, and even with the natural religion of Lord Herbert of Cherbury.

All these theological philosophies sprang from a faith in human reason (however that word might be understood) which sometimes almost threatened the supernatural premisses of religion. In his *Sacred Philosophy of the Holy Scripture* (1635) Alexander Gill carried Christian rationalism to the extreme limits of orthodoxy, limits which his quondam pupil Milton was to overstep. Chillingworth, said the horrified Cheynell, 'was not ashamed to print and publish this destructive tenet, That there is no necessity of Church or Scripture to make men faithfull men'; and Chillingworth admitted that Scripture could not prove that there is a God or that it is the word of God. When good Christians could go so far, the natural light of reason might take others still farther. The current of rationalism had been rising for centuries, fed by many Christian writers and many ancient and modern sceptics. Chillingworth, for instance, knew Montaigne and, according to Aubrey, was devoted to Sextus Empiricus. The pestilent heresy of Socinianism was denounced by Donne and Chillingworth as well as by Cheynell, and the epithet 'Socinian' was readily flung at anyone who tried to link reason with religion. We may deplore the attitude of those narrow-minded ecclesiastics and fundamentalists who abused even the orthodox latitudinarians in the name of religion and yet, like their modern counterparts, they had some glimmering of the danger which was to attend the growth of modern liberal Protestantism, the danger, not to put it profanely, of pouring out the baby with the bath-water. In 1652 Walter Charleton, the disciple of Gassendi, declared that England had lately produced more swarms of 'Atheisticall monsters' than any age or nation had been infected with. In 1659 the sophisticated Francis Osborn, whose own *Advice to a Son* the Vice-Chancellor of Oxford tried to suppress, observed that 'God and the Magistrate lies blasphemed on every Stall'.

In addition to all the rational and mystical, sceptical and scientific ideas in the air, there was a marked interest in study of the various religious creeds, contemporary and historical. It fostered a spirit of tolerance and a desire for Christian unity in such men as Sir Edwin Sandys, Edward Brerewood, Sir Thomas Browne, the orientalist John Lightfoot, and that attractive Leveller and lover of Montaigne, William Walwyn. Donne, and Henry More (for whom, as for Ficino, Plato was 'Moses Atticus'), could, at times, see diverse faiths as virtual beams of one sun. Yet contemplation of religious and sectarian chaos might also lead, as it had already led in Italy and France, either to complete scepticism or to the natural theology of Lord Herbert.

Lord Herbert (1583–1648) has commonly been christened the father of deism, and through the century after him he was both echoed and attacked as such. But deism of a kind may be said to have been alive since thought began. Although its modern origins were as various as its manifestations, it was on the negative side the child of scepticism, on the positive of Stoicism, that very malleable Stoicism which could also be fused with Arminianism and Puritanism. It was Lord Herbert who explicitly formulated the principles of natural religion, at the end of his *De Veritate* (1624); he expanded them in *De Religione Laici* (published with *De Causis Errorum* in 1645) and the posthumous *De Religione Gentilium* (1663). Herbert's five articles were these: that a supreme and providential Deity exists; that He ought to be worshipped; that virtue and piety are the essentials of worship; that men should repent of their sins; and that rewards and punishments are dispensed in a future life. These articles, based on the common notions and natural instincts of mankind, Herbert found among the ancient pagans, although, as in modern times, truth had been corrupted by the priesthood. Thus, like Anglicans and Puritans and Platonists, Herbert was trying in his way to strip off the adventitious wrappings of religion and lay bare the kernel of universal truth supplied by reason; and he reflected the controversies of his age in his anti-Calvinist assertion of free-will and in his plea for the one infallible catholic 'church' of his five articles. To scriptural revelation Herbert assigned the diminished value of an historical document subject to critical scrutiny, but he by no means excluded direct revelation or intuition; there was, therefore, no inconsistency in his appealing for divine sanction to publish *De Veritate*. Herbert's summary of common notions in religion, though it became his most notorious legacy, was only a particular application of his theory of knowledge and analysis of the criteria of truth. He exemplifies the position of those men who, not satisfied by traditional religion and critical of its excesses, wished to mediate between irreligious scepticism and what was often the ultimate phase of scepticism, irrational fideism. Like other transitional pioneers, Herbert was partly modern and partly not. The Bacon of metaphysics and epistemology, he stood as it were between Cicero and Kant. He was pre-scientific in identifying the principles of reason and religion, and he stopped far short of the philosophic deism of the Augustan age.

5

Orthodox champions of rational religion naturally stopped far short of Lord Herbert. Men of goodwill in all parties who, like Erasmus and Acontius, held by the New Testament as the charter of Christian liberty, could only deplore unchristian strife over non-essentials. Miscellaneous Anglicans such as Bacon, Selden, Joseph Hall, Ussher, Fuller, Browne, Hammond, and Taylor, and such Puritans as George Wither, John Durie, and Milton, and various radical groups, sought in their different ways for a faith based on fundamentals with a margin for disagreement, so that latitudinarianism cannot be too precisely defined. But the term is associated particularly with two schools, and the leaders of the first were 'the ever Memorable Mr John Hales of Eton College', William Chillingworth, and Lord Falkland, three friends who happened to be of small stature. ('It was an Age', says Clarendon, 'in which ther were many greate and wounderfull men of that size.')

John Hales (1584–1656), the oldest member of Falkland's philosophic circle, lives in common memory by his inalienable label, his eulogy of Shakespeare, and his farewell to Calvin.[1] 'He was', in Clarendon's words, 'one of the least men in the kingdome, and one of the greatest schollers in Europe.' Hales's place in his age was out of proportion to his meagre physique and meagre writings. He had more genial humanity than Chillingworth, but his religious outlook was similar. He 'exceedingly detested the tyranny of the Church of Rome', which had caused so many religious brawls, but he could also lay bare, in letters to Sir Dudley Carleton, what Clarendon summed up as 'the ignorance and passyon and animosity and injustice' of the Dutch Synod. Hales had little more trust than Selden in church councils and the Holy Ghost's attendance upon majorities. In his sermons and tracts he is always pleading for 'the unity of the Spirit in the Bond of Peace', the true unity of individual men who follow the plain guidance of Scripture and avoid vain speculation and debate about things not fundamental in the warfare of life. 'It was never the Intent of the Holy Ghost, to make it a matter of Wit and Subtilty, to know how to be saved.' 'Christ is our Aristotle.' The natural reason of the 'Ethnick Philosophers' brought them close to Christianity, and a Fabricius or a Regulus belongs as much to the Church of Christ as a Christian whose life falls short of his beliefs. Hales's emphasis on simple goodness does not forbid his use of such relatively neglected or dubious classics as Aeschylus, Thucydides, Euripides, Petronius, and Lucian. Like Chillingworth and Falkland, Hales was charged with Socinianism. Apart

---

[1] Hales was educated at the Bath Grammar School and Corpus Christi College, Oxford. He became a fellow of Merton (1605) and public lecturer in Greek (1612). He assisted Savile, the Provost of Eton, in the editing of Chrysostom, and from 1613 to 1649 he held a fellowship at Eton (Wotton was Provost during 1624–39.) He was, says Clarendon, 'the most separated from the worlde of any man then livinge', though he had visitors like Falkland and himself visited the wits in London; he has his niche in Suckling's *Sessions of the Poets*. As chaplain to Sir Dudley Carleton, Hales attended the Synod of Dort (1618–19). His *Tract Concerning Schism and Schismatics*, written about 1636 and said to have been done at Chillingworth's request, was published in 1642. It did not find entire favour with Laud, but led to a canonry at Windsor (1639). Hales was deprived by Parliament in 1642 and in 1649 was ejected from his fellowship. His last years were spent in retirement and poverty, and he had to sell most of his fine library. Hales's writings were partly collected in the *Golden Remains* (1659).

from Socinian tracts wrongly attributed to him, there was, for some minds, sufficient ground in his breadth of charity and common sense, in his linking of 'God and good Reason', in his dislike of formulated articles of faith, in his doubtful veneration for ecclesiastical history and the vested interests of religion, and in what he calls the freedom and gaiety of his 'open and uncautelous' temper. For a taste of the man let us quote a bit of nobly plain writing from his exculpatory letter to Laud. After citing Galen's assertion that he had followed truth and knowledge, not the opinion of the many, Hales says:

Some Title, some Claim I may justly lay to the Words of this excellent Person; for the Pursuit of Truth hath been my only Care, ever since I first understood the Meaning of the Word. For this, I have forsaken all Hopes, all Friends, all Desires, which might biass me, and hinder me from driving right at what I aimed. For this, I have spent my Mony, my Means, my Youth, my Age, and all I have; that I might remove from my self that Censure of Tertullian,— *Suo vitio quis quid ignorat.* If with all this Cost and Pains, my Purchase is but Error; I may safely say, to err hath cost me more, than it has many to find the Truth: And Truth it self shall give me this Testimony at last, that if I have missed of her, it is not my Fault, but my Misfortune.

Among the frequenters of Lord Falkland's house in the sixteen-thirties were Chillingworth, John Earle, Henry Hammond, George Morley, and Gilbert Sheldon (a high percentage of future bishops!), Edward Hyde, later Earl of Clarendon, and possibly Selden and Hobbes. A neighbour and friend was George Sandys, to whom Falkland wrote several poems. In a sea of passionate prejudice and conflict Great Tew was an island of informed and rational discussion, and Clarendon's pictures of the young poet-scholar and his friends convey a rare and gracious urbanity. There was, however, intellectual and spiritual distress in that semi-collegiate Arcadia. We think of Falkland as the example *par excellence* of the noble and philosophical cavalier, the moderate royalist and Anglican who saw faults on both sides, and whose heart was to be divided and broken by the civil war.[1] The personal charm and integrity of

[1] Lucius Cary (1610?–43), who became the second Viscount Falkland in 1633, was the son of a successful courtier and unsuccessful Lord Deputy of Ireland and a devoutly Catholic mother of literary, masculine, and eccentric character. He spent his boyhood in Oxfordshire, studied at Cambridge for a short time, went to Ireland with his parents in 1622, graduated from Trinity College, Dublin, in 1625,

soul which kindled an unwonted glow in the memory of Clarendon was combined with a restless desire for truth and assured conviction. It was partly inborn but, like that of Donne (whose rational faith Falkland praised in verse), it was heightened by the circumstances of his life—the domestic discord in which he grew up, his dislike of the self-seeking world of his father, the religious satisfaction of his Catholic (and argumentative) mother and of his Anglican wife, his troubled contemplation of growing religious and political strife, his aristocratic and idealistic bias towards King and Church, his instincts for both thought and action, his consciousness of personal abilities not put to use, his reasonable and ineffectual devotion to a policy frustrated by extremists. But Falkland's *Of the Infallibility of the Church of Rome* (printed in 1645), while it testifies to his serious study, is less important than *The Religion of Protestants a Safe Way to Salvation* (1637), on which Chillingworth worked at Great Tew and in which he expounded views similar to his host's.

In politics Chillingworth was an absolute royalist, though in a sermon to the court at Oxford he boldly condemned the sins of the cavaliers.[1] In religion he had even more cause than Falk-

was knighted by his father in 1626, and returned to England in 1628–9. His friendship with Sir Henry Morison (d. 1629), son of an official in Ireland and nephew of Fynes Moryson, was celebrated in Jonson's famous ode, and Cary himself paid tribute in elegies. Early in 1630 Cary married his friend's sister Lettice. Estranged thereby from his father, he tried military service in Holland, and then retired to the country to read Greek. His father's death (1633) took him to London, where he renewed his friendship with the wits and 'his Noble Father, Mr Jonson', but most of the time from 1631 to 1639 he lived at Great Tew, studying religious problems and discoursing with friends from Oxford and London. Falkland left this retreat to take part in the Bishops' War (1639), and in 1640 he entered Parliament. With Hyde he laboured in vain to preserve constitutional monarchy, a reformed Church of England, and peace. He was persuaded to become, in January 1642, a Privy Councillor and Secretary of State. When war broke out Falkland lost all desire to live, and he found a welcome death at the battle of Newbury (20 September, 1643).

[1] William Chillingworth (1602–44) was the son of an Oxford citizen and the godson of Laud. He became a scholar and fellow of Trinity College, Oxford (1618, 1628). Under the persuasions of the Jesuit Fisher he turned Catholic and went to Douai (1630). Laud exerted tactful influence, and the next year Chillingworth returned to England and later to Protestantism, though he did not subscribe to the Articles until he accepted preferment at Salisbury in 1638. His book was written in defence of Christopher Potter of Queen's College, who had been in controversy with Edward Knott, a Jesuit. Chillingworth's change of heart, and his book, drew a number of Romanist attacks. In 1643 he was at the siege of Gloucester and invented 'an Engyne' with the pacifistic notion of hastening the end of the war. Then, like Fuller, he joined Hopton's army. He fell ill, was captured at Arundel Castle, and died at Chichester early in 1644. In his last days he was tended, and

land to seek authority, since he for a time had gone over to Rome. He was perhaps in part the victim of his own dialectical instinct and skill, yet his religious shifts were made, as the not wholly sympathetic Clarendon bore witness, with entire sincerity and candour; 'all his doubtes grew out of himselfe' and he was 'in all his Sallyes and retreits his owne converte'. As a philosophic theologian Chillingworth is no Hooker, but he brings earnest conviction, trenchant logic, and exemplary controversial fairness, to a denial of Roman authority and infallibility and a plea for scriptural Christianity. 'The Bible, I say, The Bible only is the Religion of Protestants!' 'Universall Tradition directs you to the Word of God, and the Word of God directs you to Heaven.' The difference between a Papist and a Protestant is 'that the one judges his guide to be infallible, the other his way to be manifest', and the way to heaven is no narrower now than Christ left it. Like Andrewes, Laud (in his *Conference with Fisher*), and Hales, Chillingworth refuses an exact formulation of the fundamentals of faith, since

it is sufficient for any mans salvation, to beleeve that the Scripture is true, and containes all things necessary for salvation; and to doe his best endeavour to find and beleeve the true sense of it.

So Chillingworth is not a special apologist for the Church of England (though he later wrote in defence of episcopacy), and on his death-bed, tormented by the Presbyterian Cheynell, he would neither absolve nor condemn Turks, Papists, and Socinians. Against the tyrannous and specious unity of Rome he sets the flexible diversity of biblical Protestantism, 'For why should men be more rigid than God?' If we wonder at the charge of Socinianism, we must recognize that Knott and Cheynell alike were right in their sense of the dangers latent in Chillingworth's constant appeals to reason. While he thinks reason will convince all but the perverse that the Bible is God's word, we can imagine the perverse carrying beyond the author's premises such dicta as these:

Now nothing is more repugnant, than that a man should be required to give most certain credit unto that which cannot be made appear

badgered, by the Presbyterian Francis Cheynell, who in a recent treatise had (like Knott) accused him of Socinianism; Cheynell threw a copy of *The Religion of Protestants* into Chillingworth's grave as a prelude to a polemical sermon. All this Cheynell himself recounted in a pamphlet.

most certainly credible. . . . And for you to require a strength of credit beyond the appearance of the objects credibilitie, is all one as if you should require me to goe ten miles an houre upon a horse that will goe but five.

In fact Hobbes, who admired Chillingworth's intellectual powers and doubtless his plain, vigorous prose, exclaimed to Aubrey: 'But by God, he is like some lusty fighters that will give a damnable back-blow now and then on their owne party.'

Tillotson saw in Chillingworth 'the glory of this Age and Nation', a martyr in the cause of reasonable religion against 'Fancy and Enthusiasm'. Although Chillingworth, Hales, and Falkland attacked Rome, they were not welcomed as allies by Puritans. The Puritan attitude towards the Church of England was parallel to that of orthodox Anglicans towards Rome. From the first the Puritans, whether conformists or not, also appealed to Scripture and antiquity and demanded a Church purified from the Roman abuses, the Roman ritual, the Roman hierarchy, and, in Laud's time, the Roman Inquisition, of the Establishment. Doubtless nothing could have averted the sectarian revolt, but its force and extent might have been lessened if the national genius for compromise, of which the *via media* has been on the whole an illustrious example, had been working sympathetically. Puritan zeal, whatever its errors, was a rebuke to the Anglican lethargy which Andrewes deplored. His friend Bacon, in the *Better Pacification of the Church of England* (1604; reprinted in 1641), the earlier *Advertisement* (published in 1640), and the essay 'Of Unity in Religion' (1612–25), urged internal reform of the Church and conciliation on both sides. But the gulf grew too wide to be bridged. It was not easy for men who had inherited the idea of absolute truth and its corollary, uniformity, to think of the seamless robe as a coat of many colours. Hence, as Taylor said, every sect damned all but itself and it was damned by 499 other sects. Too many men in all parties fell short of even that measure of tolerance attained by the perhaps apocryphal modern clergyman who remarked to the dissenting minister: 'After all, we both serve the same Master, you in your way and I in His.' To Puritan extremists the Anglican appeal to ecclesiastical tradition and the beauty of order meant as little as the sacred abstractions of Burke meant to Paine; and to many Anglicans and Presbyterians the sectaries were what Paine was to Theodore

Roosevelt. Yet not all 'enthusiasm' was dogmatical. There was the leaven, especially potent from about 1640 onward, of more or less mystical thought and feeling represented by some of the sects, notably the Quakers, by the diffusion of Boehme's and kindred books, and by such individuals as John Everard, John Saltmarsh, and Gerrard Winstanley; and theological and ecclesiastical differences melted away before the inner light. But our concern is with the more central line of argument. We have seen the broad basis for toleration laid down by Chillingworth and his fellows, and that of the Cambridge Platonists we shall soon see; here we may observe the effect of the struggle to survive carried on by two large minority groups, the Presbyterians and Independents.

The battle for religious freedom may be said to have become a bitter and conspicuous fact in 1637, with the brutal punishment of John Bastwick, Henry Burton, and William Prynne. Especially after 1640 there was a flood of pamphlets, from the Smectymnuus group, Milton, Lord Brooke, Henry Parker, Thomas Goodwin and his fellows, Henry Robinson, Roger Williams, John Goodwin, John Lilburne, Richard Overton, William Walwyn, Samuel Richardson, and others. Some of these names have appeared in our chapter on political thought, and they indicate how far the tide of agitation spread beyond anti-prelacy. Whatever their particular and often conflicting aims, Puritans in general were inspired by the vision of a Christian society, and the first steps towards realization were the purifying or abolishing of the Laudian Church. We must skip the somewhat dusty conflict with the bishops, though its larger implications were visible at least to Milton and Lord Brooke (who, by the way, seem to have echoed each other). A little later toleration, which, as distinguished from comprehensive unity, had had few proponents, appeared as a definite and prominent issue. There is irony in the fact that this battle was not against the Establishment but against the Presbyterians who had overthrown it. When the Westminster Assembly settled down, in the latter half of 1643, to consider the reorganization of the Church, the Presbyterians' confident plans for national uniformity received a jolt. Five 'dissenting brethren', who had conducted self-governing congregations abroad and had the prestige of religious exiles, asked, with no thought of starting trouble, that they be allowed to carry on their old ways under the new régime. Their leader was Thomas Goodwin, a notable disciple of John Preston and Richard Sibbes. Failing in the Assembly, the five Independent divines appealed to public opinion in *An Apologetical Narration* (January 1644). Roger Williams, in his *Queries of Highest Consideration* (February), promptly opposed their admission of civil interference and their limited view of toleration. Henry Robinson, a friend of Hartlib and Walwyn, a travelled man of business, and an apostle of commercial expansion and free trade, in *Liberty of Conscience* (March) and other tracts urged the necessity of Christian liberty and peace and the wicked folly of coercion, whether Presbyterian or civil. In July Williams contributed his bold and famous statement of the natural rights of man, *The Bloody Tenent of Persecution.* The Presbyterians, including Milton's Adam Stewart, Rutherford, and 'shallow Edwards', and of course the heroic, indefatigable, and exasperating Prynne, busily defended their position, now and later; to most of them toleration meant anarchy and libertinism. One of the ablest pleas for Independent liberty and toleration was the *Theomachia* (October) of John Goodwin, 'the great Red Dragon of Coleman streete'. In proclaiming, like others, the right of discussion and inquiry, the right of divine truth to be heard, even at the risk of error, Goodwin approached a greater man who had been learning that new presbyter was but old priest writ large. In *Areopagitica* (November) Milton turned aside from his main theme, freedom of the press, to plead for charity in matters of conscience. The contemporary indifference, even among the pamphleteers, to *Areopagitica*—and to most of Milton's other tracts—is one indication of the popular style that paper warfare had as usual developed; Milton, though he moved in that direction, was rather too academic and isolated to catch the public ear. In 1645 appeared *The Ancient Bounds*, a remarkably broad and humane argument for toleration. As the debate went on it was given a stronger political and democratic turn by the Levellers, Lilburne, Walwyn, and Overton, but that does not concern us here. The Independent campaign for toleration, even if its early motive was only anti-Presbyterian, soon resulted, through Cromwell, in more security for various religious groups than they enjoyed until 1689. Despite the setback after 1660, it may be said that by that date toleration had been firmly established as both a religious and a secular principle, thanks to these writers and others from D'Ewes to Jeremy Taylor, from Vane to Harrington.

6

During these turbulent years the mainly Puritan company of Cambridge Platonists were trying to reopen a broad and solid road between controversial dogmatism and enthusiasm. But before we come to them we may look at a minor and a major Platonist who, as philosophic essayists rather than philosophers, made no very positive contribution to the movement, although they are more familiar to most of us than the Cambridge men. The first is William Drummond of Hawthornden (1585–1649). *A Cypress Grove* (1623) was a half-poetical and often beautiful meditation on death inspired by the author's serious illness, doubtless by lingering grief for the loss of his prospective bride, and by the more immediate fact of famine in Scotland. Being the work of Drummond, and an elaborate mosaic of the great commonplaces of the theme, the essay constantly reminds us of other authors, from Seneca to *Hamlet* and Ralegh's *History*, and it has clear echoes of Bacon and especially Donne. There are borrowings from Montaigne and Charron, but Drummond's picture of the frailty and misery of human life does not end in naturalism or even in Stoicism. He finds the true relief from the fear of death in Christian Platonism, in rhapsodical contemplation of 'the Arts-master of the World' and the soul's return to its beatific source, its escape from the pain and mutability of earth to 'a vision of the Divine essence' and a changeless eternity.

The second of our irregular Platonists, Sir Thomas Browne (1605–82), we have met before in his strictly, but not too strictly, scientific capacity. Browne took a place in literature— even to the extent of receiving an immediate commentary, Sir Kenelm Digby's—with his first and central book, the *Religio Medici*, which he wrote in Yorkshire in 1635, when his pulse had not yet 'beat thirty years'. It circulated in manuscript and in 1642 was printed in two surreptitious editions; an authorized edition appeared in 1643. But for references to his age and a kind of winning *naïveté*, one might suppose the gravely reflective and rambling author to be near three-score and ten. While most young physicians would be absorbed in professional concerns, Browne is intent upon taking stock of his relations with God and man. Although he was not writing for publication, his antipathy to theological and sectarian strife links him in spirit with the writers who were trying to call men back to the fundamentals of faith. He warned his readers that *Religio Medici* was 'a private Exercise directed to my self', not a guide for others nor 'an immutable Law' even to his own advancing judgement; that many things in it were 'delivered Rhetorically' or 'meerly Tropical' and were 'not to be called unto the rigid test of Reason'; and he more than once affirmed his entire deference to the 'maturer discernments' of the learned. In *Pseudodoxia Epidemica*, three years later, Browne was a scientist exploring his own domain and he did not need to be so apologetic, but in the *Religio* he was making an amateur metaphysician's contribution to the problem of the century, the problem of knowledge and ignorance, authority and faith. We might, however, still expect a religious and philosophic man of science, fresh from continental study and writing while the *Discours de la Méthode* was being incubated, to grapple directly with the primary questions which had long been coming to the front. But, apart from its atmosphere, there is little in the book that might not have been uttered generations, even centuries, before. There is, too, more caprice than systematic reasoning; allusions to science are relatively few and casual; and many of the questions Browne loves to raise are of the kind propounded by the village atheist. Yet the book remains not only a literary treasure but a religious testimony far more truly alive than many more pretentious and sophisticated works that historians of philosophy discuss. Its emotional, poetic, and spiritual power and beauty are not impaired by any 'defects' in method or matter.

Browne's attitude, of course, is not that of either the village atheist or the philosophic sceptic. Men like Montaigne and Donne might push on into libertine naturalism, but Browne's reason is much too 'soft and flexible', 'extravagant and irregular' a vehicle to arrive anywhere; his favourite image is a circle. He has, nevertheless, breathed the air of a sceptical age, and his consciousness of the *Zeitgeist*, while it does not disturb his faith, is just strong enough to demand a positive statement of it. We are (to echo Bottom) put out of fear at the beginning, for we are assured that the *medicus* is not a Pyrrhonist but Browne the believer. Despite the general scandal of his profession and his religious pacifism, he is a thoroughly orthodox Christian; a Protestant, though he would prefer a less belligerent name and though he can never hear the Ave-Mary bell without an elevation; an Englishman who feels at home in any foreign land— because he is 'in England, every where'!—and an Anglican who feels completely at home in a church that seems to have been framed to his particular devotion. It is no wonder that he can let his reason 'play and expatiate' in the realm of 'opinion', boldly challenging windmills, while his soul goes its serene way. 'In Philosophy, where Truth seems double fac'd, there is no man more Paradoxical than my self; but in Divinity I love to keep the Road; and though not in an implicite, yet an humble faith, follow the great wheel of the Church, by which I move, not reserving any proper Poles or motion from the Epicycle of my own brain.' So far from falling into any modern scientific infidelities, Browne cannot charge his youth with anything worse than three old, innocent, and generous errors. Though he regards his reason as a highly critical instrument, one of its chief functions is to start birds for faith to shoot down, and they are mostly tame birds. One must quote the most familiar and illuminating passage in the book:

As for those wingy Mysteries in Divinity, and airy subtleties in Religion, which have unhing'd the brains of better heads, they never stretched the *Pia Mater* of mine; methinks there be not impossibilities enough in Religion, for an active faith; the deepest Mysteries ours contains, have not only been illustrated, but maintained by Sylogism, and the rule of Reason: I love to lose my self in a mystery, to pursue my Reason to an *O altitudo*! 'Tis my solitary recreation to pose my apprehension with those involved Ænigma's and riddles of the Trinity, with Incarnation and Resurrection. I can answer all the Objections of Satan and my rebellious reason, with that odd resolution I learned of Tertullian, *Certum est quia impossibile est.* I desire to exercise my faith in the difficultest point; for to credit ordinary and visible objects, is not faith, but perswasion.

This is not quite 'The Religion of Protestants'. And Browne's ultra-fideism is the easier for him, and the more intelligible to us, because he is 'naturally inclined to that, which misguided Zeal terms Superstition'.

The modern rationalist may be disappointed when our man of science so willingly subdues his reason to the will of faith, when he refuses 'to prie into the maze' of God's counsels and prefers to wait for the ultimate revelation of heaven. But in that 'obscurantist' attitude he is at one with most religious—and scientific—Englishmen from Donne to Milton. He differs, however, from many of these in the positive and even genial delight with which he faces mysteries just because they are mysteries. For Browne more truly than for Donne, all divinity is love or wonder. He is 'content to understand a mystery without a rigid definition, in an easie and Platonick description'. The word of God is both a final authority and a book of riddles, and Browne's religious meditations are both a sober confession of belief and a solemn game. He can speak, with the accent of experience, of the battle of Lepanto raging within him, but amorous passion can hardly have been troublesome, and the conquest of his other passions has left him unheated and unscarred. His religious faith, though earnest, spacious, and exalted, is not itself an intense passion. He loves to contemplate things mystical, but he is not a mystic. The firmness of his faith and the limitations of his reason, his common sense and equanimity, perhaps also the consciousness of both his own merits and his own insignificance, forbid his moving into either extreme scepticism or extreme evangelicalism. So he does not perceive, or at any rate does not discuss philosophically, the central problems of reason and faith. And yet his instinctive intuitional idealism contains an all-embracing answer. What occasion for doubt, argument, agitation, and strife can offer itself to a placid but God-possessed scholar and scientist for whom man is a true microcosm, 'this visible World is but a Picture of the invisible', the whole variegated universe a divine symphony, the scale of being a mighty diapason, and even vulgar tavern music a reminder of the First Composer?

Browne pursues the study of God in His works with much more active zeal than Bacon, who also could quote 'O altitudo'— to indicate a blind alley. And Browne is distinguished from romantic pantheists in that he can never 'so forget God as to adore the name of Nature'. He does not need to be stirred by miraculous contraventions of nature when the whole normal order is a stupendous mystery and his own quiet life a miracle of thirty years. 'We carry with us the wonders we seek without us: There is all Africa and her prodigies in us.' 'There is surely a piece of Divinity in us, something that was before the Elements, and owes no homage unto the Sun.' The Platonic light which is 'but the shadow of God' casts a clear beam through every winding passage of Browne's soul. All things begin and end in God. Browne's imagination can inhabit the universe, but he has a special fondness for little things. Like Du Bartas, he thinks the Geometrician's skill more wonderfully displayed in the 'curious Mathematicks' of bees, ants, and spiders than in the 'Majestick' creatures. The supreme example of the significance of the minute, and one of the supreme flights of Browne's poetic symbolism, is the passage in the fourth chapter of *The Garden of Cyrus*, where seeds that lie in perpetual shades inspire a hymn to light and shadow, life and death.

However much Browne owes to Stoicism, scholasticism, and other philosophies, and to his study of comparative religion, it is the Platonic strain (with all its 'impurity') which broadens, deepens, and sweetens his religious thought and feeling. To an even greater degree than in other men, Christian Platonism fosters in him a charitable, undogmatic tolerance. It is man, not God, who has multiplied articles of belief and dispute. 'The Foundations of Religion are already established, and the Principles of Salvation subscribed unto by all; there remains not many controversies worth a Passion.' Although the centre of Browne's religion is salvation through Christ, it is the Christian Platonist who sees hell not as a fiery gulf but as the heart of man when Lucifer inhabits it, and who sees heaven, not as a city of 'Emerals, Chrysolites, and precious Stones', but in the soul that is filled with God, 'though within the circle of this sensible world'. It is the Christian Platonist who thinks continually of the soul imprisoned in its earthy house: 'Certainly there is no happiness within this circle of flesh, nor is it in the Opticks of these eyes to behold felicity.' And Browne is very truly Platonic in seeing humanity as 'a composition of Man and Beast; wherein we must endeavour to be as the Poets fancy that wise man Chiron, that is, to have the Region of Man above that of Beast, and Sense to sit but at the feet of Reason'. This ethical seriousness unites with religious faith to give Browne the four-square solidity of traditional Christian humanism, so that, no matter where his faculty of wonder may lead him, he never loses himself in a cloud like Wordsworth or Whitman. It is because his view of God and man and the world is Christian and ethical as well as metaphysical that Browne's Platonism is not 'too thin breathing', that his vision is not fed by shimmering rainbows; 'there is an edge in all firm belief'.

Another element in Browne which prevents his mystical impulses from evaporating in mist is his wit, which ranges from pregnant ingenuity to sublimity: 'for all this mass of flesh which we behold, came in at our mouths; this frame we look upon, hath been upon our trenchers; in brief, we have devour'd our selves'; 'And in this sense, I say, the World was before the Creation, and at an end before it had a beginning; and thus was I dead before I was alive; though my grave be England, my dying place was Paradise; and Eve miscarried of me, before she conceiv'd of Cain.' In *Hydriotaphia* a strange yet commonplace item from the pharmacopœia of London apothecaries is at once particularized and transcendentalized: 'Mummie is become Merchandise, Mizraim cures wounds, and Pharaoh is sold for balsoms.' Such metaphysical wit is by definition an instinct for paradoxical contrasts and, as in the poets, realistic particularity barbs the imaginative and emotional arrow. The astringent as well as the intensifying value of the wit in Browne's ecstasies can be measured by the lack of it in romantic pantheists.

Finally, those ecstasies are not merely introspective expansiveness, they are conditioned by Browne's immense and eclectic reading. His originality is in the chemical, or alchemical, results of his curious and loving assimilation. His ideas may become 'important' when expounded by other men; in him they are important as the revelation of a temperament, a temperament both individual and typical. Browne seems to be 'a mass of Antipathies'—love of life and disdain of life, devout piety and innocent scepticism, encyclopaedic thirst and obscurantist 'superstition', scientific exactness and figurative vagueness, sublime imagination and eccentric fàncy, cosmopolitan breadth and English insularity, unambitious modesty and amiable egotism, bookish pedantry and bookish humour. . . . But beneath the surface Browne is a completely harmonious microcosm of his paradoxical age.

Religio Medici quickly won fame abroad as well as at home. In 1646 Browne gave birth to his Colossus, *Pseudodoxia Epidemica*, and then for a dozen years he forsook authorship. Those years at Norwich, devoted to his profession and his wide-ranging private studies, his family and his learned friends, were the years of Cromwell's rise and reign, but the royalist physician and antiquary was living in a timeless world of his own. In 1658, the troubled year of the Protector's death, Browne published *Hydriotaphia: Urn-Burial* and *The Garden of Cyrus*. In the latter, combining horticulture with the general premisses of many allegorical and cabbalistic occultists (including Kepler), Browne traces the figure of the quincunx and the number five through all things in earth and heaven until the reader feels delirious, and the garden of Cyrus is choked with the weeds and tares of the author's extraordinary brain. The complete Brownist, certainly, 'shall not passe his hours in vulgar speculations' or 'fall on trite or triviall disquisitions', but most people are content to know, by heart, the conclusion. In that marvellous announcement that it is bed-time Browne leaves the 'elegant ordination of vegetables' for the ghost of a rose, and soars from 'inexcusable Pythagorisme' to the mystical mathematics of the city of heaven.

In *Hydriotaphia*, inspired by the discovery of some 'sad and sepulchral Pitchers' in a field of old Walsingham, Browne unrolled a tapestry of curious lore about the burial customs of all times and countries, and here his exotic learning and prodigal imagination and fancy were restrained, ordered, and solemnized by a greatly traditional and uniquely congenial theme. Against a sumptuously ironic background of funeral pomps, Browne contemplates death, the vanity of the world and earthly monuments, and the glory of Christian immortality. The grand and magical note is sounded in the first words of the dedication, 'When the Funerall pyre was out, and the last valediction over. . . .' (The second sentence—a prophetic one—points clearly to one major influence on Browne's style, the Bible: 'But who knows the fate of his bones, or how often he is to be buried? who hath the Oracle of his ashes, or whether they are to be scattered?') The theme evokes the ripest thoughts and emotions of a Christian, a poet, and a doctor whose study was life and death and who daily beheld examples of mortality. Many men of Browne's own century, to go no further back, had written greatly of death, but the last chapter of *Urn-Burial* is surely, as many readers have said, the most magnificent thing of its kind, outside the Bible, in English prose. It may be called the last great outcry of the dying Renaissance against devouring Time. And yet, in yielding to the intoxication of Browne's words and music, we should not fail to observe the profoundly

Christian character of his prose poetry. De Quincey and Landor, for instance, weave romantic visions and artificial harmonies about the theme of death, but Browne, like Shakespeare, Ralegh, and their fellows, has a far more robust, more religious, and, in a good sense, more prosaic heritage. The Christian humanist of the Renaissance feels the pull of both earth and heaven, and sees at the same time the greatness and the littleness of the sons of Adam: 'But man is a Noble Animal, splendid in ashes, and pompous in the grave, solemnizing Nativities and Deaths with equall lustre, nor omitting Ceremonies of bravery, in the infamy of his nature.'

Another discourse on life and death was *A Letter to a Friend*, written probably about 1672 and posthumously printed in 1690. This letter, recording the scientific observations of a doctor at the bedside, contains strands of Brownesque purple, the immortal commonplaces of mortality set off with bits of 'strange Pathology' from Hippocrates, Pliny, Cardan, and the rest, and Dante. It is unique as a medical report, and in its physical basis and metaphysical glosses it shows perhaps even more distinctly than other works the amphibian character of the author, who moves so readily, half-unconsciously, between divided and distinguished worlds. In style the *Letter* is far from the spontaneous homeliness of Browne's correspondence. The deceased friend is 'by this time no Puny among the mighty Nations of the Dead'. Even the most humbly realistic statement may approach an incantation· 'Omnibonus Ferrarius in mortal Dysenteries of Children looks for a Spot behind the Ear'; 'but too certain it is, that the Rickets encreaseth among us; the Small-Pox grows more pernicious than the Great: the Kings Purse knows that the King's Evil grows more common'. The diction may be plain or heavily latinized, but the rhythm commonly moves on Browne's middle level between relative simplicity and elaboration. In the last chapter of *Hydriotaphia* Browne had written: 'But the long habit of living indisposeth us for dying; When Avarice makes us the sport of death; When even David grew politickly cruell; and Solomon could hardly be said to be the wisest of men.' In the *Letter* he writes: 'The long habit of Living makes meer Men more hardly to part with Life, and all to be nothing, but what is to come.'

The injunctions of the second part of the *Letter* were incorporated in *Christian Morals* (printed in 1716). This book seems to have been put together a little earlier than the *Letter* and designed as a continuation of *Religio Medici*. The belated sequel offers the fruit of age and experience (and the commonplace book) in aphoristic, objective, and oracular wisdom, practical in aim and unpractical in effect, and, if we still find wit, we miss the intimate charm, the questionings, the imagination, emotion, and inlaid beauty of the early work. There Browne had remarked that 'truely there are singular pieces in the Philosophy of Zeno, and doctrine of the Stoicks, which I perceive, delivered in a Pulpit, pass for current Divinity'. The didactic purpose of *Christian Morals* brings out the strain of Christian Stoicism which was strong in Browne as in most writers of his time. But the biblical and Senecan moralist and stylist largely obscure the metaphysical poet.

Even this sketch has indicated that Browne's style did not steadily evolve from comparative plainness of language and rhythm to mature richness, and it is better considered in terms of decorum than of chronology. The style varies with the matter and the desired tone. In such a personal utterance as *Religio Medici* or such a scientific treatise as *Pseudodoxia Epidemica* the normal texture, however deliberate in composition, has a 'libertine' naturalness, though threads of gold are not excluded. *Christian Morals* is a sort of Christianized version of Proverbs, and is in the tradition of Felltham's *Resolves* and Quarles's *Enchiridion*, so that clipped parallel and antithetical clauses are as appropriate as flowing and majestic simplicity and ornateness in a soliloquy on death and human vanities. Not to go into the technicalities of Browne's varied cadences, most of his prose may be described as a very individual fusion of Senecan, Baconian, and biblical qualities, and our few quotations have exemplified some of them. The slow, stately, balanced movement of Browne's loftier writing is to that of Taylor, for instance, as the organ to the piano. For one simple basic pattern we might take a short sentence from the *Religio*: 'Every man is not a proper Champion for Truth, nor fit to take up the Gauntlet in the cause of Verity.' The second half is not needed, but it contributes more than half of the total effect. The sentence also illustrates, though very inadequately, one of the chief features of Browne's diction, the inspired combination of Saxon and classical derivatives. Here, as in more elaborate passages, 'Truth' supplies the plain sense and the phrase ending

with 'Verity' adds the emotional overtones—'Emphatically
extending that Elegant expression of Scripture, Thou hast
curiously embroydered me'. Sometimes Browne's classicized
diction is technical; one of his most useful coinages was 'electricity'. Sometimes it is only the product of bilingual habit; in 'the
Pensill or hanging gardens of Babylon' he is taking over the
pensiles of Lipsius (book two of *De Constantia*) and other writers.
When the language overtops the idea we have inflation and
'quaintness', though even then Browne has his own vitality and
colour. At its best his feeling for words and rhythms touches
that of the *Book of Common Prayer* and the Bible. Who can speak
of it without a solecism, or think thereof without an ecstasy?
Browne's polysyllables carry at once an aura of traditional
human associations and of august remoteness and pomp. We
are gathered with him into the artifice of eternity. 'But to subsist
in bones, and be but Pyramidally extant, is a fallacy in duration.' Yet Browne's most splendid effects owe much to the
strength and homeliness of Saxon, and it is his purest and
simplest English which yields the slow organ-music—'Grave-
stones tell truth scarce fourty years'.

7

The manifestations of Platonism in our period, as in every
other, were of a protean diversity and an essential similarity.
Sir Thomas Browne and the Puritan Lord Brooke, Henry More
and Milton were unwitting allies. There was a Platonic strain
in Lord Herbert, in his conception of the universe as a harmonious organism and of the correspondences between it and
man, and his 'common notions' are akin to the 'truths of natural
inscription' of the Cambridge Platonists. But the main Platonist
movement was strongly Christian and to a large degree Puritan.
Some Puritan divines approached Platonism through their
rationalistic adaptation of Ramist logic to Calvinist theology.
The seventeenth century inherited an eclectic Platonic tradition
which was generally more rational and ethical than mystical,
and once again Platonism helped to fuse theology and philosophy, Christian faith and humanistic reason, and to uphold
idealism against scepticism and 'enthusiasm', empiricism and
dogmatism. In *The Nature of Truth* (1640), Lord Brooke (1608–
43) found his way out of the apparent disunity and multiplicity
of the soul and knowledge and the world through trust in right

reason and comprehension of the single, all-embracing reality, God, and the divine unity and harmony of all being, which is but one emanation from Him. Brooke's range of reference is almost as broad as his theme—Galileo, Kepler, and Copernicus, the Bible, Plato, and Ficino, Bacon and Lord Herbert, Sir John Davies and Suckling, Thomas Goodwin and John Cotton. And, with such a spacious and unifying vision, Brooke could not be intolerant; he saw all spiritual rivers flowing towards the infinite sea.

A similar vision of divine unity was proclaimed by the more rhapsodical Peter Sterry (1613–72), Lord Brooke's chaplain and later Cromwell's, and a noted Independent preacher. Sterry has philosophic and latitudinarian affinities with the Cambridge Platonists and is commonly grouped with them. He was one of their generation at Emmanuel College, and he retained the esteem of Whichcote till his death; and he was named by Baxter as a representative of that 'mixture of Platonisme, Origenisme & Arianisme' which was more rational than scriptural. Yet Sterry stands somewhat apart. In his chief work he opposes free-will, and his argument is inspired much less by reason than by a Christian and Platonic passion for the reality and ideal beauty of the divine love and goodness which unifies all creation, which is the very principle of being, and in which 'liberty and necessity meet in one'. This doctrine leads him towards the Coleridgean view of the imagination as the faculty which 'espouseth in it self the spiritual and corporeal world to each other'; God Himself is the supreme Poet. Like some other men of his time, Sterry is on the borderland between mysticism and enthusiasm. He has a remarkably wide knowledge of literature and philosophy ancient and modern, religious and secular, and his central idea gives a kind of sanction for drawing his imagery not only from the Bible but from the classics and allegorized myth, from painting and other arts, and from nature. His luxuriantly figurative utterance is quite instinctive, as his letters show, and it has beauty, but it may become oppressive.

Whether or not we include Sterry among the Cambridge Platonists, Christian Platonism owed its characteristic temper and philosophic importance to the academic group—Benjamin Whichcote (1609–83), Henry More (1614–87), John Smith (1616?–52), Ralph Cudworth (1617–88), and Nathanael

Culverwel (1618/19–51?); and such allied figures as John Worthington (1618–71), the editor of Joseph Mede and John Smith and a translator of Thomas à Kempis, and Jeremy Taylor's friend, George Rust (c. 1626?–70). Except More, who entered Christ's College just before Milton left it, and Rust, who graduated from St. Catherine's Hall and became a fellow of Christ's, all of these men were educated in the great nursery of Puritan thought, Emmanuel College. Like the scientists who formed the nucleus of the Royal Society, the Cambridge divines were brought into fuller personal association by the civil war; later the centre of gravity moved from Emmanuel to Christ's. These latitudinarian Platonists shared with Lord Falkland's Oxonian group the desire to find a peaceful *via media*, but the Cambridge men tried to lay a broader philosophic foundation in ground which was more and more dangerously undermined. Illuminated by belief in the unity of truth, the ordered harmony of God's universe, the active reality of spirit, and the 'deiform' nature and freedom of man, they found in these conceptions a fullness, strength, and inwardness of rational faith which raised them above bitter contention, above both enthusiasm and ritualism, above the hard determinism first of Calvin and later of Hobbes. Some of these ideas appeared in *A Greek in the Temple* (1641) by John Sherman, who preached at Trinity about 1635–40.

Whichcote, the seminal spirit if one can be named, was more of a scriptural latitudinarian than a positive Platonist.[1] The admiring Bishop Burnet recorded that Whichcote had sent his students to 'Plato, Tully, and Plotin', and in 1651 his former tutor, Tuckney, made such interests a ground of reproach. In reply Whichcote avowed his debt to the philosophers but declared that he had given much more time to Calvin, Perkins, and Beza. He stands, in fact, with Hales, in the line of Christian

[1] Benjamin Whichcote (1609–83) graduated from Emmanuel College in 1629–30 (M.A., 1633; B.D., 1640). He soon made his influence felt both as a college tutor and a preacher. In 1643 he retired to a country living, but in 1644 he accepted, reluctantly, a parliamentary appointment as Provost of King's College in place of an ejected royalist. Whichcote was not a party man and did not subscribe to the Covenant. In 1651 his former tutor, Anthony Tuckney, now Master of Emmanuel, who had long viewed his old pupil's liberalism with keen though loving anxiety, took him to task, and they exchanged letters which illustrate two types of religious thought. In 1660 Whichcote was deprived of his academic post, but he complied with the Act of Uniformity and held several cures. He died at Cudworth's house in Cambridge. Whichcote himself published nothing. The sermons printed in 1698 and later years were apparently delivered in the period after 1660.

humanists that goes back through Hooker and Erasmus. Whichcote brings his own pure, strong, and winning spirituality to a rational, ethical, and practical religion, the knowledge, love, and imitation of God. He is typical of the main tradition of Christian humanism in expressly repudiating the 'Mystical, Symbolical, Ænigmatical, Emblematical'. Whichcote was fond, as Tuckney complained, of the phrase from Proverbs xx. 27, 'The spirit of man is the candle of the Lord', the phrase which became the hall-mark of the Cambridge Platonists. And the candle of the Lord is not simply the gift of divine grace arbitrarily bestowed upon the impotent elect, nor is it a private and uncertain inner light (still less is the whole verse what Bacon, at the beginning of the *Advancement of Learning*, had taken it to be, Solomon's inspired endorsement of free inquiry into nature). The candle of the Lord is the *recta ratio* of the humanistic tradition, and *recta ratio* is found, Whichcote says to Tuckney, where *vera fides* is found. There is no conflict between reason and faith, because God is perfect reason and goodness and because reason and goodness are natural to man, whatever his unnatural lapses. Nothing truly religious is irrational and nothing truly rational is irreligious. The meanings of 'reason' in seventeenth-century thought 'admit a wide solution', but for Whichcote, as for Taylor and Milton and others, reason signifies not the mere logical and critical faculty but the Platonic capacity for attaining divine truth, the whole unified personality of the well-disposed man. Since man's fall, however, his natural reason and natural religion ('Truths of first Inscription') need to be fortified and restored through revelation, through Christ 'as a principle of divine life within us, as well as a Saviour without us', and through man's own earnest effort. Like Matthew Arnold, Whichcote was charged, in Tuckney's words, with 'A kinde of a Moral Divinitie minted; onlie with a little tincture of Christ added: nay, a Platonique faith unites to God'. It is easy to see that Whichcote's version of humanistic optimism, his natural supernaturalism, might well draw from the undiscriminating those horrid epithets, Arminian and Socinian—and later win the eulogies of Tillotson, Locke, Shaftesbury, and Burnet. With a view of religion based on 'Reason and Scripture', Whichcote has little to say of the Church and ecclesiastical tradition; he urges Christian liberty and agreement in the few and clear fundamentals of Protestant faith. He believes, to use a phrase of Taylor's, that 'Theologie is rather a Divine life than a Divine knowledge', but he insists, much more strongly than Taylor, that the mind must be convinced along with the heart. The modern religious reader may not find much spiritual nourishment in the evangelical eloquence of Donne; he will find a great deal in the quiet, forceful *Aphorisms* of Whichcote.

The younger Cambridge Platonists developed, with varying emphasis, the principles taught by Whichcote, but they all have their individual genius, and to try to characterize them briefly is to burn their wings, and our fingers, in the candle of the Lord. John Smith, by his own account, 'lived upon Dr. Whichcote', and he also harmonizes 'common notions' or 'Truths of Natural Inscription' with revelation and exalts the unity and beauty of undogmatic truth, the divinity of human reason, the soul's dominion over the body, the quest of divine knowledge and participation in the divine life.[1] But while his master avowed his preference for meditation over reading, Smith reveals himself on almost every page as a learned Platonist and Neoplatonist, and he has a more rich and ample style. He constantly and beautifully celebrates the living spirit of Christ, but his hungry imagination reaches out to the supramundane and the infinite, from the Many to the unstained and unchanging One. He is preoccupied with immortality as the great fact of religion, and he reminds us of Vaughan in his Plotinian visions of 'the land of Light', of the soul's escape from fleshly contagion to the Divine Essence. Smith seems to have been one of the purest spirits in the history of English religious thought.

Nathanael Culverwel bears the generic label of latitudinarian and Platonist, and he was also a Calvinist and an Aristotelian.[2] Indeed his eclectic and critical detachment evades any too precise appellation. In the *Discourse of the Light of Nature* (1652) his main object was to vindicate the harmony of reason and faith against both fideists and Socinians. His major premiss, of course, is that of other Christian 'rationalists', that reason is

[1] John Smith (1616?–52) was educated at Emmanuel College (B.A., 1640; M.A., 1644) and received a fellowship at Queens' College (1644). He was a pupil of Whichcote and a friend certainly of Cudworth and presumably of Culverwel. His *Select Discourses* were edited by Worthington in 1660.
[2] Nathanael Culverwel (1618/19–51?) entered Emmanuel College in 1633 (B.A., 1636; M.A., 1640). He received a fellowship at Emmanuel in 1642 and, like Smith, spent his brief maturity in study, teaching, preaching, and writing. The *Discourse* and other remains were printed in 1652.

subordinate only 'to God himself, and those Revelations that
come from God', and it is 'expresse blasphemy to say that either
God, or the Word of God did ever, or ever will oppose Right
Reason'. Along with philosophic sophistication Culverwel has
a spiritual fire and figurative utterance which justify the phrase
of his editor of 1652, 'cloth of gold . . . weaved of Sunne-beams',
though for the most part the gold shines intermittently through
a tissue of learned quotations. Indeed to all the Cambridge
Platonists except Whichcote learning was a handicap as well as
an inspiration; it hurt their influence with an age disposed to
welcome the bareness of Hobbes and, in spite of their many
passages of power and beauty, it has hurt them with posterity.

Henry More's difficult verse and voluminous prose come from
a very earnest and subtle mind which faces more fundamental
problems than most men perceive, and which in its search for
proofs of the reality of spirit is apt to pursue spirits.[1] More's
weakness for the occult, though common enough in the century, is a liability in a serious philosopher who has nothing
of Browne's invincible charm and literary beauty, and it is
conspicuous enough in More to repel the unsympathetic reader
and evoke the hasty opinion that no true Platonic light can be
reflected from such a muddy pool. But the quality of his mind
and the direction of his thought are in a way independent of

---

[1] Henry More (1614–87) was the son of a prosperous and cultivated Calvinist
(and cavalier) family in Lincolnshire. He went from Eton to Christ's College,
Cambridge, in 1631. The renowned and well-loved Joseph Mede, author of
Clavis Apocalyptica (1627), was an antidote to scholastic narrowness if not to darkly
allegorical ways of thought. In Cambridge also were Whichcote and the younger
Platonists. In 1639 More received his M.A. degree and a fellowship. When in
1643–5 Parliament ejected many masters and fellows, including Joseph Beaumont,
Cowley, Crashaw, and Cleveland, Whichcote was installed at King's and Cudworth, a fellow of Emmanuel, was nominated to the mastership of Clare Hall.
More, who was always attached to the Church of England and the monarchy,
remained in his place; he did not sign the Covenant but apparently accepted the
later Engagement. Although he took orders, he steadily declined preferment and
devoted his life to study, writing, and conversation. Except for visits at Ragley, the
Warwickshire seat of the Conways, More lived in his beloved Cambridge, nourishing
his high speculations on 'the College Small Beer'. Among his many friends and
correspondents were Cudworth and other Platonists, Lady Conway and her circle,
Descartes, Jeremy Taylor, Hartlib, Joseph Glanvill (who shared his occult
interests) and other fellow-members of the Royal Society, William Penn, and John
Norris of Bemerton. More's early verse was noticed above, in Chapter III. His
chief works in prose were: *An Antidote against Atheism* (1653), *Conjectura Cabbalistica*
(1653), *Enthusiasmus Triumphatus* (1656), *The Immortality of the Soul* (1659), *An
Explanation of the Grand Mystery of Godliness* (1660), *Enchiridion Ethicum* (1667),
Divine Dialogues (1668), and *Enchiridion Metaphysicum* (1671).

his particular ideas, whether fanciful or respectable. More's troubled quest began in childhood. At Eton, where he breathed the air of Hales (in the literal sense and perhaps in the metaphorical), he had already formed a conviction of 'the Divine Justice and Goodness', and rebelled against 'that hard Doctrine concerning Fate' which he had imbibed in his Calvinist home. The dry studies of Cambridge and his own eager explorations of 'natural' knowledge, far from bringing relief to his thirsty soul, seemed to lead to 'mere Scepticism'. But More found what he needed in Ficino, Plotinus, the Hermetic writings, and other mystical works, especially the *Theologia Germanica*. He now perceived the end of life to be not in the 'Knowledge of things' but in the merging of his will with the Divine. His first efforts to describe his illumination, struggle, and assurance were made in verse. Through the veil of sense More the poet could see, more clearly than his readers do, 'that bright Idee Of steddie Good' which irradiated his soul and the infinite world. His fusion of Neoplatonism and Christianity enabled him to face the new science without misgiving.

As a religious thinker in prose, More feared two great enemies, enthusiasm and atheism, and from the central position of the rational Christian humanist he fought stoutly against both, not without results. Especially after the appearance of his bold and much-discussed book, *The Grand Mystery of Godliness* (1660), the term 'latitude-men' began to be used by some 'Cholerick gentlemen' as equivalent to 'heretics'. In 1664 More published an *Apology* in reply to the criticisms of Joseph Beaumont, author of *Psyche* (1648) and now Master of Peterhouse. Here More nobly reaffirmed the creed of his school, that 'there is no real clashing at all betwixt any genuine Point of Christianity and what true Philosophy and right Reason does determine or allow, but that . . . there is a perpetual peace and agreement betwixt Truth & Truth, be they of what nature or kind so ever'. The many eminent men named in this sketch of the problem of reason and faith have all been on the side of the angels, and almost all, from Hales to Sir Thomas Browne, are Christian humanists whose approach to the problem is pre-scientific. Others might be added to the same list, such as John Bramhall, whose dispute with Hobbes over liberty and necessity became a public affair in 1654, or the great poet of the age who was about that time beginning his justification of God's ways to men. In our special group Culverwel at least was aware of Galileo and Descartes as well as of Lord Herbert, but he died in 1650-1 without realizing that a philosophic revolution was in progress. More and Cudworth, though rooted in the same traditions, lived longer and saw further, and they laboured to bring scientific thought into line with Christian Platonism, to reinterpret in modern terms the nature of God, the soul of man, and the soul of the world. If the last phrase sounds naïve, it needs no apology when it becomes *élan vital*; and if we regard More's thought as unimportant, Newton did not. The campaign required more scientific and philosophic equipment than had sufficed for earlier champions of rational faith and ethics. Edward Davenant, Fuller's cousin, could not endure, says Aubrey, to hear of the new philosophy, for if that was brought in, a new divinity would shortly follow. Davenant spoke more wisely than he knew. But More, like his fellow Platonists, believed with Whichcote that 'To go against Reason, is to go against God'. It is one of the ironies frequent in the age-old controversy that the defender of liberal religion began by seizing upon the two-edged sword of Cartesianism.

The influence of Descartes in England may be said to date from 1637, when Sir Kenelm Digby sent to Hobbes, from Paris, a copy of the *Discours*. Digby cited Descartes in his *Two Treatises* (1644). Hobbes's relations with Descartes are a familiar story. Browne quoted him in 1646. To the English translators of the *Discours* and the *Passions* (1649, 1650) the philosopher's universal fame was an established fact, and they, with More's young Cantabrigian friend John Hall (in his tract on education, 1649), saluted him as the great gaol-deliverer of the modern mind. Cartesian ideas appeared in More's *Democritus Platonissans* (1646); in 1648 the disciple commenced writing to the master; and in 1650 he took up the defence of Descartes against the mystagogue Thomas Vaughan. At first Descartes appeared as a modern Plotinus or Plato who, like More himself, had found in conventional philosophy a blind alley, and had created a new synthesis of divine and natural knowledge in harmony with both religion and science. Thus in a battle against mechanistic materialism Descartes, the champion of God and the thinking mind with its innate ideas, might well seem a powerful and heaven-sent ally. To the end More expounded Cartesian physics; but as Cartesian metaphysics looked less and less

Platonic and Christian, his early 'transported Admiration' gave way by degrees to doubt and distrust and, in his last books, to open antagonism. Descartes came to represent, as the Church of Rome had already decided, mere atheistic materialism—a verdict opposed by the religious Boyle. We cannot go into the complex technicalities of More's thought—though it is unjust to his philosophic power not to do so, and Hobbes himself, according to More's early biographer, declared that if his own philosophy was not true he would have liked More's next best!—but we can understand something of his evolution if we recall Wordsworth's changing reactions to a system no less fatal to a spiritual view of man and the world. The universe of Descartes, even if maintained by a mathematical Creator, depended too simply upon matter and motion, while More saw in such phenomena as gravity the evidence of a 'Spirit of Nature', the vicarious power of God exerted upon matter. In short, a cool intellectual, mechanical, and dualistic system could not satisfy the soul of a man like More, whose religious and ethical faith was a vital flame, who with all his rationalism had, as he confessed, a strain of 'enthusiasm', and whose profound intuition of the divine, coupled with a philosophic belief in the 'extension' of spirit, led him to find the omnipresence of God in infinite and indwelling space.

Ralph Cudworth (1617–88) was in some ways a more modern, systematic, and important thinker than his brother-in-arms. He seems to have coined the phrase 'philosophy of religion', but there is nothing of the coldness we associate with it in the famous sermon he delivered before the Parliament of 1647, one of the noblest and most eloquent of latitudinarian pleas for the religion of the heart, the 'inward Soul and Principle of Divine Life'. Thirty years later, in 1678, came his first great broadside against atheistic materialism, *The True Intellectual System of the Universe*. In this, and in the posthumous *Treatise concerning Eternal and Immutable Morality* (1731), Cudworth laboured, with a philosophic power somewhat blunted by encyclopaedic and digressive learning, to assert the existence and providential goodness of God, the reality of mind and its priority over things, and a rational, humanistic, and immutable standard of values. But these works, philosophically and chronologically, lie too far beyond our limits for discussion here.

'Nature', said Ralegh, near the end of his first chapter, 'is nothing, but as Plato calleth it, *Dei artem, vel artificiosum Dei Organum*, The art, or artificiall Organ of God.' 'Nature is the Art of God' is Browne's text. And *Leviathan* opens with the words, 'Nature (the Art whereby God hath made and governes the World)'. But it was Hobbes, the new Protagoras, who made absolute Bacon's divorce between philosophy and religion, who finally severed the golden chain that bound nature and man to God. The attempt of the later Cambridge Platonists—and of Milton—to reunite them was made in the spirit of their ancient, medieval, and Renaissance heritage, the Christian and Platonic belief in the oneness of a divine world. Because the attempt failed, and scientific empiricism and mechanism continued their triumphal advance, Cambridge Platonism has often been dismissed as only an interesting eddy in the stream of modern thought. But, whatever their philosophic inadequacies, the Platonists were in the main stream. More specifically, they were the founders of British idealism. Their anticipations of later philosophy, British and continental, have been recognized and, since our concern is with literature, we may remember that after men had had enough of the egoistic human animal, sensationalist psychology, and a clock-like universe, there was a return to the Platonist conceptions, to 'The native grandeur of the human soul' and 'the one Spirit's plastic stress'. If in the end the romantic religions of man and nature proved nebulous and unsatisfying, it was because they were cut loose, perhaps inevitably, from the seventeenth-century Platonists' deep roots of Christian faith and right reason.

XI

HEROIC VERSE

THIS heading may be for many readers an invitation to
'Turne over the leef and chese another tale'. Yet from
Petrarch to Milton—or the hapless Blackmore—almost all the
serious poets of Europe dreamed of writing the great modern
heroic poem, and many of them, like the orator in the House
of Lords, woke up to find that they were doing it. For three
centuries Europe was strewn with epics which, as Porson said
of Southey's, will be read when Homer and Virgil are forgotten.
In England the one great heroic poem between Spenser and
Milton was Chapman's *Homer*; the most popular was Sylvester's
version of Du Bartas. Most of our material is, except in bulk,
small beer, but even the bulk warrants some attention. And
when we think of the long life and potency of the heroic impulse,
not to mention the fact that Milton awaits us, the attenuation
and ultimate death of the heroic poem mark a change of
general significance. The causes include the decline of patriotic
and ethical fervour, in the Renaissance meaning of the terms,
and the rise of scientific and satirical rationalism.

Conceptions of the heroic poem in the Renaissance and later
were so elastic and comprehensive—Dryden referred to *Cooper's
Hill* as an epic—that one is driven back to the invulnerable
title of Du Bellay's chapter, 'Du long poëme francoys'. Most
of the poems we can afford to name may be roughly grouped
as historical, classical, romantic, and biblical.

For the Elizabethans 'historical' and 'heroic' were almost
synonyms. Our early historical narratives, such as those of
Drayton and Daniel which we have met before, were the last
sturdy offshoots of the Elizabethan patriotic chronicle. Warner's
Albion's England and the *Mirror for Magistrates* received their
final enlargements in 1606 and 1610 respectively. In 1609
Thomas Heywood (1574?-1641), the very active dramatist who
was to be an active popularizer of history, produced *Troia Britannica*, a vigorous and sometimes fine poem of about 13,000
lines on the story of Troy, with digressions and with glances
at Elizabethan naval heroes, hypocritical Puritans, and Guy

Fawkes. The last two of the seventeen cantos bring Brute to
England and chronicle the English sovereigns down to James.
The main source was Caxton's *Recuyell*, though Heywood preferred to cite Homer and Virgil (and did use them), and he
took a good deal from Ovid. *Troia Britannica* may be called
the last of the 'historical' leviathans, since it stands somewhat
apart from *Poly-Olbion* and is quite different from such a short
narrative as Sir John Beaumont's *Bosworth-Field* and from the-
versified histories of Henry II and Edward III (1633, 1635) by
the translator of Lucan, Thomas May.

The Italianate Ovidian genre continued to spawn mythological tales, generally in imitation of *Hero and Leander* or Shakespeare's poems; Marlowe especially was constantly echoed. The
narratives of Drayton, Chapman, Francis Beaumont, Basse,
Phineas Fletcher, and Shirley have been mentioned already,
and many others cannot be mentioned at all. But if no single
poem rivals those written before 1600, a few have some intrinsic or adventitious interest. Leonard Digges's decorative
paraphrase, *The Rape of Proserpine* (1617), written 'as a Patterne
for a piece of Needle-work', was given a threefold allegory
borrowed from that printed with Bevilacqua's version of
Claudian. Patrick Hannay's *The Nightingale* (1622), a poem of
nearly seventeen hundred lines on Philomela, was 'to be sung
(by those that please) to the tune set downe before in the
frontispice'. Ten years later the same theme (in George Pettie's
English) tempted Martin Parker, the balladist, to an un-
accustomed flight. Henry Reynolds, the friend of Drayton and
the exponent, in *Mythomystes*, of the allegorical-mystical theory
of poetry, published tales of Ariadne and Narcissus (1628, 1632)
taken from Anguillara's free version of Ovid; *Narcissus* was
provided with a quadruple allegory. And we might mention
the schoolboy Cowley's embellishment of Golding's tale of
Pyramus and Thisbe (1633). The longest and best of these
poems is the 'Epick', *Cupid and Psyche* (1637), by Shakerley
Marmion (1603–39), the playwright and 'son of Ben'. This
first of many poetical versions of the tale, in a style as loose as
its couplets, does not suffer in comparison with the more refined
luxuriance of William Morris or the preciousness of Bridges.
Marmion used Adlington (and Heywood's masque, *Love's
Mistress*, printed in 1636) as well as Apuleius, and his verse
has a robust Elizabethan colour. With lapses of taste go

felicities, such as the literal rendering of *Veneris inevitabiles oculos*:

> What darknesse can protect me? what disguise
> Hide me from her inevitable eyes?

Marmion gives an allegorical exposition, derived from Fulgentius and Heywood, but his heart is in expansive story-telling.

This Ovidian genre had been European and it shared in the European reaction against excessive veneration for things classical. Though ancient tales had received comic handling from Shakespeare and Jonson, and Nashe and Dekker, and though mythological poems had contained more or less humorous seasoning, the first real burlesque was the jovial James Smith's 'Innovation of Penelope and Ulysses. A Mock-Poem'. This was first printed in *Wit Restored* (1658), but was apparently written in or before 1640—before Scarron's famous *Typhon* (1644) and *Virgile travesti* (1648). Then came the very scurrilous *Loves of Hero and Leander* (1651). Thus a fashion which in England was signalized by Cotton's *Scarronides* (1664) did not have to wait for the Restoration.

The Ovidian tradition contributed something to the purely romantic narrative which grew out of Elizabethan courtly and pastoral romance. This type, like the other, developed sophisticated and sometimes mock-heroic humour—as in the *Albino and Bellama* (1637) of the eccentric Cambridge wit, Nathaniel Whiting, who became a Puritan divine—but, in spite of the rise of the psychological French romance in prose, it remained on the whole invincibly old-fashioned. At the outset—to ignore here such tales as the plebeian Samuel Rowlands's *Guy of Warwick* (1608)—we meet the long pastoral, *Thealma and Clearchus*, by the obscure John Chalkhill, who was said by Izaak Walton, when he first printed the poem in 1683, to have been a friend of Spenser. William Bosworth's *Chaste and Lost Lovers*, published in 1651 but written about 1626, was a labyrinthine maze of tales contrived by a youth intoxicated with Ovid, Marlowe, Sidney, and Spenser. Sidney's *Arcadia* was the obvious source of Quarles's one, and very popular, venture into secular romance, *Argalus and Parthenia* (1629). The relatively lucid plot of Sir Francis Kynaston's *Leoline and Sydanis* (1642) will serve to indicate the kind of material used in these romances. The scene is ancient Wales and Ireland—though the Irish court can produce an elaborate Caroline masque.

The consummation of Leoline's marriage with Sydanis being
frustrated by the spell of a wicked French nobleman, the
heroine, who is thought to have killed her husband, escapes to
Ireland disguised as a page, enters the service of the Princess
Mellefant, becomes the intermediary in an affair between the
princess and Leoline, and takes her mistress's place at an
assignation; after further complications, all turns out well.
Even this brief summary, which does not take account of mock-
heroic elements, recalls the plots of Shakespeare's comedy and
Shakespeare's sources. And though Kynaston the lyrist could
catch the magical note of the half-metaphysical Caroline love
lyric, the narrative poet—as became the latinizer of *Troilus and
Criseyde*—was Spenserian and Chaucerian, and he could cite
Dares. Pure heroic romance ended, not by succumbing to
travesty but by outdoing its serious self in bulk, narrative
complexity, and energetic exuberance of fancy and metaphor,
in the shape, or shapelessness, of *Pharonnida* (1659), by the
Dorsetshire physician, William Chamberlayne (1619–89). He
has been rashly linked with the young Keats, and Saintsbury
pronounced the huge poem 'a Sinbad's Valley of poetic jewels',
but few readers have the courage to seek or explore the happy
valley. If Sidney's *Arcadia* had been versified by Chapman,
the result would have been something like *Pharonnida*. At the
end of the second book Chamberlayne had been interrupted
by the civil war and, though in his prefatory remarks on 'the
Title of Heroick' he seems to glance at Davenant and Hobbes,
even if he had begun after 1650 he would have gone his
own way.

Two heroic poems, Davenant's *Gondibert* (1650) and Cowley's
Davideis (1656), are scarcely more read nowadays than the
Caroline romances, but they are important in themselves and
in the critical theory they represented. They are among the
many foot-hills which lead up towards both *Paradise Lost* and
Religio Laici. The Reformation and the Counter-Reformation
had alike opposed the paganizing strain in the Renaissance
and had fostered the ideal of the Christian epic. In addition
to the poems of Du Bartas, Tasso, and Spenser, there were such
others as Marino's *La Strage degli Innocenti*, which Crashaw
partly translated, and Chapelain's *La Pucelle*, which appeared
in the year of *Davideis* and was one of twenty or more Christian
epics in French written in the third quarter of the century.

This more or less positive concern for religious and moral edification and genuine truth was assisted at some points by two parallel movements, the first sober maturing of neo-classicism and the rise of new critical conceptions of reality. The two latter movements accomplished a great civilizing process all over Europe, but Cartesian and Hobbesian acid was to eat at the roots as well as the rank growths of the imagination. Finally, the more immediate background of *Gondibert* was the array of heroic tapestries in prose, narrative verse, and drama produced in England and France.

Davenant's long, serious, and ambitious *Discourse upon Gondibert* and Hobbes's *Answer*, which were published together in 1650, some months before the poem appeared with them, are landmarks on the road from the Renaissance to the Augustan age.[1] Whatever may have been Davenant's debt to Hobbes, and the debt of both to English and continental writers, they set forth an eclectic, empirical, and unpedantic theory of the heroic poem. It should be, not an imitation of the ancients, but a courtly and martial work which holds up to courtly and martial readers ideal patterns of active Christian virtue, yet permits the display of love and ambition in their bad excess. Davenant sees heroic poetry (in Arnoldian phrase) as the great *magister vitae*, more needful than ever because the Church and other traditional agencies have failed. He is more intent than

---

[1] The versatile and enterprising Davenant (1606–68) was the son of an Oxford tavern-keeper of good family. Tradition made him the godson, and Aubrey the son, of Shakespeare. He became a page to the Duchess of Richmond and then to Fulke Greville. His marital career began in 1623–4, his theatrical and military careers in 1627. In various difficulties, from syphilis (which was to occasion endless jokes about his nose) to homicide, he had a good friend in Endymion Porter. Davenant's first court masque was produced in 1635. The year 1638 yielded two masques, two plays, a volume of poems called *Madagascar*, a pardon for homicide, and appointment as Jonson's successor to what was virtually the office of Poet Laureate. Davenant took part in the two Bishops' Wars, was involved in the Army Plot of 1641, and served on land and sea in the civil war. He was knighted in 1643. During 1646–50 he was mostly in Paris with Hobbes, Cowley, Waller, and the other exiles. In 1650 he sailed for Maryland, of which Charles II had made him governor, but was captured and imprisoned. Part of a third book of *Gondibert* was written in prison. Against the story, derived from good sources, that Davenant owed his life to Milton's influence must be set the fact that four of the five other royalists named in the indictment were not executed either. He was released in 1652 and pardoned in 1654. He managed to carry on theatrical performances and produced the famous 'opera', *The Siege of Rhodes*, in 1656. In 1660 Davenant was granted one of the two theatrical patents and he became among other things the chief reviver of Shakespeare. He himself wrote two dozen dramatic works. He was buried in the Abbey.

Hobbes upon didactic utility. (Davenant favours, by the way, what Hobbes rejects as epic indecorum, metaphors taken from the language of 'men of any science, as well mechanicall as liberall'.) On the whole, both men retain a good measure of orthodoxy, yet their prevailing tone, compared with that of Chapman or Greville or Jonson, shows as much as anything how far the religious, ethical, and imaginative fire of the Renaissance has been cooled by critical rationalism, literary and scientific. Bacon had exalted 'poesy parabolical' because he liked to rationalize myth and, though capable of a larger vision, he had commonly revealed a scientist's matter-of-factness and a scientist's distrustful and escapist view of the imagination. Hobbes's account of the poetic faculties begins with a commonplace schematized in terms of his psychology, and he goes on with unusual eloquence to celebrate the workmanship of fancy guided by the precepts of true philosophy; Davenant seems to expound a similar conception of wit, with a generous rhapsodical vagueness. But while Hobbes desiderates the fruitful union of imagination and judgement, his whole manner of thinking proves the division between them. And the critics' banishment of the supernatural, and even of conceits, goes beyond the words of the proscription. The praise bestowed upon *Gondibert* by Cowley and Waller and, more oddly, by Vaughan underlines for us the new emphasis on the rationalistic presentation of human nature and 'the manners of men'. This standard of nature and truth, the simple clarity of style that it enjoins, and the dichotomy between wit and judgement, mark the end of the older poetry and herald the Augustan.

Davenant, who in his grander moments claimed Lombard ancestry, saw himself as an heroic bard modernizing the tradition that led from Homer to Spenser, and he was no less sanguine in hoping that his several thousand stanzas might be sung. Even if the story, for which he got a few hints from Belleforest, had been carried through its second half, it would have been, as a story, hardly less dull than long, 'Calme as Rose-leafes, and coole as Virgin-snow', to pervert the spirit of Vaughan's eulogy. Against a background of civil war and the court of medieval Lombardy—the scene of Davenant's early play, *Albovine*—move various warriors and women. The all-embracing motives of love and honour seem to affect even a hunted stag. The noble Gondibert, proclaimed the betrothed of the perfect Rhodalind, the heiress of a kingdom, loves the no less perfect Birtha, daughter of the philosophic scientist Astragon, and the dilemma remains unsolved. In the last canto Davenant finished, the seventh of the third book, we meet a variation on the well-worn plot most familiar through *Much Ado About Nothing*. Thus *Gondibert*, though written for the most part with a masculine, weighty, and level plainness of statement, is obviously related to the heroic romances in prose and verse and to the early and later heroic plays of which Davenant the playwright was a progenitor; indeed, the narrative in its full five books was planned, like May's earlier *Henry the Second*, to follow dramatic structure. But though the poem has arresting episodes, the story was on the whole an encumbrance. If the author had been able to cut loose from the convention of heroic romance and rely upon his real gift for massive and dignified reflection, he would have remained a more vital link between Sir John Davies (whose *Nosce Teipsum* was the chief exemplar of the stanza of *Gondibert*) and his old patron Fulke Greville on the one hand and Dryden and Gray on the other. One passage which shows Davenant's philosophic and poetic power is the account of Astragon's house, a scientific—and religious— college partly derived from *The New Atlantis* (an institution Cowley was to set in ancient Judaea). Another is the fragment first published in 1673, 'The Philosopher's Disquisition directed to the Dying Christian' with 'The Christian's Reply', a noble treatment of the problem which exercised so many minds, the relations of knowledge, reason, and faith.

The paraphrase or elaboration of a biblical tale had a venerable tradition behind it, a tradition revivified by Du Bartas's large work and by his smaller epics like *Judith*. Sir William Alexander's unfinished 'Jonathan: An Heroic Poem Intended' was printed in his *Recreations with the Muses* (1637); this volume, by the way, included the much enlarged version of the early *Dooms-day* which, if it did not, like a later Scotsman's *Lives of the Chancellors*, add a new sting to death, at least shortens the life of the literary historian. Other works were Drummond's fragment, 'The Shadow of the Judgement' (1630), Drayton's several efforts (1604, 1630), Fuller's *David's Heinous Sin* (1631), and Quarles's stories of Jonah, Esther, Job, and Samson (1620–31). The veteran Thomas Heywood's *Hierarchy of the Blessed Angels* (1635) has much interest for the student both

in its poetical survey of mystical theology and occult lore
(and brief roll-call of English poets) and in the prose sections
containing 'Theologicall, Philosophicall, Poeticall, Historicall,
Apothegmaticall, Hierogliphicall and Emblematicall Observations'. Cowley was severe upon the last two writers: 'For if any
man design to compose a Sacred Poem, by onely turning a
story of the Scripture, like Mr. Quarles's, or some other godly
matter, like Mr. Heywood of Angels, into Rhyme; He is so far
from elevating of Poesie, that he onely abases Divinity.' Finally,
George Sandys's 'Paraphrase Upon Job' (1638) was named by
Pope as one of Waller's models, and the couplets have much of
the antithetical balance displayed in his *Ovid*.

Cowley's *Davideis, a Sacred Poem of the Troubles of David* (1656)
was begun at Cambridge about 1638 (when Milton was beginning to think of King Arthur), and was enlarged in later
years, though the author grew bored and finished only four of
the projected twelve books. In the critical preface he was in
agreement with many Puritans and others in vigorously condemning mythological fables and urging the claims of biblical
history; and although in his miscellaneous verse he helped to
bring back the exiled train of gods and goddesses, he excluded
from *Davideis* what the Puritan Milton poured abundantly into
Paradise Lost. Cowley's exaltation of sacred themes, as his elegy
on Crashaw also shows, was mainly based on sincere religious
feeling, but it included two other motives, a poet's desire for
fresh material and what he emphasized in his praise of *Gondibert*,
the realistic standards of truth and human life held by a modern
rational mind. For a poet of Cowley's nature and inheritance,
however, these several motives were not incompatible with one
another or with devotion to ancient art. His avowed model
was the patron saint of the neoclassical epic, whom he calls
'the most judicious and divine Poet', 'Virgil the Wise, Whose
Verse walks highest, but not flies'. So we have constant imitations of Virgil, from infernal and celestial agencies and a prophetic vision down to similes and half-lines; Cowley's learned
notes attest his concern for heroic precedent and propriety in
technique and style. He also owed a good deal to Sylvester and Tasso and something to Crashaw's translation from
Marino. When he tells us that Goliath's

> Spear the Trunk was of a lofty Tree,
> Which Nature meant some tall ships Mast should be.

he carries a phrase of Sylvester's in the Miltonic direction. Milton's esteem for Cowley we may presume to have been built largely on *Davideis*, and even the literary, theological, historical, and scientific notes, on everything from inverted adjectives to Moloch and Dagon, would have been congenial.

Earlier narratives do not much weaken Cowley's claim that he had written the first neoclassical religious epic in English. *Davideis* was also, unless we except the translations of Du Bartas's large and smaller works, the first neoclassical epic in the heroic couplets which Milton so vehemently damned. Coming in the middle of a long line of practitioners from Sylvester onward, and starting before Denham, Cowley was a not unskilful master of the closed couplet, though he took no great pains to harmonize the metrical movement with the sense and tone. Nor do couplets check his hyperboles; the picture of Lucifer with his iron teeth and fire-darting eyes is only less bad than Tasso's and Marino's. And they encourage antithetical wit perhaps as much Ovidian and Augustan as metaphysical. Envy saw Cain

> fling the stone, as if he meant,
> At once his Murder, and his Monument.

Bits of nature and oriental life and of psychological analysis, and the ideal friendship of David and Jonathan which appealed to Dorothy Osborne, are not enough to give life to 'the Cold-meats of the Antients', and we are more attracted, as the poet was, by such peripheral matters of topical and philosophic interest as the ideal college and the question of monarchy or republic, physical phenomena and metaphysics. Though aware of modern views and of 'endless space', Cowley accepts the Ptolemaic system for his Hebrew story, and his cosmology is a mixture of old and new, of Neoplatonism and science. The world was created 'From Nothing' by the triune God of Christianity, who with His angels combats Lucifer and his demons. The primal elements ranged themselves in order under the compulsion of Music and Love. The universe is 'Gods Poem', 'the æternal minds Poetick Thought'. It is also 'Great Natures well-set Clock', but a clock which, 'the School-men all agree' (if not the law of inertia), requires the 'immediate concurse of God'.

XII

MILTON

WHOEVER the third of English poets may be, Milton's place has been next to the throne, and for most of us he still stands there, 'Like Teneriff or Atlas unremov'd'. But to the defeatism of the 'Armistice' period, 1918–39, the naturalistic passion and irresponsibility of Donne appealed much more than a passion for order and righteousness, and devotion to one kind of writing necessitated a zealous dislike of all other kinds. The supreme English artist, the only one to be matched with Virgil and Dante in what Arnold called 'the sure and flawless perfection of his rhythm and diction', became the rhetorician who had crushed the fruitful metaphysical movement, divorced thought and feeling, and imposed an artificial style and prosody upon English poetry for over two hundred years, until it was freed from bondage by the 'metaphysical' poets of our time. In addition to such recent detractors Milton has always had dubious friends. The admiration for the great rebel felt by men like Blake and Shelley was mixed with antipathy for the theological system to which he was supposedly committed, and nineteenth-century critics in general were inclined to save his 'poetry' by casting his ideas overboard. In our day, while a few critics were reacting violently against him, Milton's thought began to be seriously explored and appreciated by scholars; they invoked a broader formula to unify and save the artist and thinker, and the rigid son of the Reformation became the bold son of the Renaissance. This conception, however, gained ground just as its ideological parent, Burckhardt's popular theory of the Renaissance, was being abandoned, and the new Milton, though he embodied some significant and amiable features which had been lacking in the grim Puritan, looked decidedly too much like a nineteenth-century liberal. This brief and unqualified summary indicates at least that Milton's poetic and philosophic character is less simple and obvious than friends as well as foes have often assumed it to be. Our present view of Milton is not unanimous or final but, with a better understanding of his background, roots, and evolution, we have perhaps struck a juster balance between the Renaissance humanist and the Puritan. Milton may be called the last great exponent of Christian humanism in its historical continuity, the tradition of classical reason and culture fused with Christian faith which had been the main line of European development. His Christian humanism, intensified and somewhat altered by the conditions of his age and country and by his own temperament, becomes as he grows old a noble anachronism in an increasingly modern and mundane world.

I

The most valuable insights into Milton's life and mental growth are given at large in the whole body of his works and, more specifically, in the autobiographical passages in the *Reason of Church Government* (1642), the *Apology for Smectymnuus* (1642), and the *Defensio Secunda* (1654). Here we can mention only a few facts and dates. Milton was born in 1608, in London, not far from the Mermaid tavern, and Shakespeare and Jonson may have heard his infant cries, if such an infant did cry. John Milton senior, the disinherited son of a Catholic recusant, was a prosperous scrivener and a composer of some note even in that Golden Age of English music. He transmitted to his namesake independence of mind and a love of music, and gave him the best preparation for a literary career that education, travel, and leisure could supply. Voracious private study accompanied Milton's formal training at St. Paul's School (1620?-5?) and at Christ's College, Cambridge (1625-32). Among his Cambridge contemporaries were Roger Williams, Fuller, Randolph, and Jeremy Taylor; John Cleveland was at Christ's during 1627-31 and Henry More entered in 1631. Though Milton's early encounters with academic routine led to rustication, he passed his seven years at the University 'with the approbation of the good, and without any stain' upon his character. Most of the next six years (1632-8) he spent at his father's house in Buckinghamshire. The Horton period was not a prolonged rural holiday but a voluntary postgraduate course of hard reading and thinking which gave historical background and critical direction to Milton's maturing views on all manner of civil and religious problems. One interlude was the writing of *Comus*, which was acted in 1634. In 1638-9 Milton enjoyed some fifteen months abroad, chiefly in Italy. He returned to set up in London as a private schoolmaster and to follow with eager interest the climactic stages in the struggle between King and Parliament, Anglican and Puritan.

Milton's refusal to 'subscribe slave' by taking holy orders had been combined with a growing consciousness of his literary genius and vocation. Now, with notable achievements in minor genres behind him (though his collected poems did not appear until 1645), and with plans for a major poem revolving in his mind, he felt compelled to put aside his craving for poetic fame. With mingled ardour and reluctance he devoted his energies from 1641 to 1660 largely to the prose tracts that form the great bulk of his works. *The Tenure of Kings and Magistrates*, which followed close upon the king's execution, was followed by Milton's appointment (March 1649) as Secretary for Foreign Tongues to the Council of State. The impairment of his eyesight had begun about 1644–5 and was aggravated by his fierce labour upon the *Pro Populo Anglicano Defensio* (1651). He became completely blind early in 1652, when, as we are apt to forget, he was still in his prime; it needed all Milton's courage and faith in Providence to rally from such a blow. The *Defensio Secunda* was published in 1654, and Milton may have begun *Paradise Lost* about that time, in the same heroic mood. After the Restoration the apologist for the regicides, though imprisoned for a few days, was spared through the good offices, according to different stories, of Davenant or Marvell, or because he was regarded as harmless. *Paradise Lost* was offered to the town in 1667 and *Paradise Regained* and *Samson Agonistes* appeared together in 1671.

Milton had been married three times: in 1642 to Mary Powell, who died ten years later; in 1656 to Katherine Woodcock, who died in 1658, her husband's 'late espoused Saint'; and in 1663 to Elizabeth Minshull. In the lesser sonnets of his middle years we have glimpses of friendships untroubled by external stress. Apart from memories of the good old cause, loss of property, some friction with his daughters, blindness and the pains of gout, Milton seems to have had a fairly cheerful old age. We know his simple routine and can see him walking in his garden, playing on his organ and singing, or, often with one leg thrown over the arm of his chair, meditating, listening to readers, dictating, talking with English and foreign visitors who sought him out, and finishing the day, like the heroic poet he had pictured in his youth, with a glass of water—and the

unheroic but genial addition of a pipe. In 1674 'he died by a
quiet and silent expiration'.

2

The larger part of Milton's early writing was, after the
university fashion, in Latin, and he was a master of Latin verse
before he was of English—though he displayed a Miltonic
amplitude of ambition and style in 'At a Vacation Exercise'
(1628). Further, while the disciple of Ovid and the neo-
Latinists could lament the death of bishops and celebrate the
fifth of November, the obscurity of a learned language encouraged more spontaneous and sensuous self-revelation than he
allowed himself in his native tongue. The beauty of girls in the
parks dazzles him and the reawakening of nature in the spring
kindles positive intoxication, both sexual and cosmic. But the
young Christian Ulysses clings to the magical herb, moly, and
in the sixth elegy he goes on from playful praise of vinous and
amorous verse to extol the ascetic poet of truly heroic themes.

This aspiration yielded its first fruit in the same month,
December 1629. 'On the Morning of Christ's Nativity' an-
nounces Milton's coming of age, literally, poetically, and re-
ligiously. It registers a self-consecration which is to be renewed
three years later, in more personal and positive terms, in the
seventh sonnet. After the prelude the ode proceeds in three
movements, which describe the setting, the angelic song, and
the flight of the pagan gods at the birth of a new and diviner
Deity. The artist and the Christian are interfused, as the
Pythagorean and Platonic music of the spheres is blended with
the angels' song in a mystical symbol of the divine order and
harmony of earth and heaven. The traditional notion of the
eastern gods as demons Milton exploits with aesthetic joy in
their sonorous names and exotic associations and with militant
joy in their overthrow. In comparison with Crashaw, Milton's
infant Saviour and the simple human story almost disappear
behind the sumptuous baroque background. Like his mature
poems, this one suggests innumerable 'sources'—a canzone
of Tasso, Virgil's Messianic eclogue, and so on—and it is a
uniquely Italianate beginning for the great English classicist,
yet it bears already the unmistakable stamp of its author in
its sweet or clangorous music, virginal purity of feeling, and
thematic and architectural unity.

The extent of Milton's knowledge of Elizabethan and contemporary verse is a question. He offers open tributes to Shakespeare and Jonson and seems to pay allusive homage to Spenser, and these and almost every major and minor poet have yielded echoes and analogues to the commentators. At any rate the main line of his early development is the main line of the Renaissance tradition, and he is scarcely touched by the metaphysical current. A subdued Elizabethan and Jacobean richness and sweetness of colour and fancy, with the attendant uncertainty of taste, give way by degrees to the disciplined classical sobriety of the Jonsonian lyrical style. The change is not of course unwavering, and at all times Milton is Milton. The first clear evidence of a finer gift than Jonson's appears in 'L'Allegro' and 'Il Penseroso'. These companion poems were probably written in the summer of 1631, and they have some links with Milton's first prolusion on the comparative superiority of day or night. The cheerful, social man and the thoughtful solitary are much alike in their pleasures, since they are two sides of the author. For the first and the last time he celebrates 'Merry England' and the Anglican ritual. With perfect tact, economy, and charm, and in flowing melody, Milton weaves together native and pagan folk-lore and literature, civilized rusticity and romantic suggestion, and even the ascetic ecstasy of mystical contemplation. Pastoral, 'character', and 'encomium' contribute to the observance of lyrical decorum. In generalized ideal pictures designed to express contrasted moods, realistic particularity like that of Breton's pastoral catalogue would be quite out of place.

In the spring of 1632, probably, Milton wrote the brief, conventional, and wholly graceful masque, *Arcades*, which was presented before the aged Countess of Derby (once the Amaryllis of Spenser). Here a monologue spoken by a partly Jonsonian Genius of the Wood is flanked by lyrics which echo Jonson.

The aesthetic Platonism of *Arcades* is far from the intense Christian Platonism of *Comus* (1634), and Milton's altered direction is explained by the sonnet 'How soon hath Time', written apparently in December 1632. This may be called a record of Milton's 'conversion', in the entirely authentic sense of matured religious development and earnest submission to the divine will. He had been a distinguished figure at Cambridge, and now, while his contemporaries are making visible progress, he is an obscure and solitary student at Horton, and he feels the contrast. But both friendly remonstrance and his own self-searching only strengthen the resolve to prepare himself as best he can for the unknown future and inspire a renewed consecration of his powers to God's service—a consecration none the less devout for its echo of Pindar's fourth Nemean ode.

We must pass by several ensuing attempts at exalted religious poems and come to the great testimony of Milton's spiritual and poetical rebirth. In *Comus* the 'Dorique delicacy' of the songs and odes displays richer mastery of the cool, translucent, sophisticated art of the earlier masque, and—not merely in the epilogue, where more is meant than meets the ear—Milton has a vision of heavenly beauty beyond the range of Jonson. That vision gives poetic magic to the concluding moral couplet, and even the Ovidian Echo, in the Lady's first song, is translated to the skies. In *Comus* as a whole, underneath the Miltonic unity and harmony of feeling and style, we find specimens of descriptive sensuousness and expository bareness, juvenile conceits and dramatic realism, Greek, Jonsonian, and Augustan classicism, and, in Comus's speech on the bounties of nature, something like Shakespearian or metaphysical complexity. A more characteristic kind of complexity, that of open or concealed allusion, is amply illustrated in the first dozen lines; Wotton might have said that he had seen nothing parallel to them in our language. The speech is a Euripidean prologue, delivered by a guardian angel, about angels and the souls of the good, who live on the Olympus of Homer and Lucretius, above the *fumum et opes strepitumque* of Horace's Rome, among the white-robed elders of Revelation seated round God's throne. But no part of Milton is more completely Miltonic; literary reminiscences are fused in a pure clear flame of religious and moral passion. After the fourth line of this speech there is, in the Trinity College manuscript, a passage of fourteen lines beginning:

> amidst the Hesperian gardens, on whose bancks
> bedew'd with nectar, and celestiall songs
> aeternall roses grow, and hyacinth
> and fruits of golden rind, on whose faire tree
> the scalie-harnest dragon ever keeps
> his uninchanted eye . . .

Milton's artistic conscience compelled the removal of this

beautiful passage—though he salvaged bits of it later in the masque—apparently because its sensuous luxuriance blurred his main idea, the contrast between the pure world of angelic spirits and the world of Comus.

We cannot discuss the changes Milton made in the text, nor the countless particular beauties, nor such sources and analogues as Ovid, Peele's *Old Wife's Tale*, Spenser's story of Amoret and Busyrane, Fletcher's *Faithful Shepherdess*, and other things. In place of the Circe of Homer and Ovid, Milton borrowed and refined the Comus who had appeared in Jonson's *Pleasure Reconciled to Virtue* and in the Latin *Comus* of Erycius Puteanus. The traditional masque appealed to the eye and ear. Jonson, the chief practitioner in the form, had given it a frequent didactic note, but Milton went far beyond him. The moral lesson of Circe and her spells, doubtless present to Homer himself, was a commonplace from Horace down to George Sandys's *Ovid* (1632), and it had been fully worked out by Milton's great exemplar in the poetic handling of ethical ideas, the sage and serious Spenser. The gospel of libertine naturalism which Spenser, Sidney, and others set forth and condemned was set forth with sympathy by Marlowe, Donne, and such contemporaries of Milton as Randolph; Comus is in fact a cultivated gentleman, a cavalier poet. The best approach to the young Milton's conception of chastity is the retrospective account of its development given in the *Apology for Smectymnuus* (1642). Captured at first by the smooth elegiac poets of Rome, Milton had found their sensuality less satisfying than their art. He had passed on to the two famous renowners of Beatrice and Laura. There grew the belief that 'he who would not be frustrate of his hope to write well hereafter in laudable things, ought him selfe to bee a true Poem, that is, a composition, and patterne of the best and honourablest things'. From Dante and Petrarch Milton had turned to the fables and romances of knighthood (especially, no doubt, Tasso and Spenser), and such works proved, not the fuel of wantonness, but incitements to virtue. Next came Plato, with his ethical idealism, his conception of the Eros which leads to divine knowledge and virtue. 'Last of all not in time, but as perfection is last', there were the precepts of Christian religion, the doctrine that 'the body is for the Lord and the Lord for the body'. And along with St. Paul Milton put that apocalyptic book of the Bible which sheds an unearthly light over so many of his pages from first to last. *Comus* ends, like 'Lycidas' and the *Epitaphium Damonis*, with what is for the young Puritan the beatific vision. It is temperance and chastity, not their opposites, which are rational and natural, and true chastity, beginning in the order of reason and nature, attains its fullness in the Christian order of grace. This alone possesses the beauty, joy, and freedom which the blind and perverted Comus thinks are to be found in slavery to sense. And it is this religious motive, the heavenly marriage of the virgin soul, which adds a mystical glow of adoration to Milton's rational statement of the free security of the virtuous mind. His youthful ideal of virginity was to become a richer ideal of wedded love, but his ideal of chastity is even now a positive and all-embracing way of life. Perhaps the best proof of that appears not so much in the exposition of Christian and Platonic ethics as in the crystal purity of tone which irradiates the whole. No didactic prolusion from the Elder Brother or the Lady bears truer testimony than the opening lines to the author's apprehension of 'those chaste and high mysteries', his passionate faith in invisible things.

So far, except for the self-questioning resolved in the seventh sonnet, Milton's poetry has embodied a studiously contemplative happiness, a youthful idealism, serene or fervent, unmarred by outward or inward trouble. The soul of the young poet-priest, and the natural and supernatural worlds he inhabits, have been a celestial harmony. If we have any fear that study and religious and moral zeal may dry up sensuous impulses, we may move on to Milton's letter, written to Diodati in 1637, declaring his God-given love of beauty in all the forms and appearances of things; the words—which include a phrase from Euripides—are both an aesthetic and a religious affirmation.

In this same year 1637, however, we have the first testimony of genuine spiritual disturbance. In 'Lycidas' the conflict that Keats discerned in Milton, between the pleasures and the ardours of song, appears as a bitter reality; the poem might have been called 'A Faith on Trial'. It is not to be read primarily as an elegy, and the degree of the author's sorrow for Edward King is quite irrelevant. 'Lycidas' achieves its emotional power because the drowning of a virtuous young man at once crystallizes and releases all Milton's thoughts and feelings about his own past, present, and future and about the great Task-Master's will. And this inexplicable event adds its heavy weight to the ennui, the paralysing doubts, which may attack the most zealous student after five long years of hard and outwardly unprofitable toil. What is the value of the laborious and consecrated life of learning if it is to be cut off before fame is won? The answer, that true fame can be assessed only by God and enjoyed only in heaven, is to be Milton's final answer, yet what we have at this point is half-conventional faith, the will to believe rather than emotional conviction, and doubt remains. God allows a blameless young cleric to die and hireling shepherds to infest His church, the church Milton had refused to enter. The lovely passage on flowers is a temporary escape, not a solution. The problem returns in the picture of the dead youth's body washed beyond the stormy Hebrides or toward Namancos and Bayona's hold; here the volume of sound heightens the idea—which, like many of Milton's chief ideas, is conveyed indirectly—of the littleness of man in a world of forces that God does not seem to control. But the answer returns, the definition of true achievement and true fame, and now Milton rises above Apollo and Jove to the imagery of Revelation. The vision of the virgin soul of Lycidas received into heaven banishes the last shadow of doubt. Thus beneath the smooth surface of a conventional elegy, ebbing and flowing with the motives of the pastoral pattern, the waves of regret, anger, despair, and resolution roll upon one another. The spiritual struggle goes on before our eyes, rising steadily in intensity, momentarily assuaged or aggravated by the irregularly sweet or thunderous music, until the last movement asserts the victory of faith in a triumphant glimpse of the sure glory of heaven. Life is vindicated and serenity is won.

There is no more miraculous example in poetry of the way in which a great theme, artistic power, and complete sincerity can transform a supposedly dead convention. The pastoral device had early proved its usefulness as a dramatic mask, and Milton found in it both a disguise for personal utterance and a form which imposed order upon his surging emotions. Even the very Miltonic attack on the clergy has pastoral precedents from Petrarch to Mantuan and Spenser. The poem is infinitely complex in the associations it awakens, but all things, landscape and sea, Cambridge and Paradise, British lore and classic myth, Christian and pagan symbols, are wrought into an harmonious

whole, an almost epic whole. Through this complexity and
objective solidity Milton's personal struggle becomes universal.
The entirely simple last line is an example of potent ambiguity.
Does it mean that Milton will soon be crossing the sea, or that
he is done with minor poetry, or that he must turn his back
upon death and face life with renewed faith and energy?

On his way home from abroad in 1639 Milton learned of
the death of Charles Diodati, his oldest friend. To express
real sorrow he resorted not only to the pastoral convention
but to Latin. In the *Epitaphium Damonis*, which was written
and privately printed in 1640, some main themes of 'Lycidas'
reappear, the questioning of Providence, the author's ambitions
(here the British epic), and the reception of the virgin soul into
the upper world 'where the festal orgies rage under the heavenly
thyrsus'. There are touching moments, as when Milton recalls
his friend's cultured wit and gaiety poured out on summer
walks and by the winter fire, but as a whole the elegy moves,
slowly, on a level of pastoral artifice and suggests a Renaissance
poet falling back, in the apathy of grief and vague personal
discontent, on literary habit.

3

Milton settled in London at a time when it was reserved only
for God and angels to be lookers-on. The lover of contemplation, with an heroic poem in his mind, shrank from embarking
'in a troubl'd sea of noises and hoars disputes'; but he had
loved 'the honest liberty of free speech' from his youth and the
trumpet-call of his great Task-Master left him no choice. He
would not have been Milton if he had not been able to sacrifice
his poetic hopes to the claims of public duty and his own
broadening interests. He belongs to that tradition which
stretches back through the Renaissance to antiquity, the tradition of the poet who not only writes what is doctrinal and
exemplary to a nation but takes his place as an active citizen
and leader. What course Milton would follow in the crisis of
English liberty might not, perhaps, have been confidently predicted from his early poems, but it could have been from his
seventh prolusion. It was partly as a young Baconian, partly as
a young Platonist, that he had attacked the sterile Aristotelian-
ism of Cambridge and had pleaded for real and fruitful examination of man's outer and inner world. That discourse, on the text

that learning brings more blessings to men than ignorance, seems at first sight only a tissue of the commonplaces of Christian humanism. But it embodies an intensely personal faith, the boundless dreams of a young idealist of genius who feels himself standing on the threshold of a new era, who sees no obstacle in the way of man's conquest of nature and of all human problems. And he aspires, with a half-concealed but proud self-confidence, to be one of the makers of that new era, to be the oracle of many nations, whose home will be honoured as a shrine. We cannot measure the depth of Milton's later pessimism unless we appreciate the fervid and, as we say, unrealistic optimism of his youth and early manhood.

If Milton had not written a line of verse his prose works would be important as the commentary of a great and growing mind on the complex issues of a stirring epoch, and they are still more important as a commentary on his major poems. Passing by some late pieces, the *De Doctrina Christiana*, and such miscellaneous works as the *History of Britain* noticed in an earlier chapter, we have five pamphlets against prelacy (1641–2); four on divorce (1643–5), with the letter on education and *Areopagitica* coming respectively after the first and second; in the political field, the *Tenure of Kings and Magistrates* and *Eikonoklastes* (1649), the two Latin defences of the English people (1651, 1654), and *A Ready and Easy Way to Establish a Free Commonwealth* (1660). Of these works two or three stand among the great possessions of the race, two or three more are at least required reading, and the rest, except for scholars, are mostly dead. Writing in the heat of the moment, and with his own views in process of change, Milton too seldom rose to philosophic principles of enduring wisdom; but that is not to say that his breathless exhortations do not contain much judicious and liberal thought on the problems of his time. They contain also, along with inevitable wrangling and an equally inevitable excess of citation, spontaneous jets both of the prophetic sublimity that we expect and of satirical wit that we may not expect. Though his tracts are built on rhetorical canons, the prose of the most disciplined of poets seems remarkably undisciplined. But the man who mocked at the 'spruce fastidious oratory' of the Senecan Hall is full of racy Saxon vigour, and on all levels, 'lofty, mean, or lowly', whether he is praying, arguing, or snorting down opponents, he gives the

effect of the living voice. When we remember how amiable a
quality in that turbulent age was the true-born Anglican's love
of his Church and some royalists' devotion to their king, we
may wish that Milton's zeal for purer spirituality in religion
and truer liberty in civil affairs had carried less of the common
harshness with it. But if in controversy Milton's manners were
not above the average, and sometimes below, it is clear that
he was moved, as bookish idealists—and Church Fathers—
often have been, by a genuinely impersonal fury against the
enemies of a sacred cause, a kind of fury which left him quite
honestly amazed and indignant when victims returned the
attack.

While special occasions called forth Milton's pamphlets, the
first principles of his liberal creed, as we know from his Commonplace Book, developed out of prolonged study and reflection, and they developed most rapidly during his years of
public activity. Milton's Christian humanism had two sides,
one completely orthodox, the other only partly so—or orthodox
in a new way. Milton the artist accepted as his natural heritage
the great literary tradition of antiquity and the Renaissance,
and applied the whole force of his genius to the enrichment
of that tradition. In the mode and substance of his thought
Milton also owed much to the classics, but whereas traditional
Christian humanism, Catholic or Protestant, had been in the
main a bulwark of authority, the violent conflicts of Milton's
age, the Puritan ideal of the holy community, and the impetus
of Puritan individualism led him—he being what he was—from
Anglicanism to Presbyterianism, from Presbyterianism to Independency, and from Independency to independence. It has
been said that Milton himself '*was* a sect'. Yet it was the
humanist in Milton who could neither stand still with the rigid
Presbyterians nor accompany radical Puritans all the way.
We must, however, turn to the tracts themselves and, facing
that array of works on religious, domestic, and civil liberty, we
cannot do more than recall a few familiar signposts, although
a brief summary of his opinions makes his mind appear much
more simple and static than it was.

The anti-episcopal pamphlets of 1641–2, which we now
cherish mainly for their personal passages, were Milton's contribution to the debate which raged around the Root and
Branch Bill. The author of 'Lycidas' naturally allied himself

with the 'Smectymnuus' group of ministers, which included his old tutor, Thomas Young, against Bishops Hall and Ussher. But, despite his full assurance for the moment, Milton could be no more than a temporary fellow-traveller. In the light of his vision of a great regeneration, Presbyterianism *iure divino* quickly proved itself no less intolerable than episcopacy *iure divino*, and the Long Parliament seemed no nucleus for the holy community. Such disinterested disillusionment was not lessened, as some angry sonnets testify, by the Presbyterian reception of the pamphlets on divorce. These brought Milton his first real notoriety; even James Howell called him 'a poor shallow-brain'd puppy'. Comment on the divorce tracts must be limited to a miniature 'tetrachordon'. First, modern research has freed Milton from the odium of having begun the series during his honeymoon; it appears certain that he was married over a year before the first tract was printed. Secondly, while a personal grievance furnished a special motive and heightened the anguished pictures of an inexperienced man bound to an image of earth and phlegm, Milton was treating a subject he had thought about in earlier years. Thirdly, his appeal for easier divorce was based on a high ideal of marriage, of that marriage of minds which the Bible and the law did not recognize. Finally, notwithstanding the common prejudice against Milton's 'Turkish contempt of females', he did not ignore the right of women as well as men to release from unworthy mates. If he always gave man a higher rank in the scale of being, so did everyone else; and in exalting the husband Milton exalts the wife who is to be the true companion of such a man.

The wrestlings of Milton's individual reason with Hebraic pronouncements on divorce, and his violent reaction against a new tyranny, quickened the natural evolution of his progressive thinking and carried him out of the Presbyterian ranks into the van of liberalism. The testimony of his emancipation is his most famous and in some respects, though it embodied only a part of his final outlook, his most central work in prose. In *Areopagitica* (1644) we breathe the true, large Miltonic air, the air of his admired Lord Brooke and other Platonists and latitudinarians. The tract is a signal reminder of its author's double affiliations. In form it is a classical oration, and classical liberty is one of its themes, but its background was the Independent-Presbyterian controversy over religious toleration. It was ignored by the controversialists, and it was indeed off the main line of argument, since Milton concentrated upon the licensing ordinance revived by the predominantly Presbyterian Parliament in its effort to control the press. (He dealt more directly with the problem of toleration in later tracts and in the *Christian Doctrine*.) Since *Areopagitica* has often been loosely taken as a plea for complete freedom of speech, it should be observed that Milton does in fact accept the necessity of guarding fundamentals and hence of judicious censorship of dangerous books after publication. We need not be disappointed in recognizing that Milton, like his fellows, assumed the necessity of maintaining certain absolute values, that he was a liberal of the seventeenth century, not of the nineteenth or twentieth—and even the modern liberal has to readjust his principles in war-time. But nowhere in Milton, or in English, have we a mightier plea for free discussion, a more splendid confidence in the invincible power of reason and truth, or a greater faith in England as the mansion house of liberty.

The brief sketch of Milton's political theory in an earlier chapter may be briefly amplified here. The hammer of bishops (and foe of Arians) had been, or thought himself, a true monarchist, but the close of the civil war found him on the left. In the *Tenure of Kings and Magistrates* (February 1649) he condemned shallow sympathy for a tyrant and upheld the principles of popular sovereignty and resistance with an array of authorities from the Bible and the classics down to Reformation divines. Marked out as an able spokesman for the regicides, Milton was assigned the task of answering *Eikon Basilike*. *Eikonoklastes* (1649) was inevitably ineffectual. Milton's next opponent was the great scholar Salmasius, who had been employed to state the royalist case. The Latin *Defence of the English People* (1651) discredited Salmasius but was hardly worth the remnants of Milton's sight. The *Second Defence* (1654), a reply to an anonymous and able royalist attack, included a drubbing of Alexander More (though the actual author was Peter Du Moulin), but Milton rose to a noble celebration of the liberty won, and the further liberty still to be won, by the Commonwealth, and gave a noble testimony to his own renewed faith and strength. Cromwell and Fairfax received the Miltonic praise of having proved their right to rule by ruling their own passions. It was a testimony also to the sincerity of Milton's convictions that even in eulogizing the Protector the staunch republican felt uneasy over symptoms of dictatorship.

Six years later, in very different circumstances, Milton made a last bold appeal for a free commonwealth. In the *Ready and Easy Way* (1660) he took account of ancient and modern republican constitutions and of political theorists from Plato to Bodin and Harrington, but with all its detailed plans the tract was an admission of defeat, how crushing a defeat we can understand if we realize what Milton had sacrificed to the cause of liberty. The sheltered idealist had believed that England was full of John Miltons who had only to be shown the right path to follow it. The early pamphlets had been aflame with hope of complete and immediate triumph:

Methinks I see in my mind a noble and puissant Nation rousing herself like a strong man after sleep, and shaking her invincible locks: Methinks I see her as an Eagle muing her mighty youth, and kindling her undazl'd eyes at the full midday beam; purging and unscaling her long abused sight at the fountain it self of heav'nly radiance. . . .

At times since 1640 that ecstatic vision of a noble and puissant nation had grown dim, but Milton's hopes had rallied in 1654. Now, in 1660, the vision has faded into the light of common day, and men worthy to be for ever slaves are rushing to put their heads under the yoke. The good old cause is dead; God's new and greater reformation has ended in the Restoration.

Yet Milton's career as a publicist was not wholly a loss, for him or for us. From the first he knew what he was giving up, since poetry was his right hand and prose his left, but he had always desired the fame of a great leader, an oracle of nations, and his work in prose, if in one sense a forced betrayal of his destiny, was also a large part of its fulfilment. It consoles him in his blindness to recall his defence of liberty, of which, he thinks, 'all Europe talks from side to side'. The monumental sonnets on public men and events, so different in theme and style from the mass of Elizabethan and later verse in that form, were soul-animating strains beyond the power of Tasso, and parallel rather to the exalted odes in which Horace reminded decadent Rome of the old Roman virtues—or, on the occasion of the massacre in Piedmont, to the comminatory thunders of a Hebrew prophet. The chief fruit of the author's experience in the arena was the infinite strengthening and enrichment of

the major poems. In addition to the heroic poet's 'insight into
all seemly and generous arts and affaires', Milton gained the
insight into less seemly arts which contributed to the human
reality of the rebel angels; the Secretary to the Council (to
echo Gibbon) was not useless to the historian of Pandemonium.
But the great gain was on another level. If the British or
biblical epic had been written when it was first planned, doubtless, as allusions in the early prose suggest, it would have been
a song of triumph; we cannot regret the endurance of dust and
heat, the tragic frustration and disillusionment, which deepened
and saddened its wisdom. However cheerful Milton's old age,
the stress and stimulus of imaginative effort heightened his
realization of heroic past and ignoble present. *Paradise Lost* is
a divine comedy in which good grows out of evil, but the
author's optimism is far from facile; it must be measured by the
strength of the pessimism it has to overcome. Milton can
declare himself still able to sing with voice unchanged,

> though fall'n on evil dayes,
> On evil dayes though fall'n, and evil tongues;
> In darkness, and with dangers compast round,
> And solitude,

but his voice is changed, even in these very lines. He tries to
find ground for hope in the vision of future history revealed to
Adam, but Adam hears no such story of national courage and
high destiny as Aeneas heard from Anchises:

> Truth shall retire
> Bestuck with slandrous darts, and works of Faith
> Rarely be found: so shall the World goe on,
> To good malignant, to bad men benigne,
> Under her own waight groaning, till the day
> Appeer of respiration to the just,
> And vengeance to the wicked. . . .

Pessimism reaches its depth in *Samson.* God's chosen hero is
'Eyeless in Gaza at the Mill with slaves', and his victory over
despair may not for us quite cancel the dramatic arraignment
of divine justice. Yet—and this is Milton's last message, the
indestructible remnant of his once boundless dreams of a new
age—if his faith in men and action has proved vain, there is
still hope for individual man; he can at least, with divine grace,
rule himself. The kingdom of Christ is not of this world. So

when Adam has learned the Christian way of life, he has no
need of an earthly paradise, he has a paradise within him,
happier far. So Christ, man's perfect model, maintains His
integrity against the allurements of ambition. So Samson,
resisting selfish and sensual temptations, wins a new strength
and internal peace which make his outward fate of no account.

4

The central articles of Milton's ethical and religious creed
were developed in his prose, and we may here take both a
backward and a forward glance, remembering that that creed
was always growing under the pressure of thought and experience, and that some of the most significant developments, at
least in tone and emphasis, appeared only in the late poems.

If the first article was liberty, it was the liberty achieved
through religious discipline, through education in the fullest
sense of the word. In his letter (1644) to Hartlib, the Baconian
and Comenian reformer, Milton showed, as he had in his prolusions, some affinity with Baconian critics of the prescribed
methods and materials of education, both scholastic and linguistic, and—partly perhaps because of the demands of war—
he gave a larger importance to the study of science than many
of the older humanists had given. In the main, however, he
wrote in the orthodox tradition of Renaissance and medieval humanism. His view is aristocratic (later he was to feel
more strongly the need of popular education); he aims at the
production of useful and cultivated citizens and leaders, not
scholars; and he assumes that the classics are the fundamental
literature of knowledge as well as of power. In stressing religion
and virtue, the training of the moral judgement and the will,
he only adds a personal earnestness to what had been the chief
object of Christian humanism in all ages and countries. Of the
two definitions of education in the tract, what might be called
the 'modern' one is constantly quoted, but the 'medieval' one
is even more truly Miltonic:

The end then of learning is to repair the ruins of our first parents by
regaining to know God aright, and out of that knowledge to love
him, to imitate him, to be like him, as we may the neerest by possess-
ing our souls of true vertue, which being united to the heavenly grace
of faith makes up the highest perfection.

That is the substance of the last words between Michael and
Adam, and by that time the author had gained a fuller comprehension of their meaning.

It was inevitable that Milton should break with Calvinism
as Erasmus had broken with Luther. A humanist believing in
human and divine reason could not uphold the depravity of man
and the arbitrary will of an inscrutable God. No ordinance,
human or from heaven, Milton declared in *Tetrachordon*, can
bind against the good of man. And in the tracts on divorce,
in *Areopagitica*, and most fully and explicitly in the *Christian
Doctrine*, Milton evolved that enlarged conception of Christian
liberty of which he was in his day the great exponent. That
conception of the self-directing independence of the regenerate
man, of his freedom from external prescription, could be both
aristocratic and revolutionary; it was, of course, far removed
from the licence of the unregenerate and irresponsible. Man's
guide is not the letter of civil or biblical law but the law of
the Spirit written in the hearts of believers; for Milton as for
Hooker and Taylor and other Christian humanists the law of
God is the law of right reason and of nature. With Christian
values and motives are fused ancient, aristocratic, and rational
ideals of private and republican freedom. Both the right reason
of the individual and the saving remnant of the regenerate are,
like the created universe, worlds of divine order in the midst
of chaos.

A good deal, though not all, of the purpose and substance
of Milton's chief works is crystallized in some eloquent and
familiar sentences of *Areopagitica*:

I cannot praise a fugitive and cloister'd vertue, unexercis'd &
unbreath'd, that never sallies out and sees her adversary, but slinks
out of the race, where that immortall garland is to be run for, not
without dust and heat. Assuredly we bring not innocence into the
world, we bring impurity much rather: that which purifies us is triall,
and triall is by what is contrary. That vertue therefore which is but
a youngling in the contemplation of evill, and knows not the utmost
that vice promises to her followers, and rejects it, is but a blank
vertue, not a pure; her whitenesse is but an excrementall whitenesse;
Which was the reason why our sage and serious Poet Spencer, whom
I dare be known to think a better teacher then Scotus or Aquinas,
describing true temperance under the person of Guion, brings him
in with his palmer through the cave of Mammon, and the bowr of
earthly blisse that he might see and know, and yet abstain. . . .

Many there be that complain of divin Providence for suffering Adam to transgresse, foolish tongues! when God gave him reason, he gave him freedom to choose, for reason is but choosing; he had bin else a meer artificiall Adam, such an Adam as he is in the motions. We our selves esteem not of that obedience, or love, or gift, which is of force: God therefore left him free, set before him a provoking object, ever almost in his eyes; herein consisted his merit, herein the right of his reward, the praise of his abstinence. Wherefore did he creat passions within us, pleasures round about us, but that these rightly temper'd are the very ingredients of vertu? . . .

This justifies the high providence of God, who though he command us temperance, justice, continence, yet powrs out before us ev'n to a profusenes all desirable things, and gives us minds that can wander beyond all limit and satiety.

This last sentence, with its verbal anticipations of *Paradise Lost*, is a particular reminder of Milton's method of justifying God's ways to men, his emphasis on human freedom of choice and human responsibility. The unwary Eve falls through 'pride And wandring vanitie', the credulous and mistaken desire for an apparent good, which mislead her reason, and Adam, whose reason is not deceived, allows uxorious passion to sway his will and break his higher tie with God. In putting the simple biblical story on a partly humanistic and rational basis, in making it a many-sided conflict between reason and unreason, 'knowledge' and 'ignorance', temperance and excess, hierarchic order and anarchic disorder, Milton had behind him the whole tradition of Christian humanism; two contemporary examples are the first chapter of Browne's *Pseudodoxia Epidemica* and Henry More's *Conjectura Cabbalistica*. But Milton has also risen above —some might say he had fallen below—the bold confidence of *Areopagitica* and *Tetrachordon*. If the zealous pamphleteer had not quite fully realized that reason and rectitude could partake of self-sufficient human pride, the ageing poet has had the lesson proved on his pulses. He has not abandoned the principles of Christian liberty and right reason, for these are religious and fundamental, but he has a new understanding of the prime need of humility and obedience. Irreligious pride and religious humility are indeed the one great theme of his major poems.

In *Paradise Lost*, even in exalting human reason and freedom, Milton stresses human weakness and the dangers of pride, which ruin Eve and Adam as well as Satan. The fallen angels lose themselves in the mazes of philosophic debate. The whole temptation of Eve is an appeal to the desire for godlike knowledge and power. In the long astronomical discussion of the eighth book, and with reiterated emphasis at the end of the poem, Adam is warned to check his roving fancy and to learn that the sum of wisdom is not scientific learning but everyday Christian goodness. We may be surprised at such 'obscurantism' in the man who had been kindled by Baconian ideas, who had given science a large place in his educational scheme, and who had written the great defence of free inquiry. But Milton is not condemning science in itself (he pays tribute to Galileo in the epic as well as in *Areopagitica*), he is only taking scientific knowledge and speculation as a cardinal example of the pride and presumption which obscure the true ends and values of life. Like all Christian humanists from Petrarch to Matthew Arnold, he feared the confusing of wisdom and knowledge, law for man and law for thing. In the *Reason of Church Government* (1642) he had distinguished between the lower wisdom of natural science and the only high valuable wisdom of religion, and in the following decades it might well seem that the rising tide of scientific thought threatened to sweep away religious and ethical values altogether. For Milton as for the Cambridge Platonists, the physical and metaphysical worlds were a divine order with a divine purpose, and man was made in the image of God, with a spark of divine reason and divine will.

We may notice here a parallel case in *Paradise Regained*. Many readers, knowing Milton's lifelong devotion and infinite debt to classical literature and thought, feel a shock when they come upon Christ's repudiation of the philosophy, poetry, and oratory of Greece, which has just received through Satan the poet's beautiful and heart-felt praise. The shock is unwarranted. Like other Christian humanists, Milton had always set the Bible above all other writings, and he gave still higher authority to 'the Spirit and the unwritten word'. It is only in comparison with the divine light of humble Christian faith and virtue that Greek philosophy, like science, appears as the product of arrogant human pride. In itself, so far as it goes, it is good; Christ Himself, earlier in the poem, had ranked Socrates next to Job. Milton's favourite secular authors up to the end were ancients, and this very poem—not to mention its companion, *Samson Agonistes*—owes much to them. His condemnation is relative rather than absolute. At the same time his vehemence here is a mark of the growing inwardness of his thought; in his age he turns more and more from a degenerate world and secondary aids to cling to ultimate truth. He is saying, as his old opponent Bishop Hall, the Christian Stoic, had said, that true light and peace of mind are to be won not at Athens but at Jerusalem.

The briefest survey of Milton's religious thought and feeling makes sufficiently absurd the romantic idea that he was of the devil's party without knowing it, that Satan was the real hero of *Paradise Lost*. But the idea is not yet dead in the popular or sometimes in the scholarly mind. The magnificent vitality of Satan has occasioned much idle discussion as well as wrong-headed eulogy. It is a matter of course that Shakespeare, though not a villain, could create heroic villains; why it should be a wonder and a problem that Milton could is not clear. The Satanist fallacy starts from complete misunderstanding of Satan's first speech. Here no less than later he shows himself in every word as a mighty outlaw, a great embodiment of pride and passion and a false ideal of liberty, and the intelligent reader, who does not need the poet's guiding comments, reacts as he reacts to the lawless speeches of Iago, Edmund, or Macbeth. Milton was of course a doctrinal poet as Shakespeare was not (though he often uses the technique of dramatic objectivity), but his beliefs and principles, however much philosophized by learning and heightened by Puritan fervour, were in the same tradition as Shakespeare's—and Hooker's and many other men's. It is not altogether his fault if readers debauched by sentimental and romantic liberalism and natural-ism are incapable of either intellectual or emotional response to the classical, Christian, medieval, and Renaissance doctrines of law and order in the soul, in society, and in the cosmos.

Those moderns who cannot comprehend or feel Milton's religious and ethical thought have no better understanding of a poetic method based also on law and order, so that the self-imposed limitations of all classical art become in him a simple-minded ignorance of the complexities of human nature and life. But Milton is at least no more naïve than Aeschylus and Sophocles, and the complexities and passions of mankind are the stuff of his major poems. Adam and Eve are condemned, as they must be; but the poet's acceptance of God's just punish-ment carries with it an enlarged charity towards His erring creatures. We follow with dramatic fullness the process by which the regal pair, created perfect, become Everyman and Everywoman, and we see them on the way to regeneration. The compassion that Milton feels for them culminates in the marvellously simple and suggestive close, the picture of two human beings alone in the world, with 'Providence thir guide'. Whether or not Milton justified the ways of God, his belief in a divinely ordered world did not impose a superficial unity and harmony upon his profoundly human and poetical sense of division and conflict, evil strength and evil weakness.

5

To speak briefly, as we must, of Milton's theological thought is to recognize his essential orthodoxy and to slight particular heresies. The explicit statement of his views, ethical and social as well as theological, is the *De Doctrina Christiana* (first printed in 1825) which, however early it originated, had reached virtually final form by about 1658–60 and was later amplified only in some details. Starting from such models as Ames and Wollebius, Milton was at great pains, with much discussion of the commentators, to systematize his own beliefs, and he sought also, apparently, to draw up a body of biblical teaching which all Protestants might accept. In such a biblical compilation the humanistic ethic so important in Milton's thought is not conspicuous, much less the imaginative action of his poetic fable. But the *Christian Doctrine* provides chapter and verse for the theological concepts of *Paradise Lost* and, since seventeenth-century theology was seldom flaccid, something of the hardness of the treatise is carried over into parts of the poem. At least Milton's metaphysical theology seems hard to those who consider egocentric emotionalism the highest level of religious experience.

Christ, God's executive agent in the heavenly war and in the creation and judgement of man, is the Logos, the Creative Word, and, in contrast with Satan, the incarnation of supreme love and right reason. He is also the Redeemer and the Mediator through whom man becomes regenerate. Milton not only accepts but glorifies the Atonement in both verse and prose, though his more instinctive emphasis seems to be, like that of the Cambridge Platonists, on the imitation of Christ, the divine life. The Arian or anti-Trinitarian view of the inferiority of Christ and the Holy Spirit to the Father, while clearly set forth in the treatise, is less distinct and obvious in the poem (which did not disturb generations of orthodox readers), but no doctrinal passage in the poem is inconsistent with the Arianism of Milton's formal theology.

Like Christ, God is Divine Love and much more. If at times He seems to resemble an almighty cat watching a human mouse, the trouble lies in the somewhat legal character of Christian theology itself and in the inevitable effects of dramatization. God suffers, paradoxically, through being the mouthpiece for the very doctrines which clear Him of arbitrary cruelty and justify His ways to men, the Arminian and Miltonic doctrines of free grace extended to all believers and of the right reason, free will, and responsibility of man. Against the Absolute Will of Calvinism Milton sets up Absolute Reason, the ultimate source and guarantee of life, order, justice, all the values comprehended by the spark of divine reason in man. There may be artistic defects in Milton's presentation, but there is nothing thin or cold in the conception. In the great words of Hooker,

of lawe there can be no lesse acknowledged, then that her seate is the bosome of God, her voyce the harmony of the world, all thinges in heaven and earth doe her homage, the very least as feeling her care, and the greatest as not exempted from her power, but Angels and men and creatures of what condition so ever, though ech in different sort and maner, yet all with uniforme consent, admiring her as the mother of their peace and joy.

That is the divine and natural harmony, the hierarchical order, which Satan seeks to overthrow in the universe and in the soul of man.

To enlarge a little upon Milton's metaphysics, his conception of the infinity, omnipresence, and omnipotence of God lies behind some ideas which may seem to approach pantheism, though Milton is no pantheist; he does not confound the Creator with Creation. God includes all causes, even the material. God did not create the world out of nothing, as orthodox tradition maintained, but out of the eternal substance which is a part of Himself. Uncircumscribed by necessity or chance, God communicates His goodness by manifesting Himself throughout the great scale of being which descends from Christ and the angels through the creatures and things of earth.

All things proceed from God and, unless depraved by evil, return to Him. Chaos is Chaos because He has not chosen to put forth His creative virtue upon it. (The germ of this idea is perhaps what in the *Timaeus* is called 'the absence of God'.) Milton affirms the reality and the goodness of matter; matter is not distinct from spirit but is for ever passing into it. The optimism inherent in such metaphysical monism receives characteristic expression from the poet-musician in half-mystical celebrations of cosmic harmony. It is obviously related to the ethical optimism that Milton shared also with the Cambridge Platonists, and for him it is a partial bulwark against the pessimism of experience. This metaphysical monism is not incompatible with the ethical dualism that is Christian and Platonic. What God is in the universe the divine faculty of reason is in man, and when man's reason is not in active control his nature becomes a chaos of passions. An ethical corollary of Milton's belief in the essential oneness of matter and spirit is his mature conception of human love, a conception which retains his early Christian and Platonic idealism without his early asceticism. Another logical consequence is the belief that man dies wholly until the day of resurrection; in this Milton is allied with contemporary 'mortalists'.

If this outline of some of Milton's central ideas has taken space which should have been given to 'the poetry', it is still the merest sketch of the creed he devoted his life and art to proclaiming. If the fundamental part of the creed be dismissed as elementary and commonplace, it was for Milton as for other great men and great writers the armour of a Christian soldier. And, it may be added, there is very little of the specifically Puritan in *Paradise Lost*, or indeed in the whole body of Milton's poetry. Finally, what we think of as Milton's theology belongs mainly to the *Christian Doctrine* and *Paradise Lost*, and his particular and changing beliefs are much less significant than his progress towards belief, in a deeper sense of the word. His earlier Christian humanism had been largely directed towards militant action; the decline and collapse of that external hope left him feeling the need of a closer walk with God. In his late poems, in place of the old ardent confidence in public reform, we find an 'un-Miltonic' emphasis on private experience, on humility, obedience, faith, and divine help.

6

We have had incidental hints of the epic ambitions which no Renaissance poet cherished more ardently than Milton. He had long contemplated the British theme which critical theory and poetic example prescribed, and his final choice was evidently determined by various causes, the scepticism induced by his own and others' study of early history, the cleavage in sentiment between 'Saxon' parliamentarians and 'British' royalists, the general European reaction in favour of biblical subjects, and chiefly, no doubt, his desire for a fable which would carry all that he now wished to say about God and man. The British and biblical subjects listed in the Cambridge manuscript (c. 1639–42) were planned as dramas, and Milton made four dramatic outlines of Adam's fall; indeed, the tale of Adam and Eve is in its very nature the pattern of a morality play. However, Milton did not give up his original and more satisfying project of an heroic poem. Having elected his subject and form, he still faced a problem which had existed in a smaller degree for Virgil and not at all for Homer, that is, the treatment of abstract spiritual ideas in the concrete terms of the heroic epic. As occasional apologies in the text indicate, Milton was conscious of the problem, if less fully conscious than the modern reader who feels that he has outgrown the epic tradition. The battles in heaven, the account of Creation, and the survey of Hebrew history, to mention three cardinal examples, remain more or less potent symbols of the contrast between chaotic passion and divine order, between destruction and the creative works of peace, between man's sinfulness and God's providence, yet the protracted and realistic treatment of such material, which early readers could enjoy for its own sake, means for us, in spite of many fine passages, an obscuring of symbolic values. Above all, the anthropomorphic and 'royalist' presentation of God, which was almost unavoidable in a heroic poem, has misled many readers and critics into seeing only the trappings of a tyrant and not the religious and metaphysical ideas He embodies.

In the elaboration of his narrative and drama Milton had two main resources, the plastic materials of classical story and, more directly, the whole Bible and the body of extra-biblical lore accumulated in Jewish and Christian commentary and in imaginative treatments of the Creation and the fall of Lucifer and of man. How many works of this last kind Milton had read we do not know; the *Adamus Exul* (1601) of Grotius and the *Adamo* (1613) of Andreini are perhaps the closest to *Paradise Lost*. Milton's poem is the great surviving monument of the immense mass of Renaissance writing, exegetical and poetical, which dealt with the matter of Genesis. God Himself hardly knew more about the beginnings of the world than the Du Bartas whom the young Milton had admired in Sylvester's popular translation and whose Protestant epic his own super-seded. Imaginative versions of religious 'history' were bound to keep within the limits of orthodoxy (a flexible orthodoxy, to be sure), so that they all have a degree of family resemblance, and very many items, large and small, in Milton's fable are inevitably conventional. A Renaissance poet, like a Greek dramatist, was expected to show his originality in the reworking of traditional themes, and to appreciate Milton's re-creative power we have only to think of Satan.

On the classical side Milton followed especially Virgil, the supreme model of epic decorum, and, like Virgil, he gave a new meaning to the devices he imitated—celestial machinery, the roll-call and council of leaders, epic games, the recapitula-tory narrative after the plunge *in medias res*, and the unfolding of future events. To mention a few items from various sources, the revolt of the angels blends theological tradition with the wars of giants and Titans and gods; the rebel army in hell marches like the Spartans in Plutarch's *Lycurgus*; Satan and Gabriel confront each other like Turnus and Aeneas in their last combat; Eve gives the first hint of her 'facile' nature by admiring her reflection in a pool, like Narcissus; the biblical description of the flood invites expansion from Ovid and Du Bartas; and so on. But with all his diverse means of amplifica-tion Milton remains so close to the original fable that many readers cannot feel certain where the Bible leaves off and the poet begins.

When various cosmological theories were current it was natural for a layman and a poet to follow what is called the Ptolemaic system. Milton knew enough science to discuss the old and familiar notions of the diurnal rotation of the earth and the plurality of worlds, and to treat Copernican ideas with respect, but the actual universe of *Paradise Lost* was a Miltonic

mixture of the traditional and the imaginative, and was modern
chiefly in its immensity. He was, as we have seen, too much
of a Christian humanist to let scientific speculation divert him
from the problems of direct importance to man and society. It
has been said that Shakespeare lived in a world of time, Milton
in a world of space, but for Milton space is not parallel to the
spectre of devouring Time which haunted so many minds of
the Renaissance. In his medieval scale of values, science, so
far as it is a description of God's works, is a branch of theology
and as such he, like Du Bartas, can make use of it. Hence too,
unlike some men of his century, Milton was apparently at no
time bewildered and dismayed by a consciousness of the silence
of infinite space. The axis of his faith rested on God and the
soul of man, and if that faith was sometimes shaken, the cause
was not any trepidation of the spheres. Without misgiving he
accepts the universe as his scene and his imagination triumph-
antly expands to fill it. No other English poet has such a God-
like vision of the world, a vision revealed in the great pictures
of boundless chaos and warring elements and in the constant
suggestion of vast distances. Such imperial command of space
doubtless belongs to the age of the telescope, yet we may
remember that no poet of the same age rivals the blind Milton
and, further, that a sense of space was not wholly lacking in
earlier men, among them such ancients as Lucretius, Ovid,
and Manilius.

If Milton's 'unhuman' fable and unlocalized setting invite
austere grandeur of treatment, he achieves passionate warmth
and organic unity through his profound concern with 'man,
the heart of man, and human life'; all his epic machinery and
decoration are subservient to that. But there are, apart from
the general interrelations of plot and character, various special
devices by which his story is integrated and linked with the
human and familiar. The action in heaven and hell is knit
together by such contrasted parallels as the infernal and celestial
assemblies and the 'merit' of Satan and Christ and details like
the march of the angels and the opening of the gates. A more
subtle kind of symbolism, already conspicuous in Spenser,
involves a continual antithesis between natural simplicity,
goodness, love, light, and life on the one hand and artificial
luxury, evil, hate, darkness, and death on the other. While
Homeric similes in the main keep us aware of a normal pastoral

life beyond the roar of battle and the waves, Milton's allusive-
ness takes of course a much wider range, from Galileo to 'the
Sons Of Belial' and the burglar. His geographical names are
not merely incantation but an economical as well as sonorous
way of calling up great events and great tracts of space and time.
In becoming less familiar—since it takes a world war to stir
the modern reader out of his geographical illiteracy—Milton's
allusions have become less realistic than they were in his own
age. The investing of Satan with oriental pomp and power was
not glamorous tinsel for men whose grandfathers had feared
the mighty Turk and coveted 'the wealth of Ormus and of Ind'.
But if Milton's references are commonly prompted by substantial reasons, they may also be vague enough to sustain and
heighten our sense of remoteness or mystery or grandeur or
horror. And that is in keeping with his fable and purpose.
His vast stage and superhuman action demand, not the minute
realism of Dante, but the constant use of the general and
suggestive, whether in the pictures of hell or of the 'enormous
bliss' of Eden. But that goes with and is controlled by a fundamental concreteness of thought and vision. Keats observed
Milton's habit of 'stationing' characters in relation to solid
objects; we see Adam 'under a Platan' and Satan disfigured
'on th'Assyrian mount'. Unlike the true romantic, Milton
never surrenders to the vague and unearthly. One remarkable
instance is that magnificently romantic island salt and bare,
'The haunt of Seales and Orcs, and Sea-mews clang', which
disproves the special sanctity of what George Fox called steeple-
houses.

Classical generality and romantic suggestion are never more
perfectly fused than in Milton's images from ancient myth.
They are the culmination of Renaissance art. They are, too,
an index to Milton's own artistic and spiritual evolution; his
successive allusions to Orpheus, for instance, reflect the lyrical
serenity of 'L'Allegro' and 'Il Penseroso', the troubled disenchantment of 'Lycidas', the noble fortitude of the invocation
to light, and the bitterness of the strident outburst against
Bacchus and his revellers. While Milton's classical mythology
shared in his general evolution from Elizabethan luxuriance
through a chastened splendour to bare severity, and while the
later books of *Paradise Lost* and the two last poems largely
forbade the use of myth, this more than any other element in

his writing retained the old sensuous warmth. In Milton generally, as in the Renaissance tradition, the unique value of the mythological symbol is its ideal beauty. Like such moderns as Arnold and T. S. Eliot, Milton instinctively turns away from the ugly present to the freshness and fecundity of the early world. The finest of all his similes, 'Not that faire field Of Enna', owes its complex magic to the musical and structural pattern, to the pathos of familiarity in the phrase 'all that pain', and to the implication that another innocent and lovely—and motherless—Proserpine is about to be gathered by the prince of darkness. Both the myth and the image of the flower are recalled, with a mixture of tragic irony and pity, in the description of Eve just before the temptation, when she goes forth like Ceres in her prime and when she is tying up the drooping stalks,

> Her self, though fairest unsupported Flour,
> From her best prop so farr, and storm so nigh.

The various pictures of the 'Silvan Scene', in which Milton lets himself go, though not beyond control, in the evocation of an earthly paradise, are not merely a gorgeous exercise in a Renaissance convention (still less an attempt to render the sensation of being in a garden), they spring from the poet's half-unconscious desire to believe in some ideal perfection unmarred by evil. Yet Milton is no poet of escape and he never loses his hold upon reality; over the idyllic beauty of Eden lies the ironic shadow of the tempter.

Milton's classical mythology may, in his most solemn moods, be blended with Hebraic or Christian feeling, as in the allusion to Proserpine and the prayers into which he transformed addresses to the epic Muse, or in the sonnet on his dead wife. But although tradition had reconciled classical and Hebrew story, and although the mature Milton could still link myth with religious and moral truth, he always claimed Christian superiority to 'th'Orphean Lyre' and he could feel, as Spenser did not, a conflict. His anti-pagan scruples, so often incorporated in the text of *Paradise Lost*, illustrate the dilemma of a sacred poet and a Puritan bred in the congenial air of Renaissance classicism. For one example, the lines about Mulciber's fall from heaven—which are, incidentally, a romantic transmutation of Homeric humour and embody an un-Homeric sense of space—begin and end with expressions of hostile disbelief yet they contain a richness of detail and of sound notable even in Milton.

The use of blank verse for an heroic poem was a great innovation, and Milton's handling of it added, not a new province, but a new world, to English prosody. But we cannot touch upon technicalities or even go very far into generalities. Milton's versification is of course inseparable from his diction and tone, and in recent years the organ-voice of England has been charged with an inorganically monotonous elevation of style and movement remote from the language and rhythms of common speech. There are always people who complain that Poussin is not Picasso or that Bach is not Prokofiev. Milton's poetic and critical heritage and his own purpose prescribed a long poem, and in a long poem the reader must be made to feel the continuity, 'the enormous onward pressure of the great stream' on which he is embarked. It is rather idle to compare bits of *Paradise Lost* with the short pieces of the metaphysical poets or with the dramatic texture of Shakespeare, or with such a totally different kind of epic as Dante's. Standing before the altar, as Milton habitually stood, he would have been profane if he had not worn his singing robes. A ritualistic elevation of style and movement may be as essential to an heroic subject as colloquial realism to realistic subjects and, on the Miltonic level, is a much rarer phenomenon. We can hardly imagine the gap there would be in English poetry, or in our own experience, if *Paradise Lost* were not there.

Critics who dismiss Milton on these grounds must also dismiss his models and peers, almost the whole array of Greek and Roman poets. Those poets in general created a dominant but not a simple impression by eliminating or subordinating peripheral detail; otherwise they would have been reproducing the disorder of nature and evading the artist's proper task. Their complexity of texture and reference is an ordered not a tangential complexity. Not feeling the need to tell all they know, and not believing that all the facts of experience are born free and equal, they would not have understood that their method betrayed a limitation, or a divorce, of thought and sensibility. Poetry, Milton conceived, should be 'lesse suttle and fine, but more simple, sensuous and passionate' than logic and rhetoric. For one example of sensuous and passionate writing which is far from 'simple' in the derogatory sense, an example of the

purest classical art and one of the most moving things in English
poetry, there is the invocation to light:

> Thus with the Year
> Seasons return, but not to me returns
> Day, or the sweet approach of Ev'n or Morn,
> Or sight of vernal bloom, or Summers Rose,
> Or flocks, or heards, or human face divine. . . .

Then the ancient poets commonly used an artificial 'poetical' style which, like Milton's, raised the mind above everyday
things. Milton's style is no more remote from popular English
than Virgil's is from popular Latin, or Homer's from popular
Greek. Besides, much of what in Milton is loosely condemned
as classical idiom is rather an effect of condensation. If 'Adam
the goodliest man of men since borne' is an odious Miltonic
classicism, what shall we say of Dekker's apostrophe to London,
'Thou art the goodliest of thy neighbors, but the prowdest'?
Milton may, in the interest of logical and emotional design
and emphasis, place words and phrases with something of the
freedom of an inflected language, but the attentive reading to
which he is entitled—and seldom receives from counsel for
the prosecution—will reveal the continual gain in fullness of
texture and communication. As for his syntax, it never troubles
those who leave it alone.

Granted an inevitable and fitting stylization in *Paradise Lost*,
the poem has far more variety of manner and movement than
is commonly appreciated. Its length and general clarity encourage the vague assumption that Milton splashes at a ten-
league canvas with brushes of comets' hair, that his smallest
unit is the paragraph with its planetary wheel, that his art is
too simply rhetorical for the subtler effects of phrase and
rhythm. The sensitive and unprejudiced reader may discover
for himself what there is no space to illustrate, the perpetual
and significant variations, both broad and minute, in narrative
of action, in description, in exposition, in oratory; and, within
these categories, the further variations in manner between, say,
the descriptions of chaos and of Eden, the speeches of Moloch
and of Belial. One large contrast, exemplified in countless
details as well as in the prevailing tone, separates the epic
narrative and drama of the opening books from the intimate
drama of the garden. The great archangel who had opposed

the Almighty becomes a sardonic Richard III or malignant Iago; the mother of mankind becomes a very feminine woman, much more concerned about Adam's reactions than about God's. In accordance with Milton's view of the fall as comprehending many sins, Adam and Eve pass through the phases of disobedience and levity, sensual passion, shame, fear, mutual recrimination, despair, reunited love and loyalty to each other, and finally true penitence. And the stately speech which had been appropriate to regal innocence gives place to the broken, realistic accents of human experience. Readers spoiled by the heroic energy, spaciousness, and colour of the epic books neglect the story of the fall, the centre around which all other events and characters are so greatly ordered, yet the one achievement is hardly less remarkable in its way than the other, and reveals a dramatic power and depth of pity that Milton is seldom allowed. Nor is there in English poetry a more suggestive complexity of feeling, conveyed as much by rhythm as by words, than in the last lines of the poem—an indescribable blend of sadness and hope, frailty and trust.

7

In the *Reason of Church Government* (1642), in setting forth his conception of poetry as the teacher of religion and virtue, Milton had specified three principal forms, epic, drama, and ode or hymn. He had stressed biblical along with classical models and for the epic, in addition to Homer, Virgil, and Tasso, had named the book of Job. Among many general subjects were 'the victorious agonies of Martyrs and Saints'. Much later, in the proem to the ninth book of *Paradise Lost*, Milton contrasted traditional epic themes with 'the better fortitude Of Patience and Heroic Martyrdom'. *Paradise Regained* and *Samson Agonistes* (1671) may be called the fulfilment of some of these aspirations, though we do not know when the two works were conceived. The 'Eden rais'd in the wast Wilderness' by the second Adam is the supreme type of the 'paradise within' partly regained by the first. It is in keeping with epic theory, as enunciated in the *Second Defence*, that Milton treats one 'particular action' in the life of his hero, and in keeping with his conception of poetry that the subject should be the temptation, not the crucifixion, a uniquely tragic story remote from normal experience. The book of Job makes its

contribution to the brief epic (and to *Samson* also). Unlike Job,
however, the sinless divine protagonist of *Paradise Regained*
cannot falter, much less fall, and the loss of dramatic tension
means some loss of human appeal, though a measure of tension
is given by Satan's ignorance of his adversary's true character
and by Christ's own lack of entire certainty.

On the other hand, Milton's general view of Christ encouraged what his special aim required, the presentation of his
hero not as a Deity untouched by common trials but as a man
facing such trials with man's resources, chief among them
'Light from above'. His virtues may be superhuman in degree,
but they are not in kind; they may be attained in some proportion by every Christian soul. Further, the conception of a
perfect hero was not repugnant to writers of the Renaissance,
and for not unworthy reasons. The names of Sidney and
Spenser and Chapman sufficiently attest the humanistic belief
in both the didactic value of ethical models and the ethical
intentions of the long line of heroic authors. Milton's Christ
is the last great figure in a procession which includes Arthur
and Guyon, Rinaldo and Godfrey, Orlando and Ruggiero,
Aeneas, Ulysses, Agamemnon, and Achilles. If the perfection
of Christ is more complete than that of these heroes, it is not at
all the perfection of Shelley's Prometheus and other products
of romantic and sentimental idealism. Milton's hero sternly
resists evil through the power of conscious reason guided and
strengthened by humble and obedient trust in God. Modern
readers, indifferent to the exalted didacticism, the heroic ideal
of Christian 'magnanimity', developed by Renaissance poetry
and criticism, have often seen in *Paradise Regained* the faults
without the grand beauties of *Paradise Lost*. But if ever any
artist knew what he was doing, it was Milton, and he was
writing a very different kind of poem. Even in the long epic
the major action had gone on in the souls of Adam and Eve,
and *Paradise Regained*, like the book of Job, may be called a
closet drama with a prologue and stage directions. The theme
and the form dictate the elimination of much that attracts us
in *Paradise Lost*; in interior drama—almost interior monologue
with an objectified tempter—everything, including rhythm,
must be pitched in a more subdued key.

When we first see Him, Christ has already gained one
Miltonic victory. His view of His mission has changed from

patriotic action to preaching and now, with no thought of self
or glory, He awaits God's guidance. The young and disillusioned Shelley withdrew from active reform to dream of the
millennium; the old and disillusioned Milton fortified his citadel, the upright heart and pure, in the midst of this world of
evil. His *contemptus mundi* has purged away all hopes except
in man's religious humility and his reign over himself. The
tests embraced in the second temptation go beyond those of
Spenser's book of temperance, which made so deep an impression upon his greatest disciple. Christ cannot be moved by a
luxurious feast or the promise of wealth or glory or empire, but
the noblest spirit might be swayed by Satan's appeal to the
duty of rescuing Israel from servitude and the need of the
wisdom of Greece. It is not merely Satan who misunderstands
Christ's nature and purposes; even His followers look for the
establishment of an earthly kingdom, even His mother's confidence is troubled. The wilderness is the symbol of His spiritual
isolation; He can share His thoughts with none but God. If
the first temptation had suggested at least the possibility of
self-distrust, it is by overcoming evil that Christ really proves
His divinity. A generation which has been stirred by *Murder in
the Cathedral* should not be unmoved by the victory of Milton's
'saint' over the unspiritual temptations which thrust themselves upon the possessor of spiritual power.

The poem has its purple patches. We may forget the modi-
cum of epic machinery—apart from Belial's leering suggestion
—but not the great panorama of the Roman Empire or the
eulogy of Athenian culture. Nor has Milton entirely curbed
his sensuous instincts; the magical banquet inspires the last and
one of the loveliest of his evocations of myth and romance.
But the characteristic beauty of *Paradise Regained*, a kind of
beauty present in *Paradise Lost* though obscured by surrounding
splendours, is that of simple and perfect statement, the style
almost of the gospels themselves. An occasional touch of the
old sublimity, or an occasional lapse, only heightens our sense
of the normal texture of speech and rhythm. A Miltonic and
therefore a decorous nakedness of thought and emotional force
make the prosaic poetic. It was not a 'tired' Milton who wrote
'For in the Inn was left no better room', or the image that
Donne anticipated and Newton echoed, 'As Children gathering
pibles on the shore', or the final quiet assertion of the triumph

of solitary inward strength over the glories of the world—'hee
unobserv'd Home to his Mothers house private return'd'.

8

If *Paradise Regained* expressed the settled faith and fortitude
of Milton's old age, *Samson Agonistes* expressed the moods in
which faith and fortitude contended with defiance and bitterness. Episodes in Samson's career were among the biblical
subjects in the Cambridge manuscript; the *Reason of Church
Government* contained a parallel between the Hebrew leader and
King Charles; in *Areopagitica* the militant England of Milton's
hopes was 'rousing herself like a strong man after sleep, and
shaking her invincible locks'; and in *Paradise Lost* the sensual
indulgence of Adam and Eve was likened to that of 'Herculean
Samson'. When Milton came at last to write a tragedy he was
naturally led to the Greek pattern by a scholar's admiration,
by a strong feeling for decorum, and by indifference to the
popular stage. His method, whatever his degree of consciousness, resulted in an eclectic and original adaptation both of
the common elements of Greek tragedy and of various special
features characteristic of the several dramatists. The opening
soliloquy, the pervasive strain of philosophic ratiocination, and
the characterization of Dalila, remind us of Euripides. The
constant use of dramatic irony (which begins with the suggestion
of the whole theme in the simple first line, 'A little onward lend
thy guiding hand'), the treatment of the chorus and of the
denouement, and the subjecting of the hero's will to a series of
tests, are mainly Sophoclean. The limitation of actors and plot,
the dominance of the protagonist, and the prophetic fervour
and passion for righteousness which animate the whole, are in
the vein of Aeschylus. But of such parallels the more important
spring from essential affinity rather than imitation. Among
particular plays the nearest to *Samson* are *Prometheus Bound* and
Oedipus at Colonus.

Until the final catastrophe reported by the messenger *Samson*
has no physical action, and some critics from Dr. Johnson down
have complained that it is almost static. But the drama takes
place in the soul of Samson, and the psychological progression
can perhaps be shown best by a short outline. In his early
speeches Samson laments chiefly the immediate bodily and
mental torments of captivity, degradation, and blindness, and

his pride is bitterly hurt by the manner of his fall. He is conscious of personal guilt, yet he defends his two marriages as undertaken with a feeling of divine approval, and he contrasts his heroic service with the pusillanimity of the Israelites who have forgotten him and accepted bondage. As the drama proceeds all these motives recur, but by degrees self-pity and self-assertion give way to religious humility and a single-hearted conviction of his own responsibility for his lot. Manoa's reference to the feast of Dagon enlarges the consequences of Samson's sin. With a new access of contrition he sinks the thought of his own fate in the contest between God and Dagon, a contest which, he vaguely feels, must end with him, and soon. Manoa's eagerness to arrange a ransom evokes the captive's further emphasis on his pride and sensuality. With self-knowledge grows spiritual loneliness; even his father does not understand the real nature of his present anguish. Samson has got beyond the temptation of physical freedom and other selfish motives, but it is much harder to resist despair. Tortured by his own thoughts, and by his sense of Heaven's desertion, he longs for the release of death. The effect is prolonged by the chorus, which is moved to question God's dealings with man, above all with such a man as His chosen champion. 'Just or unjust, alike seem miserable.'

The chorus breaks off to announce the approach of Dalila in all her finery. (The nautical image apparently came from Harrington's description of the Commonwealth, and apparently passed from Milton into the picture of Millamant!) Roused out of his apathy, Samson angrily repels her specious excuses and hints of sensual invitation, and when his Circe tries to reassert her spell with a touch he is stirred to sudden fury. Abandoning her wiles, Dalila turns upon him and departs. If her change of front seems to confuse the motives behind her visit, her appearance is an obvious dramatic necessity, both as a reminder of Samson's former weakness and as a test of his recovery. The latter point is underlined by the chorus's acknowledgement of the power of beauty and passion, though it goes on to a compendious censure of the female sex.

Samson has shown his conquest of pride and sensuality; he has still to conquer despair. In the fourth Act his responses to the taunts of the Philistine giant record a new and fearless confidence born of inward victory and peace. He can now affirm

'My trust is in the living God', and he challenges Dagon's
champion to combat. The chorus rejoices in this outward proof
of the renewed strength of Israel's defender and still more in
the patient fortitude he has displayed as a man. Samson refuses
a summons to entertain the Philistines, but then, impelled by
divine prompting, he goes of his own accord. A major instance
of tragic irony, the 'false dawn' before the denouement, is
furnished by Manoa's joy over his success in ransoming his son.
When the messenger bursts in and describes the scene at the
feast, the chorus exults in Samson's heroic martyrdom and
the father pronounces a eulogy of quieter nobility—though
neither chorus nor father understands Samson's real victory.
The quiet tone is continued in the last words of the chorus,
which, beginning on the Euripidean note, turn into an assertion
of God's oft-hidden but unwavering support of His faithful
champion.

Samson Agonistes could not be purely Greek (if it were it would
be only another museum piece), but Milton does not force his
material into a theologically Christian mould. The hero, compared with Adam and Christ, is wholly and merely human and,
if his sense of Heaven's desertion and his recovery are Hebraic
and Christian, we still feel ourselves in the atmosphere of
ancient rather than of modern romantic tragedy. For the
catharsis is attained not only through the triumph of character
over circumstance; there is also, as in Aeschylus and Sophocles,
a vindication of divine law and justice, though the Christian
poet does not, any more than the ancients, offer an easy formula
in solution of the mystery of pain and evil and tragic waste.

One obvious reason for the dynamic inspiration of the drama
is that it was the last retrospective and prophetic utterance of a
great soul to an ignoble nation which he had laboured in vain
to serve and save. Yet in his grand testament Milton remains a
classical artist who sublimates and generalizes his private and
public emotions. Samson may be, in his sins, the English
people; he is—and is not—John Milton. Knowing what we do,
we see autobiography in the whole picture of Israel in willing
subjection to a godless race and of the great rebel and deliverer
now blind, helpless, racked by physical and mental pains, while
the bodies of other heroes are a prey to dogs and fowls, unjust
tribunals, and the ungrateful mob; in the reasoned defence of
rebellion; in the condemnation of the oppressors' idolatry,

levity, and *hybris*; and, some would add, in the hero's fatal
marriage to a Philistine woman and the censure of her sex.
Such knowledge, if not pressed too far, may at times heighten
the poignancy of the drama, yet all that material is dramatically
logical and relevant. In any case *Samson* far transcends personal
and particular facts. Its living power is in its direct and searching treatment of human experience, the hard struggle of
humility, integrity, and faith against pride, sin, misery, and
despair. If we have any doubts of the modernity—or the
Christianity—of *Samson*, we may think again of *Murder in the
Cathedral*. With all their differences, we have in both works a
proud national leader brought low, fighting a solitary inward
battle against temptation, and, when he has made his will
perfect, meeting martyrdom with a mingled humility and selfless
spiritual exaltation which no one around him comprehends.

The difficulty and the doubtful issue of that battle are reflected
in the rugged irregularities of rhythm and rugged strength of
style. The irregular lines are not free verse, they are controlled
arrangements of metrical feet, with much of what Gerard
Hopkins called counterpoint. In the realistic licences of *Samson*
Milton's dramatic evolution reaches full maturity. But in plain
statement and broken, colloquial rhythms there is still Miltonic
grandeur and sublimity, a new kind of 'classical' writing:

> Nothing is here for tears, nothing to wail
> Or knock the breast, no weakness, no contempt,
> Dispraise, or blame, nothing but well and fair,
> And what may quiet us in a death so noble.

In general, the massive and sinewy dramatic idiom is the
instrument not merely of thought but of thinking. In style as
in form and spirit *Samson* gives the non-Grecian reader a truer
feeling for Greek tragedy than most English translations of
Greek plays. Verbal beauty is not lacking, but the real beauty
is in the full yet bare statement of a noble theme. The touch
of stiffness is not un-Greek, not even the 'tame villatic Fowl'.
One phrase which has been termed sharply Dantesque, 'whence
Gaza mourns', is rather Aeschylean—'ὡς στένειν πόλιν Περσῶν'.

9

To survey Milton's work from the beginning to *Samson* is to
be impressed by both the uniformity and the variety of style.
Always sensitively aware of critical theory and poetic practice,

he was a disciple of Ovid, of the Elizabethans, of Jonson, and in those early stages he showed himself a more and more independent master of his craft. *Comus* looked both backward and forward. In 'Lycidas' and the heroic sonnets began the forging of the grand style, which was to be the medium of *Paradise Lost*. That grandeur, however uncommon, is not un-English. In Milton as in Bacon, Browne, and other representatives of ornate sublimity, the main texture is pure English. It would be odd if it were not, since in all the essential features of his personality and work Milton was one of the most thoroughly English of English authors. What is more important is that he was a man, and 'So far from being granite, his verse is a continual spring of beauty, of goodness, of tenderness, of humility'. The word 'Miltonic', commonly applied to *Paradise Lost* or to the three major works of the poet's last phase, really includes three very different styles, and within *Paradise Lost* itself there are large variations. Those several styles were dictated by the principle of decorum, which was for Milton the artist what religious and philosophic principles were for the man and the thinker, and the principle of decorum, like the others, united liberty and discipline. But in Milton's general movement away from epic grandeur towards plain, undecorated, dramatic speech it is not altogether fanciful—after we have given decorum its large due—to see a parallel to his inward evolution, his arrival at a deeper and more personal understanding of God and human experience.

Milton's style was the natural accompaniment of his view of the function of poetry. He was the last English poet whose unified mastery of learning might fairly justify the claim of the *vates* to be a teacher of his age. For him as for Spenser poetry embraced learning on the one side and action on the other. But Milton's knowledge, though much greater than Spenser's, was essentially of the same kind. During his lifetime the mere widening of knowledge, especially in science, had gone beyond the grasp of any one man, and through the division of labour the unacknowledged legislators of mankind were losing their leadership. Milton was a poet; Dryden was a man of letters. The inspiration and purposes of knowledge had changed also. While the humanistic values of the classical tradition were united with the religious and ethical force of medieval and reformed Christianity, Milton was still possible. But the philosophy of the seventeenth century had been steadily undermining the ground on which Milton stood, had been destroying the soul of Christian humanism and of poetry. Milton's partial consciousness of that movement only fortified his religious and ethical faith. In spite of his public career, his immersion in the problems of his time, he became more and more an isolated figure, like Abdiel, Christ, and Samson.

The militant prophet of the revolution rallied from defeat

> With plain Heroic magnitude of mind
> And celestial vigour arm'd,

with a purer and humbler need of God. If the spirit of the revolutionary Milton partook of Constantine's vision, 'τούτῳ νίκα', the theme of his major poems is 'E la sua volontate è nostra pace'. Unless our faculties have been vitiated by gross and violent stimulants, or by ultra-sophisticated negations, we cannot open Milton without an access of both strength and humility, a feeling that we are greater, and weaker, than we know. And that tonic power comes not merely from beauty of phrase and rhythm but from Milton's magnanimous concern with the highest issues and values in life, from his recognition of the intellectual and irreligious pride which, as of late we have more clearly realized, has been the undoing of modern man, and from his positive and passionate faith in God and goodness. In the twentieth century many men have undergone a kind of Miltonic disillusionment; Milton himself did not stop there.

CONCLUSION

MILTON's major poems were less typical of the thought and feeling of a large part of the nation than, say, the popular *Satire Against Hypocrites* (1655) by his nephew John Phillips. Milton might have relished Phillips's anti-Presbyterian wit, but not his use of the great phrase 'Christian Liberty' as a mocking gloss on the picture of a Commonwealth Stiggins kissing his 'sisters'. To the country as a whole the restoration of Church and King and Parliament did not bring religious unity or even toleration, nor did it bring a full measure of political unity, yet things moved towards the order and security of 1689. Throughout our period order of some sort had been a main object of such various men as King James and King Charles, Strafford and Cromwell, Laud and Prynne and Selden and Winstanley, Bacon and Jonson, Hobbes and Milton. The desire for order comprehended the civil and ecclesiastical spheres, the soul and the sentence, the cosmos and the couplet. That order, of course, had not been achieved, at least in public affairs, and the great body of great literature was the product of an age of unceasing controversy and conflict. The first sentence of Clarendon's *History of the Rebellion* echoes the first sentence of Hooker's preface to the *Ecclesiastical Polity*; it is almost as if the intervening time had appeared as a bad dream, a unique outbreak of feverous passions. In the latter part of the century, with all its disturbances, we breathe the cool air of Harrington and Locke, the air of modern secular liberalism. The State is not the feudal or humanistic or paternal hierarchy of 'degrees' bound by mutual obligations, still less the holy community of Puritan dreams, but an oligarchy of property-owners whose activities and privileges government exists to protect, and whose service is perfect freedom.

In other domains, from literature and thought to music and gardening, there is a similar movement towards rational and ordered regularity. All the tendencies that we call Augustan were at work before 1660, some of them before 1600, but during the years 1600–60 individuality of spiritual vision and expression was not reduced to decorous uniformity by a highly

civilized ideal of restraint. There were many signs of vigorous
health. The age was the most erudite in English history, yet in
no age has literature been at once so close to learning and .
philosophy on the one hand and to life and action on the other.
The English language and idiom had attained its first disciplined maturity without losing its youthful freshness and colour.
The diction of both prose and verse was a free and flexible
mixture of the plain and the purple, the learned and the colloquial. It was only after 1660 that critical rationalism got
definitely rid of individual eccentricity and excess. 'Spend no
time', advised Francis Osborn, 'in reading, much less writing
Strong-lines: which like tough meat, aske more paines and time
in chewing, then can be recompensed by all the nourishment
they bring.' And having achieved in prose and verse an urbane
and mundane directness and clarity, free from metaphorical
thought and feeling, the reformers did not boggle at the price
they paid. There were of course great gains, but our concern
is with the loss.   When we think of the dynamic humanism
of most serious writers from Chapman and Jonson to Milton,
Augustan classicism appears, with some notable exceptions, as
a pretty thinly diluted ideal of order. It would not be easy to
name a major or even a minor writer of the earlier period who
has received or deserved the verdict of thinking justly but
faintly.
   In the process of dilution an attenuated classicism was largely
assisted by scientific rationalism, so that some might prefer the
word 'enlightenment' to 'dilution'. To the thoroughly modern
mind the period 1600–60 may seem to have belonged to the
kingdom of darkness. Yet it was a period of conflict over great
issues in the abstract as well as the national sphere, over the
nature of reality and of God and man, the very foundations of
knowledge and faith. For the first time in England many men
were compelled to go behind the rubrics and formulas and work
out their own philosophy. The results ranged from various
types of mystical thought to sceptical naturalism. These philosophies were in the main outgrowths of, or—very rarely—
reactions against, the all-embracing tradition of Christian
humanism which the age inherited, the tradition of the rational
wisdom and culture of antiquity purified and exalted and
intensified by the Middle Ages, the Renaissance, the Reformation, and the Counter-Reformation.   For the last time in

England all these forces, in differing degrees but in climactic
concentration, made up the basic texture of men's thinking.
The consequence was rich variety and strength, almost wholly
within the Christian frame. Around 1600 the traditional
patterns of thought and belief encountered little or no opposition; by 1700 the traditionalist could take little or nothing for
granted. It could be increasingly taken for granted that the
traditions of two thousand years did not provide adequate
answers for the problems of the modern world and the modern
mind. The types of 'truth' which satisfied Milton, More,
Cudworth, Browne, Vaughan, Traherne, Baxter, and George
Fox (to name a few men who lived into the Restoration
period) did not appeal to thoughtful or thoughtless disciples
of Descartes and Hobbes and Charles II. The 'rationalism' of
Milton and the Cambridge Platonists was no longer rationalism. Reason was not *recta ratio*, the candle of the Lord, but a
much drier light.

In the decade of *Leviathan* it was still possible for the researches of Lightfoot, Ussher, and Pearson to establish the date
of Creation as Sunday, 23 October 4004 B.C. (and the year at
least remained an article of popular faith well through the
nineteenth century), but in general, science had begun its slow
eradication of all things irrational, supernatural, and intangible
from the world and the mind of man. As the star of Bethlehem
had put to flight the pagan gods, science—though its full
victory was long delayed—banished fairies and witches, angels
and devils. With superstition went the mythological and
symbolic imagination, the capacity for 'an *O altitudo*'. With
superstition, too, went the active belief in human life enveloped
by divine power, and the whole traditional conception, in its
old dynamic form, of man as a creature between the beasts
and the angels, of man's relations with himself, with society,
with the universe, and with God. The year after Vaughan's
death appeared Toland's *Christianity Not Mysterious*. Men had
fought and died for their way of worshipping God; no one
was called upon, or was ready, to die for deism. Nor did confident deism and mechanistic cosmology nourish the religious
conviction of man's inescapable weakness and sin which, in
times past, had sobered Platonic humanists as well as biblical
Calvinists.

These paragraphs are not, it need hardly be said, a rounded

estimate of the Augustan age; they are only a brief, exaggerated, and foreshortened statement of some general contrasts and tendencies and a reminder of some values and qualities of vision which grew dimmer after 1660. The poets and critics of the Romantic age, rebelling against effete classicism and mechanistic philosophies, rediscovered many neglected writers of the earlier seventeenth century, but that revival on the whole took too little account of those writers' religious and philosophic seriousness and made too much of literary 'quaintness'. While the number of readers and scholarly students multiplied throughout the nineteenth century, our own time has witnessed a second great revival, rich in interpretative learning and rich in its effects upon contemporary literature. This revival may be said to have been inaugurated, if a starting-point can be named, by Sir Herbert Grierson's edition of Donne's poems (1912), and it was especially conspicuous during the 'Armistice' period; whatever changes in taste the future may bring, it can hardly be supposed that a body of literature containing so much of peculiar value for us will lose its present high place. The years 1912–39 may also be said to have witnessed the final bankruptcy of Baconian optimism, the scientific pride and self-sufficiency which had been the dominant creed of the modern world. The positive antidote to that creed, however, is to be found, not in the 'Armistice' literature of disillusionment and defeat, but in the religious and philosophic literature of Bacon's own century. Contrasting the two bodies of writing, we might be tempted to echo the nostalgic words of Renan: 'Je le dis franchement, je ne me figure pas comment on rebâtira, sans les anciens rêves, les assises d'une vie noble et heureuse.' But, if an historian may moralize a moment longer, we might remember that the modern 'defeatist' literature was largely the product of sophisticated coteries and was not, as it was often taken to be, the mirror and full measure of the modern or the national temper. A Jacobean reader of the contemporary literature of discontent might have felt that Englishmen had sunk far below their fathers and grandfathers, and might have denied the existence of the resolute beliefs and high passions and energies which were to bring about the civil war. And historians of the future will not be able, in the literature of the 1920's and 1930's, to discern much of the greatness of popular courage which in 1940 was displayed in trials and perils infinitely greater than those of 'the year eighty-eight' to which seventeenth-century men looked back with pride and thankfulness. Both the writers and the readers of literature, who come to see people and life in terms of words, might find there a large lesson of humility.

CHRONOLOGICAL TABLES
AND
BIBLIOGRAPHY

Date	Public Events	Literary History	Verse
1600	Disgrace of Essex. Mountjoy in Ireland. Battle of Nieuport. Charles I b. East India Company founded.	Thomas Deloney d. Richard Hooker d. Thomas Nashe d.? John Earle b.? John Ogilby b. William Prynne b.? William Walwyn b. Hayward in prison for his *Henry IV*.	Marlowe (d. 1593), *Lucan's First Book*, tr. Breton, *Melancholic Humours*; *Pasquil* pieces. Fairfax, *Godfrey of Bulloigne*, tr. Tasso. Rowlands, *Letting of Humour's Blood*. Song-books by Dowland, Jones, Morley, Weelkes. Miscellanies: *Belvedere*; *England's Helicon*; *England's Parnassus*.
1601	Rising and execution of Essex. English victory in Ireland. Parliament attacks monopolies; Elizabeth revokes many patents but asserts prerogative. Poor Law.	William Lambarde d. Sir Thomas North d.? Donne married.	Breton, *Divine Poem*; *No Whipping, Nor Tripping*. Daniel, *Works* (enlar.). Rosseter and Campion, *Book of Airs*. R. Chester et al., *Love's Martyr* (incl. 'Phoenix and Turtle'). T. Morley, ed., *Triumphs of Oriana*.
1602	Irish campaign. B. Gosnold's voyage to New England. Bodleian Library opened.	William Perkins d. William Chillingworth b. Sir Simonds D'Ewes b. Owen Felltham b.? William Lilly b. William Strode b.	Basse, *Sword and Buckler*; *Three Pastoral Elegies*. Breton, *Soul's Harmony*. Davies of Hereford, *Mirum in Modum*. Rowlands, '*Tis Merry when Gossips Meet*. F. Davison, ed., *Poetical Rhapsody*.
1603	Mountjoy completes conquest of Ireland. Elizabeth d. (March 24). Accession of James. Cecil chief minister. Millenary Petition. Monopolies revoked. Recusancy fines remitted. Watson's plot. Cobham's plot. Plague.	Thomas Cartwright d. William Gilbert d. Thomas Morley d. Edward Benlowes b.? Sir Kenelm Digby b. Shakerley Marmion b. Sir John Davies in Ireland (1603–19). Ralegh sentenced for treason, imprisoned.	Daniel, *Panegyric* . . . *Certain Epistles*. Davies of Hereford, *Microcosmos*. Dowland, *Third Book of Songs*. Drayton, *Barons' Wars* (rev. from *Mortimeriados*).

Prose

Barclay, W., *De Regno et Regali Potestate.* Coke, *Reports* (1600 ff.). Cornwallis, *Essays,* i (ii, 1601). Gilbert, *De Magnete.* Hakluyt, *Principal Navigations,* iii (2nd ed.). Holland, *Roman History,* tr. Livy. Kemp, W., *Kemp's Nine Days' Wonder.* Perkins, *Golden Chain* (works). Vaughan, Sir W., *Golden Grove.*

Drama (date of acting)[1]

Anon., 1 *Return from Parnassus.* Dekker et al., *Patient Grissill.* Jonson, *Cynthia's Revels.* Shakespeare, *Hamlet'* (1601?); *Merry Wives of Windsor* (1601?); *Twelfth Night* (1601/2?).

Bacon, *Practices and Treasons Committed by late Earl of Essex.* Chamber, J., *Treatise against Judicial Astrology.* Dent, *Plain Man's Pathway to Heaven.* Dolman, R., *French Academy,* iii, tr. La Primaudaye. Holland, *History of the World,* tr. Pliny. Johnson, R., *Essays.* Wright, T., *Passions of the Mind.*

Dekker and (?) Marston, *Satiromastix.* Jonson, *Poetaster.* Marston, *What You Will.*

Brereton, J., *Discovery of the North Part of Virginia.* Breton, *Post with a Mad Packet of Letters.* Campion, *Observations in the Art of English Poesy.* Lodge, *Works of Josephus,* tr. Patericke, S., *Means of Well Governing against N. Machiavel,* tr. Gentillet.

Lindsay, Sir D. (d. 1555), *Satire of Three Estates* pr. Anon., 2 *Return from Parnassus.* Chapman, *Gentleman Usher; May-Day.* Middleton, *Family of Love.* Shakespeare, *Troilus and Cressida; All's Well That Ends Well.*

Perkins (d. 1602), *Treatise of the Vocations.* Barclay, J., *Euphormionis Satyricon,* i (ii, 1607). Daniel, *Defence of Rhyme.* Dekker, *Wonderful Year.* Florio, *Essays of Montaigne,* tr. Holland, *Morals,* tr. Plutarch. Knolles, *General History of the Turks.* Lodge, *Treatise of the Plague.* Tofte (?), *Bachelor's Banquet.*

Anon., *Merry Devil of Edmonton.* Heywood, *Woman Killed with Kindness.* Jonson, *Sejanus.* Marston, *Dutch Courtesan.* Shakespeare, Q1 of *Hamlet* pr.

---

[1] The question-mark used after titles of uncertain date is ordinarily omitted in the Drama column, since so many of the dates of acting are conjectural and disputed. The list of plays is meagre in proportion to the output because the drama of this period is being treated in a separate volume. The latest and fullest chronological guide is A. Harbage, *Annals of English Drama* (1940).

Date	Public Events	Literary History	Verse
1604	Hampton Court Conference. Whitgift d. Bancroft Archbishop. Commons claim right to deal with Church and State. Investigation of monopolies. Acts against priests and recusants. Anglican canons; enforcement of conformity. Peace with Spain.	Thomas Churchyard d. Edward de Vere, Earl of Oxford, d. Philip Hunton b.? Jasper Mayne b. Henry Parker b. Edward Pococke b.	Alexander, *Aurora*. Bateson, *First Set of English Madrigals*. Breton, *Passionate Shepherd*. Dekker, *News from Gravesend*. Drayton, *Moses*; *Owl*; *Paean Triumphal*. M. East, *Madrigals*. Rowlands, *Look to It, for I'll Stab Ye*.
1605	Some Puritan clergy ejected. Repression of Puritans and Catholics. Amnesty for Irish rebels. King tries to stifle Scottish General Assembly. Gunpowder Plot.	John Stow d. Sir Thomas Browne b. Sir William Dugdale b. John Gauden b. William Habington b. Henry Hammond b. Thomas Randolph b. Henry Robinson b. Bulstrode Whitelocke b. Chapman, Jonson, and Marston in trouble over *Eastward Ho*.	Breton, *Soul's Immortal Crown*; *Honour of Valour*. Daniel, *Certain Small Poems, with Philotas*. Davies of Hereford, *Wit's Pilgrimage* (?). Drayton, *Poems* (coll.). Rowlands, *Hell's Broke Loose*. Sylvester, *Divine Weeks and Works*, tr. Du Bartas.
1606	Penal legislation against recusants, with new oath of allegiance. Judges support king's right to levy impositions. Coke Chief Justice of Common Pleas. Common-law judges appeal to Parliament against ecclesiastical courts. Charter for Virginia.	Arthur Golding d. John Lyly d. Sir William Davenant b. Sir William Killigrew b. Edmund Waller b.	J. Barclay, *Sylvae*. Dekker, *Double PP*. Drayton, *Poems Lyric and Pastoral*. Owen, *Epigrammata*. H. Parrot, *Mouse-Trap*. Warner, *Albion's England* (books 14–16 added).
1607	King forces bishops upon Scottish Church. Flight of Tyrone and Tyrconnell. Conflicts between Coke and Bancroft. Jamestown founded.	Henry Chettle d. (1603/7?). Sir Edward Dyer d. Thomas Legge d. John Reynolds (Rainolds) d. William Bosworth b. Bacon Solicitor-General.	Daniel, *Certain Small Works* (rev. and enlar.). Davies of Hereford, *Summa Totalis*. Drayton, *Legend of Great Cromwell*. Rowlands, *Democritus*.

Prose

Bacon, *Better Pacification of the Church of England*; *Apology concerning the late Earl of Essex.* Breton, *Grimello's Fortunes*; *Fantastics* (?). Dallington, *View of France.* King James, *Counterblast to Tobacco.* Middleton, *Father Hubburd's Tales*; *Black Book.* Rich, *Soldier's Wish to Britain's Welfare.*

Drama (date of acting)

Alexander, *Monarchic Tragedies* pr. (enlar. 1607). Chapman, *All Fools* (rev.?); *Bussy D'Ambois.* Daniel, *Philotas*; *Vision of the Twelve Goddesses.* Dekker and Middleton, 1 *Honest Whore.* Marston, *Malcontent.* Shakespeare, *Measure for Measure*; *Othello*; Q2 of *Hamlet* pr.

Bacon, *Advancement of Learning.* Camden, *Remains concerning Britain.* Hall, *Mundus Alter et Idem* (?). Sandys, Sir E., *Relation of the State of Religion.* Verstegan, *Restitution of Decayed Intelligence.*

Chapman, Jonson, and Marston, *Eastward Ho.* Daniel, *Queen's Arcadia.* Dekker and Middleton, 2 *Honest Whore.* Jonson, *Masque of Blackness.* Marston, *Sophonisba.* Middleton, *Trick to Catch the Old One.* Shakespeare, *King Lear* (1606?).

Perkins (d. 1602), *Whole Treatise of Cases of Conscience.* Bryskett, *Discourse of Civil Life*, tr. Giraldi. Dekker, *Seven Deadly Sins of London.* Holland, *Twelve Caesars*, tr. Suetonius. Knolles, *Six Books of a Commonweal*, tr. Bodin. Rich, *Faults, Faults.*

Anon., *Yorkshire Tragedy.* Jonson, *Volpone*; *Hymenaei.* Middleton, *A Mad World my Masters.* Shakespeare, *Macbeth.* Tourneur (?), *Revenger's Tragedy.*

Anon., *Dobson's Dry Bobs.* Cleland, J., *Institution of a Young Noble Man.* Cowell, *Interpreter.* Dekker, *Knight's Conjuring* (rev. from *News from Hell*, 1606). King James, *Apology for the Oath of Allegiance.* Lennard, *Of Wisdom* (1607/12), tr. Charron. Markham, *Cavelarice*; *English Arcadia*, i (ii, 1613). Topsell, *Four-footed Beasts*, tr. Gesner.

Beaumont (and Fletcher?), *Knight of the Burning Pestle.* Campion, *Lord Hay's Masque.* Day et al., *Travels of Three English Brothers.* Shakespeare, *Antony and Cleopatra* (1606?); *Timon of Athens* (1605/8?).

Date	Public Events	Literary History	Verse
1608	Failure of plan for union with Scotland. *Post-nati* naturalized. Deficit reduced by new impositions. League with Dutch. O'Dogherty's rebellion crushed. Separatist congregation moves to Holland.	John Dee d. Sir Geoffrey Fenton d. Thomas Sackville, Earl of Dorset, d. Sir Aston Cokayne b. Sir Richard Fanshawe b. Thomas Fuller b. Robert Greville, Lord Brooke, b. John Milton b. Captain John Smith President of Virginia.	H. Parrot, *Epigrams*. H. Peacham, *The More the Merrier*. Sylvester, *Divine Weeks and Works*, tr. Du Bartas (1st complete ed.). R. Tofte, *Ariosto's Satires*.
1609	Continued conflicts over ecclesiastical jurisdiction. King entails Crown lands. New charter for Virginia. Virginian commissioners wrecked at Bermuda.	Barnabe Barnes d. William Warner d. Sir Matthew Hale b. Edward Hyde, Earl of Clarendon, b. Sir John Suckling b. Benjamin Whichcote b. Gerrard Winstanley b.	Spenser (d. 1599), *Fairy Queen* (1st folio ed., with 1st ed. of *Mutability*). Chapman, *Tears of Peace*; *Iliad* (i–xii) (?). Daniel, *Civil Wars* (8 bks.). Heywood, *Troia Britannica*. Rowlands, *Knave of Clubs*. Shakespeare, *Sonnets*; *Lover's Complaint*. Wilbye, *Second Set of Madrigals*.
1610	Commons' Petition of Right and Petition of Grievances. Great Contract falls through. Judicial decision against royal proclamations. Bancroft d. Plantation of Ulster. Hudson's last voyage.	Alexander Montgomerie d.? Robert Parsons d. Lucius Cary, Lord Falkland, b.? Henry Glapthorne b. Sidney Godolphin b. Casaubon in England (1610–14). Cowell's *Interpreter* (1607) suppressed by king. Shakespeare retires to Stratford (1611?).	Davies of Hereford, *Scourge of Folly* (1611?). G. Fletcher, *Christ's Victory and Triumph*. J. Heath, *Epigrams*. R. Niccols, ed., *Mirror for Magistrates* (last enlar. ed.).
1611	Abbot Archbishop. Parliament dissolved.	Giles Fletcher the elder d.	Spenser (d. 1599), 1st folio of coll. works.

Prose

Perkins (d. 1602), *Damned Art of Witch-craft.* Dekker, *Bellman of London; Lanthorn and Candlelight.* Hall, *Characters of Virtues and Vices; Epistles* (1608–11). Heywood, *Two Notable Histories* (1608–9), tr. Sallust. Smith, Captain J., *True Relation of Virginia.* Topsell, *History of Serpents.*

Drama (date of acting)

Armin, *Two Maids of More-clack.* Chapman, *Charles Duke of Byron.* Fletcher, *Faithful Shepherdess.* Jonson, *Masque of Beauty.* Shakespeare, *Coriolanus;* (and G. Wilkins?), *Pericles.*

Jewel (d. 1571), *Works.* Bible (R. C. version of O.T., 1609–10). Bacon, *De Sapientia Veterum.* Dekker, *Four Birds of Noah's Ark; Gull's Hornbook.* Healey, *Discovery of a New World* (?), tr. Hall's *Mundus.* Holland, *Roman History,* tr. Ammianus Marcellinus. T., I., *Philosophical Comfort,* tr. Boethius.

Beaumont and Fletcher, *Philaster.* Greville, *Mustapha* pr. Jonson, *Epicoene; Masque of Queens.* Shakespeare, *Cymbeline* (1610?). Tourneur, *Atheist's Tragedy* (1610/11?).

Donne, *Pseudo-Martyr.* Guillim, *Display of Heraldry.* Healey, *City of God,* tr. Augustine; *Epictetus. Cebes,* tr. Holland, *Britain,* tr. Camden. Jourdain, *Discovery of the Bermudas.* Strachey, *True Repertory of the Wreck upon the Bermudas* (pr. 1625).

Chapman, *Revenge of Bussy D'Ambois.* Daniel, *Tethys' Festival.* Dekker and Middleton, *Roaring Girl.* Jonson, *Alchemist.*

King James Bible. Cartwright, J., *Preacher's Travels.* Coryate, *Coryate's*

Beaumont and Fletcher, *King and No King; Maid's Tragedy.* Jonson,

Date	Public Events	Literary History	Verse
	Activity against recusants. Sale of baronetcies. Robert Carr advanced. Enlarged powers given Court of High Commission. Friction with Dutch over spice trade.	Richard Mulcaster d. William Cartwright b. James Harrington b. Robert Leighton b. Sir Thomas Urquhart b.	Brathwait, *Golden Fleece.* Byrd, *Psalms, Songs and Sonnets.* Daniel, *Certain Small Works.* Donne, *Anatomy of the World.*
1612	Legate and Wightman burned for heresy. Lancashire witches hanged. Alliance with German Protestant princes. Salisbury and Prince Henry d. Continued friction with Spain over trade. Scottish Parliament ratifies episcopacy. Improved charter for Virginia.	Lodowick Bryskett d.? Sir John Harington d. Samuel Butler b. Richard Crashaw b. (1613?). James Graham, Marquis of Montrose, b. Thomas Killigrew the elder b.	Chapman, *Iliad* (i–xxiv) (?). Davies of Hereford, *Muse's Sacrifice.* Donne, *Second Anniversary.* Drayton, *Poly-Olbion* (Songs 1–18). O. Gibbons, *First Set of Madrigals and Motets.* Owen, *Epigrammata.* Peacham, *Minerva Britanna.* John Taylor, *The Sculler.*
1613	Princess Elizabeth married to Elector Palatine. Coke Chief Justice of King's Bench. Countess of Essex divorced, married to Somerset. Sarmiento (later Gondomar) Spanish ambassador.	Sir Thomas Bodley d. Henry Constable d. John Cleveland b. John Pearson b. Peter Sterry b. Jeremy Taylor b. Sir Henry Vane b. Dekker in debtors' prison (1613–19). Overbury d. in Tower. Wither imprisoned for satires.	Browne, *Britannia's Pastorals,* i. Campion, *Two Books of Airs* (?). Wither, *Abuses Stript and Whipt.* Elegies on Prince Henry by Campion, Chapman, Donne, Drummond, Herbert, Heywood, Sylvester, Tourneur, Webster, Wither, et al. (1612–13).
1614	Parliament protests against impositions. Dissolved without grant of supply. Some members imprisoned. Benevolence imposed. Somerset at height of power. Villiers at court. Renewed proposals for Spanish marriage. Discontent in Ireland.	Sir William Cornwallis d. William Hammond b. Henry More b. John Wilkins b. Fulke Greville Chancellor of Exchequer (1614–21).	Overbury (d. 1613), *A Wife.* Alexander, *Dooms-day.* Chapman, *Andromeda Liberata.* Drummond, *Poems* (?). Sir A. Gorges, *Lucan's Pharsalia,* tr. Browne, C. Brooke, Wither, and Davies of Hereford, *Shepherd's Pipe.*

Prose

Crudities. Cotgrave, *Dictionary of French and English Tongues.* Donne, *Ignatius his Conclave.* Florio, *Queen Anna's New World of Words.* Speed, *Theatre* and *History of Great Britain.*

Drama (date of acting)

Catiline; Oberon. Middleton, *Chaste Maid in Cheapside.* Shakespeare, *Winter's Tale* (1610?); *Tempest.*

Bacon, *Essays* (enlar. from 1597). Bayly, *Practice of Piety* (?). Brinsley, *Ludus Literarius.* Daniel, *History of England,* i. Heywood, *Apology for Actors.* Lok, *De Novo Orbe,* tr. P. Martyr (contin. of R. Eden). Shelton, *Don Quixote,* i, tr. Smith, Captain J., *Map of Virginia.*

Webster, *White Devil* (1610/11?).

Dallington, *Aphorisms.* Dekker, *Strange Horse-Race.* Hayward, *Lives of the Three Normans.* Purchas, *Purchas his Pilgrimage.* Savile, ed., *Chrysostomi Opera* (1610–13). Spelman, *De non temerandis Ecclesiis.* Whitaker, *Good News from Virginia.*

Beaumont, *Inner Temple Masque.* Campion, *Lords' Masque; Masque at Marriage of Somerset.* E. Cary, *Mariam* pr. Chapman, *Chabot.* Shakespeare and Fletcher, *Henry VIII; Two Noble Kinsmen.*

Overbury (d. 1613) et al., *Characters.* Barclay, J., *Icon Animorum.* Lodge, *Works of Seneca,* tr. Napier, *Mirifici Logarithmorum Canonis Descriptio.* Ralegh, *History of the World.* Rich, *Honesty of this Age.* Selden, *Titles of Honour.*

Daniel, *Hymen's Triumph.* Jonson, *Bartholomew Fair.* Webster, *Duchess of Malfi* (1613?).

Date	Public Events	Literary History	Verse
1615	King at Cambridge. Roe sent to India to investigate commercial situation. Failure of negotiations with Dutch for sharing spice trade. Trial of Overbury's murderers.	Robert Armin d. Richard Baxter b. Sir John Denham b. John Lilburne b.? John Donne ordained.	Harington (d. 1612), *Epigrams* (enlar. 1618). Brathwait, *Strappado for the Devil.* Chapman, *Odyssey* (1614–15). Rowlands, *Melancholy Knight.* Wither, *Fidelia; Shepherd's Hunting.*
1616	Cautionary towns surrendered to Dutch for cash. Trial of Earl and Countess of Somerset. Advancement of Villiers. Sale of peerages. Coke dismissed.	Francis Beaumont d. Richard Hakluyt d. William Shakespeare d. Joseph Beaumont b. Nicholas Culpeper b. Sir Roger L'Estrange b. John Smith b.? John Wallis b. Jonson given royal pension.	Browne, *Britannia's Pastorals,* ii. Chapman, *Whole Works of Homer; Divine Poem of Musaeus,* tr. Drummond, *Poems.* Jonson, *Epigrams; Forest* (in *Works*).
1617	Pocahontas presented at court. Negotiations for Spanish marriage. King in Scotland. Conflicts with Dutch in East Indies.	Thomas Coryate d. Barnabe Rich d. Elias Ashmole b. Ralph Cudworth b. Seth Ward b. Bacon Lord Keeper. Ralegh sails for Orinoco.	Campion, *Third and Fourth Book of Airs* (?). Davies of Hereford, *Wit's Bedlam.* L. Digges, *Rape of Proserpine,* tr. Claudian. Drummond, *Forth Feasting.* Rowlands, *The Bride.*
1618	Cranfield's financial reforms. *Declaration of Sports.* Clerical opposition to it and to Selden's *History of Tithes.* King's Articles pressed on Scottish Assembly. Beginning of Thirty Years War.	Thomas Bastard d. John Davies of Hereford d. Josuah Sylvester d. Abraham Cowley b. Nathanael Culverwel b. (1619?). Richard Lovelace b. Sir Edward Sherburne b. Bacon Lord Chancellor and Baron Verulam. Jonson in Scotland (1618–19). Ralegh executed.	Harington (d. 1612), *Epigrams* (enlar.). Chapman, *Georgics of Hesiod,* tr. H. Fitzgeffrey et al., *Certain Elegies. With Satires and Epigrams.*

Prose	*Drama (date of acting)*
Adams, T., *Mystical Bedlam*. Breton, *Characters upon Essays*. Camden, *Annales*, i. Markham, *Country Contentments*. Sandys, G., *Relation of a Journey*. Stephens, J., *Satirical Essays, Characters*. Swetnam, *Arraignment of Lewd Women*.	Browne, W., *Inner Temple Masque*. Fletcher, P., *Sicelides*. Jonson, *Mercury Vindicated*. Ruggle, *Ignoramus*.
Cornwallis (d. 1614), *Essays or Encomions*; *Essays of Certain Paradoxes*. Healey (d.?), *Characters*, tr. Theophrastus. Breton, *Good and the Bad*. Cotta, *Trial of Witchcraft*. Goodman, *Fall of Man*. King James, *Works*. Selden, ed., Fortescue's *De Laudibus Legum Angliae*. Smith, Captain J., *Description of New England*.	Jonson, *Golden Age Restored; Devil is an Ass; Works* pr.
Brathwait, *Law of Drinking*. Fennor, *Compter's Commonwealth*. Hall, J., *Quo Vadis?* Moryson, *Itinerary*. Selden, *De Diis Syris*.	Middleton and W. Rowley, *Fair Quarrel*.
Bolton, *Hypercritica* (written ?). Breton, *Court and Country*. Daniel, *History of England*, ii. Munday, *Amadis de Gaule*, iii–iv, tr. Mynshul, *Characters and Essays*. Selden, *History of Tithes*. Taylor, J., *Penniless Pilgrimage*.	Anon., *Swetnam the Woman-Hater* (?). Burton, R., *Philosophaster*. Jonson, *Pleasure Reconciled to Virtue*.

Date	Public Events	Literary History	Verse
1619	Queen Anne d. Calvinism triumphs at Synod of Dort. Agreement with Dutch for one-third of spice monopoly. First Colonial Parliament at Jamestown. Elector Frederick chosen king of Bohemia. James's prestige high. Buckingham all-powerful.	Samuel Daniel d. Nathan Field d. (1620?). William Chamberlayne b. Sir Edward Herbert ambassador to France.	Campion, *Epigrammata,* &c. Drayton, *Poems* (coll. folio ed.). J. Vicars, *Epigrams of John Owen,* tr.
1620	Spinola invades Palatinate. Frederick loses Bohemia. English feeling against Spain. King vacillates. Proclamation forbids discussion of State affairs. 'New England' officially named. Voyage of *Mayflower.*	Thomas Campion d. Richard Carew d. Robert Tofte d. (1619?) Alexander Brome b. John Evelyn b. Lucy (Apsley) Hutchinson b. Marchamont Needham b. George Herbert Public Orator at Cambridge(1620–7).	Overbury (d. 1613), *Remedy of Love,* tr. Ovid. Dekker, *Dekker his Dream.* Peacham, *Thalia's Banquet.* Quarles, *Feast for Worms.* Rowlands, *Night Raven.* Wither, *Works* (pirated?).
1621	First Parliament since 1614. Impeachment of monopolists and of Bacon. Commons oppose king's continental policy. Protestation on liberties of the House. Williams Bishop of London and Lord Keeper. Sir William Alexander given charter for Nova Scotia.	John Barclay d. Thomas Harriot d. Mary Herbert, Countess of Pembroke, d. Roger Boyle, Earl of Orrery, b. Andrew Marvell b. Donne Dean of St. Paul's (1621–31).	Brathwait, *Nature's Embassy.* Quarles, *Hadassa.* Wither, *Songs of the Old Testament; Wither's Motto.*
1622	Parliament dissolved. Impositions and Benevolence. King treats with Spain for marriage and recovery of Palatinate. Popular zeal for Protestant cause. Gondomar recalled. King restricts preaching. Banqueting House at Whitehall completed.	William Gager d. John Owen d. Sir Henry Savile d. Algernon Sidney b. Henry Vaughan b. (1621?) Thomas Vaughan b. (1621?)	Drayton, *Poly-Olbion,* ii. P. Hannay, *Nightingale,* &c. Rowlands, *Good News and Bad News.* T. Tomkins, *Songs.* Wither, *Fair Virtue; Juvenilia.*

Prose

Napier (d. 1617), *Mirifici Logarithmorum Canonis Constructio.* Gill, A., *Logonomia Anglica.* Gorges, Sir A., *Wisdom of the Ancients,* tr. Bacon's *De Sapientia Veterum.* Purchas, *Purchas his Pilgrim.*

Drama (date of acting)

Shakespeare (d. 1616): quartos of ten authentic and ascribed plays pr. by Jaggard, mainly with false dates. Field and Massinger, *Fatal Dowry.* Fletcher, *Humorous Lieutenant.* Fletcher and Massinger, *Sir John Barnavelt.*

Anon.: *Astrea,* i, tr. D'Urfé; *Decameron,* tr.; *Westward for Smelts.* Bacon, *Novum Organum.* Brent, *History of the Council of Trent,* tr. Sarpi. Cavendish, Sir W., *Horae Subsecivae.* Shelton, *Don Quixote,* ii, tr. Smith, Captain J., *New England's Trials.*
Earliest English newsbooks pr. in Holland.

Fletcher and Massinger, *Custom of the Country.* May, *Heir.* Webster, *Devil's Law Case.*

Barclay, J., *Argenis.* Burton, *Anatomy of Melancholy.* Carpenter, N., *Philosophia Libera.* Heylyn, *Microcosmus.* Mun, *Discourse of Trade unto the East Indies.* Wroth, Lady M., *Urania.*
Newsbooks pr. in London.

Fletcher, *Wild Goose Chase.* Jonson, *News from the New World discovered in the Moon; Metamorphosed Gypsies.*

Bacon, *Historia Naturalis et Experimentalis;* *Henry VII.* Brinsley, *Consolation for our Grammar Schools.* Hawkins, Sir R., *Observations in his Voyage into the South Sea.* Mabbe, *Rogue,* tr. Alemán. Misselden, *Free Trade.* Peacham, *Complete Gentleman.*

Carlell, *Osmond the Great Turk.* Fletcher and Massinger, *Spanish Curate.* Jonson, *Masque of Augurs.* Middleton and W. Rowley, *Changeling.*

Date	Public Events	Literary History	Verse
1623	Charles and Buckingham in Madrid. Failure of Spanish negotiations. Massacre of Amboyna. Calvert receives grant in Newfoundland.	Nicholas Breton d.? William Byrd d. William Camden d. Giles Fletcher the younger d. Thomas Weelkes d. Margaret (Lucas) Cavendish, Duchess of Newcastle, b.? Sir William Petty b. Kenelm Digby and James Howell in Madrid. Jonson's MSS. lost in fire.	Daniel (d. 1619), *Whole Works*. Drummond, *Flowers of Sion*. Wither, *Hymns and Songs of the Church*.
1624	New Parliament set on war with Spain, king on recovery of Palatinate. Treaties with Spain cancelled. Marriage arranged between Charles and Henrietta Maria. Recusancy laws suspended. Monopolies Act.	Stephen Gosson d. George Fox b. Samuel Sheppard b.? Sir Edward Herbert recalled from France.	Chapman, *Crown of All Homer's Works* (?). Quarles, *Job Militant*; *Sion's Elegies*.
1625	James d. Accession and marriage of Charles. Plague. Failure of Mansfeld's expedition. Parliament hostile to Buckingham's continental projects. War with Spain. Failure of Cadiz expedition. Alliance with Holland and Denmark. King re-annexes Crown and Church lands in Scotland.	John Fletcher d. John Florio d. (1626?). Orlando Gibbons d. Thomas Lodge d. John Norden d.? Thomas Stanley b. Nicholas Ferrar retires to Little Gidding. Commons censure R. Montagu's High-Church writings.	Bacon, *Certain Psalms*. Quarles, *Sion's Sonnets*.
1626	Second Parliament, led by Eliot, impeaches Buckingham, declares tonnage and poundage illegal. Dissolved. King resumes non-parliamentary levies.	Lancelot Andrewes d. Francis Bacon d. Sir John Davies d. John Dowland d. Samuel Purchas d. William Rowley d. Cyril Tourneur d. John Aubrey b. Sir Robert Howard b.	Parrot, *Cures for the Itch*. Sandys, *Ovid's Metamorphoses*, tr.

Prose

Ames, *Medulla Sacrae Theologiae.* Bacon, *De Dignitate et Augmentis Scientiarum; Historia Vitae et Mortis.* Drummond, *Cypress Grove.* Felltham, *Resolves* (?). Lisle, *Saxon Treatise.*

Drama (date of acting)

Shakespeare (d. 1616), First Folio pr. Massinger, *Bondman.*

Alexander, *Encouragement to Colonies.* Donne, *Devotions.* Herbert, Lord, *De Veritate.* Heywood, *Gunaikeion.* Montagu, R., *New Gag for an Old Goose.* Smith, Captain J., *General History of Virginia.* Wotton, *Elements of Architecture.*

Davenport, *City Nightcap.* Fletcher, *Rule a Wife and Have a Wife.* Heywood, *Captives.* Jonson, *Neptune's Triumph; Pan's Anniversary.* Massinger, *Renegado.* Middleton, *Game at Chess.*

Camden (d. 1623), *Annales,* ii. Bacon, *Essays* (enlar.); *Apophthegms.* Carpenter, N., *Geography.* Dekker, *Rod for Runaways.* Montagu, R., *Appello Caesarem.* Purchas, *Purchas his Pilgrims.* Wither, *Scholar's Purgatory* (?).

Beaumont, Sir J., *Theatre of Apollo* (written). Heywood, *English Traveller.* Jonson, *Fortunate Isles.* Massinger, *New Way to Pay Old Debts.*

Overbury (d. 1613), *Observations.* Roper (d. 1578), *Life of Sir T. More.* Bernard, *Isle of Man.* Donne, *Five Sermons.* Prynne, *Perpetuity of a Regenerate Man's Estate.* Spelman, *Archaeologus,* i. Vaughan, Sir W., *Golden Fleece.*

Jonson, *Staple of News.* Massinger, *Roman Actor.* Shirley, *Wedding.*

Date	Public Events	Literary History	Verse
1627	Resistance to forced loan. Expedition to Isle of Rhé. Passive obedience preached by Sibthorp and Manwaring. Archbishop Abbot sequestered for refusing to license Sibthorp's sermon for the press.	Richard Barnfield d. Sir John Beaumont d. Lucy Russell, Countess of Bedford, d. Sir John Hayward d. Thomas Middleton d. Robert Boyle b. John Hall b. Dorothy Osborne b. John Ray b.	Drayton, *Battle of Agincourt*, *Nymphidia*, &c. P. Fletcher, *Locustae*. May, *Lucan's Pharsalia*, tr. R. Niccols, *Beggar's Ape*.
1628	Third Parliament. Petition of Right becomes law. Laud Bishop of London. Buckingham assassinated. Failure of second expedition to Rochelle. Laudian *Articles of Religion*.	John Chamberlain d. Fulke Greville murdered. John Preston d. John Bunyan b. Sir William Temple b. George Villiers, second Duke of Buckingham, b. Sir K. Digby's victory at Scanderoon. Richard Montagu Bishop of Chichester.	P. Fletcher, *Britain's Ida*. May, *Virgil's Georgics*, tr. Wither, *Britain's Remembrancer*.
1629	Commons' resolutions against popery, Arminianism, impositions. Eliot and others imprisoned. Impositions exacted. Laudian censorship of press and restriction of lecturers. Peace with France. Charter to Company of Massachusetts Bay.	Sir Edwin Sandys d. John Speed d. Montagu's *Appello Caesarem* called in.	Sir John Beaumont (d. 1627), *Bosworth-Field*. Chapman, *Fifth Satire of Juvenal*, tr. May, *Selected Epigrams of Martial*, tr. Milton, 'Nativity' (written). Quarles, *Argalus and Parthenia*.
1630	Knighthood fines and impositions. Laud Chancellor of Oxford. Charles II b. Plague. Peace with Spain. Commissions for relief of poor and debtors. Drainage of fens (1630 ff.). 'Great Migration' to New England (1630 ff.).	Thomas Bateson d. Gabriel Harvey d. Fynes Moryson d. Samuel Rowlands d.? Isaac Barrow b. Charles Cotton b. John Tillotson b. George Herbert rector of Bemerton. Alexander Leighton pilloried and imprisoned for attacking prelacy. Roger Williams sails for America.	Drayton, *Muses' Elysium*, &c. Quarles, *Divine Poems*. John Taylor, *Works* (verse and prose).

Prose

Drama (date of acting)

Bacon (d. 1626), *Sylva Sylvarum*; *New Atlantis*. Cosin, *Devotions*. Cotton, Sir R., *Henry III*. Hakewill, *Apology*. Mede, *Clavis Apocalyptica*. Sanderson, *Ten Sermons*.

Davenant, *Cruel Brother*. Ford, '*Tis Pity She's a Whore* (?). Massinger, *Great Duke of Florence*.

Ralegh (d. 1618), *Prerogative of Parliaments*. Coke, *Institutes*, i. Earle, *Microcosmography*. Drake the younger, Sir F., ed., *World Encompassed by Sir Francis Drake*. Harvey, *De Motu Cordis et Sanguinis*. Leighton, A., *Appeal to the Parliament*. Selden, *Marmora Arundelliana*.

Brome, R., *City Wit*. Ford, *Lover's Melancholy*. Shirley, *Witty Fair One*.

Andrewes (d. 1626), *XCVI Sermons*; *Opuscula*. Bacon (d. 1626), *Certain Miscellany Works*. Adams, T., *Works*. Godwin, F., *Nuncius Inanimatus*. Hobbes, *Thucydides*, tr. Parkinson, *Paradisi in Sole*.

Brome, R., *Northern Lass*. Davenant, *Just Italian*. Ford, *Broken Heart* (?). Jonson, *New Inn*. Massinger, *Picture*. Randolph, *Aristippus*.

Hayward (d. 1627), *Edward VI*. Ames, *De Conscientia*. Brathwait, *English Gentleman*. Norton, R., *History of Elizabeth*, tr. Camden's *Annales*. Sibbes, *Bruised Reed*. Smith, Captain J., *True Travels*.

Randolph, *Amyntas*; *Muses' Looking Glass*. Wilson, A., *Inconstant Lady*.

Date	Public Events	Literary History	Verse
1631	King vacillates between Spain and Gustavus Adolphus. Laud enforces conformity at Oxford and elsewhere. Wentworth subdues northern gentry.	Sir Robert Cotton d. John Donne d. Michael Drayton d. Captain John Smith d. Richard Cumberland b. John Dryden b. John Phillips b. Falkland at Great Tew (1631–9).	Fuller, *David's Heinous Sin.* W. Lisle, *Fair Ethiopian*, tr. Heliodorus. Milton, 'L'Allegro', 'Il Penseroso' (written?) Quarles, *History of Samson.*
1632	King's offers rejected by Gustavus. Futile negotiations with Dutch and Richelieu. Gustavus and Elector Frederick d. Van Dyck settles in England. Maryland charter.	Thomas Dekker d. Sir John Eliot d. (in Tower). John Locke b. Katherine (Fowler) Philips b. Anthony Wood b. Milton at Horton (1632–8).	Quarles, *Divine Fancies.* Sandys, *Ovid's Metamorphoses* (with allegorical commentary) and *Aeneid* i, tr. J. Vicars, *Aeneid*, tr. Wither, *Psalms of David.*
1633	King in Scotland. Wentworth begins administration in Ireland. Abbot d. Laud Archbishop. Ordination of lecturers forbidden, chaplaincies restricted. Paul's Walk purified. *Declaration of Sports* reissued. James II b. Large migration to New England.	William Ames d. Francis Godwin d. George Herbert d. Anthony Munday d. Samuel Rowley d.? Samuel Pepys b. George Savile, Marquis of Halifax, b. Lady Davies imprisoned for prophecies.	Donne (d. 1631), *Poems.* Greville (d. 1628), *Works.* G. Herbert (d. 1633), *The Temple.* Cowley, *Poetical Blossoms.* P. Fletcher, *Purple Island*, &c. May, *Henry II.*
1634	Laud enforces conformity, revives visitations. Witch trials in Lancashire. Crown's forest claims revived. King secretly negotiates with Spain for naval alliance against Dutch. Ship-money levied on maritime districts. Anglican canons forced upon Irish Convocation. Massachusetts Bay establishes self-government.	George Chapman d. Sir Edward Coke d John Marston d. Robert South b. Nathaniel Wanley b. Prynne pilloried, imprisoned (till 1637).	Crashaw, *Epigrammatum Sacrorum Liber.* Habington, *Castara.*

Prose

Brathwait, *English Gentlewoman*; *Whimsies*. Dekker, *Penny-Wise Pound-Foolish*. Lenton, *Characterismi*. Mabbe, *Spanish Bawd*, tr. de Rojas. More, Cresacre, *Sir Thomas More* (?). Powell, T., *Tom of All Trades*. Saltonstall, W., *Picturae Loquentes*. Smith, Captain J., *Advertisements for Unexperienced Planters*.

Drama (date of acting)

Marmion, *Holland's Leaguer*. Massinger, *Believe As You List*. Shirley, *Traitor*. Wilson, A., *Swisser*.

Donne (d. 1631), *Death's Duel*. Ralegh (d. 1618), *Instructions to his Son*. Holland, *Cyropaedia*, tr. Xenophon. Lithgow, *Rare Adventures*. Lupton, *London and the Country Carbonadoed*. Prynne, *Histriomastix*. Reynolds, H., *Mythomystes*.

Lyly (d. 1606), *Six Court Comedies* pr. Shakespeare (d. 1616), Second Folio pr. Jonson, *Magnetic Lady*. Massinger, *City Madam*. Milton, *Arcades* (1630/3). Nabbes, *Covent Garden*. Randolph, *Jealous Lovers*. Shirley, *Hyde Park*. Townshend, *Albion's Triumph*; *Tempe Restored*.

Donne (d. 1631), *Juvenilia*. Spenser (d. 1599), *View of Ireland*. Fludd, *Clavis Philosophiae et Alchymiae*. Grimeston, *History of Polybius*, tr. James, T., *Voyage*.

Jonson, *Tale of a Tub* (rev.). Marston, *Tragedies and Comedies* pr. Massinger, *Guardian*. Montagu, W., *Shepherd's Paradise*. Nabbes, *Tottenham Court*. Shirley, *Bird in a Cage*; *Young Admiral*; *Gamester*.

Donne (d. 1631), *Six Sermons*. Casaubon, M., *Marcus Aurelius his Meditations*, tr. Herbert, Sir T., *Description of the Persian Monarchy*. Hickes, F., *Certain Dialogues... True History*, tr. Lucian. Ross, A., *Commentum de Terrae Motu Circulari*.

Brome, R., and Heywood, *Late Lancashire Witches*. Carew, *Coelum Britannicum*. Davenant, *Wits*; *Love and Honour*. Heywood, *Love's Mistress*. Milton, *Masque* [*Comus*]. Shirley, *Triumph of Peace*.

Date	Public Events	Literary History	Verse
1635	Diplomatic relations with Vatican. Ship-money extended to inland counties and approved by judges.	Richard Corbet d. Edward Fairfax d. Sir Robert Naunton d. Thomas Randolph d. Richard Sibbes d. Thomas Burnet b.? Sir George Etherege b.? Thomas Flatman b. Thomas Sprat b. Edward Stillingfleet b. Roger Williams banished from Massachusetts.	Donne (d. 1631), *Poems* (2nd ed., rev.). Heywood, *Hierarchy of the Blessed Angels*. Kynaston, *Amorum Troili et Creseidae*, tr. Chaucer, i–ii. May, *Edward III*. Quarles, *Emblems*. Wither, *Collection of Emblems*.
1636	Failure of negotiations regarding Palatinate. Judges affirm king's superiority to law. Royal charter for Oxford Press. Laudian Statutes for Oxford. King and Laud at Oxford. Third writ of ship-money. Plague.	John Eachard b.? Joseph Glanvill b. Sir George Mackenzie b.?	Cowley, *Sylva* (in *Poetical Blossoms*, 2nd ed.). W. Saltonstall, *Ovid's Heroical Epistles*, tr. (2nd ed.). Sandys, *Psalms of David*. Drayton, Jonson, et al., *Annalia Dubrensia*.
1637	Catholic proselytizing at Court. Judges reaffirm king's right to levy ship-money at discretion. Trial of Hampden. Censorship of press re-enforced. Scottish resistance to Prayer Book and new canons.	Nicholas Ferrar d. Robert Fludd d. Philemon Holland d. Ben Jonson d. Gervase Markham d. Wentworth Dillon, Earl of Roscommon, b. Thomas Ken b. Dr. Thomas Browne settles at Norwich. Star Chamber sentences Prynne, Bastwick, Burton, Bishop Williams.	Alexander, *Recreations with the Muses*. Heywood, *Pleasant Dialogues and Dramas*. Marmion, *Cupid and Psyche*. Whiting, *Albino and Bellama*.
1638	Seven of twelve judges decide against Hampden. General resentment over royal exactions and Laudian policy. Scottish Covenant.	Sir Robert Aytoun d. John Hoskyns d. Joseph Mede d. John Webster d.? John Wilbye d. Philip Ayres b. Thomas Traherne b. (1637/9). Davenant pensioned as virtual Laureate. Milton abroad (1638–9).	Randolph (d. 1635), *Poems*. Brathwait, *Barnabe's Journal* (enlar.). Davenant, *Madagascar*. Quarles, *Hieroglyphics of the Life of Man*. Sandys, *Divine Poems*. *Justa Edouardo King* (incl. 'Lycidas'). B. Duppa, ed., *Jonsonus Virbius*.

Prose

Drama (date of acting)

Fox, Luke, *North-West Fox*. Scott, W., *Essay of Drapery*. Selden, *Mare Clausum*. Swan, J., *Speculum Mundi*.

Brome, R., *Sparagus Garden*. Cartwright, *Ordinary*. Davenant, *News from Plymouth*; *Platonic Lovers*; *Temple of Love*. Marmion, *Antiquary*. Shirley, *Lady of Pleasure*.

Blount, *Voyage into the Levant*. Burton, H., *For God, and the King*. Dacres, *Machiavel's Discourses*, tr. Heylyn, *History of the Sabbath*. Peacham, *Coach and Sedan*. Prynne, *News from Ipswich*.

Cartwright, *Royal Slave*. Davenant, *Triumphs of the Prince d'Amour*. Glapthorne, *Hollander*. Kynaston (?), *Corona Minervae*. May, *Old Couple*. Strode, *Floating Island*.

Bastwick, J., *Litany*. Chillingworth, *Religion of Protestants*. Monro, R., *Expedition with Scots Regiment*. Morton, T., *New English Canaan*.

Mayne, *City Madam*. Milton, *Masque [Comus]* pr.

Bacon (d. 1626), *Operum Moralium et Civilium Tomus*. Fludd (d. 1637), *Philosophia Moysaica*. Godwin, F. (d. 1633), *Man in the Moon*. Lilburne, *Work of the Beast*. Peacham, *Truth of our Times*. Wilkins, *Discovery of a World in the Moon*.

Brome, A., *Cunning Lovers*. Brome, R., *Antipodes*. Cowley, *Love's Riddle* pr. Davenant, *Luminalia*; *Unfortunate Lovers*. Suckling, *Aglaura*; *Goblins*.

Date	Public Events	Literary History	Verse
1639	War with Scotland (First Bishops' War). Treaty of Berwick. King pursues his old Scottish policy. Wentworth becomes king's adviser.	Thomas Carew d.? Shakerley Marmion d. Sir Henry Wotton d. Sir Charles Sedley b. Davenant, Falkland, Lord Herbert, Lovelace, Earl of Newcastle, Suckling, Wither, et al., in Bishops' War.	Glapthorne, *Poems*.
1640	Refractory 'Short Parliament'. Convocation grants Benevolence, issues Laudian canons. London refuses forced loan and ship-money. Second Bishops' War. Long Parliament impeaches Strafford and Laud, declares ship-money and canons illegal. Root and Branch Petition.	William Alabaster d. William Alexander, Earl of Stirling, d. Robert Burton d. John Day d. John Ford d. (1640/53?). Thomas Jackson d. Philip Massinger d. Aphra (Johnson) Behn b. Bastwick, Burton, Prynne, Lilburne, Leighton released from prison.	F. Beaumont (d. 1616), *Poems*. Carew (d. 1639?), *Poems*. Jonson (d. 1637), *Underwoods* (in *Works*, 1640–1). C. Harvey, *Synagogue*. R. Mather et al., 'Bay Psalm Book'. Miscellanies: *Academy of Complements*; *Wit's Recreations*.
1641	Laud imprisoned. Army Plot. Strafford executed. Sweeping reforms by Parliament. Princess Mary married to William of Orange. Scottish army withdrawn from England. Irish rising. Grand Remonstrance.	Augustine Baker d. Thomas Heywood d. Thomas Mun d. Sir Henry Spelman d. Thomas Rymer b. William Sherlock b. William Wycherley b. Baxter called to Kidderminster. Comenius in England. Davenant arrested for Army Plot; Suckling escapes to France. Hobbes in Paris (1641–51).	Beedome (d. 1641?), *Poems*. Urquhart, *Epigrams*. Wither, *Hallelujah*.
1642	King tries to arrest five members, leaves London. Bishops' Exclusion Bill passed.	Sir Francis Kynaston d. Henry Peacham d.? Sir John Suckling d.	Denham, *Cooper's Hill*. Kynaston, *Leoline and Sydanis*, &c. More, *Psychodia Platonica*.

Prose

Sibbes (d. 1635), *Beams of Divine Light.* Fuller, *Holy War.* Hurst, R., *Endimion*, tr. Gombauld. Laud, *Conference with Fisher.* Spelman, *Concilia, Decreta*, i. Ussher, *Britannicarum Ecclesiarum Antiquitates.*

Drama (date of acting)

Cowley, *Naufragium Joculare.* Davenant, *Spanish Lovers.* Glapthorne, *Wit in a Constable.* Shirley, *Politician.* Suckling, *Brennoralt.*

Bacon (d. 1626), *Advertisement touching Controversies of the Church of England.* Donne (d. 1631), *LXXX Sermons*, with Walton's *Life* (rev. 1658 ff.). Jonson (d. 1637), *Timber*; *English Grammar.* Brooke, Lord, *Nature of Truth.* Dacres, *Prince*, tr. Machiavelli. Hall, *Episcopacy by Divine Right.* Howell, *Dodona's Grove.* Quarles, *Enchiridion.* Wilkins, *Discourse concerning a New Planet.*

Jonson (d. 1637), *Works* (1640-1), vol. ii (cf. 1616), incl. later plays, masques, verse, and prose. Fane, M., *Raguaillo d'Oceano.* Habington, *Queen of Aragon.* Sandys, *Christ's Passion*, tr. Grotius, pr.

Cavendish, G. (d. 1561/2?), *Thomas Wolsey.* Naunton (d. 1635), *Fragmenta Regalia.* Brooke, Lord, *Discourse of Episcopacy.* Hall, *Humble Remonstrance.* Hartlib, *Description of Macaria.* Milton, *Reformation touching Church Discipline*; *Prelatical Episcopacy*; *Animadversions upon Remonstrant's Defence.* Robinson, H., *England's Safety in Trade's Increase.* 'Smectymnuus', *Answer to Humble Remonstrance*; *Vindication.* Ussher, *Original of Bishops and Metropolitans.*

Brome, R., *Jovial Crew.* Denham, *Sophy.* Fane, M., *Candy Restored.* Killigrew, T., *Parson's Wedding* (?). Quarles, *Virgin Widow* (?). Shirley, *Cardinal.*

Ames (d. 1633), *Marrow of Sacred Divinity*, tr. *Medulla.* Coke (d. 1634), *Institutes*, ii. Ralegh (d. 1618), *Prince.* Browne, *Religio Medici* (unauth.). Fuller, *Holy State.*

Cowley, *Guardian.* Shirley, *Sisters.* Theatres closed, 2 September.

Date	Public Events	Literary History	Verse
	Parliament's militia ordinances and Nineteen Propositions. Suppression of Irish; Adventurers' Act. King refused admission to Hull. Navy declares for Parliament. Essex parliamentary general. King raises standard (22 August). Edgehill. TurnhamGreen. Oxford the king's head-quarters (1642–6).	George Hickes b. Sir Isaac Newton b. Thomas Shadwell b. Davenant, Denham, Falkland, Wither, et al., in war. Howell in prison (1642–50). Lovelace in prison. Milton's first marriage.	
1643	Episcopacy abolished. Cromwell in eastern counties. Waller's plot. Ordinance for licensing the press. Hampden dies of wounds. Many royalist victories. Solemn League and Covenant. Irish cessation; troops sent to king. Westminster Assembly; controversy over toleration. Pym d.	Lord Brooke killed. William Browne d.? William Cartwright d. Lord Falkland killed. Sidney Godolphin killed. Gilbert Burnet b. Charles Sackville, 6th Earl of Dorset, b. John Strype b. Chillingworth, Cleveland, Cowley, et al., at Oxford. Evelyn abroad (1643–7). George Fox begins his wanderings. Lovelace mostly abroad (1643–6). Waller imprisoned.	Cowley, *The Puritan and the Papist.* Martin Parker, 'When the King Enjoys His Own Again'.
1644	Scots enter England. Ordinance imposes Covenant on all adults. Royalists ejected from Cambridge. Committee of Both Kingdoms. First decisive parliamentary victory at Marston Moor. Trial of Laud. Montrose's victories. Parliamentary army in Cornwall	William Chillingworth d. Francis Quarles d. George Sandys d. William Penn b. Bunyan in militia (1644–7). Cowley and Crashaw abroad. Lord Herbert surrenders Montgomery Castle to Parliament.	Quarles, *Shepherd's Oracle.*

Prose   *Drama (date of acting)*

Hales, *Schism and Schismatics.* Hobbes, *De Cive.* Howell, *Instructions for Foreign Travel.* Milton, *Reason of Church Government*; *Apology for Smectymnuus.* Parker, H., *Observations upon his Majesty's Late Answers.* Many diurnals (1641–2 ff.).

                                         ..

Baker, Sir R., *Chronicle.* Browne, *Religio Medici* (auth. ed.). Digby, *Observations upon Religio Medici.* Hunton, *Treatise of Monarchy.* Milton, *Doctrine and Discipline of Divorce.* Prynne, *Sovereign Power of Parliaments.* Walwyn (?), *Power of Love.*

   Mercurius Aulicus (1643–5), *Mercurius Britannicus* (1643–6), *Mercurius Civicus* (1643–6), and many other newsbooks.

                                         ..

Coke (d. 1634), *Institutes,* iii, iv. Cleveland, *Character of a London Diurnal.* Digby, *Two Treatises.* Edwards, T., *Antapologia.* Goodwin, J., *Theomachia.* Goodwin, T., et al., *Apologetical Narration.* Milton, *Of Education*; *Judgement of Martin Bucer concerning Divorce*; *Areopagitica.* Overton, *Man's Mortality.* Robinson, H., *Liberty of Conscience.* Walwyn, *Compassionate Samaritan.* Williams, *Bloody Tenent of Persecution.*

                                         ..

Date	Public Events	Literary History	Verse
	surrenders. Friction between Manchester and Cromwell. Uxbridge Propositions.	L'Estrange condemned as royalist spy. Newcastle besieged in York; abroad (1644–60). Waller fined, banished; abroad (1644–51). Whichcote Provost of King's College.	··
1645	Prayer Book abolished. Laud executed. New Model Army. Self-Denying Ordinance. Naseby (14 June) and many other parliamentary victories. Montrose loses Philiphaugh. King tries to get Irish and foreign troops (1644–6). Witchhunting (1645–7).	Sir Richard Baker d. William Lithgow d.? William Strode d. Baxter chaplain in parliamentary army. Sir K. Digby queen's agent in Rome. Lilburne arrested several times. Scientists meet at Gresham College (c. 1645).	Quarles (d. 1644), *Solomon's Recantation*. Milton, *Poems*. Waller, *Poems*. Wither, *Vox Pacifica*.
1646	Ordinance for Presbyterianism. Hopton surrenders to Fairfax. King takes refuge with Scots. Oxford surrenders. Virtual end of war. Newcastle Propositions. Friction between Presbyterians and Independents.	Anthony Hamilton b.? Davenant in Paris (1646–50). Hyde begins *History of the Rebellion* in Scilly and Jersey.	Quarles (d. 1644), *Shepherd's Oracles*. Suckling (d. 1642), *Fragmenta Aurea*. Crashaw, *Steps to the Temple*. Lluelyn, *Men-Miracles*. Sheppard, *Times Displayed*. Shirley, *Poems*. H. Vaughan, *Poems*.
1647	King given up to Parliament. Beginning of Presbyterianroyalist alliance. Army seizes King. Parliament disregards army's proposals. Army occupies London. King treats with both Parliament and army; escapes to Isle of Wight; makes secret engagement with Scots. Putney debates.	Thomas Farnaby d. Francis Meres d. John Saltmarsh d. John Wilmot, Earl of Rochester, b. George Fox begins public ministry. Joseph Hall expelled from bishopric of Norwich. Herrick ejected from Dean Prior.	Corbet (d. 1635), *Poems*. Cleveland, *Poems* (with *Character of a London Diurnal*). Cowley, *The Mistress*. John Hall, *Poems*. C. Harvey, *Schola Cordis*. More, *Philosophical Poems*. Stanley, *Poems and Translations*. Stapylton, *Juvenal*, tr.

Prose   *Drama (date of acting)*

..   ..

..

Falkland, Lord (d. 1643), *Of the Infallibility
of the Church of Rome.* Fuller, *Good Thoughts
in Bad Times.* Herbert, Lord, *De Causis
Errorum.* Howell, *Epistolae Ho-Elianae,* i.
Lilburne, *England's Birth-Right Justified.*
Milton, *Tetrachordon; Colasterion.* Prynne,
Truth Triumphing. Ross, *Medicus Medicatus.*
Sparrow, J., et al., works of Boehme tr.
(1645–62).

Donne (d. 1631), *Biathanatos.* Browne,   Robert Cox, drolls (1646–53).
Pseudodoxia Epidemica. Edwards, T., *Gan-
graena.* Hall, John, *Horae Vacivae.* Ross,
New Planet No Planet. Saltmarsh, *Smoke in
the Temple.* Taylor, *Discourse concerning
Prayer Ex tempore.* Wilkins, *Ecclesiastes.*

Andrewes (d. 1626), *Private Devotions.*   Beaumont (d. 1616) and Fletcher
Bodley, Sir T. (d. 1613), *Life.* Browne, W., (d. 1625), *Comedies and Tragedies* pr.
Polexander, tr. Gomberville. Cudworth,   Fanshawe, *Pastor Fido,* tr. Guarini,
Sermon before House of Commons. Fuller,   pr.
*Cause and Cure of a Wounded Conscience; Good Parliamentary ordinances (1647–8)
Thoughts in Worse Times.* Howell, *Epistolae*   for suppressing plays.
Ho-Elianae, ii. Lilly, *Christian Astrology.*
May, *History of the Parliament.* Taylor, *Lib-
erty of Prophesying.*
  Mercurius Melancholicus(1647–9),*Mercurius
Pragmaticus* (1647–50), *Mercurius Elencticus*
(1647–9), and other journals.

Date	Public Events	Literary History	Verse
1648	Second civil war. Parliament negotiates with king. Leveller Petition. Army seizes king, enters London. Pride's Purge. End of Thirty Years War.	Lord Herbert of Cherbury d. Robert Barclay b. Nathaniel Lee b.? Elkanah Settle b. John Sheffield, Earl of Mulgrave, b. Lovelace in prison. Hammond, Sanderson, et al. ejected from Oxford. John Wilkins Warden of Wadham (1648–59).	Corbet (d. 1635), *Poetica Stromata*. Joseph Beaumont, *Psyche*. M. Fane, Earl of Westmorland, *Otia Sacra*. Herrick, *Hesperides*; *Noble Numbers*.
1649	King's trial and execution (30 January). Charles II proclaimed in Scotland. Rump abolishes House of Lords and monarchy, proclaims Commonwealth, disregards army's constitutional scheme. Cromwell in Ireland. Act for relief of poor debtors. Diggers. Act concerning Religion in Maryland.	Richard Crashaw d. William Drummond d. George Hakewill d. Sir Anthony Weldon d.? Benlowes fined for share in Essex rising. Evelyn abroad (1649–52). Lilburne tried, acquitted. Milton Secretary for Foreign Tongues to Council of State.	Lovelace, *Lucasta*. J. Ogilby, *Works of Virgil*, tr. R. B., ed., *Lachrymae Musarum* (elegies on Lord Hastings by Dryden, Marvell, Herrick, et al.).
1650	Engagement imposed. Montrose executed. Charles accepts Scottish Covenant. Battle of Dunbar. Acts on Sunday observance, adultery, swearing, blasphemy. Recusancy penalties repealed. Trade with royalist colonies prohibited.	William Bosworth d.? Sir Simonds D'Ewes d. John Everard d.? Phineas Fletcher d. Thomas May d. Jeremy Collier b. Davenant in prison (1650–2).	Anne Bradstreet, *Tenth Muse*. Davenant, *Gondibert* (1650–1). R. Heath, *Clarastella*. Marvell, *Horatian Ode* (written). Vaughan, *Silex Scintillans, i.*
1651	Charles crowned at Scone. Blake completes extermination of royalist privateers. Battle of Worcester. Charles a fugitive. Scotland subdued. Confiscation of royalist estates in England and Scotland. Navigation Act.	Nathanael Culverwel d.? Aurelian Townshend d.? Cowley in Jersey. Hobbes returns to England. Milton associated with *Mercurius Politicus*.	Bosworth (d. 1650?), *Chaste and Lost Lovers*. Cartwright (d. 1643), *Poems* (in *Comedies*, &c.). P. Cary, *Trivial Poems and Triolets* (written). Cleveland, *Poems*. Sherburne, *Salmacis*, &c. Stanley, *Poems*. Vaughan, *Olor Iscanus*.

Prose	Drama (date of acting)
Bacon (d. 1626), *Remains.* Hooker (d. 1600), *Ecclesiastical Polity,* books vi, viii. Duncon, *Viscountess Falkland.* Filmer, *Anarchy of a Limited or Mixed Monarchy.* Gage, *New Survey of the West Indies.* Gott, *Nova Solyma.* Petty, *Advice to Hartlib.* Wilkins, *Mathematical Magic.*	Sherburne, *Medea,* tr. Seneca, pr.
Donne (d. 1631), *Fifty Sermons.* Herbert, Lord (d. 1648), *Henry VIII.* Gauden (?), *Eikon Basilike.* Hall, John, *Humble Motion concerning Advancement of Learning.* Lilburne, *England's New Chains Discovered.* Milton, *Tenure of Kings and Magistrates;* *Eikonoklastes.* Taylor, J., *Great Exemplar.*	..
Baxter, *Saints' Everlasting Rest.* Davenant and Hobbes, *Discourse upon Gondibert. With an Answer.* Fuller, *Pisgah-Sight of Palestine.* Hobbes, *Human Nature;* *De Corpore Politico.* Howell, *Epistolae,* iii. Taylor, J., *Holy Living.* Ussher, *Annales Veteris Testamenti* (1650–4). Vaughan, T., *Anthroposophia Theomagica,* &c. *Mercurius Politicus* (1650–60).	..
Donne (d. 1631), *Essays in Divinity; Letters to Several Persons of Honour.* Ralegh (d. 1618), *Sceptic.* Wotton, Sir H. (d. 1639), *Reliquiae Wottonianae,* with Walton's *Life.* Harvey, *De Generatione Animalium.* Hobbes, *Leviathan; Philosophical Rudiments,* tr. *De Cive.* Milton, *Pro Populo Anglicano Defensio.* Taylor, J., *Holy Dying; XXVIII Sermons.*	Cartwright (d. 1643), *Comedies, Tragicomedies, With Other Poems,* pr.

Date	Public Events	Literary History	Verse
1652	Commission for legal reforms. Proposals for national Church with toleration. Royalist colonies submit. Army petitions Parliament. End of twelve years' war in Ireland; confiscation of land and transplantation (1652–7). Dutch war.	Richard Brome d.? Henry Parker d. Martin Parker d. John Smith d. William Dampier b. Thomas Otway b. Nahum Tate b. Milton's blindness complete.	Crashaw (d. 1649), *Carmen Deo Nostro*. Ashmole, ed., *Theatrum Chemicum Britannicum*. Benlowes, *Theophila*. Milton, several sonnets (written).
1653	Army seeks toleration, parliamentary and legal reforms. Parliament expelled by Cromwell. Nominated ('Barebones') Parliament. Dutch defeated by Blake and Monk. Instrument of Government establishes Protectorate.	William Basse d.? Sir Robert Filmer d. John Taylor d. Thomas D'Urfey b. Roger North b. John Oldham b. Lilburne tried, acquitted; a popular hero.	M. Cavendish, Duchess of Newcastle, *Poems and Fancies*. Cleveland, *Poems*. N. Hookes, *Amanda*. H. Lawes, *Airs and Dialogues*. Marvell, *Character of Holland* (written). Denham et al., *Certain Verses* (satires on *Gondibert*).
1654	Royalist and Leveller plots (1654 ff.). Reforms in law, manners, and education. Commission to examine clergy. Peace with Holland. Treaties with Sweden, Portugal, Denmark. French forts in Acadia seized. Parliament restricts power of Cromwell and Council.	Nicholas Culpeper d. William Habington d. Alexander Ross d. John Selden d. Cowley returns to England.	..
1655	Proclamation on religious liberty. Penruddock's rising. Blake subdues Algerian pirates. Massacre of Vaudois. Jamaica captured; West Indian colonies secured against Spain. War with	Samuel Sheppard d.? Sir Richard Blackmore b. Andrew Fletcher b. Cleveland and Cowley in prison.	*Caedmonis Paraphrasis Poetica Genesios*, ed. F. Junius. Denham, *Cooper's Hill* (auth. ed.). Fanshawe, *Lusiad*, tr. Camoens. Marvell, *First Anniversary of . . . the Lord Protector*.

Prose   *Drama (date of acting)*

Culverwel (d. 1651?), *Light of Nature.*   ..
Donne (d. 1631), *Paradoxes, Problems,*
Essays, Characters. Greville (d. 1628), *Life*
of Sidney. Herbert, G. (d. 1633), *Remains.*
Cogan, H., *Ibrahim,* tr. Scudéry. Cotterell,
Sir C., *Cassandra,* tr. La Calprenède. Fell-
tham, *Brief Character of the Low Countries*
(unauth. ed., 1648). Filmer, *Aristotle's*
Politics; Original of Government. Hall, John,
Longinus, tr. Heylyn, *Cosmography.* Love-
day, R., et al., *Hymen's Praeludia* (1652–9),
tr. La Calprenède's *Cléopâtre.* Vaughan,
H., *Mount of Olives.* Winstanley, *Law of*
Freedom.

Bacon (d. 1626), *Scripta.* Cavendish, M.,   Brome, R. (d. 1652?), *Five New*
Duchess of Newcastle, *Philosophical Fancies.*   *Plays* pr. Shirley, *Six New Plays* pr.
Everard, J., *Some Gospel Treasures Opened.*
G., F., *Artamenes or the Grand Cyrus* (1653–
5), tr. Scudéry. More, *Antidote against*
Atheism; Conjectura Cabbalistica. Ross,
Leviathan Drawn out with a Hook; Pansebeia.
Taylor, J., *XXV Sermons.* Urquhart,
Rabelais, i–ii, tr. Walton, *Complete Angler.*

Boyle, *Parthenissa* (1651–69). Hobbes, *Of*   Governmental repression of plays.
Liberty and Necessity. Milton, *Defensio*
Secunda. Vaughan, H., *Flores Solitudinis.*
Ward, S., and Wilkins, J., *Vindiciae Acade-*
miarum. Webster, J., *Examen Academiarum.*
Worthington, *Christian's Pattern,* tr. à
Kempis.

Bramhall, *Defence of True Liberty.* Davies,   Lower, Sir W., *Polyeuctes,* tr. Cor-
J., and Havers, G., *Clelia* (1655–61), tr.   neille, pr.
Scudéry. Dugdale, *Monasticon Anglicanum,*
i. Fuller, *Church History of Britain,* &c.
Hobbes, *De Corpore.* Howell, *Epistolae,* iv.
Milton, *Pro Se Defensio.* Stanley, *History of*
Philosophy (1655–62). Taylor, J., *Golden*
Grove; Unum Necessarium. Vane, *Retired*
Man's Meditations.
Seven independent newspapers suppressed;

Date	Public Events	Literary History	Verse
	Spain. Treaty with France. Rule of major-generals.	..	J. Phillips, *Satire against Hypocrites.* Vaughan, *Silex Scintillans*, i–ii. Waller, *Panegyric to my Lord Protector.* Miscellanies: *Marrow of Complements; Musarum Deliciae; English Treasury of Wit and Language*, ed. J. Cotgrave; *Wit's Interpreter, The English Parnassus*, ed. Cotgrave.
1656	Blake blockades Spanish coast. Anglican and Catholic worship connived at. Virtual toleration of Jews. Second Protectorate Parliament; about 100 members excluded by government. End of major-generals' rule.	John Hales d. John Hall d. Joseph Hall d. James Ussher d. Gerard Langbaine the younger b. Jacob Tonson b.?	Drummond (d. 1649), *Poems.* Collop, *Poesis Rediviva.* Cowley, *Poems* (coll., with *Davideis* and odes). Denham, *Destruction of Troy*, tr. *Aeneid* ii. Evelyn, *First Book of Lucretius*, tr. Miscellanies: *Choice Drollery; Cupid's Masterpiece* (?); *Parnassus Biceps*, ed. A. Wright; *Wit and Drollery.*
1657	Alliance with France against Spain. Spain crippled by Blake. Humble Petition and Advice. Cromwell declines kingship; reinvested as Protector by parliamentary authority. Quakers protected. New charter for East India Company.	William Harvey d. John Lilburne d. Richard Lovelace d. (1656?). John Dennis b. Thomas Killigrew the younger b. John Norris b. Matthew Tindal b.	King, *Poems.* J. Poole, ed., *English Parnassus.*
1658	Republican opposition to Cromwell and second chamber. Parliament dissolved. Battle of the Dunes; England acquires Dunkirk. London merchants hostile to Spanish war. Increase in public debt. Cromwell d. (3 September). Richard Cromwell Protector.	John Cleveland d. Gerard Langbaine the elder d. Edward Sexby d. Sir Henry Slingsby executed.	John Hall (d. 1656), *Emblems.* Cokayne, *Poems.* Waller and S. Godolphin (d. 1643), *Passion of Dido*, tr. *Aeneid* iv. Miscellanies: *Naps upon Parnassus; Wit Restored; Mysteries of Love and Eloquence*, ed. E. Phillips.

Prose	*Drama (date of acting)*
Needham's government papers, *Mercurius Politicus* and *Public Intelligencer*, excepted.	..

Bunyan, *Some Gospel-Truths Opened.* Cavendish, M., Duchess of Newcastle, *Nature's Pictures.* Charleton, *Epicurus's Morals.* Dugdale, *Antiquities of Warwickshire.* Harrington, *Oceana.* Hobbes, *Questions concerning Liberty, Necessity, and Chance.* More, *Enthusiasmus Triumphatus.* Osborn, *Advice to a Son* (ii, 1658). Vane, *Healing Question.*

Davenant, *First Day's Entertainment at Rutland House*; 1 *Siege of Rhodes.* Lower, Sir W., *Horatius*, tr. Corneille, pr.

Bacon (d. 1626), *Resuscitatio.* Baker, A. (d. 1641), *Sancta Sophia.* Vere, Sir F. (d. 1609), *Commentaries.* Baxter, *Call to the Unconverted.* Bunyan, *Vindication.* Howell, *Londinopolis.* Sexby, *Killing No Murder.* Taylor, J., *Discourse of Friendship.* Thornley, *Daphnis and Chloe*, tr. Longus. Walton, B., et al., *Biblia Sacra Polyglotta.*

..

Bacon (d. 1626), *Opuscula.* Ralegh (d. 1618), *Cabinet Council*, ed. Milton. Allestree (?), *Whole Duty of Man.* Bramhall, *Castigations of Mr. Hobbes.* Browne, *Hydriotaphia*; *Garden of Cyrus.* Digby, *Powder of Sympathy.* Harrington, *Prerogative of Popular Government.* Hobbes, *De Homine.* Phillips, E., *New World of English Words.*

Chamberlayne, *Love's Victory* pr. Davenant, *Cruelty of the Spaniards in Peru*; *Sir Francis Drake.*

Date	Public Events	Literary History	Verse
1659	Third Protectorate Parliament. Army officers force dissolution. End of Protectorate. Rump recalled, expelled by Lambert, again restored. Monk leads army from Scotland. Rota Club (1659–60).	Francis Osborn d. Thomas Creech b. John Dunton b.	Suckling (d. 1642), *Last Remains*. Chamberlayne, *Pharonnida*. Waller, Dryden, and Sprat, *Three Poems upon the Death of . . . Oliver Lord Protector*. E. Williamson, ed., *J. Cleveland Revived*.
1660	Monk recalls Presbyterian members excluded in 1648. Dissolution. Declaration of Breda. New Parliament recalls Charles II. King enters London (29 May). Punishment of regicides living and dead. Legislation of Cromwell and Long Parliament regarded as void. Royal Society organized.	Henry Hammond d. Sir Thomas Urquhart d.? Daniel Defoe b. Peter Motteux b. Thomas Southerne b. Bunyan in prison. Return to England of Earle, Newcastle, et al. Pepys begins diary. Wither arrested.	Lovelace (d. 1656/7), *Lucasta. Posthume Poems* (dated 1659). Dryden, *Astraea Redux*. Pordage, *Poems*. Robert Wild, *Iter Boreale*. Poems on Restoration by Cowley, Davenant, Waller, et al. Miscellanies: *Rats Rhymed to Death*; B. Rudyerd et al., *Le Prince d'Amour*.

Prose

Hales (d. 1656), *Golden Remains*. Baxter, *Holy Commonwealth*. Evelyn, *Character of England*. Fuller, *Appeal of Injured Innocence*. Milton, *Civil Power in Ecclesiastical Causes*; *Likeliest Means to Remove Hirelings out of the Church*; *Ruptures of the Commonwealth*. More, *Immortality of the Soul*. Pearson, *Exposition of the Creed*. Rushworth, *Historical Collections* (1659–1701). Somner, *Dictionarium Saxonico-Latino-Anglicum*.

Donne (d. 1631), *XXVI Sermons*. Smith, J. (d. 1652), *Select Discourses*. Boyle, *New Experiments Physico-Mechanical*. Fuller, *Mixed Contemplations in Better Times*. Hoole, *Old Art of Teaching School*. Milton, *Ready and Easy Way*. More, *Grand Mystery of Godliness*. Taylor, J., *Ductor Dubitantium*. Winstanley, W., *England's Worthies*.

Drama (date of acting)

Brome, R. (d. 1652?), *Five New Plays* pr. Davenant, 2 *Siege of Rhodes*. Shirley, *Contention of Ajax and Ulysses* pr.

Pordage, S., *Troades*, tr. Seneca, pr. Tatham, *Rump*.
Theatre patents granted to Thomas Killigrew the elder and Davenant.

BIBLIOGRAPHY

This bibliography is arranged in six sections:

 I. General Bibliographies and Works of Reference.
 II. General Collections and Anthologies.
 III. General Literary History and Criticism (general history and criticism; rhetorical theory and prose style; history and criticism of poetry).
 IV. Special Literary Studies and Literary Forms (language; popular literature; journalism; fiction; essays and characters; historical and biographical literature; classical and foreign relations; translations; contemporary criticism; printing and bookselling).
 V. The Background of Literature (political history and political thought; religion and religious thought; science and scientific thought; travel; social life; education and culture; music and the arts).
 VI. Individual Authors.

Since the bibliography is to be 'selective and directive', a great deal of more or less important material is necessarily omitted; and a general reference to the bibliographies in the *BMC* and *CBEL* (*infra*) must suffice.

The following abbreviations are used in the citing of some works of reference and current periodicals:

BMC	*British Museum General Catalogue of Printed Books*
CBEL	*Cambridge Bibliography of English Literature*
CHEL	*Cambridge History of English Literature*
DNB	*Dictionary of National Biography*
ELH	*English Literary History*
ESEA	*Essays and Studies by Members of the English Association*
HLB	*Huntington Library Bulletin*
HLQ	*Huntington Library Quarterly*
JEGP	*Journal of English and Germanic Philology*
JHI	*Journal of the History of Ideas*
MLN	*Modern Language Notes*
MLQ	*Modern Language Quarterly*
MLR	*Modern Language Review*
MP	*Modern Philology*
NQ	*Notes and Queries*
OBS	*Oxford Bibliographical Society Proceedings & Papers*

PMLA   *Publications of the Modern Language Association of America*
PQ   *Philological Quarterly*
RES   *Review of English Studies*
SP   *Studies in Philology*
STC   *Short-Title Catalogue*, ed. Pollard and Redgrave
TLS   *London Times Literary Supplement*

In sections I–V the place of publication is ordinarily given for books published outside of Great Britain, but not in section VI if such books are there cited again.

I. GENERAL BIBLIOGRAPHIES AND WORKS OF REFERENCE

Some of the older and still useful bibliographical aids are the descriptive compilations of Sir Egerton Brydges and J. P. Collier and, for its subject-index, Robert Watt's *Bibliotheca Britannica* (4 vols., 1824); W. T. Lowndes, *Bibliographer's Manual of English Literature* (rev. ed. by H. G. Bohn, 6 vols., 1869); and such works by W. C. Hazlitt as the *Hand-Book to the Popular, Poetical, and Dramatic Literature of Great Britain* (1867) and *Collections and Notes* (6 vols., 1876–1903), with the *Index* to both by G. J. Gray (1893).

Other and mainly later works of reference for original texts are: *British Museum General Catalogue of Printed Books* (new ed. in progress, 1931 ff.); E. Arber, *Transcript of the Registers of the Company of Stationers of London, between 1554–1640 A.D.* (5 vols., 1875–94); the *Transcript* of the same (1640–1708) by G. E. B. Eyre and H. R. Plomer (3 vols., Roxburghe Club, 1913–14); C. E. Sayle, *Early English Printed Books in the University Library Cambridge (1475 to 1640)* (4 vols., 1900–7); Grolier Club *Catalogue of Original and Early Editions*, &c. (3 vols., New York, 1905); *Catalogue of the Pamphlets, Books, Newspapers, and Manuscripts . . . Collected by George Thomason, 1640–61*, ed. G. K. Fortescue (2 vols., 1908), a valuable guide to chronology; A. W. Pollard, G. R. Redgrave, et al., *Short-Title Catalogue of Books Printed in England, Scotland, & Ireland . . . 1475–1640* (1926); the continuation of this invaluable work, 1641–1700, now being edited by D. Wing; C. K. Edmonds, 'Huntington Library Supplement to the Short Title Catalogue' (*HLB*, 1933); *Catalogue of the McAlpin Collection of British History and Theology*, ed. C. R. Gillett (5 vols., New

York, 1927–30); *The Britwell Handlist* (2 vols., 1933); the *Carl H. Pforzheimer Library: English Literature 1475–1700*, ed. W. A. Jackson (3 vols., New York, 1940); and further items cited below in IV. 10.

The bibliographies of texts and scholarship in the *CHEL*, vols. iii–ix (1909–12) are still of use, though superseded by the massive *CBEL*, ed. F. W. Bateson (4 vols., 1941), the most useful single work, if inevitably uneven; it covers material up to 1935. C. S. Northup's *Register of Bibliographies of the English Language and Literature* (Yale, 1925) may be supplemented by T. P. Cross, *Bibliographical Guide to English Studies* (8th ed., University of Chicago, 1943), and J. W. Spargo, *Bibliographical Manual* (2nd ed., Chicago, 1941). V. de Sola Pinto's *The English Renaissance 1510–1688* (1938) is a serviceable bibliographical compendium.

Indispensable annual bibliographies are: *The Year's Work in English Studies*, published by the English Association since 1919–20; the *Annual Bibliography of English Language and Literature*, published by the Modern Humanities Research Association since 1920; the bibliography included in the *PMLA* since 1922; 'Recent Literature of the English Renaissance' (in *SP* since 1922), which includes the period 1600–60; and 'English Literature of the Restoration and the Eighteenth Century' (in *PQ* since 1926).

Some miscellaneous works of reference are: W. W. Greg, *English Literary Autographs 1550–1650* (3 vols., 1925–32); Halkett and Laing, *Dictionary of Anonymous and Pseudonymous English Literature*, rev. by James Kennedy et al. (7 vols., 1926–34); J. C. Ghosh and E. G. Withycombe, *Annals of English Literature 1475–1925* (1935); Sir Paul Harvey, *Oxford Companion to English Literature* (2nd ed., 1937–8), and the abridgement, the *Concise Oxford Dictionary of English Literature* (1939).

Almost all of the authors mentioned in the text have a place in the *DNB* and a few in the more recent *Dictionary of American Biography*. Among early biographers of varying authority are Thomas Fuller, Samuel Clarke, who compiled several works of ecclesiastical biography, William Winstanley, and especially John Aubrey (1626–97), whose *Brief Lives* are edited by Andrew Clark (2 vols., 1898), and the less genial and picturesque Anthony Wood (1632–95), who in his later years called himself à Wood. Wood's *Athenae Oxonienses* (2 vols., 1691–2), which

included the *Fasti*, is quoted in this book from the revised and
enlarged edition of 1721.

II. GENERAL COLLECTIONS AND ANTHOLOGIES

1. PROSE

Special collections and anthologies are cited in appropriate
places. To pass by general anthologies of prose, some which
especially concern our period are: Henry Craik, *English Prose*,
vols. i–iii (1893–4); *A Book of English Prose . . . 1387–1649*, ed.
W. E. Henley and C. Whibley (1894); and the college anthologies of seventeenth-century prose edited by J. Zeitlin (Modern
Student's Library, 1926), R. P. T. Coffin and A. Witherspoon
(New York, 1929), and C. A. Moore and D. Bush (New York,
1930).

Two large treasuries of rare pamphlets are *The Harleian
Miscellany*, which first appeared in 1744–6 and was edited by
T. Park (10 vols., 1808–13), and the *Somers Tracts* (1748–52),
edited in an enlarged edition by Scott (13 vols., 1809–15).
E. Arber's *English Garner* (8 vols., 1877–96) was rearranged
under the general editorship of T. Seccombe (12 vols., 1903–4);
this includes *Stuart Tracts*, ed. Firth (1903). *Complaint and
Reform in England 1436–1714*, ed. W. H. Dunham and S. Pargellis (New York, 1938), contains many more or less rare pieces
on various subjects.

2. VERSE

This list comprises early miscellanies, modern collections and
general anthologies, and anthologies of lyrical, pastoral, and
religious verse. Collections of broadside ballads are listed
under Popular Literature in IV. 2.

A. E. Case's *Bibliography of English Poetical Miscellanies
1521–1750* (1935), supplemented by lists in *CBEL*, is almost
exhaustive. Some early miscellanies are: *Englands Helicon* (1600,
1614), ed. A. H. Bullen (1887, 1899), H. Macdonald (1925),
and definitively by H. E. Rollins (2 vols., Harvard, 1935);
Englands Parnassus (1600), ed. T. Park, *Heliconia*, iii (1815),
C. Crawford (1913); *Bel-vedere* (1600), reprinted for the Spenser
Society (1875); *A Poetical Rapsody* (1602–21), ed. Bullen
(2 vols., 1890–1), and definitively by H. E. Rollins (2 vols.,
Harvard, 1931–2); *Witts Recreations* (1640), &c., ed. by T. Park
as *Musarum Deliciae* (2 vols., 1817), reprinted under the same

title by J. C. Hotten (2 vols., 1874); and *Parnassus Biceps* (1656), ed. G. Thorn-Drury (1927). Some special collections are *Annalia Dubrensia* (1636; ed. A. B. Grosart, 1877; ed. E. R. Vyvyan, 1878), *Jonsonus Virbius* (1638), and *Justa Edouardo King* (1638); the last two are cited under Jonson and Milton in VI below.

Of the early modern collections on a large scale the most useful is Chalmers's *Works of the English Poets* (21 vols., 1810). The first two volumes of T. H. Ward's *English Poets* (1880) are canonical, though not always in line with modern taste. The best general anthology for the student is the richly annotated *Poetry of the English Renaissance 1509–1660* of J. W. Hebel and H. H. Hudson (New York, 1929). Two standard volumes are the *Oxford Book of Sixteenth Century Verse*, ed. Sir E. K. Chambers (1932), and the *Oxford Book of Seventeenth Century Verse*, ed. Sir H. J. C. Grierson and G. Bullough (1934). A large gap was partly filled by Saintsbury's *Minor Poets of the Caroline Period* (3 vols., 1905–21). R. G. Howarth's Everyman volume, *Minor Poets of the 17th Century* (1931), contains Lord Herbert, Carew, Suckling, and Lovelace.

Such Scottish poets as concern us are represented in the general anthologies, English and Scottish. The chief special anthology is G. Eyre-Todd's *Scottish Poetry of the Seventeenth Century* (1895).

Wholly or mainly lyrical anthologies of seventeenth-century verse have been edited by H. J. Massingham (Golden Treasury Series, 1919), A. C. Judson (University of Chicago, 1927), R. F. Brinkley (New York, 1936; rev. 1942), and M. W. Black (Philadelphia, 1938). An anthology which seems to have had a large share in forming modern taste is Grierson's *Metaphysical Lyrics & Poems of the Seventeenth Century* (1921). Norman Ault's *Elizabethan Lyrics* (1925) and *Seventeenth Century Lyrics* (1928) are arranged chronologically and embody fresh work on printed and manuscript sources. Two additional anthologies are L. B. Marshall, *Rare Poems of the Seventeenth Century* (1936) and N. Ault, *A Treasury of Unfamiliar Lyrics* (1938).

English Song-Books 1651–1702: A Bibliography (1940), by C. L. Day and E. B. Murrie, obviously covers only the end of our period. A. H. Bullen edited *Lyrics from the Song-books of the Elizabethan Age* (1887), *More Lyrics* (1888), and a selection from the two volumes (1889), and the kindred *Shorter Elizabethan*

Poems (1903). *English Madrigal Verse 1588–1632* (1920) has been edited by E. H. Fellowes, to whom we owe the great collections of Elizabethan and Jacobean music and song (*infra*, V. 7).

Pastoral verse can be best enjoyed in *Englands Helicon*. Two modern anthologies are *English Pastorals*, ed. Sir E. K. Chambers (1895), and *The Pastoral Elegy*, ed. T. P. Harrison and H. J. Leon (University of Texas, 1939), which is especially useful for its continental authors.

Two of the older collections of religious verse are R. Cattermole's *Sacred Poets of the Seventeenth Century* (2 vols., 1835–6) and E. Farr's *Select Poetry Chiefly Sacred of the Reign of King James the First* (1847). Some later anthologies, general and special, are: *Treasury of Sacred Song*, ed. Palgrave (1889); *Lyra Sacra*, ed. H. C. Beeching (1895); *Oxford Book of English Mystical Verse*, ed. D. H. S. Nicholson and A. H. E. Lee (1917); *Devotional Poets of the XVII Century*, ed. Sir H. Newbolt (1929); *Recusant Poets*, ed. L. I. Guiney (1939); and *Oxford Book of Christian Verse*, ed. Lord D. Cecil (1940).

III. GENERAL LITERARY HISTORY AND CRITICISM

This section comprises: (1) General literary history and criticism; (2) Rhetorical theory and prose style; (3) General and special history and criticism of poetry.

1. GENERAL LITERARY HISTORY AND CRITICISM

The fullest history is of course the *CHEL*, of which vols. iii–ix (1909–12) deal partly or wholly with the period 1600–60. Of the shorter but substantial histories the best are those of E. Legouis and L. Cazamian (Paris, 1924; trans. 1926–7, and later edns.), W. F. Schirmer (*Geschichte der englischen Literatur*, Halle, 1937), and George Sampson, whose *Concise Cambridge History of English Literature* (1941), if not always up to date in details, is a feat of compression and revision. Our period is well covered in two older books often reprinted, *The Age of Shakespeare* (2 vols., 1903), by T. Seccombe and J. W. Allen, and *The Age of Milton* (1897), by J. H. B. Masterman. J. J. Jusserand's *Literary History of the English People* (1894–1904; trans., 3 vols., 1895–1909, and later edns.), which comes down to the civil war, stresses the background of national life. Sir Herbert Grierson's *First Half of the Seventeenth Century* (1906) has a European scope.

Under the loose heading of selective interpretations may be put such books as these: E. Dowden, *Puritan and Anglican* (1900); G. N. Clark, *The Seventeenth Century* (1929), a compressed analysis of the whole outer and inner world of the European man; Sir Herbert Grierson, *Cross Currents in English Literature of the XVIIth Century, or The World, the Flesh & the Spirit, their Actions & Reactions* (1929); P. Meissner, *Die geistesgeschichtlichen Grundlagen des englischen Literaturbarocks* (Munich, 1934), an ambitious but too agile and facile work; Basil Willey, *The Seventeenth Century Background* (1934), an admirable outline of philosophic cross-currents; Hardin Craig, *The Enchanted Glass* (New York, 1936), a learned analysis of the Elizabethan and Jacobean mind and its furniture; D. Mathew, *The Jacobean Age* (1938), a sensitive Catholic view of special aspects; a substantial *Festschrift, Seventeenth Century Studies Presented to Sir Herbert Grierson* (1938); F. P. Wilson's studies of transition, *Elizabethan and Jacobean* (1945); and some of the general works named below under V. 2 and 3.

Histories of Scottish literature have less to say of the period 1600–60 than of the periods before and after. Some general works are: Hugh Walker, *Three Centuries of Scottish Literature* (2 vols., 1893); T. F. Henderson, *Scottish Vernacular Literature* (3rd ed., 1910); J. H. Millar, *Literary History of Scotland* (1903) and *Scottish Prose of the Seventeenth and Eighteenth Centuries* (1912); G. G. Smith, *Scottish Literature* (1919); and A. M. Mackenzie, *Historical Survey of Scottish Literature to 1714* (1933).

For Wales there are J. C. Morrice, *Wales in the Seventeenth Century: Its Literature and Men of Letters and Action* (1918), and W. J. Hughes, *Wales and the Welsh in English Literature from Shakespeare to Scott* (1924).

2. RHETORICAL THEORY AND PROSE STYLE

G. P. Krapp's *Rise of English Literary Prose* (1915) stops early in the seventeenth century. The evolution of prose has been fruitfully studied in connexion with the related anti-Ciceronian and scientific movements. Anti-Ciceronian theory and practice have been analysed by M. W. Croll in a series of important articles in the *Revue du seizième siècle*, ii (1914), *SP* xvi and xviii (1919 and 1921), the *Schelling Anniversary Papers* (New York, 1923), *PMLA* xxxix (1924), and *Studies in English Philology*, ed. K. Malone and M. B. Ruud (University of Minnesota, 1929).

With these may be linked G. Williamson's 'Senecan Style in the Seventeenth Century' (*PQ* xv, 1936). The scientific and philosophic quest of precise and simple expression has been most fully studied by R. F. Jones (*PMLA* xlv, 1930; *JEGP* xxx and xxxi, 1931-2; *Studies in Honor of F. W. Shipley*, Washington University, 1942). Joan Bennett has treated the same theme (*RES* xvii, 1941) and Hugh Macdonald 'another aspect' (*RES* xix, 1943).

Some other studies of rhetorical tradition and theory are: W. P. Sandford, 'English Rhetoric Reverts to Classicism, 1600-1650' (*Quarterly Journal of Speech*, xv, 1929; *English Theories of Public Address, 1530-1828*, Columbus, Ohio, 1931); W. G. Crane, *Wit and Rhetoric in the Renaissance: The Formal Basis of Elizabethan Prose Style* (Columbia, 1937); and Karl R. Wallace, *Francis Bacon on Communication & Rhetoric* (University of North Carolina, 1943), which includes a full bibliography of the subject. The potent influence of Ramist logic and rhetoric has received its fullest exposition in Perry Miller, *The New England Mind: The Seventeenth Century* (New York, 1939). Studies of pulpit style are noticed below under V. 2.

Among general studies of prose rhythm, of varying scope, are those of Saintsbury (1912), Albert C. Clark (1913), W. M. Patterson (Columbia, 1916), and N. R. Tempest (1930), and articles by Oliver Elton (*ESEA* iv, 1913; *A Sheaf of Papers*, 1922) and M. W. Croll (*SP* xvi, 1919).

3. HISTORY AND CRITICISM OF POETRY

This section covers general history and criticism; lyrical verse; sonnets; pastoral, religious, metaphysical, and heroic verse; diction; and prosody. Broadside ballads are under Popular Literature in IV below.

An early book of interest is Edward Phillips's *Theatrum Poetarum* (1675).

W. J. Courthope's *History of English Poetry*, vols. ii and iii (1897-1904, 1903), if somewhat outmoded, retains a spacious philosophic value. Two later works, compressed but distinctive, are Oliver Elton, *The English Muse* (1933) and Sir H. J. C. Grierson and J. C. Smith, *A Critical History of English Poetry* (1944).

A number of more or less general works, bearing more or less on the poetry of our period, may be mentioned. Gosse's *Seventeenth-Century Studies* (1883) and *Jacobean Poets* (1894) have sometimes a pioneer interest, sometimes more. Some later writings are: Henry W. Wells, *Poetic Imagery, Illustrated from Elizabethan Literature* (Columbia, 1924); Elizabeth Holmes, *Aspects of Elizabethan Imagery* (1929); Charles Williams, *The English Poetic Mind* (1932); E. M. W. Tillyard, *Poetry Direct and Oblique* (1934); W. Empson, *Seven Types of Ambiguity* (1930) and *Some Versions of Pastoral* (1935); C. Brooks and R. P. Warren, *Understanding Poetry* (New York, 1938), a general anthology with much acute comment; B. Ifor Evans, *Tradition and Romanticism* (1940); L. Jonas, *The Divine Science* (Columbia, 1940), which outlines the various poets' theories of poetry; and R. Tuve, 'Imagery and Logic' (*JHI* iii, 1942).

Two books of a special kind are F. Delattre, *English Fairy Poetry* (1912), and M. W. Latham, *Elizabethan Fairies* (Columbia, 1930).

Three general books, E. B. Reed's *English Lyrical Poetry* (1912), E. Rhys's *Lyric Poetry* (1913), and F. E. Schelling's *English Lyric* (1913), need to be supplemented, especially in regard to metaphysical verse, by critical writings mentioned below under that head. A later, substantial, and intelligent survey of many poets of our period is W. P. Friederich's *Spiritualismus und Sensualismus in der englischen Barocklyrik* (Wiener Beiträge, lvii, 1932). The period is touched in John Erskine's *Elizabethan Lyric* (Columbia, 1903) and in G. Bontoux's massive work, *La Chanson en Angleterre au temps d'Élisabeth* (1936). Other items are mentioned below under Music (V. 7).

Some of our men come into the chief books on the Elizabethan sonnet: J. G. Scott, *Les Sonnets élisabéthains: les sources et l'apport personnel* (Paris, 1928); L. E. Pearson, *Elizabethan Love Conventions* (University of California, 1933); and L. C. John, *The Elizabethan Sonnet Sequences: Studies in Conventional Conceits* (Columbia, 1938). An exact study of the large mass of seventeenth-century sonnets is that of C. B. Mitchell (Harvard *Summaries of Theses 1939*). L. B. Salomon's *The Devil Take Her* (University of Pennsylvania, 1931) deals with 'the Rebellious Lover in English Poetry'.

The chief works on pastoral literature are W. W. Greg, *Pastoral Poetry and Pastoral Drama* (1906), and H. Genouy, *L'Élément pastoral dans la poésie narrative et le drame en Angleterre, de 1579 à 1640* (Montpellier, 1928). There are essays by Sir E. K. Chambers (*English Pastorals*, 1895, and *Sir Thomas*

Wyatt and Some Collected Studies, 1933) and H. E. Cory (*PMLA* xxv, 1910). The poetical treatment of nature is surveyed by F. W. Moorman, *William Browne* (Strassburg, 1897), and A. von der Hcide, *Das Naturgefühl in der englischen Dichtung im Zeitalter Miltons* (Heidelberg, 1915).

The chief religious poets figure largely in the criticism cited in the next paragraph. Anthologies of religious verse listed in II above contain introductory essays. F. E. Hutchinson has a chapter in the *CHEL* vii, and F. E. Schelling an essay in his *Shakespeare and "Demi-Science"* (University of Pennsylvania, 1927). P. H. Osmond's *Mystical Poets of the English Church* (1919) is a consecutive survey, stronger on the religious than on the literary side. A good introduction to our period, which includes some of the earlier poets, is Joseph B. Collins's *Christian Mysticism in the Elizabethan Age* (Johns Hopkins, 1940). The best account of emblem books is M. Praz, *Studies in Seventeenth-Century Imagery* (1939); there is a good essay in E. N. S. Thompson, *Literary Bypaths of the Renaissance* (Yale, 1924).

Studies in Metaphysical Poetry (Columbia, 1939), by T. Spencer and M. Van Doren, contains two essays and a useful list of criticism from 1912 to 1938. The greatest critique, with all its shortcomings, is Dr. Johnson's *Cowley* (*Lives of the Poets,* 1779). Later criticism includes Grierson's introductions to his edition of Donne (1912) and his *Metaphysical Lyrics & Poems* (1921); various essays by T. S. Eliot, the leader of the return to the metaphysicals, which are mostly gathered in his *Selected Essays* (1932); K. M. Lea, 'Conceits', *MLR* xx (1925); Herbert Read, *Reason and Romanticism* (1926) and *Phases of English Poetry* (1928); E. Holmes (*supra*); J. Smith, in *Scrutiny,* ii (1933–4) and *Determinations,* ed. F. R. Leavis (1934); F. R. Leavis, in *Scrutiny,* iv (1935–6) and *Revaluation* (1936); C. Brooks, *Modern Poetry and the Tradition* (University of North Carolina, 1939). The chief larger studies are: George Williamson, *The Donne Tradition* (Harvard, 1930) (and 'Strong Lines', *English Studies,* xviii, 1936); R. C. Bald, *Donne's Influence in English Literature* (Morpeth, 1932); J. B. Leishman, *Metaphysical Poets* (1934), a good introductory volume; Joan Bennett, *Four Metaphysical Poets* (1934), which is addressed to more sophisticated readers; and Helen C. White's *Metaphysical Poets* (New York, 1936), the fullest and most philosophic study of the religious poets.

R. L. Sharp's *From Donne to Dryden: The Revolt Against*

Metaphysical Poetry (University of North Carolina, 1940) is a consecutive account of changing theory and practice. With this may be linked G. Williamson's 'Rhetorical Pattern of Neo-classical Wit' (*MP* xxxiii, 1935–6). The reputation of the meta-physical poets down through the nineteenth century has been traced by A. H. Nethercot in a series of articles (*MLN* xxxvii, 1922; *JEGP* xxiii, 1924; *PQ* iv and *SP* xxii, 1925; *MLR* xxv, 1930). The later fortunes of pre-Restoration verse in general have been followed by E. R. Wasserman (*MLN* lii, 1937; *MP* xxxvii, 1939–40) and R. C. Boys (*ELH* vii, 1940).

Of the narrative verse of our period W. M. Dixon's *English Epic and Heroic Poetry* (1912) naturally takes a broad view. Heroic theory and practice are analysed by C. M. Dowlin in his study of *Gondibert* (University of Pennsylvania, 1934), by L. F. Ball in *ELH* i (1934), and by E. M. W. Tillyard in his *Miltonic Setting* (1938). The continental background is sketched in the works of Spingarn (*infra*, IV. 9). There are studies of the heroic poem and religious inspiration by L. B. Campbell (*HLB*, 1935) and C. D. Baker (*ELH* vi, 1939).

On the poetic uses and qualities of language some general studies, of different kinds, are *Studies in English Rhymes from Surrey to Pope* (1923) and *Some Aspects of the Diction of English Poetry* (1933) by H. C. Wyld, Owen Barfield's *Poetic Diction* (1928), G. H. W. Rylands's *Words and Poetry* (1928), and F. W. Bateson's *English Poetry and the English Language* (1934). V. L. Rubel's *Poetic Diction in the English Renaissance* (New York, 1941) is a concrete study of the men whose language our poets inherited. There are suggestive essays on Shakespeare's lan-guage by G. S. Gordon (S.P.E. Tract xxix, 1928) and F. P. Wilson (*Proceedings of the British Academy*, xxvii, 1941). G. Til-lotson's *On the Poetry of Pope* (1938) has some important pages on the influence of Sylvester and Sandys.

The fullest account of metrics is Saintsbury's *History of English Prosody* (3 vols., 1906–10). Our period figures more or less in the smaller treatises and manuals, such as those of R. M. Alden (New York, 1903), Saintsbury (1910), P. F. Baum (Harvard, 1922), L. Abercrombie (1923 and 1932), William Thomson (1923), whose book is not small, J. C. Andersen (1928), E. Hamer (1930), and G. R. Stewart (New York, 1930). There are chapters by A. H. Thompson on writers of the couplet, and by Saintsbury on seventeenth-century prosody, in the *CHEL* vii and viii. The best study of the evolution of the couplet is by R. C. Wallerstein (*PMLA* l, 1935).

IV. SPECIAL LITERARY STUDIES AND LITERARY FORMS

This section comprises: (1) Language; (2) Popular literature; (3) Journalism; (4) Fiction; (5) Essays and characters; (6) Historical and biographical literature; (7) Classical and foreign relations; (8) Translations; (9) Contemporary criticism; (10) Printing and bookselling.

1. THE LANGUAGE

A. G. Kennedy has compiled *A Bibliography of Writings on the English Language* (Harvard, 1927). Some general histories are: O. Jespersen, *Growth and Structure of the English Language* (7th ed., 1933); H. C. Wyld, *History of Modern Colloquial English* (1920, 1936); G. H. McKnight, *Modern English in the Making* (New York, 1928); and A. C. Baugh, *History of the English Language* (New York, 1935).

Some special studies of the period 1600–60 are: J. L. Moore, *Tudor-Stuart Views on the Growth Status and Destiny of the English Language* (Halle, 1910); R. E. Zachrisson, *English Pronunciation at Shakespeare's Time as Taught by William Bullokar* (Upsala, 1927); H. M. Flasdieck, *Der Gedanke einer englischen Sprachakademie in Vergangenheit und Gegenwart* (Jena, 1928); Margaret Williamson, *Colloquial Language of the Commonwealth and Restoration* (1929); H. G. Fiedler, *A Contemporary of Shakespeare on Phonetics* (1936); M. Lehnert, *Die Grammatik des englischen Sprachmeisters John Wallis* (Breslau, 1936); William Matthews, *Cockney Past and Present* (1938); *Die Frühzeit der englischen Grammatik ... von Bullokar bis Wallis* (Berne, 1941), by O. Funke, who has also written *Zum Weltsprachenproblem in England im 17. Jahrhundert* (*Anglistische Forschungen*, lxix, 1929).

The great treasury for diction and usage is of course the *New English Dictionary*, ed. Sir J. A. H. Murray et al. (1884–1928; corrected reissue, 13 vols., 1933). There is a *Glossary of Tudor and Stuart Words, Especially from the Dramatists* (1914) by W. W. Skeat and A. L. Mayhew. With Sir J. A. H. Murray's *Evolution of English Lexicography* (1900) goes M. M. Mathews's *Survey of English Dictionaries* (1933). On dictionaries of the seventeenth century there are articles by D. T. Starnes (*PMLA* lii, 1937, and University of Texas *Studies in English*, 1937) and G. E. Noyes (*PMLA* liv, 1939; *SP* xxxviii, 1941).

2. POPULAR LITERATURE

This section covers London, the literature of roguery, broadside ballads, almanacs and prognostications, witchcraft, tobacco, and jestbooks.

The best bibliographies are in the *CBEL*. The *CHEL* has chapters on London and popular literature by H. V. Routh (vols. iv and vii), and one by H. G. Aldis concerning writers on country pursuits and pastimes (vol. iv). The most comprehensive survey of popular writing, in the broadest sense of the word, is Louis B. Wright's *Middle-Class Culture in Elizabethan England* (University of North Carolina, 1935), which has much on the early seventeenth century.

Stow's *Survay of London* has been edited, from the text of 1603, by C. L. Kingsford (2 vols., 1908). Some modern works are: *London Past and Present* (3 vols., 1891) by H. B. Wheatley, who contributed a chapter on the city to *Shakespeare's England* (1916); Sir W. Besant, *London in the Time of the Tudors* (1904) and *London in the Time of the Stuarts* (1903); and books entitled *Shakespeare's London* by T. F. Ordish (rev. ed., 1904) and H. T. Stephenson (New York, 1905). The most impressive work is the *London County Council Survey of London* (1900 ff.). A similar work on a smaller scale is W. Page's *Victoria History of London* (1909). N. Zwager's *Glimpses of Ben Jonson's London* (Amsterdam, 1926) gives a naturally heightened picture of urban life. Two standard books on their respective subjects are F. P. Wilson's *The Plague in Shakespeare's London* (1927) and N. G. Brett-James's *Growth of Stuart London* (1935). There are countless other books.

An excellent anthology of the literature of roguery is A. V. Judges's *The Elizabethan Underworld* (1930). The chief discussions of the subject, small and large, are the chapters in the *CHEL* iv and *Shakespeare's England*; F. W. Chandler, *The Literature of Roguery* (2 vols., Boston, 1907); F. Aydelotte, *Elizabethan Rogues and Vagabonds* (1913); and Judges's introduction.

The best guide to balladry is H. E. Rollins's *Analytical Index* of registered ballads in *SP* xxi (1924). Some of the collections are: *Political Ballads Published in England during the Commonwealth*, ed. T. Wright (Percy Society, iii, 1841); *Political Ballads of the Seventeenth and Eighteenth Centuries*, ed. W. W. Wilkins (2 vols., 1860); *Roxburghe Ballads*, ed. W. Chappell (3 vols., 1871–80) and J. W. Ebsworth (6 vols., 1881–99); *Shirburn Ballads 1585–1616*, ed. A. Clark (1907); and the long series expertly edited by H. E. Rollins—*Old English Ballads 1553–1625* (1920); *A Pepysian Garland . . . 1595–1639* (1922); *Cavalier and Puritan* (1923); *The Pack of Autolycus . . . 1624–1693* (1927); and *The Pepys Ballads* (8 vols., 1929–32). Two special anthologies are J. W. Draper's *Century of Broadside Elegies . . . of the seventeenth century* (1928) and J. Lindsay's *Loving Mad Tom. Bedlamite Verses Of the XVI and XVII Centuries* (1927).

Besides the introductions and notes in the volumes he has edited, Rollins has a monograph on the broadside in *PMLA* xxxiv (1919). Other general accounts are Sir C. Firth's chapter in *Shakespeare's England* (1916) and E. von Schaubert's long article in *Anglia*, l (1926). Firth described the ballad history of the reigns of James and Charles in *Transactions of the Royal Historical Society*, 3rd series, vols. v and vi (1911–12). With this account may be linked M. Austermann's *Die grosse englische Revolution im Spiegel der zeitgenössischen Lyrik* (Düsseldorf, 1935) and H. F. Brooks's index of 'Rump Songs' in *OBS*, vol. v, part iv, 1939 (1940).

The bibliographical history of prognostications has been written by E. F. Bosanquet, *English Printed Almanacks and Prognostications* (1917). This, with additions and corrections in the *Library*, viii (1927–8) and xviii (1937–8), comes down to 1600, and is continued in the same journal, x (1929–30). Some other discussions are: C. Camden, *Library*, xii (1931–2); F. R. Johnson, *Astronomical Thought in Renaissance England* (Johns Hopkins, 1937); F. P. Wilson, 'Some English Mock-Prognostications', *Library*, xix (1938–9); M. Nicolson, 'English Almanacs and the "New Astronomy"', *Annals of Science*, iv (1939); a chapter in D. C. Allen's *Star-Crossed Renaissance* (Duke University, 1941); and Allen's edition of *The Owles Almanacke* (Johns Hopkins, 1943).

The most learned and massive studies of witchcraft are G. L. Kittredge, *Witchcraft in Old and New England* (Harvard, 1929), and H. C. Lea and A. C. Howland, *Materials Toward a History of Witchcraft* (3 vols., University of Pennsylvania, 1939).

Some less formidable accounts, general and special, are: W. Notestein, *History of Witchcraft in England from 1558 to 1718* (Washington, 1911); sections in the *CHEL* vii and *Shakespeare's England*; several works by Montague Summers, such as *The Discovery of Witches: A Study of Master Matthew Hopkins* (1928), which includes a reprint of Hopkins's tract of 1647; C. L'Estrange Ewen, *Witch Hunting and Witch Trials* (1929); *The Trial of the Lancaster Witches*, ed. G. B. Harrison (1929); M. E. Prior, 'Joseph Glanvill, Witchcraft, and Seventeenth-Century Science', *MP* xxx (1932–3); and Charles Williams, *Witchcraft* (1941).

Among the older histories of tobacco and its literature are F. W. Fairholt's *Tobacco: Its History and Associations* (1859, 1876) and W. Bragge's bibliography, *Bibliotheca Nicotiana* (1880). The fullest recent study is R. J. Kane's manuscript thesis, *Tobacco in English Literature to 1700* (Harvard *Summaries of Theses 1929*). The most sumptuous tribute ever paid to the fragrant theme is J. E. Brooks's *Tobacco. Its History Illustrated by The Books, Manuscripts and Engravings In the Library of George Arents, Jr.*, vol. i, 1507–1615, vol. ii, 1615–1698 (New York, 1937, 1938). This work gives a facsimile of the title-page of every book described.

John Ashton's *Humour, Wit, & Satire of the Seventeenth Century* (1883) is a miscellaneous anthology of jests and ballads. Some of the jestbooks named in the text are reprinted in vols. ii, vii, ix, and xxii of the Percy Society and in W. C. Hazlitt's *Shakespeare Jest-Books* (3 vols., 1864). Thomas Brewer's *The Life and Death of the merry Devill of Edmonton* (1608) was reprinted in 1819 and is included in W. A. Abrams's edition of the play (Duke University, 1942). Fuller references are given in two scholarly studies of the genre, Ernst Schulz's *Die englischen Schwankbücher bis herab zu "Dobson's Drie Bobs" (1607)* (Berlin, 1912) and F. P. Wilson's 'English Jestbooks of the Sixteenth and Early Seventeenth Centuries', *HLQ* ii (1938–9).

3. JOURNALISM

W. P. Van Stockum has edited *The First Newspapers of England Printed in Holland 1620–1621. A Faithful Reproduction Made from the Originals* (The Hague, 1914).

A History of English Journalism to the Foundation of the Gazette (1908), by J. B. Williams (i.e. J. G. Muddiman), remains a good consecutive account, though corrected in details by later writers and in part superseded by M. A. Shaaber, *Some Forerunners of the Newspaper In England 1476–1622* (University of Pennsylvania, 1929). Some bibliographies and descriptive studies are: G. K. Fortescue's *Catalogue* of the Thomason Collection (I, *supra*); Muddiman's chapter in the *CHEL* vii; R. H. Griffith, *TLS*, 4 and 11 December, 1924; E. N. S. Thompson, 'War Journalism of the Seventeenth Century', *Literary Bypaths of the Renaissance* (Yale, 1924); R. S. Crane, F. B. Kaye, and M. E. Prior, 'Census of British Newspapers and Periodicals, 1620–1800', *SP* xxiv (1927) and separately; A. J. Gabler, 'Check List of English Newspapers and Periodicals before 1801 in the Huntington Library', *HLB* (1931); M. A. Shaaber, 'The History of the First English Newspaper', *SP* xxix (1932); W. M. Clyde, *The Struggle for the Freedom of the Press from Caxton to Cromwell* (1934); F. S. Siebert, 'Regulation of the Press in the Seventeenth Century', *Journalism Quarterly*, xiii (1936); R. T. Mitford and D. M. Sutherland, 'A Catalogue of English Newspapers and Periodicals in the Bodleian Library 1622–1800', *OBS*, vol. iv, part ii, 1935 (1936), and separately; L. Hanson, 'English Newsbooks, 1620–1641', *Library*, xviii (1937–8); F. Dahl, 'Short-Title Catalogue of English Corantos and Newsbooks 1620–1642', *Library*, xix (1938–9).

4. FICTION

The standard bibliography is Arundell Esdaile's *List of English Tales and Prose Romances Printed Before 1740* (1912). The fullest history is Ernest A. Baker's *History of the English Novel*, ii and iii (1929). J. J. Jusserand's *English Novel in the Time of Shakespeare* (1890) goes on through the seventeenth century. Some more special studies are: Charlotte E. Morgan, *Rise of the Novel of Manners* (Columbia, 1911); Henry Thomas, *Spanish and Portuguese Romances of Chivalry* (1920); T. P. Haviland, *The Roman de Longue Haleine on English Soil* (Philadelphia, 1931); C. W. Miller, 'The Influence of the French Heroico-historical Romance on Seventeenth Century English Prose Fiction' (University of Virginia *Abstracts of Dissertations 1940*). Some other books are cited below under Classical and Foreign Relations. On the place of fiction in life there is L. B. Wright's *Middle-Class Culture* (1935).

5. Essays and Characters

In addition to the bibliographies of both types in the *CBEL*, there is G. Murphy's *Bibliography of English Character-Books 1608–1700* (1925). A fuller bibliography of characters, compiled by the late C. N. Greenough, is being prepared for publication by J. M. French.

Essays and characters are included in the general anthologies cited in II above. To them may be added R. Withington's *Essays and Characters: Montaigne to Goldsmith* (New York, 1933), and the following: *Books of Characters*, ed. J. O. Halliwell [-Phillipps] (1857), which is mainly devoted to several rare works; *Character Writings of the Seventeenth Century*, ed. H. Morley (1891); *A Book of 'Characters'*, ed. R. Aldington (1924); *A Cabinet of Characters*, ed. G. Murphy (1925); *A Book of Characters*, ed. W. H. D. Rouse (1930); and H. Osborne's *Mirror of Charactery* (1933), which includes an unusual proportion of minor writers. The minor essayists have not found an anthologist.

Hugh Walker's *English Essay and Essayists* (1915) takes a broad view of our period. The most detailed and comprehensive studies are W. L. MacDonald's *Beginnings of the English Essay* (University of Toronto, 1914) and 'The Earliest English Essayists' (*Englische Studien*, lxiv, 1929), and E. N. S. Thompson's *Seventeenth-Century English Essay* (University of Iowa, 1926). There is some discussion in W. G. Crane's *Wit and Rhetoric in the Renaissance* (Columbia, 1937). H. V. Routh has a suggestive comparison of early English and French essays in *MLR* xv (1920).

Paradoxes and problems may be approached through a chapter in Thompson's monograph and through studies of Donne, such as Mrs. Simpson's article in *A Garland for John Donne*, ed. T. Spencer (1931). Some items are cited in VI below, under Cornwallis. 'The *Paradossi* of Ortensio Lando' have been described by W. G. Rice (*Essays and Studies in English*, University of Michigan, 1932), and ancient mock-encomiums by A. S. Pease in *Classical Philology*, xxi (1926).

Discussions of character-writing are given in some of the anthologies, in accounts of the essay, and in E. N. S. Thompson's *Literary Bypaths of the Renaissance* (Yale, 1924). A large history of the genre, begun by the late C. N. Greenough, is being written by B. Boyce. The influence of Theophrastus has been treated by E. C. Baldwin (*MLN* xvi, 1901; *PMLA* xviii, 1903), by G. S. Gordon in an attractive essay (*English Literature and the Classics*, ed. Gordon, 1912), and most fully by K. Lichtenberg (*Der Einfluss des Theophrast*, &c., Berlin, 1921). The relation of the character to the later periodical essay has been discussed by E. C. Baldwin (*PMLA* xix, 1904). Other items are given under the chief writers in VI below.

6. HISTORICAL AND BIOGRAPHICAL LITERATURE

This section comprises historical writing, biography, autobiographies and diaries, and letters.

White Kennett's *Complete History of England* (3 vols., 1706) includes Milton, Daniel, Habington, Sir George Buc, Bacon, Lord Herbert, Hayward, Francis Godwin, Camden, and Arthur Wilson. The *Secret History of the Court of James the First*, ed. Scott (2 vols., 1811), includes Francis Osborn, Sir Anthony Weldon, &c. Sir Thomas Wilson's interesting *State of England* (in 1600) has been edited by F. J. Fisher in the *Camden Miscellany*, xvi (1936).

The latest large account of historiography, James W. Thompson's *History of Historical Writing* (2 vols., New York, 1942), has a summary review of the Tudor and Stuart periods. There are discussions by C. Whibley and Sir A. W. Ward in the *CHEL* iii and vii, by G. N. Clark, *The Seventeenth Century* (1929), L. B. Wright, *Middle-Class Culture in Elizabethan England* (1935), and L. Strauss, *Political Philosophy of Hobbes* (1936). Among more special studies is L. F. Dean, 'Bodin's *Methodus* in England before 1625' (*SP* xxxix, 1942).

The study of Old English and of English and British antiquities grew together. Three solid works are: E. N. Adams, *Old English Scholarship in England from 1566-1800* (Yale, 1917); H. Arneke, *Kirchengeschichte und Rechtsgeschichte in England (von der Reformation bis zum frühen 18. Jahrhundert)* (Halle, 1937); and D. C. Douglas, *English Scholars* (1939), which, though focused on the period 1660-1730, has much on the earlier age. With these books may go two solid articles, J. Butt's 'Facilities for Antiquarian Study in the Seventeenth Century' (*ESEA* xxiv, 1939), and R. Tuve's 'Ancients, Moderns, and Saxons' (*ELH* vi, 1939). Some studies of one important set of traditions are: G. S. Gordon, 'The Trojans in Britain' (*ESEA* ix, 1924); R. F. Brinkley, *Arthurian Legend in the Seventeenth Century* (Johns Hopkins, 1932); and M. Schütt's article in *Britannica*, xiii (1936).

An attractive and useful anthology of biographical portraits is D. Nichol Smith's *Characters from the Histories & Memoirs of the Seventeenth Century* (1918). The standard study is D. A. Stauffer's *English Biography before 1700* (Harvard, 1930), which has a full bibliography.

There is a long list of autobiographies, diaries, and correspondence in the *CBEL*, and one must refer to that without attempting to cite scores of records no less fascinating than the few mentioned in the text. There is a bibliography of *New England Diaries 1602–1800* (Topsfield, Mass., 1923) by H. M. Forbes. Extracts are given in Arthur Ponsonby's three volumes running from the sixteenth to the twentieth century, *English Diaries* (1923), *More English Diaries* (1927), and *Scottish and Irish Diaries* (1927). J. G. Fyfe has edited *Scottish Diaries and Memoirs 1550–1746* (1928). Approaches to a general survey have been made by D. Hendrichs, *Geschichte der englischen Autobiographie von Chaucer bis Milton* (Leipzig, 1925), and J. C. Major, *The Role of Personal Memoirs in English Biography and Novel* (Philadelphia, 1935), and in Stauffer. The wealth of Puritan diaries is indicated in W. Haller's *Rise of Puritanism* (Columbia, 1938).

Some collections of letters are: Sir Henry Ellis, *Original Letters, Illustrative of English History* (11 vols., 1824–46), and *Original Letters of Eminent Literary Men of the Sixteenth, Seventeenth, and Eighteenth Centuries* (Camden Society, 1843); J. O. Halliwell[-Phillipps], *A Collection of Letters illustrative of the Progress of Science in England from the Reign of Queen Elizabeth to that of Charles the Second* (1841); S. J. Rigaud, *Correspondence of Scientific Men of the Seventeenth Century* (2 vols., 1841); two works compiled by T. Birch and edited by R. F. Williams, *The Court and Times of James the First* (2 vols., 1848), and *The Court and Times of Charles the First* (2 vols., 1848); and sections of such books as F. Bickley's *English Letter Book* (1925). Two short accounts of letter-writing are the essay in E. N. S. Thompson's *Literary Bypaths of the Renaissance* (Yale, 1924) and R. W. Ramsey's paper in *Essays by Divers Hands*, xiv (1935). The best studies of epistolary theory and formal practice are K. G. Hornbeak's *Complete Letter-Writer in English 1568–1800* (Smith

College, 1934) and Jean Robertson's *Art of Letter Writing* (1942).

7. CLASSICAL AND FOREIGN RELATIONS

F. Watson's chapter in the *CHEL* vii is a good survey of ecclesiastical, theological, Hebrew, and classical learning. Mark Pattison's *Isaac Casaubon* (2nd ed., 1892) gives intimate pictures of scholarship in England and abroad. Sir J. E. Sandys's *History of Classical Scholarship*, ii (1908) is the standard work in its field.

Neo-Latin writing is described by F. A. Wright and T. A. Sinclair, *A History of Later Latin Literature* (1931), and L. Bradner, *Musae Anglicanae: A History of Anglo-Latin Poetry 1500–1925* (New York, 1940).

The stylistic influence of Lipsius is discussed in the articles by M. W. Croll cited above in III. 2. Some references for his Stoic thought and its influence are: L. Zanta, *La Renaissance du stoïcisme au XVIe siècle* (Paris, 1914); B. Anderton, *Sketches from a Library Window* (1922); and R. Kirk's edition of Stradling's translation, *Two Bookes Of Constancie* (Rutgers, 1939). The Stoic strain in English literature of the period is outlined by P. A. Smith (*Harvard Summaries of Theses 1940*).

H. Brown's 'Classical Tradition in English Literature' (*Harvard Studies and Notes in Philology and Literature*, xviii, 1935) is a comprehensive bibliography which, with the *CBEL*, obviates the need of listing many titles here.

The general background of classical influence is furnished in the numerous volumes of the series 'Our Debt to Greece and Rome', ed. G. D. Hadzsits and D. M. Robinson (Boston, 1922 ff.). An important interpretative study of the sixteenth and seventeenth centuries in England is W. F. Schirmer's *Antike, Renaissance und Puritanismus* (rev. ed., Munich, 1933). Our period is touched at some points in *English Literature and the Classics*, ed. G. S. Gordon (1912). Of the many studies of the individual influence of ancient authors, and of classical influences upon individual English authors, a few are cited elsewhere in appropriate places.

One set of relations has been much studied, in E. S. Duckett, *Catullus in English Poetry* (Smith College, 1925), J. B. Emperor, *Catullian Influence in English Lyric Poetry, Circa 1600–1650* (University of Missouri, 1928), J. A. S. McPeek, *Catullus in Strange and Distant Britain* (Harvard, 1939), and K. A. McEuen's more comprehensive *Classical Influence upon the Tribe of Ben* (Cedar Rapids, 1939). Some other traditions are represented by: J. 'S. Harrison, *Platonism in English Poetry of the Sixteenth and Seventeenth Centuries* (Columbia, 1903); R. Shafer, *The English Ode to 1660* (Princeton, 1918), and G. N. Shuster, *The English Ode from Milton to Keats* (Columbia, 1940); T. K. Whipple, *Martial and the English Epigram From Sir Thomas Wyatt to Ben Jonson* (University of California, 1925); and D. Bush, *Mythology and the Renaissance Tradition in English Poetry* (University of Minnesota, 1932).

For continental literature and relations, in addition to material cited here and under Translations, there are the current bibliographies in *SP.*

Two general sketches of foreign influence are T. G. Tucker, *The Foreign Debt of English Literature* (1907), and L. Magnus, *English Literature in its Foreign Relations* (1927). D. Hannay's *The Later Renaissance* (1898) and Grierson's *First Half of the Seventeenth Century* (1906) deal with English as a part of European literature.

For France, the most comprehensive survey is A. H. Upham, *The French Influence in English Literature from the Accession of Elizabeth to the Restoration* (Columbia, 1908). The period is touched in Sir S. Lee's *French Renaissance in England* (1910) and in L. Charlanne's *L'Influence française en Angleterre au XVIIᵉ siècle* (Paris, 1906), which covers social and literary relations chiefly in the second half of the century. There is not much of literature proper in C. Bastide, *Anglais et français du XVIIᵉ siècle* (Paris, 1912; translated as *The Anglo-French Entente in the Seventeenth Century*, 1914), or G. Ascoli, *La Grande-Bretagne devant l'opinion française au XVIIᵉ siècle* (2 vols., Paris, 1930). A solid special work is K. Lambley's *The Teaching and Cultivation of the French Language in England during Tudor and Stuart Times* (1920). There are many studies of particular authors, such as H. Ashton, *Du Bartas en Angleterre* (Paris, 1908), and Huntington Brown, *Rabelais in English Literature* (Harvard, 1933). Some books, though not concerned with England, are of value for the student of English, such as M. Magendie's *La Politesse mondaine et les théories de l'honnêteté, en France, au XVIIᵉ siècle, de 1600 à 1660* (Paris, 1925) and *Le Roman français au XVIIᵉ siècle de l'Astrée au Grand Cyrus* (Paris, 1932), and René Bray's *La Formation de la doctrine classique en France* (Paris, 1927).

There is for the seventeenth century no such survey of Anglo-Italian relations as exists for other periods. Some items are mentioned under Translations, Travel, and individual authors such as Fairfax. There are of course many special studies, such as H. M. Priest, 'Tasso in English Literature, 1575–1675' (Northwestern University *Summaries of Dissertations*, i, 1933).

J. G. Underhill's *Spanish Literature in the England of the Tudors* (Columbia, 1899) hardly goes beyond 1600. There are pages on the period in Martin Hume's *Spanish Influence on English Literature* (1905). The fullest account is E. G. Mathews's unpublished *Studies in Anglo-Spanish Cultural and Literary Relations, 1598–1700* (Harvard *Summaries of Theses 1938*). One area is treated in Henry Thomas's *Spanish and Portuguese Romances of Chivalry* (1920) and some writings cited under Munday. Some further items are cited under Mabbe, Shelton, and others. Spanish mysticism has been elaborately studied by E. Allison Peers in three volumes (1924–7–30).

Some books facing in various directions are: G. Waterhouse, *The Literary Relations of England and Germany in the Seventeenth Century* (1914); T. de Vries, *Holland's Influence on English Language and Literature* (Chicago, 1916); E. J. Simmons, *English Literature and Culture in Russia (1553–1840)* (Harvard, 1935); and Ethel Seaton, *Literary Relations of England and Scandinavia in the Seventeenth Century* (1935).

8. TRANSLATIONS

This section covers translations from ancient and modern literature, Hebrew scholarship, the Bible, and versions of the Psalms. Many of the books cited in the preceding section are important here also.

A number of our translators are reprinted in the large series of Tudor Translations. A. F. Clements's *Tudor Translations* (1940) includes, from our period, brief excerpts from Hobbes, Heywood, Holland, Shelton, Florio, and Urquhart.

Some critical studies are: the introductions to the various works reprinted in the Tudor Translations; Whibley's chapter in the *CHEL* iv; F. R. Amos, *Early Theories of Translation* (Columbia, 1920); and F. O. Matthiessen, *Translation: An Elizabethan Art* (Harvard, 1931), which has minutely documented essays on Hoby, North, Florio, and Holland. The cultural importance of translations is shown by L. B. Wright (*supra*, IV. 2).

Bibliographical guides to translations from the ancient classics are: H. R. Palmer, *List of English Editions and Translations of Greek and Latin Classics Printed before 1641* (1911); F. M. K. Foster, *English Translations from the Greek* (Columbia, 1918); F. Seymour Smith, *The Classics in Translation* (1930); and H. Brown (*supra*, IV. 7). The· fullest critical study, which stops early in our period, is H. B. Lathrop, *Translations from the Classics into English from Caxton to Chapman, 1477–1620* (University of Wisconsin, 1933).

Translations from the French are listed and more or less discussed by A. H. Upham (*supra*, IV. 7).

For Italy the standard bibliography, which covers our period, is Mary A. Scott, *Elizabethan Translations from the Italian* (Boston, 1916).

For Spain the latest work is R. U. Pane, *English Translations From The Spanish 1484–1943: A Bibliography* (Rutgers, 1944).

Hebrew scholarship receives a short bibliography in the *CBEL* and is dealt with more or less in books on the Bible, notably that of D. Daiches cited below, and in such special works as H. Fletcher's *Milton's Semitic Studies* (University of Chicago, 1926) and *Milton's Rabbinical Readings* (University of Illinois, 1930), and in H. J. Todd's *Memoirs and Writings of . . . Brian Walton* (2 vols., 1821).

On learned and imaginative writing about the Creation materials may be found in F. E. Robbins, *The Hexaemeral Literature, a Study of the Greek and Latin Commentaries on Genesis* (University of Chicago, 1912); in articles by A. Williams in *SP* xxxiv (1937), *MP* xxxvii (1939–40), and *PMLA* lvi (1941); and in G. McColley's *Paradise Lost* (Chicago, 1940).

The standard bibliography of the English Bible is the *Historical Catalogue of the Printed Editions of Holy Scripture in the Library of the British and Foreign Bible Society*, by T. H. Darlow and H. F. Moule (2 vols., 1903–11). There are smaller bibliographies such as H. Guppy's *Catalogue of an Exhibition Illustrating the History of the Transmission of the Bible* (1935), and the full list of editions in the *BMC* and, to 1640, in the *STC*.

Editions especially useful to the literary student are Bagster's *English Hexapla Exhibiting the Six Important English Translations of the New Testament Scriptures* (1841), and the Authorized

Version in the Tudor Translations (6 vols., 1903–4), the Cambridge English Classics, ed. W. A. Wright (5 vols., 1909), and the tercentenary edition, in reduced facsimile, with illustrative documents, ed. A. W. Pollard (1911).

Pollard has edited *Records of the English Bible: The Documents Relating to the Translation and Publication of the Bible in English, 1525–1611* (1911). A valuable early account of the prices of Bibles, M. Sparke's *Scintilla* (1641), is reprinted in Arber's *Transcript*, iv, and in Darlow and Moule.

There are so many good studies, long and short, of the history and character of the English Bible that a fair number must be named: H. W. Hoare (3rd ed., 1911); B. F. Westcott (3rd ed., rev. by W. A. Wright, 1905); I. M. Price, *The Ancestry of Our English Bible* (1907; 12th ed., 1940); A. S. Cook, *CHEL* iv; chapters in G. P. Krapp (*supra*, III. 2) and F. R. Amos (*supra*, IV. 8); E. J. Goodspeed, *Making of the English New Testament* (University of Chicago, 1925); E. E. Kellett, 'The Translation of the New Testament' (*Reconsiderations*, 1928), an exception to the common eulogies of the 1611 version; J. L. Lowes's essay in his *Of Reading Books* (1930) and *Essays in Appreciation* (Boston, 1936) and in the following volume; *The English Bible*, ed. V. F. Storr (1938), containing essays by H. H. Henson, J. L. Lowes, W. M. Dixon, A. Clutton-Brock, and Sir A. Quiller-Couch; two studies by J. Isaacs, which make probably the best short account, in *The Bible in its Ancient and English Versions*, ed. H. W. Robinson (1940); and two good recent books, *The Literary Lineage of the King James Bible 1340–1611* (University of Pennsylvania, 1941), by C. C. Butterworth, and *The King James Version of the English Bible* (University of Chicago, 1941), by David Daiches.

A concrete special study is James G. Carleton, *The Part of Rheims in the Making of the English Bible* (1902). H. Pope has given a history of the Rheims New Testament in the *Library*, xx (1939–40).

No book could approach an adequate account of the influence of the English Bible. Among attempts are A. S. Cook's chapter (*supra*) and *The Bible and Its Literary Associations*, ed. M. B. Crook (New York, 1937).

John Holland's *Psalmists of Britain* (2 vols., 1843) gives accounts of versifiers, with specimens. W. T. Brooke's *Old English Psalmody . . . 1557–1660* (1916) is a good short history.

The best is P. von Rohr-Sauer's *English Metrical Psalms from 1600 to 1660* (Freiburg, 1938). The subject is sketched in Louis F. Benson, *The English Hymn* (1915) and H. W. Foote, *Three Centuries of American Hymnody* (Harvard, 1940).

9. CONTEMPORARY CRITICISM

The standard collections are: G. G. Smith, *Elizabethan Critical Essays* (2 vols., 1904); J. E. Spingarn, *Critical Essays of the Seventeenth Century* (3 vols., 1908–9); and A. H. Gilbert, *Literary Criticism: Plato to Dryden* (New York, 1940), which is especially valuable for continental writers. R. P. Cowl's *Theory of Poetry in England* (1914) is an anthology of pronouncements from critics and poets. C. Gebert's *Anthology of Elizabethan Dedications and Prefaces* (University of Pennsylvania, 1933) goes up to 1623.

Saintsbury's *History of Criticism and Literary Taste in Europe* (3 vols., 1900–4) and *History of English Criticism* (1911) display their author's usual virtues and defects. A general picture is supplied by the introductions of Smith and Spingarn and the latter's *Literary Criticism in the Renaissance* (2nd ed., Columbia, 1908) and chapter in the *CHEL* vii. More special studies are: P. Hamelius, *Die Kritik in der englischen Literatur des 17. und 18. Jahrhunderts* (Leipzig, 1897); G. M. Miller, *The Historical Point of View in English Literary Criticism from 1570–1770* (Heidelberg, 1913); Guy A. Thompson, *Elizabethan Criticism of Poetry* (Menasha, 1914); Donald L. Clark, *Rhetoric and Poetry in the Renaissance* (Columbia, 1922); H. O. White, *Plagiarism and Imitation during the English Renaissance* (Harvard, 1935); and the books by Dowlin, L. Jonas, and Sharp cited above in III. 3. Theories of the imagination inherited by our period have been discussed by M. W. Bundy (*JEGP* xxix and *SP* xxvii, 1930). Neoclassical theories are viewed in different ways by G. Williamson (*SP* xxx, 1933), D. F. Bond (*PQ* xiv, 1935 and *ELH* iv, 1937), C. D. Thorpe, *Aesthetic Theory of Thomas Hobbes* (University of Michigan, 1940), and T. G. Steffan (University of Texas *Studies in English*, xxi, 1941).

10. PRINTING AND BOOKSELLING

Many of the bibliographical works cited above in I are indispensable here. To them may be added two early items,

Jaggard's *Catalogue of English Books* (1619), ed. O. M. Willard (*Stanford Studies in Language and Literature*, 1941), and William London's *Catalogue of The most vendible Books in England* (1657–8). A standard work is A. Growoll and W. Eames, *Three Centuries of English Booktrade Bibliography* (New York, 1903).

Printing and publishing are treated by H. G. Aldis in the *CHEL* iv and xi (1909, 1914) and by R. B. McKerrow in *Shakespeare's England* (1916), and in such books as H. R. Plomer, *Short History of English Printing* (2nd ed., 1915); F. A. Mumby, *Publishing and Bookselling* (1930); *A History of The Printed Book*, ed. L. C. Wroth (*Dolphin* No. 3, New York, 1938); and especially Marjorie Plant, *The English Book Trade* (1939). J. C. Reed has an account of the most literary of publishers, Humphrey Moseley, in *OBS*, vol. ii, part ii, 1928 (1929). Many special studies are to be found in *Transactions of the Bibliographical Society* (1893 ff.) and the *Library* (Fourth Series, 1920 ff.). E. L. Klotz made a statistical analysis of books published during 1480–1640 in *HLQ* i (1937–8).

For some of the chief publishing centres outside London there are such guides as: F. Madan, *Oxford Books* (3 vols., 1895–1931); R. Bowes, *Catalogue of Books Printed at or Relating to the University, Town, or County of Cambridge* (1894); S. C. Roberts, *A History of the Cambridge University Press 1521–1921* (1921); H. G. Aldis, 'A List of Books Printed in Scotland before 1700' (*Edinburgh Bibliographical Society*, vii, 1904); and E. R. McC. Dix, *Books Printed in Dublin in the 17th Century* (4 parts, Dublin, 1898–1912).

Two valuable guides to technical bibliography are R. B. McKerrow's *Introduction to Bibliography* (2nd ed., 1928) and A. Esdaile's *Student's Manual of Bibliography* (2nd ed., 1932). With these may be put P. Simpson's *Proof-reading in the Sixteenth, Seventeenth, and Eighteenth Centuries* (1935). Among works of reference are the *Dictionary of Printers and Booksellers . . . 1557–1640* (1910) by McKerrow et al. and H. R. Plomer's *Dictionary* (1907), covering 1641–67.

Aspects of fraudulent enterprise may be seen in C. B. Judge's *Elizabethan Book-Pirates* (Harvard, 1934) and in articles in the *Library*, &c.

The relations of authors, patrons, and public are surveyed by D. Nichol Smith in *Shakespeare's England* and at length in P. Sheavyn's *The Literary Profession in the Elizabethan Age* (1909).

S. L. Clapp has studied 'The Beginnings of Subscription Publication in the Seventeenth Century' (*MP* xxix, 1931–2).

Studies of censorship have been mainly concerned with the stage and those are passed over here. Non-dramatic writings are treated in some items mentioned above in IV. 3, and in C. R. Gillett, *Burned Books* (2 vols., Columbia, 1932).

V. THE BACKGROUND OF LITERATURE

This section comprises: (1) Political history and political thought; (2) Religion and religious thought; (3) Science and scientific thought; (4) Travel; (5) Social life; (6) Education and culture; (7) Music and the arts.

1. POLITICAL HISTORY AND POLITICAL THOUGHT

The standard works of reference are Conyers Read, *Bibliography of British History, Tudor Period* (1933), and Godfrey Davies, *Bibliography of British History, Stuart Period, 1603–1714* (1928), supplemented by the briefer bibliography in Davies's *The Early Stuarts 1603–1660* (Oxford History of England, 1937) and, for 1934 ff., by A. T. Milne's annual *Writings on British History*.

A few important collections are: S. R. Gardiner, *Constitutional Documents of the Puritan Revolution 1625–1660* (1889; 3rd ed., 1906); *Clarke Papers*, ed. Firth (Camden Society, 4 vols., 1891–1901); J. R. Tanner, *Constitutional Documents of the Reign of James I* (1930); William Haller, *Tracts on Liberty in the Puritan Revolution 1638–1647* (3 vols., Columbia, 1934); M. James and M. Weinstock, *England During The Interregnum (1642–1660)* (1935); A. S. P. Woodhouse, *Puritanism and Liberty: Being the Army Debates (1647–9) from the Clarke Manuscripts with Supplementary Documents* (1938); Don M. Wolfe, *Leveller Manifestoes of the Puritan Revolution* (New York, 1944); and W. Haller and G. Davies, *The Leveller Tracts 1647–1653* (Columbia, 1944). These books have important introductions.

Three histories of Europe are the *Cambridge Modern History*, iii and iv (1904, 1906), D. Ogg's *Europe in the Seventeenth Century* (1925), and G. N. Clark's *The Seventeenth Century* (1929); this last survey of civilization assumes a knowledge of ordinary 'history'. The best one-volume histories of England are G. M. Trevelyan's *England under the Stuarts* (1904; 15th ed., 1930), and G. Davies's *Early Stuarts (supra)*, which embodies later researches. The most detailed account of public affairs is given in the several works of S. R. Gardiner: *History of England from the Accession of James I. to the Outbreak of the Civil War* (1863–82 and later edns., 10 vols.); *History of the Great Civil War* (3 vols., 1886–91; 4 vols., 1893); and *History of the Commonwealth and Protectorate* (3 vols., 1894–1901; rev. ed., 4 vols., 1903). This last was continued in Sir C. Firth's *Last Years of the Protectorate* (2 vols., 1909). The beginning of our period is included in such works as E. P. Cheyney, *History of England From the Defeat of the Armada to the Death of Elizabeth* (2 vols., 1914–26), which has a notably full 'Account of English Institutions', and J. B. Black, *The Reign of Elizabeth* (Oxford History of England, 1936). For the beginnings of a larger growth one may mention the *Cambridge History of the British Empire*; A. D. Innes, *The Maritime and Colonial Expansion of England under the Stuarts (1603–1714)* (1932); and some books cited below under Travel.

There are general histories of Scotland by P. H. Brown (3 vols., 1899–1909) and Andrew Lang (4 vols., 1900–7), and shorter ones by R. S. Rait (1911), C. S. Terry (1920), P. H. Brown (1924), and others. An attractive book is John Buchan's *Montrose* (1928). P. H. Brown edited two collections, *Early Travellers in Scotland* (1891) and *Scotland Before 1700 from Contemporary Documents* (1893).

A recent history of Ireland is that of E. Curtis (1936; rev. ed., 1937). A full special work is Richard Bagwell, *Ireland under the Stuarts and during the Interregnum* (3 vols., 1909–16).

In the economic and social history of England two books of special interest to the literary student are L. C. Knights, *Drama & Society in the Age of Jonson* (1937), and Margaret James, *Social Problems and Policy During the Puritan Revolution 1640–1660* (1930). Since these books cite standard economic authorities, only very few can be mentioned here: W. Cunningham, *Growth of English Industry and Commerce* (6th ed., 3 vols., 1915–19); Lord Ernle, *English Farming Past and Present* (1912; last ed., 1936); R. H. Tawney, *The Agrarian Problem in the Sixteenth Century* (1912), which goes well into the seventeenth century, and *Religion and the Rise of Capitalism* (1926); chapters in G. N. Clark (*supra*); J. Viner, 'English Theories of Foreign Trade before Adam Smith' (*Journal of Political Economy*, xxxviii, 1930; *Studies in the Theory of International Trade*, 1937); E. Lipson, *Economic History of England. The Age of Mercantilism* (vols. ii and iii, rev. ed., 1943);

E. F. Heckscher, *Mercantilism* (2 vols., trans. 1935); J. U. Nef, *Industry and Government in France and England, 1540–1640* (Philadelphia, 1940); P. W. Buck, *The Politics of Mercantilism* (New York, 1942); and Mildred Campbell, *The English Yeoman Under Elizabeth and the Early Stuarts* (Yale, 1942).

There is a *Bibliography of English Law* by W. H. and L. F. Maxwell (3 vols., 1925–33, with supplements). F. J. C. Hearnshaw has a chapter on early legal literature in the *CHEL* viii. Sir W. S. Holdsworth has written the fullest *History of English Law* (vols. iv–vi, 1924), *Sources and Literature of English Law* (1925), and *Some Makers of English Law* (1938). The best study of legal and ecclesiastical antiquarianism and historiography is by H. Arneke (*supra*, IV. 6). G. Smith has discussed 'The Reform of the Laws of England, 1640–1660' (*University of Toronto Quarterly*, x, 1941).

In the field of constitutional history some general works are: a *Bibliography* by H. M. Cam and A. S. Turberville (Historical Association Leaflet lxxv, 1929); D. J. Medley, *Student's Manual of English Constitutional History* (1894; 6th ed., 1925); the constitutional histories of England by F. W. Maitland (1908), D. L. Keir (1938), and Mark A. Thomson (1938); Holdsworth's *History of English Law*; and many biographies. In addition to the general histories named above, some histories and interpretations of the political and constitutional struggle are: F. C. Montague, *History of England . . . 1603–1660* (1907); J. Mackinnon, *History of Modern Liberty*, vols. iii and iv (1908–41); K. Feiling, *History of the Tory Party 1640–1714* (1924) and *England under the Tudors and Stuarts* (Home University Library, 1927); J. R. Tanner, *English Constitutional Conflicts of the Seventeenth Century 1603–1689* (1928); J. D. Mackie, *Cavalier and Puritan* (rev. ed., 1936); Sir J. A. R. Marriott, *The Crisis of English Liberty* (1930); I. Deane Jones, *The English Revolution . . . 1603–1714* (1931); and F. D. Wormuth, *The Royal Prerogative 1603–1649* (Cornell, 1939).

Political thought comes more or less into these books and is the main subject of many others. Perhaps the best general survey is G. H. Sabine's *History of Political Theory* (New York, 1937), which has on our period the chapters of a specialist. Some other general works are those of Otto von Gierke; W. A. Dunning, *History of Political Theories from Luther to Montesquieu* (1902; repr. 1938); and J. W. Gough, *The Social Contract* (1936).

Of the books more fully focused on our period some are: G. P. Gooch, *Political Thought in England from Bacon to Halifax* (Home University Library, 1915) and *English Democratic Ideas in the Seventeenth Century* (rev. by H. J. Laski, 1927); *The High Court of Parliament and Its Supremacy* (Yale, 1910), the introduction to *Political Works of James I* (Harvard, 1918), and other writings of C. H. McIlwain; J. N. Figgis, *The Divine Right of Kings* (rev. ed., 1922); *Social & Political Ideas of Some Great Thinkers of the Sixteenth and Seventeenth Centuries*, ed. F. J. C. Hearnshaw (1926), and the companion volumes for the Renaissance and Reformation (1925) and the Augustan age (1928); Yung Chi Hoe, *The Origin of Parliamentary Sovereignty or 'Mixed' Monarchy* (Shanghai, 1935); J. W. Allen, *English Political Thought 1603–1660. Vol. I, 1603–44* (1938); and Z. S. Fink, *The Classical Republicans: An Essay in the Recovery of a Pattern of Thought in Seventeenth Century England* (Northwestern University, 1945).

Many of the books already cited, such as J. W. Allen's, have to do with ecclesiastical and religious problems, and more will be named in the next section. H. M. Gwatkin's *Church and State in England to the Death of Queen Anne* (1917) is a good general survey. Important recent discussions are Haller's introduction to his *Tracts on Liberty*, and his *Rise of Puritanism* (Columbia, 1938); Don M. Wolfe's *Milton in the Puritan Revolution* (1941); and especially the books by Woodhouse and Barker cited below (V. 2) among studies of Puritanism.

T. C. Pease's *The Leveller Movement* (Washington, 1916) is a standard work. Some more or less leftist books are: E. Bernstein, *Cromwell & Communism* (trans. 1930); H. Holorenshaw, *The Levellers and the English Revolution* (1939); C. Hill, M. James, and E. Rickword, *The English Revolution 1640* (1940); and some books cited in VI under Winstanley.

2. RELIGION AND RELIGIOUS THOUGHT

This section covers Roman Catholicism; the Church of England; Puritanism and the sects; toleration; Latitudinarianism and Cambridge Platonism; preaching; devotional literature and mysticism. Since religion is inseparable from politics, many books cited in the preceding section are relevant here.

Hastings's *Encyclopaedia of Religion and Ethics* (13 vols., 1908–27) is an invaluable work of reference.

To J. P. Whitney's *Bibliography of Church History* (Historical

Association Leaflet lv, 1923) may be added the bibliographies in many of the books and articles named below. Much material is to be found in the files of such journals as *Church History*.

H. Bettenson's *Documents of the Christian Church* (World's Classics, 1943) contains Anglican and Nonconformist documents.

For Roman Catholicism there are the general histories of England and general studies of politics and religion. Among special books are: Joseph Gillow, *Bibliographical Dictionary of the English Catholics* (5 vols., 1885–1902); D. Mathew, *Catholicism in England 1535–1935* (1936); Brian Magee, *The English Recusants* (1938); and some publications of the Catholic Record Society. A bibliographical survey of European scope is R. M. Huber's 'Recent Important Literature Regarding the Catholic Church During the Late Renaissance Period, 1500–1648', *Church History*, x (1941).

For the Church of England, some collections are: R. Cattermole, *Literature of the Church of England* (2 vols., 1844), in which our men are well represented; H. Gee and W. J. Hardy, *Documents Illustrative of English Church History* (1896); and the large but not wholly satisfactory body of extracts in P. E. More and F. L. Cross, *Anglicanism: The Thought and Practice of the Church of England, Illustrated from the Religious Literature of the Seventeenth Century* (Milwaukee, 1935).

Fuller's *Church-History of Britain* (1655) is of course a first-hand authority on our period. Two histories are *The English Church in the Reigns of Elizabeth and James I* (1904) by W. H. Frere, and the sequel, *The English Church from the Accession of Charles I to the Death of Anne* (1903), by W. H. Hutton, who has a chapter on the Caroline divines in *CHEL* vii. Smaller books are C. S. Carter, *The English Church in the Seventeenth Century* (1909), and A. Plummer, *English Church History from the Death of Archbishop Parker to the Death of King Charles I* (2nd ed., 1914). Some large and special works are: F. Makower, *Constitutional History and Constitution of the Church of England* (trans. 1895); J. Stoughton, *History of Religion in England, from the Opening of the Long Parliament to 1850* (rev. ed., 8 vols., 1901); R. G. Usher, *The Reconstruction of the English Church* (2 vols., 1910), an important study of the early Jacobean age; and two accounts of the Church in the Puritan period, W. A. Shaw's *History of the English Church . . . 1640–1660* (2 vols., 1900), and G. B. Tatham's *The Puritans in Power* (1913).

Some studies of religious thought are: John Hunt, *Religious Thought in England*, i (1870); John Dowden, *Outlines of the History of the Theological Literature of the Church of England* (1897); H. H. Henson, *Studies in English Religion in the Seventeenth Century* (1903); C. S. Carter, *The Anglican Via Media* (1927); A. W. Harrison, *Arminianism* (1937); some essays in *Masters in English Theology*, ed. A. Barry (1877), and *Typical English Churchmen*, ed. W. E. Collins (1902); and a number of books mentioned below. Of a more literary cast are E. Dowden's *Puritan and Anglican* (1900) and the essay on literary churchmen in H. C. Beeching's *Religio Laici* (1902). *Liturgy and Worship*, ed. W. K. L. Clarke and C. Harris (1932) includes 'The History of the Book of Common Prayer down to 1662'. G. W. O. Addleshaw's *High Church Tradition* (1941) is strictly liturgical.

The Puritans, ed. Perry Miller and T. H. Johnson (New York, 1938) is a large, fresh, and varied anthology of Puritan writing, hardly less valuable for England than for New England.

Of the older works on Puritanism the largest and most influential has been Daniel Neal's *History of the Puritans* (4 vols., 1732–8; later enlarged edns., e.g., 3 vols., 1837). Some representative modern works are: Douglas Campbell, *The Puritan in Holland, England, and America* (2 vols., New York, 1892; rev. 1902); H. M. and M. Dexter, *The England and Holland of the Pilgrims* (Boston, 1905), with an index of Separatist publications; Henry W. Clark, *History of English Nonconformity* (2 vols., 1911–13); C. Burrage, *The Early English Dissenters . . . (1550–1641)* (2 vols., 1912). Some smaller books are: James Heron, *Short History of Puritanism* (1908), John Brown, *The English Puritans* (Cambridge Manuals, 1910), and H. H. Henson, *Puritanism in England* (1912). The best historical introduction to our period is M. M. Knappen, *Tudor Puritanism* (University of Chicago, 1939). The best account of Puritan writing in the period is W. Haller, *The Rise of Puritanism* (Columbia, 1938). The most solid and discriminating analyses of the attitudes of various parties and persons are in A. S. P. Woodhouse's *Puritanism and Liberty* (1938) and Arthur Barker's *Milton and the Puritan Dilemma* (University of Toronto, 1942). Two fresh books, with institutional and intellectual emphasis respectively, Perry Miller's *Orthodoxy in Massachusetts 1630–1650* (Harvard, 1933) and *The New England Mind: The Seventeenth Century* (New York, 1939), are important for England as well as New England.

Two corrective doctrinal studies are Herbert D. Foster's 'Liberal Calvinism', on the Synod of Dort (*Harvard Theological Review*, xvi, 1923; *Collected Papers*, priv. pr., 1929), and P. Miller's 'The Marrow of Puritan Divinity' (*Publications of The Colonial Society of Massachusetts*, xxxii, 1937).

The character and origins of the sects are treated in some books already named and in the books by R. M. Jones and Robert Barclay cited near the end of this section. There are accounts in vols. ii and iii of Masson's *Milton* and in C. E. Whiting's *Studies in English Puritanism . . . 1660–1688* (1931). W. B. Selbie's *Nonconformity* (Home University Library, 1912) is a brief and broad survey. There are many histories of the chief sects and biographies of leaders. Histories of Presbyterianism range from Heylyn's *Aerius Redivivus* (1670) to A. H. Drysdale (1889); a recent special study is S. W. Carruthers, *Everyday Work of the Westminster Assembly* (1943). A few bibliographical and historical works are: Joseph Smith, *Descriptive Catalogue of Friends' Books* (2 vols., 1867), W. C. Braithwaite, *Beginnings of Quakerism* (1912), and L. M. Wright, *Literary Life of the Early Friends 1650–1725* (Columbia, 1932); B. Hanbury, *Historical Memorials relating to the Independents* (3 vols., 1839–44); H. M. Dexter, *Congregationalism of the Last Three Hundred Years, As Seen In Its Literature* (New York, 1880); W. T. Whitley, *Baptist Bibliography* (2 vols., 1916–22), and Louise Brown, *Political Activities of the Baptists and Fifth Monarchy Men in England during the Interregnum* (Washington, 1912).

An early work on Scottish religious history was the *History of the Church of Scotland*, published in abridged form in 1678, by David Calderwood (1575–1650). Two recent books are G. D. Henderson, *Religious Life in Seventeenth-Century Scotland* (1937), and Duncan Anderson, *The Bible in Seventeenth-Century Scottish Life and Literature* (1936).

Many of the chief documents in the controversy on toleration are collected and discussed in Haller's *Tracts on Liberty* (3 vols., Columbia, 1934) and Woodhouse's *Puritanism and Liberty* (1938). The fullest history, which takes in almost everyone who wrote at all, is Wilbur K. Jordan's *Development of Religious Toleration in England* (4 vols., 1932–40); vols. ii–iv cover 1603–60. Two shorter books are Michael Freund, *Die Idee der Toleranz im England der grossen Revolution* (Halle, 1927), and T. Lyon, *Theory of Religious Liberty in England 1603–39* (1937).

The fullest study of the religious outlook of Falkland and his circle is in John Tulloch, *Rational Theology and Christian Philosophy in England in the Seventeenth Century* (2 vols., 1872; rev. ed., 1874). Among shorter accounts are those in the *Cambridge Modern History*, v; E. A. George, *Seventeenth Century Men of Latitude* (New York, 1908); K. B. Murdock's long essay, with a bibliography, in *The Sun at Noon* (New York, 1939); and items mentioned in VI under Falkland, Hales, and Chillingworth.

E. T. Campagnac's anthology, *The Cambridge Platonists* (1901), has selections from Whichcote, Smith, and Culverwel. The fullest study of the group is Tulloch's second volume. They are included in the 'shorter accounts' (except Murdock) noticed just above, and in Mullinger's *University of Cambridge*, iii (1911), W. R. Sorley's *History of English Philosophy* (1920), and W. R. Inge's sketch, *The Platonic Tradition in English Religious Thought* (1926). F. J. Powicke's *Cambridge Platonists* (1926) is a semi-popular introduction, G. P. H. Pawson's *Cambridge Platonists* (1930) is a compact summary of religious ideas, and W. C. de Pauley's *Candle of the Lord* (1937) has a theological emphasis. A distinctive work is E. Cassirer, *Die platonische Renaissance in England und die Schule von Cambridge* (Leipzig, 1932). There are special studies by S. P. Lamprecht, on innate ideas (*Philosophical Review*, xxxv, 1926); M. Nicolson, 'Christ's College and the Latitude-Men' (*MP* xxvii, 1929–30); J. J. De Boer, *The Theory of Knowledge of the Cambridge Platonists* (Madras, 1931); E. M. Austin, *Ethics of the Cambridge Platonists* (Philadelphia, 1935). Affinities between More and Cudworth and the romantic age are shown by J. W. Beach, *The Concept of Nature in Nineteenth-Century English Poetry* (New York, 1936).

There are many sermons in Cattermole and specimens of Donne, Hales, Adams, and Taylor in H. H. Henson, *Selected English Sermons* (World's Classics). C. F. Richardson's *English Preachers and Preaching 1640-70* (1928) deals chiefly with the character and background of the clergy. Our preachers receive chapters in the *CHEL* iv, vii, and viii, and some pages in Charles Smyth's *Art of Preaching* (1940). The fullest and best critical study is W. Fraser Mitchell, *English Pulpit Oratory from Andrewes to Tillotson* (1932). If Mitchell is somewhat inadequate on Puritans, the deficiency is made good in John Brown's *Puritan Preaching in England* (1900) and especially in Haller's *Rise of Puritanism* (1938) and Miller's *New England Mind* (1939).

Among articles are two on political sermons by E. W. Kirby (*American Historical Review*, xliv, 1938–9) and G. Davies (*HLQ* iii, 1939–40), and one by R. F. Jones on the Restoration attack on pulpit eloquence (*JEGP* xxx, 1931).

On the character of mysticism the most familiar books are those of Evelyn Underhill and W. R. Inge. Some other general studies are: C. F. Spurgeon, *Mysticism in English Literature* (Cambridge Manuals, 1913); an essay by A. H. Thompson, *ESEA* viii (1922); G. F. Hodgson, *English Mystics* (1922); C. A. Bennett, *Philosophical Study of Mysticism* (1923); Dom David Knowles, *The English Mystics* (1927); and M. A. Ewer, *Survey of Mystical Symbolism* (1933). Some studies focused on our period are: Robert Barclay, *The Inner Life of the Religious Societies of the Commonwealth* (1876); Rufus M. Jones, *Spiritual Reformers in the 16th and 17th Centuries* (1914) and *Mysticism and Democracy in the English Commonwealth* (Harvard, 1932); E. N. S. Thompson, 'Mysticism in Seventeenth-Century Literature', *SP* xviii (1921); Helen C. White, *English Devotional Literature (Prose), 1600–1640* (University of Wisconsin, 1931); Joseph B. Collins (*supra*, III. 3); H. F. Thoma's unpublished thesis, *The Hermetic Strain in Seventeenth Century English Mysticism* (Harvard, 1941); and numerous studies cited under individual writers in VI below.

The best studies of Boehme and his influence are part of Jones's *Spiritual Reformers* and W. Struck, *Der Einfluss Jakob Boehmes auf die englische Literatur des 17. Jahrhunderts* (Berlin, 1936). Convenient lists of the translations of Boehme are in the *BMC* and *CBEL* ii.

3. SCIENCE AND SCIENTIFIC THOUGHT

This section comprises general histories of science and of several sciences; alchemy and astrology; origins of the Royal Society; general and special works on scientific thought and philosophy; the influence of Descartes; Jacobean melancholy.

In addition to the brief list which follows, references are supplied in many of the books and articles cited, in a critical survey of the literature of Renaissance science by F. R. Johnson and S. V. Larkey (*MLQ* ii, 1941), and in the current bibliographies in *Isis* (1913 ff.).

Collections of scientific correspondence were mentioned above in IV. 6.

Broad outlines are given in such books as W. T. Sedgwick and H. W. Tyler, *Short History of Science* (rev. ed., 1939), H. T. Pledge, *Science since 1500* (1939), and Charles Singer, *Short History of Science* (1941). Brief surveys of science (and pseudo-science) in our period are given in Traill's *Social England*, iv, in *Shakespeare's England*, in the *CHEL* viii, and in the *Cambridge Modern History*, v. The most comprehensive work is A. Wolf, *History of Science, Technology, and Philosophy in the 16th and 17th Centuries* (1935). A full though more special work is R. K. Merton's *Science, Technology and Society in Seventeenth Century England* (*Osiris*, iv, 1938). Much varied material is furnished in the numerous volumes of R. T. Gunther's *Early Science in Oxford* (1920 ff.) and in his *Early Science in Cambridge* (1937). Important articles are W. E. Houghton's 'History of Trades' (*JHI* ii, 1941) and E. Zilsel's 'Genesis of the Concept of Physical Law' (*Philosophical Review*, li, 1942).

There are short histories of chemistry by J. M. Stillman (New York, 1924), I. Masson (1925), and J. R. Partington (1937); of physics by F. Cajori (rev. ed., 1929). Less formidable than K. Lasswitz's *Geschichte der Atomistik vom Mittelalter bis Newton* (2 vols., Hamburg, 1890) is J. C. Gregory's *Short History of Atomism from Democritus to Bohr* (1931). Atomism in our period has been studied by G. B. Stones (*Isis*, x, 1928), C. T. Harrison (*Harvard Studies and Notes in Philology and Literature*, xv, 1933, and *Harvard Studies in Classical Philology*, xlv, 1934), and J. R. Partington (*Annals of Science*, iv, 1939).

Mathematical history has fared well in such general works as those of F. Cajori (1894; rev. ed., 1919) and David E. Smith (2 vols., Boston, 1923–5), and such special books as E. W. Hobson, *John Napier and the Invention of Logarithms* (1914), the *Napier Tercentenary Memorial Volume*, ed. C. G. Knott (1915), F. Cajori, *William Oughtred* (1916), and J. F. Scott, *Mathematical Work of John Wallis* (1938).

A Source Book in Astronomy, ed. H. Shapley and H. E. Howarth (1929) has selections from Copernicus, Brahe, Kepler, Galileo, and others. Some books on astronomy are: J. L. E. Dreyer, *History of the Planetary Systems from Thales to Kepler* (1906); Dorothy Stimson, *The Gradual Acceptance of the Copernican Theory of the Universe* (New York, 1917); K. B. Collier, *Cosmogonies of our Fathers* (Columbia, 1934); and especially Francis R. Johnson, *Astronomical Thought in Renaissance England* (Johns Hopkins, 1937). G. McColley has a long series of articles, such as 'The Seventeenth-Century Doctrine of a Plurality of Worlds' (*Annals of Science*, i, 1936), and others cited in VI under John Wilkins. Some of Marjorie Nicolson's studies are: 'The Telescope and Imagination' (*MP* xxxii, 1934–5), 'The "New Astronomy" and English Literary Imagination' (*SP* xxxii, 1935), *The Microscope and English Imagination* and *A World in the Moon* (Smith College, 1935, 1936), and 'Cosmic Voyages' (*ELH* vii, 1940).

Two of the best general histories of biology are by W. C. Locy (New York, 1925) and C. Singer (1931). There is a good account of the Tradescants and their museum of natural history, the first in England, in R. T. Gunther, *Early Science in Oxford*, iii (1925).

Among the many histories of medicine are those of A. H. Buck (1917), F. H. Garrison (4th ed., 1929), Sir W. Osler (1921), C. G. Cumston (1926), C. Singer (1928) and Singer's *Evolution of Anatomy* (1925), and A. Castiglioni (trans. 1941). Two more special books are Sir Michael Foster, *Lectures on the History of Physiology during the Sixteenth, Seventeenth and Eighteenth Centuries* (1901, 1924), and Sir Norman Moore, *History of the Study of Medicine in the British Isles* (1908). Some other special works are cited in VI under Harvey. An important monograph by W. Pagel is 'Religious Motives in the Medical Biology of the XVIIth Century' (*Bulletin of the Institute of the History of Medicine*, iii, 1935).

A. E. Waite has done a number of books on alchemy and related matters. Lynn Thorndike's *History of Magic and Experimental Science* covers the sixteenth century in vols. v and vi (1941). For alchemy in particular there are a bibliography by G. Heym (*Ambix*, i, 1937–8) and John Read's *Prelude to Chemistry* (New York, 1937). A recent and authoritative study of astrology is Don C. Allen's *Star-Crossed Renaissance* (Duke University, 1941), which covers the Jacobean age.

Scientific societies in general have been described by M. Ornstein, *The Rôle of Scientific Societies in the Seventeenth Century* (New York, 1913; University of Chicago, 1928), and Harcourt Brown, *Scientific Organizations in Seventeenth Century France* (Baltimore, 1934). Histories of the Royal Society began with Sprat's famous book (1667). The early stages of the Society's growth are dealt with in C. R. Weld's *History* (2 vols., 1848), I. Masson, *Three Centuries of Chemistry* (1925), the *Record of the Royal Society of London* (4th ed., 1940), Sir Henry Lyons, *The Royal Society 1660–1940* (1944), and such important special discussions as: Robert F. Young, *Comenius in England* (1932); D. Stimson, 'Dr. Wilkins and the Royal Society' (*Journal of Modern History*, iii, 1931), 'Comenius and the Invisible College' (*Isis*, xxiii, 1935), 'Puritanism and the New Philosophy in 17th Century England' (*Bulletin of the Institute of the History of Medicine*, iii, 1935), and 'Amateurs of Science in 17th Century England' (*Isis*, xxxi, 1939); F. R. Johnson, 'Gresham College: Precursor of the Royal Society' (*JHI* i, 1940); J. B. Conant, 'The Advancement of Learning during the Puritan Commonwealth' (*Proceedings of the Massachusetts Historical Society*, lxvi, 1942); and W. E. Houghton, 'The English Virtuoso in the Seventeenth Century' (*JHI* iii, 1942), a study of broad scope.

Among historical surveys and philosophic analyses, with more or less on scientific thought, are such books as: A. N. Whitehead, *Science and the Modern World* (1925); J. H. Randall, *Making of the Modern Mind* (rev. ed., Boston, 1940); E. A. Burtt, *Metaphysical Foundations of Modern Physical Science* (1925); G. N. Clark, *The Seventeenth Century* (1929); A. Lalande, *Les Théories de l'induction et de l'expérimentation* (Paris, 1929); Preserved Smith, *History of Modern Culture. I. The Great Renewal 1543–1687* (New York, 1930); B. Willey, *The Seventeenth Century Background* (1934), for the literary student the most suggestive introductory work; Richard F. Jones, *Ancients and Moderns* (Washington University, 1936), the fullest study of Baconian influence; A. O. Lovejoy, *The Great Chain of Being* (Harvard, 1936), a major achievement in the history of ideas; E. W. Strong, *Procedures and Metaphysics* (University of California, 1936), in part a reply to Burtt; M. Taube, *Causation, Freedom and Determinism* (1936); and Michael Roberts, *The Modern Mind* (1937). Theodore Spencer's *Shakespeare and the Nature of Man* (New York, 1942) and E. M. W. Tillyard's *Elizabethan World Picture* (1943) give lucid outlines of the Renaissance ideas of religious, ethical, social, and cosmic order inherited by the seventeenth century.

Andrew D. White's *History of the Warfare of Science with*

Theology (2 vols., 1896, and later edns.) is the standard work in its field and is also a valuable analysis of scientific thought. A similar double purpose is attained, on a smaller scale, by Sir W. Dampier(-Whetham) in his *History of Science and its Relations with Philosophy and Religion* (1929; 3rd ed., 1942). C. Singer has a brief survey, *Religion & Science Considered in their Historical Relations* (1929). We may include here F. A. Lange's *History of Materialism* (trans., 3 vols., 1877–81; 3rd ed., 1925).

P. O. Kristeller and J. H. Randall have a critical survey of modern studies of Renaissance philosophy in the *JHI* ii (1941). There is more or less on English thought in such formal histories of modern or seventeenth-century philosophy as H. Höffding (trans. Meyer, i, 1900), G. Sortais (2 vols., Paris, 1920–2), and E. Bréhier (Paris, 1929). There are histories of English philosophy by Charles de Rémusat (2 vols., Paris, 1875), who goes from Bacon to Locke, and by James Seth (1912) and W. R. Sorley (1920); this last is based on chapters in the *CHEL*.

Some studies of Cartesianism in England are the articles by M. Nicolson (*SP* xxvi, 1929), S. P. Lamprecht (*Studies in the History of Ideas*, iii, Columbia, 1935), and J. Laird (*Revue philosophique*, cxxiii, 1937), and parts of A. J. Snow's *Matter & Gravity in Newton's Physical Philosophy* (1926). Other items appear under Henry More and Cudworth.

A few special items on melancholy may be added here: G. B. Harrison, in his edition of Breton's *Melancholike humours* (1929); Sir E. K. Chambers, 'The Disenchantment of the Elizabethans', *Sir Thomas Wyatt and Some Collected Studies* (1933); L. C. Knights, *Criterion*, xiii (1933–4) and *Drama & Society in the Age of Jonson* (1937); G. Williamson, 'Mutability, Decay, and Seventeenth-Century Melancholy', *ELH* ii (1935); R. F. Jones, 'The Decay of Nature', *Ancients and Moderns* (1936); articles by D. C. Allen and K. Koller, *SP* xxxv (1938), and L. Babb, *HLQ* iv (1940–1); many studies of Shakespeare's problem plays and malcontents, e.g., those of O. J. Campbell; and the volumes by Spencer and Tillyard cited in a preceding paragraph.

4. TRAVEL

This section covers general bibliographies, collections, and histories; England; Europe and the east; America.

The fullest bibliography is E. G. Cox, *Reference Guide to the*

Literature of Travel: *1, The Old World, 2, The New World*
(University of Washington, 1935–8). There are extensive
bibliographies in E. G. R. Taylor (*infra*).

Purchas appears in VI below. Early modern collections
which remain valuable are those of A. and John Churchill (4
vols., 1704; v and vi, 1732; 6 vols., 1744–6; vii and viii by
Thomas Osborne, 1745, repr. 1747); John Harris (2 vols.,
1705; 2nd ed., 1744–8); and John Pinkerton (17 vols., 1808–14).
The records of many travellers and voyagers to east and west
have been edited separately for the Hakluyt Society, for the
Argonaut Press series, ed. N. M. Penzer (1925 ff.), and for the
Broadway Travellers series, ed. Sir D. Ross and E. Power
(1926 ff.).

Two books of large scope are J. N. L. Baker, *History of
Geographical Discovery and Exploration* (1931), and E. Heawood,
*History of Geographical Discovery in the Seventeenth and Eighteenth
Centuries* (1912). Much the best book for our period is E. G. R.
Taylor, *Late Tudor and Early Stuart Geography 1583–1650* (1934),
with a full bibliography. Among short surveys are the chapters
in Traill's *Social England*, iv; the *Cambridge Modern History*, iv;
the *CHEL* iv; *Shakespeare's England*; and the *Cambridge History
of the British Empire*.

Travel in England in the Seventeenth Century (1925), by Joan
Parkes, is a standard and attractive book. More special works
are: *An Historical Geography of England before A.D. 1800*, ed.
H. C. Darby (1936); G. E. Fussell, *Exploration of England* (1935),
a bibliography of travel and topography, 1570–1815, enlarged
from an article in the *Library*, xiii (1932–3); and Sir H. G.
Fordham's accounts of road-books (1924) and surveyors and
map-makers (1929).

Two general books on foreign travel are E. S. Bates, *Touring
in 1600* (Boston, 1911), and Clare Howard, *English Travellers of
the Renaissance* (1914). B. Penrose's *Urbane Travellers 1591–1635*
(University of Pennsylvania, 1942) has full sketches of Moryson,
Coryate, Sandys, and others. Travellers figure in some of the
books already cited on foreign relations.

The fullest account of eastern things and travellers is S. C.
Chew, *The Crescent and the Rose* (New York, 1937). Sir William
Foster has done work of special authority, such as *Letters
Received by the East India Company From its Servants in the East*,
which covers 1602–17 (with F. C. Danvers, 6 vols., 1896–1902);

The English Factories in India (1906 ff.); *Early Travels in India 1583–1619* (1921), a collection which includes Coryate; *England's Quest of Eastern Trade* (1933); and editions of individual narratives. Among less detailed and more popular books are E. F. Oaten, *European Travellers in India* (1909), and F. R. Dulles, *Eastward Ho!* (1931). Of special interest to literary students is W. G. Rice's 'Early English Travellers to Greece and the Levant' (*University of Michigan Publications*, x, 1933).

For America the fullest bibliography is Cox's second volume. A short survey, up to 1638, is G. W. Cole's 'Elizabethan Americana', in *Bibliographical Essays: A Tribute to Wilberforce Eames* (Harvard, 1924).

Some collections are: *Tracts*, ed. Peter Force (4 vols., Washington, 1836–46); *The Genesis of the United States*, ed. Alexander Brown (2 vols., Boston, 1890); Original Narratives of Early American History, ed. J. F. Jameson, a series which includes volumes like L. G. Tyler's *Narratives of Early Virginia 1606–1625* (New York, 1907); *Chronicles of the Pilgrim Fathers*, ed. J. Masefield (Everyman, 1910); *Forerunners and Competitors of the Pilgrims and Puritans*, ed. C. H. Levermore (2 vols., New York, 1912); *Colonising Expeditions to the West Indies and Guiana, 1623–1667*, ed. V. T. Harlow (1925).

There are books on the quest of the western ocean by P. F. Alexander (1915), N. M. Crouse (New York, 1928), and L. J. Burpee (rev. ed., 2 vols., Toronto, 1935). J. B. Brebner has written *The Explorers of North America 1492–1806* (1933). Some books on early voyages and settlements are: Justin Winsor, *Narrative and Critical History of America*, iii (Boston, 1884); L. G. Tyler, *England in America 1580–1652* (1904; vol. iv of *The American Nation*, ed. A. B. Hart); C. M. Gayley, *Shakespeare and the Founders of Liberty in America* (New York, 1917); V. L. Parrington, *The Colonial Mind* (New York, 1927); S. E. Morison, *Builders of the Bay Colony* (Boston, 1930); C. M. Andrews, *Colonial Period of American History*, i–ii (Yale, 1934–6); and M. P. Andrews, *The Soul of a Nation: The Founding of Virginia and the Projection of New England* (New York, 1943). N. M. Crouse analysed 'Causes of the Great Migration 1630–1640' (*New England Quarterly*, v, 1932). Two recent studies are Louis B. Wright's *Religion and Empire: The Alliance between Piety and Commerce in English Expansion 1558–1625* (University of North Carolina, 1943) and F. Mood's more special 'English Geographers

and the Anglo-American Frontier in the Seventeenth Century'
(*University of California Publications in Geography*, vi, no. 9, 1944).
The literary fruits of travel have been studied by R. R.
Cawley in numerous articles and in *The Voyagers and Elizabethan
Drama* (1938) and *Unpathed Waters: Studies in the Influence of the
Voyagers on Elizabethan Literature* (Princeton, 1940). J. E. Gilles-
pie embraces social life and literature in *The Influence of Oversea
Expansion on England to 1700* (Columbia, 1920). As usual,
L. B. Wright's *Middle-Class Culture in Elizabethan England*
(1935) must be mentioned. R. W. Frantz's *English Traveller and
the Movement of Ideas* (*University of Nebraska Studies*, 1932–3),
though concerned with the period 1660–1732, has suggestions
for the preceding age.

5. SOCIAL LIFE

Contemporary memoirs, diaries, and letters have been
touched upon in IV. 6. Some collections of original texts are:
Andrew Lang, *Social England Illustrated. A Collection of XVIIth
Century Tracts* (1903); R. B. Morgan, *Readings in English Social
History from Contemporary Literature*, vol. iv, 1603–1688 (1922);
M. St. C. Byrne, *The Elizabethan Home* (2nd ed., 1930); G. B.
Harrison, *England in Shakespeare's Day* (1928) and, if they may
be included here, Harrison's unique series of *Elizabethan
Journals* (1928 ff.; collected 1939) and *A Jacobean Journal . . .
1603–1606* (1941); D. Hartley and M. M. Elliot, *Life and Work
of the People of England . . . The Seventeenth Century* (1928), an
attractive pictorial record; A. V. Judges, *The Elizabethan Underworld* (1930); and W. H. Dunham and S. Pargellis, *Complaint
and Reform in England 1436–1714* (New York, 1938).

The standard large survey is *Social England*, ed. H. D. Traill
and J. S. Mann (6 vols., 1893–7; rev. 1901–4). There is much
information in the *Victoria History of the Counties of England*
(1900 ff.). G. M. Trevelyan's *English Social History* (New
York, 1942; 1944) runs from Chaucer to Queen Victoria.
Shakespeare's England, ed. Sir Sidney Lee and C. T. Onions
(2 vols., 1916) is a comprehensive picture of many aspects
of life. A short account is M. St. C. Byrne's *Elizabethan Life
in Town and Country* (2nd ed., 1934). Books on the next age
are Mary Coate's *Social Life in Stuart England* (1924) and E.
Godfrey's *Home Life under the Stuarts 1603–1649* (1903, 1925).
Condensed accounts are given by Sir A. W. Ward in the *CHEL*
v, in Trevelyan's *England under the Stuarts* (1904; many edns.),

and in G. Davies's *The Early Stuarts* (1937); the last has bibliographies. L. B. Wright's *Middle-Class Culture in Elizabethan England* (1935), which covers much of our period, is a very full account of *bourgeois* interests and reading. Many relevant books have been cited in earlier sections.

Of the many special books a few are: W. B. Rye, *England as Seen by Foreigners in the Days of Elizabeth and James the First* (1865), and M. Letts, *As the Foreigner Saw Us* (1935); R. Withington, *English Pageantry* (2 vols., Harvard, 1918–20); M. and C. H. B. Quennell, *History of Everyday Things in England* (1918 ff.); Joan Parkes (*supra*, V. 4); *Englishmen at Rest and Play . . . 1558–1714*, ed. R. Lennard (1931); Gladys S. Thomson, *Life in a Noble Household, 1641–1700* (1937); J. C. Drummond and A. Wilbraham, *The Englishman's Food. A History of Five Centuries of English Diet* (1939).

The strong religious colouring of social and family life may be seen best in diaries, letters, and conduct books. Modern studies range from E. Troeltsch's *Social Teaching of the Christian Churches* (trans., 2 vols., 1931) to L. L. Schücking's *Die Familie im Puritanismus* (Leipzig, 1929) and H. Reinhold's *Puritanismus und Aristokratie* (Berlin, 1938). That peculiarly English phenomenon, the Puritan Sunday, has evoked many books, e.g., Robert Cox, *Literature of the Sabbath Question* (2 vols., 1865), Max Levy, *Der Sabbath in England* (Leipzig, 1933), and W. B. Whitaker, *Sunday in Tudor and Stuart Times* (1933). Storm Jameson's *Decline of Merry England* (1930) is a popular and hostile survey of the workings of Puritanism. For the northern part of the island a recent book is G. D. Henderson's *Religious Life in Seventeenth-Century Scotland* (1937).

In addition to books already cited, some special studies of the domestic and cultural status of women are: Rose M. Bradley, *The English Housewife in the Seventeenth & Eighteenth Centuries* (1912); Chilton L. Powell, *English Domestic Relations 1487–1653* (Columbia, 1917); Alice Clark, *Working Life of Women in the Seventeenth Century* (1919); Myra Reynolds, *The Learned Lady in England 1650–1760* (Boston, 1920); Violet Wilson, *Society Women of Shakespeare's Time* (1924); M. Phillips and W. S. Tomkinson, *English Women in Life & Letters* (1927); and Dorothy Gardiner, *English Girlhood at School* (1929). Either in this paragraph or the last might be mentioned W. and M. Haller's 'The Puritan Art of Love', *HLQ* v (1941–2).

6. EDUCATION AND CULTURE

This section comprises anthologies; general histories; universities; schools; the modernist movement and Comenius; books of conduct and courtesy; and libraries.

Henry Barnard's *English Pedagogy* (2 vols., 2nd ed., Hartford, 1876) has extracts from Bacon, Wotton, Milton, Hoole, Cowley, Hartlib, and Petty. Extracts from many writers are given in E. Rowland, *A Pedagogue's Commonplace Book* (1925). A large collection of educational tracts is being prepared by W. E. Houghton.

Some outlines of educational history which take account of our period are the books of S. S. Laurie (1903); J. W. Adamson (1919; and *infra*); and H. Wodehouse (1924). There are chapters on the period by Woodward in the *CHEL* iii and by Sandys in *Shakespeare's England* (1916).

To Sir Charles Mallet's *History of the University of Oxford* (3 vols., 1924–7) may be added the histories of the colleges. And to Anthony Wood's *Athenae Oxonienses* and *Fasti* (I, *supra*), which have more than Oxonian value, may be added his *History and Antiquities of the University of Oxford*, ed. J. Gutch (2 vols., 1792–6), and *The Life and Times of Anthony Wood . . . 1632–1695, described by Himself: Collected from his diaries and other papers by Andrew Clark* (5 vols., 1891–1900). A full account of academic disruption is given by M. Burrows, *The Register of the Visitors of the University of Oxford from A.D. 1647 to A.D. 1658* (Camden Society, 1881). Another side is presented in F. J. Varley's *The Siege of Oxford* (1932) and *A Supplement* (1935). Some works of reference are: C. W. Boase and A. Clark, *Register of the University of Oxford* (5 vols., 1885–9); John Griffiths, *Statutes of the University of Oxford Codified in the Year 1636* (1888); Joseph Foster, *Alumni Oxonienses 1500–1714* (4 vols., 1891–2); and Strickland Gibson, *Statuta Antiqua* (1931).

J. Bass Mullinger followed up his *Cambridge Characteristics in the Seventeenth Century* (1867) with the standard history, *The University of Cambridge* (3 vols., 1873–1911). There are again the histories of the individual colleges. University organization around 1600 is well described in George Peacock, *Observations on the Statutes of the University of Cambridge* (1841). Some other histories and works of reference are: J. Heywood and T. Wright, *Cambridge University Transactions during the Puritan*

Controversies of the 16th and 17th Centuries (2 vols., 1854); C. H. and
T. Cooper, *Athenae Cantabrigienses* (3 vols., 1858–1913); D.
Masson, *Milton*, i (1859; rev. ed., 1881); John and J. A. Venn,
Alumni Cantabrigienses (4 vols., 1922–7); and F. J. Varley,
Cambridge During the Civil War (1935).

One of the best pictures of life and work at the English
universities is given in S. E. Morison's *Founding of Harvard
College* (Harvard, 1935). There is much material in contemporary memoirs, letters, and tracts, and in modern biographies.
College Life in the Time of James the First (1851), by J. H. Marsden,
is drawn from D'Ewes's diary.

The chief original documents on schools are the books of
Brinsley and Hoole cited under their names in VI below.
Mullinger has a chapter on schools in the *CHEL* vii. Standard
large accounts are Foster Watson's *English Grammar Schools to
1660* (1908), and T. W. Baldwin, *William Shakspere's Small
Latine & Lesse Greeke* (2 vols., University of Illinois, 1944).
J. Howard Brown's *Elizabethan Schooldays* (1933) and Irene
Parker's *Dissenting Academies in England* (1914) touch on the
beginning and end of our period. Many of the famous public
schools have had historians.

The best general history of the modernist movement is
Pioneers of Modern Education 1600–1700 (1905) by J. W. Adam-
son, who has a chapter in the *CHEL* ix. Another good survey
is B. Dressler, *Die Entwicklung der englischen Erziehung im 17. Jahr-
hundert* (Leipzig, 1927). A full and concrete study is F. Watson,
The Beginnings of the Teaching of Modern Subjects in England (1909).
Baconian influence is described in R. F. Jones's *Ancients and
Moderns* (Washington University, 1936).

Comenius's *Great Didactic* was translated and edited, with a
long introduction, by M. W. Keatinge (1896; enlarged 1910).
Of the many books on Comenius a few are those of W. S.
Monroe (1900), A. Heyberger (Paris, 1928), and R. F. Young,
whose *Comenius in England* (1932) receives some discussion from
D. Stimson in *Isis*, xxiii (1935). Comenius's visit to England
evoked a number of tercentenary articles and books in 1941–2,
among them *The Teacher of Nations*, ed. J. Needham (1942),
which includes a bibliography. The question of his having
been invited to Harvard was fully examined by A. Matthews in
Publications of The Colonial Society of Massachusetts, xxi (Boston,
1920).

For the literature of courtesy the fullest bibliographies are G. E. Noyes, *Bibliography of Courtesy and Conduct Books in Seventeenth-Century England* (New Haven, 1937), and V. B. Heltzel, *Check List of Courtesy Books in the Newberry Library* (Chicago, 1942). There is no adequate anthology.

The fullest study of books of conduct and courtesy, with a full survey of scholarship, is John E. Mason's *Gentlefolk in the Making* (University of Pennsylvania, 1935). Other important studies are: an essay in E. N. S. Thompson, *Literary Bypaths of the Renaissance* (Yale, 1924); Ruth Kelso, *The Doctrine of the English Gentleman in the Sixteenth Century*, with a bibliography to 1625 (University of Illinois, 1929); articles by W. L. Ustick, *SP* xxix (1932) and *MP* xxx (1932–3); and sections of C. L. Powell and L. B. Wright (*supra*, V. 5) and of W. E. Houghton, *The Formation of Thomas Fuller's Holy and Profane States* (Harvard, 1938).

A good brief account of libraries is Mullinger's chapter in the *CHEL* iv. Older and fuller accounts are Edward Edwards's *Memoirs of Libraries* (2 vols., 1859) and *Libraries and Founders of Libraries* (1865). Some references for Oxford are given below under Sir Thomas Bodley. Some other items are: W. D. Macray, *Annals of the Bodleian Library Oxford* (2nd ed., 1890); G. W. Wheeler, *The Earliest Catalogues of the Bodleian Library* (1928); and occasional articles in the *Bodleian Quarterly Record*, such as those of S. Gibson (i, 1916) and J. P. R. Lyell (vii, 1933). C. Sayle compiled *Annals of Cambridge University Library* (1916).

7. MUSIC AND THE ARTS

This section covers collections and histories of music; the graphic arts; antiquities; architecture; decoration, furniture, and dress; and gardening.

W. Chappell's *Popular Music of the Olden Time* (2 vols., 1855–9) was revised by H. E. Wooldridge as *Old English Popular Music* (2 vols., 1893). The great modern editions of Tudor and early Stuart music are: *The English Madrigal School*, ed. E. H. Fellowes (36 vols., 1913–24); *The English School of Lutenist Song Writers*, ed. Fellowes (32 vols., 1920–32); and *Tudor Church Music*, ed. P. C. Buck, Fellowes, et al. (10 vols., 1923–9). 'Peter Warlock' and P. Wilson edited a selection, *English Ayres Elizabethan and Jacobean* (1927–31).

Shakespeare's England includes a section on music by W. B. Squire. General histories of English music especially good for our period are those of Henry Davey (1895; rev. ed., 1921) and Ernest Walker (2nd ed., 1924). Sir Hubert Parry's volume on the seventeenth century, in the *Oxford History of Music*, has been revised by E. J. Dent (1938). Pinto's *English Renaissance 1510–1688* (1938) has a chapter on music by B. Pattison. The chief modern authority, Dr. Fellowes, has written *The English Madrigal Composers* (1921), *The English Madrigal* (1925), books on Orlando Gibbons (1925) and Byrd (1936), and *English Cathedral Music* (1941). Some other books are: 'Peter Warlock', *The English Ayre* (1926), E. Brennecke, *John Milton the Elder and His Music* (Columbia, 1938), M. C. Boyd, *Elizabethan Music and Musical Criticism* (University of Pennsylvania, 1940), and W. M. Evans, *Henry Lawes* (New York, 1941). P. A. Scholes has devoted a large volume, *The Puritans and Music in England and New England* (1934), to the destruction of 'a calumny'. The life and work of individual musicians is summarized in some of these books and in *Grove's Dictionary of Music and Musicians* (3rd ed., ed. H. C. Colles, 5 vols., 1927–8) and J. Pulver, *A Biographical Dictionary of Old English Music* (1927). Sir F. Bridge has a series of sketches, *Twelve Good Musicians From John Bull to Henry Purcell* (1920).

L. Cust has a section on painting, sculpture, and engraving in *Shakespeare's England* (1916). Some books are: G. C. Williamson, *History of Portrait Miniatures* (2 vols., 1904), and B. S. Long's biographical dictionary, *British Miniaturists* (1929); Sir S. Colvin, *Early Engraving & Engravers in England (1545–1695)* (1905); C. H. C. Baker, *Lely & the Stuart Portrait Painters . . . before & after Van Dyck* (2 vols., 1913); and C. H. C. Baker and W. G. Constable, *English Painting of the Sixteenth and Seventeenth Centuries* (Florence; New York, 1930).

The chief descriptive catalogue of classical antiquities is Adolf Michaelis, *Ancient Marbles in Great Britain* (trans. C. A. M. Fennell, 1882). The activities of the greatest of collectors are described in M. F. S. Hervey's *Life, Correspondence & Collections of Thomas Howard Earl of Arundel* (1921).

Some works on architecture are: Sir Reginald Blomfield, *History of Renaissance Architecture in England, 1500–1800* (2 vols., 1897), and a *Short History* (1900; many reprints); a number of later books by J. A. Gotch, who has a section in *Shakespeare's*

England (1916); H. A. Tipping's sumptuous *English Homes*, Periods III and IV (1920–7); and the earlier part of B. S. Allen's *Tides in English Taste* (2 vols., Harvard, 1937). Exteriors and interiors are treated in A. Vallance, *Art in England during the Elizabethan and Stuart Periods* (*Studio*, Spring Number, 1908). There are also Tipping and books on decoration by M. Jourdain (1924) and F. Lenygon (rev. ed., 1927). The standard *History of English Furniture* (4 vols., 1919) is by P. Macquoid, who has a chapter on costume in *Shakespeare's England*. Among histories of dress are: D. C. Calthrop, *English Costume*, iii (1906); Iris Brooke, *English Costume of the Seventeenth Century* (1934); M. C. Linthicum, *Costume in the Drama of Shakespeare and his Contemporaries* (1936); and Herbert Norris, *Costume & Fashion*, whose 3rd volume (1938) has reached 1603.

One of the two most famous books on gardening, John Parkinson's *Paradisi In Sole Paradisus Terrestris* (1629), was handsomely reproduced in 1904. The other, William Lawson's *New Orchard and Garden* (1618), was edited by E. S. Rohde (1927) from the 3rd edition. *The Garden Book of Sir Thomas Hanmer* was first printed from the manuscript of 1659 and edited by Mrs. Rohde in 1933. Mrs. Rohde has also edited an inviting anthology, *The Old-World Pleasaunce* (1925).

Some accounts of gardening are: Sir R. Blomfield, *The Formal Garden in England* (1892); Alicia Amherst, *History of Gardening in England* (rev. ed., 1910); Lord Ernle's section in *Shakespeare's England* (1916); Sir Frank Crisp, *Mediæval Gardens* (2 vols., 1924), which comes up into the Stuart period; E. S. Rohde, *The Story of the Garden* (1932); parts of B. S. Allen's *Tides in English Taste* (2 vols., 1937); and R. E. Clarkson, *Green Enchantment* (New York, 1940). The best introduction to the literature is Mrs. Rohde's *Old English Gardening Books* (1924), with a bibliography.

Accounts of herbals have been written by Agnes Arber (rev. ed., 1938) and Mrs. Rohde (1922). M. Woodward has abridged Gerard's *Herball* from T. Johnson's ed. of 1636 (1927).

VI. INDIVIDUAL AUTHORS

THOMAS ADAMS, *c.* 1580–*ante* 1660.

Adams's 'Sermons, Meditations, and other Divine and Morall Discourses' were collected in the *Workes* of 1629. The modern edition is that of J. Angus (3 vols., 1861–2). Twelve sermons were edited by John Brown (Cambridge Devotional Series, 1909); one is in Bishop Henson's *Selected English Sermons* (World's Classics, 1939). Some characters are in G. Murphy's *Cabinet of Characters* (1925). Adams is discussed in the books on preaching by J. Brown (1900) and C. Smyth (1940) and most fully in that of W. F. Mitchell (1932).

SIR WILLIAM ALEXANDER, EARL OF STIRLING, 1577?–1640.

The standard edition of the verse is by Kastner and Charlton (2 vols., 1921–9), who give a full history of Senecan drama, a brief introduction to the non-dramatic works, and bibliographical data. *An Encouragement To Colonies* (1624) was reprinted in *Royal Letters, Charters, and Tracts* (Bannatyne Club, 1867) and by the Prince Society (Boston, 1873). *Anacrisis,* an essay on poetry, first printed in the 1711 edition of Drummond's works, is reprinted in Spingarn's collection. T. H. McGrail's *Sir William Alexander* (1940) is an authoritative biography.

RICHARD ALLESTREE, 1619–81.

The Whole Duty of Man, the first and most popular of a series of books of conduct, appeared anonymously in 1658; it was reprinted into the nineteenth century. Some discussions of the problem of authorship are: C. E. Doble's several articles in the *Academy,* xxii (1882); E. Solly et al., *Bibliographer,* ii (London, 1882); the *DNB* on Lady Dorothy Pakington and Allestree; F. Madan, *Bodleian Quarterly Record,* iv (1924); and W. Jaggard, London *Bookman,* lxxxi (1931–2).

WILLIAM AMES, 1576–1633.

Ames's best-known books were *Medulla Sacræ Theologiæ* (Franeker, 1623), translated as *The Marrow of Sacred Divinity* (1638? 1642), and *De Conscientia, et Eius Iure, vel Casibus* (Amsterdam, 1630). In 1643 appeared his *Workes ... Translated out of Latine for publike use.* The fullest and best account of Ames's thought and influence is in Perry Miller's *New England Mind: The Seventeenth Century* (1939).

LANCELOT ANDREWES, 1555–1626.

XCVI. Sermons, published in 1629 by the king's command, was edited by Bishops Laud and Buckeridge. An imperfect edition of the *Private Devotions* was issued in 1647 by Moseley, who in 1648 put out a better edition translated by R. Drake. These and the controversial and other works were edited in the Library of Anglo-Catholic Theology (11 vols., 1841–54). Other reprints are *Seventeen Sermons on the Nativity* (last ed., 1898) and *Two Sermons of the Resurrection* (Cambridge Plain Texts, 1932). The *Private Devotions* has had many translators and editors, such as Newman (1840) and F. E. Brightman (1903). There are books by R. L. Ottley (1894) and D. Macleane (1910). Among shorter studies are those of R. W. Church, in *Masters in English Theology*, ed. A. Barry (1877); W. H. Frere's lecture (1898); A. W. Fox, *A Book of Bachelors* (1899); K. N. Colvile, *Fame's Twilight* (1923); T. S. Eliot, *For Lancelot Andrewes* (1928; repr. in *Selected Essays*, 1932); and W. F. Mitchell, *English Pulpit Oratory* (1932). M. M. Knappen has discussed Andrewes's 'Early Puritanism' in *Church History*, ii (1933).

ROBERT ARMIN, *c.* 1568 1615.

Armin's *Works* were edited by Grosart (1880). Information about the actor and playwright is given in the works on the Elizabethan stage by Sir E. K. Chambers and T. W. Baldwin, in E. Nungezer's *Dictionary of Actors* (Yale, 1929), in articles by E. Denkinger (*PMLA* xli, 1926) and F. P. Wilson (*HLQ* ii, 1938–9), and in the full account by A. K. Gray (*PMLA* xlii, 1927).

ELIAS ASHMOLE, 1617–92.

Ashmole's fame rests more solidly on the Oxford museum of natural history than on his antiquarian and occult labours, most of which belong to the Restoration. Two early books were *Theatrum Chemicum Britannicum*, which he edited in 1652, and *The Way to Bliss* (1658). His *Diary* was edited in 1717 and 1774, and lately by R. T. Gunther (1927). There are sketches of him by Dudley Wright (1924) and A. L. Humphreys (1925; repr. from *Berks, Bucks & Oxon Archaeological Journal*, xxviii, 1924). Ashmole's translation of the *Prophecies of Merlin*, the first in English, is edited by C. B. Millican in *SP* xxviii (1931).

Sir Robert Aytoun or Ayton, 1570–1638.

Most of Aytoun's verse was not printed in the seventeenth century. It was edited in the *Bannatyne Miscellany*, i (1827); by Charles Roger in 1844 (revised 1871); and also in *Transactions of the Royal Historical Society*, i (1875). Selections are given in G. Eyre-Todd (*supra*, II. 2) and other anthologies.

Francis Bacon, 1561–1626.

Some of the writings published in Bacon's lifetime were: *Essayes. Religious Meditations. Places of perswasion and disswasion* (1597; enlarged 1612, 1625); *Certaine Considerations touching the better pacification, and Edification of the Church of England* (1604); *The Twoo Bookes . . . Of the proficience and advancement of Learning, divine and humane* (1605); *De Sapientia Veterum* (1609; translated in 1619 as *The Wisedome of the Ancients*); *Instauratio Magna* (1620); *Historie of the Raigne of King Henry The Seventh* (1622); *De Dignitate & Augmentis Scientiarum* (1623), the enlarged Latin version of the *Advancement*; and *Apophthegmes* (1625). William Rawley edited an elegiac *Memoriae* (1626) and these volumes of remains: *Sylva Sylvarum or A Naturall History*, with *The New Atlantis* (1627); *Certaine Miscellany Works* (1629); *Operum Moralium et Civilium Tomus* (1638); *Resuscitatio* (1657; enlarged 1661, 1671); and *Opuscula Varia Posthuma* (1658). Some other early publications were: *A Collection of Some Principall Rules and Maximes of the Common Lawes* (1630); *The Confession of Faith* (1641); *Remaines* (1648); *Scripta in Naturali et Universali Philosophia*, ed. I. Gruter (Amsterdam, 1653); *Baconiana*, ed. T. Tenison (1679); *Letters*, ed. R. Stephens (1702), *Letters and Remains* (1734).

A facsimile of the *Essayes* of 1597 was printed in *The Bibliographer*, ii (1903) and issued separately (New York, 1904).

The great modern edition of the works is by J. Spedding, R. L. Ellis, and D. D. Heath (7 vols., 1857–9), supplemented by Spedding's *The Letters and the Life* (7 vols., 1861–74), in which the occasional writings are reprinted.

Of volumes of selections the most substantial is that of J. M. Robertson (1905).

Bacon's poems, chiefly the *Translation Of Certaine Psalmes into English Verse* (1625), were edited by Grosart (*Miscellanies of The Fuller Worthies' Library*, i, 1870).

Of the countless editions of the *Essayes* some of the most useful are those of W. A. Wright (Golden Treasury Series, 1862),

E. A. Abbott (2 vols., 1876), S. H. Reynolds (1890), and M. A. Scott (Modern Student's Library, 1908). Arber's *Harmony of the Essays* (1871) facilitates comparison of the several editions. The *Advancement of Learning* has been annotated by W. A. Wright (1868) and F. G. Selby (2 vols., 1892–5). The Latin text of the *Novum Organum* was edited with a full commentary by T. Fowler (1889). *Henry VII* was edited by J. R. Lumby (Pitt Press Series, 1876), *The New Atlantis* by G. C. M. Smith (Pitt Press Series, 1900) and A. B. Gough (1915).

Rawley's short *Life*, from the *Resuscitatio* of 1657, is reprinted in Spedding's first volume of the *Works* and in Arber's *Harmony of the Essays*. Spedding's exhaustive *Letters and Life*, which he himself abridged in *An Account of the Life and Times of Francis Bacon* (1878), has been the quarry of later and usually less worshipful and less learned biographers. Dean Church's *Bacon* (English Men of Letters, 1884) is a well-rounded sketch. The *DNB* article, by S. R. Gardiner and T. Fowler, is full and solid. The biographies of M. Sturt (1932) and C. Williams (1933) neglect the writer and thinker for the man.

The history of Bacon's fame is summarized in the judgements given by Sortais in the work cited below. Of early modern critiques the best-known is Macaulay's essay (1837), which is of interest now chiefly to the student of Macaulay and early Victorian thought. T. Fowler's *Bacon* (1881) and the second volume of J. Nichol's *Francis Bacon: His Life and Philosophy* (1888–9) are still useful primers. In recent decades English-speaking writers have been mostly content with writing articles in disparagement of Bacon's scientific importance, and most of the major studies are Italian and German. E. Wolff's *Francis Bacon und seine Quellen* (2 vols., Berlin, 1910–13) is a solid piece of research. C. D. Broad's *Philosophy of Francis Bacon* (1926) is a compendious review of the *Instauratio Magna*. There are short but important discussions by A. N. Whitehead (*Science and the Modern World*, 1925) and A. E. Taylor (*Proceedings of the British Academy*, xii, 1926). Perhaps the best full analysis of Bacon's thought and its Renaissance background is Adolfo Levi's *Il Pensiero di Francesco Bacone* (Turin, 1925). Bacon's scientific influence has been treated from various angles by G. Sortais, *La Philosophie moderne depuis Bacon jusqu'à Leibniz* (2 vols., Paris, 1920–2), Basil Willey, *The Seventeenth Century Background* (1934), and R. F. Jones, *Ancients and Moderns* (1936). That Bacon's defence of learning was not otiose is made clear by G. Bullough (*Seventeenth Century-Studies Presented to Sir Herbert Grierson*, 1938). The *New Atlantis* figures in histories of utopian thought and has been the special theme of E. D. Blodgett (*PMLA* xlvi, 1931), K. Sternberg (*Rivista di Filosofia*, xxv, 1934), and H. Minkowski (*Die Neu-Atlantis des Francis Bacon*, Jena, 1936).

The essays of Bacon and Montaigne have often been contrasted, most solidly by J. Zeitlin (*JEGP* xxvii, 1928). This last study may be set against P. Villey's elaborate argument for Montaigne's general influence on Bacon's thought (*Revue de la Renaissance*, xii and xiii, 1911–12). An important article is R. S. Crane's 'The Relation of Bacon's *Essays* to His Program for the Advancement of Learning' (*Schelling Anniversary Papers*, New York, 1923). A recent comment on the *Essays* is G. Tillotson's 'Words for Princes' (*TLS*, 6 February, 1937; *Essays in Criticism and Research*, 1942). The early influence of the *Essays* is treated in the monographs by W. L. MacDonald and E. N. S. Thompson cited above in IV. 5. *De Sapientia Veterum* is analysed in C. W. Lemmi's *Classic Deities in Bacon* (Johns Hopkins, 1933).

There are estimates of Bacon the historian by F. J. C. Hearnshaw (*Contemporary Review*, cxxiii, 1923) and in the *TLS*, 8 April, 1926. Bacon's theory of historical writing is expounded by L. F. Dean (*ELH* viii, 1941). The sources of *Henry VII* are set forth by W. Busch, *England under the Tudors. Vol. I. King Henry VII* (trans. 1895).

Bacon's political outlook is discussed by such historians of political thought as G. P. Gooch and J. W. Allen (*supra*, V. 1), and more fully by W. Richter (*Bacon als Staatsdenker*, Berlin, 1928) and H. Bock (*Staat und Gesellschaft bei Francis Bacon*, Berlin, 1937). The fullest study of one affiliation is N. Orsini, *Bacone e Machiavelli* (Genoa, 1936). Bacon's ecclesiastical policy is reviewed in W. K. Jordan, *Development of Religious Toleration*, ii (1936).

Bacon's legal work is dealt with in Holdsworth (*supra*, V. 1) and in Lord Birkenhead's *Fourteen English Judges* (1926). J. Ritchie has edited *Reports of Cases Decided by Francis Bacon . . . in the High Court of Chancery* (1932).

M. W. Croll's important articles on Bacon and the anti-Ciceronian movement in prose, and K. R. Wallace's full and solid *Francis Bacon on Communication & Rhetoric* (1943), were cited above under III. 2. Bacon's theory of poetry and the imagination is discussed in Spingarn's *Critical Essays of the Seventeenth Century* (1908) and more fully by M. W. Bundy in *SP* xxvii (1930) and L. C. Knights in *Scrutiny*, xi (1943). Bacon's poem, 'The World', is placed in its background by Grierson (*MLR* vi, 1911; *Essays and Addresses*, 1940).

Bibliographical material concerning Bacon's works is scattered through Spedding's edition and conveniently summarized in the *CBEL*. G. W. Steeves's *Francis Bacon: A Sketch of his Life, Works and Literary Friends* (1910) is a useful bibliographical guide with facsimiles of title-pages. Bibliographies of philosophic criticism are supplied in various modern books of that kind, such as some of those named above.

AUGUSTINE BAKER, 1575–1641.

David (in religion Augustine) Baker, the chief Roman Catholic mystic of our period, is identified with the posthumous *Sancta Sophia. Or Directions for the Prayer of Contemplation, &c. Extracted out of more then XL. Treatises written by the late Ven. F. Augustin Baker . . . And Methodically digested by the R. F. Serenus Cressy* (2 vols., Douai, 1657). This has been edited (1876; rev. 1932 as *Holy Wisdom*) by J. N. Sweeney, who also wrote a *Life* (1861). Some other books by or about Baker are: volumes of selections, ed. B. Weld-Blundell (1907–33); *Confessions*, ed. J. McCann (1922); *The Cloud of Unknowing . . . With A Commentary on the Cloud by Father Augustine Baker*, ed. McCann (1924); *Memorials*, ed. McCann and H. Connolly (Catholic Record Society, vol. xxxiii, 1933); and the *Life* by P. Salvin and S. Cressy, ed. McCann (1933), with a bibliography. There is an essay in David Knowles's *English Mystics* (1927).

JOHN BARCLAY, 1582–1621.

Barclay's chief works were: *Euphormionis Lusinini Satyricon* (Paris, 1603–7) and *Euphormionis Satyrici Apologia pro se* (Paris, 1610); some Latin poems, *Sylvae* (1606); *Icon Animorum* (1614), translated by T. May as *The Mirrour of Mindes* (1631); and *Argenis* (Paris, 1621; London, 1622), translated by Kingesmill Long (1625) and Sir Robert Le Grys (1628), with the verse rendered by May. It was translated by Clara Reeve as *The Phoenix* (4 vols., 1772). The vast European fame of *Argenis* in its own century has long been eclipsed among English-speaking readers (as Coleridge lamented), but it has inspired many monographs by continental scholars, such as A. Collignon (Paris, 1902), who wrote also *Notes sur l'"Euphormion"* (Nancy, 1901); K. F. Schmid (Berlin, 1904); P. Kettelhoit (Bottrop i. W., 1934); and L. Bardino (Palermo, 1939). Among the few English accounts are those of E. Bensly (*CHEL* iv), who has a good bibliography in the *CBEL*; G. Waterhouse, *Literary Relations of England and Germany* (1914); K. N. Colvile; *Fame's Twilight* (1923); E. A. Baker, *History of the English Novel*, iii (1929); and G. Langford, University of Virginia *Abstracts of Dissertations 1940*.

WILLIAM BASSE, c. 1583–1653?

The standard edition of the *Poetical Works* is by R. W. Bond (1893). What was to be a popular book, *A Helpe to Discourse . . . By W. B. & E. P.* (1619), contained the poem 'A memento for mortalitie' which was reprinted many times before the abridged version was assigned, without reason, to Francis Beaumont (*Poems*, 1653) under the title 'On the Tombes in Westminster'. The matter is set forth by N. Ault in the *TLS*, 12 January, 1933.

RICHARD BAXTER, 1615–91.

Although some of Baxter's most famous works are *The Saints Everlasting Rest* (1650; ed. W. Young, 1907), *A Call to the Unconverted* (1657), and the *Holy Commonwealth* (1659), he belongs rather to the next age and the next volume. For the general reader, at least, he lives in the memoir of his wife, the *Breviate* of 1681 (ed. J. T. Wilkinson, 1928), and the autobiography which, abridged from the *Reliquiæ Baxterianæ* (1696), has been edited by J. M. Lloyd Thomas (1925; Everyman's Library, 1931). *The Reformed Pastor* (1656) has been edited by Wilkinson (1939). The standard biography is by F. J. Powicke (2 vols., 1924–7). There are bibliographies of the voluminous Baxter by Grosart (1868) and A. G. Matthews (1932).

LEWIS BAYLY, 1565–1631.

The earliest extant edition of the immensely popular *Practise of Pietie* is the third, of 1613. It had been entered in January 1612. There is a good account of the author and the book by J. E. Bailey in *Papers of the Manchester Literary Club*, ix (1883).

FRANCIS BEAUMONT, 1584?–1616.

Under Beaumont's name were published *Poems . . . The Hermaphrodite. The Remedie of Love. Elegies. Sonnets, with other Poems* (1640) and an enlarged edition (1653), but a number of the poems were not his. One item is noticed above, under Basse. Poems were reprinted in Chalmers's *English Poets* (1810), vi, and in *Works of Beaumont and Fletcher*, ed. Dyce, xi (1846). *Salmacis and Hermaphroditus* (1602) was edited for the *Shakespeare Society's Papers*, iii (1847). E. H. Fellowes has edited *Songs & Lyrics, from the Plays of Beaumont and Fletcher. With Contemporary Musical Settings* (1928). Beaumont's mock 'Grammer Lecture', given at the Inner Temple revels (1601–5?), is edited by M. Eccles in the *RES* xvi (1940). A general study is C. M. Gayley's *Beaumont, the Dramatist* (New York, 1914). There is a *Concise Bibliography* by S. A. Tannenbaum (New York, 1938).

SIR JOHN BEAUMONT, 1583?–1627.

The anonymous *Metamorphosis of Tabacco* (1602) was reprinted in Collier's *Illustrations of Early English Popular Literature*, i (1863). The unprinted *Theatre of Apollo* has been edited by W. W. Greg (1926). The manuscript of the supposedly lost *Crowne of Thornes*, Beaumont's major work, has been apparently identified in the British Museum (B. H. Newdigate, *RES* xviii, 1942). Beaumont's other verse, collected by his son in the volume *Bosworth-field* (1629), was reprinted in Chalmers's *English Poets* (1810), vi, and edited, with additions, by Grosart (Fuller Worthies' Library, 1869). Beaumont is discussed in the standard histories, by G. Williamson in *MP* xxxiii (1935–6), and by R. L. Sharp in *From Donne to Dryden* (1940). M. Eccles gives a full biography in *HLQ* v (1941–2).

JOSEPH BEAUMONT, 1616–99.

Psyche: or Loves Mysterie In XX. Canto's: Displaying the Intercourse Betwixt Christ, and the Soule (1648) had a 'second' edition (1702) which contained four new cantos and had received 'Corrections throughout'. This second edition, with some minor poems, was edited by Grosart (Chertsey Worthies' Library, 2 vols., 1880). The *Minor Poems* were edited by E. Robinson in 1914. Beaumont is discussed in Miss Robinson's introduction, by H. E. Cory in 'Spenser, the School of the Fletchers, and Milton' (*University of California Publications in Modern Philology*, ii, 1912), by P. H. Osmond in his *Mystical Poets of the English Church* (1919), and by Austin Warren in his *Richard Crashaw* (Louisiana State University, 1939). *Memoirs* of Beaumont by

John Gee (d. 1772) have been edited from a manuscript by T. A. Walker (1934).

THOMAS BEEDOME, 1613–41?

Poems Divine, And Humane appeared posthumously in 1641, edited by Henry Glapthorne. Francis Meynell edited *Select Poems* in 1928. Some new biographical facts are given by C. L. Shaver in *MLN* liii (1938).

EDWARD BENLOWES, 1603/4–76.

Theophila (1652) was a handsome book which reflected its author's interest in the arts. The Harvard copy has an inscription from Benlowes to a fellow poet, Mildmay Fane, Earl of Westmorland. Benlowes was satirized in Butler's character of 'A Small Poet'. *Theophila* is reprinted in Saintsbury's *Minor Poets of the Caroline Period*, i (1905). There are critical discussions in G. Williamson, *The Donne Tradition* (1930), and R. L. Sharp, *From Donne to Dryden* (1940). C. Niemeyer and H. Jenkins contributed important biographical articles to *RES* xii (1936) and *MLR* xxxii (1937). There is some bibliographical discussion by G. and A. Tillotson in the *Library*, xiv (1933–4). Some of Benlowes's poetical borrowings were noted by H. J. L. Robbie in *MLR* xxiii (1928) and 'Hibernicus' in the *TLS*, 22 August, 1929. A piece attributed to Benlowes, *A Buckler against the fear of Death* (1640), reissued as *Midnights Meditations of Death* (1646), was the work of a preacher, Edward Buckler (1610–76). This has been discussed by C. A. Moore (*MLN* xli, 1926), W. H. Buckler (*Library*, xvii, 1936–7), and H. R. Mead (ibid., xxi, 1940–1).

RICHARD BERNARD, 1568–1642.

Bernard's best-known book, *The Isle of Man: or, The Legall Proceeding in Man-shire against Sinne*, appeared in 1626. His work is described in W. Haller's *Rise of Puritanism* (1938) and studied most fully in Max Müller, *Richard Bernard: The Isle of Man* (Markneukirchen, 1933). There is a bibliography, *The Writings of Richard Bernard*, by J. I. Dredge (priv. pr., 1890).

SIR HENRY BLOUNT, 1602–82.

A Voyage into the Levant . . . With particular observations concerning the moderne condition of the Turkes, and other people under that

Empire (1636) was reprinted in the collections (cited above under Travel) of Churchill and Osborne and in the 10th volume of Pinkerton. There is some discussion in S. C. Chew, *The Crescent and the Rose* (1937), and a fuller account in B. Penrose, *Urbane Travellers* (1942).

SIR THOMAS BODLEY, 1545–1613.

The short *Life*, written in 1609 and printed at Oxford in 1647, was included in Hearne's *Reliquiæ Bodleianæ* (1703), the *Harleian Miscellany*, ed. Park, iv (1809), and *Trecentale Bodleianum* (1913), and was reprinted by itself at Edinburgh (1894) and Chicago (1906). Bodley's letters to Thomas James, the first Keeper, were mostly printed by Hearne and have been edited by G. W. Wheeler (1926). Wheeler has also edited *Letters of Sir Thomas Bodley to the University of Oxford, 1598–1611* (1927). Bodley's draft of the statutes was printed by Hearne; with the 1906 edition of the *Life*; and in the *Trecentale Bodleianum*. *Pietas Oxoniensis* (1902) contains much matter about Bodley and the Library. J. D. Doty has an article in *Faculty Papers of Union College*, i (1930). Some other references are given above, in V. 6.

EDMUND BOLTON, 1575?–*post* 1634.

Hypercritica; or A Rule of Judgment for writing, or reading our History's, completed *c.* 1618, was first printed in 1722 and is reprinted in Spingarn's *Critical Essays*. Bolton's proposal to King James for an English academy is described by J. Hunter in *Archaeologia*, xxxii (1847) and by E. M. Portal in *Proceedings of the British Academy*, vii (1915–16).

ROGER BOYLE, BARON BROGHILL AND EARL OF ORRERY, 1621–79.

Parthenissa was published in Ireland and England chiefly during 1654–6, but some of it appeared in 1651 and a last instalment in 1669; the work was issued 'Compleat' in 1676. The bibliographical problems are summarized by C. W. Miller (University of Virginia *Abstracts of Dissertations 1940*). The romance is set in its background by E. A. Baker, *History of the English Novel*, iii (1929). Boyle's *Dramatic Works* have been edited, with a full biographical and critical introduction, by W. S. Clark (2 vols., Harvard, 1937).

JOHN BRAMHALL, 1594–1663.

The collected *Works* were printed in folio (Dublin, 1676) and reprinted in 5 vols. (1842–5). Jeremy Taylor's funeral sermon is of course in editions of Taylor. The fullest account of Bramhall is the book by W. J. Sparrow Simpson (1927). There are essays by W. E. Collins, *Typical English Churchmen,* ed. Collins (1902); T. S. Eliot, *For Lancelot Andrewes* (1928; repr. in *Selected Essays,* 1932); C. Nye, *Church Quarterly Review,* cxvii (1933–4); and M. Taube's acute analysis of Bramhall's controversy with Hobbes in his *Causation, Freedom and Determinism* (1936). Another side is discussed by W. K. Jordan, *Development of Religious Toleration,* iv (1940).

RICHARD BRATHWAIT, 1588?–1673.

Barnabæ Itinerarium (*c.* 1636, completed 1638) was reprinted frequently in the eighteenth century and edited three times (1805, 1818, 1820) by Joseph Haslewood, who discovered its authorship; it was last reprinted in 1932. Only a few other things from Brathwait's large and uncertain canon have had modern editions, e.g. *Essaies upon the Five Senses* (1620), ed. Brydges, *Archaica,* ii (1815); *Whimzies: Or, A New Cast of Characters* (1631), ed. J. O. Halliwell[-Phillipps] (1859); *Natures Embassie* (1621) and *A Strappado for the Divell* (1615), ed. J. W. Ebsworth (1877, 1878); and *The Law of Drinking* (1617), ed. W. B. Hooker (Yale, 1903). The one full study is M. W. Black, *Richard Brathwait* (Philadelphia, 1928). The *English Gentleman* (1630) and the *English Gentlewoman* (1631) are discussed by the writers on conduct books, such as J. E. Mason, *Gentlefolk in the Making* (1935), and W. E. Houghton (v. Fuller below).

NICHOLAS BRETON, 1551?–c. 1623.

Grosart's edition of the *Works in Verse and Prose* (2 vols., Chertsey Worthies' Library, 1879) is comprehensive but not complete. In the selection, *A Mad World My Masters And Other Prose Works,* ed. U. Kentish-Wright (2 vols., 1929), Breton owes more to the publisher than to the editor. Some of the separate reprints are: *The Passionate Shepheard* (1604), ed. F. Ouvry (1877); *Characters upon Essaies* (1615) and *The Good and the Badde* (1616), in H. Morley, *Character Writings of the Seventeenth Century* (1891), and specimens in later anthologies; *No*

Whippinge, nor Trippinge (1601), ed. C. Edmonds (Isham Reprints, 1895); *Melancholike humours* (1600), ed. G. B. Harrison (1929); *Grimellos Fortunes* (1604) and *An Olde Mans Lesson* (1605), ed. E. G. Morice (1936); *The Court and Country* (1618), in *Complaint and Reform in England*, ed. W. H. Dunham and S. Pargellis (1938). *Fantasticks* (1604?) has had a number of reprints. Breton's verse has appeared in many anthologies, especially since Bullen's *Poems, Chiefly Lyrical, from Romances and Prose-Tracts of the Elizabethan Age* (1890).

There are appreciative essays by Bullen (*Elizabethans*, 1924), Edmund Blunden (*TLS*, 22 August, 1929; *Votive Tablets*, 1931), and M. B. Whiting (*Fortnightly Review*, May, 1929). The most comprehensive studies are E. M. Tappan's article on the verse (*PMLA* xiii, 1898) and Nellie E. Monroe's *Nicholas Breton as a Pamphleteer* (University of Pennsylvania, 1929), and especially F. H. McCloskey's unpublished thesis (Harvard *Summaries of Theses 1929*). Breton's essays, characters, letters, and fiction are noticed in the general accounts of those genres. C. N. Greenough's 'Nicholas Breton, Character-Writer and Quadrumaniac' (*Kittredge Anniversary Papers*, 1913) is reprinted in his *Collected Studies* (Cambridge, Mass., 1940). Special studies, mainly on problems of the canon, have been made by H. E. Rollins in his editions (1933, 1936) of two small miscellanies, *Brittons Bowre of Delights* (1591) and *The Arbor of amorous Devises* (1594), in his edition of *Englands Helicon* (1935), and in *HLB* (1936) and *SP* xxxiii (1936); by F. T. Bowers, *MLN* xlv (1930); F. Flournoy, *RES* xvi (1940); J. Robertson, *HLQ* iii and iv (1939–41), *MLR* xxxvi and xxxvii (1941–2), *RES* xvii (1941), and *NQ* clxxx and clxxxi (1941).

JOHN BRINSLEY, 1564/5?–1653/63?

Ludus Literarius (1612) has been edited from the 1627 edition by E. T. Campagnac (1917), *A Consolation for our Grammar Schooles* (1622) by T. C. Pollock (*Scholars' Facsimiles & Reprints*, 1943). Brinsley's educational ideas are discussed in F. Watson's *English Grammar Schools to 1660* (1908), by G. W. McClelland in the *Schelling Anniversary Papers* (New York, 1923), and incidentally by W. F. Mitchell, *English Pulpit Oratory* (1932).

SIR THOMAS BROWNE, 1605–82.

The two unauthorized editions of *Religio Medici* (1642) were followed by an authorized edition in 1643. A Latin version appeared at Leyden and Paris in 1644. The last edition supposedly revised by Browne was the eighth (1682). *Pseudodoxia Epidemica: or, Enquiries into Very many received Tenents, And commonly presumed Truths* (1646) reached its sixth edition, the last 'Corrected and Enlarged by the Author', in 1672. The running title was 'Enquiries into Vulgar and Common Errors'. In 1658 appeared *Hydriotaphia, Urne-Buriall, Or, A Discourse of the Sepulchrall Urnes lately found in Norfolk. Together with The Garden of Cyrus.* After Browne's death came *Certain Miscellany Tracts*, ed. T. Tenison (1683); the folio *Works* of 1686; *A Letter to a Friend, Upon occasion of the Death of his Intimate Friend* (1690); *Posthumous Works* (1712), with a *Life* and J. Whitefoot's personal portrait; and *Christian Morals*, ed. J. Jeffery (1716). The second edition of this last (1756) contained the *Life* by Samuel Johnson.

There are facsimiles of the 1642 *Religio* (ed. W. A. Greenhill, 1883) and of the *Hydriotaphia* and *Garden of Cyrus* (Noel Douglas Replicas, 1927), and a number of *de luxe* editions.

Modern editorial foundations were well and truly laid by Simon Wilkin, who edited Browne's works and letters in 4 volumes in 1835-6 (Bohn ed., 3 vols., 1852). A commentary like Wilkin's was not attempted in C. Sayle's edition (3 vols., 1904-7), nor in the standard edition of the complete works and correspondence by G. Keynes (6 vols., 1928-31). Greenhill produced valuable annotated editions of the *Religio Medici*, *Christian Morals*, and *Letter to a Friend* (1881) and *Hydriotaphia* and *The Garden of Cyrus* (1896); and there have been other small editions.

The only modern English biography is that of Gosse in the English Men of Letters series (1905). The latest work is O. Leroy, *Le Chevalier Thomas Browne (1605–82), médecin, styliste & métaphysicien* (Paris, 1931). The traditional distortion of Browne's share in the witch-trial, heightened in Gosse, was corrected by M. Letts (*NQ*, 23 March, 1912), who was followed by W. P. Dunn (*Sir Thomas Browne*, Menasha, 1926) and Leroy; the history of the tradition was reviewed by D. Tyler in *Anglia*, liv (1930). With biography may be included M. L. Tildesley's *Sir Thomas Browne: His Skull, Portraits, and Ancestry* (1923).

Criticism began with Digby's *Observations* (1643) and Alexander Ross's *Medicus Medicatus* (1645) and *Arcana Microcosmi* (1651). Coleridge's comments are in his *Miscellaneous*

Criticism, ed. T. M. Raysor (1936). Some modern essays are those of Sir Leslie Stephen, *Hours in a Library, Second Series* (1876); Walter Pater, *Appreciations* (1889); Edward Dowden, *Puritan and Anglican* (1900); Sir William Osler, *Library*, vii (1906; repr. in *An Alabama Student*, 1908, 1929); P. E. More, *Shelburne Essays, Sixth Series* (1909); C. Whibley, *Essays in Biography* (1913); and L. Strachey, *Books and Characters* (1922). The best analyses of Browne's mind and world are contained in the books by Dunn and Leroy already cited, and in B. Willey's *Seventeenth Century Background* (1934).

In *Outflying Philosophy* (Hildesheim, 1924), R. Sencourt stresses Browne's religious and scholastic thought. A. C. Howell stresses the influence of Bacon and Descartes (*SP* xxii, 1925). A solid and corrective article is G. K. Chalmers's 'Sir Thomas Browne, True Scientist' (*Osiris*, ii, 1936). Among other special studies are R. R. Cawley's full investigation of Browne's reading (*PMLA* xlviii, 1933), J. M. Cline's essay on *Hydriotaphia* (*University of California Publications in English*, viii, 1940), and J. S. Finch's account of the quincunx (*SP* xxxvii, 1940). D. K. Ziegler (*In Distinguished and Divided Worlds*, Harvard, 1943) argues that Browne divorced reason and faith.

Browne's style is of course discussed by many of the critics already named, and he has a prominent place in Saintsbury's *History of English Prose Rhythm* (1912). More technical studies have been made by B. Anderton, *Sketches from a Library Window* (1922); N. R. Tempest, *RES* iii (1927); and E. L. Parker, *PMLA* liii (1938). Many autograph corrections have been collected by J. Carter and J. S. Finch, in the former's sumptuous edition of *Urne Buriall and The Garden of Cyrus* (1932), in the *Colophon*, xiii (1933), and elsewhere; references are given in the *TLS*, 16 March, 1940 and 27 February, 1943.

G. Keynes compiled a *Bibliography* in 1924 and Leroy *A French Bibliography* in 1931.

WILLIAM BROWNE, 1590/1?–1643/5?

The first book of *Britannia's Pastorals* appeared in 1613, the second, with a second edition of the first, in 1616, and the two books again in 1625. The unfinished third book was first printed for the Percy Society (xxx, 1852). *The Shepheards Pipe* (1614) included seven eclogues by Browne and four by C. Brooke, Wither, and Davies of Hereford. The *Inner Temple*

Masque was first printed in the 1772 edition of Browne's *Works*. Modern editions of the works are those of W. C. Hazlitt (2 vols., 1868–9) and G. Goodwin (Muses' Library, 2 vols., 1894). It is uncertain whether the poet was the William Browne whose translation of *Polexandre* appeared in 1647.

The fullest critical study is F. W. Moorman's *William Browne* (Strassburg, 1897). There are briefer discussions by Bullen (in Goodwin's edition), in the books on pastoral literature by W. W. Greg (1906) and H. Genouy (1928), and in H. Ashton's *Du Bartas en Angleterre* (1908). The epitaph on the Countess of Pembroke is the subject of a brochure by Philip Sidney (1907) and an article by Grierson (*MLR* vi, 1911). G. Tillotson has bibliographical studies in *RES* vi and vii (1930–1) and the *Library*, xi (1930–1). Milton's annotations in his copy of *Britannia's Pastorals* are printed in vol. xviii of the Columbia edition. Some parallels with Milton are recorded by H. C. H. Candy in *NQ* clviii (1930).

ROBERT BURTON, 1577–1640.

The Anatomy of Melancholy was first published at Oxford in 1621 and reissued, with more or less augmentation and revision, in 1624, 1628, 1632, and 1638. The posthumous 6th edition (1651) included the author's few last revisions; he never corrected a number of slips and multiplying misprints. The 7th and 8th editions appeared in 1660 and 1676, the 9th not until 1800; then came a rapid succession of editions and reprints. In what has been the standard modern edition (3 vols., 1893, and various reprints), A. R. Shilleto did valuable pioneer work in tracing Burton's sources; he unfortunately based his text on the 7th edition, and numerous errors were pointed out by E. Bensly (*NQ*, Ser. 9, vols. xi and xii, Ser. 10, vols. i–vii and x). The Nonesuch edition (2 vols., 1925) is not complete or accurate. The two-volume edition of Floyd Dell and P. Jordan-Smith (New York, 1927; reissued in 1 vol., 1929) translates the Latin quotations and has a new index. The Everyman edition, ed. Holbrook Jackson (3 vols., 1932) is based on the 6th edition, collated with the 5th, and takes account of Shilleto and Bensly.

There is no extant manuscript of the *Anatomy* but there are two manuscripts, both now in America, of Burton's Latin play, *Philosophaster*. The play was first printed, along with Burton's

Latin verses from Oxford anthologies, by W. E. Buckley (Roxburghe Club, 1862). This has been re-edited by P. Jordan-Smith (Stanford, 1931), with a translation of the play. In her *John Florio* (1934) F. A. Yates suggests that Burton collaborated with Florio and Sir William Vaughan in *The New-found Politicke* (1626), a version of selections from Boccalini's *Ragguagli di Parnaso*.

Among appreciations of Burton are the essays of A. W. Fox, *A Book of Bachelors* (1899); C. Whibley, *Literary Portraits* (1904); E. Bensly, *CHEL* iv; Sir W. Osler, *Yale Review*, N.S., iii (1913–14), and *OBS*, vol. i, part iii, 1925 (1926); J. M. Murry, *TLS*, 28 April, 1921; repr. in *Countries of the Mind* (1922); L. Powys, *Thirteen Worthies* (1923); *TLS*, 21 January, 1926; some good pages in Hardin Craig, *The Enchanted Glass* (1936); and H. W. Taeusch, *Democritus Junior Anatomizes Melancholy* (Cleveland, 1937).

The first special study of the *Anatomy* was John Ferriar's *Illustrations of Sterne* (1798). Lamb's relation to Burton was discussed by Bernard Lake, *General Introduction to Charles Lamb* (Leipzig, 1903). Three recent special studies are H. J. Gottlieb's pamphlet, *Robert Burton's Knowledge of English Poetry* (New York University, 1937), S. B. Ewing's *Burtonian Melancholy in the Plays of John Ford* (Princeton, 1940), and Bergen Evans's *The Psychiatry of Robert Burton* (Columbia, 1944). There is a bibliographical study of the 5th edition by E. G. Duff, *Library*, iv (1923–4). The *OBS* volume already cited contains, in addition to Osler's essays, valuable bibliographical articles by Duff and Bensly and other things, including a list of the books Burton bequeathed to the Bodleian and Christ Church libraries. Much useful matter about the sources and editions of Burton is collected by P. Jordan-Smith in *Bibliographia Burtoniana* (Stanford, 1931).

WILLIAM BURTON, 1575–1645.

Burton's translation of Achilles Tatius, *The Most Delectable and Plesant Historye of Clitophon and Leucippe* (1597), has been handsomely edited by Sir S. Gaselee and H. F. B. Brett-Smith (1923). His *Description of Leicester Shire* appeared in 1622.

WILLIAM CAMDEN, 1551–1623.

Camden's long-lived Greek grammar appeared in 1595.

Britannia . . . Chorographica descriptio (1586) was enlarged in later editions and translated by Holland in 1610. It was translated and enlarged by E. Gibson in 1695 and had further editions. *Remaines of A Greater Worke, Concerning Britaine* (1605) was often reprinted, most recently in the Library of Old Authors (1870). *Annales Rerum Anglicarum, et Hibernicarum, regnante Elizabetha, ad annum salutis M.D.LXXXIX* was published in 1615. A second part, covering 1589–1603, with the first part revised, was issued by the Elzevir press in 1625. The whole work was edited by T. Hearne (3 vols., 1717). The first three books (1558–88) were translated by A. Darcie, from a French version of Camden's Latin, as *Annales. The True and Royall History of the famous Empresse Elizabeth* (1625); the fourth book was done by T. Browne (1629). R. Norton made a complete translation (1630); selections are in Sir H. Newbolt's *Noble English*, ii (1925). A translation of the *Annales*, and of Camden's notes on the reign of James, is in White Kennett's *Complete History of England* (1706), ii. Camden's *Epistolæ* were printed in 1691. L. B. Wright gives a general discussion in his *Middle-Class Culture* (1935) and R. B. Gottfried has studied the Irish aspect of Camden's scholarship in *ELH* x (1943).

THOMAS CAMPION, 1567–1620.

The only book reprinted was the treatise on counterpoint, which was included in the many editions of J. Playford's *Brief Introduction to the Skill of Musick* (1655 ff.). Campion's verse remained almost unknown after his own time until it was revived by Arber (*English Garner*, iii, 1880) and especially by Bullen in his several volumes of lyrics from Elizabethan song-books (1887–9) and his editions of Campion (1889, 1903). P. Vivian edited the English poems and masques (Muses' Library, 1907) and the standard edition of the complete works (1909). The *Observations* (1602) are in Bullen, in Vivian's large edition, and, with Daniel's reply, in G. G. Smith's *Elizabethan Critical Essays* (1904) and G. B. Harrison's Bodley Head Quartos (1925). Campion's music was edited by E. H. Fellowes in *The English School of Lutenist Song Writers* (1920 ff.).

The fullest critical study is *England's Musical Poet: Thomas Campion* (Columbia, 1938), by M. M. Kastendieck, who stresses the musical side. There are shorter discussions in the general histories of poetry and music and essays by Vivian (editions and *CHEL* iv), Bullen (editions and *Elizabethans,* 1924), and Robert Lynd (*Athenæum,* 26 September, 1919; *The Art of Letters,* 1920), and a discursive brochure by T. Mac-Donagh (1913). To these may be added G. D. Willcock's article on Elizabethan classical metres (*MLR* xxix, 1934) and R. W. Short's study of Campion's metrics (*PMLA* lix, 1944). Among other special studies in which Campion appears are J. A. S. McPeek's *Catullus in Strange and Distant Britain* (1939) and L. Bradner's *Musae Anglicanae* (1940). Rosseter's author-ship of the second part of *A Booke of Ayres* (1601) is supported by R. W. Berringer (*PMLA* lviii, 1943).

RICHARD CAREW, 1555–1620.

Godfrey of Bulloigne (1594; ed. Grosart, 1881), Carew's version of Tasso's first five books, is examined by R. E. N. Dodge and W. L. Bullock in *PMLA* xliv and xlv (1929–30). A translation from Spanish, by way of Italian, was *Examen de Ingenios. The Examination of mens Wits . . . By John Huarte* (1594). Carew's *Excellencie of the English tongue* (1595–6?), printed in the 1614 edition of Camden's *Remaines,* was an avowed imitation of tracts by H. Estienne and others; it is reprinted in G. G. Smith's *Elizabethan Critical Essays* (1904). The *Survey of Cornwall* (1602; edns. in 1769 and 1811) was an early piece of county history and topography.

THOMAS CAREW, 1594/5–1639?

The *Poems,* including the masque, *Cœlum Britanicum* (pr. 1634), were published in 1640 and enlarged in 1642 and 1651; the 1651 edition was reprinted in 1670. Errors of attribution in these and in the editions of W. C. Hazlitt (1870) and J. W. Ebsworth (1893) were mostly set right in the edition of A. Vincent (Muses' Library, 1899). Evidence from many manu-scripts concerning doubtful poems was assessed by C. L. Powell in *MLR* xi (1916). The poems, including manuscript pieces (but without a few of Powell's corrections), are re-printed in full in R. G. Howarth's *Minor Poets of the 17th Century* (Everyman, 1931). Carew gets his share, or perhaps less than his share, in the older anthologies and discussions of the cavalier poets, and more discriminating criticism in such books as Grierson's *Metaphysical Lyrics & Poems* (1921), G. Williamson's *Donne Tradition* (1930), and F. R. Leavis's *Revaluation* (1936).

One side of Carew is illustrated in K. A. McEuen, *Classical Influence upon the Tribe of Ben* (1939).

NATHANAEL CARPENTER, 1589–1628?

Carpenter's books were *Philosophia Libera* (Frankfort, 1621, Oxford, 1622; 2nd English ed., 1636) and *Geography Delineated* (1625; 2nd ed., 1635). The chief discussions are by F. Watson, *Beginnings of the Teaching of Modern Subjects* (1909), E. G. R. Taylor, *Late Tudor and Early Stuart Geography* (1934), W. S. Howell, *Speech Monographs*, i (1934), R. F. Jones, *Ancients and Moderns* (1936), F. R. Johnson, *Astronomical Thought in Renaissance England* (1937), and G. McColley, *Popular Astronomy*, xlviii (1940).

WILLIAM CARTWRIGHT, 1611–43.

Comedies, Tragi-Comedies, With other Poems . . . The Ayres and Songs set by Mr Henry Lawes was published by Moseley in 1651, with a great array of commendatory verses. The poems have been edited by R. C. Goffin (1918). The complete works have been elaborately edited, with a full critical study, by G. B. Evans (Harvard *Summaries of Theses 1940*). Some poems from manuscripts have been edited and assigned to Cartwright by W. M. Evans (*PMLA* liv, 1939). One clement in his work is discussed in the books on classical influence (*supra*, IV. 7) by J. B. Emperor, J. A. S. McPeek, and K. A. McEuen. There are bibliographical studies by G. B. Evans (*Library*, xxiii, 1942) and J. P. Danton (*Library Quarterly*, xii, 1942).

ELIZABETH CARY, VISCOUNTESS FALKLAND, 1585?–1639.

The *Tragedie of Mariam* (1613) was edited by A. C. Dunstan (Malone Society, 1914). A *History* of Edward II, 'Written by E. F. in the year 1627', of which two versions appeared in 1680, is fully discussed by D. A. Stauffer (*Parrott Presentation Volume*, Princeton, 1935). The chief biographical source is *The Lady Falkland: Her Life* (1861). There is a substantial essay in K. B. Murdock, *The Sun at Noon* (New York, 1939).

LUCIUS CARY, VISCOUNT FALKLAND, 1610?–43.

Of the Infallibilitie of the Church of Rome (1645) was reprinted with Henry Hammond's *View of Some Exceptions*, &c. (1646, 1650), and edited, with Thomas White's *Answer* and Falkland's

Reply, by T. Triplet in 1651 (enlarged 1660). Biography begins with Clarendon's two portraits (and the companion sketches of Falkland's friends), which are reprinted in D. Nichol Smith's *Characters . . . of the Seventeenth Century* (1918). Two Victorian estimates are Arnold's (*Mixed Essays*, 1879) and Goldwin Smith's reply to Arnold (*Lectures and Essays*, New York, 1881). Sir John Marriott's *Life and Times* (1907) has a political emphasis. The elaborate study in K. B. Murdock's *The Sun at Noon* (New York, 1939) combines public affairs with religious thought. Kurt Weber's *Lucius Cary, Second Viscount Falkland* (Columbia, 1940) stresses literary and philosophic interests. The fullest account of the Latitudinarianism of Great Tew is in Tulloch's *Rational Theology* (1872), i; a recent analysis, in addition to Murdock and Weber, is in W. K. Jordan, *Development of Religious Toleration*, ii (1936). To Grosart's edition of the poems (*Miscellanies of the Fuller Worthies' Library*, 1871) should be added an appendix in Weber and the elegy on Morison edited by Murdock (*Harvard Studies and Notes in Philology and Literature*, xx, 1938). Murdock and Weber give full bibliographies.

PATRICK CARY, 1624–56.

Cary, a younger brother of Lord Falkland, grew up abroad as a Catholic, led a disturbed and migratory life, religious and secular, and wrote *Trivial Poems, and Triolets* in 1651. These were first printed in 1771, edited by Scott in 1820, and again in Saintsbury's *Minor Poets of the Caroline Period*, ii (1906). There is a full appendix given to him in Weber's *Lucius Cary, Second Viscount Falkland* (Columbia, 1940).

MARGARET CAVENDISH, DUCHESS OF NEWCASTLE, 1623?–73.

There is no need of naming the prolific lady's publications, except *Natures Pictures* (1656), which contained 'A true Relation of my Birth, Breeding, and Life', and *The Life of . . . William Cavendishe* (1667). The first reliable modern edition of these two portraits, by M. A. Lower (1872), was superseded by that of Sir C. Firth (1886; rev. ed., 1906). The two texts are contained in an Everyman volume (1915). *The Cavalier and his Lady*, ed. E. Jenkins (Golden Treasury Series, 1872) gives selections from the work of the duke and duchess. The standard biographical and critical study is H. T. Perry, *The First Duchess of Newcastle and her Husband as Figures in Literary History* (Boston,

1918). There are sketches in C. Whibley's *Essays in Biography* (1913) and Virginia Woolf's *Common Reader* (1925).

WILLIAM CAVENDISH, SECOND EARL OF DEVONSHIRE, 1591?–1628.

The volume of essays called *Horæ Subsecivæ* (1620) has been assigned to either Grey Brydges, Lord Chandos, or Gilbert Lord Cavendish, as the *DNB* article on the former indicates. But Leo Strauss (*Political Philosophy of Hobbes*, 1936) describes a Chatsworth MS., written between 1612 and 1620 and apparently in Hobbes's hand, containing an earlier and shorter version of the published book. The author was evidently Hobbes's pupil, William Cavendish (to whom Malone and Park had attributed the work). It may be added that scholars seem to have missed the references in the *Stationers' Register* (29 March, 1619–20 and 1 July, 1637) to '*A Discourse against flattery* and *of Rome*, with Essaies' and 'Lord Cavendishes Essaies'. 'Discourse against flattery, by William Cavendish Knight' is also listed in Jaggard's *Catalogue* of 1619 (ed. O. M. Willard, *Stanford Studies in Language and Literature*, 1941).

WILLIAM CECIL, LORD BURGHLEY, 1520–1598.

Burghley's *Certaine Precepts*, published anonymously in 1616–17 and often reprinted in the seventeenth, eighteenth, and early nineteenth centuries, is conveniently accessible in Craik's *English Prose*, i, and G. B. Harrison's edition of *Henry Percy's Advice to his Son* (1930).

JOHN CHALKHILL, *fl.* 1600.

Thealma and Clearchus was first printed in 1683 by Izaak Walton, who had quoted songs of Chalkhill in the *Angler*, and reprinted by Singer (1820) and by Saintsbury in *Minor Poets of the Caroline Period*, ii (1906). In addition to the editors' remarks, some discussions of the author's identity or the poem are: an article in the *Retrospective Review*, iv (1821); two letters by F. S. Merryweather in the *Gentleman's Magazine* (March, April, 1860); some pages in Stapleton Martin's *Izaak Walton and his Friends* (2nd ed., 1904); and the *DNB*.

JOHN CHAMBERLAIN, 1554–1628.

The full and standard edition of Chamberlain's letters is by Norman McClure (2 vols., Philadelphia, 1939).

WILLIAM CHAMBERLAYNE, 1619–89.

Pharonnida: A Heroick Poem (1659) was reprinted in 1820 by Singer (along with the play of 1658, *Loves Victory*), and in Saintsbury's *Minor Poets of the Caroline Period*, i (1905). The play has been edited by C. K. Meschter (Bethlehem, Pa., 1914). Some critical discussions are articles in the *Retrospective Review*, i (1820); Saintsbury's preface; and a dissertation by Ernst Kilian (Königsberg, 1913).

GEORGE CHAPMAN, 1559?–1634.

Chapman's chief non-dramatic writings are cited in the text. The defective *Poems and Minor Translations* (1875) has been replaced by P. B. Bartlett's edition of the *Poems* (New York, 1941). Havelock Ellis's *Chapman. With Illustrative Passages* (1934) is a good introduction. *Hero and Leander* is minutely annotated in Marlowe's *Poems*, ed. L. C. Martin (1931), as well as in Miss Bartlett's volume. Reprints of the *Homer* extend from those of R. Hooper (Library of Old Authors, 5 vols., 1857–8) and R. H. Shepherd (1875) to the sumptuous Shakespeare Head edition (5 vols., 1930–1); a handy text is in the Temple Classics (4 vols., 1897–8).

There is a biographical sketch in R. L. Hine, *Hitchin Worthies* (1932). Chapman's relations with Somerset are examined by N. D. Solve, *Stuart Politics in Chapman's Tragedy of Chabot* (University of Michigan, 1928).

Among the older critiques are Swinburne's essay, prefixed to *Poems and Minor Translations* and issued by itself as *George Chapman* (1875), and Bullen's (*Elizabethans*, 1924). The most important commentary is F. L. Schoell's masterly investigation of Chapman's humanistic sources, ancient and modern, *Études sur l'humanisme continental en Angleterre* (Paris, 1926), with which go his related studies in the *Revue germanique*, ix (1913), and *MP* xiii (1915–16). Other critical and scholarly studies of Chapman's poetic theory and practice are those of Janet Spens, 'Chapman's Ethical Thought', *ESEA* xi (1925); E. Holmes, *Aspects of Elizabethan Imagery* (1929); G. Williamson, *The Donne Tradition* (1930); J. Smith, *Scrutiny*, iii and iv (1934–6); M. C. Bradbrook, *The School of Night* (1936); M. Bottrall, *Criterion*, xvi (1936–7); L. A. Rutledge (Harvard *Summaries of Theses 1938*); N. von Pogrell, *Die philosophisch-poetische Entwicklung George Chapmans* (*Britannica*, xviii, 1939); Roy W. Battenhouse,

'Chapman and the Nature of Man', *ELH* xii (1945). A special study is *Technik und Stil von Hero und Leander* (Bonn, 1915) by G. Lazarus.

Some notable comments on Chapman's *Homer* are those of Ben Jonson (printed by P. Simpson, *TLS*, 3 March, 1932), Coleridge (*Miscellaneous Criticism*, ed. T. M. Raysor, 1936), and Arnold, *On Translating Homer*. There is a German thesis by A. Lohff (Berlin, 1903). Chapman is discussed in H. B. Lathrop's *Translations from the Classics* (1933). Some fresh and important articles are three by P. B. Bartlett, on Chapman's revisions in the *Iliad* (*ELH* ii, 1935), his heroes (*RES* xvii, 1941), and his stylistic devices in the *Iliad* (*PMLA* lvii, 1942); and D. Smalley's 'Ethical Bias of Chapman's *Homer*' (*SP* xxxvi, 1939). G. G. Loane contributed many notes to *NQ* and the *TLS* during 1935–42.

There is a *Concise Bibliography* by S. A. Tannenbaum (New York, 1938).

KING CHARLES I, 1600–49.

The *Εἰκὼν Βασιλικὴ* is noticed under Gauden. *Reliquiæ Sacræ Carolinæ* ('Hague', 1650), which included the *Εἰκὼν*, had many editions. Three modern collections are: *Charles I in 1646. Letters of King Charles the First to Queen Henrietta Maria*, ed. J. Bruce (Camden Society, lxiii, 1856); *Trial of King Charles the First*, ed. J. G. Muddiman (1928); and *The Letters, Speeches and Proclamations of King Charles I*, ed. Sir C. Petrie (1935). Of the countless contemporary pamphlets and memoirs listed in the *BMC*, a few are mentioned here under Sir Thomas Herbert, W. Lilly, Milton, H. Parker, and Sir A. Weldon. In addition to the general histories, there are biographies by C. W. Coit (1924), F. M. G. Higham (1932), H. Belloc (1933), Evan John (1933), and E. Wingfield-Stratford (1937). To these may be added G. M. Young's 'essay', *Charles I and Cromwell* (1935). Among special works are Sir Claude Phillips, *The Picture Gallery of Charles I* (1896); G. Albion, *Charles I and the Court of Rome* (1935); and M. B. Pickel, *Charles I as Patron of Poetry and Drama* (1936). P. Simpson has discussed the king's opinions on the drama in the *Bodleian Quarterly Record*, viii (1936–7). There are lives of the queen by Carola Oman (1936), Janet Mackay (1939), and Jane Oliver (1940).

WALTER CHARLETON, 1620–1707.

Sir H. Rolleston has a general sketch in the *Bulletin of the History of Medicine*, viii (1940). Different sides of Charleton are discussed by F. Manning in his edition (1926) of *Epicurus's Morals* (1656) and T. F. Mayo, *Epicurus in England* (Dallas, 1934); by G. Williamson, *SP* xxxii (1935) and *RES* xii (1936); and by C. D. Thorpe, *Aesthetic Theory of Thomas Hobbes* (1940). There are bibliographies in W. Munk, *Roll of the Royal College of Physicians* (rev. ed., 1878), i, and in Manning and Rolleston.

ROBERT CHESTER, *fl.* 1601.

Loves Martyr: or, Rosalins Complaint. Allegorically shadowing the truth of Love, in the constant Fate of the Phœnix and Turtle (1601; ed. Grosart, 1878) contained an appendix of poems subscribed 'Vatum Chorus', 'Ignoto', 'William Shake-speare', 'John Marston', 'George Chapman', and 'Ben Johnson'. These 'Poeticall Essaies' have had separate editions, e.g. B. H. Newdigate (1937). Carleton Brown edited *Poems by Sir John Salusbury and Robert Chester* (E.E.T.S., Extra Series, cxiii, 1914). The endless discussion of Shakespeare's poem is summarized by H. E. Rollins in his variorum edition, *Shakespeare: The Poems* (1938).

KATHERINE CHIDLEY, *fl.* 1641–5.

This vigorous preacher, who failed of a place in the *DNB*, replied to Thomas Edwards in *The Justification Of The Independant Churches of Christ* (1641), which is summarized and excerpted in B. Hanbury's *Historical Memorials relating to the Independents*, ii (1841), and in *A New-Yeares-Gift* (1645). She is noticed in Masson's *Milton*; by E. M. Williams, 'Women Preachers in the Civil War', *Journal of Modern History*, i (1929); by W. Haller, *Tracts on Liberty* (1934), i; and A. Barker, *Milton and the Puritan Dilemma* (1942).

WILLIAM CHILLINGWORTH, 1602–44.

The Religion Of Protestants A Safe Way To Salvation appeared at the end of 1637. The *Works* were edited in 3 vols. in 1820 and 1838. Cheynell's hostile tract was *Chillingworthi Novissima* (1644); a happier early sketch was that of Clarendon. The first and only biography is the *Historical and Critical Account* of P. Des Maizeaux (1725). The fullest analysis of Chillingworth's thought is in J. Tulloch's *Rational Theology* (1872).

Other old but good discussions are by E. H. Plumptre, in *Masters in English Theology*, ed. A. Barry (1877); Sir James Stephen, *Horae Sabbaticae, First Series* (1892); and H. Rashdall, in *Typical English Churchmen*, ed. W. E. Collins (1902). Later accounts are in the books on toleration by M. Freund (1927), W. K. Jordan, ii (1936), and T. Lyon (1937); in W. F. Mitchell, *English Pulpit Oratory* (1932); and in the studies of Falkland by K. B. Murdock and K. Weber (*supra*, Lucius Cary).

JOHN CLEVELAND, 1613–58.

Cleveland's several prose 'characters' (1644 ff.) are reprinted in H. Morley's and other anthologies of characters. *The Character Of A London-Diurnall: With severall select Poems* (1647) had many enlarged editions, especially as *Poems* (1651 ff.), before the *Clievelandi Vindiciæ; or, Clieveland's Genuine Poems* (1677), edited by Bishop Lake and S. Drake, who tried to carry out a purge, since numerous pieces had been mixed with his work, notably in E. Williamson's anthology, *J. Cleaveland Revived* (1659 ff.). The bibliographical problems are outlined in the edition of J. M. Berdan (New York, 1903; Yale, 1911). The poems are reprinted also in Saintsbury's *Minor Poets of the Caroline Period*, iii (1921). Fresh biographical data are given by S. V. Gapp in *PMLA* xlvi (1931). For criticism, there are editorial prefaces, G. Williamson's *Donne Tradition* (1930), and H. Levin's essay (*Criterion*, xiv, 1934–5).

LADY ANNE CLIFFORD, 1590–1676.

Lives of Lady Anne Clifford . . . and of her Parents, Summarized by Herself, ed. J. P. Gilson (Roxburghe Club, 1916), was followed by V. Sackville-West's edition, from an eighteenth-century transcript, of *The Diary of the Lady Anne Clifford* (1923). The extant diary, which may be incomplete, covers, with gaps, the years 1603–19. Further information about Lady Anne and her background is given in G. C. Williamson's *George, Third Earl of Cumberland* (1920) and *Lady Anne Clifford* (1922), and V. Sackville-West's *Knole and the Sackvilles* (1923).

SIR EDWARD COKE, 1552–1634.

The *Reports* appeared in 13 parts (1600–15, and later). The still more famous *First Part Of The Institutes Of The Lawes of England* ('Coke on Littleton') appeared in 1628 (rev. 1629), the second part in 1642, the third and fourth in 1644. There are sketches by Lord Birkenhead (*Fourteen English Judges*, 1926) and Sir W. Holdsworth (*Some Makers of English Law*, 1938), and books by H. Lyon and H. Block (Boston, 1929) and C. W. James (1929), who deals largely with Coke's family and descendants. Coke is treated, *passim*, in the general histories, such as S. R. Gardiner's, in Holdsworth's *History of English Law*, vols. i–xii (1903–38), and in H. Arneke (*supra*, IV. 6). Among special studies is D. O. Wagner's 'Coke and the Rise of Economic Liberalism', *Economic History Review*, vi (1935–6).

JOHN COLLOP, 1625–*post* 1660.

Poesis Rediviva (1656) was revived, with copious extracts, in an essay by John Drinkwater (*A Book for Bookmen*, 1926). Some poems are printed in L. B. Marshall, *Rare Poems of the Seventeenth Century* (1936). Collop's irenical *Medici Catholicon* (1656) is noticed by W. K. Jordan, *Development of Religious Toleration*, iv (1940).

LADY CONWAY, 1631–79.

We meet many figures and ideas of the age in *Conway Letters: The Correspondence of Anne, Viscountess Conway, Henry More, and their Friends, 1642–1684*, edited from manuscripts by Marjorie Nicolson (Yale, 1930). Lady Conway's notorious medical case is discussed by G. R. Owen, *Annals of Medical History*, N.S., ix (1937).

RICHARD CORBET or CORBETT, 1582–1635.

Two posthumous volumes were *Certain Elegant Poems, written by Dr. Corbet, Bishop of Norwich* (1647) and *Poëtica Stromata* (? The Hague, 1648). O. Gilchrist edited a 'fourth edition' in 1807. Corbet was included in Chalmers's *English Poets* (1810), v. He was the subject of one of Aubrey's best lives. Important articles are J. E. V. Crofts's 'Life of Bishop Corbett 1582–1635', *ESEA* x (1924), and H. H. Wood's 'A Seventeenth-Century Manuscript of Poems by Donne and Others', ibid., xvi (1931). C. W. Brodribb had several notes in *NQ* cl (1926).

SIR WILLIAM CORNWALLIS, 1579?–1614.

Cornwallis wrote *Essayes* (two parts, 1600–1); *Discourses upon Seneca the Tragedian* (1601), included in the 1610 and 1632 editions of the *Essayes*; a tract on the union with Scotland

(1604); and two posthumous volumes, *Essayes Or rather, Encomions* (1616) and *Essayes Of Certaine Paradoxes* (1616). The 'Praise of King Richard the Third', in this last volume, was not by Cornwallis (W. G. Zeeveld, *PMLA* lv, 1940). R. E. Bennett has edited 'Four Paradoxes' in *Harvard Studies and Notes in Philology and Literature*, xiii (1931). A few essays are reprinted in some of the college anthologies (*supra*, II. 1). The essays are discussed in the monographs (*supra*, IV. 5) by W. L. Mac-Donald and E. N. S. Thompson. A full study of Cornwallis's life and work has been made by R. E. Bennett (*Harvard Summaries of Theses 1931*), who has discussed the publication of the essays and paradoxes (*RES* ix, 1933) and the essayist's use of Montaigne (*PMLA* xlviii, 1933). Traditional errors in the biography were corrected by Bennett and others in the *TLS*, 23 October–4 December, 1930, and by P. B. Whitt in *RES* viii (1932).

THOMAS CORYATE, 1577?–1617.

Coryats Crudities Hastily gobled up in five Moneths travells (1611; repr. in 2 vols., 1905) was accompanied by two small pieces, also of 1611, *Coryats Crambe* and *The Odcombian Banquet. Thomas Coriate Traveller for the English Wits: Greeting. From the Court of the Great Mogul* (1616) was included, with other things, in the 1776 edition of the *Crudities* (3 vols.). Fragments on Coryate's eastern travels are also in *Purchas His Pilgrimes* and in Sir William Foster's *Early Travels in India* (1921); they are discussed by W. G. Rice and S. C. Chew (*supra*, V. 4). There are sketches of Coryate by A. W. Fox, *A Book of Bachelors* (1899); L. Powys, *Thirteen Worthies* (1923); and T. Spencer, *Harvard Graduates' Magazine*, xl (1931–2); and a fuller account by B. Penrose, *Urbane Travellers* (1942).

JOHN COTTON, 1584–1652.

For the writings of this eminent Puritan divine one can only refer to the *BMC*, *STC* (Wing), and J. H. Tuttle's article in *Bibliographical Essays: A Tribute to Wilberforce Eames* (Harvard, 1924). There is a brief account, with references, in the *Dictionary of American Biography*, and more or less discussion in such books as Perry Miller's *Orthodoxy in Massachusetts* (1933) and *New England Mind: The Seventeenth Century* (1939), W. Haller's *Rise of Puritanism* (1938), and studies of Roger Williams.

SIR ROBERT COTTON, 1571–1631.

Cotton's writings were less important than his library, which is described in *Catalogus Librorum Manuscriptorum Bibliothecae Cottonianae*, ed. T. Smith (1696), *Catalogue of the Manuscripts in the Cottonian Library*, ed. J. Planta (1802), and *A Guide to a Select Exhibition of Cottonian Manuscripts*, ed. H. I. Bell (1931), and in E. Edwards's *Memoirs of Libraries* (1859), i, and the books on Old English scholarship by E. N. Adams and D. C. Douglas which were cited above in IV. 6. Many of Cotton's tracts were collected by James Howell in *Cottoni Posthuma* (1651; ed. E. Goldsmid, *Collectanea*, iii, 1884–8). Some pieces are reprinted in *Smeeton's Historical & Biographical Tracts* (1820), ii; *Harleian Miscellany*, ed. Park, ii (1809); and *Somers Tracts*, ed. Scott, iv (1810).

ABRAHAM COWLEY, 1618–67.

Most of Cowley's writings are mentioned in the text. His collected—though not complete—*Works* were edited in 1668 by Thomas Sprat, who edited the Latin poems in the same year. There was no complete edition after the 12th (1721)—though Cowley was included in the several large series of English poets—until that of Grosart (Chertsey Worthies' Library, 2 vols., 1881). This was in part superseded by A. R. Waller's edition of the English works (Cambridge English Classics, 2 vols., 1905–6). The best modern anthology is J. Sparrow's *The Mistress With Other Select Poems* (1926). Cowley's essays, which belong to the next volume, have been frequently edited. Though Cowley has not received the *apparatus criticus* which modern scholarship has bestowed upon a number of his fellows, he has been the subject of two standard biographies, by A. H. Nethercot (1931) and J. Loiseau (Paris, 1931).

The curve of his reputation, which has been traced by Nethercot in his book and in *PMLA* xxxviii (1923) and in a monograph by Loiseau (Paris, 1931), is roughly parallel to the record of editions. Formal criticism as well as biography began with Sprat. The neoclassical reaction, registered by the aged Dryden, by Pope and Addison, culminated in Dr. Johnson's 'Cowley' (*Lives of the Poets*, 1779). But Cowley's immense seventeenth-century fame gave him a momentum which, assisted by congenial elements in his verse and by his prose, carried him, in spite of much critical hostility, through the eighteenth and early nineteenth centuries, where so many metaphysical poets sank. After fifty years of neglect came Gosse's essay (*Cornhill Magazine*, xxxiv, 1876; *Seventeenth-Century Studies*, 1883), which is a minor landmark but quite unreliable. Skipping other essays, and taking Courthope and the *CHEL* for granted, we may trace Cowley's return through such items as these: Havelock Ellis, *New Statesman*, xiii (1919); K. N. Colvile, *Fame's Twilight* (1923); Sparrow's introduction (1926); 'Cowley's Lyrics', *TLS*, 18 November, 1926; H. W. Garrod, 'Cowley, Johnson, and the "Metaphysicals" ', *The Profession of Poetry* (1929); G. Williamson, *The Donne Tradition* (1930); R. C. Wallerstein, 'Cowley as a Man of Letters', *Transactions of the Wisconsin Academy*, xxvii (1932); G. Walton, *Scrutiny*, vi (1937–8); and T. S. Eliot, 'A Note on Two Odes of Cowley', *Seventeenth Century Studies Presented to Sir Herbert Grierson* (1938). There is some criticism in Nethercot's biography, which incorporates the author's numerous articles, and an exhaustive critical study in Loiseau.

The odes are minutely examined in R. Shafer's *English Ode to 1660* (Princeton, 1918). J. M. McBryde's 'Study of Cowley's *Davideis*' (*JEGP* ii, 1899) is modified and enlarged by Loiseau and by H-H. Krempien, *Der Stil der Davideis von Abraham Cowley im Kreise ihrer Vorläufer* (*Britannica*, xi, 1936). Loiseau gives a very full bibliography, the *CBEL* a brief one. A bibliography of criticism, 1912–38, is provided by T. Spencer and M. Van Doren in *Studies in Metaphysical Poetry* (1939).

RICHARD CRASHAW, 1612/13–49.

Crashaw's published volumes were *Epigrammatum Sacrorum Liber* (1634), *Steps to the Temple* (1646; enlarged 1648), and *Carmen Deo Nostro* (Paris, 1652). While much less popular than Herbert in the seventeenth century, he did not in the eighteenth drop quite so completely out of sight, thanks in part to Cowley's elegy and Pope's faint praise. He was edited in 1785 and included in several collections. Grosart's edition (Fuller Worthies' Library, 2 vols., 1872–3) and the editions of A. R. Waller (Cambridge English Classics, 1904) and J. R. Tutin (Muses' Library, 1905), were superseded by that of L. C. Martin (1927), which has a full apparatus.

Among critical essays are those of Gosse, *Seventeenth-Century*

Studies (1883); F. Thompson, *Academy*, 20 November, 1897 and *Works*, iii (1913); H. C. Beeching, in Muses' Library edition; R. A. E. Shepherd, in his edition of the *Religious Poems* (1914); Lord Chalmers, *In Memoriam Adolphus William Ward* (1924); T. S. Eliot, *For Lancelot Andrewes* (1928); F. E. Hutchinson, in the *CHEL* vii and *Church Quarterly Review*, cvi (1928); E. I. Watkin, in *The English Way*, ed. M. Ward (1933); T. O. Beachcroft, *Criterion*, xiii (1933–4); and sections in the books on the metaphysical poets by G. Williamson (1930), Joan Bennett (1934), and especially Helen C. White (1936). M. Praz's *Secentismo e Marinismo in Inghilterra* (Florence, 1925) retains its special value. R. C. Wallerstein's *Richard Crashaw* (University of Wisconsin, 1935) is an able 'Study in Style and Poetic Development'. The newest, fullest, and best book is Austin Warren's *Richard Crashaw, A Study in Baroque Sensibility* (Louisiana State University, 1939). There is a bibliography of criticism, 1912–38, in T. Spencer and M. Van Doren, *Studies in Metaphysical Poetry* (1939).

OLIVER CROMWELL, 1599–1658.

Carlyle's *Letters and Speeches of Oliver Cromwell* (2 vols., 1845) retains its special place, but the standard collection is now W. C. Abbott's *Writings and Speeches of Oliver Cromwell* (4 vols.; vols. i–iii, Harvard, 1937–45). There is a massive *Bibliography of Oliver Cromwell* (Harvard, 1929) by Abbott, who has reviewed the course of Cromwell's fame in *Conflicts with Oblivion* (Yale, 1924; 2nd ed., Harvard, 1935). Some of the biographies, representing various points of view, are those of Sir C. Firth (1900), Lord Morley (1900), G. R. Stirling Taylor (1928), John Buchan (1934), F. H. Hayward (1934), and M. Ashley (1937).

RALPH CUDWORTH, 1617–88.

Cudworth's great *Sermon Preached before the Honourable House of Commons, At Westminster, March 31. 1647* has been reproduced by the Facsimile Text Society (New York, 1930). His chief works were *The True Intellectual System of the Universe* (1678; ed. T. Birch, 2 vols., 1743, 4 vols., 1820; ed. J. Harrison, with full notes, 3 vols., 1845) and *A Treatise concerning Eternal and Immutable Morality* (1731). Light is thrown on Cudworth's background by M. Nicolson in 'Christ's College and the Latitude-Men', *MP* xxvii (1929–30). Among the older critics are

J. Tulloch (*Rational Theology and Christian Philosophy*, 1872), C. de Rémusat (*Histoire de la philosophie en Angleterre*, 1875), and C. E. Lowrey (*Philosophy of Ralph Cudworth*, New York, 1884). More recent critics are Powicke, Pawson, De Boer, and De Pauley, in their books on the Cambridge Platonists; J. C. Gregory, 'Cudworth and Descartes', *Philosophy*, viii (1933); B. Willey, *Seventeenth Century Background* (1934); and Joseph Beyer, *Ralph Cudworth als Ethiker, Staats-philosoph und Aesthetiker* (Bottrop, 1935). The most solid and acute analysis is in J. Muirhead, *Platonic Tradition in Anglo-Saxon Philosophy* (1931).

NICHOLAS CULPEPER, 1616–54.

Among the works of the physician, herbalist, and astrologer were *A Physicall Directory* (1649), a translation of the College of Physicians' 'dispensatory' which outraged vested interests, and *The English Physician* (1652, unauthorized; enlarged and corrected, 1653). The latter has been issued, with more or less revision, ever since; there were editions in 1922 and 1932 and a small volume of extracts in 1930. Culpeper's works were edited by G. A. Gordon (3 vols., 1802). L. Powys's *Thirteen Worthies* (1923) has a pleasant essay. A more scholarly account by B. Chance is in *Annals of Medical History*, N.S., iii (1931). And one should not forget the story in Kipling's *Rewards and Fairies*.

NATHANAEL CULVERWEL, 1618/19–51?

W. Dillingham edited *Spiritual Opticks* (1651) and *An Elegant And Learned Discourse Of the Light of Nature, With several other Treatises* (1652; other edns., 1654, 1661, 1669). The *Discourse* has been edited by John Brown and John Cairns (1857) and, abridged, by E. T. Campagnac (*The Cambridge Platonists*, 1901). Rémusat has a full analysis in his *Histoire de la philosophie en Angleterre* (1875). Later discussions are contained in the books on the Cambridge Platonists by Powicke (1926), Pawson (1930), De Boer (1931), and De Pauley (1937), and in W. F. Mitchell's *English Pulpit Oratory* (1932).

EDWARD DACRES, *fl.* 1636–40.

The first printed English translations of Machiavelli's chief works were those of Dacres, *Machiavels Discourses. upon the first Decade of T. Livius* (1636) and *Nicholas Machiavel's Prince* (1640; Tudor Translations, 1905; ed. W. E. C. Baynes, 1929).

SIR ROBERT DALLINGTON, 1561–1637.

The informative and entertaining *View of Fraunce*, written largely in 1598, was pirated in 1604 and reissued, with an introduction, by the author (in 1604–5?) as *A Method for Travell* (ed. W. P. Barrett, Shakespeare Association Facsimiles, 1936). Two other books were *A Survey of the Great Dukes State of Tuscany* (1605) and *Aphorismes Civill and Militarie: Amplified with Authorities, and exemplified with Historie, out of the first Quarterne of Fr. Guicciardine* (1613).

SAMUEL DANIEL, 1563?–1619.

Daniel was included in Chalmers's *English Poets* (1810), iii. His complete works were edited by Grosart (5 vols., 1885–96). *Poems and A Defence of Ryme* (Harvard, 1930) is a selection carefully edited by A. C. Sprague. The *Defence of Ryme* has been reprinted in G. G. Smith's *Elizabethan Critical Essays* (1904), G. B. Harrison's Bodley Head Quartos (1925), and elsewhere.

Daniel has a not always adequate place in the histories of literature and poetry. There are introductory essays by H. C. Beeching (*A Selection*, 1899) and Sprague, and an essay in A. H. Bullen's *Elizabethans* (1924). A large proportion of the scholarly work has been concerned with the sonnets and dramatic pieces, and that is omitted here. Coleridge's praise of the *Civil Wars* may be found in his *Miscellaneous Criticism*, ed. T. M. Raysor (1936). That poem has been treated in a thesis by A. Probst (Strassburg, 1902); by J. H. Roberts, University of Chicago *Abstracts of Theses, Humanistic Series*, ii (1926), and *MLN* xli (1926); and in L. F. Ball's study of historical epics (*ELH* i, 1934). Among other special studies are: G. R. Redgrave, 'Daniel and the Emblem Literature', *Transactions of the Bibliographical Society*, xi (1909–11); J. I. M. Stewart, 'Montaigne's *Essays* and *A Defence of Ryme*', *RES* ix (1933); M. Eccles, 'Samuel Daniel in France and Italy', *SP* xxxiv (1937); and B. Stirling, 'Daniel's *Philotas* and the Essex Case', *MLQ* iii (1942). There is a full *Bibliography* of Daniel's works, with an appendix of letters, by H. Sellers, in *OBS*, vol. ii, part i, 1927 (1928). Sellers printed additions to the text of Daniel in *MLR* xi (1916). There is a *Concise Bibliography* (New York, 1942) by S. A. Tannenbaum.

Sir William Davenant or D'Avenant, 1606–68.

This note ignores Davenant the playwright. *Madagascar,* a volume of poems (1638; repr. 1648), was followed by the *Discourse upon Gondibert* or *Preface to Gondibert* which, with Hobbes's *Answer,* appeared in two editions at Paris in 1650. The unfinished poem, with these critical pieces, was issued in London in two editions dated 1651; one of these at least came out in 1650. Both old and unpublished poems were included in the folio *Works* (1673). *Gondibert* and some other poems were reprinted in Anderson's *British Poets* (1793), iv, and Chalmers's *English Poets* (1810), vi. Another canto of *Gondibert,* published in 1685, has been edited by J. G. McManaway (*MLQ* i, 1940). *Selected Poems* have been printed by G. Bush (Cambridge, Mass., 1943). The *Discourse* and Hobbes's *Answer* are in Spingarn's *Critical Essays of the Seventeenth Century.* There are standard biographies by Alfred Harbage (University of Pennsylvania, 1935), who has a chapter on *Gondibert,* and A. H. Nethercot (University of Chicago, 1938), whose longer work stresses biography and the theatre. There are theses on *Gondibert* by G. Gronauer (Erlangen, 1911) and C. M. Dowlin (University of Pennsylvania, 1934), who emphasizes the English tradition behind the critical theory of Davenant and Hobbes. That theory is discussed also by R. L. Sharp, *From Donne to Dryden* (1940), and fully by C. D. Thorpe, *The Aesthetic Theory of Thomas Hobbes* (1940).

Lady Eleanor Davies, *c.* 1590–1652.

Lady Eleanor is more commonly known by the name of her first husband, Sir John Davies (d. 1626), the poet and jurist, than by that of her second, Sir Archibald Douglas. Her prophetic instinct asserted itself in 1625. One specimen, *Strange and Wonderfull Prophesies* (1649), is reprinted in W. C. Hazlitt's *Fugitive Tracts, Second Series* (1875). T. Spencer has an amusing account of her in *Harvard Studies and Notes in Philology and Literature,* xx (1938). Briefer sketches are given by S. G. Wright in the *Bodleian Quarterly Record,* vii (1932), and by C. J. Hindle in his valuable bibliography of her pamphlets in *Edinburgh Bibliographical Society Transactions,* vol. i, pt. i (1936). The 53 items run from 1625 to 1652.

JOHN DAVIES of Hereford, 1565?–1618.

The complete works were edited by Grosart (Chertsey Worthies' Library, 2 vols., 1878). The chief studies are: H. Heidrich, *John Davies of Hereford* (Leipzig, 1924), which had a partly corrective review from R. B. McKerrow (*RES* i, 1925); R. L. Anderson, 'A French Source for John Davies of Hereford's System of Psychology' (*PQ* vi, 1927), and *Elizabethan Psychology and Shakespeare's Plays* (University of Iowa, 1927); and C. D. Murphy, *John Davies of Hereford* (Cornell *Abstracts of Theses 1940*), and an article on Davies's use of Mornay (*PQ* xxi, 1942). Davies's epigrams are discussed by T. K. Whipple, *Martial and the English Epigram* (1925), and by L. Enñis in *HLB* (1937).

THOMAS DEKKER, 1572?–1632.

The only comprehensive edition of Dekker's non-dramatic works, that of Grosart (5 vols., 1884–6), will be superseded by that of F. P. Wilson, whose editions of *Foure Birds of Noahs Arke* (1924) and *The Plague Pamphlets of Thomas Dekker* (1925) made the larger task inevitable. *The Guls Horne-booke*, since it was first reprinted by Nott (1812), has had several reprints, e.g. Temple Classics; the standard edition is by R. B. McKerrow (1904). *The Wonderfull yeare* is reprinted in G. B. Harrison's Bodley Head Quartos (1924) and in Wilson's *Plague Pamphlets*. *The Belman Of London* and *Lanthorne and Candle-light* are included in the Temple Classics volume and, abridged, in A. V. Judges's *Elizabethan Underworld* (1930). Other reprints are: *A Knights Conjuring*, Percy Society, v (1842); *Penny-Wise Pound-Foolish*, ed. W. Bang, *Materialien*, xxiii (1908); and *The Seven deadlie Sinns of London*, ed. H. F. B. Brett-Smith (Percy Reprints, 1922).

Besides the introductions of Wilson and other editors, there are essays in Swinburne's *Age of Shakespeare* (1908) and A. H. Bullen's *Elizabethans* (1924). The fullest study is Mary L. Hunt's *Thomas Dekker* (Columbia, 1911). A special discussion is K. L. Gregg's *Thomas Dekker: A Study in Economic and Social Backgrounds* (University of Washington, 1924). The tracts on roguery are treated in the books by F. W. Chandler (Boston, 1907) and F. Aydelotte (1913) and in Judges's introduction. Grobianism is described in C. H. Herford's *Studies in the Literary Relations of England and Germany* (1886) and E. Rühl's *Grobianus in England* (Berlin, 1904). Dekker's 'characters' are discussed by M. L. Hunt (*JEGP* xi, 1912) and W. J. Paylor (*MLR* xxxi,

1936; *The Overburian Characters*, 1936). His authorship of the famous lyrics in *Patient Grissill* has been questioned, e.g. by H. Jenkins (*Henry Chettle*, 1934, and *TLS*, 25 October, 1941). There are biographical notes by F. P. Wilson in *MLR* xv (1920). There is a *Concise Bibliography* (New York, 1939) by S. A. Tannenbaum.

WILLIAM DELL, c. 1607?–70.

Several Sermons and Discourses (1652) was reprinted in 1709; *Select Works* appeared in 1773; and the *Works* in 1816 (Philadelphia) and 1817 (2 vols., London). *The Tryal of Spirits* (1653) included a discourse on 'The right Reformation of Learning, Schools, and Universities, according to the state of the Gospel'. The same theme was touched in *The Stumbling-Stone* (1653). These pieces are included in the collections mentioned and in part in *A Collection of Devotional Tracts* (Philadelphia, 1760). A portion of *The Way of True Peace and Unity* (1649) is reprinted in A. S. P. Woodhouse, *Puritanism and Liberty* (1938). Dell receives more or less space in Mullinger, *University of Cambridge*, iii (1911); Rufus M. Jones, *Studies in Mystical Religion* (1909); R. F. Jones, *Ancients and Moderns* (1936); W. K. Jordan, *Development of Religious Toleration*, iii (1938); and Woodhouse. There is a biographical account in John Venn's *Caius College* (1901).

SIR JOHN DENHAM, 1615–69.

The Sophy was printed in 1642. The piratical first edition of *Coopers Hill* (1642) was reissued four times before the first authorized and enlarged text of 1655. Some things, like *The Destruction of Troy* (1656) and the elegy on Cowley (1667), appeared separately. The *Version of the Psalms* was not printed until 1714. The first collected edition of Denham's verse came out in 1668, the tenth in 1780. He was reprinted in various large collections. The standard edition of T. H. Banks (Yale, 1928) provides full biographical, critical, and bibliographical matter. The chief early critics were Dryden, in various essays, and Johnson in the *Lives of the Poets* (1779). B. Dobrée's *Sir John Denham* (1927; repr. in *As Their Friends Saw Them*, 1933) is a pleasant essay in the form of a dialogue between Bishop King and Waller. Important articles are R. C. Wallerstein's study of the heroic couplet in *PMLA* l (1935) and G. Williamson's 'Rhetorical Pattern of Neo-classical Wit' in *MP* xxxiii (1935–6). The genre which *Coopers Hill* re-created is fully described in R. A. Aubin's *Topographical Poetry in XVIII-Century England* (New York, 1936).

ARTHUR DENT, *c.* 1553–1601.

The enormously popular *Plaine Mans Path-way to Heaven* (1601) is discussed in H. C. White's *English Devotional Literature* (1931) and L. B. Wright's *Middle-Class Culture* (1935) and, in relation to Bunyan, by J. B. Wharey in *MLN* xxxvi (1921).

SIR SIMONDS D'EWES, 1602–50.

The *Journals of all the Parliaments During the Reign of Queen Elizabeth* was published in 1682. The *Journal . . . from the Beginning of the Long Parliament to the Opening of the Trial of the Earl of Strafford* has been edited by W. Notestein (Yale, 1923), the *Journal . . . from the First Recess of the Long Parliament to the Withdrawal of King Charles from London* by W. H. Coates (Yale, 1942). The *Autobiography and Correspondence* were edited by J. O. Halliwell[-Phillipps] (2 vols., 1845). J. H. Marsden's *College Life in the Time of James the First* (1851) was compiled from the autobiography.

SIR KENELM DIGBY, 1603–65.

Some of Digby's writings were: *Observations upon Religio Medici* (1643); *Observations on the 22. Stanza in the 9th. Canto of the 2d. Book of Spencers Faery Queen* (1643); *Two Treatises . . . The Nature of Bodies . . . The Nature of Mans Soule* (Paris, 1644; London, 1645), his chief scientific and philosophic work; *A Late Discourse . . . Touching the Cure of Wounds by the Powder of Sympathy* (1658), translated from the French *Discours* of the same year; *A Discourse Concerning the Vegetation of Plants* (1661). The *Private Memoirs* were edited by Sir H. Nicolas (1827); the *Journal of a Voyage into the Mediterranean* by J. Bruce (Camden Society, xcvi, 1868); and *Poems from Sir Kenelm Digby's Papers* by H. A. Bright (Roxburghe Club, 1877). The cookery book attributed to Digby, *The Closet of . . . Sir Kenelm Digbie Kt. opened* (1669), was edited by A. Macdonnell in 1910.

Criticism began with Alexander Ross's *Philosophicall Touch-Stone* (1645) and *Medicus Medicatus* (1645), and biography with Aubrey. Digby flits through contemporary memoirs and letters, such as the *Conway Letters*, ed. M. Nicolson (Yale, 1930). Some biographical books are T. Longueville's *Life* (1896),

H. M. Digby's *Sir Kenelm Digby and George Digby, Earl of Bristol* (1912), and E. W. Bligh's *Sir Kenelm Digby and his Venetia* (1932). C. Whibley's *Pageant of Life* (2nd ed., 1910) has a sketch. Two scholarly portraits are Allardyce Nicoll's lecture (*Johns Hopkins Alumni Magazine*, xxi, 1933) and J. F. Fulton's *Sir Kenelm Digby* (New York, 1937); the latter has a bibliography. Shirley's *The Wedding* was linked with Digby's marriage by A. Harbage (*PQ* xvi, 1937). W. G. A. Robertson discussed 'The Powder of Sympathy' in *Annals of Medical History*, vii (1925), and R. G. Grenell a more modern scientific idea in the *Bulletin of the History of Medicine*, x (1941).

LEONARD DIGGES, 1588–1635.

The Rape of Proserpine (1617) reappeared in 1628 as *Claudian Translated out of Latine into English Verse.* Two poems in praise of Shakespeare are reprinted in Sir E. K. Chambers, *William Shakespeare* (1930), ii. Digges—a friend of Mabbe—translated a Spanish novel, *Gerardo* (1622); the translation is fully discussed by E. G. Mathews (*supra*, IV. 7). There is some account of Digges in L. Hotson's *I, William Shakespeare* (1937).

JOHN DONNE, 1571/2–1631.

Donne's chief writings in prose were (in the order of publication, not of composition): *Pseudo-Martyr* (1610); *Ignatius his Conclave* (1611), in both Latin and English editions; *Devotions Upon Emergent Occasions* (1624); *Five Sermons* (1626); single sermons at various times, notably *Deaths Duell* (1632); *Juvenilia: or Certaine Paradoxes, and Problemes* (1633); *Six Sermons* (1634); *LXXX Sermons* (1640), with Walton's *Life*; *BIAΘANATOΣ* (1646); *Fifty Sermons* (1649); *Essayes in Divinity* (1651); *Letters to Severall Persons of Honour* (1651); and *XXVI. Sermons* (1660/1).

Among the very few poems printed in Donne's lifetime the important ones were *An Anatomy of the World* (1611) and *The Second Anniversarie. Of the Progres of the Soule* (1612), with which the *Anatomy* was reissued. The first collected edition was *Poems, By J. D. With Elegies on the Authors Death* (1633). In the 1635 edition the poems were arranged by genres and many, by Donne and others, were added. Further editions appeared in 1639, 1649, 1650, 1654, 1669 (the last which enlarged the canon and had manuscript authority), and 1719. All these editions are described by Grierson (*infra*), who took the first as most authoritative, though subject to correction.

The Facsimile Text Society has published facsimiles of *Biathanatos*, ed. J. W. Hebel (1930); the two *Anniversaries* (1934;
Noel Douglas Replicas, 1926); *Juvenilia*, ed. R. E. Bennett (1936);
and *Ignatius his Conclave*, ed. C. M. Coffin (1941).

Donne's poems were included in the large collections from
Bell (1779) onward. The editions of Grosart (Fuller Worthies'
Library, 2 vols., 1872–3), J. R. Lowell and C. E. Norton (Grolier
Club, 2 vols., 1895), and Sir E. K. Chambers (Muses' Library,
2 vols., 1896), were superseded by that of Sir Herbert Grierson
(2 vols., 1912), which opened a new era in Donne scholarship.
Two valuable small editions are Grierson's one-volume text with
a new introduction (first printed in 1929), which has a few
changes from 1912, and that of R. E. Bennett (Chicago, 1942),
which embodies recent scholarship and original work on the
manuscripts.

The only large edition of Donne's sermons is the *Works*, ed.
H. Alford (6 vols., 1839). Recent volumes of selections are:
Donne's Sermons: Selected Passages, ed. L. P. Smith (1919); *Ten
Sermons*, ed. G. Keynes (1923); *Donne's Sermon of Valediction at his
going into Germany*, ed. E. M. Simpson (1932). Some other
editions are: *Essays in Divinity*, ed. A. Jessopp (1855); *Letters to
Severall Persons of Honour*, ed. C. E. Merrill (New York, 1910);
Paradoxes and Problemes, ed. G. Keynes (1923); *Devotions*, ed.
J. Sparrow (1923), the standard edition; and *The Courtier's
Library*, edited with a translation by E. M. Simpson (1930).

A compendious and scholarly volume, first published in 1929,
is J. Hayward's *Complete Poetry and Selected Prose*.

Walton's *Life* (1640; enlarged 1658) remains the foundation of
biography. Jessopp in his *John Donne* (1897) also dealt with the
divine. Gosse's *Life and Letters* (2 vols., 1899), the standard book,
has the virtues and defects of a pioneer work and of its author.
Some of the countless corrections have to do with the date of
Donne's birth (F. P. Wilson, *RES* iii, 1927; H. W. Garrod, *TLS*,
30 December, 1944); the date of his travels (J. Sparrow, *A
Garland for John Donne*, 1931); and his terms in the Inns of Court
and in Parliament (I. A. Shapiro, *TLS*, 16 and 23 October,
1930, and 10 March, 1932).

Recorded criticism began with Jonson's remarks to Drummond. The most significant estimate in the seventeenth century
was Carew's 'Elegie'. The curve of Donne's fame may be
roughly suggested by the names of Dryden, Johnson ('Cowley'),

and Coleridge (*Literary Remains*, i and iii, 1836–8; *Notes on English Divines*, 1853). In the century of the Oxford Movement the reputation of Dr. Donne assisted that of Jack Donne and the opinions of Coleridge, Lamb, and Browning were increasingly shared. Towards 1900 came two editions, Gosse's *Life*, and a crop of essays such as those of Gosse (*Jacobean Poets*, 1894), Saintsbury (in Chambers's edition; reprinted in *Prefaces and Essays*, 1933), and Arthur Symons (*Fortnightly Review*, N.S., lxvi, 1899). Grierson's chapter in the *CHEL* iv (1909), his edition (1912), and perhaps especially his *Metaphysical Lyrics & Poems* (1921), did much to extend Donne's fame from the scholarly to the literary public. The chief critical agent in changing standards of taste from the romantic to the metaphysical was T. S. Eliot, whose writings hardly need citation. Essays by Eliot and others appeared in *A Garland for John Donne*, ed. T. Spencer (Harvard, 1931). In addition to chapters in the books on the metaphysical poets by J. B. Leishman (1934), Joan Bennett (1934), and H. C. White (1936), who deals mainly with the religious verse, there are essays by J. E. V. Crofts (*ESEA* xxii, 1937) and by C. S. Lewis and J. Bennett, who oppose each other in *Seventeenth Century Studies Presented to Sir Herbert Grierson* (1938). Among longer studies are M. Praz, *Secentismo e Marinismo in Inghilterra* (Florence, 1925), P. Legouis, *Donne the Craftsman* (Paris, 1928), which is concerned with the 'Songs and Sonets', and M. A. Rugoff, *Donne's Imagery* (New York, 1939). A popular biographical interpretation is E. Hardy's *Donne* (1942). Donne's poetic influence in the seventeenth century has been analysed most fully by G. Williamson, *The Donne Tradition* (1930), and R. C. Bald, *Donne's Influence in English Literature* (1932).

E. M. Simpson's standard *Study of the Prose Works of John Donne* (1924) has been supplemented by the author in numerous articles. Donne the preacher, on whom Coleridge made extensive comments (*supra*), has been studied especially by J. Sparrow (*ESEA* xvi, 1931), W. F. Mitchell (*supra*, V. 2), and H. H. Umbach (*PMLA* lii, 1937; *ELH* xii, 1945).

Studies of Donne's ideas, naturalistic, scientific, and religious, include M. P. Ramsay's *Les Doctrines médiévales chez Donne* (1917; 2nd ed., 1924), an able pioneer work with an unwarranted Plotinian bias; R. Sencourt's suggestive *Outflying Philosophy* (Hildesheim, 1924); L. I. Bredvold's solid articles in

JEGP xxii (1923) and *Studies in Shakespeare, Milton and Donne* (New York, 1925); M. Y. Hughes, in *Essays in Criticism, Second Series* (University of California, 1934); G. Williamson's article on *Biathanatos* in *PQ* xiii (1934); C. M. Coffin's *John Donne and the New Philosophy* (Columbia, 1937), which, though not altogether reliable in regard to astronomy, contains much able analysis of Donne's reactions; I. Husain's *Dogmatic and Mystical Theology of John Donne* (1938); and M. F. Moloney's *John Donne: His Flight from Mediaevalism* (University of Illinois, 1944).

This note necessarily omits a multitude of important articles on every aspect of Donne. For these one must refer to the current bibliographies, to *Studies in Metaphysical Poetry* (1939) by T. Spencer and M. Van Doren, who list items published during 1912–38, and to William White's *John Donne since 1900: A Bibliography of Periodical Articles* (Boston, 1942; reprinted from the *Bulletin of Bibliography*, xvii, 1941–2).

The standard bibliography (incomplete concerning early editions extant) is by G. Keynes (1914; 2nd ed., 1932). H. C. Combs and Z. R. Sullens have compiled a *Concordance* (Chicago, 1940).

MICHAEL DRAYTON, 1563–1631.

Although *Englands Heroicall Epistles* continued to be read, the general eclipse of Drayton is indicated by the lack of any full edition between 1637 and 1748; the 1748 folio was reprinted in 4 vols. in 1753. Among signs of Drayton's slow return were his inclusion in the collections of Anderson (1793) and Chalmers (1810). The best modern selection is C. Brett's *Minor Poems* (1907). The standard edition of the complete works is that of J. W. Hebel, which was finished by K. Tillotson and B. H. Newdigate (5 vols., 1931–41). So much scholarly and critical material is there cited, digested, and augmented that only a few items need be mentioned. The best biographical account is Newdigate's *Michael Drayton and His Circle* (1941). Among critical discussions are those of Courthope, iii (1903); Oliver Elton, *Michael Drayton* (1905); Brett; H. H. Child, *CHEL* iv; A. H. Bullen, *Elizabethans* (1924); Edmund Blunden's tribute to *Poly-Olbion*, 'The Happy Island' (*TLS*, 17 August, 1922; *Votive Tablets*, 1931); and R. L. Sharp, *From Donne to Dryden* (1940). Some special studies are in the books on pastoral literature by W. W. Greg (1906) and H. Genouy (1928); R. Shafer, *The English Ode to 1660* (1918); the books on the sonneteers by J. G. Scott (1929), L. E. Pearson (1933), and L. C. John (1938); and L. F. Ball's article on 'Minor English Renaissance Epics', *ELH* i (1934). Drayton's theory of poetry is outlined by L. Jonas, *The Divine Science* (1940), his literary vogue since 1631 by R. Noyes, *Indiana University Studies*, xxii (1935). Bibliographies of Drayton's works are given in Elton, of works and scholarship in the Hebel edition. There is a *Concise Bibliography* (New York, 1941) by S. A. Tannenbaum.

WILLIAM DRUMMOND of Hawthornden, 1585–1649.

Drummond's *Poems* were edited by Milton's nephew, Edward Phillips, in 1656, his *Works* by Bishop Sage and T. Ruddiman in 1711. W. C. Ward's edition of the poems (Muses' Library, 2 vols., 1894) has good literary and philosophical notes. The standard edition is by L. E. Kastner (Scottish Text Society, 2 vols., 1913). Both editors supply bibliographies of Drummond's publications. Masson's copious account of the writer and his age (1873) has been in part superseded by A. Joly's concise, critical, and documented *William Drummond de Hawthornden* (Lille, 1934). Kastner's notes, which gathered up his own numerous studies (chiefly in *MLR* iii–vi), emphasized the poet's lack of originality. The balance is righted by J. G. Scott (*Les Sonnets élisabéthains*, 1929), by Joly, and by R. C. Wallerstein's discriminating critique in *PMLA* xlviii (1933).

A Cypresse Grove is included in the editions of Ward and Kastner and was reprinted separately by S. Clegg (1919). The borrowings noted by these editors, and by A. H. Upham (*French Influence*, 1908), were supplemented with echoes of Donne and Bacon by G. S. Greene and M. Rugoff in *PQ* xi (1932) and xvi (1937) and *MLN* xlviii (1933). The *Conversations* with Jonson, since their first appearance in very garbled form in the 1711 folio, have been printed with increasing accuracy by D. Laing in *Archaeologia Scotica*, iv (1833) and *Shakespeare Society Papers* (1842); by R. F. Patterson (1923); and by G. B. Harrison in the Bodley Head Quartos (1923). The most accurate text is that in Herford and Simpson's *Ben Jonson*, i (1925).

SIR WILLIAM DRUMMOND, 1636–1713.

Drummond's *Diary* for 1657–9 was printed for the first time by H. W. Meikle in the *Miscellany of The Scottish Historical Society*, vii (1941).

SIR WILLIAM DUGDALE, 1605–86.

Some of the great antiquarian's chief works appeared before 1660: *Monasticon Anglicanum* (3 vols., 1655–73), for which a good deal had been compiled by Roger Dodsworth; *The Antiquities of Warwickshire* (1656); and *The History of St. Pauls Cathedral in London* (1658; ed. Sir H. Ellis, 1818). W. Hamper edited the *Life, Diary, and Correspondence* (1827). The best accounts of the man and his work are by D. C. Douglas (*History*, xx, 1935–6; *English Scholars*, 1939) and E. S. Scroggs (*Journal of the British Archaeological Association*, 3rd Series, ii, 1937). There is an article on Dodsworth and his circle in the *Bodleian Quarterly Record*, vii (1934).

JOHN DURIE or DURY, 1596–1680.

As the *BMC* testifies, Durie's writings on religious and public questions were many and various; some of them were published by his friend Hartlib. The broad channel of much of his activity has been described briefly by H. R. Trevor-Roper, *Archbishop Laud* (1940), and most fully by G. Westin, *Negotiations about Church Unity 1628–1634* (Upsala, 1932), and J. M. Batten, *John Dury Advocate of Christian Reunion* (University of Chicago, 1944), who give bibliographies. Durie's educational writings (1642–50) are most amply discussed by H. J. Scougal, *Die pädagogischen Schriften John Durys* (Jena, 1905); they come into the books by J. W. Adamson, R. F. Young, and R. F. Jones cited above (V. 6) among studies of modernist education. Durie's *Reformed Librarie-Keeper With a Supplement to the Reformed-School* (1650) was partly incorporated in an essay in A. W. Pollard's *Old Picture Books* (1902) and edited, without the 'Supplement', by R. S. Granniss (Chicago, 1906).

JOHN EARLE, 1600?–65.

Micro-cosmographie. Or, A Peece of the World Discovered; In Essayes and Characters had three or four editions in 1628, the year of publication, and was enlarged in 1629 and 1633. The twelve editions of the seventeenth century were all issued anonymously. Bliss's edition (1811) includes Earle's occasional verse. The latest editions are by G. Murphy (1928) and H. Osborne (1933). The work is also included in the anthologies of characters by H. Morley (1891) and R. Aldington (1924). Clarendon's sketch of Earle is reprinted in Arber's edition and D. Nichol Smith's *Characters . . . of the Seventeenth Century* (1918). Critical matter is provided by Earle's editors and in the general studies of character-writing. Editions are described in G. Murphy's *Bibliography of English Character-Books 1608–1700* (1925).

SIR JOHN ELIOT, 1592–1632.

Grosart edited several works and letters, from manuscripts, in 6 vols. (1879–82). The view of Eliot set forth in such books as John Forster's biography (2 vols., 1864) has been somewhat altered by modern scholars, e.g. H. Hulme (*Journal of Modern History*, iv, 1932), and Yung Chi Hoe (*supra*, V. 1). Public and private aspects of his life are presented by M. B. Fuller (*Smith College Studies in History*, iv, 1919) and Hulme (*Camden Miscellany*, xvi, 1936; xvii, 1940).

JOHN EVERARD, 1575?–1650?

Everard left a number of translations of mystical works in manuscript. Two published ones were *The Divine Pymander of Hermes Mercurius Trismegistus* (1650) and *The Single Eye* (1646), the latter (from Nicholas of Cusa's *De Visione Dei*) probably by Everard and Giles Randall. Extracts from translations were included with Everard's sermons in *Some Gospel-Treasures Opened* (1653). The fullest account of him (and of Randall) is in Rufus M. Jones, *Spiritual Reformers in the 16th & 17th Centuries* (1914). He is discussed also by Jones in *Mysticism and Democracy in the English Commonwealth* (Harvard, 1932), by W. Haller in *The Rise of Puritanism* (1938), and by W. K. Jordan in *HLQ* iii (1939–40).

ADAM EYRE, 1614–61.

A Dyurnall, or Catalogue of all my Accions and Expences from the 1st of January, 1646 [i.e. 1647], which runs to 1649, was edited by H. J. Morehouse in Charles Jackson's *Yorkshire Diaries and Autobiographies in the Seventeenth and Eighteenth Centuries*, i (Surtees Society, lxv, 1877). Eyre receives an essay in W. Notestein's *English Folk* (1938) and is cited in Mildred Campbell's *English Yeoman* (1942).

EDWARD FAIRFAX, d. 1635.

Godfrey of Bulloigne, or The Recoverie of Jerusalem, Fairfax's Spenserian translation of Tasso's *Gerusalemme Liberata,* appeared in 1600, had other editions in 1624 and 1687, and was reprinted by H. Morley (Carisbrooke Library, 1890). It is more or less prominent in the studies of Tasso in England by E. Koeppel, *Anglia,* xi–xiii (1888–90); Sir Sidney Lee, *Elizabethan and Other Essays* (1929); and A. Castelli, *La Gerusalemme Liberata nella Inghilterra di Spenser* (Milan, 1936). Fairfax and R. Carew are discussed by R. E. N. Dodge in *PMLA* xliv (1929), Fairfax's metrical technique and significance by R. C. Wallerstein in *PMLA* l (1935). His tract on a case of witchcraft in his own family (1621) was printed in *Miscellanies of the Philobiblon Society,* v (1858–9) and edited, with two eclogues by Fairfax, by W. Grainge, as *Dæmonologia* (1882). W. W. Greg edited the eighth eclogue in the *Modern Language Quarterly,* iv (1901).

MILDMAY FANE, EARL OF WESTMORLAND, 1602–66.

Otia Sacra (1648) was edited by Grosart (1879). There are selections in Brydges's *Restituta,* ii (1815), and L. B. Marshall's *Rare Poems of the Seventeenth Century* (1936). M. C. Bradbrook has some comments on Fane's verse in her essay on Marvell in *RES* xvii (1941). Two plays, *Raguaillo d'Oceano* (1640) and *Candy Restored* (1641), have been edited from manuscripts by C. Leech, with a full introduction (Louvain, 1938). Fane's dramatic work had been discussed by A. Harbage in *SP* xxxi (1934).

SIR RICHARD FANSHAWE, 1608–66.

Il Pastor Fido (1647), from Guarini, reappeared in 1647–8 with other translations, including that of the 4th book of the *Aeneid,* and original pieces. *Selected Parts of Horace* (1652) was followed in 1655 by Fanshawe's largest work, the *Lusiad* of Camoens. Translations from Antonio Hurtado de Mendoza were printed in 1670, Fanshawe's *Original Letters* in 1701. His widow's *Memoirs,* with some of his letters, were first printed in 1829 and have been edited by B. Marshall (1905) and, more elaborately, by H. C. Fanshawe (1907). The Virgilian translation has been edited by A. L. Irvine (1924), the *Lusiad* by J. D. M. Ford (Harvard, 1940). There is an essay in J. W.

Mackail's *Studies of English Poets* (1926) and an article by H. Thomas in the *Revue Hispanique*, xlviii (1920).

OWEN FELLTHAM, 1602?–68.

The 1st edition of *Resolves* (1623?) contained a hundred essays; the 2nd (1628) had a second century; in the 3rd (1628–9) and later impressions the order of the two centuries was reversed. Further changes were made in number and content. The folio of 1661 contained, besides the 8th edition of the *Resolves*, 41 poems, some of which had been printed long before, letters, and the *Brief Character of the Low-Countries*. Of this last piece unauthorized editions had appeared in 1648 and 1652, an authorized one in 1652. The *Resolves* reached a 12th and last edition in 1709. Revival came in the early nineteenth century with a volume of *Beauties* (1800, 1818), J. Cumming's garbled edition (1806, 1820), and Pickering's reprint (1840). There is a handy text in the Temple Classics (1904). Selections are given in anthologies cited above in II. 1. E. N. S. Thompson has some discussion in his *Seventeenth-Century English Essay* (1926). The *DNB* has had biographical and bibliographical supplements from M. D. Cornu (University of Washington *Digests of Theses*, i, 1931); J. Robertson (*NQ* clxxiii, 1937; *MLN* lviii, 1943; *MLR* xxxix, 1944); and F. S. Tupper (*MLN* liv, 1939).

NICHOLAS FERRAR, 1592–1637.

Ferrar's translation, *The Hundred and Ten Considerations of Signior John Valdesso* (1638), was edited by F. Chapman (1905). J. E. B. Mayor edited *Nicholas Ferrar. Two Lives by his brother John and by Doctor Jebb* (1855). The first and part of the second of five manuscript books were edited by E. C. Sharland as *The Story Books of Little Gidding* (1899). Two recent standard books are A. L. Maycock's *Nicholas Ferrar of Little Gidding* (1938) and B. Blackstone's *The Ferrar Papers* (1938). There is a sketch by H. Collett (1925). One cannot overlook the special quality of J. H. Shorthouse's picture in *John Inglesant* (1880–1).

SIR ROBERT FILMER, c. 1588?–1653.

Thomason assigned to Filmer *The Necessity of the Absolute Power of all Kings* (1648), a book largely compiled from Knolles's translation of Bodin. In addition to sensible tracts on witchcraft (1653) and usury (1653), Filmer wrote *The Anarchy of a Limited or Mixed Monarchy* (1648), a critique of Hunton; *Observations upon Aristotles Politiques* (1652); *Observations concerning the Originall of Government* (1652), which contained criticism of Hobbes, Milton, and Grotius; and *Patriarcha* (1680). A number of the political tracts were reprinted in *The Free-holders Grand Inquest* (1679); the title-piece was apparently not Filmer's. H. Morley edited a popular reprint of *Patriarcha* (1884). The critique of Milton is reprinted in W. R. Parker, *Milton's Contemporary Reputation* (Ohio State University, 1940). Thanks chiefly to Locke, Filmer has commonly been under a cloud in histories of political thought, but he is vigorously rehabilitated by J. W. Allen in *Social & Political Ideas of Some English Thinkers of the Augustan Age*, ed. F. J. C. Hearnshaw (1928).

GILES FLETCHER, 1585/6–1623.

Christs Victorie, and Triumph (1610) reappeared in 1632 and 1640. A prose work, *The Reward of the Faithfull*, was printed in 1623. Grosart's edition of Giles's poems (Fuller Worthies' Library, 1868; rev. ed., 1876) was superseded by F. S. Boas's standard edition of the *Poetical Works* of the brothers (Cambridge English Classics, 2 vols., 1908–9). The fullest and best critique is Arno Esch's *Giles Fletchers „Christs Victorie and Triumph": Eine Studie zum Epenstil des englischen Barock* (Bottrop, 1937). Giles Fletcher figures in critical discussions cited below under Phineas.

PHINEAS FLETCHER, 1582–1650.

Besides the works mentioned in the text Fletcher published two pieces of devotional prose, *The Way to Blessednes* and *Joy in Tribulation* (1632), and *Sylva Poetica* (1633). *A Fathers Testament*, a prose work containing verse, appeared in 1670. Grosart's edition of the poems (Fuller Worthies' Library, 4 vols., 1869) was superseded by F. S. Boas's (see Giles Fletcher, *supra*). A manuscript containing *Venus and Anchises (Brittain's Ida)* and other poems was discovered by Ethel Seaton in 1923 and edited by her in 1926. Earlier scholarly material is gathered up and enlarged in A. B. Langdale's *Phineas Fletcher, Man of Letters, Science and Divinity* (Columbia, 1937). The Fletchers' influence on Milton is summarized in J. H. Hanford's *Milton Handbook* (1939).

John Florio, 1553–1625/6.

In 1580 Florio translated, from the Italian, Cartier's account of his first two voyages; the work had been commissioned by Hakluyt, who reprinted it in the *Voyages* (1600). The Italian phrase-books and readers, *Florio His firste Fruites* and *Florios Second Frutes*, appeared in 1578 and 1591; the former has been elaborately edited by A. del Re (Formosa, 1936). The Italian–English dictionary, *A Worlde of Wordes* (1598), was much enlarged as *Queen Anna's New World of Words* (1611). Florio had a share in Sir William Vaughan's *New-found Politicke* (1626), taken from Boccalini's *Ragguagli di Parnaso*. The *Essayes* of Montaigne were licensed in 1600 and printed in 1603. There are many modern editions, e.g. Everyman and World's Classics. The text edited by J. I. M. Stewart (2 vols., 1931) is the first based on a collation of the editions of 1603, 1613, and 1632. The standard book is F. A. Yates, *John Florio* (1934). Among studies of the *Essayes* are Saintsbury's introduction in the Tudor Translations (3 vols., 1892–3), a chapter in F. O. Matthiessen's *Translation: An Elizabethan Art* (1931), and two articles on Florio's language by A. Koszul (*Revue Anglo-Américaine*, ix, 1931–2). The influence of Montaigne and Florio on Bacon, Jonson, and Burton is the subject of a monograph by F. Dieckow (Strassburg, 1903); their influence on Marston and Webster is studied by Charles Crawford, *Collectanea, Second Series* (1907). Another line of generally exaggerated claims, represented by G. C. Taylor's *Shakspere's Debt to Montaigne* (Harvard, 1925), is questioned by A. Harmon (*PMLA* lvii, 1942).

Thomas Floyd, c. 1572?–?

Floyd's *Picture of a Perfit Common Wealth* (1600) is discussed by D. T. Starnes (University of Texas *Studies in English*, xi, 1931), who shows the author's large use of Elyot's *Governour* (1531) and N. Ling's *Politeuphuia*. *Wits Commonwealth* (1597).

Robert Fludd, 1574–1637.

'His Books written in Latine', said Fuller, 'are great, many and mystical', and there is no strong reason to recite titles. J. B. Craven's *Doctor Robert Fludd . . . The English Rosicrucian* (1902) may be supplemented by F. Freudenberg, *Paracelsus und Fludd* (Berlin, 1918), and by parts of A. E. Waite's *Brotherhood of the Rosy Cross* (1924) and *Secret Tradition in Alchemy* (1926), Saurat's *Milton: Man and Thinker* (1925; section on Fludd enlarged in 1944 edition) and *Literature and Occult Tradition* (trans. 1930), and K. B. Collier's *Cosmogonies of our Fathers* (Columbia, 1934). An important discussion of Fludd is contained in W. Pagel's monograph on religious motives in medical biology (*supra,* V. 3).

EMANUEL FORD or FORDE, *fl.* 1598 ff.

Parismus, The Renoumed Prince of Bohemia (1598), which had a sequel, *Parismenos* (1599), went through more than twenty reprints up to 1740; brief extracts are in R. Brimley Johnson's *Birth of Romance* (1928). *Ornatus and Artesia,* which was written before 1598 and is extant in an edition of 1607, is reprinted in P. Henderson's *Shorter Novels,* ii (Everyman's Library, 1930). The earliest extant edition of *The Famous Historie of Montelyon, Knight of the Qracle* is that of 1633. Ford's works are chronicled in A. Esdaile's *List of English Tales and Prose Romances* (1912) and discussed in E. A. Baker's *History of the English Novel,* ii (1929).

THOMAS FULLER, 1608–61.

Some of Fuller's works are: *Davids Hainous Sinne* (1631), edited, with his other verse, by Grosart (1868); *Historie of the Holy Warre* (1639), reprinted by Pickering (1840); *The Holy State* (1642), ed. J. Nichols (1841), ed. in facsimile, with elaborate apparatus, by M. G. Walten (2 vols., Columbia, 1938); *A Sermon of Reformation* (1643); *Good Thoughts in Bad Times* (1645); *Good Thoughts in Worse Times* (1647); *A Pisgah-Sight of Palestine* (1650); *Abel Redevivus* (1651; ed. W. Nichols, 2 vols., 1867), a collection of biographies of modern divines, edited and partly written by Fuller; *The Church-History of Britain;* . . . *The History of the University of Cambridge* (1655), ed. J. Nichols (3 vols., 1837), ed. J. S. Brewer (6 vols., 1845); *A Collection of Sermons* (1656); *The Appeal of Injured Innocence* (1659), Fuller's reply to Heylyn; *Mixt Contemplations in Better Times* (1660); and *The History of the Worthies of England* (1662), ed. J. Nichols (2 vols., 1811), ed. P. A. Nuttall (3 vols., 1840). *Collected Sermons* were edited by J. E. Bailey and W. E. A. Axon (2 vols., 1891). Anthologies of different sorts have been edited by A. Jessopp (1892), A. R. Waller (1902), and E. K. Broadus (1928).

The anonymous *Life* (1661) is reprinted in Brewer's edition of the *Church-History* and in Broadus. The standard biography is by J. E. Bailey (1874). An authoritative short one is D. B. Lyman, *The Great Tom Fuller* (University of California, 1935).

Coleridge's comments are in his *Literary Remains*, ii (1836), *Notes on English Divines* (1853), i, and *Miscellaneous Criticism*, ed. T. M. Raysor (1936). Broadus reprints criticism from Lamb, J. Crossley (*Retrospective Review*, iii, 1821), and Sir Leslie Stephen (*Cornhill Magazine*, xxv, 1872). Among modern essays are those of E. N. S. Thompson (*Literary Bypaths of the Renaissance*, Yale, 1924) and E. E. Kellett (*London Quarterly Review*, cxlv, 1926; *Reconsiderations*, 1928). The most solid and suggestive study of Fuller's mind and sources is W. E. Houghton's *The Formation of Thomas Fuller's Holy and Profane States* (Harvard, 1938). Fuller the character-writer and essayist figures in the general studies of those genres. Particular parts of his work are discussed in such books as D. A. Stauffer, *English Biography before 1700* (1930), W. F. Mitchell, *English Pulpit Oratory* (1932), H. Arneke, *Kirchengeschichte und Rechtsgeschichte*, &c. (1937), and W. K. Jordan, *Development of Religious Toleration*, iv (1940).

There is a full bibliography of Fuller's works by S. Gibson, with a biographical essay by G. Keynes, in *OBS*, vol. iv, part i, ii, 1934 (1936).

JOHN GAUDEN, 1605-62.

Whatever small interest there may be in Gauden's religious and miscellaneous writings, or in his edition, with a *Life*, of Hooker (1662), his fame hangs on the question whether he was the author of Εἰκὼν Βασιλική. *The Pourtraicture of His Sacred Majestie in his Solitudes and Sufferings* (1649). Modern opinion seems in general to support his claim. Some references for the history of the book and the long debate are: C. E. Doble's articles in the *Academy*, xxiii (1883); E. Almack's *Bibliography of The King's Book, or Eikon Basilike* (1896) and his edition of the book (1903); E. N. S. Thompson, *John Milton: Topical Bibliography* (Yale, 1916); S. B. Liljegren, *Studies in Milton* (Lund, 1918); David H. Stevens, *Reference Guide to Milton* (University of Chicago, 1930); G. W. Whiting's summary of opinion in *NQ* clxii (1932); and the bibliography under Charles in the *BMC*. The charge, elaborated by Liljegren, that Milton and Bradshaw had the prayer of Sidney's Pamela inserted in some editions, in order to damage the book by the exposure of such an item, was answered by J. S. Smart (*RES* i, 1925), and revived by P. P. Morand (*The Effects of his Political Life upon John Milton*, Paris, 1939). We may hope that this fabrication has been finally killed by the vigorous common sense of R. W. Chambers ('Poets and their Critics', *Proceedings of the British Academy*, xxvii, 1941).

WILLIAM GILBERT, 1540–1603.

Gilbert's great work was *De Magnete, Magneticisque Corporibus, et de magno magnete tellure, Physiologia nova, plurimis & argumentis, & experimentis, demonstrata* (1600; facsimile ed., Berlin, 1892). *De Mundo nostro Sublunari Philosophia Nova* appeared at Amsterdam in 1651. *De Magnete* has been translated by P. F. Mottelay (New York, 1893) and, with valuable notes, by S. P. Thompson (1900–1). Gilbert is discussed in general histories of science and astronomy and in Mottelay's *Bibliographical History of Electricity & Magnetism* (1922), E. G. R. Taylor's *Late Tudor and Early Stuart Geography* (1934), and F. R. Johnson's *Astronomical Thought in Renaissance England* (1937). A recent important study is E. Zilsel's 'The Origins of William Gilbert's Scientific Method' (*JHI* ii, 1941).

ALEXANDER GILL the elder, 1565–1635.

Gill is best known as Milton's headmaster at St. Paul's School and as the author of *Logonomia Anglica* (1619; ed. O. L. Jiriczek, *Quellen und Forschungen*, xc, 1903). Gill's interest in the English language has been studied by Jiriczek (op. cit. and *Studien zur vergleichenden Literaturgeschichte*, ii, 1902) and H. Kökeritz (*Studia Neophilologica*, xi, 1938–9). *The Sacred Philosophie Of the Holy Scripture* (1635) was, as A. Barker has shown (*MLR* xxxii, 1937), an interesting attempt at a rational Christian theology. There is an account of Gill, in addition to the *DNB*, in Masson's *Milton*.

SIDNEY GODOLPHIN, 1610–43.

Godolphin's poems, first collected in Saintsbury's *Minor Poets of the Caroline Period*, ii (1906), were edited by W. Dighton (Tudor and Stuart Library, 1931). Clarendon's sketch of him is reprinted in D. Nichol Smith's *Characters . . . of the Seventeenth Century* (1918).

FRANCIS GODWIN, 1562–1633.

Bishop Godwin's solid works were *A Catalogue of the Bishops of England* (1601) and the Latin *Annales* (1616; trans. 1630) of the reigns of Henry VIII, Edward VI, and Mary. His much livelier *Man in the Moone* (1638) may have been written between 1601 and 1630, perhaps after 1620. The full text was first edited, along with Godwin's *Nuncius Inanimatus* (1629), by G. McColley (Smith College, 1937), who has given extracts in his *Literature and Science* (Chicago, 1940). McColley has supplementary articles in *MP* xxxv, *Library*, xvii, and *PQ* xvi (all of 1937). An important study by H. W. Lawton appeared in the *RES* vii (1931). The romance is discussed also by M. Nicolson in *A World in the Moon* (Smith College, 1936) and 'Cosmic Voyages' (*ELH* vii, 1940) and by F. R. Johnson in his *Astronomical Thought in Renaissance England* (1937).

GODFREY GOODMAN, 1583–1656.

The Fall of Man, Or the Corruption of Nature Proved by the light of our naturall Reason (1616) is a rare book, but its argument may be followed in the 5th and 6th books of the 3rd edition (1635) of Hakewill's *Apologie*. Modern discussions are mentioned in the note on Hakewill below. In reply to Weldon, Bishop Goodman was defensively concerned with another kind of corruption in his *Court of King James the First*, which was first printed in 1839 (ed. J. S. Brewer, 2 vols.).

JOHN GOODWIN, 1594?–1665.

Anti-Cavalierisme (1642) and *ΘΕΟΜΑΧΙΑ* (1644) are reproduced in W. Haller, *Tracts on Liberty* (1934), and parts of *Independencie Gods Veritie* (1647) and *Right and Might well met* (1649) are given in A. S. P. Woodhouse, *Puritanism and Liberty* (1938). One of Goodwin's services to religious freedom was his sponsoring (with Durie) a translation (1648) of part of Jacobus Acontius's *Stratagemata Satanae* (1565). There is an unsatisfactory life of Goodwin by T. Jackson (rev. ed., 1872). His thought is discussed by Haller in his *Tracts* and *Rise of Puritanism* (1938), by Woodhouse, by W. K. Jordan, *Development of Religious Toleration*, iii (1938), by D. M. Wolfe, *Milton in the Puritan Revolution* (1941), and by Arthur Barker, *Milton and the Puritan Dilemma* (1942).

THOMAS GOODWIN, 1600-80.

The *Works* were issued in 5 vols. (1681–1704) and reprinted in 6 vols. (1861). The *Apologeticall Narration* (1644), by Goodwin and others, is reproduced in W. Haller, *Tracts on Liberty* (1934). Goodwin is discussed by John Brown, *Puritan Preaching in England* (1900), by Haller in his two works, and by Jordan (see preceding note).

SAMUEL GOTT, 1614-71.

Gott was a lawyer, M.P., country gentleman, and liberal Puritan. His chief work, the utopian romance *Novæ Solymæ Libri Sex* (1648), was translated by W. Begley (2 vols., 1902), who attributed it to Milton. The author was identified by S. K. Jones (*Library*, Third Series, i, 1910). The book is discussed by F. E. Held in his edition of Andreae's *Christianopolis* (1916). J. M. Patrick has a full account of Gott and his writings in the *University of Toronto Quarterly*, viii (1939).

WILLIAM GOUGE, 1578-1653.

The life and works of this Puritan divine are discussed in W. Haller's *Rise of Puritanism* (1938), his *Of Domesticall Duties* (1622) in C. L. Powell, *English Domestic Relations* (1917), L. B. Wright, *Middle-Class Culture* (1935), and W. E. Houghton's book cited under Fuller.

JAMES GRAHAM, MARQUIS OF MONTROSE, 1612-50.

The two famous pieces, 'Montrose to his Mistress' and the lines on the dead Charles I, were printed as broadsides, the latter also in the 1653 edition of Cleveland's poems. These two and six others appeared in the third part of James Watson's *Choise Collection* (Edinburgh, 1711) and were frequently reprinted thereafter. The latest edition (1938) is by J. L. Weir, who had printed the texts in *NQ* clxxiii (1937) and early tributes to Montrose in *NQ* clxxiv (1938). Montrose's letter on sovereignty, written in 1640-1, is printed in the standard modern biography by John Buchan (1928) and in Mark Napier's *Memorials* (2 vols., 1848-50) and *Memoirs* (2 vols., 1856).

JOHN GREENE, 1616-59.

Selections from Greene's diary (1635-57) were printed by

E. M. Symonds in the *English Historical Review*, xliii and xliv (1928-9).

FULKE GREVILLE, FIRST LORD BROOKE, 1554-1628.

Greville himself published none of his writings, though a few pieces from *Caelica* got into anthologies and a version of *Mustapha* was printed in 1609. His poems and minor pieces of prose were printed in *Certaine Learned and Elegant Workes* (1633) and *Remains* (1670). *The Life Of the Renowned Sir Philip Sidney*, published in 1652, was edited by Nowell Smith in the Tudor and Stuart Library (1907). Grosart's edition of the complete works (Fuller Worthies' Library, 4 vols., 1870) has been partly superseded by G. Bullough's *Poems and Dramas* (2 vols., 1939). *Caelica* was included in M. F. Crow's *Elizabethan Sonnet Cycles*, iv (1898), and has been edited by U. Ellis-Fermor (1936). The best biographical account is given by Bullough in *MLR* xxviii (1933). M. W. Croll's *The Works of Fulke Greville* (Philadelphia, 1903) remains a valuable study. This and other contributions are revised and amplified in Bullough's edition. One special study is M. Kupffer, *Fulke Grevilles "Poems of Monarchy" als Spiegel seiner politischen Ansichten* (Riga, 1929). A recent critique is William Frost's *Fulke Greville's Caelica* (priv. pr., U.S.A., 1942).

ROBERT GREVILLE, SECOND LORD BROOKE, 1608-43.

Brooke wrote *The Nature of Truth Its Union and Unity with the Soule, Which is One in its Essence, Faculties, Acts; One with Truth* (1640) and *A Discourse opening the Nature of that Episcopacie, which is exercised in England* (1641; 2nd ed., 1642). The latter is reproduced in W. Haller's *Tracts on Liberty* (1934). Brooke is discussed by C. de Rémusat, *Histoire de la philosophie en Angleterre* (1875), i; J. Freudenthal, *Archiv für Geschichte der Philosophie*, vi (1892-3); W. Haller, *Tracts* and *The Rise of Puritanism* (1938); W. K. Jordan, *Development of Religious Toleration*, ii (1936); and Arthur Barker, *Milton and the Puritan Dilemma* (1942). A mutual debt between Brooke and Milton is suggested in G. W. Whiting, *Milton's Literary Milieu* (University of North Carolina, 1939).

EDWARD GRIMESTON, ?-1640.

There are articles on Grimeston by F. S. Boas (*MP* iii, 1905-6) and G. N. Clark (*English Historical Review*, xliii, 1928), who gives a detailed bibliography.

ELIZABETH GRYMESTON, *ante* 1563–1601/4.

Miscelanea. Meditations. Memoratives, compiled for the guidance of the author's son, appeared in 1604 and was reissued in 1605–6, *c.* 1608, and *c.* 1618. A few pages are reprinted in Michael Roberts's *Elizabethan Prose* (1933). There is a full and careful account of Mrs. Grymeston in the *Library,* xv (1934–5), by R. Hughey and P. Hereford, who show among other things that all her bits of verse are taken from *Englands Parnassus,* Southwell, and R. Verstegan's *Odes* (Antwerp, 1601).

WILLIAM HABINGTON, 1605–54.

Habington published a play, *The Queene of Arragon* (1640; reprinted in Dodsley's *Collection,* ed. Hazlitt, xiii), and two prose works, *The Historie of Edward the Fourth* (1640; repr. in W. Kennett, *Complete History of England,* 1706), in which his father had had a large share, and *Observations upon Historie* (1641). *Castara* (1634) was enlarged in 1635 and again, with a religious section which contains some of the poet's best pieces, in 1640. The 3rd edition was included in Chalmers's *English Poets* (1810), vi, and reprinted by C. A. Elton (1812) and by Arber (1870). H. C. Combs has a bibliographical study of *Castara* in Northwestern University *Summaries of Doctoral Dissertations,* vii (1939).

GEORGE HAKEWILL, 1578–1649.

Hakewill's monument is *An Apologie of the Power and Providence of God in the Government of the World. Or An Examination and Censure of the Common Errour Touching Natures Perpetuall and Universall Decay* (1627; rev. and enlarged, 1630, 1635). The chief discussions are by G. Williamson (*ELH* ii, 1935) and R. F. Jones (*Ancients and Moderns,* 1936). Earlier writers on degeneration and mutability are analysed by D. C. Allen and K. Koller (*SP* xxxv, 1938). J. I. Dredge listed Hakewill's works and editions in *A Few Sheaves of Devon Bibliography . . . The Second Sheaf* (1890).

JOHN HALES, 1584–1656.

Some publications, chiefly posthumous, were: *Oratio Funebris* on Sir Thomas Bodley (1613); *A Tract Concerning Schisme And Schismatiques* (1642); *Golden Remains* (1659), enlarged in 1673 and 1688; *Sermons* (1660); *Several Tracts,* to use the later title, first published in 1677 and enlarged in 1716 by the 'Letter to Archbishop Laud'; *Works,* ed. Lord Hailes (3 vols., 1765).

There are large selections in Jared Sparks's *Collection of Essays and Tracts*, v (Boston, 1825), a few pages in Craik's *English Prose*, and one sermon in Bishop Henson's *Selected English Sermons* (World's Classics, 1939). Walton's biographical notes are edited by J. Butt in *MLR* xxix (1934). Clarendon's portrait is reprinted in D. Nichol Smith's *Characters . . . of the Seventeenth Century* (1918). There is a biography by P. Des Maizeaux (1719). Some discussions, of varying length and solidity, are in J. Tulloch, *Rational Theology and Christian Philosophy* (1872); A. C. Benson, *Essays* (1895); E. A. George, *Seventeenth Century Men of Latitude* (1908); N. E. Scott, *Harvard Theological Review*, x (1917); W. F. Mitchell, *English Pulpit Oratory* (1932); and the books on toleration (*supra*, V. 2) by Freund, Jordan (ii), and Lyon.

JOHN HALL, 1627–56.

Some of the many products of Hall's short and irregular life were his essays, *Horæ Vacivæ* (1646); *Poems* (1647); *An Humble Motion To The Parliament Of England Concerning The Advancement of Learning: And Reformation of the Universities* (1649); Περὶ ὕψους, *Or Dionysius Longinus of the Height of Eloquence* (1652); *A Letter written to a Gentleman in the Country* (1653), a piece of Cromwellian journalism which Thomason and Masson ascribed to Milton; *Hierocles upon the Golden Verses of Pythagoras* (1657), which contains an unusually concrete biographical sketch of Hall by John Davies of Kidwelly; and *Emblems* (1658), taken from Michael Hoyer's *Flammulae Amoris S. P. Augustini*. Brydges reprinted extracts from the essays in *Restituta*, iii (1815). The poems, edited by Brydges in 1816, are in Saintsbury's *Minor Poets of the Caroline Period*, ii (1906). Besides the *DNB*, there is some account of Hall in Mullinger's *University of Cambridge*, iii (1911). Hall's place in the educational controversy is shown by R. F. Jones, *Ancients and Moderns* (1936).

JOSEPH HALL, 1574–1656.

The standard modern edition is that of P. Wynter (10 vols., 1863). Hall's poems were reprinted in Chalmers's *English Poets* (1810), v, and edited by Grosart (1879); the satires were edited by K. Schulze with a full commentary (Berlin, 1910). Healey's translation of the *Mundus*, *The Discovery of A New World* (1609?), has been elaborately edited by H. Brown (Harvard,

1937). The *Characters* are reprinted in the anthologies of H. Morley (1891) and R. Aldington (1924) and represented in the other anthologies. Hall's autobiographical writings are assembled in Wynter's first volume. There is a life by George Lewis (1886). The fullest literary study is the Harvard thesis (1921) of S. M. Salyer, who has printed a study of the *Mundus* (*PQ* vi, 1927). The *Characters* figure in the accounts of that genre; parallels with Theophrastus are given by E. C. Baldwin in *PMLA* xviii (1903) and in K. Lichtenberg's *Der Einfluss des Theophrast* (1921). Some of Hall's work is discussed in W. F. Mitchell's *English Pulpit Oratory* (1932) and W. Haller's *Rise of Puritanism* (1938). His popularity in Germany is shown in G. Waterhouse, *Literary Relations of England and Germany* (1914).

PATRICK HANNAY, *fl.* 1619–22.

Hannay's poems are reprinted by Saintsbury, *Minor Poets of the Caroline Period*, i (1905).

SIR JOHN HARINGTON, 1561?–1612.

There is a bibliographical account of the translation of *Orlando Furioso* (1591; slightly rev., 1607, 1634) by W. W. Greg (*Library*, iv, 1923–4), a full critical study by T. Rich, *Harington & Ariosto* (Yale, 1940). Harington's preface is reprinted in G. G. Smith, *Elizabethan Critical Essays* (1904). The *Metamorphosis of Ajax* (1596) was reprinted by Singer (1814) and the Fanfrolico Press (1927). Harington's more conventional contribution to hygiene, the popular translation *The Englishmans Doctor. Or, the Schoole of Salerne* (1607), was edited by F. R. Packard and F. H. Garrison (New York, 1920; London, 1922). Some letters and papers were printed in *Nugæ Antiquæ* (2 vols., 1769–75; enlarged, 3 vols., 1779; ed. Park, 2 vols., 1804). Other prose tracts have been edited separately. The *Epigrams* appeared in 1613, 1615, 1618 ff. N. E. McClure's *Letters and Epigrams* (University of Pennsylvania, 1930) is the standard edition, with a standard account of Harington (*The Prayse of Private Life*, which McClure includes, is possibly Daniel's work). Two general essays are in Sir Walter Raleigh's *Some Authors* (1923) and Lytton Strachey's *Portraits in Miniature* (1931). Harington's Rabelaisian strain is studied in G. Rehfeld, *Sir John Harington* (Halle, 1914), and Huntington Brown, *Rabelais in English Literature* (Harvard, 1933). A. E. M. Kirkwood has an article on the *Ajax* and its sequels in the *Library*, xii (1931–2). Some of the works are touched on in R. Hughey's account of the Harington MS. at Arundel Castle (*Library*, xv, 1934–5).

JAMES HARRINGTON, 1611–77.

The Common-Wealth of Oceana (1656) and smaller related writings were edited by Toland in 1700. H. Morley's popular reprint of *Oceana* (1887) was superseded by S. B. Liljegren's elaborate edition (Heidelberg, 1924). Harrington has his place in the histories of political thought cited in V. 1, such as those of G. P. Gooch, Sabine, and Fink. The fullest study of his thought and influence is H. F. R. Smith's *Harrington and his Oceana* (1914). There are shorter studies by A. E. Levett (*Social & Political Ideas of Some Great Thinkers of the Sixteenth and Seventeenth Centuries*, ed. F. J. C. Hearnshaw, 1926), R. Koebner (*Englische Studien*, lxviii, 1933–4), and R. H. Tawney (*Proceedings of the British Academy*, xxvii, 1941). One of Liljegren's supplementary studies, on maritime and utopian ideas, is in *Festschrift Johannes Hoops* (Heidelberg, 1925); another is an edition of *A French Draft Constitution of 1792 modelled on . . . Oceana* (1932). The special problem of Church and State is discussed in the books on toleration by M. Freund (1927) and W. K. Jordan, iv (1940).

THOMAS HARRIOT, 1560–1621.

A briefe and true report of the new found land of Virginia (1588), the second original English book about America, was reprinted by Hakluyt. It has been published several times in facsimile (ed. L. S. Livingston, *Bibliographer*, i, 1902, and separately, New York, 1903; ed. R. G. Adams, Ann Arbor Facsimile Series, 1931). The text was edited by Henry Stevens (1900). T. de Bry's illustrated edition (Frankfort, 1590) has also been issued in facsimile (New York, 1871; ed. W. H. Rylands, 1888); and, with the illustrations and Hakluyt's version of the Latin letterpress, was reprinted by Quaritch (1893). The background of the book is supplied by the editors; by Stevens's *Thomas Harriot and his Associates* (1900); by G. P. Winship's chapter in the *Cambridge History of American Literature*, i (1917); by G. W. Cole, 'Elizabethan Americana', *Bibliographical Essays: A Tribute to Wilberforce Eames* (Harvard, 1924); and by G. B. Parks,

Richard Hakluyt and the English Voyages (New York, 1928). Harriot's friend Walter Warner edited a mathematical work (1631), but there is a mass of unpublished manuscripts in the British Museum and perhaps elsewhere. Stevens's account of Harriot's intellectual importance, and the *DNB*, have been amplified by M. Nicolson (*SP* xxxii, 1935), M. C. Bradbrook, *The School of Night* (1936), F. R. Johnson, *Astronomical Thought in Renaissance England* (1937), Eleanor G. Clark, *Ralegh and Marlowe* (Fordham University, 1941), and the historians of mathematics.

SAMUEL HARTLIB, 1596/1600–1662.

Hartlib himself almost fulfilled the functions of the intellectual clearing-house that he desired. A few examples of the many and varied writings which he composed or sponsored or inspired are: *A Description of the famous Kingdome of Macaria* (1641; *Harleian Miscellany*, ed. Park, i, 1808); *A further Discovery of The Office of Publick Addresse For Accommodations* (1648; *Harleian Miscellany*, vi, 1810); *Londons Charity inlarged* (1650); *The Reformed Virginian Silk-Worm* (1655; P. Force, *Tracts*, iii, 1844). Hartlib's correspondence with Robert Boyle is in Boyle's *Works*, ed. Birch (1744), v or (1772), vi. His correspondence with Worthington is cited under the latter. H. Dircks's account (1865) is supplemented by G. H. Turnbull, *Samuel Hartlib: A Sketch of his Life and his Relations to J. A. Comenius* (1920), by R. F. Jones, *Ancients and Moderns* (1936), and by other studies, cited in V. 3 and 6, of the progressive movement in science and education. L. M. Wulcko has biographical notes in *NQ* cliii (1927). Dircks gives a bibliography of Hartlib's publications.

CHRISTOPHER HARVEY, 1597–1663.

Harvey, a cleric and friend of Izaak Walton, wrote *The Synagogue* (1640), a small volume of sacred poems in avowed imitation of Herbert (with whose *Temple* it was commonly bound up), and *Schola Cordis* (1647), a collection of emblems (based on Van Haeften's) which, up into the nineteenth century, was attributed to Quarles. Harvey's poems were edited by Grosart (Fuller Worthies' Library, 1874).

WILLIAM HARVEY, 1578–1657.

The *Exercitatio Anatomica de Motu Cordis et Sanguinis in Animalibus*

(Frankfort, 1628) was printed in facsimile by G. Moreton (1894) and in several tercentenary editions, a facsimile (Florence, 1928), *Anatomical Exercises . . . The first English text of 1653*, ed. G. Keynes (1928), and a facsimile with a translation by C. D. Leake (Springfield, Illinois, and Baltimore, 1928; 3rd ed. of translation, 1941). Harvey's other major work was *Exercitationes de Generatione Animalium* (London and Amsterdam, 1651). The *Works* were translated in 1847 by R. Willis, whose version of the *De Motu* is reprinted, with letters, in Everyman's Library. There are biographical studies by Sir D'Arcy Power (1897), who has two essays in his *Selected Writings* (1931), R. B. H. Wyatt (1924), A. Malloch (New York, 1929), and Sir Wilmot Herringham, *Annals of Medical History*, N.S., iv (1932). In addition to the histories of medicine, some special studies are: Sir W. Osler, *The Growth of Truth* (1906), reprinted in *An Alabama Student* (1908, 1929); C. Singer, *The Discovery of the Circulation of the Blood* (1922); Sir W. Hale-White, *Bacon, Gilbert and Harvey* (1927), who has a tenuous argument for Bacon's influence; articles on Harvey's experiments on circulation, by J. J. R. Macleod, and on Elizabethan ideas of circulation, by I. I. Edgar, in *Annals of Medical History*, x (1928) and N.S., viii (1936); and the series of articles by H. P. Bayon in *Annals of Science*, iii and iv (1938–9). Harvey's other treatise is discussed in Joseph Needham, *History of Embryology* (1934), and most fully in A. W. Meyer, *Analysis of the De Generatione Animalium of William Harvey* (Stanford, 1936). G. Keynes compiled a *Bibliography of the Writings of William Harvey* (1928).

SIR JOHN HAYWARD, 1564?–1627.

Parts of Hayward's historical writings are in W. Kennett's *Complete History of England* (1706) and the *Harleian Miscellany*, ed. Park, ii (1809) and supplemental vol. i (1812), and another part was edited by J. Bruce for the Camden Society (1840). M. Dowling has described 'Sir John Hayward's Troubles over His *Life of Henry IV*' in the *Library*, xi (1930–1). This and more general questions are considered in L. B. Campbell's 'Use of Historical Patterns in the Reign of Elizabeth' (*HLQ* i, 1937–8), where further references are given.

JOHN HEALEY, *c.* 1585/6–*post* 1609.

Healey translated Hall's *Mundus Alter et Idem* as *The Dis-*

covery of A New World (1609?), which has been elaborately edited by H. Brown (Harvard, 1937); *St. Augustine, of the Citie of God* (1610), which has had several modern editions (2 vols., 1890, repr. 1909; Temple Classics, 3 vols., 1903; ed. E. Barker, 1931); and *Epictetus his Manuall. And Cebes his Table* (1610), to which Healey's version of Theophrastus's *Characters* was added in 1616. The Theophrastian translation is reprinted in the Temple Classics edition of Earle's *Microcosmographie*.

EDWARD LORD HERBERT OF CHERBURY, 1583–1648.

The standard edition of the autobiography (first printed by Horace Walpole in 1764) is that of Sir Sidney Lee (1886; rev. ed., 1906). A handsome reprint (1928) has an introduction by C. H. Herford. There are some pages on the book and the man by Sir Leslie Stephen ('Autobiography', *Hours in a Library*), essays by E. Blunden (*Votive Tablets*, 1931) and B. Willey (*ESEA* xxvii, 1942), and a bibliographical article by R. I. Aaron (*MLR* xxxvi, 1941).

The Life and Raigne of King Henry the Eighth (1649) is in W. Kennett's *Complete History of England* (1706), ii.

Occasional Verses (1665) was edited, badly, by Churton Collins (1881). The standard edition of the English and Latin poems is by G. C. M. Smith (1923). R. G. Howarth's *Minor Poets of the 17th Century* (Everyman, 1931) contains the English verse. Herbert's poetry is discussed by his editors and by G. Williamson, *The Donne Tradition* (1930).

De Veritate (Paris, 1624) has been translated by M. H. Carré (1937). *De Causis Errorum* and *De Religione Laici* appeared together in 1645; the latter has been edited and translated by H. R. Hutcheson (Yale, 1944). A manuscript in Herbert's hand, called *Religio Laici* but different from the published work, is edited by H. G. Wright in *MLR* xxviii (1933). Two other works were *De Religione Gentilium* (Amsterdam, 1663; trans. W. Lewis, 1705) and *A Dialogue between A Tutor and his Pupil* (1768). H. Scholz edited selections from *De Veritate* and *De Religione Gentilium* in *Studien zur Geschichte des neueren Protestantismus*, v (1914).

Recent accounts of Herbert's philosophy are the introductions of Carré and Hutcheson. Some other modern studies are: C. C. J. Webb, *Studies in the History of Natural Theology* (1915); A. Carlini, *R. Accademia dei Lincei*, xxvi (1917); W. R. Sorley,

CHEL iv and his *History of English Philosophy* (1920); B. Willey, *Seventeenth Century Background* (1934); C. Lyttle, *Church History*, iv (1935); and W. K. Jordan, *Development of Religious Toleration*, ii (1936).

C. J. Fordyce and T. M. Knox have listed the books Herbert bequeathed to Jesus College, Oxford, in *OBS*, vol. v, part ii, 1937 (1937).

Hutcheson gives a full bibliography of texts and scholarship.

GEORGE HERBERT, 1593–1633.

The Temple (1633), printed posthumously under the supervision of Nicholas Ferrar, had 13 editions by 1709. There are facsimiles, ed. J. H. Shorthouse (1883) and Grosart (1885). *Herbert's Remains* (1652) contained *A Priest to the Temple, Jacula Prudentum* (an enlarged form of *Outlandish Proverbs*, first printed in 1640), &c., and a biographical discourse by B. Oley; the book was partly reprinted with a new title and preface in 1671, 1675, and 1701. From the early eighteenth century to the early nineteenth Herbert was pretty well ignored, except by John Wesley and Cowper. The first edition of *The Temple* since 1709 appeared at Bristol in 1799. In 1835–6 Pickering published the collected *Works* (2 vols.), with some notes from the hand of Coleridge, Herbert's critical rediscoverer. Grosart's edition (Fuller Worthies' Library, 3 vols., 1874) was superseded by G. H. Palmer's edition of the English works (Boston, 3 vols., 1905; rev. 1907; 1 vol., 1916); Palmer's valuable work was marred by an arbitrary view of the poet's spiritual evolution. The standard edition of the complete works is now that of F. E. Hutchinson (1941). The Nonesuch edition of *The Temple* (1927) printed the Bodleian MS. and included a short bibliography by G. Keynes. There have been countless popular editions. H. C. Beeching edited *A Priest to the Temple* as *George Herbert's Country Parson* (1898).

Walton's *Life* (1670) has of course unique value. The scope of A. G. Hyde's *George Herbert and His Times* (1906) is obvious. Among the older modern critics are E. Dowden (*Puritan and Anglican*, 1900), Beeching (*Religio Laici*, 1902), Palmer, and P. E. More (*Shelburne Essays, Fourth Series*, New York, 1906). Herbert has shared in the modern revival of the metaphysical poets and in the books on them by G. Williamson (1930), J. B. Leishman (1934), J. Bennett (1934), and H. C. White (1936).

Among modern essays are those of T. O. Beachcroft (*Criterion*, xii, 1932–3); T. S. Eliot (*Spectator*, 12 March, 1932); articles in the *TLS*, 2 March, 1933 and 12 July, 1941; F. L. Lucas (*Studies French and English*, 1934); Austin Warren (*American Review*, vii, 1936); F. E. Hutchinson, in *Seventeenth Century Studies Presented to Sir Herbert Grierson* (1938) and in his edition; and L. C. Knights, *Scrutiny*, xii (1943–4).

There are studies of Herbert's Latin verse by E. Blunden (*ESEA* xix, 1934), of *Jacula Prudentum* by H. G. Wright (*RES* xi, 1935), of his metrical technique by A. Hayes (*SP* xxxv, 1938), and of his relation to the emblem books by R. Freeman (*RES* xvii, 1941).

G. H. Palmer's *Herbert Bibliography* (Cambridge, Mass., 1911) is a catalogue of the compiler's collection. In addition to the *CBEL*, a useful list of critical writings, 1912–38, is in T. Spencer and M. Van Doren, *Studies in Metaphysical Poetry* (1939). There is a *Concordance* by Cameron Mann (Boston, 1927).

SIR THOMAS HERBERT, 1606–82.

A Discription of the Persian Monarchy Now beinge, of which the inner title was *A Relation of Some Yeares Travaile, Begunne Anno 1626*, appeared in 1634. Later editions were increasingly swollen with second-hand material. From the 1677 edition Sir W. Foster has edited the attractive original matter as *Thomas Herbert: Travels in Persia 1627–1629* (Broadway Travellers, 1928). Herbert receives a chapter in M. H. Braaksma, *Travel and Literature* (Groningen, 1938) and in B. Penrose, *Urbane Travellers* (1942). In his old age Herbert, who had attended Charles I in 1647–9, wrote *Memoirs of the Two last Years of . . . King Charles I*, which were first printed in full in 1702. They have been edited, with contemporary documents, by Allan Fea, *Memoirs of the Martyr King* (1905), and G. S. Stevenson, *Charles I in Captivity* (1927).

ROBERT HERRICK, 1591–1674.

Since the volume of 1648 was first reprinted as a whole by Thomas Maitland (2 vols., Edinburgh, 1823; London, 1825), there have been many editions, popular, expensive, and critical. That of A. W. Pollard (Muses' Library, 2 vols., 1891; rev. 1898) contained a preface by Swinburne. The standard edition is by F. W. Moorman (1915; reprinted in 1921 in the series of Oxford Poets, with the apparatus and most of the epigrams omitted).

Herrick had a very small place in nineteenth-century anthologies until H. Morley's *The King and the Commons* (1868) and Ward's *English Poets*, ii (1880).

The standard biographical and critical works are Moorman's *Robert Herrick* (1910) and Floris Delattre's exhaustive *Robert Herrick* (Paris, 1912). Pollard's *Old Picture Books* (1902) has essays on 'Herrick and his Friends' and 'A Poet's Studies'. Among essays in appreciation are those of Gosse (*Seventeenth-Century Studies*, 1883), Swinburne, Saintsbury (Aldine *Herrick*, 2 vols., 1893), T. B. Aldrich (Century Classics, New York, 1900; *Ponkapog Papers*, Boston, 1903); and Edmund Blunden (*Votive Tablets*, 1931). Herrick's classical affinities have been treated by J. B. Emperor, J. A. S. McPeek, and K. A. McEuen (*supra*, IV. 7) and in a monograph by P. Aiken (University of Maine, 1932). His bibliographical and critical vicissitudes are outlined by Delattre, by E. M. Cox (*Library*, Third Series, viii, 1917), and by N. Roeckerath, *Der Nachruhm Herricks und Wallers* (Leipzig, 1931). Poems which appeared in miscellanies and song-books are listed in Delattre, in Moorman's 1915 edition, and by N. Ault (*TLS*, 20 April, 1933). There is a *Concordance* by M. MacLeod (1936).

PETER HEYLYN, 1599–1662.

Ecclesia Restaurata (1661) was edited by J. C. Robertson (2 vols., 1849), with the life by Heylyn's son-in-law, J. Barnard. His geographical work is noticed by F. Watson, *Beginnings of the Teaching of Modern Subjects* (1909), and by E. G. R. Taylor and F. Mood (*supra*, V. 4).

THOMAS HEYWOOD, 1574?–1641.

Heywood's version of Sallust (1608–9) has been edited by C. Whibley (Tudor Translations, 1924). Some other non-dramatic works were: *Troia Britanica* (1609), which is discussed by J. S. P. Tatlock, 'The Siege of Troy in Elizabethan Literature', *PMLA* xxx (1915); *An Apology For Actors* (1612), edited for the Shakespeare Society (1841) and by R. H. Perkinson (Scholars' Facsimiles & Reprints, 1941); *Englands Elizabeth* (1631), reprinted in the *Harleian Miscellany*, ed. Park, supplemental vol. ii (1813); *The Life of Merlin* (1641; repr. 1812, reissued 1813); *The Hierarchie of the blessed Angells* (1635), which is described in P. H. Osmond, *Mystical Poets of the English Church* (1919); and *Pleasant Dialogues and Dramma's* (1637), ed. W. Bang (*Materialien*, iii,

1903). The non-dramatic work is treated in A. M. Clark's *Thomas Heywood* (1931) and L. B. Wright's *Middle-Class Culture* (1935). The complexities of Heywood's quarrel with Jaggard over piracy are disentangled by H. E. Rollins in his edition (1940) of the 1612 edition of *The Passionate Pilgrime*. Clark has a full bibliography of Heywood's works in *OBS*, vol. i, part ii, 1924 (1925). Scholarly studies are included in S. A. Tannenbaum's *Concise Bibliography* (New York, 1939).

NICHOLAS HILL, 1570?–1610.

Philosophia Epicurea, Democritiana, Theophrastica (Paris, 1601; Geneva, 1619) is noticed in T. F. Mayo's *Epicurus in England* (*1650–1725*) (Dallas, 1934) and discussed by F. R. Johnson (*Astronomical Thought in Renaissance England*, 1937) and especially by G. McColley in *Annals of Science*, iv (1939).

THOMAS HOBBES, 1588–1679.

Hobbes's chief works were listed in the biographical note in Chapter viii. Sir W. Molesworth edited the complete works in Latin and English (16 vols., 1839–45). *Leviathan* has been edited by A. R. Waller (Cambridge English Classics, 1904) and by W. G. P. Smith (1909), and in popular series. F. Tönnies edited *Behemoth* (1889) and *Elements of Law Natural & Politic* (1889; Cambridge English Classics, 1928). Hobbes's *Answer* to Davenant is in Spingarn's *Critical Essays of the Seventeenth Century* (1908). A recent volume of selections is that of F. J. E. Woodbridge (New York, 1930).

Perhaps the best biographical and critical introductions are still the books by G. C. Robertson (1886) and Sir Leslie Stephen (English Men of Letters, 1904). Hobbes has of course a prominent place in histories of philosophy, some of which are cited above in V. 3, and in B. Willey's *Seventeenth Century Background* (1934). Of the general studies of his thought the best is John Laird's minutely documented *Hobbes* (1934). Other good general works are *Thomas Hobbes: Leben und Lehre* (3rd ed., Stuttgart, 1925) by F. Tönnies, and A. Levi's *La Filosofia di Tommaso Hobbes* (Milan, 1929). Hobbes's scientific thought is placed in its setting in E. A. Burtt's *Metaphysical Foundations of Modern Physical Science* (1925); an important study of its development is F. Brandt's *Thomas Hobbes' Mechanical Conception of Nature* (Copenhagen, 1928). Hobbes's atomism is fully discussed by K. Lasswitz, *Geschichte der Atomistik vom Mittelalter bis Newton* (1890) and, along with Bacon and Boyle, by C. T. Harrison in *Harvard Studies and Notes in Philology and Literature*, xv (1933).

Hobbes the ethical and political thinker figures largely of course in the general studies of him and in histories of political theory; some of the latter have been cited in V. 1. Some other discussions, short and long, are the essays in Sir J. F. Stephen's *Horae Sabbaticae, Second Series* (1892); essays by John Dewey and others in *Studies in the History of Ideas*, i (1918), by the Department of Philosophy, Columbia University; R. Hönigswald's solid *Hobbes und die Staatsphilosophie* (Munich, 1924); E. L. Woodward's essay in *Social & Political Ideas of Some Great Thinkers of the Sixteenth and Seventeenth Centuries*, ed. F. J. C. Hearnshaw (1926); J. Lips, *Die Stellung des Thomas Hobbes zu den politischen Parteien*, &c. (Leipzig, 1927); B. Landry, *Hobbes* (Paris, 1930); Z. Lubienski, *Die Grundlagen des ethisch-politischen Systems von Hobbes* (Munich, 1932); J. Vialatoux, *La Cité de Hobbes, théorie de l'état totalitaire* (Paris, 1935); a symposium on 'La Pensée et l'Influence de Th. Hobbes' by J. Souilhé, Laird, Tönnies, and others, in *Archives de philosophie*, xii (1936); Leo Strauss's *Political Philosophy of Hobbes* (trans. 1936), a notably fresh study of the evolution of Hobbes's ideas; M. Oakeshott's critique of Strauss in *Politica*, ii (1936-7); A. E. Taylor's articles in *Seventeenth Century Studies Presented to Sir Herbert Grierson* (1938) and *Philosophy*, xiii (1938); G. P. Gooch's lecture (*Proceedings of the British Academy*, xxv, 1939; *Studies in Diplomacy and Statecraft*, 1942); S. P. Lamprecht's 'Hobbes and Hobbism' (*American Political Science Review*, xxxiv, 1940); and W. K. Jordan's *Development of Religious Toleration*, iv (1940).

The impact of Hobbes's thought on society and literature belongs chiefly to the Restoration, but reference may be made to L. I. Bredvold, *Intellectual Milieu of John Dryden* (University of Michigan, 1934), and articles by G. Williamson (*SP* xxx, 1933), L. Teeter (*ELH* iii, 1936), M. E. Hartsook (*Seventeenth Century Studies, Second Series*, ed. R. Shafer, Princeton, 1937), and T. B. Stroup (*SP* xxxv, 1938). Hobbes and Milton are contrasted by M. Nicolson (*SP* xxiii, 1926) and D. M. Wolfe (*SP* xli, 1944).

Hobbes's literary and aesthetic doctrines are discussed by Spingarn; by C. M. Dowlin, in the monograph cited under Davenant and in *RES* xvii (1941); by D. F. Bond (*ELH* iv,

1937); and most elaborately, and defensively, by C. D. Thorpe, *The Aesthetic Theory of Thomas Hobbes* (1940).

The most convenient bibliographies of Hobbes's works are in the *DNB* and *CBEL* and especially that in Laird.

MARGARET LADY HOBY, 1571–1633.

The *Diary of Lady Margaret Hoby 1599–1605*, the earliest extant diary by an Englishwoman, has been edited from the manuscript in the British Museum by D. M. Meads (1930), with a full introduction.

PHILEMON HOLLAND, 1552–1637.

Holland's major translations are listed in the text. A. F. Clements's *Tudor Translations* (1940) has brief excerpts from Livy's *Romane Historie* (1600), Pliny's *Historie of the World* (1601), and Suetonius's *Historie of Twelve Cæsars* (1606). Selections from the *Livy* are given in W. H. D. Rouse's *Hannibal in Italy* (1905), selections from the *Pliny* in M. St. C. Byrne's *Elizabethan Zoo* (1926) and H. N. Wethered's *Mind of the Ancient World* (1937). The *Suetonius* has been reprinted in the Tudor Translations (2 vols., 1899), the Broadway Translations (1923), and the Haslewood Books (1931). Selected essays from Plutarch's *Morals* (1603) have been edited by F. B. Jevons (1892) and E. H. Blakeney (Everyman's Library). The *Cyropaedia* (1632) has been reprinted by the Gregynog Press (1936). One of several medical pieces, *Regimen Sanitatis Salerni* (1617), was reprinted in Sir John Sinclair's *Code of Health and Longevity*, iii (1807).

C. Whibley's *Literary Portraits* (1904) contains an appreciation reprinted from the Tudor Translations *Suetonius*. The fullest study of Holland's workmanship is in F. O. Matthiessen's *Translation: An Elizabethan Art* (1931). There is some discussion in H. B. Lathrop's *Translations from the Classics* (1933). Alfred Schäfer made a detailed study of the *Livy* (Burgstädt, 1910). H. Silvette's *Catalogue of the Works of Philemon Holland . . . 1600–1940* (Charlottesville, 1940) is enlarged from his *Short-Title List* (1939). Some biographical details are furnished by Silvette and by C. L. Shaver (*Annals of Medical History, Third Series*, iv, 1942).

CHARLES HOOLE, 1610–67.

One notable work was Hoole's translation (1659) of the

famous illustrated text-book, Comenius's *Orbis Sensualium Pictus*. This was reprinted even in the nineteenth century, was edited by C. W. Bardeen (Syracuse, 1887), and was described by A. W. Holland in the *Contemporary Review*, cliv (1938). Hoole's own treatise, *A New Discovery Of the old Art of Teaching Schoole* (1660), first written *c.* 1637, was edited by T. Mark (Syracuse, 1912) and E. T. Campagnac (1913). Hoole is discussed in F. Watson's *English Grammar Schools to 1660* (1908) and *The Beginnings of the Teaching of Modern Subjects in England* (1909).

JOHN HOSKYNS, 1566–1638.

Full material by and about Hoskyns is contained in H. H. Hudson's edition of *Directions for Speech and Style* (Princeton, 1935) and L. B. Osborn's *Life, Letters, and Writings of John Hoskyns* (Yale, 1937). Grierson discussed 'Absence, heare thou my Protestation' in *MLR* vi (1911) and in his edition of Donne's poems (1912).

JAMES HOWELL, 1593/4–1666.

Two well-known specimens of Howell's large and varied output were *ΔΕΝΔΡΟΛΟΓΙΑ. Dodona's Grove* (1640; second part, 1650), a political allegory which won rapid popularity, and *Instructions for forreine Travell* (1642; enlarged 1650; ed. Arber, 1869). The first two volumes of *Epistolæ Ho-Elianæ* appeared in 1645 and 1647. The 2nd edition, with a third volume of new letters, and with dates added, was issued in 1650. The third edition (1655), the last in Howell's lifetime, had a fourth volume of new letters. Nine other editions were published between 1673 and 1754; then the book was obscured by the eighteenth-century essayists. The next edition, the standard one, with full apparatus, was that of J. Jacobs (2 vols., 1890–2). Other modern editions are those of W. H. Bennett (2 vols., 1890) and Agnes Repplier (2 vols., Boston, 1907), and the one in the Temple Classics (3 vols., 1903).

Howell is discussed in some studies of familiar letters cited in IV. 6, and by Ward in the *CHEL* vii. There is a thesis on the *Epistolæ* by G. Jürgens (Marburg, 1900), and Jacobs's notes are corrected and extended in a series of articles by E. Bensly, *Aberystwyth Studies*, iii–vi and viii–ix (1922–7). Howell's linguistic works and knowledge are discussed by E. H. Mensel (*JEGP* xxv, 1926). W. H. Vann's *Notes on the Writings of James*

Howell (Baylor University, 1924) gives a full bibliography with a biographical sketch.

PHILIP HUNTON, 1604?–82.

Hunton published *A Treatise of Monarchie* in 1643, a *Vindication* (against Dr. Ferne) in 1644. The *Treatise* was reprinted twice in 1689; one edition contained most of the *Vindication*. The *Treatise* is in the *Harleian Miscellany*, ed. Park, vi (1810). The significance of Hunton's thought has been stressed by C. H. McIlwain in *Politica*, i (1934–5), and *Constitutionalism and the Changing World* (1939), and by Yung Chi Hoe (*supra*, V. 1).

KING JAMES I, 1566–1625.

James's *Workes* appeared in 1616. Groups of miscellaneous writings have been edited by Arber (1869), R. S. Rait (*A Royal Rhetorician*, 1900; *Lusus Regius*, 1901), and A. F. Westcott (*New Poems by James I of England*, Columbia, 1911). The tract on 'Scottis Poesie' is in G. G. Smith's *Elizabethan Critical Essays* (1904), and *Daemonologie* (1597) is reprinted in G. B. Harrison's Bodley Head Quartos (1924). C. H. McIlwain has edited the *Political Works* (Harvard, 1918), with an introduction which is one of the classical studies of political thought. J. Craigie is editing *Basilikon Doron* for the Scottish Text Society (vol. i, 1944).

A few of the contemporary histories are cited here under Goodman, Osborn, Weldon, and Arthur Wilson. The standard modern histories are cited above in V. 1. John Nichols's *Progresses, &c. of King James the First* (4 vols., 1828) has unique value. There are biographies of varying length by T. F. Henderson (1904), Charles Williams (1934), and H. R. Williamson (1935). What will be an authoritative political biography is being prepared by D. H. Willson. There are essays, mainly political, by H. M. Chew, *Social & Political Ideas of Some Great Thinkers of the Sixteenth and Seventeenth Centuries*, ed. F. J. C. Hearnshaw (1926); C. J. Sisson, *Seventeenth Century Studies Presented to Sir Herbert Grierson* (1938); and G. Davies, *HLQ* v (1941–2). More special studies are H. G. Stafford, *James VI of Scotland and the Throne of England* (New York, 1940), H. Witte, *Die Ansichten Jakobs I. von England über Kirche und Staat* (Berlin, 1940), and Willson, *HLQ* viii (1944–5).

Basilikon Doron is touched in the studies of conduct books cited above in V. 6, and receives the last chapter in W.

Kleineke's *Englische Fürstenspiegel* (Halle, 1937). James's attitude towards witchcraft is treated with corrective authority by G. L. Kittredge, *Witchcraft in Old and New England* (1929). Sir G. F. Warner catalogued 'The Library of James VI. 1573–1583' in *Publications of the Scottish History Society*, xv (1893).

RICHARD JOHNSON, 1573–1659?

Johnson's chief works were: *The nine Worthies of London* (1592), which is reprinted in the *Harleian Miscellany*, ed. Park, viii (1811); the very long-lived romance, *The Seaven Champions of Christendome* (1596–7), which has had editions and abridgements even in the last century and a half; *Tom a Lincolne* (1599, 1607), reprinted in W. J. Thoms, *Early English Prose Romances* (3 vols., 1828 and 1858, 1 vol., 1907); *The Pleasant Conceites of Old Hobson* (Percy Society, ix, 1844); *A Crowne-Garland of Goulden Roses*, a book of ballads reprinted by the Percy Society, vi and xv (1842, 1845); two tracts on London life reprinted in Collier's *Illustrations of Early English Popular Literature*, ii (1864); and *The History of Tom Thumbe* (1621), which is commonly assigned to Johnson. His writings in general are described in L. B. Wright, *Middle-Class Culture* (1935). His most famous romance is the subject of a thesis by H. W. Willkomm (Berlin, 1911) and is touched upon in G. E. Dawson's edition of *The Seven Champions of Christendome by John Kirke* (Western Reserve, 1929). *Old Hobson* has a place in the studies of jestbooks by E. Schulz and F. P. Wilson (*supra*, IV. 2).

ROBERT JOHNSON, *fl.* 1601 ff.

Essaies, Or Rather Imperfect Offers (1601) had several other editions, 1607–38. Johnson is also credited with *The Travellers Breviat* (1601), taken from G. Botero's *Relationi Universali*, and with *Nova Britannia* (1609) and its second part, *The New Life of Virginea* (1612). The American pieces are reprinted in P. Force's *Tracts*, i (1836), and G. P. Humphrey's *American Colonial Tracts*, Nos. 6 and 7 (Rochester, N.Y., 1897). The essayist and propagandist were probably different persons.

BENJAMIN JONSON, 1572–1637.

Epigrammes and *The Forrest*, and of course the lyrics in a number of plays and masques, appeared in the folio *Workes* (1616). This was reprinted as the first volume of the second folio edition, the *Workes* of 1640–1, edited by Sir Kenelm Digby. The second volume of the 1640 edition contained more plays and masques, *Under-woods* (properly *Under-wood*), *Horace, His Art of Poetrie, The English Grammar,* and *Timber: or, Discoveries.* Some poems had been printed before and some appeared in two small volumes issued separately in 1640.

A facsimile of *Epigrammes, The Forrest,* and *Under-wood* has been edited by H. H. Hudson (Facsimile Text Society, 1936).

The Gifford-Cunningham edition of Jonson's works (3 vols., 1871; 9 vols., 1875) has been superseded by the edition of C. H. Herford and P. Simpson (1925 ff.); this has not yet (1944) reached the non-dramatic writings.

There are annotated editions of *Timber* by F. E. Schelling (1892) and M. Castelain (Paris, 1906); the latter quotes the sources. The text is in the Bodley Head Quartos, ed. G. B. Harrison (1923). The *English Grammar* has been edited by A. V. Waite (New York, 1909) and S. Gibson (1928). The complete *Poems* have been edited by B. H. Newdigate (1936). H. Levin's *Ben Jonson* (New York, 1938) includes non-dramatic selections.

Biography began with Drummond's *Conversations,* which is reprinted by Harrison with *Timber*; the standard text is in the first volume of Herford and Simpson. Two of the smaller biographical and critical surveys are by G. G. Smith (English Men of Letters, 1919) and John Palmer (1934). The largest and best works are Castelain's *Ben Jonson: l'homme et l'œuvre* (Paris, 1907) and the first volume of Herford and Simpson. Some biographical problems have been elucidated by M. Eccles (*RES* xii and xiii, 1936–7) and F. T. Bowers (*SP* xxxiv, 1937).

Formal criticism began with the elegiac *Jonsonus Virbius* (1638), which is reprinted in Cunningham's 9th volume and in J. F. Bradley and J. Q. Adams, *The Jonson Allusion-Book* ... *1597–1700* (Yale, 1922). Jonson's early fame is studied by G. E. Bentley, *Shakespeare and Jonson* (2 vols., University of Chicago, 1945). Victorian criticism may be represented by the books of J. A. Symonds (1886) and Swinburne (1889). The fullest criticism of the non-dramatic writing is in Castelain, Herford and Simpson (ii), and G. B. Johnston, *Ben Jonson: Poet* (Columbia, 1945). Some other discussions of Jonson's poetic theory and practice are: F. E. Schelling, 'Ben Jonson and the Classical School' (*PMLA* xiii, 1898; *Shakespeare and*

"Demi-Science", University of Pennsylvania, 1927); E. C. Dunn, *Ben Jonson's Art* (Northampton, Mass., 1925); W. M. Evans, *Ben Jonson and Elizabethan Music* (Lancaster, Pa., 1929); R. S. Walker, 'Ben Jonson's Lyric Poetry' (*Criterion*, xiii, 1933–4); and R. L. Sharp, *From Donne to Dryden* (1940).

Much scholarly and critical work has been done on Jonson's classical debts and affinities. He has a place in the books (cited in IV. 7) by R. Shafer on the ode, T. K. Whipple on the epigram, J. B. Emperor and J. A. S. McPeek on Catullus, and K. A. McEuen on miscellaneous classical influences. Some special studies are: Hugo Reinsch, *Ben Jonsons Poetik und seine Beziehungen zu Horaz* (Leipzig, 1899); W. D. Briggs's valuable articles on sources of the poems, in *MP* x and xv (1912–13, 1917–18) and *Classical Philology*, xi (1916); C. B. Hilberry, *Ben Jonson's Ethics in Relation to Stoic and Humanistic Ethical Thought* (University of Chicago, 1933); J. E. Hankins, on the Pindaric ode and Seneca (*MLN* li, 1936); and C. F. Wheeler, *Classical Mythology in the Plays, Masques, and Poems of Ben Jonson* (Princeton, 1938). Much fresh mythological material is supplied by E. W. Talbert (*SP* xl, 1943; *PQ* xxii, 1943) and in a forthcoming book on the masques by A. H. Gilbert.

Some heterogeneous items may be added. Jonson's use of Greek 'characters' is shown by E. C. Baldwin in *MLN* xvi (1901). His echo of Micanzio was observed by A. T. Shillinglaw (*TLS*, 18 April, 1936; *Englische Studien*, lxxi, 1936–7). The latest discussion of the problem of Jonson's or Donne's authorship of the group of elegies is by E. M. Simpson (*RES* xv, 1939). The hallowed name of S. Pavy was regretfully corrected by G. E. Bentley in the *TLS*, 30 May, 1942. Jonson's English and the *English Grammar* have been studied by J. H. Neumann (*PMLA* liv, 1939) and O. Funke (*Anglia* lxiv, 1940).

Among bibliographical studies are several articles by W. D. Briggs in *Anglia*, xxxvii–xxxix (1913–16) and by W. W. Greg in the *Library*, vi and xi (1925–6, 1930–1), H. L. Ford's *Collation of the Ben Jonson Folios 1616–31–40* (1932), and the discussion in *The Carl H. Pforzheimer Library*, ed. W. A. Jackson (1940), ii. There is a *Concise Bibliography* (New York, 1938) by S. A. Tannenbaum.

SILVESTER JOURDAIN or JOURDAN, *d.* 1650.

A Discovery of the Barmudas (1610) had a second edition, *A*

Plaine Description of the Barmudas (1613), which was edited by
'W.C.', perhaps William Crashaw (father of the poet), who
edited Alexander Whitaker's *Good Newes from Virginia* in the
same year. The pamphlet of 1610 was included in the Aunger-
vyle Society Reprints, Second Series (1884), and has been
edited by J. Q. Adams (Scholars' Facsimiles & Reprints, 1940).
The *Plaine Description* is reprinted in P. Force, *Tracts*, iii (1844).
The Shakespearian importance of the work is discussed by
editors of *The Tempest*, by Adams, and by C. M. Gayley,
Shakespeare and the Founders of Liberty in America (New York, 1917).

HENRY KING, 1592–1669.

King's metrical version of the Psalms appeared in 1651,
Poems, Elegies, Paradoxes, and Sonnets in 1657. Unsold copies of
the latter were reissued with new title-pages in 1664 (this with
38 pages of additional elegies) and 1700. There was no other
edition until J. Hannah's selection, *Poems and Psalms* (1843).
The modern editions, which include poems from miscellanies
and manuscripts, are those of L. Mason (Yale, 1914), Saintsbury
(*Minor Poets of the Caroline Period*, iii, 1921), and John Sparrow
(1925). The best critical discussions are Sparrow's introduction
and some pages in G. Williamson's *Donne Tradition* (1930). The
fullest biographical and bibliographical account is L. Mason's
'Life and Works of Henry King', in *Transactions of the Connecti-
cut Academy of Arts and Sciences*, xviii (1913). Sparrow's edition
includes a bibliography by G. Keynes. Percy Simpson has
described the Bodleian MSS. in the *Bodleian Quarterly Record*, v
(1929).

RICHARD KNOLLES, 1550–1610?

The *Generall Historie of the Turkes* appeared in 1603 and was
brought up to date in editions of 1610, 1621, &c. It is discussed
in S. C. Chew, *The Crescent and the Rose* (1937). Knolles also
translated Bodin's *Les six livres de la Republique* (1576) as *The Six
Bookes of a Commonweale* (1606).

SIR FRANCIS KYNASTON, 1587–1642.

Kynaston's productions were: *Amorum Troili et Creseidæ
Libri duo priores Anglico-Latini* (1635), the translation from
Chaucer; *Leoline & Sydenis An Heroick Romance*, with amatory

poems (1642; unsold copies reissued with a new inner title-page, 1646); and the account of his academy, *Constitutions of the Musaeum Minervae* (1636). The English poems are reprinted in Saintsbury's *Minor Poets of the Caroline Period*, ii (1906). H. G. Seccombe has biographical and bibliographical notes in *RES* viii (1932).

SIR JAMES LANCASTER, 1554/5–1618.

The Voyages of Sir James Lancaster, Kt., to the East Indies were edited from Hakluyt and Purchas by Sir C. Markham (Hakluyt Society, 1877) and have been augmented and re-edited by Sir William Foster (1940).

WILLIAM LAUD, 1573–1645.

Perhaps the best statement of Laud's liberal theology was *A Relation of The Conference betweene William Lawd . . . And Mr. Fisher the Jesuite* (1639; ed. C. H. Simpkinson, 1901), which had been sketched, over the initials of Laud's chaplain, Richard Baylie, in Francis White's *Replie to Jesuit Fishers answere* (1624). H. Wharton edited Laud's diary and *The History of the Troubles and Tryal of William Laud*, written by himself in the Tower, in 1695, and a *Second Volume of the Remains* in 1700. The *Autobiography* published in 1839 was compiled from the diary, the *History*, and the history of Laud's chancellorship. The complete *Works* were edited in the Library of Anglo-Catholic Theology (7 vols. in 9, 1847–60). Among the many contemporary attacks (listed in the *BMC* and Collins, *infra*) were several by Prynne, notably the *Breviate* (1644), a garbled version of Laud's stolen diary. His chaplain, Heylyn, produced a eulogistic biography, *Cyprianus Anglicus* (1668). In modern times Laud's character and work have evoked antithetical opinions from 'liberal' and ecclesiastical writers. Among essays are those by J. B. Mozley (*Essays Historical and Theological*, 1878), Sir James Stephen (*Horae Sabbaticae, First Series*, 1892), the discourses in *Archbishop Laud Commemoration*, ed. W. E. Collins (1895), and E. R. Adair's article in *Church History*, v (1936). Among biographies are those by the churchmen W. H. Hutton (1895) and A. S. Duncan-Jones (1927), a popular book by R. P. T. Coffin (New York, 1930), and H. R. Trevor-Roper's large work (1940), which is more political than ecclesiastical. Collins includes a full bibliography.

JOHN LILBURNE, 1615?–57.

Several tracts and portions of others are reproduced in W. Haller, *Tracts on Liberty* (1934), A. S. P. Woodhouse, *Puritanism and Liberty* (1938), and D. M. Wolfe, *Milton in the Puritan Revolution* (1941). Two new collections of Leveller tracts, edited by W. Haller and G. Davies and by D. M. Wolfe, have been cited above (V. 1). Besides discussions in the books already named, there are Firth's article in the *DNB*, T. C. Pease, *The Leveller Movement* (1916), E. Bernstein, *Cromwell & Communism* (trans. 1930), and Haller, *Rise of Puritanism* (1938). There are bibliographical lists and notes in Haller's books and in Wolfe.

WILLIAM LILLY, 1602–81.

Some of Lilly's many publications were: *Merlinus Anglicus Junior: The English Merlin revived* (1644); *A Collection Of Ancient And Moderne Prophesies Concerning these present Times* (1645); *The Starry Messenger* (1645); *Christian Astrology* (1647); and *Monarchy Or No Monarchy in England* (1651). This last included *Several Observations upon the Life and Death of Charles late King of England*. The very interesting *Mr. William Lilly's History of His Life and Times* (1715) was edited by C. Burman in *Lives of . . . Elias Ashmole . . . and William Lilly, Written by Themselves* (1774) and reprinted several times in the early nineteenth century. The *Several Observations* was reprinted with the autobiography in 1715 and some later editions, and is included in F. Maseres, *Select Tracts* (1815). A valuable bibliography of astrology is the catalogue of Lilly's library at the end of his *Easie and plain Method Teaching How to judge upon Nativities* (1658).

WILLIAM LISLE or L'ISLE, 1569?–1637.

The Faire Æthiopian (1631; 2nd ed., 1638) was a verse translation of Heliodorus. Lisle's chief work was *A Saxon Treatise Concerning The Old And New Testament* (1623), reissued as *Divers Ancient Monuments in the Saxon Tongue* (1638). His labours in Old English are discussed by E. N. Adams, *Old English Scholarship in England from 1566–1800* (1917), and R. Tuve, 'Ancients, Moderns, and Saxons' (*ELH* vi, 1939).

WILLIAM LITHGOW, 1582?–1645?

A Most Delectable, And True Discourse, of an admired and painefull peregrination (1614; enlarged, 1623) was used by Purchas and by Lithgow in his larger work, *The Totall Discourse, Of the Rare Adventures, and painefull Peregrinations of long nineteene Yeares Travayles, from Scotland, to the most Famous Kingdomes in Europe, Asia, and Affrica* (1632 and later edns.). J. Maidment edited Lithgow's *Poetical Remains* (1863). The *Totall Discourse* has been reprinted by MacLehose (1906) and abridged by B. I. Lawrence as *Rare Adventures and Painefull Peregrinations* (1928). There is a general sketch of Lithgow in B. Penrose, *Urbane Travellers* (1942). His eastern travels are discussed by W. G. Rice and S. C. Chew (*supra*, V. 4).

MARTIN LLUELYN, 1616–82.

Lluelyn's one book was *Men-Miracles. With other Poemes* (1646), which reappeared in 1656, 1661 (as *The Marrow of the Muses*), and 1679. He contributed a poem to the English translation (1653) of Harvey's *De Generatione Animalium.* Some poems are reprinted in Brydges, *Censura Literaria*, x (1809); Corser, *Collectanea Anglo-Poetica*, Part 8 (Chetham Society, cii, 1878); and the anthologies of N. Ault and L. B. Marshall. There is a good critical study by R. C. Wallerstein (*JEGP* xxxv, 1936).

THOMAS LODGE, 1557/8–1625.

Lodge's original works, which came before 1600, were collected for the Hunterian Club (4 vols., 1875–88), with an essay by Gosse which is reprinted in his *Seventeenth-Century Studies* (1883); a number of things have had separate editions. The literary fruit of his medical degree (1598) was a *Treatise of the Plague* (1603). Other works of our period, and of the author's sober maturity, were translations: *The Flowers of Lodowicke of Granado* (1601); *The Famous And Memorable Workes of Josephus* (1602); *The Workes both Morrall and Natural of Lucius Annaeus Seneca* (1614; rev. 1620); and *A Learned Summary Upon the famous Poeme of William of Saluste Lord of Bartas* (1621), a version of Simon Goulart's commentary. The standard biographical and critical studies are those of N. B. Paradise (Yale, 1931) and E. A. Tenney (Cornell, 1935). Much biographical matter was brought forward by C. J. Sisson in *Thomas Lodge and Other Elizabethans* (Harvard, 1933) and by Alice Walker in *RES* ix and x (1933–4). There is a *Concise Bibliography* (New York, 1940) by S. A. Tannenbaum.

RICHARD LOVELACE, 1618–56/7.

Only the prologue and epilogue of Lovelace's Oxford comedy reached print. *Lucasta* (1649) was published by him; the inferior *Lucasta. Posthume Poems*, dated 1659 but issued in 1660, was edited by his brother and E. Revett. Except for 'To Althea, From Prison', Lovelace had no great fame in his century (though he received intelligent praise from Edward Phillips in 1675), and he was largely forgotten until a revival began with Percy's *Reliques* (1765). The original two volumes had no second edition until Singer's (1817–18). The standard edition is that of C. H. Wilkinson (1930), based on his own two-volume edition of 1925. The handiest text is in R. G. Howarth's *Minor Poets of the 17th Century* (Everyman's Library, 1931). The fullest picture of the poet, C. H. Hartmann's *The Cavalier Spirit and its Influence on the Life and Work of Richard Lovelace* (1925), receives some correction in Wilkinson. Wilkinson has contributed biographical and bibliographical data to the *TLS*, 14 August, 1937. The question of Lucasta's actuality or identity has been discussed by Hartmann, Wilkinson, and A. C. Judson (*MP* xxiii, 1925–6).

JAMES MABBE, 1572–1642?

Mabbe translated *The Rogue: or The Life of Guzman de Alfarache. Written in Spanish by Matheo Aleman* (1622), which is reprinted in the Tudor Translations (4 vols., 1924), with an essay by J. Fitzmaurice-Kelly; *The Spanish Bawd, Represented in Celestina: or, The Tragicke-Comedy of Calisto and Melibea* (1631), from F. de Rojas (ed. Fitzmaurice-Kelly, Tudor Translations, 1894; ed. H. W. Allen, 1908 and, in the Broadway Translations, 1923); and Cervantes's *Exemplarie Novells* (1640). This last has been edited by S. W. Orson (2 vols., 1900), and three tales reprinted as *The Spanish Ladie and Two Other Stories* (1928). In addition to Fitzmaurice-Kelly's critical eulogies there is a study of 'Mabbe's Paganization of the *Celestina*' by H. P. Houck (*PMLA* liv, 1939).

SIR GEORGE MACKENZIE, 1636?–91.

The first part of *Aretina; Or, The Serious Romance* appeared in 1660; it was never finished. Brief excerpts are given in R. B. Johnson's *Birth of Romance* (1928). Mackenzie's legal and miscellaneous writings are beyond our limits. There is a biography by Andrew Lang (1909), a bibliography by F. S. Ferguson, *Edinburgh Bibliographical Society Transactions*, i, pt. i (1936).

GERVASE MARKHAM, 1568?–1637.

Among Markham's 'literary' works were religious poems (1600–1), which were edited by Grosart (*Miscellanies of The Fuller Worthies' Library*, ii, 1871). His many books on the arts of country life were published separately and in collections. His bibliography, which is much complicated by his cumulative and repetitious habits, is more or less clarified in the *STC*; G. E. Noyes, *Bibliography of Courtesy and Conduct Books* (1937); G. E. Fussell, *NQ* clxxv (1938); and especially C. F. Mullett, *Isis*, xxxv (1944). Markham gets some space in Donald McDonald, *Agricultural Writers . . . 1200–1800* (1908), and Lord Ernle, *English Farming Past and Present* (1912; 5th ed., 1936). Markham's agreement with the booksellers is printed in Arber's *Stationers' Register*, iii, 679.

SHAKERLEY MARMION, 1603–39.

The *Legend of Cupid and Psyche* (1637; another issue, 1638) was reissued in 1666 as *Cupid's Courtship*. It was reprinted by Singer (1820) and in Saintsbury's *Minor Poets of the Caroline Period*, ii (1906). The only minute study of the poem is in Adolf Hoffmann, *Das Psyche-Märchen des Apuleius in der englischen Literatur* (Strassburg, 1908). Marmion's plays were edited by J. Maidment and W. H. Logan (1875).

ANDREW MARVELL, 1621–78.

The first collection of verse, which did not include the late satires, was *Miscellaneous Poems* (1681; reprinted 1923). Marvell's poems were edited by T. Cooke (2 vols., 1726, 1772) and his complete works by E. Thompson (3 vols., 1776), but he did not appear in the large collections down to and including Chalmers's (1810); for the eighteenth century—and for Landor in the *Imaginary Conversations*—Marvell was wholly or mainly a publicist. Appreciation of his lyrical verse is represented by Bowles, Hazlitt, Campbell, Lamb, Hartley Coleridge, Emerson, Poe, and Tennyson. Marvell first won recognition (without the aid of the 'Coy Mistress') in Palgrave's *Golden Treasury* (1861 ff.). Grosart edited the complete works (Fuller Worthies' Library, 4 vols., 1872–5). The standard edition is the *Poems and Letters*, ed. H. M. Margoliouth (2 vols., 1927), which has to be completed with a volume of prose. The best small edition is by G. A. Aitken (Muses' Library, 2 vols., 1892, 1901).

Augustine Birrell's *Andrew Marvell* (English Men of Letters, 1905), R. Poscher's *Andrew Marvells poetische Werke* (Vienna, 1908), and smaller studies were superseded by the exhaustive critical biography of P. Legouis, *André Marvell, poète, puritain, patriote* (Paris, 1928). The year 1921 brought many appreciations, such as those of T. S. Eliot, Cyril Falls, H. J. Massingham, and others, in *Tercentenary Tributes*, ed. W. H. Bagguley (1922). Eliot's essay was reprinted in his *Homage to John Dryden* (1924) and *Selected Essays* (1932). Among other discussions are those of F. L. Lucas, *Authors Dead and Living* (1926); G. Williamson, *The Donne Tradition* (1930); W. Empson, 'Marvell's Garden', in *Scrutiny*, 1 (1932), in *Determinations*, ed. F. R. Leavis (1934), and in Empson's *Some Versions of Pastoral* (1935); F. R. Leavis, in *Scrutiny*, iv (1935), and *Revaluation* (1936); and C. Brooks and R. P. Warren, *Understanding Poetry* (1938). In her brief *Andrew Marvell* (1929), V. Sackville-West has a not wholly congenial subject. A freshly suggestive, and sometimes inaccurate and fanciful, critical study is *Andrew Marvell* (1940) by M. C. Bradbrook and M. G. Lloyd Thomas. Miss Bradbrook has an article on 'Marvell and the Poetry of Rural Solitude' in *RES* xvii (1941).

The mystery of the 'Mary Marvell' who supposedly edited the *Miscellaneous Poems* of 1681 is cleared up by F. S. Tupper in *PMLA* liii (1938). A full bibliography is given by Legouis. Critical writings of the years 1912–38 are listed by T. Spencer and M. Van Doren in their *Studies in Metaphysical Poetry* (1939).

THOMAS MAY, 1595–1650.

In addition to his plays May wrote a popular translation, *Lucan's Pharsalia* (3 books in 1626, the whole in 1627), an also popular *Continuation* of Lucan (1630), versions of *Virgil's Georgicks* (1628) and *Selected Epigrams of Martial* (1629), and two historical poems, *The Reigne Of King Henry the Second* (1633) and *The Victorious Reigne Of King Edward the Third* (1635). In prose he translated Barclay's *Icon Animorum* in 1631 as *The Mirrour Of Mindes* (he had done the verses in Long's and Le Grys's versions of *Argenis*) and produced a *History of the Parliament Of England* (1647; repr. 1812, 1854). The standard book is A. G. Chester's *Thomas May: Man of Letters* (University of Pennsylvania, 1932). G. W. Whiting has argued for Milton's use in *Eikonoklastes* of May's history of the Long Parliament (*Milton's Literary Milieu*, University of North Carolina, 1939).

JOSEPH MEDE or MEAD, 1586–1638.

Mede's chief work, *Clavis Apocalyptica* (1627), was translated in 1643 by R. More as *The Key of the Revelation*; there were translations also in 1831 and 1833. Mede's works were edited in 1664 and 1672 by John Worthington. Letters are printed in *The Court and Times of James the First* (2 vols., 1848) and *The Court and Times of Charles the First* (2 vols., 1848), ed. T. Birch and R. F. Williams, and in J. Heywood and T. Wright, *Cambridge University Transactions* (1854), ii. A *Life* was included in the *Works* of 1664–72; better accounts are in the *DNB* and Mullinger's *University of Cambridge*, iii (1911). M. Nicolson has suggested Mede as the original of Milton's 'old Damoetas' and Henry More's Mnemon (*MLN* xli, 1926). The influence of his love of precise expression is noted by W. F. Mitchell (*English Pulpit Oratory*, 1932).

SIR JAMES MELVILLE, 1535–1617.

Melville's *Memoires* were first printed in 1683 by G. Scott, whose text, a translation from the original Scots, has been followed in subsequent editions, including that of A. F. Steuart (1929). The Scots text, which Steuart made some use of, was printed for the Bannatyne Club (1827) and reprinted for the Maitland Club. There are selections in J. G. Fyfe's *Scottish Diaries and Memoirs* (1928).

JAMES MELVILLE, 1556–1614.

The *Diary* was printed for the Bannatyne Club (1829), the *Autobiography and Diary* for the Wodrow Society (2 vols., 1842). The diary proper ends in 1601; the *Continuation*, 1596–1610, is more heavily ecclesiastical and political. Melville's record was largely used by David Calderwood in his *True History of the Church of Scotland* (pr. 1678). There are selections in J. G. Fyfe's *Scottish Diaries and Memoirs* (1928). M. A. Bald has an essay on Melville in *MLR* xxi (1926).

SIR JOHN MENNES, 1599–1671.

The names of Mennes, a seaman and soldier, and of the unclerical divine, James Smith, appeared in the miscellanies *Musarum Deliciae* (1655), *Wit and Drollery* (1656), and *Wit Restor'd* (1658). The pair have also been associated with *Witts Recreations* (1640). These last two books, with *Musarum Deliciae*, were edited by T. Park as *Musarum Deliciae* (2 vols., 1817) and reprinted by J. C. Hotten (2 vols., 1874). The numerous early editions are described by A. E. Case, *Bibliography of English Poetical Miscellanies* (1935).

GRACE LADY MILDMAY, *c.* 1552–1620.

Lady Mildmay's unpublished journal is described, with excerpts, by R. Weigall in the *Quarterly Review*, ccxv (1911).

JOHN MILTON, 1608–74.

The chief poetical publications in Milton's lifetime were: *A Maske Presented At Ludlow Castle* (1637), now known as *Comus*; 'Lycidas', in *Justa Edouardo King naufrago* (1638); *Epitaphium Damonis*, privately printed in 1640 (?); *Poems* (1645), reprinted with additions in 1673; *Paradise lost* (1667; 2nd ed., 1674); *Paradise Regain'd* with *Samson Agonistes* (1671). Of the prose works published in his lifetime the most important are: *Of Reformation Touching Church-Discipline in England* (1641); *The Reason of Church-governement* (1642; dated 1641); the tract commonly cited as *An Apology for Smectymnuus* (1642); *The Doctrine and Discipline of Divorce* (1643; rev. ed., 1644); *Of Education* (1644); *Areopagitica* (1644); *The Tenure of Kings and Magistrates* (1649); *EIKONOKΛΑΣΤΗΣ* (1649); *Joannis Miltoni Angli Pro Populo Anglicano Defensio* (1651, the *Defensio Prima*); the *Defensio Secunda* (1654); *A Treatise of Civil power in Ecclesiastical causes* (1659); *The Readie & Easie Way to Establish a Free Commonwealth* (1660); *The History of Britain* (1670); *Epistolae Familiares* and *Prolusiones* (1674).

Of the surviving manuscripts the most important is that of the minor poems, mostly in his own hand, in the library of Trinity College, Cambridge; it has been published in facsimile by W. A. Wright (1899) and in part by F. A. Patterson (Facsimile Text Society, 1933). Other valuable manuscripts, not autograph, are: the Bridgewater MS. of *Comus* or so-called stage-copy, in the possession of the Egerton family (printed 1910); *De Doctrina Christiana*, in the Public Record Office, first published with a translation by C. Sumner (2 vols., 1825); the Pierpont Morgan MS. of *Paradise Lost*, Book I, ed. with facsimile by Helen Darbishire (1931).

There are facsimiles of *Comus*, 1637 (ed. L. S. Livingston, New York, 1903); of *Justa Edouardo King*, 1638 (Facsimile Text Society, 1939); of *Areopagitica* (Noel Douglas, 1927); of the

Poems of 1645 (Oxford, 1924; Noel Douglas, 1926, omitting the Latin and Greek poems); and of *Paradise Lost,* 1667 (ed. R. H. Shepherd, 1873; ed. D. Masson, 1877). H. F. Fletcher is editing in 4 vols. a notable facsimile edition of the complete poetical works; vol. i (University of Illinois, 1943) contains the minor poems.

The Columbia University edition in 18 vols. (1931–8) is the only complete edition in the original spelling with generally full collations. Though the editing is sometimes uneven, the edition is a great achievement; and the two-volume Index (1940) is alone an invaluable work of reference. The only other attempt at a complete edition is Mitford's (8 vols., 1851), and this omits the *De Doctrina Christiana.*

There are library editions of the poems: by H. J. Todd (1st ed., 6 vols., 1801; 5th ed., 4 vols., 1852), a variorum edition which makes full use of some of the best-known eighteenth-century work, for example, R. Bentley's eccentric edition of *Paradise Lost* (1732), T. Newton's editions of *Paradise Lost* (2 vols., 1749) and of *Paradise Regain'd, Samson Agonistes,* and the minor poems (1752), and T. Warton's edition of the minor poems (*Poems upon Several Occasions,* 1785; rev. ed., 1791); by D. Masson, with full introductions and commentary (2nd ed., 3 vols., 1890); by Sir Herbert Grierson (2 vols., 1925). Of smaller editions of the poems the best are by D. Masson (Globe, 1877); H. C. Beeching (1900; rev. ed., 1938), preserving the old spelling; W. A. Wright (1903), with excellent textual notes; W. V. Moody (Boston, 1899; rev. ed., 1924), with introductions; F. A. Patterson (rev. ed., New York, 1933), with the early biographies; M. Y. Hughes (2 vols., New York, 1935–7), with fresh and valuable apparatus; J. H. Hanford (New York, 1937); and H. F. Fletcher (Boston, 1941).

The Bohn edition of the prose works (5 vols., 1848–53) is still useful, though superseded by the more reliable Columbia text and by *The Student's Milton (infra).* Groups of prose works have been edited in various popular series. M. Y. Hughes is preparing an annotated volume of selections.

The one-volume *Student's Milton,* ed. F. A. Patterson (rev. ed., New York, 1933), contains the poems and most of the prose. Among similar but smaller collections is that of E. H. Visiak (Nonesuch Press, 1938).

Among the many editions of particular works some are

the richly annotated editions of most of the minor poems and of *Paradise Lost* and *Samson Agonistes* by A. W. Verity; the elaborate editions of several prose works by Yale scholars; the *Sonnets*, ed. J. S. Smart (1921); *Latin Poems*, ed. W. MacKellar (Cornell, 1930); and *Private Correspondence and Academic Exercises*, ed. P. B. and E. M. W. Tillyard (1932).

Six lives written by men who knew Milton or who knew men who knew him (Aubrey, an anonymous writer, Anthony Wood, Edward Phillips, Toland, and Jonathan Richardson) are collected as *Early Lives of Milton* (1932) by H. Darbishire; her attribution of the anonymous life to John Phillips (q.v.) has been disputed by other scholars. Masson's *Life* (6 vols., 1859–80, with rev. edns. of the first 3 vols., and an Index, 1881–96) is indispensable for the fullness of its biographical evidence and of its account of the political and religious life of the times. Some recent more or less biographical books are: J. S. Diekhoff, *Milton on Himself* (1939), an annotated collection of personal passages from the works; J. M. French, *Milton in Chancery* (New York, 1939), a definitive account of the Miltons' financial affairs; W. R. Parker, *Milton's Contemporary Reputation* (Ohio State University, 1940), which contains an essay, a list of allusions, and facsimiles of five pamphlets written in answer to Milton.

Much eighteenth-century criticism is now of more interest to the student of that period than to the student of Milton, but Johnson's in his *Lives of the Poets* (1779) is, with all its prejudices, of the kind that can never be out of date. The best-known nineteenth-century criticism (Coleridge, Landor, Hazlitt, Macaulay, Emerson, Arnold, Bagehot) was published in occasional form, especially as essays. The two outstanding books of the century are Mark Pattison's (1879) and Sir W. Raleigh's (1900). In the twentieth century more or less conservative criticism is represented by J. W. Mackail (*Springs of Helicon*, 1909), John Bailey (*Milton*, Home University Library, 1915), Sir Herbert Grierson (*Cross Currents in English Literature of the XVIIth Century*, 1929; *Milton and Wordsworth*, 1937), and E. E. Stoll (*Poets and Playwrights*, University of Minnesota, 1930; *From Shakespeare to Joyce*, New York, 1944).

Modern scholars have been mainly interested in the analysis of Milton's personality and in placing him in his setting as thinker and artist. An important pioneer work was D. Saurat's *Milton: Man and Thinker* (1925; enlarged 1944). Much has been done towards a more judicious reinterpretation by J. H. Hanford, in many articles (such as those in *Studies in Shakespeare, Milton and Donne,* New York, 1925) and in *A Milton Handbook* (3rd ed., New York, 1939), the most compendious summary of modern scholarship and criticism.

A good deal of recent criticism has been stimulated by the 'metaphysical' anti-Miltonism of T. S. Eliot (*Selected Essays,* 1932, and *ESEA* xxi, 1936) and his followers, such as F. R. Leavis (*Revaluation,* 1936). Two sympathetic, penetrating, and solid books are E. M. W. Tillyard's *Milton* (1930) and *The Miltonic Setting* (1938). Distinctive if somewhat oracular criticism appears in books by Charles Williams (1932, 1933) and in his introduction to the World's Classics edition of Milton's English poems (1940). W. Empson's suggestive 'Milton and Bentley' is in his *Some Versions of Pastoral* (1935). Logan Pearsall Smith's *Milton and his Modern Critics* (1940) was a lively foray, though rather slight. Two expositions which approach *Paradise Lost* by way of the whole epic tradition, C. S. Lewis's *Preface to Paradise Lost* (1942) and the elaborate essay in C. M. Bowra's *From Virgil to Milton* (1945), contain much that is illuminating.

A few of the books on special aspects of Milton are: C. G. Osgood, *Classical Mythology of Milton's English Poems* (New York, 1900); Robert Bridges, *Milton's Prosody* (rev. ed., 1921); R. D. Havens, *The Influence of Milton on English Poetry* (Harvard, 1922); H. F. Fletcher's studies of Milton's Hebrew learning (*supra,* IV. 8); W. R. Parker, *Milton's Debt to Greek Tragedy in Samson Agonistes* (Johns Hopkins, 1937) ; G. McColley, *Paradise Lost* (Chicago, 1940), a study of sources and literary patterns; D. M. Wolfe, *Milton in the Puritan Revolution* (1941); *Milton and the Puritan Dilemma* (University of Toronto, 1942), a very discriminating study of Milton's growth as revealed in his prose works, by Arthur Barker, who is engaged on a history of Miltonic criticism; and Maurice Kelley's *This Great Argument* (Princeton, 1941), the nearest approach to a definitive account of Milton's theology, though A. Sewell's *Study in Milton's Christian Doctrine* (1939) retains interpretative value. Some smaller special studies are: Sir C. Firth, 'Milton as an Historian' (*Proceedings of the British Academy,* iii, 1907-8; *Essays Historical & Literary,* 1938); J. H. Finley, 'Milton and Horace: A Study of Milton's Sonnets' (*Harvard Studies in Classical*

Philology, xlviii, 1937); and A. S. P. Woodhouse's articles on Milton and Christian liberty, *Comus*, and the early poems (*University of Toronto Quarterly*, iv, 1935; xi, 1941; xiii, 1943). But for countless important articles the reader must be referred to the bibliographies in books and periodicals.

Some bibliographical articles are those of A. W. Pollard (*Library*, x, 1909), F. Madan (ibid. iv, 1923–4), W. R. Parker (ibid. xvi, 1935–6), J. H. Pershing (ibid. xxii, 1941–2), and H. Darbishire (*RES* xvii, 1941). Guides to eighteenth-century work on Milton are the apparatus in Todd's edition, with the list of 'detached pieces of criticism' at the end, and A. Oras, *Milton's Editors and Commentators . . . 1695–1801* (1931). For later writings there are D. H. Stevens, *Reference Guide to Milton from 1800 to the Present Day* (Chicago, 1930), and H. Fletcher's supplementary *Contributions* (University of Illinois, 1931), and the current bibliographies.

Among works of reference are concordances to the English poems by J. Bradshaw (1894) and to the Latin, Greek, and Italian poems by Lane Cooper (Halle, 1923), and a *Lexicon to the English Poetical Works* by L. Lockwood (New York, 1907).

HENRY MORE, 1614–87.

More's chief works are cited in the text. Grosart's *Complete Poems* (Chertsey Worthies' Library, 1878) has been partly superseded by G. Bullough's *Philosophical Poems* (1931), which contains large selections and a full critique. Two early collected editions of prose were *A Collection* (2nd ed., 1662; 4th ed., 1712) and *Theological Works* (1708). The prose works have not attracted modern editors, but the English translation (1690) of *Enchiridion Ethicum* has been reproduced by the Facsimile Text Society (1930), and F. I. MacKinnon has edited useful selections as *Philosophical Writings of Henry More* (New York, 1925). More's letters to Descartes are in *Œuvres de Descartes*, ed. C. Adam and P. Tannery, v (Paris, 1903), and are partly translated by L. D. Cohen in *Annals of Science*, i (1936). Richard Ward's vague *Life* (1710; ed. M. F. Howard, 1911) has had a concrete supplement in M. Nicolson's *Conway Letters* (Yale, 1930). Coleridge's comments are in his *Notes on English Divines* (1853), i. There are semi-popular sketches by E. A. George (*Seventeenth Century Men of Latitude*, 1908) and F. J. Powicke (*Cambridge Platonists*, 1926), and closer analyses in the books on Cambridge Platonism by G. P. H. Pawson (1930) and W. C. de Pauley (1937). The fullest studies are a section of J. Tulloch's *Rational Theology and Christian Philosophy* (1872), ii, and Paul R. Anderson's *Science in Defense of Liberal Religion* (New York, 1933). Some valuable and more or less special discussions are M. Nicolson's articles on More and Milton (*SP* xxii, 1925 and *PQ* vi, 1927) and her 'Early Stage·of Cartesianism in England' (*SP* xxvi, 1929); E. A. Burtt, *Metaphysical Foundations of Modern Physical Science* (1925); A. J. Snow, *Matter & Gravity in Newton's Physical Philosophy* (1926); and W. K. Jordan, *Development of Religious Toleration*, iv (1940). More's affinities with later thought are treated by Burtt and Snow; by J. T. Baker, *Historical and Critical Examination of English Space and Time Theories* (Sarah Lawrence College, 1930), and 'Henry More and Kant' (*Philosophical Review*, xlvi, 1937); and J. W. Beach, *The Concept of Nature in Nineteenth-Century English Poetry* (New York, 1936). There is a bibliography in MacKinnon.

FYNES MORYSON, 1566–1630.

Moryson's great work appeared in 1617 as *An Itinerary Written . . . First in the Latin Tongue, and then translated By him into English: Containing His Ten Yeeres Travell Through . . . Germany, Bohmerland, Sweitzerland, Netherland, Denmarke, Poland, Italy, Turky, France, England, Scotland, and Ireland.* This was reprinted by MacLehose in 4 vols. (1907–8). A small section was included in H. Morley's *Ireland under Elizabeth and James the First* (Carisbrooke Library, 1890). Moryson had only summarized a large portion which he omitted as not yet finished, and selections from this unprinted part of his manuscript were edited by C. Hughes, with a full account of the author, as *Shakespeare's Europe* (1903). In addition to Hughes, some discussions are in the books on travel, cited in V. 4, by E. S. Bates (1911), Clare Howard (1914), and B. Penrose (1942), and in S. C. Chew's *The Crescent and the Rose* (1937). R. B. Gottfried has shown Moryson's debt to Spenser's *View* (*PQ* xvii, 1938).

THOMAS MUN, 1571–1641.

Mun's *Discourse of Trade, From England unto the East-Indies* (1621), which Purchas used, was reprinted in J. R. McCulloch, *Select Collection of Early English Tracts on Commerce* (1856), and has been reproduced by the Facsimile Text Society (1930).

England's Treasure by Forraign Trade, written *c.* 1630 and printed in 1664, is in McCulloch and A. E. Monroe, *Early Economic Thought* (Harvard, 1924), and has been reprinted by itself (1895 ff. and 1928). Mun has a place in such books on economic history and mercantilism as are cited in V. 1. The fullest study is Roger Granchet, *L'Œuvre économique de Thomas Mun* (Angers, 1921).

ANTHONY MUNDAY or MUNDY, 1553?–1633.

The standard book is Celeste Turner's *Anthony Mundy, An Elizabethan Man of Letters* (University of California, 1928). In addition to H. Thomas (*supra*, IV. 7), two short studies are M. St. C. Byrne, 'Anthony Munday and his Books' (*Library*, i, 1920–1), and G. R. Hayes, 'Anthony Munday's Romances of Chivalry' (ibid. vi and vii, 1925–7). There is a *Concise Bibliography* (New York, 1942) by S. A. Tannenbaum.

PETER MUNDY, *c.* 1596–1667?

The *Travels of Peter Mundy in Europe and Asia, 1608–1667* were edited by Sir R. C. Temple and L. M. Anstey for the Hakluyt Society (5 vols., 1907–36).

GEFFRAY MYNSHUL, 1594?–1668.

Certaine Characters and Essayes of Prison and Prisoners (1618) had in the same year an edition with altered title and contents; the latter was reprinted at Edinburgh in 1821. Specimens are included in such anthologies as those of G. Murphy (1925) and H. Osborne (1933). Mynshul's work is discussed in the general studies of early essays and characters and especially by M. L. Hunt in her *Thomas Dekker* (Columbia, 1911) and her article on Mynshul and Dekker (*JEGP* xi, 1912).

SIR ROBERT NAUNTON, 1563–1635.

Fragmenta Regalia, or Observations on the late Q. Elizabeth, her times and favorites (1641) was reprinted from the 1653 ed. by Arber (1870) and is included in A. C. Ward's *Miscellany of Tracts and Pamphlets* (World's Classics, 1927).

MARCHAMONT NEDHAM or NEEDHAM, 1620–78.

A few of Needham's books were: *The Case of the Common-Wealth of England, Stated* (1650); *Of the Dominion, Or, Ownership of the Sea* (1652), a translation of Selden's *Mare Clausum*; *The Excellencie of a Free-State* (1656; repr. 1767); and the pamphlet, *A Discourse Concerning Schools And School-Masters* (1663), which is reprinted in *Complaint and Reform in England*, ed. W. H. Dunham and S. Pargellis (1938). His tortuous career is described by Firth in the *DNB*, with a bibliography. One phase is illuminated by J. M. French in 'Milton, Needham, and *Mercurius Politicus*', *SP* xxxiii (1936), and E. A. Beller in *HLQ* v (1941–2).

JOHN NORDEN, 1548–1625?

Of more than a dozen religious works the first and most popular was *A Pensive Mans Practise* (1584). *A Progresse of Pietie* (1591?) was reprinted by the Parker Society (1847). The poem *Vicissitudo rerum . . . The first Part* (1600) has been edited by D. C. Collins (Shakespeare Association Facsimiles, 1931) and studied in relation to its source by K. Koller (*SP* xxxv, 1938); the theme was pursued in *The Labyrinth Of Mans Life* (1614). The division between the religious writer and the surveyor, which is made in the *DNB*, is closed in A. W. Pollard's 'The Unity of John Norden' (*Library*, vii, 1926–7). His 'historicall and topographicall' descriptions of English counties have been published over a long stretch of time, from 1593 to 1938, when C. M. Hood edited *Norfolk*, with an account of Norden's work. *The Surveyors Dialogue* (1607) is reprinted in *Architectural Publication Society. Detached Essays* (1853). Norden has a place in the books on English topography cited in V. 4; in M. St. C. Byrne's *Elizabethan Life in Town and Country* (1925; rev. 1934); and in E. G. R. Taylor's *Late Tudor and Early Stuart Geography* (1934). H. B. Wheatley contributed 'Notes upon Norden and his Map of London, 1593' to the New Shakspere Society edition (1877) of William Harrison's *Description of England*. W. B. Gerish's *John Norden* (1903) contains a biographical sketch and bibliography.

SIR JOHN OGLANDER, 1585–1655.

Extracts from Oglander's commonplace book were edited by W. H. Long as *The Oglander Memoirs* (1888). A more authoritative volume of selections is F. Bamford's *A Royalist's Notebook* (1936).

FRANCIS OSBORN, 1593–1659.

Historical Memoires on the Reigns of Queen Elizabeth, and King James (1658) were reprinted in *Secret History of the Court of James the First*, ed. Scott (2 vols., 1811). *Advice to a Son* (1656; with 2nd part, 1658) was edited by Sir E. A. Parry (1896). According to Sir William Petty (Pepys's *Diary*, 27 January, 1664), the *Advice* was one of three works most esteemed for wit—the other two being *Religio Medici* and *Hudibras*. The collected *Works* reached their 11th and last edition in 1722 (2 vols.). The *Advice* is discussed in J. E. Mason's *Gentlefolk in the Making* (1935) and most fully analysed by S. A. E. Betz in *Seventeenth Century Studies, Second Series*, ed. R. Shafer (Princeton, 1937). Osborn's religious outlook is discussed by W. K. Jordan, *Development of Religious Toleration*, iv (1940).

DOROTHY OSBORNE, 1627–95.

Temple probably destroyed his letters to Dorothy but he and his descendants preserved hers. Extracts in T. P. Courtenay's *Memoirs of . . . Sir William Temple* (1836) aroused Macaulay's enthusiasm, which inspired Judge Parry to edit them (1888; rev. 1903; reprinted in Everyman and Wayfarer's Library). The letters were also edited by Gollancz (1903). The standard edition, with full apparatus, is by G. C. M. Smith (1928). The letters have 'a sequel' in J. G. Longe's *Martha Lady Giffard* (1911). Among essays on Dorothy are those of Maurice Hewlett (*Nineteenth Century*, xciii, 1923; *Last Essays*, 1924); L. L. Irvine, *Ten Letter-Writers* (1932); Virginia Woolf, *The Second Common Reader* (1932); and F. L. Lucas, *Studies French and English* (1934).

SIR THOMAS OVERBURY, 1581–1613.

The characters are given almost in full in the anthologies of H. Morley (1891) and R. Aldington (1924) and are represented in other anthologies. The standard edition is W. J. Paylor's *The Over-burian Characters* (Percy Reprints, 1936). The thirty-two characters now assigned to John Webster are included in F. L. Lucas's ed. of Webster (1927). The Overburian characters are discussed in studies of the genre cited in IV. 5. Bibliographical data are supplied by G. Murphy in her *Bibliography* (1925) and by Paylor in his edition and in the *Library*, xvii (1936–7). Overbury's *Observations* of the Netherlands (1626) are in Arber's *English*

Garner, iv (1882) and Firth's *Stuart Tracts* (1903) and, with other things, in the *Miscellaneous Works*, ed. E. F. Rimbault (1856).

The murder of Overbury and the ensuing trials have been described and analysed by many writers from John Chamberlain and James Howell onward. The proceedings are set forth in T. B. Howell's *State Trials*, ii (1816). Among modern accounts are those of James Spedding, in *Archaeologia*, xli (1867) and in *Studies in English History* (1881), by Spedding and J. Gairdner; S. R. Gardiner, *History of England from the Accession of James I*, vol. ii; A. W. Fox, *A Book of Bachelors* (1899); C. Whibley, *Essays in Biography* (1913); W. Roughead, *The Fatal Countess and Other Studies* (1924); and the more or less fictionized *King's Favourite* (1909) by Sir Philip Gibbs, and *The Overbury Mystery* (1925) by Sir E. A. Parry.

RICHARD OVERTON, *fl*. 1642–63.

For reprints of Overton's political tracts, and for accounts of them, the reader is referred to the books cited above under Lilburne. *Mans Mortallitie* (1643–4) is discussed by Masson and Saurat in their books on Milton and by G. Williamson, 'Milton and the Mortalist Heresy', *SP* xxxii (1935).

JOHN OWEN, 1564–1622.

Owen published *Epigrammatum libri tres* and a supplementary *Liber Singularis* in 1606–7, and two volumes, each containing three books, in 1612. There were many editions and some translations. Owen is discussed by E. Bensly in the *CHEL* iv; by F. A. Wright and T. A. Sinclair, *A History of Later Latin Literature* (1931); and by L. Bradner, *Musae Anglicanae* (1940). His influence in Germany is described by E. Urban, *Owenus und die deutschen Epigrammatiker des XVII. Jahrhunderts* (Berlin, 1900), and more briefly by G. Waterhouse, *Literary Relations of England and Germany in the Seventeenth Century* (1914).

HENRY OXINDEN (1608–70) et al.

Dorothy Gardiner has edited two attractive volumes, *The Oxinden Letters 1607–1642* (1933) and *The Oxinden and Peyton Letters 1642–1670* (1937).

HENRY PARKER, 1604–52.

One of the most important of Parker's score of pamphlets,

Observations upon some of his Majesties late Answers and Expresses (1642), is reproduced in W. Haller, *Tracts on Liberty* (1934). He is discussed by Haller in his *Tracts* and *Rise of Puritanism* (1938); by M. A. Judson, 'Henry Parker and the Theory of Parliamentary Sovereignty', *Essays in History and Political Theory in Honor of Charles Howard McIlwain*, ed. C. Wittke (Harvard, 1936); by J. W. Allen, *English Political Thought . . . 1603–1644* (1938); and with thorough completeness in *Men of Substance* (University of Chicago, 1942) by W. K. Jordan, who gives a bibliography.

MARTIN PARKER, *c.* 1600?–52.

The texts of Parker's ballads may be found in the collections cited in IV. 2, especially the many volumes edited by H. E. Rollins, who has written the only authoritative account of him in *MP* xvi and xix (1918–19 and 1921–2).

HENRY PARROT, *fl.* 1606–26.

Parrot and his five books of epigrams have been studied by M. C. Pitman in *MLR* xxix (1934) and by F. B. Williams in *PMLA* lii (1937) and *Harvard Studies and Notes in Philology and Literature*, xx (1938).

LADY KATHERINE PASTON, 1578/85–1629.

The *Correspondence of Lady Katherine Paston 1603–1627* has been edited by Ruth Hughey for the Norfolk Record Society, xiv (1941).

SIR GEORGE PAULE, 1563?–1637.

Paule's *Life* of Whitgift (1612) was reprinted in Christopher Wordsworth's *Ecclesiastical Biography*, iii (3rd ed., 1839), and is noticed in D. A. Stauffer, *English Biography before 1700* (1930).

HENRY PEACHAM, 1578?–1642?

The Compleat Gentleman (1622) was enlarged in 1627 and 1634 and—not by Peacham—in 1661. The 1634 text has been edited by G. S. Gordon (Tudor and Stuart Library, 1906). Other works which have been reprinted are: *Coach and Sedan* (1636; Haslewood Books, 1925); *The Truth of Our Times* (1638; ed. R. R. Cawley, Facsimile Text Society, 1942); *The Worth Of A Peny* (1641?), in Arber's *English Garner*, vi (1883) and Lang's *Social*

England Illustrated (1903); and *The Art of Living in London* (1642; *Harleian Miscellany*, ed. Park, supplemental vol. i, 1812). There are introductory essays by Gordon and Cawley and an essay in A. W. Fox's *Book of Bachelors* (1899). M. C. Pitman has a condensed and corrective survey of Peacham's life and work in the *Bulletin of Historical Research*, xi (1934). He has a place in such studies of courtesy books as J. E. Mason's *Gentlefolk in the Making* (1935). His debt to Elyot is shown by D. T. Starnes (*MLR* xxii, 1927). In addition to the known volume of epigrams, *Thalias Banquet* (1620), Peacham's title to *The More the Merrier* (1608) has been established by Miss Pitman (*MLR* xxix, 1934).

HENRY PERCY, EARL OF NORTHUMBERLAND, 1564–1632.

The latter part of *Advice to his Son* was printed, in expurgated form, in *Archaeologia*, xxvii (1838). The whole tract was edited by G. B. Harrison in 1930.

WILLIAM PERKINS, 1558–1602.

The enormous influence of Perkins's treatises may be partly judged from the list of editions in the *STC*. The first folio edition of the collected works appeared in 1600. Fuller's sketch is a famous part of *The Holy State* (1642). There is a good general account by L. B. Wright in *HLQ* iii (1939–40). The influence of Perkins's book on preaching is shown in W. F. Mitchell, *English Pulpit Oratory* (1932). This and other sides of his work are treated in W. Haller's *Rise of Puritanism* (1938). His teaching on vocations, domestic duties, and casuistry is discussed in W. E. Houghton's study of Fuller (*supra*). The influence of Perkins's Calvinistic theology and the reaction against it are analysed by Perry Miller in *Publications of The Colonial Society of Massachusetts*, xxxii (1937) and his *New England Mind* (1939). The influence of his ideas on the damnable art of witchcraft is shown by G. L. Kittredge, *Witchcraft in Old and New England* (1929).

THOMAS PESTELL, 1585–1667.

Though some pieces have been included in modern anthologies (e.g. H. J. Massingham, 1919), much of Pestell's verse existed only in manuscript until it was edited with full apparatus by Hannah Buchan (1940).

SIR WILLIAM PETTY, 1623–87.

Petty's pioneer work in political economy lies beyond our

limits. *The Advice of W. P. to Mr. Samuel Hartlib. For The Advancement of some particular Parts of Learning* (1648) is reprinted in the *Harleian Miscellany*, ed. Park, vi (1810), and discussed by R. F. Jones, *Ancients and Moderns* (1936), and some other writers on education cited above in V. 6.

KATHERINE PHILIPS, 1632–64.

Mrs. Philips's most famous work was *Pompey* (Dublin and London, 1663), her translation from Corneille. Her unauthorized *Poems* (1664) were enlarged in 1667 with more poems and the tragedies *Pompey* and *Horace*; there were further editions in 1669, 1678, and 1710. Her *Letters from Orinda to Poliarchus* (1705; enlarged 1729) give a valuable picture of the author and her world. *Selected Poems* were published in 1904 by J. R. Tutin, with a preface by L. I. Guiney. Saintsbury reprinted the poems from the 1678 text in *Minor Poets of the Caroline Period*, i (1905). Gosse's unreliable essay in *Seventeenth-Century Studies* (1883) was superseded by Philip W. Souers's full and thorough volume, *The Matchless Orinda* (Harvard, 1931).

JOHN PHILLIPS, 1631–1706.

Apart from the very popular *Satyr Against Hypocrites* (1655), most of Phillips's writings came after 1660. In her *Early Lives of Milton* (1932) Helen Darbishire attributes the anonymous biography to Phillips, but the case for Phillips is opposed, in *PMLA* l (1935), by E. S. Parsons, who first edited the life in the *English Historical Review*, xvii (1902). The problem is further discussed by A. R. Benham and Parsons in *ELH* vi (1939) and ix (1942).

JOSHUA POOLE, *c.* 1615–ante 1657.

Poole's *English Parnassus: or, A Helpe to English Poesie* (1657), one of the books Charles Hoole recommended for schools, is discussed by Foster Watson in his *Beginnings of the Teaching of Modern Subjects* (1909) and by G. Williamson in *MP* xxxiii (1935–6). Poole's quotations from Milton are collected by A. Farrell (*MLN* lviii, 1943).

THOMAS POWELL, 1572?–1635?

Tom of All Trades. Or The Plaine Path-way to Preferment (1631) was reprinted, with an account of Powell, by F. J. Furnivall

(New Shakspere Society, Series 6, 1876), and is included in *Complaint and Reform in England*, ed. W. H. Dunham and S. Pargellis (1938). *Tom* and another social piece are in the *Somers Tracts*, ed. Scott, vii (1812).

JOHN PRESTON, 1587–1628.

Preston's sermons were mostly issued after his death by Thomas Goodwin, Richard Sibbes, John Davenport, and other friends. Some of the popular collections were *The New Covenant* (1629), *The Breast-Plate Of Faith And Love* (1630), and *Life Eternall* (1631). Preston's writings and influence are discussed by W. Haller, *The Rise of Puritanism* (1938), and Perry Miller, *The New England Mind* (1939).

WILLIAM PRYNNE, 1600?–69.

Of Prynne's nearly 200 pamphlets and books probably the best known is *Histrio-mastix*, which was dated 1633 but published at the end of 1632. It is discussed in E. N. S. Thompson's *Controversy between the Puritans and the Stage* (New York, 1903), in an essay by T. R. Lounsbury in the *Yale Review*, N.S., xii (1923), and in the general books on the Caroline stage. A few of Prynne's many ecclesiastical and political pieces are reprinted in the *Somers Tracts*, ed. Scott, iv–vi (1810–11); *Vox Populi* (1642) is in the *Harleian Miscellany*, ed. Park, vii (1811). The prominent Presbyterian martyr and pamphleteer was of less permanent importance than the Keeper of the Records under Charles II; his services in that capacity, A. F. Pollard has said, 'have never been surpassed'. S. R. Gardiner edited *Documents relating to the Proceedings against William Prynne in 1634 and 1637* (Camden Society, 1877). The article in the *DNB* is by Firth. The one full account, with a bibliography, is Ethyn W. Kirby's *William Prynne* (Harvard, 1931). The controversialist gets more or less attention in the general histories and in such special works as J. W. Allen, *English Political Thought . . . 1603–1644* (1938); W. Haller, *Tracts on Liberty* (1934) and *The Rise of Puritanism* (1938); and W. K. Jordan, *Development of Religious Toleration*, iv (1940).

SAMUEL PURCHAS, 1577–1626.

Purchas's first two works were: *Purchas his Pilgrimage. Or*

Relations Of The World And The Religions Observed In All Ages And places discovered, from the Creation unto this Present (1613; enlarged 1614 ff.); and the jeremiad *Purchas his Pilgrim. Microcosmus, or The Historie Of Man* (1619). The third one was the great collection of voyages, *Hakluytus Posthumus or Purchas His Pilgrimes* (4 vols., 1625), which has been reprinted by MacLehose in 20 vols. (1905-7). Two volumes of selections are H. G. Rawlinson's *Narratives from Purchas His Pilgrimes* (1931) and Cyril Wild's *Purchas His Pilgrimes in Japan* (1939). There are good accounts of Purchas by Sir W. Foster, *Geographical Journal*, lxviii (1926); G. B. Parks, *Richard Hakluyt and the English Voyages* (New York, 1928); E. G. R. Taylor, *Late Tudor and Early Stuart Geography* (1934); and, from a special angle, in L. B. Wright's *Religion and Empire* (1943).

FRANCIS QUARLES, 1592–1644.

The only collected edition is by Grosart (Chertsey Worthies' Library, 3 vols., 1880–1). Quarles is discussed by P. H. Osmond (*supra*, III. 3) and in studies of emblems by Thompson and Praz (*supra*, III. 3), by A. Warren, *Richard Crashaw* (v. Crashaw), and by R. Freeman (*RES* xvii, 1941). The latest and fullest study of Quarles's emblem imagery is by E. James (University of Texas *Studies in English*, 1943). One side of Quarles is shown in W. K. Jordan, *Development of Religious Toleration*, ii (1936). Quarles's play, his debt to Bacon and Machiavelli, and his royalist tracts are discussed by G. S. Haight in *RES* xii (1936). Haight contributed biographical data to the *TLS*, 11 April and 17 October, 1935. The curve of Quarles's fame was traced by A. H. Nethercot (*MP* xx, 1922–3). Bibliographical articles by W. L. Ustick, on the *Enchyridion*, and Haight, on the *Emblemes*, appeared in the *Library*, ix (1928–9) and xv and xvi (1934–6).

SIR WALTER RALEGH, 1552?–1618.

Two early pieces of prose were the *Report* (1591), on the exploit of the *Revenge*, and *The Discoverie of . . . Guiana* (1596). The *History of the World* had three issues in 1614 and a number of later editions. Among posthumous publications were: *The Prerogative of Parlaments in England* (1628); *Instructions to his Sonne* (1632); *The Prince, or Maxims of State* (1642); *Judicious And Select Essayes And Observations* (1650); *Sir Walter Raleigh's Sceptick, or Speculations* (1651; in 1657 and later edns. called *Remains*);

The Cabinet-Council, ed. Milton (1658). Miscellaneous works were edited by T. Birch (2 vols., 1751). The one complete edition, with biographies by Oldys and Birch, was published in 8 vols. in 1829.

Poems by Ralegh, or attributed to him, appeared in *The Phœnix Nest* (1593), *A Poetical Rapsody* (1602 ff.), and elsewhere, but they were not collected. The standard edition, superseding earlier editions by Sir E. Brydges (1813) and J. Hannah (1845, &c.), is by A. M. C. Latham (1929).

Selections from the verse and prose (including letters) have been edited by W. R. Macklin (King's Treasuries, 1926) and F. W. C. Hersey (Boston, 1909 ff.). G. E. Hadow edited a larger selection of prose (1917). The account of the *Revenge* is in the volumes of selections and in Hakluyt and has been edited by Arber (1871) and others. The standard edition of the *Discoverie of Guiana* is by V. T. Harlow (1928). *Instructions to his Sonne* is abridged in Macklin and has been edited by C. Whibley (1927).

Famous early biographical portraits were in Naunton's *Fragmenta Regalia* (1641), Fuller's *Worthies* (1662), and Aubrey. Of the countless modern biographies the most solid and useful to the student are still those of E. Edwards (2 vols., 1868) and W. Stebbing (1891, 1899); the latest is by Edward Thompson (1935). An important special book is V. T. Harlow's *Ralegh's Last Voyage* (1932).

Apart from editorial introductions and brief comment in biographies there is not much general criticism of Ralegh. One item is Thoreau's *Sir Walter Raleigh*, ed. H. A. Metcalf (Boston, 1905). Tucker Brooke has a picture of the poet and philosopher in *ELH* v (1938). Ralegh's poetry and literary relationships are treated by M. C. Bradbrook, *The School of Night* (1936), and Eleanor G. Clark, *Ralegh and Marlowe* (Fordham University, 1941), the poetry by E. C. Dunn, *Literature of Shakespeare's England* (New York, 1936). The latest discussion of the 'last' poem is by V. B. Heltzel (*HLB*, 1936), of *Cynthia* by A. M. Buchan (*MLQ* i, 1940). The authenticity of the farewell letter to Lady Ralegh in 1603 is upheld by A. M. C. Latham in *ESEA* xxv (1940).

The best general account of the *History* is by Sir C. Firth (*Proceedings of the British Academy*, viii, 1917–18; *Essays Historical & Literary*, 1938). Two important articles by E. Strathmann (*HLQ* iii, 1939–40 and *MLQ* i, 1940), based on the *History*, deal with Ralegh's religious and philosophic outlook. The chief analysis of his political thought is N. Kempner, *Raleghs staats-theoretische Schriften: die Einführung des Machiavellismus in England* (Leipzig, 1928). The fullest *Bibliography* of works and biographies is by T. N. Brushfield (2nd rev. ed., 1908), who contributed much miscellaneous 'Raleghana' to *Transactions of the Devonshire Association*, vols. xxviii–xlii (1896–1910).

THOMAS RANDOLPH, 1605–35.

The bulk of Randolph's non-dramatic verse was first collected in *Poems With The Muses Looking-Glasse: And Amyntas* (1638; enlarged, 1640 ff.). W. C. Hazlitt's poor edition of the works (2 vols., 1875) was partly superseded by J. J. Parry's *Poems and Amyntas* (Yale, 1917) and G. Thorn-Drury's *Poems* (1929). Two attributed plays have had recent editions, *The Drinking Academy*, ed. S. A. Tannenbaum and H. E. Rollins (Harvard, 1930), and *The Fary Knight or Oberon the Second*, ed. F. T. Bowers (University of North Carolina, 1942). There are essays by C. Falls (*London Mercury*, xiii, 1926), G. C. M. Smith (*Proceedings of the British Academy*, xiii, 1927), and E. Blunden (*Votive Tablets*, 1931), and a monograph by K. Kottas (*Wiener Beiträge*, xxix, 1909).

BARNABE RICH, 1542?–1617.

Rich's large output falls into five divisions, in the words of E. M. Hinton (*infra*), 'military tracts, romances, "books of information", social satire, and Irish chronicles'. These run from 1574 to 1617. *Riche his Farewell to Militarie profession* (1581) was reprinted by the Shakespeare Society (1846), and one story, 'Apolonius and Silla', by M. Luce (Shakespeare Library, 1912). *The Honestie of this Age* (1614) was reprinted by the Percy Society, xi (1844), with a bibliography. D. T. Starnes has a study of Rich the story-teller in *SP* xxx (1933). Two Irish pieces are edited by C. L. Falkiner (*Royal Irish Academy*, xxvi, 1906) and E. M. Hinton (*PMLA* lv, 1940), who gives an account of Rich. S. Ghall has three articles on Rich and Ireland in the *Dublin Magazine*, N.S., i–ii (1926–7). The military tracts are studied by H. J. Webb in *JEGP* xlii (1943).

HENRY ROBINSON, 1605–73?

Englands Safety, in Trades Encrease (1641) and *Certain Proposalls* (1652) are reprinted in W. A. Shaw, *Select Tracts and Documents*

Illustrative of English Monetary History 1626–1730 (1896). *Liberty of Conscience* (1644) is reproduced in W. Haller, *Tracts on Liberty* (1934). Robinson is discussed by Haller, by W. K. Jordan in his *Development of Religious Toleration*, iv (1940), and most fully in Jordan's *Men of Substance* (University of Chicago, 1942).

SIR THOMAS ROE, 1580–1644.

The standard book, Sir William Foster's *Embassy of Sir Thomas Roe to the Court of the Great Mogul, 1615–1619* (Hakluyt Society, 2 vols., 1899) was revised as *The Embassy of Sir Thomas Roe to India* (1926). Roe's parliamentary speech on the decay of trade, published in 1641, is in the *Harleian Miscellany*, ed. Park, iv (1809), and *Complaint and Reform in England*, ed. W. H. Dunham and S. Pargellis (1938). There is a sketch of Roe by D. Hannay in *Blackwood's*, ccxxi (1927). He comes into the studies of things eastern by Sir W. Foster, W. G. Rice, and S. C. Chew, which are cited above in V. 4.

ALEXANDER ROSS, 1591–1654.

Among Ross's scientific and controversial works were: *Commentum de Terræ Motu Circulari* (1634), which led to debate with John Wilkins in *The New Planet no Planet* (1646); *The Philosophicall Touch-Stone* (1645), against Digby; *Medicus Medicatus* (1645), against *Religio Medici* and Digby's *Observations*; *Arcana Microcosmi* (1651; enlarged, 1652), against Browne's *Vulgar Errors*, Bacon, and Harvey's *De Generatione*; and *Leviathan drawn out with a Hook* (1653), against an obvious monster. Some other works were *Virgilius Evangelisans, sive Historia Jesu Christi* (1634), a poem in Virgilian language on the life of Christ; *Mel Heliconium* (1642) and *Mystagogus Poeticus* (1647), handbooks of allegorized mythology; and *ΠΑΝΣΕΒΕΙΑ: Or, A View of all Religions in the World* (1653). F. Watson had an account of Ross in the *Gentleman's Magazine*, cclxxix (1895). G. McColley's articles on Ross and Wilkins are cited below under the latter.

SAMUEL ROWLANDS, 1570?–1628/30?

The *Complete Works . . . 1598–1628* were first collected by the Hunterian Club (1880), with an essay by Gosse. Some pieces have been reprinted separately, such as the 'Knave' tracts (Percy Society, ix, 1844); and the *Works* do not include *The Bride* (1617; ed. A. C. Potter, Boston, 1905). The only full study is by J. R. Bowman (Harvard *Summmaries of Theses 1933*). Some short discussions, in addition to Gosse's essay (repr. in his *Seventeenth-Century Studies*, 1883), are in R. M. Alden, *The Rise of Formal Satire in England* (Philadelphia, 1899); *CHEL* iv, by H. V. Routh; the books on the literature of roguery by F. W. Chandler (1907) and F. Aydelotte (1913), and A. V. Judges, *The Elizabethan Underworld* (1930); T. K. Whipple, *Martial and the English Epigram* (1925); and L. B. Wright, *Middle-Class Culture* (1935).

LUCY HARINGTON RUSSELL, COUNTESS OF BEDFORD, 1581–1627.

Though the Countess's own writings are few and uncertain, so notable a patroness cannot be overlooked. There is more or less about her in Grierson's edition of Donne (1912), in the edition of Jonson by Herford and Simpson, in F. A. Yates's *John Florio* (1934), and in the *TLS*, 8 October, 1938, where P. Simpson corrects the *DNB* and cites the important though neglected source, Lord Braybrooke's private edition of *The Private Correspondence of Jane Lady Cornwallis; 1613–1644* (1842), which contains letters by the Countess. B. H. Newdigate sought, not very plausibly, to connect her with 'The Phoenix and the Turtle' (*TLS*, 24 October, 1936; and ibid. 28 November, 1936, 13 and 20 February, 1937; and H. E. Rollins, *Shakespeare: The Poems*, 1938).

JOHN SALTMARSH, *c.* 1610–47.

Sparkles of Glory (1647) was reprinted in 1811 and 1847. Extracts from *The Smoke in the Temple* (1646) and a letter to the Council of War (1647) are given in A. S. P. Woodhouse, *Puritanism and Liberty* (1938); extracts from *Reasons For Unitie, Peace, and Love* (1646) in D. M. Wolfe, *Milton in the Puritan Revolution* (1941). Saltmarsh is discussed by Woodhouse and Wolfe, by Rufus M. Jones in *Studies in Mystical Religion* (1909) and *Mysticism and Democracy in the English Commomwealth* (Harvard, 1932), and by W. K. Jordan in *HLQ* iii (1939–40).

ROBERT SANDERSON, 1587–1663.

Sanderson's most popular work was *Logicæ Artis Compendium* (1615). *Ten Sermons* (1627) had by 1689 become *XXXVI. Sermons*. The works of casuistry to which he owed his special fame appeared in his later years and posthumously. The standard edition of the *Works* is by W. Jacobson (6 vols., 1854). C. Wordsworth edited, in translation, *Bishop Sanderson's Lectures on Conscience and Human Law* (1877). For most people Sanderson lives wholly in Izaak Walton, whose work appeared as *The Life of Dr. Sanderson . . . To which is added, Some short Tracts or Cases of Conscience, written by the said Bishop* (1678). George Lewis's *Robert Sanderson* (1924) is in the S.P.C.K. series. The sermons are discussed in W. F. Mitchell, *English Pulpit Oratory* (1932).

SIR EDWIN SANDYS, 1561–1629.

A Relation Of The State Of Religion . . . in . . . these westerne parts of the world had three unauthorized editions in 1605, from 'a spurious stolne Copie; in part epitomized, in part amplified', according to the preface of the 1629 edition, called *Europæ Speculum*. Sandys's version of selected Psalms appeared in 1615. His concern with the publication of Hooker is discussed by Hardin Craig (*JHI* v, 1944). Sandys's activities on behalf of Virginia are described in C. M. Gayley, *Shakespeare and the Founders of Liberty in America* (New York, 1917), and other books on colonial beginnings. There is a monograph by W. M. Wallace, *Sir Edwin Sandys and the First Parliament of James I* (University of Pennsylvania, 1940).

GEORGE SANDYS, 1578–1644.

Sandys's chief writings were: *A Relation of a Journey begun An: Dom: 1610* (1615); *Ovid's Metamorphosis* (1626), enlarged in 1632 with an allegorical commentary and a version of *Aeneid* i; *A Paraphrase upon the Psalmes of David* (1636); *A Paraphrase upon the Divine Poems* (1638); and the drama *Christs Passion* (1640), translated from Grotius. The last three works were edited by R. Hooper (2 vols., 1872). Extracts from the *Relation* are in Purchas and J. Harris. There is a full sketch of Sandys the traveller in B. Penrose, *Urbane Travellers* (1942); there are more special discussions in the studies by W. G. Rice and S. C. Chew cited in V. 4, and by E. S. De Beer (*Library*, xvii, 1936–7) and R. H. Barker (*Transactions of the Wisconsin Academy of Sciences, Art and Letters*, xxx, 1937). The story of the composition and publication of the *Ovid* is traced by R. B. Davis in *Papers of the Bibliographical Society of America*, xxxv (1941). There is a thesis on the translation of Grotius by G. H. Grüninger (Tauberbischofsheim, 1927). Sandys's versification is analysed by R. C. Wallerstein

AUTHORS: G. SANDYS—SHAKESPEARE 587

(*PMLA* l, 1935), his influence on diction by G. Tillotson, *On the Poetry of Pope* (1938).

SIR HENRY SAVILE, 1549–1622.

Savile translated parts of Tacitus (1591; 6th ed., 1640) and edited *Rerum Anglicarum Scriptores post Bedam* (1596), Xenophon's *Cyropaedia* (1613) and, his great achievement, the works of Chrysostom (8 vols., 1610–13).

JOHN SELDEN, 1584–1654.

Without disturbing the dust on *Joannis Seldeni Jurisconsulti Opera Omnia*, ed. D. Wilkins (3 vols., 1726), one may mention such particular works as *De Dis Syris* (1617), *The Historie of Tithes* (1618), *Marmora Arundelliana* (1628), and *Mare Clausum* (1635). The standard text of Selden's annotations on *Poly-Olbion* is in Hebel's edition of Drayton. Among editions of *Table-Talk*, first printed in 1689, are those by Arber (1868), S. H. Reynolds (1892), and Sir F. Pollock (1927). Among general accounts are Sir E. Fry's full article in the *DNB* and essays in Herbert Paul's *Men and Letters* (1901) and the *TLS*, 22 October, 1925. Selden's legal work is analysed by H. D. Hazeltine in *Festschrift Heinrich Brunner* (Weimar, 1910) and the *Harvard Law Review*, xxiv (1910–11), by D. Ogg in his edition of *Ioannis Seldeni Ad Fletam Dissertatio* (1925), and by H. Arneke, *Kirchengeschichte und Rechtsgeschichte* (1937). His position on Church and State is discussed in the general histories, such as Gardiner, in G. P. Gooch's books on political thought, and in the books on toleration by M. Freund (1927) and W. K. Jordan (ii, 1936). J. Sparrow has listed 'The Earlier Owners of Books in John Selden's Library' in the *Bodleian Quarterly Record*, vi (1931).

EDWARD SEXBY, d. 1658.

Killing No Murder, printed in Holland in 1657 as by 'William Allen', is reprinted in the *Harleian Miscellany*, ed. Park, iv (1809), in H. Morley's *Famous Pamphlets* (1886), and in A. C. Ward's *Miscellany of Tracts and Pamphlets* (World's Classics, 1927). In the *English Historical Review*, xvii (1902) Firth modified his *DNB* article and defined the probable extent of Silius Titus's collaboration. Sexby is noticed in some studies of the Levellers.

WILLIAM SHAKESPEARE, 1564–1616.

The *Sonnets*, though published in 1609, belong with the earlier sequences and to the preceding volume of the *Oxford History*. Some references for 'The Phoenix and the Turtle' are given above under Robert Chester.

THOMAS SHELTON, *fl.* 1612.

The first part of *The History of . . . Don-Quixote* appeared in 1612, the second part, with a second edition of the first (revised, but perhaps not by Shelton), in 1620. The complete work was reprinted in 1652 and 1675. Some modern editions have been edited by J. Fitzmaurice-Kelly (Tudor Translations, 4 vols., 1896), A. W. Pollard (Macmillan's Library of English Classics, 3 vols., 1900), and F. J. H. Darton (Navarre Society, 2 vols., 1923). Editions are listed in the *BMC* and in J. D. M. Ford and R. Lansing, *Cervantes: A Tentative Bibliography* (Harvard, 1931). A detailed and corrective account of the English reception of Cervantes is Edwin B. Knowles's *Four Articles on Don Quixote in England* (New York University, 1941); three of the articles appeared in *PQ* xx (1941), *Hispanic Review*, ix (1941), and *Hispania*, xxiii (1940). Knowles has a textual study in *Papers of the Bibliographical Society of America*, xxxvii (1943).

SAMUEL SHEPPARD, 1624?–55?

The article on Sheppard in the *DNB* is quite unreliable. A full and authoritative account, with copious excerpts, especially from his roll-calls of English poets, and with valuable information about journalism and other matters, is given by H. E. Rollins in *SP* xxiv (1927).

SIR EDWARD SHERBURNE, 1618–1702.

Sherburne, a relative and friend of Thomas Stanley, is neglected in the text because he was wholly a translator and, in that age of great translation, rather respectable than distinguished. His chief works were versions of Seneca's *Medea* (1648) and *Troades* (1679) and *Tragedies of L. Annæus Seneca* (1701), containing those two and others; a volume issued in 1651 under two titles, *Salmacis, Lyrian & Sylvia*, &c., and *Poems And Translations. Amorous, Lusory, Morall, Divine;* and *The Sphere of Marcus Manilius* (1675). The volume of 1651 was reprinted in Chalmers's *English Poets* (1810), vi, and as *Miscellaneous Poems* (1819). The sources are set forth by M. Praz in *MLR* xx (1925).

SIR ANTHONY SHERLEY (1565–*post* 1636), SIR ROBERT SHERLEY (1578/81?–1628), and SIR THOMAS SHERLEY (1564?–1633?).

Of the abundant material produced by and about the renowned trio, only a few items can be mentioned. *Sir Antony Sherley His Relation of his Travels into Persia* (1613) was abridged in Purchas. W. Parry's *Travels of sir Anthony Sherley . . . to the Persian Empire* (1601), also abridged in Purchas, is reprinted in Collier's *Illustrations of Early English Popular Literature*, ii (1864), and, with other documents and with a full introduction and bibliography, in *Sir Anthony Sherley and his Persian Adventure*, ed. Sir Denison Ross (Broadway Travellers, 1933). *Sir Robert Sherley . . . His Royall entertainement into Cracovia* (1609) is reprinted in the *Harleian Miscellany*, ed. Park, v (1810), and in Bullen's ed. of Thomas Middleton (1885–6), viii. Sir Thomas's *Discours of the Turkes*, written in 1606–7, is edited from the manuscript by Ross in the *Camden Miscellany* xvi (1936). Extracts from various narratives were given in the anonymous *The Three Brothers* (1825). Anthony Nixon's *The Three English Brothers* (1607) is discussed by Ross and by L. Ennis in his article on Nixon (*HLQ* iii, 1939–40). E. P. Shirley's *The Sherley Brothers* (Roxburghe Club, 1848) was a scholarly work which remains valuable. The most recent account is B. Penrose's *The Sherleian Odyssey* (1938). The brothers' activities are well summarized in S. C. Chew, *The Crescent and the Rose* (1937). A special study of Sir Anthony is F. Babinger's *Sherleiana* (Berlin, 1932).

JOHN SHERMAN, *c.* 1609/10–61.

Sherman is sometimes associated with the Cambridge Platonists on the strength of *A Greek in the Temple; Some Common-places delivered in Trinity Colledge Chapell in Cambridge, upon Acts xvii, part of the 28. verse* (1641). He is noticed in Mullinger's *University of Cambridge*, iii (1911) and in the same writer's chapter in the *CHEL* viii.

JAMES SHIRLEY, 1596–1666.

Shirley's *Poems &c.* (1646) were reprinted in the *Dramatic Works*, ed. Gifford and Dyce (1833), vi. The standard edition is *The Poems of James Shirley* (New York, 1941), edited by R. L. Armstrong, who gathers up the biographical and critical material of modern scholarship.

RICHARD SIBBES, 1577–1635.

Sibbes's influence was felt by many men, notably Baxter, John Cotton, and Hugh Peters. Among his many volumes (most of them posthumously edited by Thomas Goodwin and other friends) were *The Bruised Reede, and Smoaking Flax* (1630) and *Beames of Divine Light* (1639), both collections of sermons. His collected works were printed in 1809 and 1812 and were edited by Grosart (7 vols., 1862–4). Sibbes is discussed in W. Haller's *Rise of Puritanism* (1938) and W. F. Mitchell's *English Pulpit Oratory* (1932).

JAMES SMITH, 1605–67. *See* SIR JOHN MENNES.

CAPTAIN JOHN SMITH, 1579/80–1631.

Some of Smith's chief publications are cited in the text. The standard collected edition is *Travels and Works of Captain John Smith*, ed. A. G. Bradley, with a bibliography by T. Seccombe (2 vols., 1910), a revision of Arber's edition (1884; 2 vols., 1895). Of the many reprints of one or more works, one is *The True Travels, Adventures, & Observations*, ed. John Gould Fletcher and L. C. Wroth (New York, 1930). Smith has his place in numerous books on the colonization of America, such as those mentioned above in V. 4. The best biography is by J. G. Fletcher (New York, 1928). The *Dictionary of American Biography* (1935) contains a short account. J. M. Morse has a review of the attacks on Smith's veracity in the *Journal of Southern History*, i (1935). W. Eames compiled a *Bibliography* (New York, 1927).

JOHN SMITH, 1616?–52.

The *Select Discourses*, with Simon Patrick's funeral sermon, were edited by John Worthington (1660). The 2nd and 3rd editions appeared in 1673 and 1821; the 4th, edited by H. G. Williams, in 1859. Lord Hailes had published an incomplete edition (1756), and John Wesley had put extracts into his *Christian Library*. W. M. Metcalfe edited selections as *The Natural Truth of Christianity* (1882; enlarged as *The Cambridge Platonists*, 1885). The most accessible selections are in E. T. Campagnac, *The Cambridge Platonists* (1901). There are remarks in Coleridge's *Literary Remains*, iii (1838), and in Arnold's 'A Psychological Parallel' (*Last Essays on Church and Religion*, 1877). Smith is discussed in J. Tulloch, *Rational Theology and Christian Philosophy*

(1872); Rufus M. Jones, *Spiritual Reformers in the 16th & 17th Centuries* (1914); in the books on Cambridge Platonism by Powicke, Pawson, De Boer, and De Pauley, cited in V. 2; in W. F. Mitchell, *English Pulpit Oratory* (1932); B. Willey, *Seventeenth Century Background* (1934); and by E. I. Watkin, *The Catholic World*, cxlv (1937). A full bibliography of Smith's book is given in R. C. Christie's *Bibliography of . . . John Worthington* (Chetham Society, N.S., xiii, 1888).

MICHAEL SPARKE, d. 1653.

The earliest extant edition of Sparke's very popular *Crums of Comfort* (1623?) is the 7th (1628). The chief account of the Puritan publisher and author is by H. R. Plomer, *The Bibliographer*, i (New York, 1902).

JOHN SPEED, 1552?–1629.

The topographical and antiquarian *Theatre Of The Empire Of Great Britaine* (1611) was continued in the large *History Of Great Britaine* (1611), which came from the beginning to the reign of James. A very popular lesser work was an account of scriptural genealogies. Speed is discussed by C. Whibley in the *CHEL* iii and by L. B. Wright, *Middle-Class Culture* (1935).

SIR HENRY SPELMAN, 1561?–1641.

Some of Spelman's works were: *De non temerandis Ecclesiis* (1613); *Archæologus. In modum Glossarii* (2 vols., 1626–64); *Concilia, Decreta, Leges, Constitutiones, In Re Ecclesiarum Orbis Britannici* (2 vols., 1639–64); *Reliquiæ Spelmannianæ*, ed. E. Gibson (1698); *The English Works . . . Together with his Posthumous Works, Relating to the Laws and Antiquities of England* (1723). There is an account of Spelman and his work by F. M. Powicke in *Proceedings of the British Academy*, xvi (1930). The movement in which Spelman played a part is described in H. Arneke, *Kirchengeschichte und Rechtsgeschichte in England* (1937), and David C. Douglas, *English Scholars* (1939).

THOMAS STANLEY, 1625–78.

Stanley's poems and translations appeared in volumes of various titles and dates from 1647 to 1652. His lyrics were set by John Gamble in *Ayres and Dialogues* (1656). The *Poems* of 1651 was reprinted by Brydges (1814–15), the *Anacreon* by Bullen

(1893, 1906). *Kisses*, the version of Secundus, was included in the Bohn translation of Propertius and reprinted by the Nonesuch Press in 1923. The ostensibly original verse and some of the shorter translations are reprinted in L. I. Guiney's *Thomas Stanley* (1907) and Saintsbury's *Minor Poets of the Caroline Period*, iii (1921), but both texts must be read in the light of M. Praz's 'Stanley, Sherburne and Ayres as Translators and Imitators of Italian, Spanish and French Poets', *MLR* xx (1925). Stanley is discussed also by H. Thomas, 'Three Translators of Góngora', *Revue Hispanique*, xlviii (1920). The translation from Pico, *A Platonick Discourse Upon Love* (in *Poems*, 1651), has been edited by E. G. Gardner (Boston, 1914). Stanley's once famous *History of Philosophy* (1655–62) was an enlargement of Diogenes Laertius, with excerpts from the philosophers. His edition of Aeschylus (1663) seems to have been illuminated by 'borrow'd rays'. G. E. Bentley has reprinted poems by Shirley, Sherburne, and other friends on Stanley's wedding (*HLQ* ii, 1938–9).

GEORGE STARKEY, d. 1665?

Starkey, a physician of dubious quality and a born rebel, wrote medical and royalist pamphlets. *Natures Explication and Helmont's Vindication* (1657), an empiric's attack on traditional medical training and practice, is placed in its setting by R. F. Jones, *Ancients and Moderns* (1936). In *The Dignity of Kingship Asserted* (1660), 'G. S.' inveighed against Milton's *Readie and Easie Way*, and in editing the tract (Facsimile Text Society, 1942) W. R. Parker argues for Starkey's authorship and gives an account of him.

JOHN STEPHENS, *fl.* 1615.

Satyrical Essayes Characters And Others (1615) had a 2nd enlarged edition in 1615. The book was reprinted in Halliwell [-Phillipps], *Books of Characters* (1857), and extracts are given in modern anthologies. Stephens's relations with the Overburian volume are discussed by G. Murphy in her *Bibliography* (1925) and by W. J. Paylor in his *Overburian Characters* (1936). The 'Essayes' are noticed in E. N. S. Thompson's *Seventeenth-Century English Essay* (1926).

PETER STERRY, 1613–72.

A number of sermons appeared separately. Of the larger

(and posthumous) works the best known is *A Discourse of the Freedom of the Will* (1675). V. de Sola Pinto filled a gap with his *Peter Sterry, Platonist and Puritan, 1613–1672: A Biographical and Critical Study with passages selected from his Writings* (1934). Pinto's high estimate of Sterry's literary power is not wholly shared by W. F. Mitchell, *English Pulpit Oratory* (1932). Some other accounts of Sterry's religious thought are sections in R. M. Jones, *Spiritual Reformers in the 16th & 17th Centuries* (1914), F. J. Powicke, *The Cambridge Platonists* (1926), and W. K. Jordan, *Development of Religious Toleration*, iv (1940).

JOHN STOW, 1525–1605.

After his edition of Chaucer (1561) came Stow's historical and antiquarian works: *A Summarie of Englyshe Chronicles* (1565), which had abridged and enlarged editions; *The Chronicles of England* (1580), from 1592 called *Annales* and in 1615 ff. continued by E. Howes; and his best work, *A Survay of London* (1598), which was enlarged by Stow in 1603 and from 1618 by Anthony Munday and others. The standard edition by C. L. Kingsford (2 vols., 1908) gives the text of 1603, with a full account of Stow and a bibliography; Kingsford published *Additional Notes* in 1927. J. Gairdner edited *Three Fifteenth-Century Chronicles* from Stow's collection (Camden Society, xxviii, 1880) and Kingsford *Two London Chronicles* (*Camden Miscellany* xii, 1910). Stow is discussed by C. Whibley in the *CHEL* iii and in his *Essays in Biography* (1913), and in L. B. Wright's *Middle-Class Culture* (1935).

WILLIAM STRACHEY, *fl.* 1606–18.

The *Historie of Travaile into Virginia Britannia*, written *c.* 1612, was first printed for the Hakluyt Society in 1849. For *The Colony in Virginea Britannia. Lawes Divine, Morall and Martiall* (1612) is reprinted in P. Force's *Tracts*, iii (1844). *A true reportory of the wracke, and redemption of Sir Thomas Gates* appeared in Purchas (1625). Shakespearian associations are discussed by editors of *The Tempest*; by C. M. Gayley, *Shakespeare and the Founders of Liberty in America* (New York, 1917); and most minutely by R. R. Cawley in *PMLA* xli (1926). The *Dictionary of American Biography* (1936) has an up-to-date account of Strachey.

WILLIAM STRODE, 1602–45.

Strode's poems were first collected, along with the tragicomedy *The Floating Island* (pr. 1655), by B. Dobell in 1907. There is a study of the drama by E. G. Hoffsten (St. Louis, 1908).

SIR JOHN SUCKLING, 1609-42.

Aglaura (1638) and some other things were printed in Suckling's lifetime. The first collection, *Fragmenta Aurea* (1646; repr. 1648, 1658), contained poems, letters, *An Account of Religion by Reason*, and plays. The *Last Remains* (1659) appeared separately and also with the *Fragmenta Aurea* dated 1658. W. C. Hazlitt's edition of the complete works (2 vols., 1874; rev. 1892) was superseded by that of A. H. Thompson (1910). The poems are in R. G. Howarth's *Minor Poets of the 17th Century* (Everyman, 1931). Suckling figures in general accounts of the cavalier poets. He received an essay in the *TLS*, 9 May, 1942. He is discussed in K. M. Lynch's *Social Mode of Restoration Comedy* (New York, 1926) and more minutely by F. O. Henderson, 'Traditions of *Précieux* and *Libertin* in Suckling's Poetry' (*ELH* iv, 1937). P. H. Gray has emphasized the English character of 'A Sessions of the Poets' and discounted Boccalini (*SP* xxxvi, 1939). C. Niemeyer has corrected a common error by showing that 'A Ballade. Upon a Wedding' was first printed in the *Fragmenta Aurea* of 1646 (*MLN* lvi, 1941).

JOHN SWAN, *fl.* 1635.

The encyclopaedic *Speculum Mundi. Or A Glasse Representing The Face Of The World* (1635) had further editions in 1643, 1665, and 1670. Swan's scientific ideas are discussed by F. Watson, *Beginnings of the Teaching of Modern Subjects* (1909); L. B. Wright, *Middle-Class Culture* (1935); and F. R. Johnson, *Astronomical Thought* (1937).

JOSUAH SYLVESTER, 1563-1618.

Parts of Sylvester's and other men's translations of Du Bartas appeared in 1584 ff. The first collected edition of Sylvester was *Bartas His Devine Weekes & Workes* (1605; completed 1608). Editions included minor pieces translated from Du Bartas and others. Sylvester's miscellaneous publications must be skipped. Grosart edited the *Complete Works* (Chertsey Worthies' Library, 2 vols., 1880). An abridgment of the chief work was edited by

T. W. Haight as *The Divine Weeks of Josuah Sylvester* (Waukesha, Wisconsin, 1908). Study of Du Bartas and Sylvester has been advanced by the critical edition of the former edited by U. T. Holmes, J. C. Lyons, and R. W. Linker (3 vols., University of North Carolina, 1935–40). To their critical matter, and French scholarship, may be added A. E. Creore's study of Du Bartas's style (*MLQ* i, 1940). The chief accounts of Du Bartas's influence in England are H. Ashton, *Du Bartas en Angleterre* (Paris, 1908) and A. H. Upham, *French Influence in English Literature* (1908). More special studies are: P. Weller, *Joshuah Sylvesters englische Übersetzungen der religiösen Epen des Du Bartas* (Tübingen, 1902); G. C. Taylor, *Milton's Use of Du Bartas* (Harvard, 1934); L. B. Campbell, 'The Christian Muse' (*HLB*, 1935); some pages in F. R. Johnson, *Astronomical Thought* (1937); J. Arthos, *Studies in the Diction of Neo-Classic Poetry* (Harvard *Summaries of Theses 1937*); and G. Tillotson, *On The Poetry of Pope* (1938).

JEREMY TAYLOR, 1613–67.

The standard edition of the complete works is that of R. Heber (15 vols., 1822) revised by C. P. Eden (10 vols., 1847 54). *Poems and Verse-Translations* were edited by Grosart (*Miscellanies of The Fuller Worthies' Library*, i, 1870). *Holy Living* and *Holy Dying* have had many modern reprints, e.g. Temple Classics (3 vols.). Two anthologies are *Jeremy Taylor*, ed. Martin Armstrong (1923), and *The Golden Grove*, ed. L. P. Smith (1930). 'The Marriage Ring' is in H. H. Henson's *Selected English Sermons* (World's Classics, 1939).

Biography began with George Rust's funeral sermon, which is reprinted by Heber and Eden, who supplied the first and best scholarly life. The only modern biography is by Sir E. Gosse (English Men of Letters, 1903). New material on Taylor's later life is furnished by M. Nicolson in *PQ* viii (1929) and her *Conway Letters* (Yale, 1930). The puzzle of Taylor's imprisonment in 1655 is partly solved by E. S. De Beer (*NQ* clxx, 1936).

Coleridge's extensive comments are in his *Literary Remains*, iii (1838) and *Notes on English Divines* (1853), i, Hazlitt's in his *Dramatic Literature of the Age of Elizabeth* (Lecture 7) and else-where. Arnold was less eulogistic in 'The Literary Influence of Academics'. The most thorough study of Taylor the divine is W. J. Brown's *Jeremy Taylor* (1925), which makes up for Gosse's

theological and philosophical deficiencies. Some more or less full
and solid essays are those of J. Tulloch, *Rational Theology and
Christian Philosophy* (1872), i; F. W. Farrar, in *Masters in English
Theology*, ed. A. Barry (1877); Sir James Stephen, who examines
The Liberty of Prophesying and *Ductor Dubitantium* in *Horae Sabbaticae, First Series* (1892); E. Dowden, *Puritan and Anglican*
(1900); H. H. Henson, in *Typical English Churchmen*, ed. W. E.
Collins (1902); and C. J. Stranks, *Church Quarterly Review*, cxxxi
(1940–1). On the more literary side there are Gosse; L. P.
Smith's introduction to *The Golden Grove*, a fine essay by a
literary epicure; and W. F. Mitchell, *English Pulpit Oratory*
(1932). Charles Smyth has briefer remarks in his *Art of Preaching*
(1940).

Taylor's liberalism is discussed by some of the scholars named,
notably Tulloch, and in the books on toleration by M. Freund
(1927) and W. K. Jordan, iv (1940). T. G. Steffan has discussed Taylor's humanistic dislike of abstract speculation in
University of Texas *Studies in English* (1940).

Smith's *Golden Grove* contains a bibliography by R. Gathorne-
Hardy which was corrected and enlarged in the *TLS*, 25 September, 2 and 9 October, 1930, and especially 15 September,
1932.

JOHN TAYLOR, 1578?–1653.

Sixty of the pamphlets written up to 1630 were reprinted in
the *Workes* of that year; this folio was reprinted (1869) by the
Spenser Society, which reprinted Taylor's later pieces in 5 vols.
(1870–8). C. Hindley reprinted many pieces in his *Old Book
Collector's Miscellany*, ii and iii (1872–3), and 21 more, with an
introduction and bibliography, in his *Works of John Taylor*
(1872). *A Dog of War* is one of the Haslewood Books (1927).
Southey had a long account of Taylor in *Lives of the Uneducated
Poets* (1831; ed. J. S. Childers, 1925). The one full study is the
manuscript dissertation of R. B. Dow (Harvard *Summaries of
Theses 1931*). W. Thorp has an essay in the *Texas Review*, viii
(1922–3). One side of Taylor's activity is discussed in E. G. R.
Taylor, *Late Tudor and Early Stuart Geography* (1934).

'TOM TELL-TROATH'.

*Tom Tell-Troath: Or, A free Discourse touching the Manners of the
Time* was apparently written about 1622, though possibly not

published until the beginning of Charles's reign. The tract is reprinted in the *Harleian Miscellany*, ed. Park, ii (1809), and the *Somers Tracts*, ed. Scott, ii (1809), and abridged in W. H. Dunham and S. Pargellis, *Complaint and Reform in England* (1938).

SIR WILLIAM TEMPLE, 1628–99.

The works of Temple's maturity lie beyond our limits. G. C. M. Smith edited *The Letters of Dorothy Osborne to William Temple* (1928) and his *Early Essays and Romances* (1930). There are biographical and critical books by Clara Marburg (Yale, 1932) and H. E. Woodbridge (New York, 1940).

ROBERT TOFTE, 1561/2–1619/20.

Tofte was rather a translator than an original author. The chief feather in his cap would be *The Batchelars Banquet* (1603), done from *Les Quinze Joyes de Mariage*, if we accept F. P. Wilson's good but admittedly tentative internal evidence in his edition of the translation (1929). His introduction and F. B. Williams's full study (*RES* xiii, 1937) are the best accounts of Tofte.

EDWARD TOPSELL, 1572–1625.

Topsell's *Historie of Foure-Footed Beastes* (1607) and *Historie of Serpents* (1608) were drawn from Conrad Gesner. Large extracts are given in M. St. C. Byrne's *Elizabethan Zoo* (1926). The *DNB* is corrected and enlarged by Miss Byrne and by V. B. Heltzel, who gives an account of the unpublished *Fowles of Heaven* (*HLQ* i, 1937–8). M. Doran discusses Topsell in relation to Elizabethan 'credulity' (*JHI* i, 1940).

AURELIAN TOWNSHEND, 1583?–1651?

Two masques, *Albions Triumph* and *Tempe Restord* (pr. 1632), along with poems from miscellanies and manuscripts, were edited by Sir E. K. Chambers (Tudor and Stuart Library, 1912). This volume and the *DNB* received bibliographical and biographical supplements from G. C. M. Smith in *MLR* xii (1917) and the *TLS*, 23 October, 1924.

THOMAS TRAHERNE, 1637/9–74.

Some works published in Traherne's century were: *Roman Forgeries* (1673); *Christian Ethicks* (1675; two chapters, *Of Magnanimity and Charity*, ed. J. R. Slater, Columbia, 1942); and *A serious and patheticall Contemplation of the Mercies of God* (1699;

ed. R. Daniells, *University of Toronto Studies*, xii, 1941). Bertram
Dobell first printed the *Poems* (1903) and *Centuries of Meditations* (1908). In 1910 *Poems of Felicity* were edited from the
Burney MS. by H. I. Bell; these had been prepared for publication, and doctored, by the author's brother Philip, who had
made some changes in the Dobell MS. In the standard edition
of the complete poems (1932) G. I. Wade enables the reader so
far as possible to detach Philip's revisions. *Felicities*, ed. Sir A.
Quiller-Couch (1934), is a small selection of prose and verse.

Among Traherne's numerous critics have been the pioneer
Dobell; Rufus M. Jones, *Spiritual Reformers in the 16th & 17th
Centuries* (1914); G. E. Willett, *Traherne (An Essay)* (1919); E. N.S.
Thompson, *PQ* viii (1929); T. O. Beachcroft, *Criterion*, ix (1929–
30) and *Dublin Review*, clxxxvi (1930); Q. Iredale, *Thomas Traherne*
(1935); sections in the books on the metaphysical poets by J. B.
Leishman (1934) and especially H. C. White (1936); and G. I.
Wade, who in *Thomas Traherne* (Princeton, 1944) gives the
fullest possible biography, a critical discussion of all the works,
and bibliographies of texts and criticism.

BRIAN TWYNE, 1576?–1644.

As a young man Twyne wrote the first history of Oxford,
Antiquitatis Academiæ Oxoniensis Apologia (1608), and he left large
manuscript collections which were used by Wood. Some interesting correspondence, 1596–1613, was printed in the *Bodleian
Quarterly Record*, v (1927–8).

SIR THOMAS URQUHART, 1611–60?

After *Epigrams: Divine and Moral* (1641) Urquhart published
(to omit his eccentric Greek titles) a mathematical treatise
(1645), a work on chronology, including the famous Urquhart
pedigree (1652), *The Discovery of A most exquisite Jewel* (1652),
a tract on a universal language (1653), and the first two books
of Rabelais (2 vols., 1653). Urquhart's version of the 3rd book
was printed (dated 1693) in the 1694 edition of Rabelais of
which the first two books were a reprint of Urquhart, the 4th
and 5th translated by Motteux. The whole text of the translation
by Urquhart and Motteux has been often reprinted, e.g. in the
Tudor Translations, ed. C. Whibley (3 vols., 1900). Some
miscellaneous works were collected in *Tracts* (1774) and all in
the *Works* (Maitland Club, 1834). *The Life and Death of the*

Admirable Crichtoun, from the *Jewel*, has been edited by H. Miles (1927), a small volume of miscellaneous *Selections* by J. Purves (1942). There are a biography by J. Willcock (1899), essays by Whibley (repr. in *Studies in Frankness*, 1910) and other editors, and by L. Powys (*Thirteen Worthies*, 1923), and a scholarly discussion by Huntington Brown, *Rabelais in English Literature* (Harvard, 1933).

JAMES USSHER, 1581–1656.

The standard edition of Ussher's works, with a life, is that of C. R. Elrington and J. H. Todd (17 vols., Dublin, 1847–64). Richard Parr's *Life* (1686) is valuable for the scholarly background of the age as well as for the man. The modern *Life and Times* is by J. A. Carr (1895). In addition to the *DNB*, there is a sketch by E. W. Watson in *Typical English Churchmen*, ed. W. E. Collins (1902). The best account of Ussher's work is in H. Arneke, *Kirchengeschichte und Rechtsgeschichte* (1937). His preaching is dealt with by W. F. Mitchell, *English Pulpit Oratory* (1932).

SIR HENRY VANE, 1613–62.

Two of Vane's significant writings were *The Retired Mans Meditations, or the Mysterie and Power of Godliness* (1655) and *A Healing Question* (1656). The latter is reprinted in *Somers Tracts*, ed. Scott, vi (1811), in John Forster's *Sir Henry Vane* (D. Lardner's *Eminent British Statesmen*, iv, 1838), and in *Old South Leaflets*, General Series, vol. i, no. 6 (Boston, 1896). The *DNB* has a long article by Firth, the *Dictionary of American Biography* (1936) a short one by J. T. Adams. There are biographies by J. K. Hosmer (Boston, 1888), W. W. Ireland (1905), and John Willcock (1913). Vane's religious ideas are discussed by Rufus M. Jones, *Spiritual Reformers in the 16th & 17th Centuries* (1914), and in the books on toleration by M. Freund (1927) and W. K. Jordan, iv (1940).

HENRY VAUGHAN, 1621/2–95.

Vaughan's volumes of verse and prose were: *Poems* (1646); *Silex Scintillans* (1650); *Olor Iscanus* (1651); *The Mount of Olives* (1652); *Flores Solitudinis* (1654); *Silex Scintillans* (1655), a reissue of 1650 with new introductory matter and a second part; *Hermetical Physick* (1655); and *Thalia Rediviva* (1678). The only reprint in Vaughan's own century was that of *Olor*

Iscanus in 1679. After long oblivion—though Cowper owned and studied *Silex*—Vaughan crept into several anthologies in the early nineteenth century. H. F. Lyte edited *Sacred Poems* (1847); this edition was reprinted a number of times and the text was included in the Temple Classics (1900). The complete works were edited by Grosart (Fuller Worthies' Library, 4 vols., 1871), the complete *Poems* by Sir E. K. Chambers, with an introduction by H. C. Beeching (Muses' Library, 2 vols., 1896). The standard edition of the *Works* is that of L. C. Martin (2 vols., 1914), who provides a full apparatus. Among small editions are *The Mount of Olives*, &c., ed. L. I. Guiney (1902) and *Silex Scintillans*, ed. W. A. L. Bettany (1905). Volumes of selections have been issued by the Nonesuch Press (1924) and the Gregynog Press (1924).

In the way of general criticism may be mentioned L. I. Guiney, *A Little English Gallery* (New York, 1894); Lionel Johnson's essay of 1896, reprinted in *Post Liminium* (1911); E. Dowden, *Puritan and Anglican* (1900); Henry W. Wells, *Tercentenary of Henry Vaughan* (New York, 1922); F. L. Lucas, *Authors Dead and Living* (1926); Edmund Blunden, *On the Poems of Henry Vaughan* (1927); T. S. Eliot's very individual comment in the *Dial*, lxxxiii (1927); and sections in the books on the metaphysical poets by G. Williamson (1930), J. Bennett (1934), J. B. Leishman (1934), and especially H. C. White (1936). Vaughan is the hero of *The Swan of Usk* (1940), an historical novel by Helen Ashton.

Studies of philosophic and particularly Hermetic influences have been made by R. Sencourt, *Outflying Philosophy* (Hildesheim, 1924); A. C. Judson, *SP* xxiv (1927) and *PMLA* xlii (1927); Elizabeth Holmes, *Henry Vaughan and the Hermetic Philosophy* (1932); W. O. Clough, *PMLA* xlviii (1933); A. J. M. Smith, *Papers of the Michigan Academy*, xviii (1933); R. M. Wardle, *PMLA* li (1936); H. F. Thoma (*supra*, V. 2); and L. C. Martin, *RES* xviii (1942). 'The Retreate' is the special theme of H. McMaster, 'Vaughan and Wordsworth', *RES* xi (1935); L. C. Martin, *Seventeenth Century Studies Presented to Sir Herbert Grierson* (1938); and M. Y. Hughes, *Renaissance Studies in Honor of Hardin Craig* (Stanford, 1941). The question of Vaughan's service in the civil war is discussed (*JEGP* xli, 1942) by E. L. Marilla, whose study of the secular verse is summarized in Ohio State University *Abstracts of Dissertations*, No. 36 (1941). The problems of the publication and character of *Olor Iscanus* are clarified by W. R. Parker (*Library*, xx, 1939–40) and H. R. Walley (*RES* xviii, 1942). There is a bibliography of criticism, 1912–38, in T. Spencer and M. Van Doren, *Studies in Metaphysical Poetry* (1939).

RICHARD VAUGHAN, EARL OF CARBERY, 1600?–86.

Carbery was Jeremy Taylor's patron, and his third wife (1652) was the Lady Alice Egerton of *Comus*. *Advice to his Sonn*, written in 1651, was partly printed, in somewhat garbled form, in an anonymous anthology, *Practical Wisdom* (1824, 1901, 1907), where it was attributed to William, Earl of Bedford. A full and accurate text, from the Ellesmere MS., was printed by V. B. Heltzel, with a valuable introduction, in *HLB* (1937).

THOMAS VAUGHAN, 1621/2–66.

Vaughan's alchemical and mystical writings (1650–5) have been edited by A. E. Waite as *The Works of Thomas Vaughan: Eugenius Philalethes* (1919). His poems were included in Grosart's edition of Henry's works (Fuller Worthies' Library, 1871, ii) and in Waite. In the way of commentary there are Waite's introduction, an article by E. Martin in the *Fortnightly Review* (March 1924), and a number of the studies of Hermetic thought cited above under Henry Vaughan.

SIR WILLIAM VAUGHAN, *c.* 1575–1641.

Vaughan's writings belong rather to the documentary than to the literary domain, unless we except the conduct book, *The Golden-grove* (1600). Others were *The Golden Fleece* (1626), *The Newlanders Cure* (1630), and *The Church Militant* (1640). Another item is mentioned under Robert Burton and John Florio. The *DNB* is corrected and amplified by M. Eccles in *HLQ* v (1941–2); e.g. Vaughan sent colonists to Newfoundland although, at least up to 1630, he had apparently not gone there himself.

VERNEY FAMILY

We become acquainted with the interesting Verneys through the following books: *Verney Papers. Notes of Proceedings in the Long Parliament, Temp. Charles I. Printed from original pencil memoranda taken in the House by Sir Ralph Verney, Knight*, ed. J. Bruce

(Camden Society, xxxi, 1845); *Letters and Papers of the Verney Family down to the End of the Year 1639*, ed. Bruce (Camden Society, lvi, 1853); and especially *Memoirs of the Verney Family during the Civil War*, compiled by F. P. Verney (2 vols., 1892), and *Memoirs of the Verney Family During the Commonwealth 1650 to 1660*, by M. M. Verney (1894), who in a 4th volume (1899) carries the story up to 1696.

RICHARD (ROWLANDS) VERSTEGAN, *c.* 1550–*c.* 1640.

The Catholic Verstegan, whose later life was spent abroad, produced an account of English and other martyrs, *Theatrum Crudelitatum Hæreticorum Nostri Temporis* (Antwerp, 1587; French trans., 1588, repr. Lille, 19–?), and *Odes. In Imitation of the Seaven Penitential Psalmes* ([Antwerp], 1601). There are selections from the latter, with a biographical sketch, in L. I. Guiney's *Recusant Poets* (1939). Verstegan's best-known work is *A Restitution of Decayed Intelligence: In antiquities. Concerning the most noble and renowmed English nation* (Antwerp, 1605). The latest full study is E. Rombauts, *Richard Verstegen, Een Polemist der Contra-Reformatie* (Brussels, 1933).

EDMUND WALLER, 1606–87.

The first issue of the *Poems* in 1645 may have been unauthorized, but Waller seems to have been associated with the second issue and the other two editions of 1645, although the 1664 edition claimed to be the first authorized one. The notorious *Instructions to a Painter* appeared in 1666. The *Second Part of Mr. Waller's Poems* (1690) contained a critical essay by Atterbury. The *Works* were edited by E. Fenton in 1729 and by P. Stockdale in 1772. Waller was of course included in the large collections of English poets. The standard modern edition is by G. Thorn-Drury (Muses' Library, 1893; 2 vols., 1905). Of the older critiques the most famous is Johnson's, in *Lives of the Poets* (1779). Among modern discussions, in addition to Thorn-Drury, Courthope (iii, 1903), and A. H. Thompson (*CHEL* vii), there are D. C. Tovey, *Reviews and Essays* (1897); H. C. Beeching, 'A Note upon Waller's Distich', in *An English Miscellany Presented to Dr. Furnivall* (1901), and 'Atterbury on Waller', in *Provincial Letters* (1906); a thesis by S. H. Werlein (MS., Harvard, 1919); important articles by R. C. Wallerstein on the heroic couplet (*PMLA* l, 1935) and G. Williamson, 'The Rhetorical Pattern of

Neo-classical Wit' (*MP* xxxiii, 1935–6); and R. L. Sharp, *From Donne to Dryden* (1940). Waller's Virgilian translation (1658) is discussed in W. Dighton's edition of Sidney Godolphin (1931). The scope of N. Roeckerath's *Der Nachruhm Herricks und Wallers* (Leipzig, 1931) is obvious. B. Chew's account of the first editions of the poems is in the *Bibliographer*, i (New York, 1902) and *Essays & Verses About Books* (New York, 1926).

JOHN WALLIS, 1616–1703.

Wallis's mathematical and theological works cannot be itemized. With his *Defence Of the Royal Society* (1678) goes his account of his education and the beginnings of the Society (in *Peter Langtoft's Chronicle*, ed. T. Hearne, 2 vols., 1725). Wallis figures more or less in books on Hobbes. The standard work, J. F. Scott's *Mathematical Work of John Wallis* (1938), is for mathematicians, but the first two chapters deal with Wallis's life and the Royal Society. Wallis's *Grammatica Linguæ Anglicanæ* (1653) is studied by M. Lehnert, *Die Grammatik des . . . John Wallis* (Breslau, 1936).

BRIAN WALTON, 1599/1600–61.

The *Biblia Sacra Polyglotta*, the work of Walton and many collaborators, was published in six tomes dated 1657. Information about it and about the state of oriental learning is given in H. J. Todd's *Memoirs and Writings of . . . Brian Walton* (2 vols., 1821), in the biblical bibliography of Darlow and Moule (*supra*, IV. 8), in W. E. Barnes's essay in *In Memoriam Adolphus William Ward* (1924), and in Harris Fletcher's books on Milton's Semitic and biblical learning (*supra*, IV. 8).

IZAAK WALTON, 1593–1683.

The *Compleat Angler* (1653) was much enlarged and altered in 1655. The 3rd and 4th editions were issued in 1661 (repr. 1664) and 1668. The 5th (1676) included some new matter by Walton, Cotton's imitative supplement, which has often been printed with Walton's book, and Robert Venables's *Experienced Angler* (first pr. in 1662). There were 10 editions and reprints in the eighteenth century, 164 in the nineteenth, and so far the twentieth has had over 100 more (6 of these in the years 1914–18). Among the chief editors and writers of introductions have been Moses Browne (1750), Sir John Hawkins (1760), John

Major and R. Thomson (1823), Sir H. Nicolas (1836), G. W. Bethune (New York, 1847), R. B. Marston (1888), J. R. Lowell (1889), Andrew Lang (1896 and Everyman's Library, 1906), John Buchan (1901 and World's Classics, 1935), Bliss Perry (Boston, 1928), and G. Keynes, *The Compleat Walton* (1929). There is a facsimile of the 1st ed. (1928). The place of the *Angler* in the history of piscatory literature is touched in many essays and most fully treated by R. B. Marston, *Walton and Some Earlier Writers on Fish and Fishing* (1894). The bibliographical history of the book is admirably set forth by Peter Oliver, *A New Chronicle of The Compleat Angler* (1936).

The *Lives* underwent continual revision in substance and style. The life of Donne, first printed with Donne's *LXXX Sermons* (1640), was much enlarged and printed separately in 1658. Further additions were made in the collected *Lives* of 1670 and 1675. The life of Wotton, in *Reliquiæ Wottonianæ* (1651), was enlarged in the 2nd edition (1654), in the *Lives* (1670), and in the 3rd edition of the *Reliquiæ* (1672). The life of Hooker (1665) was reprinted with a few changes in Hooker's *Works* (1666) and the *Lives* (1670). The life of Herbert was issued twice in 1670, by itself and in the *Lives*; a revised version was prefixed to the 10th edition of *The Temple* (1674), and slight changes were made in the *Lives* (1675). The life of Sanderson, prefixed to a volume of Sanderson's tracts (1678), was enlarged and added to the 7th and 8th editions of Sanderson's *Sermons* (1681, 1686). The first four lives were printed together in 1670; the chief additions in the 2nd edition (called the 4th) of 1675 were in the life of Donne. Among modern editions of the five biographies are those in the Temple Classics (2 vols.), the Scott Library, and the World's Classics, the last in the original spelling, with an essay by Saintsbury.

A. W. Pollard edited the *Angler* and the *Lives* in Macmillan's Library of English Classics (1901). *The Compleat Walton*, ed. G. Keynes (1929), includes, with the major works, the anonymous tract *Love and Truth* (1680), miscellaneous notes, letters, verses, &c.

Our knowledge of Walton has grown through the labours of many editors and other devotees. Stapleton Martin's *Izaak Walton and his Friends* (2nd ed., 1904) is a pleasantly discursive miscellany. Summaries of biographical information are given by Keynes and most recently in Cornell *Abstracts of Theses 1938* by A. M. Coon, who has recorded new items in various journals (1937 ff.).

To such introductory essays as are mentioned above may be added those of Sir Leslie Stephen ('Country Books', *Hours in a Library*) and L. Powys (*Thirteen Worthies*, 1923). The best studies of the *Lives* are by D. A. Stauffer, *English Biography before 1700* (1930), and John Butt, *ESEA* xix (1934). Walton's handling of letters is illustrated by R. E. Bennett, *PQ* xvi (1937). Fresh material on one biography is given in C. J. Sisson's *Judicious Marriage of Mr. Hooker* (1940). Butt has edited Walton's notes for a life of Hales (*MLR* xxix, 1934) and compiled the fullest bibliography of the *Lives* in *OBS*, vol. ii, part iv (1930).

WILLIAM WALWYN, 1600–80.

To the references cited under Lilburne should be added W. Schenck, *Economic History Review*, xiv (1944).

SETH WARD, 1617–89.

Ward published sermons and theological and mathematical treatises, but he is perhaps best known as co-author with John Wilkins of *Vindiciæ Academiarum* (1654), a reply to John Webster, Hobbes, and Dell. The fullest account of the controversy is in R. F. Jones, *Ancients and Moderns* (1936). J. M. J. Fletcher has a discursive biographical sketch, with a bibliography, in the *Wiltshire Archæological & Natural History Magazine*, xlix (1940).

JOHN WEBSTER, 1610–82.

For the background of Webster's *Academiarum Examen* (1654) reference may be made to the note on Seth Ward just above. In another realm, the limitations of Webster's supposed scepticism in *The Displaying of Supposed Witchcraft* (1677) are displayed by G. L. Kittredge, *Witchcraft in Old and New England* (1929).

SIR ANTHONY WELDON, d. 1649?

The Court and Character of King James (1650; enlarged in 1651 with 'The Court of King Charles') was reprinted in *Secret History of the Court of James the First*, ed. Scott (2 vols., 1811), and in *Smeeton's Historical & Biographical Tracts* (1820), i. Among critics of the work were Godfrey Goodman, Sir William Sanderson (*Aulicus Coquinariæ*, 1650; repr. in *Secret History*), and Heylyn. Weldon's *Perfect Description of Scotland* (pr. 1647), often wrongly attributed to Howell, is reprinted in the *Secret History*, in Nichols's *Progresses* (1828), iii, and in P. H. Brown, *Early Travellers in Scotland* (1891).

ELIZABETH JANE WESTON, 1582–1612.

Poemata appeared at Frankfort in 1602, *Parthenicon* at Prague in 1606. *Opuscula* were edited by J. C. Kalckhoff (Frankfort, 1723). There are accounts of the author in G. Ballard, *Memoirs of Several Ladies of Great Britain* (1752; *Memoirs of British Ladies*, 1775), the *DNB*, Myra Reynolds, *The Learned Lady in England* (1920), and A. Kolář, *Humanistická Básnířka Vestonia* (Bratislavě, 1926), which has a two-page summary in English.

BENJAMIN WHICHCOTE, 1609–83.

Select Sermons, based on the author's and hearers' notes, were printed in 1698 with a preface by Shaftesbury, and re-edited by W. Wishart (1742). Larger collections were *Several Discourses*, ed. J. Jeffery (4 vols., 1701–7), and *Works* (4 vols., Aberdeen, 1751). *Moral and Religious Aphorisms*, ed. Jeffery (1703) was enlarged, with the Whichcote-Tuckney letters, by S. Salter (1753). Selections are in E. T. Campagnac's *Cambridge Platonists* (1901). The *Aphorisms* were reprinted in 1930 with a preface by W. R. Inge. Whichcote is discussed by J. Tulloch, *Rational Theology and Christian Philosophy* (1872), ii; B. F. Westcott, *Masters in English Theology*, ed. A. Barry (1877); E. A. George, *Seventeenth Century Men of Latitude* (1908); Rufus M. Jones, *Spiritual Reformers in the 16th & 17th Centuries* (1914); in the books on Cambridge Platonism by F. J. Powicke (1926), G. P. H. Pawson (1930), and W. C. De Pauley (1937); and by W. F. Mitchell, *English Pulpit Oratory* (1932), and W. K. Jordan, *Development of Religious Toleration*, iv (1940).

NATHANIEL WHITING, *c.* 1612–*post* 1662.

Le hore di recreatione: Or, The Pleasant Historie Of Albino and Bellama (1637) is reprinted in Saintsbury's *Minor Poets of the Caroline Period*, iii (1921).

RICHARD WHITLOCK, *c.* 1616?–*c.*1672.

Whitlock, who does not appear in the *DNB*, was an Oxonian who studied law and medicine and at the Restoration took orders. G. Williamson (*PQ* xv, 1936) has shown the significance of his rare and only work, *ZOOTOMÍA*, *or, Observations on the Present Manners of the English* (1654).

JOHN WILKINS, 1614–72.

Apart from sermons, Wilkins's chief works were: *The Discovery of a World in the Moone* (1638), enlarged in 1640 with a *Discourse on the earth as a planet*; *Mercury* (1641), a book on ciphers; *Ecclesiastes* (1646), a book on preaching often reprinted; *Mathematicall Magick* (1648), of which one chapter, on 'an Ark for submarine Navigations', is reprinted in Sir Hubert Wilkins's *Under the North Pole* (1931); *Vindiciæ Academiarum* (1654), cited above under Seth Ward; *An Essay Towards a Real Character, And a Philosophical Language* (1668), a part of which is reprinted in F. Techmer, *Beiträge zur Geschichte der französischen und englischen Phonetik und Phonographie* (Heilbronn, 1889); and *Of the Principles and Duties of Natural Religion* (1675). The *Mathematical and Philosophical Works* were collected in 1708 (repr., 2 vols., 1802).

P. A. W. Henderson's *Life and Times* (1910) has been superseded by many special studies, such as those of D. Stimson, R. F. Jones, M. Nicolson, F. R. Johnson, and R. K. Merton, which are cited above in V. 3, and others which follow here. G. McColley has dealt with Wilkins's astronomical ideas in *Annals of Science*, i, iii, and iv (1936–9), *PMLA* lii (1937), and *SP* xxxv (1938). Wilkins's theory of preaching is treated by W. F. Mitchell, *English Pulpit Oratory* (1932), his interest in language by E. N. Andrade (*Annals of Science*, i, 1936), L. Hogben (*Dangerous Thoughts*, 1939), and some writers listed above in IV. 1.

ROGER WILLIAMS, 1603/6–83.

The Bloudy Tenent, of Persecution, for cause of Conscience (1644) was edited by E. B. Underhill (Hanserd Knollys Society, 1848) and is of course in the standard edition of Williams's chief works (6 vols., Narragansett Club, 1866–74). Large extracts are in A. S. P. Woodhouse, *Puritanism and Liberty* (1938). Among biographies, popular or scholarly, are those of E. Easton (Boston, 1930), J. E. Ernst (New York, 1932), and S. H. Brockunier (New York, 1940). Among general discussions are V. L. Parrington, *The Colonial Mind* (New York, 1927), and essays by L. C. Wroth (*Brown University Papers*, xiv, 1937) and John Dos Passos (*The Ground We Stand On*, New York, 1941). More or less special discussions of Williams's thought are in the books on toleration by M. Freund (1927) and W. K. Jordan, iii (1938); by Ernst, *Political Thought of Roger Williams* (University of Washington, 1929) and *Rhode Island Historical Society Collections*, xxiv (1931); H. B. Parkes, *New England Quarterly*, iv (1931); Perry Miller, *Orthodoxy in Massachusetts* (1933); W. Haller, *Tracts on Liberty* (1934); F. B. Wiener, *Rhode Island Historical Society Collections*, xxviii (1935); R. E. E. Harkness, *Journal of Religion*, xv (1935); Woodhouse, *supra*; E. F. Hirsch, *Church History*, x (1941); and Arthur Barker, *Milton and the Puritan Dilemma* (1942).

ARTHUR WILSON, 1595–1652.

The History of Great Britain, Being The Life and Reign of King James the First (1653) was reprinted in White Kennett, *Complete History of England* (1706), ii. *Observations of God's Providence, in the Tract of my Life* is in Francis Peck's *Desiderata Curiosa* (2 vols., 1732–5; repr. 1779) and in Bliss's edition (1814) of Wilson's play, *The Inconstant Lady*.

GERRARD WINSTANLEY, 1609–post 1660.

G. H. Sabine has filled a gap by editing Winstanley's *Works . . . with an appendix of Documents Relating to the Digger Movement* (Cornell, 1941). A volume of selections has been edited by Leonard Hamilton (1944). The fullest and best discussions are Sabine's introduction, which stresses religious motives, and D. W. Petegorsky's *Left-Wing Democracy in the English Civil War* (1940), a scholarly Marxist study which somewhat overstresses economics. Other accounts of varying length, besides L. H. Berens's pioneer *Digger Movement* (1906), are given by G. P. Gooch, *Political Thought in England* (1915), M. James (*supra*, V. 1), D. M. Wolfe (*supra*, V. 1), and J. M. Patrick, *University of Toronto Quarterly*, xii (1942).

GEORGE WITHER, 1588–1667.

Wither was recalled from oblivion by Percy's *Reliques* and revived by Lamb, Brydges, et al. Nearly all his works were reprinted by the Spenser Society (1871–82) and several early ones in Arber's *English Garner*, iv and vi (1882–3). The best edition, chiefly of his pastoral verse, is by F. Sidgwick (2 vols., 1902). Besides Lamb's essay, remarks in his letters, and comments reproduced by Swinburne in his 'Charles Lamb and George

Wither' (*Miscellanies*, 1886), there are Sidgwick's introduction; essays in John Fyvie, *Some Literary Eccentrics* (1906), and Gosse, *Selected Essays, Second Series* (1928); some pages in the general histories and in H. Genouy, *L'élément pastoral* (Montpellier, 1928). The fullest study is the unpublished Harvard thesis (1928) of J. M. French, who has printed some Witheriana in *PMLA* xlv (1930) and *HLB* (1931) and *Wither's History of the Pestilence* (Harvard, 1932). Other sides of his work are treated in I. Tramer, *Studien zu den Anfängen der puritanischen Emblemliteratur in England: Andrew Willet—George Wither* (Berlin, 1934); W. M. Clyde, *Struggle for the Freedom of the Press* (1934); and W. K. Jordan, *Development of Religious Toleration*, ii (1936). There are bibliographical articles on the *Workes* of 1620 by P. Simpson and L. Kirschbaum (*Library*, vi, 1925–6 and xix, 1938–9).

HEZEKIAH WOODWARD, 1590–1675.

Woodward contributed many tracts to the religious controversy; his use of some of Milton's anti-episcopal ideas is suggested by G. W. Whiting, *SP* xxxiii (1936). He is perhaps best known as a friend of Hartlib and a fellow-supporter of Baconian and Comenian education. Some short extracts are given in Edith Rowland, *A Pedagogue's Commonplace Book* (1925), and in *The Beginnings of the Teaching of Modern Subjects* (1909) by Foster Watson, who discusses Woodward's views.

JOHN WORTHINGTON, 1618–71.

The most popular of Worthington's publications was *The Christians Pattern* (1654), a translation, or rather a revision of earlier translations, of à Kempis. He edited the works of John Smith (1660) and Joseph Mede (1664). His own *Miscellanies* ... *Also A Collection of Epistles, Written to Mr Hartlib* appeared in 1704. The *Diary and Correspondence*, ed. J. Crossley and R. C. Christie (Chetham Society, 3 vols., 1847–86), gives a good picture of contemporary scholarship. Christie compiled a *Bibliography* (Chetham Society, 1888). Further information is given in W. A. Copinger, *Bibliographiana No. 3. On the English Translations of the 'Imitatio Christi'* (1900).

SIR HENRY WOTTON, 1568–1639.

The first collection of prose and verse, with Walton's life, was *Reliquiæ Wottonianæ* (1651; enlarged in 1654, 1672, and 1685).

The Elements of Architecture (1624) is in the *Somers Tracts*, ed. Scott, iii (1810), and *Complaint and Reform in England*, ed. W. H. Dunham and S. Pargellis (1938), and has been reprinted separately by G. Kirkham (Springfield, Mass., 1897) and S. Prideaux (1903). H. S. Kermode has edited *A Philosophical Survey of Education or Moral Architecture and The Aphorisms of Education* (1938). The poems were edited by Dyce (Percy Society, vi, 1842) and J. Hannah (1845 and later edns.). The 'Character of a Happy Life' first appeared among the Overburian characters (4th ed., 1614). 'You meaner Beauties of the Night', written in 1620, was first printed, with music, in Michael East's *Sixth Set of Books* (1624); a discussion of variant versions and their history went on in the *TLS* (1924 and 26 February, 1925; and D. Hamer, *NQ* clxiii, 1932). The standard account of Wotton is L. P. Smith's *Life and Letters* (2 vols., 1907), which contains a selection from nearly a thousand letters and dispatches. There are essays by A. W. Fox, *A Book of Bachelors* (1899) and P. E. More, *Shelburne Essays, Fifth Series* (1908).

INDEX

Many minor names and incidental references are necessarily omitted. Main entries are in bold figures. An asterisk indicates a biographical note. Topics and seventeenth-century authors in the bibliography are indexed.